Personal Injury and Damage Ascertainment under Civil Law

Santo Davide Ferrara
Editor

Rafael Boscolo-Berto
Guido Viel
Co-Editors

Personal Injury and Damage Ascertainment under Civil Law

State-of-the-Art International Guidelines

Springer

Editor
Santo Davide Ferrara
Department of Legal and Occupational Medicine, Toxicology and Public Health
University-Hospital of Padova
Padova, Italy

Co-Editors
Rafael Boscolo-Berto
Guido Viel
Department of Legal and Occupational Medicine, Toxicology and Public Health
University-Hospital of Padova
Padova, Italy

ISBN 978-3-319-29810-8 ISBN 978-3-319-29812-2 (eBook)
DOI 10.1007/978-3-319-29812-2

Library of Congress Control Number: 2016941884

Printed on acid-free paper

This Springer imprint is published by Springer Nature
The registered company is Springer International Publishing AG Switzerland

Foreword

The assessment of personal injury and damage is an integral part of clinical forensic medicine. This is true not only for criminal justice but also for the application of civil law. Up to now, the evaluation criteria of bodily harm differ from country to country due to the variety of legal situations and national regulations. Therefore, the International Academy of Legal Medicine (IALM) under the presidency of Prof. Santo Davide Ferrara has set its sights on harmonizing the medicolegal ascertainment of personal injury and damage in order to establish international standards. This is in harmony with the Academy's aim to achieve scientific progress especially by promoting collaboration and information exchange among specialists and to recommend guidelines in the different areas of legal medicine. Against this background, an international and multidisciplinary Working Group on personal injury and damage under civil-tort law was constituted in 2014. This panel, composed of renowned representatives from all continents, incorporates the knowledge and experience of juridical, clinical, and medicolegal experts, thus guaranteeing a wide base of competence. A similar approach has already been chosen by Prof. Ferrara and his coeditors in another relevant topic of forensic medicine, namely medical malpractice and liability. In both projects, the collaborating authors initiated a consensus process aiming at common principles and evidence-based guidelines.

Insurance medicine is a special field with a long tradition. In Italy, where the editors of the monograph work, insurance medicine constitutes an essential task in daily medicolegal practice which finds expression in the designation of the postgraduate specialty ("legal and insurance medicine"). This proves the great relevance of civil and insurance issues in research, teaching, and forensic services not only in Italy but in many other countries as well.

Legal Medicine is oriented toward forensic needs, which explains that the responsibilities may differ considerably depending on the respective national law. According to a generally accepted definition, legal medicine deals with the application of medical knowledge in the administration of justice. One of its fundamental objectives is the reconstruction of events and the clarification of legally relevant circumstances. Morphological and clinical findings have to be interpreted as to their causation, which requires a detailed knowledge of traumatology and biomechanics. Otherwise, the expert would be at risk of misinterpreting bodily damage and resulting complaints especially in cases of suspected malingering (fabricating or exaggerating symptoms of mental or physical disorders). This aspect is important forinstance in the assessment of sequelae from cervical acceleration/deceleration in motor vehicle accidents.

The monograph edited by Ferrara, Boscolo-Berto, and Viel imparts comprehensive information on both juridical and medical issues of the topic. Specialists from Europe, North and South America, Africa, Asia, and Oceania give a detailed description of the medicolegal procedure in the ascertainment of personal injury and damage including remarks on the required qualification and competences of the assessing experts. A separate chapter is devoted to dental damage.

Apart from the historical development and actual conditions of personal injury compensation under the respective judicial terms, fundamental questions such as the causal relation between an incident and any consecutive impairment to health are thoroughly discussed. Based on the systematic investigation of the actual situation, the Working Group elaborated supranational recommendations which meanwhile have been adopted as official IALM guidelines defining the needed qualification of the experts and the medicolegal methodology of assessing health damage.

As the authors rightly state, future harmonization of impairment rating requires the application of standards for ascertaining and evaluating personal injury and damage. So the submitted guidelines are a big step forward in that direction. It is to be hoped that the great efforts made by the Working Group will help to propagate the presented principles of injury and damage assessment, which can be regarded as the current state of the art. It is confidently to be hoped that the monograph will find a wide acceptance within the scientific community.

Stefan Pollak

Preface

Every repetition of the ancient cultural conflict between the past and the present implies a practically ineluctable and intrinsic deictic chrono-centrism, understood as an egocentric absolutism of one's era, as if it were the only one in which values change, and as though in no other have epochal transformations occurred, lived more or less as such, if not as real "anthropological mutations": the present, more than ever, seems to be the victim of this illusion of perspective.

The issue is ancient, dating back to the affirmation of the modern around four centuries ago, when the hourglass of history was suddenly upturned, with the result that the good was no longer behind us, as man had believed for centuries, but rather on the horizon, as the distant goal orienting the spaces of man and defining his objective; destiny became challenge, adventure, risk, a search, and only sometimes discovery.

The modern return to the "ancient question" of personal injury and damage, described as long as 4400 years ago in Mesopotamia [1] when it was already defined as any injury to the body, mind, or emotions, caused by a third person, does not elude the ineffable ineluctability of "deictic chrono-centrism." The Nippur Tablets (2050 BC), Hammurabi Code (1750 BC), Talion Law, Eshnunna Law, Mishnah, and Lex Aquilia are just a few of the historical legislative examples containing references to reparation and/or compensation for personal injury and damage [2]. Among these, the Hammurabi Code, an early attempt to legislate justice in moral, social, and economic spheres, decreed punitive actions against a person causing bodily injury; the Law of Eshnunna illuminated a modern approach to personal injury, with rules and ordinances recommending monetary compensation for bodily harm, such as the loss of teeth, ears, or other physical impairments.

Personal injury and bodily harm, considered as actions necessitating punishment and/or compensation, have always presented questions concerning how and by which means personal damage caused by a third party should be punished and/or compensated, and which professionals should assess the pecuniary and non-pecuniary losses causally related to the injury, from which have always derived different responses depending on the sociocultural values and principles underpinning the respective legal systems [2].

In the postmodern era, the prevailing principle uniting the majority of different national legal frameworks is the full compensation of past, present, and future losses (restitutio in integrum) causally linked to the injury. In spite of this common principle and the various attempts to harmonize international private law, heterogeneity and divergences still exist across different national legislative systems regarding the type of pecuniary and non-pecuniary losses to be compensated ("*quantum debeatur*"), the criteria to be used for determining liability (e.g., strict liability, fault based, no-fault based), and the limitation periods for exercising individual rights.

The "*quantum,*" recognized as a proper and specific entity in almost all of the countries across the world, in addition to non-pecuniary loss related to physical or psychic impairment, and to "intangible" pain and suffering, loss of amenity, and/or psychic-existential damage, is strictly and increasingly linked to objective and scientifically sound medical evidence.

Therefore, the starting point of any current procedure should indeed be a clinical/medicolegal ascertainment, acquiring evidence on the event which caused the injury, the mechanism of injury, the preexisting health condition of the injured person, and the health consequences of that injury, in terms of temporary/permanent impairment, disability, work incapacity, loss of independence, and quality of life. Although it concerns an ascertainment of a principally medicolegal and forensic nature, and there is an absence of international recognition of a professional specialization specifically dedicated to personal injury and damage ascertainment and evaluation, in many countries, most prevalently North East Europe, Africa, and North America, specialists in insurance medicine and clinics of varying specialities (physiatrists, orthopedists, neurologists, psychiatrists, etc.) are involved in this area.

We are thus speaking of a major issue of significant existential, individual and collective, cultural, social, and economic value, so far tackled with diverse legislative and procedural perspectives, by equally diverse figures of medical and nonmedical evaluators, who apply related as much as unknown, but in any case dissimilar, ascertainment methodologies, in an era which is ever more marked by the essential nature of objective, demonstrable, and inconfutable evidence, resistant to juridical examination, according to canons and criteria of probability/near certainty, transcending the penal context and pervading the civil context.

Thus, reiterating the aforementioned "deictic chrono-centrism," that of the resurfacing of the ancient cultural conflict between past and present, and imbued with the enthusiastic presumption which the President of a planetary Scientific Society, such as that of the International Academy of Legal Medicine (IALM), must possess, I founded in 2014 an International Working Group on "Personal Injury and Damage under civil-tort law" composed of 58 juridical, clinical, and/or medicolegal experts from 21 different countries and representing all five continents (Africa, America, Asia, Europe, and Oceania).

With the implied as well as explicit Scientific aims of filling the gaps of knowledge in relation to supranational contexts, proposing legislative–juridical and insurance-related innovations arising from the cultures of the biomedical and medicolegal disciplines, and developing bio-medico-clinical-legal ascertainment methodologies of personal injury and damage, the expression of Scientific Consensus and Evidence-Based Medicine was proposed at an International level on the subject of personal damage in general, psychic-existential damage, and whiplash-associated disorders, with the supreme aim of ensuring qualitative and quantitative uniformity and specificity of the individual contexts of injuries and their temporary or permanent consequences or aftereffects.

Coherent with the aforementioned aims, this Monograph, the result of the work of the aforementioned experts, is composed of 9 Parts and offers the contents detailed below.

1. An intercontinental *Juridical and Methodological Overview* (Part I) on personal injury/damage compensation, envisioning the future evolution of Biomedicine and the Bio-medicolegal sciences in the post-genomic era (Chap. 1), describing the need for a Holistic and systematic clinical and medicolegal approach (Chap. 2), discussing the principles and rules to be used for the reconstruction of the causal value and link between the event and the injury/impairment (Chap. 3), and analyzing the different juridical and judicial frameworks, institutions, and operative roles related to personal injury compensation (Chap. 4).
2. A *detailed description of the medicolegal methods of ascertainment of personal injury and damage under civil-tort law around the world*, including four continental areas, Europe (*Part II*), North and South America (*Part III*), Africa (*Part IV*), and Asia and Oceania (*Part V*). Following a common "*Logical Structure*," the Authors, as Members of the IALM Working Group, were asked to illustrate the historical, judicial, and juridical framework of personal injury assessment and compensation in their country, describing the expert's qualification and competences and detailing the ascertainment methodology and criteria of evaluation utilized for identifying, describing, and estimating any personal injury, its temporary and permanent consequences, and the causal value/link between the event and the injury and between the injury and the impairment/disability.

   Within Europe, eleven countries have been included: Portugal (Chap. 5), Spain (Chap. 6), France (Chap. 7), Italy (Chap. 8), Belgium (Chap. 9), The Netherlands (Chap. 10), United Kingdom (Chap. 11), Germany (Chap. 12), Hungary (Chap. 13), Lithuania (Chap. 14), and Estonia (Chap. 15). Two Countries, the United States (Chap. 16) and Argentina (Chap. 17), have been included for Americas, while two other Countries, Egypt (Chap. 18) and Nigeria (Chap. 19), have been included for Africa. Finally, the methodological overview comprises six countries of the Asian and Oceanic continental areas: Turkey (Chap. 20), the Kingdom of Saudi Arabia (Chap. 21), India (Chap. 22), China (Chap. 23), Japan (Chap. 24), and Australia (Chap. 25).
3. *An International Overview and Epicrisis (Part VI)* describing the state of the art on dental damage ascertainment (Chap. 26) and proposing an international epicritical overview on the operative rules, procedures, and methods used for personal injury/damage assessment in 21 different countries (Chap. 27).

4. *A Methodology of ascertainment and International Guidelines* (*Part VII*), focusing on the biomechanical tools to be used for reconstructing the dynamics of the damaging event (Chap. 28), describing the most useful and innovative instruments for detecting malingering (Chap. 29), for ascertaining psychic-existential damage (Chap. 30), and proposing the very first methodological flowchart for the ascertainment of personal injury and damage in general (Chap. 31) and of whiplash-associated disorders in particular (Chap. 32).
5. The *Requirements and Final Recommendations* for the ascertainment and evaluation of personal injury and damage (*Part VIII*, Chap. 33).
6. A selected *Historical Iconography* on personal injury and damage from the "Vincenzo Pinali" Antique Medical Library of the University of Padova, Italy (*Part IX*, Chap. 34).

The International Guidelines (Chaps. 31 and 32), elaborated by the IALM Working Group utilizing the methodology of the Consensus Conference and revised by leading experts in the field of personal injury and damage assessment, have been adopted as Official IALM Guidelines defining the requirements and the basic skills that the professional must possess in order to carry out an assessment with regard to personal injury and damage, as well as the methods and procedures of data/evidence collection so as to guarantee the objectivity, rigor, and reproducibility required for scientific evidence to overcome the scrutiny of the civil courtroom and become scientific proof.

These Guidelines do not provide harmonized "Baremés" or "Compensation Schemes" for quantifying the impairment/disability causally related to the personal injury and refer to the national legislation for damage quantification.

Indeed, there have been several research efforts, above all in the United States and Europe, aimed at rationalizing the assessment of non-pecuniary damages by proposing evaluation Baremés, Evaluation Scales, and Tables consisting of systems of percentage points for each category of physical and/or mental impairment. As described in detail in Parts II, III, IV, and V, in the majority of countries compensation Tables developed by the Legislator or National Scientific Societies are utilized in order to translate human pathology resulting from trauma or disease into a percentage of the whole person's permanent impairment, assisting adjudicators and others in determining the financial compensation to be awarded to the individuals who, as a result of injury or illness, have suffered measurable, physical, and/or psychological losses.

In the United States, the "gold standard" for rating a permanent impairment/disability is the "*American Medical Association Guides to the Evaluation of Permanent Impairment*," now in its sixth edition [3]. These Guides, created five decades ago as a tool for adjudication of workers' compensation claims, with accumulating experience, have been increasingly used outside that specific setting in claims of personal injuries (e.g., automobile accidents, medical malpractice cases, etc.), spreading across the globe, above all in Oceania (i.e., Australia, and New Zealand).

In Europe, there are no unified official Baremés or Evaluation Scales. In several countries compensation for non-pecuniary losses is based on the discretion of the judge, with damages awarded according to legal practice, whereas in other nations Baremés and Compensation Tables are used (e.g., Belgium, France, Italy, Lithuania, Portugal, Spain, The Netherlands, and Turkey) [4].

In June of 2000, the "Trier Group," based on the results of a Consensus Conference held at the Academy of European Law (ERA) in Trier (Germany), proposed a Recommendation to the European Commission, Parliament, and Council on the "*Rationalisation of the medico-legal assessment of non-economic damage*" [4]. Similarly, in May 2003 a group of medical experts supported by the Confédération Européenne d'Experts en l'Evaluation et Réparation du Dommage Corporel (CEREDOC) presented another recommendation to the European Commission, Parliament, and Council proposing unified European Evaluation Baremés inspired by the French, Belgian, Italian, and Spanish compensation tables [5]. Both of the above efforts, although commendable, failed to be adopted, predominantly as a result of the strong resistance manifested by the "*The Pan-European Organisation of Personal Injury Lawyers—PEOPIL.*"

The above Group observed that, although being of some interest from an academic point of view, the idea of a unified medicolegal scale based upon a system of percentage points for each category of physical or mental impairment, to be adopted in all EU Member States, would imply a significant imposition where there are marked differences in respect of the medical ascertainment and evaluation approach in the diverse national realities [4].

Although commendable, these efforts at harmonization were probably premature given the absence of a shared clinical and medicolegal ascertainment methodology. Prior to setting any impairment rating criteria, indeed, it is of the utmost importance to define the quality requirements for the ascertainment methodology and the evaluation criteria (i.e., intended as "logical steps" to be followed for the assessment of any impairment and/or disability, not as a "Baréme" or "Guide" for expressing an impairment rating percentage), which are essential to guarantee the objectivity, rigor, and reproducibility of the data/evidence collection.

Currently, there are no supranational and/or national clinical/medicolegal guidelines dealing specifically with the ascertainment methodology of personal injury and damage [6]. Therefore, the Methodology and the Guidelines set out analytically in Part VII of the Monograph are the very first International Guidelines on that topic and pave the way for a future harmonization of the impairment rating and the assessment of any pecuniary and non-pecuniary losses causally related to personal injury.

The Reader and possible user of the Monograph and Guidelines, which can also be downloaded in digital format to facilitate professional use, is warmly invited to communicate to the Editor any observations, comments, and, above all, criticisms relating to the improvement of the work.

In summary, the Monograph, in pursuing and aiming to achieve the aforementioned Scientific aims, is an editorial work. Indeed, the publishing industry, from its mechanical origin in lead and printing machines, has always been entirely part of the modern context and thus obliged to coexist with it, viewing itself in relation to the public and in terms of the number of copies sold and distributed. For a monograph of scientific imprint and scope, there exist cognitive and educational needs and the expression of the community of scholars, namely devotees of the discipline and the "practice of the subject." Regardless of the specificity of personal injury and damage ascertainment, there are grounds to believe that such a work might equal the great editorial success of the previous Monograph, "Malpractice and Medical Liability" [7], which has been circulated across five continents in many thousands of copies. Because it too, as in the present work, did not aspire to reach a broad public *tout court*, nor to attach to a certain standard the "optimum model," both being operations that do not bring with them any benefits, but rather reproduce in the cultural world a map of an unequal society. It is hoped that scientists, legislators, jurists, lawyers, insurers, doctors, and other interested parties derive from the Monograph reasons and contents to meet the needs of knowledge and training in the creation of a bridge between entertainment and originality of writing.

To the coeditors, Rafael Boscolo-Berto and Guido Viel, and all of the coauthors and members of the IALM Working Group

Osama Mohammed Al Madani (Kingdom of Saudi Arabia), Viviana Ananian (Italy), Eric Baccino (France), Manal S. Bamousa (Kingdom of Saudi Arabia), Peter Banczerowski (Hungary), Daniele Bordignon (Italy), Jan Buithenius (The Netherlands), Luigi Cicinnati (Italy), Giovanni Comandè (Italy), Krisztian Csapò (Hungary), Wout E. L. De Boer (Switzerland), Katja De Munnynck (Belgium), Ranieri Domenici (Italy), Agnes Dòsa (Hungary), Uwom O. Eze (Nigeria), Javier Gorriz Quevedo (Spain), Matthias Graw (Germany), Mete Korkut Gulmen (Turkey), Wolfram Hell (Germany), Claudio Hernàndez-Cueto (Spain), Ahmet Hilal (Turkey), Ping Huang (China), Haluk Ince (Turkey), Eva Keller (Hungary), Magdy A. Kharoshah (Kingdom of Saudi Arabia), Juel Thiis Knudsen (Denmark), Adarsh Kumar (India), Marta Beatriz Maldonado (Argentina), Stefano Masiero (Italy), Danuta Mendelson (Australia), George Mendelson (Australia), Massimo Montisci (Italy), Axel Muttray (Germany), Elisabeth Mützel (Germany), Gian Aristide Norelli (Italy), William O. Odesanmi (Nigeria), Graziella Orrù (Italy), Vilma Pinchi (Italy), Mohammed Ranavaya (USA), Romas Raudys (Lithuania), Jean Sebastien Raul (France), Giuseppe Sartori (Italy), Andras Sarvary (Hungary), Toshiko Sawaguchi (Japan), Dina A. Shokry (Egypt), Vera Sterzik (Germania), Claudio Terranova (Italy), Enrico Tessitore (Switzerland), Jana Tuusov (Estonia), Marika Väli

(Estonia), Peter Vanezis (UK), Yvo Vermylen (Belgium), Duarte Nuno Vieira (Portugal), Alessia Viero (Italy), Enrique Villanueva (Spain), Ya-hui Wang (China), Peter Weiss (Germany), Andrea Zangrossi (Italy), Anna Chiara Zanuzzi (Italy), and Riccardo Zoia (Italy) in addition to the Publisher the most cordial thanks and appreciation for the distinguished individual and collegial contributions offered toward the realization of the present Monograph.

S. Davide Ferrara
President
International Academy of Legal Medicine

References

1. Margeat H (1988) La réparation du dommage corporel à l'horizon 1992. Revue Française du Dommage Corporel 14(3):403–8
2. Magalhaes T, Viera DN (2014) Personal Injury Assessment. In Madea B (Ed.) Handbook of forensic medicine. John Wiley & Sons, Inc., Hoboken, New Jersey, USA
3. Rondinelli RD, Ranavaya M (2008) American Medical Association: Guides to the Evaluation of Permanent Impairment, 6th edn, AMA Press, Chicago, USA
4. Bona M, Mead P (2003) Personal injury compensation in Europe. Kluwer, Deventer, The Netherlands
5. Chappuis G, Soltermann B (2008) Number and cost of claims linked to minor cervical trauma in Europe: results from the comparative study by CEA, AREDOC and CEREDOC. Eur Spine J 7(10):1350–1357.
6. Ferrara SD, Bajanowski T, Cecchi R, Snenghi R, Case C, Viel G (2010) Bio-medicolegal guidelines and protocols: survey and future perspectives in Europe. Int J Legal Med 124 (4):345–50
7. Ferrara SD (Ed.) (2013) Boscolo-Berto R, Viel G (Co-Eds) Malpractice and medical liability. European state of the art and guidelines. Springer, Heidelberg, Germany

Contents

List of Contributors

Osama Mohammed Al Madani Forensic Medicine, SCFHS Riyadh; Forensic Medicine Center, Dammam, Eastern Province, Kingdom of Saudi Arabia

Viviana Ananian Department of Legal and Occupational Medicine, Toxicology and Public Health, University-Hospital of Padova, Padova, Italy

Eric Baccino Service de Médecine Légale, University of Montpellier, Hôpital Lapeyronie, Montpellier Cedex, France

Manal S. Bamousa Forensic Medicine, SCFHS Riyadh; Forensic Medicine Center, Dammam, Eastern Province, Kingdom of Saudi Arabia

Peter Banczerowski Department of Neurosurgery, Semmelweis University, Budapest XIV, Hungary

Daniele Bordignon Private Medico-Legal Practice, Vicenza, Italy

Rafael Boscolo-Berto Department of Legal and Occupational Medicine, Toxicology and Public Health, University-Hospital of Padova, Padova, Italy

Jan Buitenhuis Dutch Academic Center for Insurance Medicine (DACIM), University Medical Center Groningen, Afdeling Gezondheidswetenschappen, Sectie Sociale Geneeskunde/secretariaat K623, Sector F/FA10, Groningen, The Netherlands

Luigi Cicinnati Research and Development Cincinnati Engineering – Padova, Padova, Italy

Giovanni Comandè LIDER-Lab, University Scuola Superiore Sant'Anna, Pisa, Italy

Krisztian Csapó Department of Neurosurgery, Semmelweis University, Budapest, XIV, Hungary

Wout E.L. De Boer Asim Research & Education I Department Clinical Research, University Hospital Basel, Basel, Switzerland

Katja De Munnynck MedLEx, Rotselaar, Belgium

Ranieri Domenici Department of Clinical, Surgical, and Molecular Pathology, Unit of Legal Medicine, University of Pisa, Pisa, Italy

Agnes Dósa Department of Forensic and Insurance Medicine, Semmelweis University, Budapest, IX, Hungary

Uwom O. Eze Forensic Pathology, University College Hospital Ibadan, Ibadan, Oyo State, Nigeria

Santo Davide Ferrara Department of Legal and Occupational Medicine, Toxicology and Public Health, University-Hospital of Padova, Padova, Italy

Javier Gorriz Quevedo Gorriz Hernando Médicos, Barcelona, Spain

Matthias Graw Institut für Rechtsmedizin, Ludwig-Maximilians-University of München, Munich, Germany

Mete Korkut Gulmen Department of Forensic Medicine, Medical Faculty, Cukurova University, Balcali, Adana, Turkey

Wolfram Hell Institut für Rechtsmedizin, Ludwig-Maximilians-University of München, Munich, Germany

Claudio Hernàndez-Cueto Department of Legal Medicine, Forensic Toxicology and Anthropology, University of Granada, Granada, Spain

Ahmet Hilal Medical Faculty, Department of Forensic Medicine, Cukurova University, Adana, Turkey

Ping Huang Shanghai Key Laboratory of Forensic Medicine, Institute of Forensic Science, Ministry of Justice, Shanghai, People's Republic of China

Haluk Ince Medical Faculty, Department of Forensic Medicine and Public Health, Istanbul University, Fatih/İstanbul, Istanbul, Turkey

Eva Keller Department of Forensic and Insurance Medicine, Semmelweis University, Budapest, IX, Hungary

Magdy A. Kharoshah Forensic Medicine, SCFHS Riyadh; Forensic Medicine Center, Dammam, Eastern Province, Kingdom of Saudi Arabia

Peter Juel Thiis Knudsen Institute of Forensic Medicine, University of Southern Denmark, Odense C, Denmark

Adarsh Kumar Medical Disability Evaluation Board, JPNA Trauma Centre, All India Institute of Medical Sciences, New Delhi, Delhi, India

Marta Beatriz Maldonado Faculty of Odontology, University of Buenos Aires, Buenos Aires, Argentina

Stefano Masiero Department of Neurosciences, Physical and Rehabilitation Medicine, University-Hospital of Padova, Padova, Italy

Danuta Mendelson Faculty of Business & Law, School of Law, Deakin University, Caulfield Junction, Australia

George Mendelson Department of Psychiatry, School of Clinical Sciences, Faculty of Medicine, Nursing and Health Sciences, Monash University, Melbourne, VIC, Australia

Massimo Montisci Department of Legal and Occupational Medicine, Toxicology and Public Health, University-Hospital of Padova, Padova, Italy

Axel Muttray Institute of Occupational, Community and Environmental Medicine, Johannes-Gutenberg-University of Mainz, Mainz, Germany

Elisabeth Mützel Institute of Forensic Medicine, Ludwig-Maximilians-University of München, München, Germany

Gian Aristide Norelli Department of Health Sciences, Forensic Sciences Section, Institute of Legal Medicine, University of Florence, Florence, Italy

William O. Odesanmi Forensic Pathology, Ekiti State University, Ado-Ekiti, Nigeria

Graziella Orrù Department of Psychology, University of Padova, Padova, Italy

Vilma Pinchi Department of Health Sciences, Section of Forensic Medical Sciences, University of Florence, Florence, Italy

Mohammed Ranavaya Division of Disability Medicine, Joan C. Edwards School of Medicine, Marshall University, Huntington, WV, USA

Romas Raudys State Forensic Medicine Service of Lithuania, Mykolas Romeris University, Lithuania

Jean Sebastien Raul Institut de Médecine Légale, Faculté de Médecine, Université de Strasbourg, Strasbourg, France

Giuseppe Sartori Department of Psychology, University of Padova, Padova, Italy

Andras Sarvary Department of Forensic and Insurance Medicine, Semmelweis University, Budapest, IX, Hungary

Toshiko Sawaguchi Department of Legal Medicine, Tokyo Women's Medical University, Shinjuku-ku, Tokyo, Japan

Dina A. Shokry Department of Forensic Medicine and Clinical Toxicology, Faculty of Medicine, Cairo University, Cairo, Egypt

Vera Sterzik Institute of Forensic Medicine, Kantonsspital St. Gallen, St. Gallen, Switzerland

Claudio Terranova Department of Legal and Occupational Medicine, Toxicology and Public Health, University-Hospital of Padova, Padova, Italy

Enrico Tessitore Département de Neurosciences Cliniques, Service de Neurochirurgie, Faculté de Médecine, Hôpitaux Universitaires de Genève, Geneva 14, Switzerland

Jana Tuusov Department of Pathological Anatomy and Forensic Medicine, University of Tartu, Tartu, Estonia

Marika Väli Estonian Forensic Science Institute, University of Tartu, Tartu, Estonia

Peter Vanezis Department of Clinical Pharmacology, Cameron Forensic Medical Sciences, William Harvey Research Institute, Barts and the London, Queen Mary, University of London, London, UK

Yvo Vermylen Department of Dentistry, Faculty of Medicine, The Catholic University Leuven, Leuven, Belgium

Duarte Nuno Vieira Department of Forensic Medicine, Ethics and Medical Law, Faculty of Medicine, University of Coimbra, Coimbra, Portugal

Guido Viel Department of Legal and Occupational Medicine, Toxicology and Public Health, University-Hospital of Padova, Padova, Italy

Alessia Viero Department of Legal and Occupational Medicine, Toxicology and Public Health, University-Hospital of Padova, Padova, Italy

Enrique Villanueva Department of Legal Medicine, Toxicology and Physical Anthropology, University of Granada, Granada, Spain

Ya-hui Wang Shanghai Key Laboratory of Forensic Medicine, Institute of Forensic Science, Ministry of Justice, Shanghai, People's Republic of China

Peter Weiß Department of Public Prosecution, Würzburg, Germany

Andrea Zangrossi Department of Psychology, University of Padova, Padova, Italy

Anna Chiara Zanuzzi Department of Private Law and Critique of Law, University of Padova, Padova, Italy

Riccardo Zoia Department of Health and Biomedical Sciences, Section of Legal Medicine, University of Milan, Milano, Italy

Part I
Juridical and Methodological Overview

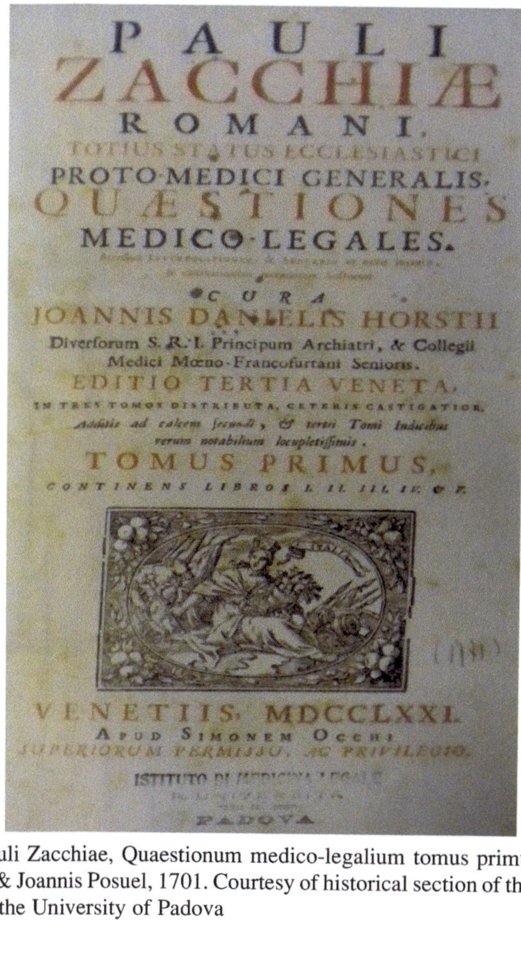

PAULI
ZACCHIÆ
ROMANI,
TOTIUS STATUS ECCLESIASTICI
PROTO-MEDICI GENERALIS,
QUÆSTIONES
MEDICO-LEGALES.

CURA
JOANNIS DANIELIS HORSTII
Diverforum S. R. I. Principum Archiatri, & Collegii
Medici Mœno-Francofurtani Senioris.
EDITIO TERTIA VENETA,
IN TRES TOMOS DISTRIBUTA, CETERIS CASTIGATIOR,
Additis ad calcem secundi, & tertii Tomi Indicibus
rerum notabilium locupletissimis.
TOMUS PRIMUS,
CONTINENS LIBROS I. II. III. IV. & V.

VENETIIS, MDCCLXXI.
APUD SIMONEM OCCHI
SUPERIORUM PERMISSU, AC PRIVILEGIO.

Zacchia Paolo—Pauli Zacchiae, Quaestionum medico-legalium tomus primus-tertius Lugduni : sumptibus Anisson & Joannis Posuel, 1701. Courtesy of historical section of the “Vincenzo Pinali” Medical Library of the University of Padova

Chapter 1
Bio-Medicolegal Sciences and Personal Injury/Damage Ascertainment in the Post-Genomic Era

Santo Davide Ferrara, Guido Viel, and Rafael Boscolo-Berto

Abstract The first part of the chapter analyzes the techno-scientific evolution of postmodern biomedicine, highlighting the pros and cons of the holistic approach of systems biology and its clinical translation in the form of individualized precision medicine, as well as the opportunity to refound the doctor–patient relationship and the healthcare organization of the third millennium on the principles of personalized slow and value medicine. In the second part, the historical development of the bio-medicolegal sciences, their progressive disintegration into specialized subdisciplines, and the related need to find a biomolecular unitariness are discussed. The chapter then deals with the problems and the current limits of personal injury and damage ascertainment, envisaging an increase in the objectivity and accuracy of the impairment and disability assessment through the medicolegal implementation of technology platforms of in vivo functional imaging and bio-analysis, developed by postmodern biomedicine. The conclusions stress the importance of investing in human capital, through teaching and education at a university level. The main responsibility of academic institutions, indeed, is to educate toward a critical mentality and a democratic citizenship of the world, safeguarding the transmission of knowledge of the past together with the defense of the idea that it is feasible to innovate such knowledge.

1.1 Introduction

Post-genomic biomedicine, also referred to as P4 Medicine, being personalized, predictive, preventive, and participative, has surpassed the traditional approach to diagnosis and treatment, in a patient-centric vision, where, thanks to new omics

S.D. Ferrara (✉) • G. Viel • R. Boscolo-Berto
Department of Legal and Occupational Medicine, Toxicology and Public Health, University-Hospital of Padova, Via Falloppio 50, 35128 Padova, Italy
e-mail: santodavide.ferrara@unipd.it; guido.viel@unipd.it; rafael.boscoloberto@unipd.it

S.D. Ferrara et al. (eds.), *Personal Injury and Damage Ascertainment under Civil Law*, DOI 10.1007/978-3-319-29812-2_1

technologies (genomics, epigenomics, proteomics, metabolomics, fragmentomics, and interactomics), it is possible to analyze and evaluate the individual biomolecular profile of the subject. This profile, providing a significant contribution to the diagnosis and the specific choice of treatment, will permit, in the near future, the minimization of a given treatment's toxicity, improve the quality of life of patients, and optimize the management of healthcare resources.

A paradigmatic example of the extraordinary potential of translational omics is the *integrative personal omics profile* (iPOP) [1], which involves a combined analysis of genomic, transcriptomic, proteomic, metabolomic, and autoantibody profiles from a single individual over a 14-month period [1].

Of the same innovative reach is the application of the "geographic information system" (GIS) [2] for mapping, in biomolecular terms and in a sort of "pre-womb to tomb assessment," the various moments in the life of a patient, from preconception to the fetal, neonatal, childhood, and adult periods [2].

Equally interesting is the recent application of micro- and nanotechnology to "single cell and spatially resolved omic analysis" that aims to collect geno-transcripto-proteomic data retaining positional information [3].

The advent of laser capture microdissection, permitting the isolation of a group of cells from a given tissue and the subsequent extraction of DNA and RNA and the development of a "mass cytometry," capable of identifying and quantifying protein at the subcellular level, will soon make it possible to reveal, through a high-dimensional data analysis, new spatiotemporal interdependencies disclosing the molecular pathways and biological interconnections of the entire biological system of the "person."

The enormous translational potentialities originating from the extraordinary progress of technological imaging and bioanalytical platforms will require intensive and rigorous validation efforts in order to determine whether individualized precision medicine is really able to improve, in a cost-effective manner, the clinical–diagnostic course and the patient outcome [3]. The extreme technologicalization of personalized medicine and the increasing reliance on algorithms and artificial intelligence will continue to change the face of postmodern biomedicine and to transfigure the therapeutic relationship [4], directing it toward "personalized slow and value medicine," in a neo-humanistic vision of the profession.

In such a framework the bio-medicolegal sciences have been experiencing, for some time now, a deep crisis of cultural and scientific impoverishment, dependent upon a variety of phenomena and factors, the leading among them being the progressive fragmentation of knowledge with the emergence of mutually independent and isolated specialist subdisciplines, the paucity of funds for international and national research, and the lack of an inter- and transdisciplinary vision, ready to assimilate and develop the technical, technological, and epistemological innovations of post-genomic biomedicine.

Some recent bibliometric studies [5–7] have highlighted a good level of publication in terms of the number of contributions and citation indices (e.g., impact factor, citation index, h-index) for specialized subdisciplines such as forensic genetics, anthropology, toxicology, and radiology, with some papers on the subject of virtopsy, personal identification, postmortem interval estimation, child sexual abuse, and wound age estimation downloaded and cited numerous times. There is a demonstration that the bio-medicolegal sciences have grasped the importance of publishing in "peer review" in journals with impact factor, surveyed by the most important international databases, such as *Scopus*, the *Journal Citation Report* of *ISI-Web of Science*, and *MEDLINE*.

From the studies carried out, however, a lack of innovation and interdisciplinary innovation has also emerged, demonstrated by the absence, in the international medicolegal literature, of inter- and transdisciplinary studies with the involvement of the basic sciences and the association of the forensic experts of various sub-disciplines, such as criminology, pathology, toxicology, and/or genetics [5–7].

In the race toward the future, biomedicine is moving at a rapid pace, like a rocket, whereas the bio-medicolegal sciences are proceeding with the speed of a hot-air balloon. Several black holes of knowledge still remain, regarding state and trait markers of disease, the reconstruction of molecular mechanisms of trauma, the dating of skin lesions, the evaluation of biological age, the hereditary and environmental factors linked to criminogenesis, etc.

To remedy and to guarantee their own survival, the bio-medicolegal sciences must trigger a cultural renewal that, taking account of the *holistic omic approach* and the *personalized value of medicine*, derives from an innovative systematic and from a new inter- and transdisciplinary unitariness based on *molecular evidence*.

This means not only importing the ethical and epistemological paradigms of omic holism and personalized value medicine into bio-medicolegal culture but also taking advantage of the main technological, bioanalytical, and biomedical imaging platforms developed for forensic applications, aimed at the measurement of the uncertainty of the acquired data and, in relation to scientific evidence, improving the quality of the system [8], through the implementation of proficiency testing programs and quality systems aimed at measuring the objectivity, robustness, and reliability of the data collected, the ascertainment methods, and the criteria of evaluation in bio-medicolegal sciences where they have not yet been developed, such as "clinical forensic–legal medicine," criminology, forensic psychiatry, and forensic pathology.

The ascertainment and evaluation of personal injury and damage under civil/tort law, a paradigmatic example of clinical and medicolegal assessment in which the measure of accuracy, precision, and robustness and the reliability of the epicritical assessment, in terms of scientific evidence, are still in its infancy, can profitably benefit from the translation of the new bioanalytical and molecular imaging technologies.

The overview set out in the following paragraphs illustrates these technologies, some of which have extraordinary potential for innovation and application in the bio-medicolegal evaluation of impairment and disability causally related to disorders that are currently difficult or impossible to objectify.

1.2 "Omics" Technologies

In the document of the European Commission entitled *Use of omics technologies in the development of personalized medicine* (2013), the developments of biomedical research permit the reevaluation of the role of diagnostics in the personalized approach to diagnosis, the determination of the prognosis, and the care of the patient affected by neoplastic, chronic inflammatory, and/or degenerative diseases. The availability of omics platforms (genomics, epigenomics, proteomics, miromics, metabolomics, etc.) therefore necessitates a process of qualification and validation of new biomarkers for their efficient and effective utilization within clinical practice and, in the future, in clinical forensic medicine. The amount of data obtained with these high-throughput platforms requires the integration, analysis, and development of methodologies and statistical algorithms suitable for the utilization of the obtained information in both the clinical and forensic environments.

The current state of the art implies the molecular characterization at the level of the tissues and/or recourse to "liquid biopsy," translatable into the possibility to identify the entirety of the molecular alterations which characterize a specific illness in biological fluids and, therefore, in a noninvasive and repeatable fashion.

The liquid biopsy involves the search, in relation to the blood or other biological fluids (e.g., urine, feces, cerebrospinal fluid), for (1) cells; (2) DNA; (3) mRNA and microRNA; (4) proteins, peptides, and protein profiles associated with a specific disease; and (5) alterations of metabolites and metabolic profiles.

The liquid biopsy requires, first of all, the acquisition and evaluation of technologies, which permit the analysis of single biotic components.

(1) Circulating Cells

The search for circulating cells can be carried out through various methodological approaches. The search for one or more specific transcript can be carried out on enriched (or non-enriched) samples of pathological cells (e.g., magnetic beads) permitting the identification of 1^{-10} cells per mL of whole blood. The quantification of disease-specific transcripts (qRT-PCR) allows the enhancement of the RT-PCR sensitivity. Besides these indirect methodologies of identification, new methodologies of analysis are currently available. These include immune-cytometric analysis of enriched samples, analysis with flow cytometry, as well as analysis through semiautomatic instrumentation, which includes an initial phase of enrichment via magnetic beads, followed by marking with specific antibodies for the pathological cells and any contaminating cells.

(2) DNA

The search for specific mutations in relation to neoplastic and/or degenerative illnesses through the analysis of circulating DNA is based on the premise that fragments of DNA are normally released by the cells following apoptosis. Freely circulating DNA is detectable in the plasma of subjects and is enriched in a variable percentage of DNA of tumoral origin in the event of neoplasia. The analysis of somatic mutations important for the prognosis and/or the choice of treatment (e.g., K-ras, BRAF V600, EGFR mutations, etc.), through the analysis of plasma DNA, is one of the most innovative frontiers of translational medicine and a representative example of what is meant by liquid biopsy. Until now this approach has not gained wide diffusion due to the sensitivity limits of the available technologies. The new technologies of analysis (e.g., digital PCR) permit the detection and quantification of up to 1 % of mutated DNA, also in the event of a minimum quantity of circulating DNA. The availability of such technologies could guarantee the rapid transfer of this form of liquid biopsy into clinical practice.

(3) mRNA and Circulating MicroRNA

The genetic and phenotypic alterations of pathological cells involve, in cascade, a complex of variations in a pattern of gene transcription (transcriptome) that affect not only the messenger RNAs but also microRNAs. Traces in the biological fluids of the alterations to the abnormal cells can be detected through analysis of specific expression profiles of messenger RNA (mRNA) and microRNA. These nucleic acids are carried in the blood by means of microvesicles with a diameter of 60–120 nm, also known as exosomes. The analysis of gene expression profiles on plasma samples enriched by exosomes is an important frontier for clinical development and for a future forensic "liquid biopsy." This innovative approach of recent introduction and development requires the operational steps of fine-tuning and validation. The verification of the specific enrichment of exosomes, carried out via ultracentrifugation or by means of precipitation and centrifugation systems, can make use of imaging instrumentations (e.g., NanoSight). The profiling of gene expression can be subsequently effected via instrumentation of microarray analysis followed by validation with RT-PCR.

(4) Proteins, Peptides, and Proteomics

Analogously to that described in paragraph (3), functional alterations in gene expression can lead to cascade/feedback variations in total proteome detectable in biological fluids or parts of these. In particular, similarly to that reported for RNA and microRNA, microvesicles can carry proteins of direct pathological derivation, representing, also in this case, a potential matrix for the identification of protein biomarkers. In the context of the protein alterations induced by specific diseases, variations in the type and degree of phosphorylation of proteins (phospho-proteomics) are another potential area for translational research. The study of phosphoproteins contained in the microvesicles offers the advantage, compared to the study of freely circulating proteins, of obtaining results that are more representative of the specific neoplastic and/or degenerative illness. The search for new protein biomarkers and phosphoproteins (free or conveyed by microvesicles) in the biological fluids can make use of mass spectrometry technologies, the productive characteristics of which must guarantee the possibility to identify the largest possible number of biomarkers in the unit of time (fast-scan high resolution, such as LTQ Orbitrap). The subsequent validation of the identified biomarkers requires quantitative methodologies that include mass spectrometry in addition to the classical methods of antigen–antibody reaction.

(5) Alterations of Metabolites and Metabolic Profiles

The study of sets of small molecules, which permit the tracking of altered metabolic profiles in chronic inflammatory, neoplastic and/or degenerative diseases, has found extensive development in the field of biomedical translational research over the last decade. Metabolic components of glycolysis; the tricarboxylic acid cycle; the urea cycle; the metabolism of some amino acids such as tryptophan, proline, or arginine; and the metabolism of fatty acids have been identified as potential biomarkers of cardiovascular, neurological, and/or neoplastic diseases. Metabolomic analysis requires the availability of high-throughput instrumentation with great analytical sensitivity, such as nuclear magnetic resonance (NMR) spectroscopy or mass spectrometry associated with liquid or gas chromatography (LC-MS or GC-MS). The application of metabolomics within the clinical and forensic context includes the study of known metabolic profiles and the identification of new metabolites or panels of metabolites in the diverse biological fluids collected from the patients.

In conclusion, there is a need for biological markers capable of objectifying a physical and/or psychic impairment/disability, especially if the symptoms and signs of the functional loss pertain to the somatosensory or psychic sphere. In the near future, the systems biology framework and its bioanalytical platforms (partly described above) will favor the development and validation of new markers of functional weakening/loss, capable of enhancing the sensitivity and specificity of the ascertainment, providing objective evidence of the existence of the impairments/disabilities, and quantifying their functional implications.

1.3 Functional Brain Neuroimaging

The current imaging techniques for examining the anatomical structure and functioning of the human brain in vivo are often referred to as *neuroimaging modalities* and comprise five main platforms: functional magnetic resonance imaging (fMRI), positron emission tomography (PET), single-photon emission computed tomography (SPECT), multichannel electroencephalography (EEG), and diffusion tensor imaging (DTI).

Over the last two decades, fMRI has emerged as the dominant technique for functional brain mapping, at least in the research arena, with increasing translational applications in clinical and forensic medicine. Functional MRI is based on the physiological principle that an increase in the neural activity of a specific brain region correlates with an increase in the blood flow of that specific region. This blood flow variation leads to the blood oxygen-level-dependent (BOLD) signal, measured by the RMN detector as the ratio between oxyhemoglobin and deoxyhemoglobin signals, which are characterized by different magnetic properties

[9]. Thousands of fMRI investigations have been published in the last two decades, particularly in the field of cognitive neuroscience, neuropsychology, experimental psychology and sociology. They focus mainly on determining the distribution and patterns of brain activity associated with specific tasks.

Cognitive and neural fMRI probes can be adapted to include tasks of memory function, visual discrimination, reaction time, spatial, auditory and somatosensory processing, and executive functioning. In order to detect any abnormality in the above functions, individual fMRI data are compared to normative reference data. One of the current main challenges for bringing fMRI into medicolegal and forensic protocols is that the sensitivity, and even more the specificity, of the diagnosis depends on the statistical power of the normative data (i.e., the number of healthy controls included in the normative database).

Recent studies, nevertheless, have shown the elevated accuracy and precision of fMRI in the identification of activation patterns collected from single individuals, thus opening the field to a variety of applications in the area of personal injury and damage ascertainment, such as the functional characterization of dementia and neurodegenerative conditions, the objective diagnosis of purely psychological disorders (e.g., post-traumatic stress disorder, reactive depression), the objective quantitation of pain, lie detection, and/or malingering identification [10].

On the other hand, the tremendous expansion in the technological ability of PET and SPECT, as well as DTI, has given rise to the possibility of objectivizing a number of psychiatric syndromes causally correlating to anatomical and functional alterations derived from cerebral trauma or neurodegenerative diseases, thanks to the generation of comprehensive brain maps, called *connectomes* [11].

The integrated application of fMRI, PET, SPECT, and DTI has led to the construction of increasingly detailed maps of brain connectivity at high resolution, offering a powerful framework for localizing pathology, tracking patterns of disease, and ascertaining the functional compromise that results from an insult.

In the near future, the development of the *connectome topology* will enormously increase the understanding of the mechanistic causes of brain pathology, permitting the objective identification and prediction of cognitive and behavioral deficits resulting from a neurological or psychiatric pathology [11].

Since 2005, neuroimaging techniques, such as fMRI, PET, SPECT, and DTI, have been introduced in several civil and criminal proceedings across the world, with diverse verdicts of the trier of fact (i.e., judge or jury) concerning the admissibility of evidence. In order to meet the Daubert or Frye criteria, at least in the United States of America, the proposed methods must have undergone a process of validation on the part of the international scientific community at the basis of the method, on the quality of the evidence deriving from peer-review studies, and on the falsification of the method itself, in terms of "error rate." This expensive and academically complex enterprise must include, among its co-protagonists of the process of scientific validation, forensic psychiatrists and medicolegal experts dealing with personal injury and damage ascertainment, who are familiar with the current forensic framework and potential repercussions in terms of innovation and increase of the quality of the system derivable from the application of objective, accurate, and precise neuroimaging methods to medicolegal issues such as personal injury, impairment, disability, and work capacity assessment.

1.4 Optical Coherence Tomography and Frequency Domain Imaging

This concerns biomedical imaging techniques that utilize light to capture micrometer-resolution three-dimensional images from within biological tissues, which, as is well known, are optical scattering media [12]. Depending on the properties of the light source (typically femtosecond lasers and supercontinuum lasers), optical coherence tomography can achieve sub-micrometer resolution (i.e., about 3–10 μm) having the following advantages in comparison to ultrasound, computed tomography, and/or magnetic resonance.

- Live subsurface images at near microscopic resolution.
- Instant imaging of tissue morphology.
- Noninvasiveness.
- Nonionizing radiation.

Currently, this technique is limited to imaging 3 mm below the surface of the biological tissue, because at greater depths the amount of light that escapes without scattering is too small to be detected. Several clinical applications have already been published regarding ophthalmology (e.g., imaging of the anterior segment of the eye and retina), neurology (e.g., assessment of axonal integrity), gastroenterology, pneumology, dermatology, interventional cardiology, and radiology.

Its second-generation implementation, called frequency domain optical coherence tomography (FD-OCT), exhibiting increased imaging resolution and acquisition speed, has been profitably applied to coronary investigation for detecting vulnerable plaques in asymptomatic patients, for investigating the morphology of the intima, the histological characteristics of the thrombus, and the thickness of the fibrous cap [13].

Thanks to its noninvasive nature and high axial (3–5 μm) and lateral (5–10 μm) resolution, FD-OCT has already been used to detect changes of the retinal tissue, particularly in macular degeneration [14].

Other interesting novel applications have been achieved thanks to the coupling of FD-OCT with endoscopy, in the field of gastroenterology for the diagnosis of precancerous lesions (i.e., early gastric cancer, Barrett's esophagus), for the study of the microscopic alterations correlated with celiac disease, in pneumology for the identification of micro neoplasms of the bronchial mucosa and in dermatology for the staging of cutaneous melanoma [14].

Furthermore, numerous clinical trials are underway aimed at testing the diagnostic utility of FD-OCT for imaging the lower gastrointestinal tract, solid organs such as the prostate, guiding needle biopsies or laparoscopic surgery, and evaluating the morpho-functional characteristics of bronchia and alveoli in allergic asthma [15].

1.5 Photoacoustic Tomography

Photoacoustic imaging falls within the category of the novel vibrational imaging techniques, which can provide volumetric images of biological tissues in vivo with high spatial resolution at depths that far exceed the penetration capacities of conventional high-resolution optical imaging modalities (i.e., 1–2 cm).

It is based on the illumination of the tissue with short light pulses (i.e., in the nanosecond range), absorption by the cells, followed by thermoelastic expansion, and emission of ultrasonic waves, which are captured by ultrasonic detectors placed around the sample. In other words, photoacoustic tomography (PAT) produces images with optical absorption-based contrast, using deeply penetrable diffused light to excite photoacoustic signals. Apart from producing high-resolution images, this technique is safe for clinical use, is broadly applicable, and can furnish precious functional information on the organ or tissue.

Currently, PAT has four major implementations: raster-scan based photoacoustic microscopy (PAM), multispectral optoacoustic tomography (MSOT), rotation scan-based photoacoustic endoscopy (PAE), and hybrid systems coupling PAT to other imaging modalities, such as conventional ultrasound, optical coherence tomography, and MRI.

In recent years, PAT has been used in a number of preclinical applications, including imaging of angiogenesis, microcirculation, drug response, brain functioning, tumor microenvironments, biomarkers, and gene expression [16]. Coupled to an endoscopic system (PAE), it has also been applied on animal models for the in vivo imaging of the upper and lower gastrointestinal tracts [17].

In particular, PAM, utilizing a scanning focused ultrasonic transducer, has been profitably applied to the anatomical reconstruction of subcutaneous melanomas, as well as their microvasculature and lymphatic drainage. Indeed, PAM can depict blood vessels at ultrahigh resolution using oxyhemoglobin and deoxyhemoglobin as different light absorbers [18].

MSOT, with multiple illumination wavelengths for separating the optical reporter of interest from the background absorption, has already been used for functional imaging of blood vessels and for characterizing the morphology of atherosclerotic plaques.

Hybrid systems, integrating PAT with conventional pulse-echo imaging, have also been implemented for the detection of early stage neoplastic tissues and for characterizing the functionality of a diseased tissue. In addition to morphological and anatomical data, this novel vibrational imaging technique can provide physiological and functional information, such as cellular temperature, blood flow, and oxygen supply.

The properties of great optical absorption contrast, abundant penetration depth, noninvasiveness, absence of ionizing radiations, and functional imaging of the above-described techniques suggest several useful future applications in the field of clinical forensic medicine.

Mindful of the great success that forensic radiology has experienced in the last decade and is still currently experiencing, it is foreseeable that the above innovative in vivo imaging techniques will have a widespread diffusion in the field of personal injury and damage ascertainment, such as in the identification and characterization of visual impairments, the objectification of post-traumatic muscle or tendon injuries (e.g., whiplash-associated disorders), and the morphometric characterization of nerve damage (e.g., hypo-anosmia) and of any other functional loss or impairment, the detection of which implies a labor-intensive and not always reliable neurophysiological examination.

All of the above novel imaging techniques and their medicolegal applications, however, will have to pass a thorough validation process, in terms of sensitivity, specificity, reproducibility, and robustness before they can be used in any forensic case and be considered as scientific evidence at trial, in a civil or criminal proceeding.

1.6 Conclusions

The unique combination of the new bioanalytical and molecular imaging technologies is predictive for the objectification of currently undetectable osteo-musculo-fascial injuries, for the morphological and functional characterization of internal organ damage, for functional brain mapping, as well as for cancer mapping and staging and, therefore, for an accurate and precise assessment of the prognosis *quoad vitam* and *quoad valetudinem* and of the related nonpecuniary damages (e.g., impairment, disability, loss of chances, psychological-existential damage, etc.).

The extraordinary scientific and technological evolution of postmodern biomedicine implies a challenge and a great opportunity for the bio-medicolegal sciences of the third millennium which, in order to survive and not lose the disciplinary unity, will have to be able to develop new conceptual paradigms with the aim of diminishing the current fallibility of the ascertainment and contestability of the evaluation.

This implies, equally, the need to modify and expand the strategies for the recruitment of international and national scientific funding to be reserved for the implementation of scientific projects, with an awareness and understanding on the part of the whole medicolegal community that change is the only way to avoid being excluded from the innovation process. The above issue cannot be taken lightly for it is of vital importance: on it hinges the very future and survival of the medicolegal discipline, whose ethical priority must include the preservation of the unitariness, the development of evidence, and the great commitment in pre- and postgraduate education and training.

It is necessary, indeed, to be aware that, without the empowerment of human capital, there is no growth, culture, or innovation. Thus, today more than ever, the essential task is to prepare young people so that they may first identify, and then perform, their role in the modern society of knowledge: a society in which economic, social, and cultural development principally depends on the creation and sharing of knowledge and expertise. Today, we can truthfully say that we are living in a "global campus," where the elaboration of contemporary culture is being developed, which is no longer—as it once was—expressed and formulated only by Western culture but also by cultural traditions and intellectual communities of other continents, which are emerging at the same pace as the respective economies of their countries. These cultures are no longer—as was the case for many years—emanations of the West, passively absorbing topics and keywords, but new subjects participating as equal protagonists in a common educational process, a process that is closely related with the economy. Indeed, education continuously represents an antidote against poverty and the descent into underdevelopment and, at the same time, a factor of growth and innovation. Already in 2007, moreover, the Conference of the Ministers of Higher Education held in London highlighted the great influence that universities exercise over the development of modern society, thanks to their tradition as centers of knowledge, research, and creativity and the transmission of knowledge; and the key role that they perform in the definition and diffusion of the values upon which society itself is founded is essential.

On the other hand, this authentic improvement in quality required of the university and other scientific communities has been rendered indispensable by the process of globalization, which has radically transformed the conditions affecting competitiveness, throwing new light on the territorial dimension. A "mobile" territory such as this, traversed by continuous flows of information, knowledge, goods, people, and financial capital, if it is to compete at a global level, will have to redefine, first of all, the very dynamics of social construction and territory, beginning not only from administrative borders but also and predominantly from those relating to cognition and relations between places.

In order to develop human capital, today it is not enough to provide a large number of students with a set of notions to be applied in a standard form during their working lives. That which educators call "expertise," namely, the ability to mobilize personal resources (meaning knowledge, know-how, approaches) and external information resources, is necessary, so as to be able to effectively respond to unfamiliar situations. It is important to teach how to proceed on a global scale, to reason in universal terms so as to become accustomed to interacting and competing within an ever more complex world, with cultural, linguistic, ethical, and religious diversity.

All of the aforementioned can act, furthermore, as an indirect and powerful invitation to refuse any form of limitation in terms of identity and locale. If the occurrence of planetary global warming is real, then there is an analogous process in relation to conscience, connected to some extent to a distorted conception of existence that assigns absolute priority to the idea of profit, subordinating everything to that, including education: with the risk, as noted by the American scholar

Martha Nussbaum, to create "generations of docile machines rather than fully fledged citizens, able to think for themselves."

If it is true that wisdom is difficult to teach, it is also true that, as Plato reminds us in *Philebus*, "wisdom is the right measure of knowledge and pleasure." Within the very DNA of the university and the scientific communities, the objective is not to "produce" as a function of the labor market but to teach "to learn how to learn," that is, by providing the tools to remain critical and at the same time competitive in the labor market but also open to cooperation in solving the major issues of humanity.

Today there is a great need to view the world from outside disciplinary limitations, with a unifying, not sectoral, perspective. And at the same time, the main current of the economy of knowledge, of strategic importance now and, even more, tomorrow, teaches us to invest in human capital, that is, in its continuous, not contingent, education. It is a message to be taken on board, since it refers directly to the responsibility of our academic institutions, and of ourselves, who are called upon to animate their foundational spirit in a modern key: which is that of educating toward a critical mentality and a democratic citizenship of the world, wherever one lives and acts. The deepest meaning of the university and scientific community is the safeguarding and transmission of knowledge of the past together with the defense of the idea that it is feasible to innovate such knowledge. A task, that of innovating knowledge with the aim of setting in motion the world, which coincides with the true identity and establishment of the university at the beginning of the last millennium, as a carrier of messages of universal value, in addition to values of freedom, pluralism, moral integrity and passion for research, expressions of the legislative autonomy of the intellect and culture.

In final conclusion and in line with the thinking of the anthropologist Marc Augé [19], the bio-medicolegal sciences of the post-genomic era will be able to "turn to the future without projecting illusions onto it but by creating hypotheses so as to test their validity."

References

1. Chen R, Mias GI, Li-Pook-Than J, Jiang L, Lam HY, Chen R et al (2012) Personal omics profiling reveals dynamic molecular and medical phenotypes. Cell 148(6):1293–1307
2. Topol EJ (2014) Individualized medicine from prewomb to tomb. Cell 157(1):241–253
3. Crosetto N, Bienko M, van Oudenaarden A (2015) Spatially resolved transcriptomics and beyond. Nat Rev Genet 16(1):57–66
4. Ferrara SD (2013) Medical malpractice and legal medicine. Int J Leg Med 127(3):541–543
5. Boscolo-Berto R, Viel G, Cecchi R, Terranova C, Vogliardi S, Bajanowski T, Ferrara SD (2012) Journals publishing bio-medicolegal research in Europe. Int J Leg Med 126(1):129–137
6. Ferrara SD, Bajanowski T, Cecchi R, Boscolo-Berto R, Viel G (2011) Bio-medicolegal scientific research in Europe: a comprehensive bibliometric overview. Int J Leg Med 125 (3):393–402
7. Viel G, Boscolo-Berto R, Cecchi R, Bajanowski T, Vieira ND, Ferrara SD (2011) Bio-medicolegal scientific research in Europe. A country-based analysis. Int J Leg Med 125 (5):717–725

8. Ferrara SD, Pfeiffer H (2010) Unitariness, evidence and quality in bio-medicolegal sciences. Int J Leg Med 124(4):343–344
9. Walhovd KB, Johansen-Berg H, Káradóttir RT (2014) Unraveling the secrets of white matter: bridging the gap between cellular, animal and human imaging studies. Neuroscience 12 (276):2–13
10. Allen MD, Owens TE, Fong AK, Richards DR (2011) A functional neuroimaging analysis of the Trail Making Test-B: implications for clinical application. Behav Neurol 24(2):159–171
11. Fornito A, Zalesky A, Breakspear M (2015) The connectomics of brain disorders. Nat Rev Neurosci 16(3):159–172
12. Zysk AM, Nguyen FT, Oldenburg AL, Marks DL, Boppart SA (2007) Optical coherence tomography: a review of clinical development from bench to bedside. J Biomed Opt 12 (5):051403
13. Gutiérrez-Chico JL, Alegría-Barrero E, Teijeiro-Mestre R, Chan PH, Tsujioka H, de Silva R, Viceconte N, Lindsay A, Patterson T, Foin N, Akasaka T, di Mario C (2012) Optical coherence tomography: from research to practice. Eur Heart J Cardiovasc Imag 13(5):370–384
14. Keane PA, de Salvo G, Sim DA, Goverdhan S, Agrawal R, Tufail A (2015) Strategies for improving early detection and diagnosis of neovascular age-related macular degeneration. Clin Ophthalmol 17:353–366
15. Carignan CS, Yagi Y (2012) Optical endomicroscopy and the road to real-time, in vivo pathology: present and future. Diagn Pathol 7:98
16. Wang LV, Hu S (2012) Photoacoustic tomography: in vivo imaging from organelles to organs. Science 335(6075):1458–1462
17. Yang JM, Favazza C, Chen R, Yao J, Cai X, Maslov K, Zhou Q, Shung KK, Wang LV (2012) Simultaneous functional photoacoustic and ultrasonic endoscopy of internal organs in vivo. Nat Med 18(8):1297–1302
18. Yoon TJ, Cho YS (2013) Recent advances in photoacoustic endoscopy. World J Gastrointest Endosc 5(11):534–539
19. Augé M (2012) The future. Verso Books, London

Chapter 2
The Holistic and Systematic Approach in Legal Medicine

Santo Davide Ferrara, Gian Aristide Norelli, and Riccardo Zoia

Abstract After an overview of the subdisciplines and topics pertaining to bio-medicolegal sciences at an international level, the chapter illustrates the need for a systematic and holistic approach for the ascertainment and evaluation of personal injury and damage.

Modern evidence-based medicine is moving toward a preventive, predictive, participatory, and personalized model of diagnosis and therapy. Bio-medicolegal sciences, following that trend, must increase precision, objectivity, and reproducibility in data/evidence collection procedures, consider the injured and damage person as a "unique" entity, and personalize the description and evaluation of any impairment, disability, handicap, and other nonpecuniary losses causally related to the damaging event. The medicolegal contribution to compensation for personal damage must look for the deepest and most complete representation of the components of a person. A holistic view does not consider the person as a sum of parts but rather a complex ensemble requiring interpretation and medicolegal representation for forensic application purposes. The challenge to face is thrilling and involves drawing maps of a new geography of knowledge, to identify the pathways and destinations to restore order, aware that the coming evolution must preserve the medicolegal tradition, while rebuilding a new system of quality and values.

S.D. Ferrara (✉)
Department of Legal and Occupational Medicine, Toxicology and Public Health, University-Hospital of Padova, Via Falloppio 50, 35128 Padova, Italy
e-mail: santodavide.ferrara@unipd.it

G.A. Norelli
Department of Health Sciences, Forensic Sciences Section, Institute of Legal Medicine, University of Florence, Largo Brambilla 3, 50134 Florence, Italy
e-mail: ganorelli@unifi.it

R. Zoia
Department of Health and Biomedical Sciences, Section of Legal Medicine, University of Milan, Via Luigi Mangiagalli 37, 20133 Milano, Italy
e-mail: riccardo.zoia@unimi.it

S.D. Ferrara et al. (eds.), *Personal Injury and Damage Ascertainment under Civil Law*, DOI 10.1007/978-3-319-29812-2_2

The strange flirtation between "reality and the impossible," precisely that of the postmodern era, brings us back to the celebrated phrases of two thinkers who have considerably influenced Western culture.

One, circular, incontestable, and insidious, is from Hegel: "what is real is rational, what is rational is real." The other, ineffable as it is elusive, is from Lacan: "The real is the impossible." Taken individually they leave one perplexed. In relation to the first, an attempt has been made and continues to be made to fashion a "sense" of life and events that is mirrored in a solidity that appertains to time and its securities—with tradition and with common sense. It answers a deep need for harmonization, both individual and collective.

The other gives voice to the unexpected that manifests itself continuously in our lives, which can render life a marvel, although this is not often the case.

In particular, in recent years, one has been subjected to the dual pressure of a rationalized world reduced to manageable and imaginable figures, in programmatic plans on the one hand, and, on the other, to a continuous form of "impossible bubbles" that rupture such plans. The unexpected is around the corner, but, as such, we know neither how nor when it will manifest itself, on the condition that it will do so in the end. The "real is the impossible" even when it is institutionalized, following the figure of the inexplicable. As if to say that one does not understand that such an occurrence is perhaps unacceptable, and yet it occurs, shuffling the cards of a game which is in itself "real."

Rationality and the impossible are involved in a continuous flirtation with one another. Thus, the rational impossible will give place to the irrational impossible that is life itself, of which in the end one knows very little. We know that it is and we traverse it with love and apprehension, as in a dream. What is required of us, in the challenge of accelerating events, is a great degree of elasticity between rationality and openness to the new, without defending the first at all costs or fearing the second. It is up to us to interpret the patterns which make up the kaleidoscope of the world, with common sense and the ability to invent new solutions to new problems, which is after all the weapon that over the millennia man has used in the face of every impossible challenge.

Real and impossible, never a fatal "flirtation" in which the systematic and holistic approach of the bio-medicolegal sciences is included, in the scientific search for innovation and education, as well as in the assessment and evaluation of personal injury and the related damage.

The growing need to resort to medicolegal services, both in relation to issues of harmfulness regarding individuals or the community and those related to medical malpractice, confirms the shared opportunity for the recognition of an international dimension (and not only) of legal medicine, to be pursued through a process of unification of the characteristics specific to its specialization; for this reason it is necessary to carry out a critical review of the operational model adopted so far, on the basis that the increasing complexity of the tasks and functions of legal medicine implies the need to restrict medicolegal activity to those who provide proof of specific skills and competencies.

To this end a common model of specialist expertise must be sought, with a common characterization in each country, analogously to that of forensic pathology, toxicology, genetics, or psychopathology.

The reference is to what might be termed general legal medicine, including that area defined by many as clinical legal medicine, which should be aimed at the consideration of personal injury in the various juridical areas (criminal, civil, public health) as well as the most specific aspects of those circumstances that the damage itself may determine (such as professional liability) in addition to the assessment of causality. Belonging essentially to that part of the forensic disciplines that, in the absence of a precise systematization and specialized denomination useful for identifying the content with precision, comes to be considered as a sort of "no man's land," which everyone, therefore, for various reasons, can sometimes inappropriately, represent.

Considering the national legislation, by way of example and thus incompletely, although in a manner sufficient to grasp the dimension of the issue within which it is called to operate, one observes straightaway how the organizational model is distorted in each individual country, thereby conditioning, in fact, the diversity that seems to permeate the medicolegal component of culture and activity. This diversity, however, is perhaps more apparent than real, since one can find, at the international level, a kind of common denominator for every specialized expertise of a medicolegal nature, aimed at the expression of a final product (as it is for pathology, toxicology, psychopathology, the odontology/forensics), applicable to every level and adaptable to the persistent evaluative differences that emanate from individual international laws.

This, moreover, is what has largely already been achieved and continues to be achieved ever more effectively, for other forensic disciplines of a more strictly biological matrix: for which the search for shared organizational and operational methods in general is the rule and has permitted the promotion of methodological guidelines which have provided a substantial unity to the subject, although maintaining, in the individual operating models, the diversity and individuality that emanate from the different national laws. Such an experience, moreover, cannot be considered foreign to the intentions of the International Academy of Legal Medicine (IALM), which has already moved in this direction by developing guidelines regarding the approach to cases of malpractice, in the same way as for medicolegal ascertainment in injuries, also due to distortion trauma of the cervical spine, and for psychic and existential damages.

A synoptic table (Table 2.1), partial and for merely illustrative purposes, however, seems useful in order to define the aforementioned preconditions in some European countries.

There can be no doubt that the scientific and cultural base of those more closely biological disciplines of the forensic matrix has for a long time been, in the broadest sense, the expression of the same language, inspired by guidelines and international protocols and supported by common and shared intentions. This is a demonstration of the fact that in each medicolegal discipline there can exist a unitary model, derived from the characteristics of the datum and the methodology useful for

Table 2.1 Synoptic preconditions

France	United Kingdom	Germany	Spain
Permanent functional deficit (*déficit fonctionnel permanent*) "the reduction of stability of physical, psycho-sensorial or intellectual potential deriving from damage to anatomical-physiological integrity, medically objectifiable and appreciable from an adequate clinical examination completed by appropriate additional studies, in addition to painful phenomena and the psychological impact normally associated and described in everyday life" It is expressed as a percentage on a scale from 1 to 100% in which each appeal court assigns a monetary value as an increasing function of the rate of disability and a decreasing one according to the age of the victim – Damage to the quality of life (*pré judices d'agrément*) compensates the suffering arising from the inability to practice specific future activities/sports, arising from the loss of smell and the ability to walk, to procreate, to carry weights, etc. – Permanent aesthetic damage (*préjudices esthétique*)	*General Damages* represent the main item of nonpecuniary losses and include damage relating to pain/suffering ("*pain and suffering*") and impaired quality of life ("*loss of amenity*"). They are expressed in a lump sum, without categorization, on the basis of the previous judgments For the calculation various factors are considered, such as the age of the injured party, sex, preexisting health condition, and effects on social life, such as the inability to play sports or engage in other pastimes, the loss of one of the five senses, the impairment of sex life, marriage prospects, vacations, etc. [The Judicial Studies Board Guidelines for each injury report a specific range of compensatory amounts for reference purposes, including both "pain and suffering" ("moral damage" in its broadest sense) as well as any other potential item of "nonpecuniary" damage] – Loss of congenial employment Specific item of damage constituted by the possibility that the injured loses, as a	*Schmerzensgeld* comprehensive figure of the "nonpecuniary" damage, to which are traced all the consequences, in terms of loss of income, of the accident In quantifying the Schmerzensgeld, the judge must take into account the followings. – The severity of the injuries – The age of the victim – The intensity of the pain – The loss of the possibility to practice hobbies or recreational activities – Possible changes in personality – The loss of a sense – Psychological consequences (anxiety, depression, etc.) – Loss of marriage prospects or sentimental relationships – Loss of the professional possibilities and earning capacity (further to the effective pecuniary loss) – The possibility, unpredictable at the time of the sentence, of future aftereffects – The significance of a preexisting damage – Factors dependent on those responsible for the damage (a) The degree of fault or intent (ordinary negligence involves a lower amount of	Permanent invalidity (*Incapacidad permanente*), with reference to *daño corporal* or "any impairment of the psychophysical integrity of the individual that interferes or threatens the health of the injured party, both organically and functionally" This is evaluated on the basis of the Baremo: it provides, firstly, the establishment of a base point, defined as *Indemnización básica*, which considers – Physical or functional sequelae of injury, such as limited mobility, loss of function, amputations, persistent pain, etc., together with the connected psychological-moral consequences (the table provides a scale of 0–100 invalidity points for each impairment with a range of possible oscillation of about 8 points) – Aesthetic damage, specifically assessed on its own with a scale of 1–50 points The quantification of the economic base point will depend on the number of points of invalidity and the age of the injured

(continued)

Table 2.1 (continued)

France	United Kingdom	Germany	Spain
– Damage to sexual function (*préjudice sexuel*) – Damage to the possibility of establishing a family (*préjudice d'établissement*) loss of hope and the opportunity to practice a normal project of family life (get married, start a family, raise children, etc.) due to the severity of the disability – Damage connected to evolving pathologies (*préjudices liés à des pathologies é volutives*) such as the reduction in life expectancy of a person infected by HIV – Permanent exceptional disability (*pré judices permanents exceptionnels*)	result of the accident, rewarding and fulfilling employment – Loss of marriage prospects This is not an item of damage in its own right but is evaluated as an increment the compensation of general damages (for impaired quality of life), and damage to the reproductive organs has a specific item in the JSB guidelines	compensation than that involving malicious intent) (b) His/her economic level (a civil lawsuit must not compromise excessively the economic state of the responsible party) (c) The potential degree of kinship between tortfeasor and the injured party (a wife suing her husband will see a reduction of compensation) (d) Delayed payment (e.g., by promoting useless legal actions and remedies) The social condition of the injured party has no significance	Besides the base point, a further item of damage to be calculated in the compensation of the *daño corporal* are the so-called factors of correction (*Factores de corrección*): additional amounts of damage are established (encroaching into pecuniary compensation) based on the net loss of income of the injured party and of particular circumstances related to impairments (e.g., the need for assistance from a third person, transportation costs, costs for medicine and rehabilitation, moral damages suffered by the relatives, cost of adapting homes or vehicles, etc.)

acquiring it, diversifying only its model of application, which must necessarily take its inspiration from the single national precept.

And it is in such a sense, in our view, that the term "holistic" should be interpreted, for a methodology to be shared at the international level and also to be pursued for general legal medicine, not only in terms of professionalism but also in terms of research and teaching, so as to arrive at a body of subjects on which it can develop the comparison, in full respect of the rules that guide scientific research; and for postgraduate training, a highly individualized professional specialization is outlined for general legal medicine, as has long been the case for other bio-medicolegal and forensic disciplines.

In considering the complex issue of the medical approach to factors of damage in humans, only at the beginning of the discussion on some essential aspects of this topic, it is very important to point out that the concept of personal damage is a reason for further investigation and medical research in every field of scientific study on individuality; the study of humans, in all their conditions as single individuals, is a type of analysis that, in addition to the specialized aspects of clinics, conceives of a person as a psychologically and physically unitary and inseparable entity, with their components and within their cultural and social context. This is a prevalent object of medical science derived from the contemporary orientation of research and widely shared by the scientific community.

The concept of prognosis itself ("quoad vitam" or "quoad valetudinem") clearly represents a technical parameter that constantly shapes, even and particularly at the present time, the methods of analysis and the meaning of the results of applied biomedical science studies, the issues of clinical indication for medical treatment, and all scientific studies aimed at human biological knowledge required to deal with human health and to preserve it as much as possible, in addition to every line of research assessing the cost-benefit ratio of different treatments.

These concepts represent, when considered in the specialized study of forensic medicine (analysis of a person as a complex but unitary psychological and physical entity by the law), an essential foundation of the bio-medicolegal disciplines since their earliest origin and are constantly emphasized in the present time.

In different systems, "legal and forensic medicine" research and the study of personal damage have always considered, of course, the point of view of civil law; in all its utterances, the law provides traces of a path that becomes due reference for forensic medicine; nonetheless, medicolegal studies have sometimes inspired jurisprudence in critical steps of its history. They have always considered as an essential line of their complicated evolution the aspiration to obtain a representation of human reality as complete as possible while being aware that neither constant reproducibility nor unconditioned predictability belongs to human reality. These assumptions, today shaping many directions of applied research within the whole of contemporary medicine, have always been valid, even in the medicolegal sciences.

In damage analysis, the holistic view of a person represents the awareness for which a unit does not simply derive from the sum of parts but is, rather, a complex ensemble requiring interpretation and medical representation for legal application purposes.

According to a purely medical view, compensation for personal damage could be defined as a factually unattainable goal; the field linking biomedical knowledge and law is "legal and forensic medicine," whose tasks are the identification of benchmarks in the dynamics of scientific knowledge and the supply of representational tools to better approach the target.

Thus, the field of scientific medicolegal research in its section related to the assessment of personal damage needs to be enhanced, restarted, and supported to find more appropriate and comparable assessment tools (Table 2.2).

Regardless of any legal systems of reference, the conceptually difficult, but essential, problem for a medicolegal consideration is the object of medical appreciation of personal damage. This means the identification of the fields of research and study that must be addressed in order to obtain necessary parameters for the detection of personal damage. An issue predominantly qualifying this cultural and technical theme, it requires a definite clarification and is even, in medical terms, independent from legal jurisdictions. Namely, it is a medical problem that then must contribute and adapt itself to different legal systems. In fact, in a holistic

Table 2.2 Scientific medicolegal research assessment and personal damage

Personal damage as the focus of contemporary medical research			
EBM			
A person as a complex and unitary system		A person in the holistic concept	
Prognosis	Clinical indications	Benefit-cost ratio	Treatment of non-amendable conditions
Medicolegal research			

approach to the assessment of personal damage, it firstly becomes important to identify components and methods for understanding a person in their individuality in the deepest and most complete way.

Evidence-based medicine provided a systemic cultural contribution that, on the one hand, dramatically transformed the categories of certainty and probability in human biology and, on the other hand, allowed us to go into the investigation of the components of a person that, though not completely unexplored, had been surveyed with a criteria of analysis not functional to a medicolegal application, i.e., search for evidence and degree of data reliability. Further, it allowed a better definition of the external components and factors influencing a person considered as an anatomical and physiological entity in their life context.

The medical contribution to compensation for personal damage cannot pursue a different direction from that of the scientific approach and the related tools typical of general medicine investigation. This means that medicolegal studies have no technical and cultural alternatives to those of looking for the deepest and most complete representation of the components of a person.

It is a central orientation, representing the foundation of developing medicolegal research guidelines on personal damage: historically, they could also influence law and jurisprudence, and in the future they must play an increasingly central role in keeping pace with the times and in enhancing the lines of scientific research on personal damage (Table 2.3).

Thus, in the field of medicolegal research about personal damage and the tools for its evaluation and representation, dignity and autonomy do exist: it can be said they go beyond and are independent of the issues of legal systems.

The first consequence of these fundamental considerations is the incompatibility of a model on indemnity for all parameters concerning the medical assessment of personal damage in civil reimbursement. Each indemnity system is based on parameters of medical quantification and of representation of human functions, as well as of the measurement of anatomical and physiological components, which are conventional, fixed, preordained, and invariable, i.e., in contrast with the definition itself of "personal damage" in its broadest and harmonious medical meaning. In any case, although the purpose of a medical ascertainment is to arrive at a correct diagnosis, the medicolegal aim, unlike that of clinical medicine, focuses on distinguishing, among the infirmities, those of a spontaneous nature from others that are not. Within the latter, regarding the component of damage that is relevant for our purposes, it is sometimes necessary to emphasize infirmities that would be

Table 2.3 Components of personal damage

Components of personal damage
Highlighted data from general medical research
↓
Person/environment relation
Medicolegal research
Application of significance and quality of data as a proof
Integral perception of a person

marginal in clinical terms (e.g., modest aesthetic impairments) or to consider, in addition to the need to take into account the possible competition of the infirmities (spontaneous or not), the significance of the resulting impairment on the various activities of the person (lucrative and non-lucrative).

In the ascertainment methodology lies the "core" of what was defined as the holistic perspective of medicolegal action, in the sense that the methodology of the ascertainment must move from the consideration that each type of injury deserves to be collected and defined, not limiting itself to the evaluative contingency in which one finds oneself operating. In other words, and without limitation, any medicolegal report should include a detailed description of the injury and disability including data on, their potential usefulness and characteristics of pain (measured according to a defined scale) or discomfort that come with injury or the quality of life, irrespective of the consideration that the single legislation reserves to them, as elements of damage deserving of a specific value (as is the case, e.g., in France) or to be considered within other predictions of a compensatory valence (as is the case, e.g., in Italy), where the moral component and the existential are not equipped with autonomous characteristics of damage but are to be encompassed within extra-patrimonial biological damage.

The expression of an ascertainment methodology shared at the international level appears to be, furthermore, the interpretive key for a unique model of culture and scientificity that gives life to the medicolegal tradition, redirecting it toward a typified specialist profession, which does not only have to compete as a very professional operation but also where education and scientific research are the appropriate apex, like any other discipline within science, reserving for them a supranational level in terms of role and interest.

The maximum objectivization in the collection of the data and the highest reproducibility in its utilization ensure the scientific nature of the subject as an essential prerequisite to systematic research on the subject and the ability to define rules, necessary for a correct diagnosis as well as for the educational standardization of practices; having as its final aim the closing of a complex circle, for which one arrives at the training of professionals through the definition of a common methodology, the application defines and qualifies the expertise of the one who is required to apply it.

This line of reasoning, then, can only tend toward the definition of the expert, to be considered as the professional who, beyond self-referentiality or demonstrations of experience, is both the bearer of the recognized title which recognizes him/her as possessor of the method that, based on standardized rules of acquisition of evidence, renders the model of reasoning objective, interpretable according to the scientific definition. The expert, in other words, is so at the time when he/she is able to proceed with the acquisition of the data, according to an ascertainment criteriology that is subject to the shared methodology, in addition to, obviously, being able to proceed to the definitive summary (evaluation of damage). It seems clear that (and this is embodied in one of the major difficulties regarding the transfer from theory to practice of the above premise), according to the indications arising from national regulations, the expert must be formed in reference to the need to translate into the practice of the country of origin that which stems from indications of a supranational character (think, e.g., as regards Italy, the complexity of assessment that is derived, for the same claim, by the intersection of the compensatory regulations of civil liability with that of private insurances and social security).

What is necessary to the state, therefore, is to strive to determine whether there is a common pathway in the training of the expert in general legal medicine, equipped with cultural characteristics, of a scientific and professional nature, helpful in the fulfillment of his/her requisite duties.

The situation, as is known, is quite varied at the international level. Just looking at Europe, one notes that while there is a substantial identity for the forensic disciplines in terms of training elements and programs as regards the most typically biological characterization, one cannot say the same for general legal medicine. In Spain, for example, the preparation on the subject of assessment of personal damage is reserved to an intensification (Valoracion of dano corporal) of the specialization in general legal medicine oriented toward "clinical forensic medicine"; in France there exists a university degree with theoretical course and practical work (120 and 30 h, respectively) in "Réparation juridique du dommage corporel," with diversified paths depending on the activities that should be provided as part of the assessment; in the UK it lies with the individual clinical specialist to draw up the certification, according to which the attorney will measure the claim; in Italy any doctor-surgeon or dentist can prepare certification evaluations, with priority given to the specialist in legal/forensic medicine who follows, moreover, a 4-year course which should render him/her an expert in all forensic disciplines.

It would be appropriate, therefore, for legal medicine to move toward a substantial uniqueness of training and scientific programs, so that, at least at the European level, specialists could be trained who have the quality and qualification of truly professional "experts" in the field of general legal medicine, that is, bearers of that apparatus, complex and structured, of culture, experience, and scientificity that must everywhere be requested of the "Qualified Expert" for each medical discipline.

General legal medicine, then, will finally be able to provide a culture of "evidence," like any other sister discipline, specifically to be understood as the ability to render objective any given particular, acquired according to a specific ascertainment methodology, subject to unambiguous interpretation on the level of causality, measurable in terms of statistical occurrence and, on that of evaluation, with or without the provision, for the latter, of the application of barèmes of reference.

The prevalence of technical guidelines, inspiring the evolution of medical thought in the contemporary age and radically marking the cultural development of sciences applied to the protection of human health (evidence-based medicine), has witnessed the emergence of a prevailing direction: acquisition of data that aims, in a prospective and controlled way, at exploring and verifying what operational direction, for each case with its own characteristics, is more correct so as to preserve the utmost individual integrity, prevent factors of damage, and assess the quality of life in consideration of every personal physiological and pathological aspect.

Awareness of the complexity of a system such as a "person," i.e., an entity with no possible comparison in nature, has more and more increased. On this basis, the holistic view confirms itself as the very essence of the principles to be proposed so that the study of any person by "legal and forensic medicine" be complete and responsive to contemporary demands; these have shown that sectoralization can only be a step aimed at contributing to global value acquisitions, which can then be referred to people according to their individual characteristics.

It is not coincidental that all multidisciplinary scientific production of medical clinical research continuously urges us to understand the biological and psychological interconnections of the human being in the diagnostic, therapeutic, rehabilitative, and prognostic aspects in each sector of study and investigation, on the lookout for "evidence" in medicine. Evidence constantly refers to principles such as "quality of life index," "social relations," "impairing impact," "functional disability," and so on, which urgently demand objects of directed study and of medicolegal assessment and research. The bio-medicolegal sciences themselves require a deep commitment toward innovation. If we accept as an applicative tool the standardization of preestablished parameters (as occurs in most indemnity fields) that includes a line of demarcation and evaluation limits as well as detailed elements of representation, the need to represent a strictly individual reality, as unique and complex as the aims of the general clinician studies in a holistic perspective are, will fail.

There is no doubt that orienting the system of compensation for personal damage in public liability toward parameters similar to those of indemnity expresses the will to make social systems as predictable and controlled as possible, especially from the economic perspective. Though being admissible parameters with valid reasons, they should not influence medical thinking, both in its research profiles and its way of self-development and practical application.

Distinctly, notwithstanding the need for a description of the elements defining the idea of personal damage in due public liability, even the etymology of the term expresses its more typical meaning starting from the medical lexicon [sarcio (latin) = heal, get back in shape; and in the broadest sense = compensation, mending; "etenim sarcire est integrum facere," S.P. Festo in De verborum significatione].

In a medical and, in particular, medicolegal perspective, this premise is essential as a basis of the meaning of research, the praxis regarding personal damage, and the objective of its assessment. We are witnesses to the justifiable fact that, in many legal systems, in terms of a cash settlement for damage, there is an attempt to consider fixed parameters that are capable of interpreting a medical assessment in a predictable and consistent way; however, this aspect should not affect any medical configuration of the assessment, i.e., the object of medicolegal research and the evaluation of an individual for compensation.

When, as in any compensation, the different aspects of human pathology are beforehand established in their method of quantification, the perspective of personal and individual reality no doubt acquires a subordinate value, and even its study is limited within determined boundaries. On the contrary, when the objectives of medical study and assessment are issues such as reparative compensation and the restoration of a preexisting reality, albeit evolutionary, then the perspectives of scientific analysis completely overlap those of all biological and clinical research that cannot compromise on invariably considering human reality as primarily unique and individual. This is the only fundamental medical principle that can support the concept of assessing personal damage in relation to compensation.

The scientific content of the analysis, object of a specific professionalism, should include and describe: (a) the content and purpose of the ascertainment; (b) the methodology useful and necessary for the performance of said ascertainment.

As regards the first aspect, in general terms it can be said that in every country, regardless of the relevant legislation, general legal medicine, in particular regarding the model of damage assessment, identifies itself through conditions not dissimilar from one another, although combined according to different modalities that are essentially represented by the functional-anatomical basis of the infirmity, the consequences of which reverberate on the various aspects of everyday life understood both in terms of the expressivity common to everybody and of that of the individual or, finally, in the context of interpersonal relationships. Everywhere, in fact, the damage to be assessed seems to express itself in similar categories, which can be more or less emphasized according to the relevant regulations, admitted to or excluded from compensation or indemnity, however, in a model of professional practice, which is uniquely connoted. Whether it is called Déficit Fonctionnel Permanent, General Damage, Schmerzensgeld, Incapacidad Permanente, or Danno Biologico or considered in a descriptive form or anchored to barèmes of reference, the model is always inspired by a "biological" component of damage (extra-patrimonial or, however, denominated) to which must correspond an economic service (indemnity and/or compensation) supplemented by expressions characterizing the individuality of the particular case (existential component, moral component, etc.) and in relation to which no implication concerning the ability of the injured party to produce income is considered. Alongside this form of damage, the other component is identified, by contrast measured in relation to the earning capacity of the person and the past and future costs, the need for which has been induced by the injury (pecuniary or, however, denominated).

It seems implicit, then, that the forensic pathologist, by necessity equipped with a profound knowledge of the doctrinal bases of the discipline, must be able to move within the ascertainment of causality between the harmful event and the relevant antecedent (human or work related) provided that the consideration of the infirmity and its corresponding assessment cannot be separated from its etiopathogenesis. This is true regardless of the evaluation system in which one operates, given that, whether it is a system of subjective liability or no fault, the traceability or lack thereof of the event and of the consequent damage to a specific genesis must always and everywhere be ascertained. The nature of the bodily damage, has to be demonstrated in medico-legal terms for the proper conclusion of the ascertainment. This is what makes and marks the difference between the medicolegal and the clinical ascertainment.

The idea of personalization of damage is stated in different legal systems in an approximately schematic way. In numerous systems it is considered as an asset, i.e., related to criteria of adapting a compensation amount to the peculiarities of a person. Clinically, it is the concept that undoubtedly shapes the medical approach toward a deep understanding of how and to what extent a person changed, or more precisely that *particular* person, on account of an unfair event. The medical assessment of personal damage as part of compensation in public liability can only be based on the complex personal and individual analysis. This analysis must derive from a repeatable method and use shared and motivated parameters while being based on the need to understand a reality that is individual and therefore unique.

These are criteria of medicolegal clinics to be established just before considering their practical application.

In this field, independence of medical knowledge and action is certainly not a simple issue, considering that in this area different legal elements are implied: it is no coincidence that it is always important to declare if there is a principal or any interest at stake in relation to one's work in the field of personal damage. However, true scientific research on the inspection and evaluation of damage can only be wide ranging in order to obtain substantive knowledge of all clinical aspects that may affect the injured person; it is essential to further identify the methods implied in formulating judgments, which may depend on legal or political elements external to medical research (Table 2.4).

From the history of medicolegal doctrine, we clearly derive the categories describing individual offense: the factors determining personal damage. They are the outline for progressive study in the field of legal medicine: (1) *cause of injury*, (2) *injury*, and (3) *impairment*, requiring a qualitative specification.

Preliminary elements are cause of damage (external etiological factor capable of acting in a non-purposive way on human biological structure) and injury (detrimental modification of human physical and mental state expressed by the effects of the damaging cause); the study of these factors can be considered methodologically comparable to the general parameters of medicolegal research and assessment.

In the logic of compensation, the study of "impairment"—temporary and permanent—represents the most difficult field because it involves, unlike all indemnity systems, dealing with each single case for the systematic representation of a person as an individual damaged entity.

Table 2.4 Damage indemnification and compensation

Indemnification	Compensation
Indemnity and private insurance	Assessment of personal damage
Fixed parameters	Personalization
System rigidity	Individual evaluation
Impairment TABLES	Indicative barèmes

In the context of the biomedical sciences, the paramount goal of legal medicine is "to discover the truth and state the justice," this being achieved by applying proper, particular "systematics." This, defined as "methodology of ascertainment" and "criteriology of evaluation," aims at acquisition of the objectivity of the datum and its translation into proof, if possessing the characteristics of evidence and irrefutability; epi-critical interpretation, aiming for evaluative conclusions of a diverse nature; and finality. "Systematics" capable of encompassing and unifying multiple budding, whose gradual innovation and sometimes pervasive extension has led to the generation, development, and definitive consolidation of disciplines such as forensic pathology, forensic genetics, forensic toxicology, forensic psychopathology, criminology, and forensic anthropology, as well as that of many other sectors of study, to in-depth investigation, which have yet to be consolidated in further disciplines. This tumultuous disciplinary budding process has led to a loss of unitariness in medicolegal knowledge, with an incurrent risk of a fall into an irreversible fragmentation and the impoverishment of the said knowledge, no longer nourished by cultural products of high interdisciplinary value. It is evident, in fact, that knowledge is enriched not through highly specialized sophistication but also, and above all, through interdisciplinarity.

The preservation of unitariness and the enhancement of the value of evidence in bio-medicolegal knowledge depend upon the implementation of quality systems, based on continuous education, shared guidelines and protocols, internal quality control, and proficiency testing systems, which, in turn, aim at the certification and the accreditation of institutions and individual professionals. The realization of this long-standing process finds a rational foundation in a context of a broad "critical mass," such as that existing in the international medicolegal community and, in particular, in the European one, characterized by a cultural affinity, yet differentiated in its structural, organizational, functional, and operative features, where interdisciplinary and supranational innovations may lead to a wide methodological and criteriological harmony.

Observing some of the main general fields of applied research in biomedical sciences, we can find a perfect accord with the areas required in relation to medicolegal research when studying personal damage.

Briefly, we can identify research on (1) biological and clinical aspects relating to the causes of damage (e.g., cellular changes following external stimuli, effects of traumatic factors on the anatomical components under all possible conditions, etc.); (2) clinical circumstances that require mastery of biometric knowledge (e.g., duration of survival related to an impaired context, aspects of deterioration in

Table 2.5 Determinants of personal damage

Determinants of personal damage		
		Impairment
Cause of injury	Injury	Temporary and/or permanent
Personalization research		
Identify categories representative of a person	Optimize medical examination	Study for standardization and repeatability of criteria of medical assessment

respect to a therapy, etc.); and (3) relevant factors of the detrimental individual changes, static or developing (link between psyche and soma, individual pathological changes compared to a preexisting personal condition, etc.).

All these areas should adopt scientific work for the evaluation of a person's impairment in a more pragmatic way than ever before (Table 2.5).

Therefore, there is an essential reason for clarification, which is an unequivocal prerequisite to any further introductory consideration.

Which personal categories can interest the medicolegal activity and are to be studied in order to obtain an assessment on impairment with the purpose of repairing damages? This is a key element for which medicine has a triple role. (a) Identify what, according to its knowledge, is of essential importance in the representation of a person: this has a further function of social and political contribution and is a source of inspiration for legal development. (b) Identify, understand, and update the methods of investigation on humans. (c) Search for shared methods and criteria to make consistent and repeatable assessments.

It is obvious that all possible medical components of personal damage provide a perspective of research and assessment. It is also true that the patrimonial aspects of a negative personal impact of an injury and impairment, according to the medicolegal point of view, necessarily originate from an assessment based on the comparison between a biological reality detrimentally changed and monetary consequences.

A principle of the medicolegal assessment of emerging damage consists in considering the necessity and justification of costs (individual, institutional, or social) already incurred or to be incurred in the future, in agreement with a clinical judgment of adequacy with respect to market parameters or to the political and social criteria of healthcare organization.

The damage due to loss of profit also needs a clinical assessment customized according to a real and present business activity, comparable to concrete economic parameters and current income paradigms; this is accomplished according to legal principles common in most national laws whose greater or minor evolution of social systems of compensation is the variable resource for a complete consideration for compensation. In this area, the medicolegal task is an extremely delicate issue even for those aspects that can be defined as "prospective." It coincides with the importance of assessing from a medico-legal point of view the limitation of future resources rather than of current ones, an assessment which is particularly difficult but fundamental in the case of young (i.e. unemployed subjects), of permanent limitations in the attitude to profitable activities different from the actual practice carried out according to a biological and cultural individual reality. This is because such an assessment is expressed according to concrete employment prospects of a socioeconomic reality, to the reduction or loss of a prospective increased income even in the same productive sector, due to biomedical interruption or limitation of applicable physiological resources.

All aspects are based on the solely medicolegal perception and assessment of the individual reality of a person in their patrimonial components.

But the most complex field in terms of scientific and applicative structures relates to nonpecuniary damage. And the interest and paroxysm from most political and legal systems do confirm it. All these functions and categories have an evident impact on present and future legal, political, and social systems. In fact, as already mentioned, one of the most acute problems constantly posed by the law on the international scene of the Western world is precisely that concerning the "totality" of indemnity in relation to personal damage in case of offense, a problem that can even have macroeconomic implications and for which medicolegal involvement plays a necessary and indispensable scientific role.

The route traced within the last 50 years of Western world history by nonpecuniary damage, especially in some countries, is precisely represented by the following evolutionary line: the attempt to identify points of convergence between legal configuration and the increment in knowledge proposed by biological sciences in the understanding of a person as a system.

As for the Italian experience, "biological damage"—in the meaning of devaluing a person in their integrity, i.e., as a global and unique entirety in their static and dynamic components—was at first a disturbing concept, problematic to implement, but certainly carrying developments which consider a concept of human beings more appropriate to a medical vision related to current and future occurrences.

Medicolegal research and its deriving thought are marked and associated with such a development in a qualifying and unquestionable way. In this scientific and cultural dynamic, the most relevant issue was the real medical forensic function assumed by the medicolegal acquisitions: a progressive improvement in knowledge and principles adding to and pushing for jurisprudential orientations that may be more consistent and relevant to a reality and that may increase the basics of legal dynamism as a parameter of representation and of social organization.

It is possible, to all intents and purposes, to define the scientific-legal progress as well as the applicable results of biomedical and anthropological social research as a collective improvement. And there is evidence of the parallel evolution of general scientific aspects, medicolegal contribution, and jurisprudence development, namely, in the fact that most Western legal systems have recognized human physical and psychological integrity itself as an indemnifiable category. It is a fact accepted by the majority. Finding ways to standardize assessment is an important objective. However, one principle is essential: the fundamental aspect of personal damage is, first, to identify how and to what extent an individuals' anatomical, physiological, psychological, and physical reality has changed temporarily and permanently, considered in itself, even irrespective of all aspects of its relationship with the world, i.e., in a static aspect. This is the first nucleus expressing the need for a holistic conception. Its roots originated from the history of medicolegal research and reached us: a person should not be considered as a collection of separate parts but as a complex unit that cannot be partitioned and that is the result of articulated components. All barèmes for indemnity purposes oriented to this result show a clear approach for which a unit is a set of interactive features that go beyond mathematical boundaries and that must always be modulated by a competent medical contribution: they can never have absolute value (as it could be in a compensation) but can be the basis of an assessment of the static and average reduction of psychophysical integrity as an expression of general medical knowledge. For this reason they are but guidelines and should be considered in dynamic terms over time (in parallel with changes in medical knowledge); it is a task of medicolegal research to establish reference values which are variable, with clinical knowledge, scientific acquisition, and evolution of human sciences.

The objective of medicolegal research is to find some common points on the basis of controlled observational results to identify levels of *static reduction* of various human components working as starting points for an assessment. Aiming at an international homogeneous reference points is surely correct, although, in a comprehensive and holistic vision of a person, absolute indications of graduation whose scientific justification is not recognizable are clearly inadequate. Therefore, the analysis must be based on wide, compared, and flexible epidemiological and ergonomic evaluations in order to understand what reference in the quantification of a psychophysical reduction can work as the most relevant and shared assessment indicator. This is certainly based on parameters that can be proposed in a repeatable manner, influenced by the analysis of all anatomical, functional, mechanical, metabolic, and physical variables, in full analogy with criteria of research in any field of medical sciences.

Further, there occurs the most delicate problem regarding *dynamic components* for which an even more individual expression is needed. On this aspect the most complex conceptual differences are observed, which are often influenced by legal reasons and by what is implied in economic terms while asserting them. This is inevitably relevant because it is linked to social and economic contexts, to the organization of the collective welfare system, and to the value of money and its purchasing power, but it should not paradoxically affect the principle of representation of the biological reality of a person.

If the components actually affecting the personalization of an impairment of mental and physical integrity are considered from a medicolegal point of view, it becomes evident that, from the clinical side, all preconditions for their detection are given. Legal and forensic medicine must reaffirm and always bear them in mind while approaching the assessment of personal damage. The particular political and legal systems of different nations may decide to make them subjects of compensation, or not, as well as to vary their criteria: what concerns medicine is recalling their existence, studying their methods of assessment and quantification standards, and always considering them as methodical principles and obligations of a correct and complete clinical assessment.

The first concerns modifying the static aspects according to age, gender, and preexisting conditions. This is part of the "biological component" of a person in terms of everything pertaining to their being. It is the first real moment of customization compared to quantifying directions based on a static arrangement. What matters here are all individual physiological and pathological variables, the essential foundation of a global vision of a person from the clinical-functional perspective. One of the goals of making the international systems of assessment homogeneous is to understand whether the reproductive and sexual functions and the aesthetic component of a given impairment are to be considered as separate domains of quantification rather than components of a medical assessment always included in the biological psychophysical integrity of a person.

When a holistic orientation is accepted as the foundation of the medicolegal approach in personal damage, both sexual and aesthetic components are no doubt regarded as full components of the biological reality of humans and thus evaluated with respect to their integrity and with full rights as components of a complex unit. Therefore, they undergo all of the peculiarities of each single component that needs to be varied according to the person.

The second are the existential, i.e., dynamic relational, components specific of a person derived from psychophysical impairment. Research on nonpecuniary components of humans, which goes beyond the static or dynamic psychophysical impairment and their role in compensation, has prompted important areas of investigation. In history, limitations in personal fulfillment within the extra-employment environment were considered even in nonmedical studies, and it is an issue that for the purposes of compensation clearly represents the need to consider a person in global terms. Soon a principle was set by which, when negative effects on these functions are determined by an unfair anatomic-physiological lesion, forensic skills are called upon to express themselves and are required for data acquisition, modulation of judgment, qualification, and quantification of the phenomenon. This is a matter in complete harmony with the cited epistemological and cognitive orientations of medicine. It is a complicated theme with potential fragile elements. For this reason certain systems may not accept it or subject it only to certain requirements.

The problem concerning proof, economic consideration, and areas of application can also be beyond medical competence. However, it is important to note that when an impairment of the psychophysical integrity gives rise to these circumstances, the role of a medicolegal assessment is unavoidable. Even this sector of medicolegal research should be enhanced, as it is a task of forensic medicine to identify cases in which it truly realizes itself, the best tools of description and graduation as well as shared benchmarks. Similarly, it can be said of the study of pain, suffering, and adaptation to new conditions as components of a harmful pathological route. These are categories of study and representation in broad areas of algological, pain management and subjective variation research that, deepening its individual psychobiological mechanisms, proposes ways of inquiry that go through the interactions among metabolic processes, psychodynamic changes, cultural and historical, as well as those linked to relational subjects.

The result is a scenario that seems to consist of several components of a person, but they are all connected by a common denominator: human health. This is the central value that medicine protects and that “legal and forensic medicine” should help to affirm as a key element in personal damage indemnification while constantly studying the tools for a repeatable evaluation of impairment due to an unfair act.

All of the above confirms that, among all medical sciences, forensic medicine is the proper and specific field of analysis, research, and operations of the sector. The indisputable interface with law and jurisprudence (in terms of mutual influence) shows what knowledge and training are specific and indispensable for this purpose. Therefore, “legal and forensic medicine” is the essential specialized field that can guarantee complete knowledge, scientific assumptions, methodological analysis, and foundations for comparability of data and social justice.

The fundamentals of any national positive law of reference are clearly an insuperable standard. In international comparison and knowledge exchange, this has long been a limit. Modern medicine must make knowledge a public good and be a leader of a progressive unity of paths whose central need is deep knowledge of human psychobiological reality. For the abovementioned reasons, forensic medicine is the field of choice for this route that is mainly scientific and whose aim is to stimulate and contribute to the legal intent of compensation.

The peculiarity of medicolegal training, culture, and research derives from the systematic framework of realization of the paths directed to the modulation of biological knowledge with concepts of positive law in the field of compensation to personal damage.

This is an important reason to consider and to which direct aims of training, international harmonization, exchange, and discussion are essential to an adequate future of biomedical forensic sciences and their role as social contributors.

All this goes together with the most rigorous independence of biomedical forensic research in fields of study that, due to their articulation, characteristics and effects are inevitably destined to include relevant interests, clearly involving organizational and economic-sensitive structures that are qualifying and of a strategic nature in a complex and developing political and social reality.

Namely the modern era, the territory of progress, in which the result is measured objectively on a scale of numerically expressed values. As in the case of the semantic destiny of “talent,” from when the balancing weight of the dish of experience appeared in order to measure it, to when it served to express the exchange *value*, becoming legal tender, before becoming a metaphor and indication of the quality of the invention and the creation. An impervious problem, beginning with the adjudication of who is to provide the definition of quality and competence, is always questionable and evasive of comparative and “imitative” models, rather than “ideological” and “prescriptive” of the goal pursued.

By now the adventure of modernity has ended, and at the beginning of the millennium, one becomes a worried and anxious witness of the transforming world, in which the yearning of the remote past, irredeemably more ideological than ideal, and the dissolution of the peculiarities of each society render the duration of canons and educational programs ephemeral.

The challenge to face is certainly thrilling, since among the mists of a present so confusing and difficult to interpret, it involves drawing maps of a new geography of knowledge, in order to identify the pathways and their destinations, to restore order, aware that there are not, nor can there be glimpsed, prophets of the future, and that, therefore, the coming evolution will be strenuous and exciting. The heir of the tradition is not restorable but it is capable of being rebuilt in renewed value systems, through the foundation of a solid and balanced culture and civilization, of which books will retain the memory of what is destined to be preserved.

Below are listed some general bibliographic sources useful to deepen the issue. They are not reported within the text as they are no cited references.

Bibliography

1. Airey CM, Chell SM, Rigby AS, Tennant A, Connelly JB (2001) The epidemiology of disability and occupation handicap resulting from major traumatic injury. Disabil Rehabil 23:509–515
2. Cazzaniga A (1928) Le basi medico-legali per la stima del danno alla persona da delitto a quasi delitto. SA Istituto Editoriale Scientifico, Milan
3. Fabra M, Stevens A, Merten T (2009) Recommendations for independent medical examinations of PTSD claimants. Versicherungsmedizin 61:111–117
4. Ferrara SD, Baccino E, Bajanowski T, Boscolo-Berto R, Castellano M, De Angel R, Pauliukevičius A, Ricci P, Vanezis P, Vieira DN, Viel G, Villanueva E, EALM Working Group on Medical Malpractice (2013) Malpractice and medical liability. European guidelines on methods of ascertainment and criteria of evaluation. Int J Leg Med 127(3):545–557
5. Ferrara SD, Bajanowski T, Cecchi R, Snenghi R, Case C, Viel G (2010) Bio-medicolegal guidelines and protocols: survey and future perspectives in Europe. Int J Leg Med 124 (4):345–350
6. Ferrara SD, Boscolo Berto R, Viel G (eds) (2013) Malpractice and medical liability—European state of the art and guidelines. Springer, Berlin
7. Ferrara SD, Pfeiffer H (2010) Unitariness, evidence and quality in bio-medicolegal sciences. Int J Leg Med 124(4):343–344
8. Ferrara SD (2013) Medical malpractice and legal medicine. Int J Leg Med 127(3):541–543
9. Gerin C (1953) Medicolegal evaluation of personal physical damage in civil liability. Riv Infort Mal Prof 40:371–424
10. Hureau J (2006) Harmonisation of personal injury compensation in the European Union. Application to medical liability case law. Bull Acad Natl Med 190:725–746
11. Jafari S, Abdollahi M, Saeidnia S (2014) Personalized medicine: a confluence of traditional and contemporary medicine. Altern Ther Health Med 20(5):31–40
12. Newmann S, Collie A, Vogel AP, Kelehr H (2014) The impacts of injury at the individual, community and societal levels: a systematic meta-review. Public Health 128:587–618
13. Norelli GA, Focardi M (2007) La medicina legale e la valutazione olistica del danno alla persona. Riv It Med Leg 2:379–404
14. Tomljenovic A (2014) Holistic approach to human health and disease: life circumstances and inner processing. Coll Antropol 38:787–792
15. Wright BW (2007) The evolution of Rogers' science of unitary beings: 21st century reflections. Nurs Sci Q 20:64–67

Chapter 3
Causal Value and Causal Link

Santo Davide Ferrara

Abstract Following on from an introduction concerning the advisable identical nature of criteria of identification in criminal and civil-tort law contexts and an overview of the evolution of concepts of truth, cause, and causation in the history of philosophy, the chapter examines the current postmodern conception of material causality in medicolegal doctrine, aimed at the identification of the core cause and the reconstruction of the causal nexus.

The theory of the "conditio sine qua non" and its subsumption under scientific laws, which constitute the common denominator for the imputation of the event, are described in detail.

The judicial inquiry and the expert's report, applicable in medicolegal practice of specific causality, are illustrated with particular reference to deductive-nomological and inductive-statistical models, as well as to the necessity of a new "evidentiary regime" for ascertaining personal injury and damage.

3.1 Introduction

Plato, in the Speech of Alcibiades [1], defined love as follows:

Love is the desire to possess the good forever.

And if this is, in general, love, what is it, in those who are in thrall to it, that living tension of the soul, that desirous act called, precisely, love? ... It is to give birth in the beautiful, both with respect to the body and to the soul ... And in truth the desire of love is not for beauty, but rather the desire to generate and give birth within beauty ... *Since generation is that which, in mortal beings, can be non-generated and immortal. And immortality necessarily loves itself, if, according to what has been agreed, love is the desire for eternal possession of the good; and thus the conclusion of the discourse is that* love is also love of immortality.

S.D. Ferrara (✉)
Department of Legal and Occupational Medicine, Toxicology and Public Health, University-Hospital of Padova, Via Falloppio 50, 35128 Padova, Italy
e-mail: santodavide.ferrara@unipd.it

S.D. Ferrara et al. (eds.), *Personal Injury and Damage Ascertainment under Civil Law*, DOI 10.1007/978-3-319-29812-2_3

Aristotle, in *Metaphysics* (I, 1, 982) [2], defined knowledge as a science of principles and first causes.

Of which causes and principles are Knowledge-Science... it is the science of that which is knowable par excellence, namely of principles and causes, because by means of these and from these one knows the rest, and these are not known by means of what is derived from them.

And science, par excellence, and above other subordinates, knows the purpose for which each thing must be implemented. The goal for each thing is its good, and, in general, the highest good of all nature. Science, therefore, is that which speculates on principles and causes, among which are precisely the good and the aim.

Following Plato's conception of "love" and Aristotle's conception of "knowledge-science" and their value in terms of divine unchangeableness and immortality, the following chapter entitled "Casual value and causal link," taken from the previously published monograph on "Malpractice and Medical Liability" [3], is reproduced here.

It deals with a subject vital for the definition and identification of "personal injury and damage," the essential nature of which assumes an indispensability in the methodological and ascertainment process of the existence and specific nature of "personal injury and damage."

An indispensability connected, moreover (according to the conviction of this author), to the advisable identical nature of the approach, namely, the demonstration of the "conditio sine qua non," rather than of the mere principal of "more probable than not." This means that, in the search for evidence in medicine, as an affirmation of "evidence-based medicine," one must not and cannot adopt criteria of identification of diverse causes and causal links and/or related to the diverse penal and civil contexts. Such diversity, belonging to juridical and judiciary protagonists, must be extraneous to the co-protagonists of the biomedical and medicolegal sciences.

3.2 Principles of Truth and Cause

The *principles* of *truth*, *cause*, *causation*, and *causal chains* are deeply rooted in the history of thought, inasmuch as expressive of the ontological need of man to give meaning to his existence. These principles evolved, in correlation with those of certainty and probability, from the naturalistic pre-Socratic school to the psychodynamic conception of Socrates to the rational-idealistic speculation of Plato to the rational-empirical-experimental, material, formal, and efficient conception of Aristotle [4–7]. According to deductive or inductive criteria of certainty or probability of truth, the speculative evolution of causal principles has been influenced by neo-Platonic or neo-Aristotelian contributions, followed by those of the Scholastics, through the certainties of faith and reason of St. Thomas, from post-Renaissance empiricism to "formal and categorical" Kantian rationality, before resulting in positivism and neopositivism [4].

In particular, in light of the Kantian vision [8], causality is a category, such as space and time, applicable to reality, science, and other related disciplines, from medicine to history, ethics, and even politics. The concept of cause is the same in any sphere and dimension of life, and causality is, conversely and for whatever purpose, the means to ascertain the relationship between one event and another.

The inherent values of causation relate to *objectivity*, *regularity*, and *knowableness*.

Reality is conceived as *objective* insofar as it exists independently of individual actions and subjective situations. Reality is such, furthermore, inasmuch as it is *regular*, where the existence of such conditions leads to similar effects in different times and places. Reality is ultimately *knowable* to the extent that the modalities of its occurrence are ascertainable. Even if things are not in themselves knowable, the mode of their way of appearing is, and in accordance with this Kantian axiom, Newton and Einstein search effectively for the modalities of appearance of reality [9].

Nevertheless, the framing of the differences in attributions regarding causation is independent of and transcends the scientific context, to the point of ignoring and excluding it. Therefore, in accordance with Hume [10] and Reichenbach [11], the cause may not be unequivocally proven in a scientific sense, but be the expression of coincidental occurrence and of a practical basis of explanation of reality, such as a reductionist, rather than holistic approach, where the cause involves the understanding of the totality of circumstances in which an event occurs [12]. Therefore, it is also the estimate of the *relative* contribution of each of the possible causal factors, or even the evaluation of the contribution of a specific factor to the totality of significant factors in the causation. So that, with a return to the Aristotelian vision of final causality, in the integral dimension of the teleological approach to the natural order of the Universe, the final search for the cause is the search for the first causes of nature, that is, the search for the *episteme*, capable of comprehending causation and identifying not only the phenomenon but the reason for the occurrence of any event.

From these apparently contradictory assumptions derive concepts of truth and cause and the theories relating to "probability" as the basis of reality, as well as the pre-chosen system, precisely that of the postmodern society of risk [13].

In these, as highlighted by Popper [14], science does not advance through the progressive and continuous accumulation of truths that are gradually acquired through the testing of the hypotheses advanced by scientists (an ideal impossible to achieve for logical reasons), but thanks to attempts to refute the theories proposed. Scientific progress takes place because an error is discovered in a generally accepted theory, and thus the discovery of errors in existing theories obliges the scientist to abandon the previously considered hypothesis in order to propose a new one which is in accordance with all of the known facts [4]. Extremely distant, therefore, from the Manichean illusion of the Enlightenment of Descartes [15] and the Scholastics of St. Thomas and Augustine, where good and evil, truth, and error were clearly distinguishable and distinct [5]. Where the development of scientific understanding, as Grmek [16] noted, one of the greatest medical historians of the last century, was envisioned as "a staircase that rises triumphantly toward the temple of science, with each step representing a new level of scientific development, a truth reached, albeit partial, which should be considered definitive" [4].

Contemporary epistemology has led to the subversion of the positivistic conception of technological and scientific progress, arriving at the conclusion that *science is nothing but a cemetery of errors* [17]. Fundamental, in this sense, are the contributions of Kuhn [18], in whose thought the idea of the foundation paradigm prevails, that is, of a formal science based on revolutionary discovery that creates a new paradigm; of Lakatos [19], for whom science is founded on research programs competing with one another and continually subject to methodological falsificationism; of Laudan [20], for whom science and the research tradition are a set of general assumptions about the extent of processes, problems, and theories of a domain of study; of Carnap [21], for whom the complete verification of a law is impossible even in the face of millions of positive examples; of Feyerabend [22], for whom scientific progress is the result of continuous violations of mandatory principles and methods; and finally, of Popper [14], for whom nothing is certain in science, based on the triad of problems-theories-criticisms, and the only concrete possibility for the scientist is to hunt for errors [4, 11].

Science, therefore, anchored by the laws and paradigms equivalent to mere hypotheses, whose truth it will never be possible to ascertain, cannot offer any certainty [23]. Almost as if to conclude a pluri-millennial historical cycle that restores value to "sophistry," a proponent of the inductive criterion of probability as synonymous with possibility and, therefore, uncertainty. Returning, with that, the value of *Art* to the science of risk, which medicine inevitably is as a matter of priority, called to govern the patchwork of differing sequences and *interconnected causes* or *contributing factors*, in particular the almost infinite variety of those factors which are *etiologic*, exogenous, endogenous, mono, poly, necessary, sufficient or insufficient, exhaustible or inexhaustible, static or dynamic, genetic, anatomical and physiological, pathological, preexisting or contemporary or supervening, concurrent, exclusive, adverse or antinomic, known or unknown, *determining a pathogenesis*, *mono or multi-specific*, of a disease, symptomatic or asymptomatic, fatal or indifferent, known or unknown and, if known, predictable and/or preventable, controllable, or not, with etiological or symptomatic therapy [4]. All of this contributes to a *chaos*, whose domain is based on descriptive data and methods (casuistry, statistical, logical-connective, formal) which show insurmountable limitations and exclusive reference to criteria of possibility [24] and where probabilistic logicism is affirmed.

According to Jeffreys [25], the unitariness of scientific knowledge is based exclusively, in fact, on elaborated and applied methods, rather than on the heterogeneity of acquirable data. Such unitariness is founded on the theory of induction, aimed at satisfying at least three logical conditions: the production of a general method, the abstraction from the world "in itself", and the use of postulates or rules that deduction cannot prove.

The rules, distinct from their empirical content, must in their turn be applied to observational data, express themselves in a formally congruent manner with regard to each other, and provide that the product of the inference may be erroneous, so as not to deny a priori the practical applicability of any empirical proposition.

In accordance with these principles, the principle of causality is defined as a "complex determinant" of the uniformity of nature or as "similar antecedents able to produce similar consequences." The "antecedents," in differentiating themselves from the categories of time and space, exclude the utilization of chronological and topographical criteria in the identification of the cause and the reconstruction of the causal relationship.

The conjugation of inductive empiricism and probabilism, in assimilating the inference to the "degree of confidence" and "probability" (both "variables" according to observed or experimental cases), involves surpassing the historical limit of philosophical and scientific empiricism [26]. All of this entails, therefore, the affirmation of the *principle of probability* as an *exclusive basis for the identification of the causative agent* and the *relationship of material causality.* As an extension of logic, including all of its principles, probability theory assumes the role of indisputable *interpreter of concrete reality.*

In contrast, and consistent with the above, the historical evolution of the principle of probability is explained by means of *classical theory*, as demonstrated by the works of Newton, Gauss, and Boyle [27, 28], and others: *frequentist theory*, of strong impact on the science of risk, from biomedicine to medicine and genetics; *logical theory*, adopted in the nonquantitative sciences, such as biology, sociology, psychology, economics, and theoretical informatics; and *subjectivist theory*, characterized by reciprocal relationships with quantum mechanics and particle physics.

Despite the apparent multiplicity of the above theories, the concept and the principle of probability preserve unitariness in their practical applications, valid in order to provide solid ideological or computational support to diverse scientific disciplines.

3.3 Juridical Construction, Evidence, and Medicine

In the juridical framework, some theories conceive the cause of an event as a necessary condition of the effect, while some view it as a sufficient condition among others. Regardless of the theory or vision adopted, the cause is a combination of factors to which one always owes an identical effect.

Human *responsibility*, correlating and linking causation to the law, offers its own close correlation and causation in the identification of natural events. Therefore, the definition of the effects of individual conduct necessitates the identification of the cause or the correlation of the reality before and after the explication of its conduct, methods, timing, and circumstances. Causation is an essential means to render the individual responsible for the modification of reality. Responsibility is a means and pragmatic value, useful for attributing and defining the history and consequential outcomes of individual actions, as well as for forming the identity and character of individuals. They are responsible as they intervene in reality, modifying it. Causation applies to individual responsibility, insofar as one is aware of the consequences that such a responsibility exerts on reality and on the life of single individualities [29, 30].

The holistic conception, or "judicial justice," finds in the judge the restoration of the right balance in the "bipolar relationship" of rights and entitlements which have been erroneously altered. It is a conception and holistic system where the identification of the material causes performs a classificatory function.

In *law*, the classification of a cause, as direct or indirect, determines the homologation of the cause of the action to the cause of the facts.

In *medicine*, the identification of efficient and precipitating causes is vital for the diagnosis and treatment of the imbalance and disease that derive from them.

In both disciplines, the causal analysis is retrospective, from the current medical condition, or the legal context of the circumstances, to the origin or the act which has caused the transition, of the psychophysical or economic well-being, to the disease, disability, and final damage. In both disciplines, moreover, the cause of the pathological process, disability, and/or damage must underlie the *evidence* arising from observation and experience, classifiable on the basis of gradation levels. In the case of *evidence-based medicine* (EBM), levels range from (1) the "Systematic Review of all reliant randomized control trials" to (2) "At least one properly designed randomized control trial" and "Cohort study, case control study" to (3) "Historical controls" up to (4) "Case series" [31]. The applicability of levels of evidence, the strength of the association between cause and disease, and the accuracy in the estimation of risk must also underlie the careful evaluation of individual variability, the diverse implications of evidence obtained from other individuals, and, therefore, the peculiarity of the individual and the specific circumstances, expressed by genetic predisposition, gender, age, comorbidity, drug use, degree of exposure, mode of survey, and identification of the disease. The manifold variability in the level of scientific information on causation, never static but always and more frequently subject to frenetic evolution, is influenced today not only by genetics but rather by systems biology, that is, by genomics, transcriptomics, interactomics, proteomics, metabolomics, and so on.

The tumultuous evolution of scientific knowledge, in comparison with the pragmatic view of the judicial system and of the parties to the proceedings, brings up the problem of selection, qualification, and the roles of the *expert witnesses*. In particular, it suggests the need for the impartiality of the expert witness, to be anchored to scientific and technical data, independent of the interests of the individual parties, that is, in the defense and representation of science, rather than of the parties involved in the proceedings. All of this is achieved through the careful evaluation of the scientific quality of the evidence produced, in the clear differentiation between fact and opinion, in addition to the *intellectual honesty to claim causal uncertainty when the cause is unknown, due to lack and/or non-reliability of the data* or for *inadequate application and/or knowledge of statistical probability*. And, therefore, with recognition of the continued validity of the assumptions of

Roman law regarding causation and fault, not deeming the latter sufficient for the assertion of responsibility, especially in the field of malpractice and medical liability. This is equivalent to affirming, even in the contemporary era, the validity of the assumption to avoid, on the subject of medical causation, reductionist or one-dimensional approaches. This, again, is equivalent to saying that the multidimensional and epistemologically impure nature of causation put forward in court involves extensive sharing, both in legislative-juridical evolution and in the development of social and private insurance regulations.

Also in light of the foregoing, there is a meeting, a *confrontation between biomedical science and law*, dominated by the erratic chaos of uncertainty and error, the second necessitating certainty, which is essential for the attribution of the damaging event, the identification of the offender, and the reconstruction of the material causal nexus between conduct and event, including a degree of conviction of the judge *beyond any reasonable doubt*. This in order to guarantee and protect victims, the innocent, safeguards inviolable individual and collective rights, good name, reputation, freedom (as understood in its broadest sense), and values transcending and founding the most advanced democratic societies. Societies in which the cause is a necessary condition, and in which recourse is wisely made to a legal construction of scientific knowledge.

Since no agreement exists between philosophers of science on a single scientific method, and as the current methodology proposes diverse and contrasting research methods, the need to ensure the highest degree of certainty has imposed the enunciation of a clear legal rule: the court must only take into consideration reliable *scientific hypotheses that have received the degree of confirmation required by the inductive* conception of the scientific method and, furthermore, which conform to the requirements set out by *the falsificationist conception*, possibly supplemented by the criterion of general consent. What is important, given that there are no certainties in science, is strict adherence to the scientific method. The judge will need to decide on the question of the reliability of the scientific hypothesis relevant to the process, making sure not only that hypothesis has received confirmations from various empirical checks but also that it has withstood the necessary attempts at falsification.

A juridical construction of science, therefore, in which scientific knowledge by hypothesis, contingently true, acquires validity according to the specific aim pursued and in which, for the sciences of risk (including biomedical), the general and/or specific (individualizing) causality is confirmed or denied, depending on the error rate and probability. Being able to recognize the value of truth (thus far resistant to falsificationist confirmation) *only* at the beginning of the causal chain based, *exclusively and uniquely*, on the confirmed corpuscularian and quantum-mechanical theory [32].

This conclusion, exposing the fragility of certainty of knowledge, reaffirms the—albeit noble—nature of the *medical art*, rather than that of science, imbued with the hyper-technological contents of the postmodern era, thereby recognizing the value of juridical knowledge, whose principles and models on the subject of causality are certainly more of a guarantee for the protection of the individual and collective primary goods, inasmuch as culminating in the rule of *beyond any reasonable doubt*, often obsolete in the ranks of the sciences of risk, to which belong medical art and any of its specialist use of adjectives, including those of legal medicine. In reality, thereby having to confirm that the nosographic classifications; the etiopathogenesis and physiopathological interpretations; the diagnoses, prognoses, and treatments; and the evaluative epicrises belong to a system of knowledge whose reliability, truth, or falsity depends on the transient systematic theory and practice of the biomedicine of the time, the progress of which lies in the discovery of errors and the development of new theories. With this, fully confirming the Hippocratic Oath of the third millennium which, *in founding the ethical role of the doctor's professionalism* across cultures and social contexts, recognizes the aforesaid assumptions and states that the new contract of the *doctor*, stipulated with the individual-patient and with society, must be based on the assumption of a new role, that of the *Researcher*, *constantly in pursuit of Errors*, the discovery of which reduces the uncertainty of science, enhances professional formation, and improves the "quality system" [4, 33].

3.4 "Conditio Sine Qua" and Scientific Laws

The *conditio sine qua non* or *but-for cause*, theory of universal use, constitutes everywhere the *indispensible minimum* for the objective allocation of individual harmful events. So it is, in effect, in European Criminal Justice Systems, starting with Germany, where the equivalence theory of causes is now accepted as the first and essential criterion for criminal charges and where it is assumed that any other causal theory (such as that of *adequate causality*) or objective criteria of importance (*i.e.*, *the increase of risk*) require as an indispensible minimum the subsistence of a condition that can withstand counterfactual reasoning, namely, that it cannot be eliminated mentally without the elimination of the event [32].

In the same situation as Germany, one finds, just to cite some of the European countries, the UK, France, Spain, and Italy. In the UK, in fact, the use of the *but-for cause* is generally accepted, both in doctrine and in case law, in line with the approach of all or nothing, which is typical and traditional in *common law*. Even in France and Spain, it is accepted that the *conditio sine qua non* constitutes the basis for criminal charges for damaging events, recognizing also the postulate of equivalence of conditions. For Spanish criminal lawyers, the triumph of the conditionalistic theory played down the significance of the causal problem, at least in the field of criminal law. The existence of causality continues, in fact, to be a requirement in all criminal offenses: in crimes of endangerment, because it is necessary that the author has caused the risk, as in a harmful offense, since these presuppose that the offender caused impairment of the legal right of the victim, the proof being insufficient that the conduct has created a risk [34]. Thus, also in the Italian legal system, where material causality has its normative foundations in the Criminal Code (art. 40–41), the causal nexus is based on the theory of the necessary condition, also known as the equivalence of causes, supported by the theory of scientific laws of coverage, and tempered by so-called causal regularity.

Even in the system of adequate causality, the *conditio sine qua non* remains the essential prerequisite, built on the following principles.

(a) The event must be a consequence of the conduct, and the behavior is considered to be the cause only when it constitutes a necessary condition for the event.
(b) The behavior of a man can only be one among many necessary conditions of the event so that, from a logical point of view, the cause must be understood as a totality of necessary conditions, not as a sufficient condition, and, from the point of view of criminal law, the cause does not coincide with the "sufficient" condition, but with the "necessary condition."
(c) Human conduct is never a necessary condition in absolute terms, but it is in contingent terms, or rather in a specific context of concrete conditions; since it is not possible to grade the effectiveness of every single condition, all those indispensable to the occurrence of the event are considered equivalent to each other and equally causal, i.e., with the same legal significance.
(d) The demonstration of the causal nexus, being a posteriori or ex post, aims to determine whether human conduct has been a contingently necessary condition for the occurrence of the event.
(e) The criterion of the adequacy of the cause—that is, of adequate randomness—operates in addition to and not as a substitute for the conditioning nexus.
(f) Counterfactual reasoning is indispensable in order to establish whether particular human conduct is actually a necessary condition for the occurrence of the event and to proceed to the mental elimination of such a condition, verifying, always mentally, if the event would have happened anyway.

3.5 From the Theory to the Practice of Specific Causality

The abovementioned theories find logical-conceptual support and corroboration in the *scientific laws of coverage*, in *universal scientific laws or statistical laws*, able to prove with certainty or various degrees of probability that a particular condition is invariably followed by the verification of a specified event. Although belonging to the category of scientific laws, the statistical laws provide propositions and offer causal links only in terms of probability, not certainty, meaning that a particular event is accompanied by another event only in a certain percentage of cases, with the consequence that such laws are much more equipped with scientific validity, inasmuch as they can find application in a high enough number of cases receiving confirmation from rational and controlled testing methods [35].

It is universally accepted in medicolegal doctrine that the subsumption under scientific laws of coverage is applicable both in terms of causality by commission or omission. In both areas, the logical procedure utilized for the causal reconstruction makes use of two fundamental explanatory models.

- The *deductive-nomological* model, in which the *explanandum* is derived through a deductively valid reasoning from the *explanans*.
- The *statistical-inductive* model, in which the *explanandum* possesses a high inductive probability with regard to the *explanans*.

The assessment based on the *deductive-nomological* model employs *universal laws* and permits deductive conclusions and, therefore, theoretically substantial *certainty*. The preliminary criterion, which should always be applied, is that of the so-called *scientific possibility* of a *causal nexus*, also defined as (ex ante) *capability of causing harm*.

The medicolegal expert, who is called upon to decide on the possible existence of a causal nexus between conduct and damage, in the absence of scientific laws of universal coverage, will often be forced to resort to the use of statistical laws, pointing out, however, that the demonstration of the nexus with a criterion of high probability-near certainty will be possible only where there is a high degree of logical probability or rational credibility [13]. In other words, one will be able to hold that the conduct of the agent constitutes a necessary condition of the event, only if, without the agent's behavior, with a high grade of logical probability, it would not have occurred or, rather, when it is possible, with any reasonableness and rational justification, to exclude the involvement of a different causal process (i.e., "counterfactual reasoning"). This model is applicable to cases which involve commissive conduct, where there is clear and convincing evidence of the applicability of the general laws of physics, chemistry and biochemistry, physiology, and knowledge of general pathology, knowledge that can well be regarded in the same manner as universal laws [33, 36].

The logical process of assessment by the *inductive-statistical probabilistic model* is based on the use of statistical laws or maxims of experience that, integrated with each other, enable a probability of a causal nexus to be inferred, almost always in terms of prevalence, which is difficult to quantify on the hypothesis of improbability. This model is very often applied in the biomedicolegal field and concerns, in particular, cases of omissive conduct typical of professional medical liability, environmental damage, and damage to the product.

The inductive-statistical explanatory model can also benefit from the application of additional and indicative medicolegal criteria of evaluation regarding the causal relationship. They are criteria that, if utilized appropriately and critically, still represent a useful applicative tool in the logical-probabilistic-inductive procedure. In the doctrine, these criteria (topographical, chronological, and phenomenological continuity and exclusion of other causes) are frequently listed without a hierarchical order and in varying numbers, while it is appropriate to use them in an articulated manner, as a guide for the organization of a case study. If the current scientific knowledge of the data of the specific case makes the accreditation of a causal link impossible from the outset, the assessment should be interrupted. Only two conclusions are possible: the exclusion of the nexus or the impossibility of its ascertainment [34].

The first and most important criterion, which is that of *harmful efficiency* or *capability of causing harm*, refers to a nomological paradigm, while the other criteria require concrete proof in order to demonstrate the appropriateness of the scientific law. Among the criteria described above, the exclusion of other causes deserves particular emphasis, being fundamental and, in general, more complex than the others, as it is potentially a harbinger of misconceptions, since it is involved both in the process of identification of the entire causal chain, necessary and sufficient, and in the assessment of the necessity of the individual causal conditions of all the etiological factors. This fundamental medicolegal criterion corresponds to the differential diagnosis in medicine, in which the hypothesis that survives among the various hypotheses put forward, through the procedure known as "modus tollens", requires, in its turn, the search for evidence in its favor, making use of an inductive approach of an eliminative type [23].

The use of customary and well-established medicolegal criteriology must, in the final analysis, be directed toward the reconstruction of the intermediate causal links, with the aim of giving concrete form to the scientific laws of coverage in the specific case, in a transition from the ambit of general causality to that of individual or specific causality. It involves, therefore, an accurate search for evidence that allows the reconstruction of the complex *causal puzzle* and the necessary transition from factorial adequacy to (almost) causal certainty. The cause, conserving and accentuating its epistemological contractions, cannot but distinguish itself as the basis of a medicolegal judgment founded on the evidence [17].

In order to identify with high probability the existence of a material causal nexus, the demonstration of damage eligibility ex ante is not sufficient, which is an error that, unfortunately, many of the various biomedicolegal and/or forensic "experts" still commit. It is a sort of inherent flaw that has considered the concept of cause in an autonomous way, detached from the point of view of the law and therefore from the concept of a necessary condition, replacing it with the concept of *capability of causing harm* or, rather, "adequate causality." It is an adequate causality which is wholly foreign to the world of biomedicine and legal medicine. The criterion of eligibility or causal adequacy is certainly not sufficient, but rather a prerequisite, for the medicolegal opinion on the existence of a causal link between the event and the damage, which is equipped with high probability-near certainty. Clearly there is a strong need to find the particularistic evidence of the nexus, seeking a mechanistic explanation by means of chains of cause and effect, in which individual events are explained in a deterministic sense.

In the absence of a transition from the general causality to the specific causality, the model of subsumption under the laws of science would remain a hollow expression: the failure to verify the concrete antecedents, including the concrete *but-for* antecedent, subsumable under the abstract antecedents, provided by the law of coverage, renders vain any reconstructive attempt. In other words, there is a need to formulate an *ex post judgment* linked to particularistic evidence of concrete expression and not based on bare statistics.

Still more difficult is the problem of the reconstruction of the causal relationship in the ambit of *omissive causation*, where the finding of real and objective data, which permit the reconstruction of the causal intermediate links, is extremely rare and the reconstruction is largely based on hypothetical and/or prognostic judgments which, supposing the dutiful act has been carried out, ask whether the harmful event would have occurred anyway. In order to recognize the causal nexus, even in the field of omission, it is necessary to achieve the highest possible degree of probability, thereby finding that the dutiful act, if accomplished, would have been able to prevent the event with a probability close to certainty [17].

In the medical-surgical area, and specifically in professional *medical*-healthcare *liability*, and *personal injury* and *damage*, the problem of omissive causality reaches the highest vertices of complexity, since the maximum part of the explanations offered is based on probabilistic laws with a low coefficient, which are not capable of providing mechanistic explanations. Therefore, when assessing by counterfactual reasoning what the consequences of the correct alternative medical conduct, omitted by the attending physician, would have been, the degree of probability by which to assess the effects on the health of the patient is not to be referred to mere statistical probability derived from previous trials but the concept of logical probability, which must be close to certainty. The logical probability, in its turn, must be constructed by epicritically assessing all the circumstances of the specific case as they appear from the collected evidence [17, 34].

Consistent with the principles of probability, the conclusions are equivalent to the assessment of the degree of probability, the expert being unable to express opinions that would compel the judge to make a decision, which is only assumable on the basis of the whole spectrum of information derived from the various sources of evidence. Applying probabilistic logicism, where the production of evidence is based on experimental or observational data, the expert interpretation must be founded on principles and expressions of probability, rather than on descriptive adjectives. In the unfolding of the production of proof, the acceptability and the utility of scientific evidence assume great importance in the trial, where the qualification, experience, and competence of the expert, as well as the "peer review" of the opinions expressed by other experts, acquire relevance.

More specifically, in relation to the criteria of procedural *acceptability* of scientific evidence, the selection of scientific concepts and methods must arise from the consensus of the scientific community as to the limits of the demonstrability of the assumptions and the evidential value of the methods and conclusions, in order to clarify in the context of the individual case the probabilistic value of the observational or experimental evidence. This is in line with the process of preordained validation of scientific evidence through "standards of acceptability" previously established on the basis of "consensus documents," or derived, rather, from judgments of significant innovatory impact (Daubert v. Merrel Dow Pharmaceutical Inc., 113 S. Ct. 2786; 1993), thereby rejecting the principle, sometimes widespread in the judicial contexts of some countries, of the proclaimed "legal and judicial autonomy" of the validation of the acceptability of scientific methods and conclusions.

The application of probabilistic logicism, the sharing of criteria of *admissibility*, and the unanimous acceptance of methods and results of scientific evidence all find common ground in margins of uncertainty, intrinsic structure, means of production, and the interpretation of the same results. All of these are subject to possible dispute and balanced debate between the parties, for which the identification of causality is the expression of degrees of probability.

It is implicit, however, that the *quality of evidence* must be supported by the degree of general and specific reliability of its production, by means of verifying (1) the assertive effectiveness of scientific data, (2) the diversification of evidence, (3) the conformity or discrepancy of knowledge arising from evidence, and (4) the availability of alternative tests capable of modifying the judgment already acquired. From the entirety of the means of production, eligibility, and acceptability of the methods and acquirable outcomes in the form of scientific evidence, there emerges indicative guidance on the explication of best conduct on the part of the judge and the expert.

It is advisable for the *judge* to keep in mind the followings.

(a) The truth cannot always arise from a single piece of evidence or a grouping of evidence.
(b) Uncertainty is desirable.
(c) The evaluation of the context "a priori" and the proof must be founded on the rules of probabilistic logicism.
(d) The weight and individual quality of each piece of evidence must be evaluated separately from the general context; the decision, never relying on a single piece of evidence (to which it would remain hostage), must be the expression of multiple reciprocally independent scientific findings.
(e) The quality of the evidence provided by the expert should be subject to verification in itself and in the general evidential context [37].

There are a number of key elements that it is advisable for the *expert* to keep in mind: (a) to prove the hypothesis and not absolute truth; (b) to ignore the procedural evidence of nonscientific value; (c) to disregard the nature of the proceedings, be they penal or civil, as well as the party (prosecution or defense) for whom one is working; (d) to express numerical evaluations of the value of evidence according to scales of shared measurement; (e) to search for and assess multiple evidence, ensuring reciprocity and independence; (f) to provide, on an exclusive basis, evaluations and opinions that correspond to one's proven expertise; (g) to show any discordance in the resulting evidence; and (h) to admit the objective impossibility or incapacity to provide evidence in the context of a specific case [37].

In spite of the trust that the public places in the scientific process, there exist many objections to the quality of evidence adduced by forensic scientists and the validity of the above guidance of probabilistic logicism. It would therefore be particularly necessary that a *new evidentiary regime* permeates the scientific evidence produced during the trial, beginning with greater uniformity between national and continental judicial systems and in particular between "North America and Europe," where, in the latter, the activity of the forensic expert is often the expression of an autonomous profession. Often there is, in fact, diversity in conceiving expert testimony and practicing rigorousness in the methods and the standards of evidence. It concerns limits which are particularly relevant in the category of medical expertise, where the ascertainment of material causality is focused on the demonstration of the cause-effect relationship between harmful means, injury, and/or death. The medical examination of the living or deceased person, in creating a collection of data, is equivalent to the obtainment of recorded rather than experiential evidence, thereby proposing a clear separation between circumstantial and medico-technical evidence as a fundamental paradigm of any inference. The expert should reason, therefore, only on the basis of medical data, leaving to others the logical combination among these and other data which are not pertinent to the medical field, avoiding the commingling of plans and consequent inferential confusion, for which it is easy to commit abuses of logic with significant consequences concerning the acceptability and admissibility of scientific evidence.

The process of formation of medical evidence finds obvious and particular significance in the category of cases of professional "medical liability" and of "personal injury and damage," where much of the nonempirical evidence is derived from the interpretation of health records. There subsists, in fact, a profound difference between the neo-production of a test (of genetic fingerprinting, toxicology, molecular-biology, etc.) and the utilization of evidence from previous clinical, instrumental, laboratory results, etc. In identifying the cause, there exists a profound difference between the phenomenic explanation, through the interventionist criterion or through the descriptive criterion of preexisting evidence. The experimental evidence is, in fact, aimed at satisfying the requirements of inference. The evidence arising from past unselected data, insofar as produced by others (but inferable, for example, from health records), is foreign to the direct satisfaction of inferential purposes, with the result that the interpretations of preexisting medical data can be characterized by a high degree of potential ambiguity and are therefore difficult to classify, with consequent extraneity to the experimental acquisition of evidence, on which the probabilistic logicism must be based. From such a limit, as well as from the difference of subjective interpretations and the frequent lack of rigor in the logical inference of the clinical-therapeutic ascertainment methodology, there arise difficulties, delays, and disagreements in the expert evaluations and opinions on the subject of alleged medical professional liability and personal injury and damage, which can be remedied only through the application of rigorous, shared, and widely applied guidelines regarding ascertainment methodology and criteria of evaluation.

References

1. Plato (1989) Symposium. Hackett, Indianapolis, IN
2. Aristotle (1989) Metaphysics. Harvard University Press, London
3. Ferrara SD, Boscolo-Berto R, Viel G (eds) (2013) Malpractice and medical liability: European state of the art and guidelines. Springer, Berlin
4. Ferrara SD (2004) Arte Medico-Legale. Unitarietà di Sapere e Qualità di Sistema. Riv It Med Leg 26:273

5. Ladyman J (2007) Filosofia della scienza. Tommaso Piazza, Carocci, Roma
6. Aristotle (1908) Nichomachean ethics. Clarendon Press, Oxford
7. Aristotle (2008) Physics. Oxford University Press, Oxford
8. Kant I (1781) Critique of pure reason. Cambridge University Press, Cambridge
9. Dobbs BJ (1994) Newton as final cause and first mover. Isis 85(4):633–643
10. Hume D (1751) An inquiry concerning human understanding. Cambridge University Press, Cambridge
11. Reichenbach H (1951) The rise of scientific philosophy. University of California Press, Berkeley, CA
12. Mill IS (1868) A system of logic ratiocinative and inductive. Lightning Source UK Ltd, Kiln Farm
13. Cohen JL (1977) The probable and the provable. Clarendon Press, Oxford
14. Popper K (1934) Logica della scoperta scientifica. Einaudi, Torino
15. Descartes R (2007) Discorso sul metodo per dirigere la propria ragione e cercare la verità nelle scienze. Barbera, Siena
16. Grmek MD (1998) Western medical thought from antiquity to the middle ages. Harward University Press, Cambridge
17. Stella F (2003) Giustizia e modernità. Giuffrè, Milano
18. Khun T (1970) The structure of scientific revolutions. University of Chicago Press, Chicago, IL
19. Lakatos I (1968) Criticism and the methodology of scientific research programmes. Proc Aristot Soc 69:149–186
20. Laudan L (1996) Beyond positivism and relativism: theory, method, and evidence. Westview Press, Boulder, CO
21. Carnap R (1950) Logical foundation of probability. University of Chicago Press, Chicago, IL
22. Horgan J (1993) Paul Karl Feyerabend: the worst enemy of science. Sci Am 268(5):36–37
23. Blaiotta R (2004) La causalità nella responsabilità professionale. Tra teoria e prassi. Giuffrè, Milano
24. Salmon W (1992) 40 anni di spiegazione scientifica. Scienza e filosofia 1948–1987. Muzzio, Padova
25. Jeffreys H (1966) Theory of probability. Clarendon Press, Oxford
26. Hacking I (2001) An introduction to probability and inductive logic. Cambridge University Press, Cambridge
27. Anstey P (2000) The philosophy of Robert Boyle. Routlege, London
28. Dunnington G, Waldo P (1955) Carl Friedrich Gauss: Titan of science. Hafner, New York, NY
29. Mendelson D (1998) The interfaces of medicine and law: the history of the liability for negligently caused psychiatric injury (nervous shock). Ashgate/Dartmouth, Farnham
30. Mendelson D (2000) Torts. Butterworths, Sydney
31. Sackett DL, Strauss SE, Richardson US, Rosenberg W, Haynes RB (2000) Evidence-based medicine. How to practice and teach. Churchill Livingstone, London
32. Freckelton I, Mendelson D (2002) Causation in law and medicine. Ashgate/Dartmouth, Farnham
33. Ferrara SD, Pfeiffer H (2010) Unitariness, evidence and quality in bio-medicolegal sciences. Int J Leg Med 124(4):343–344
34. Barni M (1995) Il rapporto di causalità materiale in medicina legale. Giuffrè, Milano
35. Barnes DW (1983) Statistics as proof. Little, Brown, Boston, MA
36. Ferrara SD, Bajanowski T, Cecchi R, Snenghi R, Case C, Viel G (2010) Bio-medicolegal guidelines and protocols: survey and future perspectives in Europe. Int J Leg Med 124 (4):345–350
37. Pascali V (2011) Causalità ed inferenza nel diritto e nella prassi giuridica. Giuffrè, Milano

Chapter 4
Compensation for Personal Injury in a Comparative Perspective: The Need to Bridge Legal and Medicolegal Knowledge

Giovanni Comandè

Abstract This chapter gives an transnational overview on the different judicial and legislative models adopted for personal injury and damage compensation. An alleged constant increase in awards and the difficulties linked to the subjectivity of the assessment and quantification of nonmaterial damages raise the need for a more harmonized model capable of providing justice and equal treatment across the world. By means of a comparative analysis, the chapter explores the lasting debate that surrounds economic and noneconomic damages for personal injury and the diverse techniques used for awarding intangible losses. It further proposes an in-depth analysis of selected common law (e.g., England, Scotland, the USA) and civil law systems (e.g., France, Germany, Italy) highlighting the pros and cons of each and prospecting a solution for increasing horizontal and vertical equality without necessarily impeding an inevitable variability of awards among different jurisdictions.

4.1 An Introduction to Different Languages

The Western legal tradition in general and the European countries have for a long time affirmed non-pecuniary loss as a proper title of damages. In the preceding decades, we have witnessed an escalation in the monetary amounts awarded for the non-pecuniary component of damages in cases of personal injury[1]. As a result of this escalation, several legal systems have embarked on a shrill debate in trying to decipher a

[1] In this sense, see [1–5]. *But see* [6]. Of course, recognition of non-pecuniary damages as a proper title of damages does not preclude this expansive trend from having experienced both misuses and abuses or, at least, misunderstandings. *See generally* [7, 8].

G. Comandè (✉)
LIDER-Lab, University Scuola Superiore Sant'Anna, Piazza Martiri della Libertà 33, 56127 Pisa, Italy
e-mail: giovanni.comande@sssup.it

S.D. Ferrara et al. (eds.), *Personal Injury and Damage Ascertainment under Civil Law*, DOI 10.1007/978-3-319-29812-2_4

definition of their concrete notions of non-pecuniary damages[2] and on their awarding methods[3]. This has often led to the revision or at least the discussion of the general classifications, the terminology used, and the concepts they reflect along the line of opposing verbal expressions: patrimonial v. non-patrimonial, economic v. noneconomic, pecuniary v. non-pecuniary, and material v. immaterial damage.

Hence, for instance, the Anglo-American expression "pain and suffering" often subsumes all damages for non-pecuniary loss [18][4], even though its technical meaning involves itself more with the restricted connotation of moral and physical suffering. On the contrary, loss of amenity of life could be defined as a material modification of the capacity to enjoy life as distinguished both from the loss of earning capacity and from pain and suffering[5].

Broadly speaking, in our view [16], noneconomic damages for personal injury are essentially an attempt to offer compensation for "limitations on the person's life created by the injury."[6] However, this attempt at pinpointing the role of noneconomic damages has resulted in a distinction within the domain of traditional non-pecuniary loss, that is, between loss of enjoyment of life[7] and pain and suffering. These two types of damage redress diverse, intangible losses[8] in personal injury cases. The latter (pain and suffering) attempts to restore entirely subjective non-economic damages for intangible loss, while the former (loss of enjoyment of life) relies upon an "objective"[9] basis for evaluation: the existence of an ascertainable medical condition[10]. In several jurisdictions—especially the European ones—this

[2] For a much more detailed clarification, see [9, 10]. *See also* [11]. For further commentary on these same issues, see [12, 13] at 138 (criticizing the UK tort system sharply). For a survey of different theories and policies on non-economic damages, see [14].

[3] For a wider account of the state of the art and of the debate, see [15, 16]. For a critical perspective on awarding pain and suffering, see [17], who argues that awarding damages for pain and suffering "without rational criteria for measuring [them undermines] the tort law's rationality and predictability" and advocates legislative intervention.

[4] Restatement (Second) of Torts § 924 (1977). For further commentary on pain and suffering awards and notions, see [19–28] (suggesting that the only jury guide-posts in its task of assessing damages for these matters are common sense and sound judgment).

[5] Sometimes the expression hedonic damages is used to signify the compensation for limitations "on the injured person's ability to participate in and derive pleasure from the normal activities of daily life, or for the individual's inability to pursue his talents, recreational interests, hobbies, or avocations." *See* Boan v. Blackwell, 541 S.E.2d 242, 244 (S.C. 2001).

[6] McDougald v. Garber, 536 N.E.2d 372, 379 (N.Y. 1989) (Titone, J., dissenting) (citing Thompson v. Nat'l R.R. Passenger Corp., 621 F.2d 814, 824 (6th Cir. 1980)).

[7] For commentary on the problem of awarding damages for loss of enjoyment of life, also known as "hedonic" damages, see, among others, [29–34].

[8] Such a distinction in the American tort system has already been acknowledged. *See, e.g.*, [29, 35].

[9] As already distinguished, "objective" means "existing independently of perception or an individual's conceptions" as opposed to "distorted by emotion or personal bias."

[10] As per Lord Justice O'Connor in Housecroft v. Burnett, 1 All E.R. 332, 337 (1986), "The human condition is so infinitely variable that it is impossible to set a tariff, but some injuries are more susceptible to some uniformity in compensation than others."

outlined distinction echoes the constitutional choice of protecting health and bodily integrity as a reaffirmed social value (e.g., in Italy or Germany) which deserves tort damages compensation in order to grant a minimum level of protection[11].

No such clear reference to the constitutional protection of health exists in other countries in the Western legal tradition (as in the USA) in awarding damages for non-pecuniary loss. This European trait must be stressed and kept in mind. What is clearly evident, however, is a distinct trend in the entire Western legal tradition (including countries such as the USA) to identify and distinguish between pain and suffering (as subjectively perceived pretium doloris) and loss of enjoyment of life as an "objective" component in non-pecuniary damages, damages Europeans would probably qualify as compensation for lost health and bodily integrity, as such. Indeed, European jurisdictions have more openly opted for a clear differentiation between pain and suffering (with the sole purpose of compensating mental-moral suffering) and loss of enjoyment of life (as a means to redress health and bodily integrity accompanying physical injury or indeed purely emotional harm generating an illness).

With the doubtless existence and increasing role of non-pecuniary damages we now turn to the main objective of this paper, that is, to offer a rapid overview of the awarding systems for non-pecuniary loss in selected European jurisdictions.

In part 4.2, a brief historical excursus on the legal terminology used in common law countries illustrates the basic elements of the notions regularly used. Part 4.3 will briefly discuss the evolution and actual state of the art of the awarding methods for loss of enjoyment of life in four European countries, thereby obtaining some challenging suggestions for further research in part 4.4.

4.2 Contrasting Oppositions: The Example of Common Law Countries

If we try to make a quick survey of the damages awarded and the concept used over time even within a single legal family, it is easy to find recurrent debates and problems. So, for instance, in England the basic distinction between pecuniary and non-pecuniary damages is that money can fully compensate the former, meaning that these damages are related to the wealth or property of the claimant. Definition of non-pecuniary damages is more complex in that they are paid in respect of the nonmonetary aspects of the harm. Pecuniary are both negative, e.g., loss of earnings, and positive, e.g., medical expenses. Non-pecuniary is anything that cannot be measured in monetary terms.

The USA have similar definitions: pecuniary loss refers to financial loss, whereas non-pecuniary damages compensate for intangible injuries sustained and, in particular, those lacking a market value.

---

[11] See for instance Corte di Cassazione 8827 8828\2003 in *Danno e responsabilità*, 2003, 816, with commentary by [36, 37].

The Scottish (a mixed jurisdiction) experience varies also in terminology to express similar concepts. Its terminology refers to patrimonial damages and solatium. The former concept derives from patrimony: i.e., it relates to a persons' estate or property, e.g., loss of earnings. The latter indicates non-patrimonial damage to the victim other than wealth or property: i.e., pain and suffering. Ireland more commonly refers to non-pecuniary damages as general and special damages. The former comprises actual or anticipated financial losses, while the latter encompasses the non-pecuniary elements such as pain and suffering, loss of amenity, and reduction of life expectancy [10].

In an historical perspective, non-pecuniary losses[12] consist of five headings:

Pain and suffering, loss of amenities, and of expectation of life. The terms "pain" and "suffering" are interchangeable in that there now seems to be no differential between the two. With this said, however, it is suggested that pain is the actual physical sensation felt when injury is sustained, whereas suffering encompasses more the emotions felt as a result of the injury, e.g., fright, fear, humiliation, sadness, etc. Damages may be recoverable under loss of amenities where the extent of the injury causes more than pain and suffering and where it further impedes a person's normal pursuits, e.g., the inability to pursue a hobby. Loss of expectation of life, established in Flint v Lovell 1935 and abolished by the Administration of Justice Act 1982, existed to compensate for the shortening of one's life. It can now be assessed under pain and suffering.

Physical inconvenience and discomfort: this is generally included under pain and suffering and loss of amenities (Sherman v. Folland 1950). If the inconvenience is not a result of a physical injury it can, in those circumstances, be assessed separately, e.g., false imprisonment.

Social discredit: injury to reputation mainly recoverable under the tort of defamation but has also been extended to malicious prosecution (Saville v Roberts 1699) and false imprisonment (Walter v Alltools 1944).

Mental distress, as a distinct claim, is not recoverable (Lynch v Knight 1861). However, in instances where it is claimed in addition to other elements of damage, then it may be recoverable, for instance, as injury to feelings as a result of libel or slander.

Loss of Society: originally it was a tort involving the infringement of family relationships which was the basis for this heading. However, with the abolishment of these torts (Law Reform (Miscellaneous Provisions) Act 1970), the only claim for recovery lay with a husband for the loss of consortium of his wife which has now also been abolished (Administration of Justice Act 1982).

In the UK, the right to bereavement damages was introduced as a sort of substitute for this claim. However, they are obviously limited to specific cases.

Even limiting ourselves to these brief historical considerations, it appears clear that legal and medicolegal languages need to find ways to converge on shared terminology and correlated concepts.

---

[12] According to McGregor On Damages Mental distress.

Yet the picture and the need for more uniformity become clearer if we move from general definitions and classifications to investigate awarding methods.

4.3 Awarding Methods: Convergencies and Divergencies in European Jurisdictions

A study of non-pecuniary loss in Europe reveals an assortment of names and definitions for non-pecuniary damages: smartengeld, pain and suffering, préjudice corporel, préjudice d'agrément, daño corporal, daño moral, danno alla salute, Schmerzensgeld, and danno morale.[13] In European jurisdictions, they stem from the same inspiring principles that guide legal protection in general [41]. In all jurisdictions we discover a quest to avoid unjustified variations within levels of injury seriousness, fulfilling the principle of horizontal justice. Equally, a will to avert divergences in the amounts awarded for the duration of the injury can be discerned, effectuating the principles of vertical justice. The equality principle is therefore the point of convergence and goes hand in hand with the search for individual justice in the courtroom. As mentioned, several European countries distinguish—at least de facto—between damage to health and bodily integrity and mere psychological alterations or subjective predispositions resulting from a personal injury. The first, damage to health and bodily integrity, amounting to documented illnesses and disabilities assessable by medical experts, is awarded under notions similar to loss of enjoyment of life. Mere psychological alterations, amounting to transient sufferings, such as anger or temporary stress, are awarded under titles easily incorporated into the notion of pain and suffering as moral suffering. Yet often European systems award a global sum encompassing both losses[14].

Considering the above, all European awarding systems[15] depend on medical description or evidence in evaluating objective noneconomic damages[16]. Medical evaluation is critical in offering an "objective" description and a uniform estimation of loss of enjoyment of life. In general terms, in Europe, once obtained, the medical description is affiliated to a monetary barème (that is, a system of standardization using scheduling) based upon age and confirmed permanent disability expressed either in percentage permanent impairment (in France and Italy) or by descriptive

[13] For information on several European Community member States, see generally [38–40].

[14] Indeed, the recent decisions of the Italian Supreme Court today require a global sum awards. See Cass., S.U. civ., 11 November 2008 n. 26972-26973-2697426975, in *Guida al diritto*, n. 47, 2008 with comment of di G. Comandé, *Un'autentica estensione di tutela che cancella solo "diritti immaginari,"* at, 34.

[15] From now on we will be referring exclusively to methods of evaluating loss of enjoyment of life as damages to health as such as opposed to pain and suffering in the sense of *pretium doloris*.

[16] *See generally* [42] (stressing the different systemic impact of medical evidence in several European Countries).

tables (in the UK and Germany). These aids offer to judges the basic parameters within which respect of the equality principle should be obtained. With this bedrock of commonalities laid out, we must turn to the differences that exist between the examined jurisdictions, of which insight is essential in relation to their applicability beyond the borders of these countries.

4.3.1 *The English Way to Intangible Loss*

A useful starting point for our comparative analysis is the English experience. This system has dramatically changed since the Court of Appeal began the process of monitoring awards[17] and setting standardized compensation amounts according to their findings. These efforts have produced brackets of values to be utilized by the courts in computing damages. This method simplifies the calculation process, attains consistency in the outcome of cases, and also aids predictability, useful both in promoting settlements and in maintaining insurability. In practice, in assessing pain and suffering and loss of amenity of life, this approach permits trial judges and the Court of Appeal to consider the severity of the injury and to equate it with an amount within the brackets. These amounts (within the brackets) are deduced from precedents on quantum and are currently produced and periodically published by the The Judicial College (formerly the Judicial Studies Board)[18]. Amounts are updated in accordance with both inflation and new increasing/decreasing trends[19].

It is rather intuitive that standardization ensued, leading to reliable tables of values based on the relative seriousness of different injuries. The guidelines and the cases referred to in them offer at least a starting point for any case[20]. Yet, these guidelines are not a fixed tariff nor are they binding even where injuries are comparatively uniform and physically very similar. Indeed, the court will have to assess damages with regard to the actual claimant, meaning that it will have to

[17] Roughly after World War II. *See, e.g.*, Ward v. James, [1966] 1 Q.B. 273, 299300 (U.K.). The background idea in this assessment of evolution is clearly summarized in Wright v. British Rys. Bd., [1983] 2 A.C. 773, 784–85 (H.L.) (U.K.).

[18] For the guidelines, see [43]. These Guidelines are not in themselves law, but are regarded with the respect accorded to the writings of any specialist legal author. *See* Arafa v Potter [1994] P.I.Q.R. 73, 79. See also [44] (using a 13-category classification system based on both the area and severity of the injury, with subcategories for more specific parts of the body); [45] (18-category classification system based on both the area and severity of the injury, with subcategories for specific parts of the body and more specific types of injuries).

[19] For instance, after a consultation paper in 1996, the English Law Reform Commission issued a report in 1999 urging the "Court of Appeal and/or the House of Lords, using their existing powers to lay down guidelines as to quantum in the course of personal injury litigation" and to adopt recommendations for increasing non-pecuniary loss awards. [46]. The invitation was answered by in Heil v. Rankin, [2000] 3 All E.R. 138 (C.A.) (Eng.); *see* [47].

[20] *See* [48].

consider their injury and its impact on their life according to their age (though decisions rarely mention age expressly), in addition to the severity and permanence of the injury. The key to the evolution of the system lies in the fact that an explanation as regards the actual amount awarded is required. Thus, only where insufficient reasoning is supplied can the court of appeal intervene[21].

The described system necessitates a significant body of case law detailing the facts of, and the reasons for, the decision, a sustained policy decision, easy accessibility to the information for all the stakeholders, and a sufficient degree of itemization of the awarded damages[22]. All the elements required to borrow from the experience of the UK are present in the USA: the only requirement is that juries are given access to information on previous awards. Note, also, that itemization has been introduced in the UK tradition and indeed in some American jurisdictions as well[23].

4.3.2 *German Tables and Descriptions*

Germany, strikingly enough, being a civil law country, has developed a system comparable to the British one, to assist in awarding loss of enjoyment of life accompanying damage to health and bodily integrity. However, contrary to English lawyers, German jurists may only refer to private compilations reciting cases and amounts awarded for noneconomic damages (so-called Schmerzensgeldtabellen). Accordingly, German practice created an indicative system of scheduling to assess non-pecuniary damages (Schmerzensgeld) in personal injury cases. As in the UK, trial courts' discretionary decisions on compensation are reviewed on appeal for their reasonableness according to the relevant circumstances of the case[24]. Indeed, the individual circumstances of each case remain decisive, but they are pigeonholed in uniform patterns emerging from practice. Indeed, the Schmerzensgeldtabellen[25] describe the injury suffered by the victim and the amounts awarded according to claimant's request in an ever growing set of actual cases decided by courts. Overall, the German model offers more structured and complex information than the English one[26]. It is perhaps more functional in relation to practitioner use. In fact, there are diverse publications of Schmerzensgeldtabellen that offer collections indexed in different ways (e.g., according to the kind of impairment suffered or

[21] For an updated description [49].

[22] *See* [50].

[23] See also [51].

[24] *See, e.g.*, [52].

[25] There are several publications available on the market. *See, e.g.*, [53–55].

[26] See [56].

on the global sum awarded) and offering both a description of the case and the specific arguments used by the parties and the judges.

4.3.3 A Franco-Italian Approach to Scheduling

The use of "objective" factors in the evaluation of loss of enjoyment of life is common to other jurisdictions. In the Franco-Italian model, medical baremes, in conjunction with monetary schedules, are used by courts. Often, monetary scheduling and models are elaborated upon by courts or by scholars, but always with reliance upon previous decisions[27]. This is important to note, since Italy and France are civil law countries. However, in relation to tort law, regarding the evolution of their legal systems and especially for the awarding of damages, case law has always played a significant role, comparable to that of a legal system developed through the decisions of judges in general.

The French equivalent[28] of loss of enjoyment of life is named préjudice physiologique (ou déficit physiologique ou déficit fonctionnel). Préjudice physiologique compensates the victim for the permanent reduction of physical, psychological, or intellectual functions. The medical expert describes and subsequently expresses, in percentage points, the loss suffered by the victim. The percentage is decided by reference to authoritative disability scorings[29]. As in some German Schmerzensgeldtabellen the disability scorings group decisions by disabilities.

As in the other experiences considered in this article, none of the medical scoring tables have an official character, although they are, so to speak, "appreciated" by the French Supreme court. Indeed, in all examined countries, medical scoring tables have gained their authoritative role in the judicial arena as a result of their scientific reputation.

Usually, parties to a case and the court itself appoint their own medical expert and the judges then assign a percentage value to the plaintiff's disability according to the evaluation provided by the medical experts. This percentage value is then multiplied by the monetary value currently assigned by the court itself for claimants in similar circumstances. Courts create their own tables of monetary values, which decrease according to age and increase according to the disability rate. In summary, the courts, by multiplying the victim's disability rate, which is expressed in percentage points, by the corresponding monetary value, obtain the monetary

---

[27] Note that in several European jurisdictions courts usually appoint their own impartial experts.

[28] For information on the French experience of awarding damages for personal injuries, see [57].

[29] This list of medical scoring points sets a rate for disabilities, by recommending either a specific rate or a scale of rates for each of them. *See* in general [58]. Galand-Carval also argues that along with objective parameters, medical experts have an important role in measuring the so-called "personal temporary incapacity" (*l'incapacité traumatique temporaire à caractère personnel*). *Id.* at 89.

damages award[30]. Another important factor to note is that in France courts update the monetary value assigned to a particular disability to reflect both inflation and different perceptions of the complained non-pecuniary loss[31]. Subsequently, any alterations find acceptance at the court of appeal level.

4.3.4 The Italian Search for a Synthesis

The French model has been adopted and developed by the Italian judiciary and scholars. The system is used for awarding the so-called danno alla salute or danno biologico, which we assimilate with loss of enjoyment of life. Indeed, the Italian judiciary, by way of judicial interpretation, has distinguished loss of enjoyment of life (danno alla salute) from pain and suffering (danno morale). Compensation for the former should ensue even though damage to health and bodily integrity neither reduced the ability to generate earnings nor caused pain and suffering[32], because danno alla salute is "a first, essential, priority compensation that conditions every other one."[33] According to the Italian Constitutional Court, damages for danno alla salute are compensatory and health "cannot suffer limits to the compensation for damage done to it."[34]

It is important to stress this last consideration, since it emphasizes the compensatory nature of awards for loss of enjoyment of life/danno alla salute. It is undeniable that a lost limb cannot literally be fully restored by any amount of money. However, social perception visualizes the award of damages as capable of making the victim whole[35]. Consequently, the use of indicative scheduling must be

---

[30] It is noteworthy to remark that the uniform descriptions of health impairments developed by medical scientists and monetary value tables based upon precedent decisions were developed by judges and scholars intending them as not binding. Indeed, they should not be binding according to the French Supreme Court. *See* Cass., 2e civ., Feb. 1, 1995, Bull. civ. II, No. 42.

[31] *See* [59]. Note also that damages for disfigurement and physical pain are assessed according to schedules calculated with reference to previous awards and judges indicate the lowest, highest, and dominant awards of the past year for each of the several scale degrees.

[32] *See* Cass., 6 june 1981, n.3675, *in* LA VALUTAZIONE DEL DANNO ALLA SALUTE 398 (M. Bargagna & F. D. Busnelli eds., 1995). In this work, most of the leading decisions on personal injury damages can be found as an appendix, in addition to other materials and commentary from members of the Research Group on *Danno Alla Salute* of Pisa under the auspices of the Italian National Research Council. *See also* [60] (analyzing over 1000 decisions).

[33] Corte cost., 14 July 1986, n.184, Foro It. I 1986, I, 2053, with commentary by Giulio. Ponzanelli, *La Corte Costituzionale, il Danno Non Patrimoniale e il Danno Alla Salute*.

[34] Corte cost., 14 July 1986, n.184, Foro It. 1986, I, 2053, "with commentary by Giulio Ponzanelli, *La Corte Costituzionale, il Danno Non Patrimoniale e il Danno Alla Salute*".

[35] *Wright*, [1983] 2 A.C. at 777: "Any figure at which the assessor of damages arrives cannot be other than artificial and if the aim is that justice meted out to all litigants should be even-handed instead of depending on idiosyncrasies of the assessor ... the figure must be 'basically a conventional figure' derived from experience and from awards in comparable cases." (per Lord

seen as an instrument used to obtain equal treatment, not as a means to reduce compensation or individual justice.

Similarly to France, the Italian awarding method finds its uniformity by carrying out a medical evaluation of the psychophysical disability and with reference to consistent monetary guidelines, developed once more, from an examination of prior awards. Again, corresponding to the French system, a medical evaluation, based upon reputed scientific and practitioners' publications, assigns to the permanent disability a percentage point. The court thereupon allocates a monetary value to this percentage point and multiplies the value by the percentage point. Needless to say, the Courts discretion remains absolute in defining the final monetary value of each point according to its previous awards. The judicial assessment of the disability is the responsibility of the court in any given case, its correspondence to a severity percentage, medical evidence being the leading guide[36].

In summary, courts in the European countries examined developed local tables of monetary values from their previous case evaluations and now use them together with scientific medical scorings to award objective noneconomic damages (danno alla salute and préjudice physiologique, loss of enjoyment of life). Local tables enable a reflection of the "local" social perception of the amount of money required to consider the victim whole. Strange as it might seem, those amounts might vary, and indeed vary significantly, from one Italian (or French) Region to another, as is probably the case in various American court districts. This somewhat awkward result illustrates once again that the European scheduling mechanisms are not a way of curtailing victims' rights, but rather a means to improve and govern the awarding of non-pecuniary loss. Indeed, medical scoring tables and monetary values used in Europe grant, at the very least, the sharing and distribution of information among all the stakeholders in personal injury cases.

In principle, it would be possible to develop a single scheduling system capable of serving horizontal and vertical justice. This notion could be realized by projecting the monetary value of the permanent impairment, defined by each court, into a conceptual uniform grid[37], which would reflect the actual perception of the relationship between different types of loss of enjoyment of life as awarded in case law and as described by medical expertise. Indeed, Italian judges developed a curve describing percentage points of permanent impairment and subsequently assigned to those percentage points an indicative monetary value, translating the points on the curve into the final monetary amounts they use to reflect (it is

---

Diplock); see also Rushton v. Nat'l Coal Bd. [1953] 1 Q.B. 495, 502 (U.K.), stating: The only way... in which one can achieve anything approaching a uniform standard is by considering cases which have come before the courts in the past and seeing what amounts were awarded in circumstances so far as may be comparable with the case which the court has to decide.

[36] Indeed, the Italian Constitutional Court expressly fostered: "a criterion fulfilling both the need for basic monetary uniformity and [the need] for elasticity and flexibility to adjust awards to reflect the actual effects of the ascertained disability on activities of daily life." See See Corte cost., 14 July 1986, n.184, Foro It. 1986, I, 2067.

[37] Further information and references available in [16].

assumed) the local, socially accepted evaluation of loss of enjoyment of life. Of course, a perfect system would require a methodology uniform to all courts[38]. Nevertheless, even a disparate approach is capable of affording predictability to the system and higher levels of horizontal and vertical equality in a given jurisdiction. Indeed, the monetary scheduling tables developed in France and Italy function simply by multiplying the value of the relevant point for each age/degree of disability combination, by the basic monetary award decided by each court. This system of calculating damages is utilized only if an amount has not already been established by averaging previous awards. Every different amount of the basic monetary award decided in a given jurisdiction respects principles of vertical and horizontal equality.

4.3.5 *Judicial Scheduling: The European Way*

The awarding methods we have briefly described improved vertical justice (among lesser and greater injuries) and horizontal justice (among similar personal injuries). Moreover, these awarding systems do not transform the personal injury victim into a faceless number but instead permit, along with a uniform base of monetary parameters, the delivery of better horizontal justice. This can be said with confidence, since the monetary values are indicative and susceptible to equitable adjustment, according to the specific case before the court. These awarding methods allow different injuries to be treated in different ways and similar injuries to be treated alike, always taking into consideration their individual and distinctive aspects. These results are mainly achieved by legal systems on a jurisdictional level. A vision of achievement of the same on a National level would indeed be ideal.

Where tables of monetary values have been developed, evidence of the personalization of awards is clear. The first avenue of personalization is offered by the combination of age and disability in the schedule. The second one allows for the adaption of these results depending on the facts of the case.

Medical-legal evaluations of psychophysical disabilities provide the basis for uniformity in the awarding process. These evaluations offer objective parameters and measurability while establishing homogeneous grounds for the evaluation of damages based on an examination of disabilities from past case law. The equitable power of each judge is safeguarded. He/she can adjust the objective measurement to the peculiarities of the case and the creation\selection of the scheduling and scoring tables, since the objective evaluation is his/her choice.

The joint effort of the judiciary and of experts (legal, medical, and economic) has produced descriptive\orientation tables. This long process of judicial experimentation has made objective non-pecuniary damages easier to ascertain and

[38] As proposed in [61].

assess. With the European situation outlined, we now turn to the question of whether or not a similar process of assessing damages could be initiated in the USA.

4.4 When Conclusions Impose Further Research

Italy, France, Germany, and the United Kingdom, by their processes of systemization, tend to reach similar results. Within the civil law and common law traditions considered, the basis for the assessment of damages for non-pecuniary loss relies on preceding cases concerning quantum, which set out the sum of money awarded and a description of the medically ascertainable condition suffered[39]. The two European models briefly described have been coined the "disability schedule and value table" model and the "precedent model."[40] A process of hybridization of the diverse models could result in an array of variations, useful for moving toward a European response to common problems.

In practice, however, the two models have diverse functionalities. "The French or Italian lawyer, having obtained medical evidence which places the injury at the relevant level of disability in terms of points, then turns to the relevant 'value' table to convert that into a sum of money. The English lawyer, having obtained evidence on the nature and effects of the injury, then tends to regard it in 'descriptive' terms and goes to the standard sources of specialist material reporting court awards, to look for something similar."[41]

When considering application at a European scale, each model presents hurdles. Though the disability schedule and value table approach would appear the simplest to implement, it would most probably result in competing expert views. This would most certainly arise in deciphering where on the matrix a particular disability should be allotted. Indeed, problems may also arise in relation to the accuracy of the scoring.

With this said, we suggest that these methods can easily function in every country in evaluating those noneconomic damages for which an objective criterion for establishing and measuring them is possible. Indeed, through medical expertise, we can objectively ascertain and score noneconomic damages for bodily and health impairment that we have compared to loss of enjoyment of life.

Drawing on the Anglo-German (use of descriptive tables)[42] and on the Franco-Italian (adoption of scoring percentages), a potential European system could achieve standardization and a more equalitarian use of resources for calculating,

---

[39] See generally [62, 63].

[40] *See* [64].

[41] *See* [65].

[42] Moreover, the Charter of Fundamental Rights of the European Union now strongly supports health, although this document has political value only. *See* Charter of Fundamental Rights of the European Union, Dec. 18, 2000, 2000 O.J. (C 364) 1.

simply by profiting more from available information. Indeed, when information is collected and shared, it becomes a theoretical starting point for evaluation both in and out of the courtroom. The information sharing process does not threaten the individualized justice which tort law promises. In fact, the search for clear guidelines reduces vertical and horizontal inequality since it enables judges to justify their departure from the guidelines.[43]

It is absolutely clear that combining reasonable predictability with the tailored assessment of damages is possible, tackling simultaneously the problem of uncertainty and justice (both vertical and horizontal). European legal systems, as shown, attain this either by using leading cases on quantum or by building upon scientific tables. Both options contribute information about past evaluations relative to both the litigating parties and the courts. Moreover, each system conserves ample discretion for decision makers (judges, juries, claim adjusters) in determining the amount of damages. Also important to note is that both systems allow for the adaption of the collated information (in the descriptive tables or in the scoring ones) to the case at hand. Every mentioned method requires rational justifications, if departure from the previous decisions occurs. The case has to be actually distinguished to avoid review on appeal[44]. Except for the UK, the European systems discussed in this article are not based on fully binding precedents, but, once elaborated in a meaningful way, they offer a preliminary informative framework that can be used repeatedly, leading to higher certainty in predicting the possible award of a given case.

The European experiences certainly demonstrate that rationalizing the awarding system for loss of enjoyment of life without taking away victims' rights and judicial powers is not a mythical chimera. In fact, it introduces rationality by supplying information and also has the potential to increase the possibilities for settlement, which would correspondingly reduce litigation.

European examples suggest that no limit to the discretion of the judicial system is required to foster these goals. The only requirement is the transformation of the judicial process into a better informed process.

In short, what the European insight suggests is the development of a shared methodology aimed at guaranteeing that similar loss of enjoyment of life, medically ascertainable, receives more similar treatment, even if the monetary value attached

---

[43] The argument is not novel. *See* [66], "An unexplained outlier should constitute a prima facie case for either remittitur or additur by the trial judge or an appellate holding of inadequacy or excessiveness of the judgment."

[44] Similar standards do exist in the USA. See, e.g., Steinke v. Beach Bungee, Inc., 105 F.3d 192, 198 (4th Cir. 1997), stating: In determining on remand whether the jury's verdict was rendered in accordance with South Carolina law, the district court should look to South Carolina cases to determine the range of damages in cases analogous to the one at hand... If the court believes a departure from the range is justified, it should provide the reasoning behind its view. If the court determines that there are no other comparable cases under South Carolina law, it should explain this determination as well. Such a decision in the district court will reduce the risk of caprice in large jury awards and will assure a reviewing court that the trial court exercised its considered discretion under the applicable state law.

to each case would still be relatively different. One must bear in mind the proverb, which states that change hurts, but stagnation kills[45].

References

1. Comandé G (1999) Risarcimento del Danno alla Persona e Alternative Istituzionali. Giappichelli, Torino, pp 3–45
2. Holding FJ, Kaye P (eds) (1993) Damages for personal injuries: a European perspective 1. Chancery Law Publishing, Chichester
3. Geerts A et al (1977) Compensation for bodily harm: a comparative study. Fernand Nathan; Labor, Brussels, pp 95–98
4. Pfenningtorf W, Gifford DG (1991) A comparative study of liability law and compensation schemes in ten countries and the United States. Insurance Research Council, Oak Brook, IL, 9–14, 77, 155–157
5. Schwartz VE, Lorber L (2002) Twisting the purpose of pain and suffering awards: turning compensation into "punishment". SC L Rev 54:47, 64
6. Geistfeld M (1995) Placing a price on pain and suffering: a method for helping juries determine tort damages for nonmonetary injuries. Cal L Rev 83:775, 777
7. Huber PW (1988) Liability: the legal revolution and its consequences. Basic Books, Inc., New York, NY
8. Olson WK (1991) The litigation explosion. Dutton, New York, NY
9. Comandé G (1999) Risarcimento del Danno alla Persona e Alternative Istituzionali. Giappichelli, Torino, p 3ff
10. Comandé G (1993) Le non pecuniary losses in common law. Rivista di diritto Civile I:453
11. Komesar NK (1974) Toward a general theory of personal injury loss. J Legal Stud 3:457, 459
12. Atiyah PS (1996) Personal injuries in the twenty-first century: thinking the unthinkable. In: Birks P (ed) Wrongs and remedies in the twenty-first century. Clarendon Press, Oxford
13. Atiyah PS (1997) The damages lottery. Hart Publishing, Oxford
14. Chapman B (1995) Wrongdoing, welfare, and damages: recovery for non-pecuniary loss in corrective justice. In: Owen DG (ed) Philosophical foundations of tort law. Clarendon Press, Oxford, p 409
15. Sugarman SD (2005) Pain and suffering: comparative law perspective. DePaul Law Review 55:399, Clifford Symposium
16. Comandé G (2005) Towards a global model for adjudicating personal injury damages: bridging Europe and the United States. Temple Int Comp Law J 19(2):241ff
17. Niemeyer PV (2004) Awards for pain and suffering: the irrational centerpiece of our tort system. Va L Rev 90:1401
18. Dobbs DB (1993) Handbook on the law of remedies, damages for personal injury (2nd ed.), § 8.1
19. Bell PA (1984) The bell tolls: toward full tort recovery for psychic injury. U Fla L Rev 36:333
20. Cohen MA (1988) Pain, suffering, and jury awards: a study of the cost of crime to victims. Law Soc Rev 22:537
21. Ingber S (1985) Rethinking intangible injuries: a focus on remedy. Cal L Rev 73:772
22. Kalionzes PN (1973) Case notes, infant pain and suffering: the valuation dilemma. Pepp L Rev 1:102
23. Leebron DW (1989) Final moments: damages for pain and suffering prior to death. New York Univ Law Rev 64:256

[45] As a great Irish student taught me.

24. O'Connell J, Simon RJ (1972) Payment for pain & suffering: who wants what, when & why? Univ Ill Leg Forum 1972:1
25. Peck CJ (1974) Compensation for pain: a reappraisal in light of new medical evidence. Mich L Rev 72:1355
26. Somerville MA (1986) Pain and suffering at interfaces of medicine and law. U Toronto L J 36:286
27. Vidmar N, Rice JJ (1993) Assessments of noneconomic damage awards in medical negligence: a comparison of jurors with legal professionals. Iowa L Rev 78:883
28. Zelermyer W (1954) Damages for pain and suffering. Syracuse L Rev 6:27, 31
29. Cramer R (1981) Comment, Loss of enjoyment of life as a separate element of damages. Pac L J 12:965, 972
30. Kriftcher EL (1988) Comment, Establishing recovery for loss of enjoyment of life apart from conscious pain and suffering: McDougald v Garber. St John's L Rev 62:332
31. Marth PE (1975) Comment, Loss of enjoyment of life: should it be a compensable element of personal injury damages? Wake Forest L Rev 11:459
32. Mishkin RJ (1969) Comment, Loss of enjoyment of life as an element of damages. Dick L Rev 73:639
33. Stolker CJJM (1990) The unconscious plaintiff: consciousness as a prerequisite for compensation for non-pecuniary loss. Int'l & Comp LQ 39:82
34. Fearon SJ (1989) Hedonic damages: a separate element in tort recoveries? Def Couns J 56:436
35. (1984) Annotation, Loss of enjoyment of life as a distinct element or factor in awarding damages for bodily injury. A.L.R. 4TH 34: 293
36. Busnelli FD (2003) Chiaroscuri d'estate. La Corte di Cassazione e il danno alla persona. Danno e resp 826
37. Ponzanelli G (2003) Ricomposizione dell'universo non patrimoniale: le scelte della Corte di Cassazione. Danno e resp 829
38. Horton Rogers WV (2001) Comparative report. In: Horton Rogers WV (ed) Damages for nonpecuniary loss in a comparative perspective. Springer, New York, NY, pp 245–296
39. Koch BA, Koziol H (2003) Comparative analysis. In: Koch BA, Koziol H (eds) Compensation for personal injury in a comparative perspective. Springer, New York, NY, p 407, 419–434
40. Comandé G (1999) Risarcimento del Danno alla Persona e Alternative Istituzionali. Giappichelli, Torino, pp 17–45
41. Busnelli FD (2000) Il danno alla salute; un'esperienza italiana; un modello per l' Europa? Responsabilità civile e previdenza, fasc. 4–5, pp 851–867
42. Horton Rogers WV (2001) Comparative report. In: Horton Rogers WV (ed) Damages for non-pecuniary loss in a comparative perspective. Springer, New York, NY, pp 268–275
43. Judicial Studies Board (2002) Guidelines for the assessment of general damages in personal injury cases, 6th edn. Oxford, Oxford University Press
44. Kemp DA et al. (2000) The quantum of damages in personal injury and fatal accident claims, 4th edn
45. Munkman J (1996) Damages for personal injury and death 130, 10th edn
46. The Law Comm'n, Damages for personal injury: non-pecuniary loss 5 (1999). http://www.lawcom.gov.uk/docs/lc257.pdf. p 7
47. Richard Lewis (2001) Increasing the price of pain: damages, the law commission and Heil v Rankin. Mod L Rev 64:100
48. Horton Rogers WV (2001) Comparative report. In: Horton Rogers WV (ed) Damages for nonpecuniary loss in a comparative perspective. Springer, New York, NY, p 246
49. Di Bona De Sarzana L (2005) L'evoluzione del modello inglese: il ruolo della Court of Appeal nel controllo dei valori liquidati e le Guidelines dello Judicial Studies Board. In: Comandé G, Domenici R (eds) La Valutazione Delle Macropermanenti: Profili Pratici E Di Comparazione. Pisa, Italy, ETS, p 97
50. Horton Rogers WV (2001) Comparative report. In: Horton Rogers WV (ed) Damages for nonpecuniary loss in a comparative perspective. Springer, New York, NY, p 276

51. Blumstein JF, Bovbjerg RR, Sloan FA (1991) Beyond tort reform: developing better tools for assessing damages for personal injury. Yale J On Reg 8 :171, 179–180
52. Magnus U (2003) Schadensersatz für Körperverletzung in Deutschland. In: Koziol H, Koch BA (eds) Compensation for personal injury in a comparative perspective. Springer, New York, NY, pp 148–176
53. Jaeger L, Luckey J (2003) Schmerzengeld
54. Hampfing W, Fehler A (1989) Schmerzensgeldtabellen
55. Hacks S, Ring A, Böhm P (2004) Schmerzensgeldbeträge
56. Wünsch S (2005) Il modello tedesco delle Schmerzensgeldtabellen. In: Comandé G, Domenici R (eds) La Valutazione Delle Macropermanenti: Profili Pratici E Di Comparazione. Pisa, Italy, ETS, p 85
57. Radé C, Bloch L (2003) La Réparation du Dommage Corporel en France. In: Koziol H, Koch BA (eds) Compensation for personal injury in a comparative perspective. Springer, New York, NY, pp 101–104
58. Galand-Carval S (2001) France. In: Horton Rogers WV (ed) Damages for non-pecuniary loss in a comparative perspective. Springer, New York, NY, p 90
59. Galand-Carval S (2001) France. In: Horton Rogers WV (ed) Damages for nonpecuniary loss in a comparative perspective. Springer, New York, NY, p 101
60. Bargagna M, Busnelli FD (eds) (1996) Rapporto Sullo Stato Della Giurisprudenza In Materia Di Danno Alla Salute
61. Turchetti G (1996) Gli sviluppi dello studio sulla determinazione del valore monetario base del punto di invalidità. In: Bargagna M, Busnelli FD (eds) Rapporto Sullo Stato Della Giurisprudenza In Materia Di Danno Alla Salute
62. Baldus D, MacQueen JC, Woodworth G (1995) Improving judicial oversight of jury damages assessments: a proposal for the comparative additur/remittitur review of awards for nonpecuniary harms and punitive damages. Iowa L Rev 80:1109
63. Bovbjerg RR, Sloan FA, Blumstein JF (1989) Valuing life and limb in tort: scheduling "pain and suffering". Nw U L Rev 83:908
64. Horton Rogers WV (2001) Comparative report. In: Horton Rogers WV (ed) Damages for nonpecuniary loss in a comparative perspective. Springer, New York, NY, p 274
65. Horton Rogers WV (2001) Comparative report. In: Horton Rogers WV (ed) Damages for nonpecuniary loss in a comparative perspective. Springer, New York, NY, pp 274–275
66. Blumstein JF, Bovbjerg RR, Sloan FA (1991) Beyond tort reform: developing better tools for assessing damages for personal injury. Yale J On Reg 8(171):179

Part II
Medico-Legal Ascertainment of Personal Injury and Damage Under Civil-Tort Law: Continental Overview – Europe

Paulus Zacchia s. aetatis anno LXVI Joanes Dominicus Cerrinus delin., Joanes Baptis. Bonacina mediolanen. sculp. Romae [S.l.: s.n., 1650–1657]. Courtesy of historical section of the "Vincenzo Pinali" Medical Library of the University of Padova

Chapter 5
Methods of Ascertainment of Personal Damage in Portugal

Duarte Nuno Vieira

Abstract The chapter illustrates the historical, judicial, and juridical framework of personal injury assessment and compensation in Portugal, describing the expert's qualification and competences and detailing the ascertainment methodology and criteria of evaluation utilized for identifying, describing, and estimating any personal injury, its temporary and permanent consequences, and the causal value/link between the event and the injury and between the injury and the impairment/disability.

5.1 Historical, Judicial, and Juridical Overview

Despite the Resolution (75) 7 of the Council of Europe—Committee of Ministers, concerning the assessment and compensation for damages suffered in cases of personal injury and death—the features of personal injury compensation within the European Community are still diverse. The different modalities for the assessment and compensation result from social and legislative diversities and reflect the profound philosophy of societies.

Several attempts to harmonize personal injury and damage assessment have been performed in the past. For example, in 1998, the "European Confederation of Specialised in the Assessment and Compensation of Physical Injury" (CEREDOC), which brings together the national associations of legal doctors working in judicial and insurance fields of several European countries (Belgium, France, Italy, Spain, and Portugal), has made a valuable effort for defining the damages to be assessed and the evaluation methodology, harmonizing the qualification of medical experts and creating a guide for the evaluation of permanent impairment.

D.N. Vieira (✉)
Faculty of Medicine, Department of Forensic Medicine, Ethics and Medical Law, University of Coimbra, Pólo das Ciências da Saúde - Unidade Central, Azinhaga de Santa Comba, Celas, 3004-504 Coimbra, Portugal
e-mail: dnvieira.pt@gmail.com; dnvieira@fmed.uc.pt

S.D. Ferrara et al. (eds.), *Personal Injury and Damage Ascertainment under Civil Law*, DOI 10.1007/978-3-319-29812-2_5

However, despite the abovementioned and other similar initiatives aimed at establishing an international harmonization, there are still numerous differences regarding the ascertainment methodology, the barémés for the evaluation, the terminology, and the training of forensic specialists in the evaluation of personal injury/damage at an international level.

Under the Portuguese juridical system, civil responsibility takes place when the injured individual files a lawsuit claiming patrimonial and/or non-patrimonial damages derived from a tort committed by another individual. The aim of civil law is to reestablish, as precisely as possible, the equilibrium destroyed by the injury and return the victim, at expenses of the person responsible of the tort, to the state that she/he would have been had if the event causing the injury did not occur.

In Portugal, full compensation shall be awarded for all injuries and losses to legitimate interests suffered by the victim (i.e., both material and nonmaterial losses). The assessment is traditionally based on objective considerations (medical expenses, loss of income, occupational disability, permanent total or partial incapacity) and subjective considerations (pain, aesthetic detriment and loss of amenity). Ultimately, the judge must decide what sum is adequate (exercising his discretion).

5.2 Description of Medicolegal Expert's Qualifications

In Portugal, there are two kinds of medical experts expected to ascertain and evaluate personal injury/damage suffered by an individual: (1) specialists in forensic medicine and (2) private experts with a specific demonstrable competence on personal injury assessment.

These experts (1 and 2) have to prove that they received a solid medical and legal preparation and a domain of medicolegal expertise.

However, following the Portuguese law, anyone with a degree in medicine (MD) is allowed to assess personal injury/damage and to testify in court as an expert.

In Portugal, forensic medicine services are concentrated in a single National Institute of Legal Medicine (INML), with headquarters in Coimbra, three delegations (in Lisbon, Coimbra and Porto) and a network of 31 medicolegal offices spread around the country. These are located in central hospitals and are answerable to one of the INML delegations, in accordance with geographic area.

5.3 Ascertainment Methodology

The medical forensic expert who will examine cases of personal injury/damage has access to all of the clinical data included in the civil process and may also request further information deemed relevant to the case. In the case of expert investigations ordered by the court, experts from the INML have direct access to all relevant clinical information, which they may request directly from hospitals, private doctors, clinical departments of insurance companies, or any other institution involved in the situation under examination. These bodies are then obliged to send a copy of the requested documents to the INML within 15 working days under penalty of legal sanctions.

It should also be pointed out that the forensic medical experts from the INML have, by law, total autonomy to order any complementary tests deemed scientifically justifiable for an accurate understanding of the situation, without having to seek prior approval from the court.

The parties involved and the court may of course also request further clarification from the INML concerning the investigation being conducted or may seek the answers to concrete questions about any aspect of the medicolegal investigation (about the methods used, complementary tests, scientific interpretation, conclusions, etc.) or even about merely scientific aspects.

During the course of the investigation and subsequent preparation of the report, the medical expert must consider all prior clinical information (clinical history, hospital records, etc.), as well as opinions and testimonies issued by private experts, and should interview and examine the patient and undertake any complementary diagnostic tests deemed necessary.

5.3.1 Collection of Circumstantial and Clinical Data

The first operation, which the expert must carry out, is the collection of clinical and documentary data, retrieving all medical and healthcare information believed to be useful for a diagnostic framework, for later identification of the pathological features, injuries and damages.

The documents of prime importance to be collected and examined are as follows: authorization for admission, anamnesis and physical examination, patient's journal, medical orders sheet, consent documents, emergency room assistance sheet or emergency room report, inter-consultation sheet, reports of complementary examinations, presurgery examination sheet, anaesthesia report, operating room report, postsurgery evolution sheet, pathological anatomy report, nursing journal, graph of vital signs and clinical discharge report.

It is of utmost importance to collect also any circumstantial documents useful for the reconstruction of the event/accident which caused the injury and, in particular, the mechanism which caused the injury.

5.3.2 Medical Case History

The expert must recon a detailed medical history, including familial anamnesis, physiological anamnesis (with a description of the particular/specific daily recreational activities) and work-related, remote and recent anamnesis.

Special attention must be paid in recording the exact circumstances of the event/accident, all the complaints attributed by the victim to the sequelae resulting from the trauma (i.e. familial, daily activities, recreational activities, social activities, work-related activities, etc.). Particularly in posttraumatic cases, the expert must be able to understand the full impact of the trauma upon the injured party, considering the type and characteristics of the trauma, the victim's reaction in the peri- and posttraumatic periods, the injuries and impairments resulting from the trauma, the perception that the damaged person has of the event and its consequences. This latter perception is related not only to the resulting personal injury but also to the justice system and to personal factors, such as previous experience of other traumatic situations, former health status, consumption habits, cultural and religious characteristics, the victim's responsibility and his or her resilience and motivation for rehabilitation. The expert must collect information also on the economic, family, social and cultural contexts where the victim lives because all these factors may influence the impairments and disabilities causally related to the traumatic event.

5.3.3 Systematic Clinical and Medicolegal Visit

This part involves a careful systematic collection of objective clinical data including internal medicine, neurological and clinic-objective tests aiming at specific problems.

In view of the possibility that the patient being examined may simulate non-existent injuries or accentuate the severity of injuries already present, proper medicolegal semeiotics must be applied in all clinic-objective examinations.

An exhaustive local examination of the injured region of the body must be performed, with an analytic study of simple movements and a global study of complex gestures.

5.3.4 Additional Investigations

If after the examination of medical and healthcare documentation and clinical objective signs, the available anatomo-functional data are not sufficient for a diagnostic picture, the possibility of further diagnostic tests, non-invasive and/or invasive, must be evaluated.

5.4 Evaluation Criteria

The first step for the medicolegal expert is to verify if, after the injury, the victim has gained the maximal medical improvement or, in other words, if the lesion is stabilized/consolidated.

It is possible that the victim, after receiving proper treatment, has been cured, that is, experienced a full anatomical, functional and/or psychosensorial recovery (i.e. the victim is not affected by any permanent impairment or damage).

It is also possible, more often, that after an evolution of the injury/disorder, the victim is still affected by a sequela with a permanent impairment, which does not require any other medical treatment unless those aimed at preventing a further deterioration of the *sequelae*.

Using all circumstantial evidence and the data collected at medical anamnesis, the expert must reconstruct the event/accident that could have caused the injury, focusing on the followings.

- Circumstances and mechanism of the trauma/injury.
- Symptoms in the immediate period after the event/injury.
- Symptoms in the interval between the event/injury and the ascertainment.
- Treatment(s) and/or medication(s) administered in the interval between the event/injury and the ascertainment.
- Outcomes of treatments already performed.

Basing on the circumstantial and clinical data previously collected, the medico-legal expert must then reconstruct the *pre-existing psychic and somatic state* of the victim prior to the event/injury.

5.4.1 Personal Injury Identification

The expert identifies the physiopathological features of the injury/disorder reconstructing the initial, intermediate and final stages of the disorder/disease. This reconstruction must be based on scientific references, following a proper source hierarchy.

- Guidelines.
- Consensus documents.
- Evidence-based publications.
- National literature.

In Portugal, the expert must classify the disorder using the *International Classification of Functioning, Disability and Health* (ICF).

This classification, created by the World Health Organization (WHO), provides a unifying framework for classifying the health components of functioning and disability.

The ICF classification complements WHO's International Classification of Diseases (ICD), which contains information on diagnosis and health condition, without details on the functional status.

The ICF is structured around body functions and structure, activities related to tasks and actions by an individual and involvement in a specific life situation.

After depicting the initial, intermediate and final status of the injury/disorder from a clinical point of view, the expert must identify the medicolegal equivalents, in terms of temporary/permanent impairment, and their repercussion on professional and social/leisure activities.

5.4.2 Temporary Impairment

The temporary impairment represents the detriment to good health caused by the injury/disorder in its initial and intermediate phases. It manifests first and foremost as a perturbation of the normal existence, being accompanied by physiopathological disturbances and subjective suffering.

In Portugal, the medicolegal expert, in order to describe and evaluate the temporary impairment, takes into account the followings.

- The characteristics of the traumatic injuries.
- The nature and severity of the lesions.
- The location, extent, depth and number of lesions.
- The treatment methods.
  - Type and number of treatments.
  - Number and nature of surgical interventions.
  - Time spent in continuous extension.
- The evolution of the injuries.
  - Incidents of immobilization and evolutionary.
  - Number and length of hospital admissions.
  - Number and nature of the exams.

In order to assess the *quantum doloris*, which is a particular noneconomic temporary damage, in Portugal, the medicolegal expert uses a "scale" divided into 7 subcategories: from very slight pain (1/7) to light (2/7), moderate (3/7), average (4/7), considerable (5/7), important (6/7) and very important (7/7) pain.

5.4.3 Permanent Impairment

The permanent impairment starts when the injury has stabilized and the maximal medical improvement has been achieved.

The expert must furnish a detailed and motivated description of the permanent functional deficit, the permanent repercussion upon the generic and specific professional activity and upon the leisure and social activities, the aesthetic damage and the eventual impairment of the sexual function.

In order to assess the damage in the most global and personalized manner and promote integral reparation, the expert should consider the person as a whole, rather than as the sum of his or her body parts, including capacities/functions and life situations/participation and activities.

These three levels may be the body and biological aspects (1) with their morphological, anatomical, histological, physiological and genetic particularities; (2) the functions and capacities; and (3) the life situations and activities. Regarding this latter point, in particular, the expert should carefully evaluate the repercussions on the work capacity and the leisure/social activities, explaining the followings.

- The eventual impossibility of performance of a particular profession.
- The difficulties of performance in a particular profession.
- The compatibility of a potential professional reclassification with the existing sequelae.
- The impossibility of performance of any work.

The medicolegal report should describe the injuries, impairments, disabilities and losses in a way that is clear, rigorous, objective, detailed, systematic and comprehensible to non-medical practitioners, even though medical terminology should always be respected. Sources of information and references should be provided.

5.4.4 *Causal Value/Link Between Event, Injury and Impairment*

The causal value/link and the relationship of an actual causal link must be evaluated by means of a "criterion of scientific probability", such as universal law, statistical law or criterion of rational credibility.

In Portugal, the medicolegal expert uses the criteria by Muller and Cordonnier (1925), focusing on the followings.

- The adequate nature of the event to produce the observed injuries/sequelae.
- The adequate nature of injuries/sequelae to the concerned aetiology.
- The exclusion of pre-existing damage.
- The adequacy between the region affected by the trauma and the seat of the lesion.
- The time adequacy.
- The anatomo-clinical chaining.
- The exclusion of causes strange to trauma.

In the medicolegal report, the expert must clarify whether the causal link between the trauma and the injury/impairment is certain or hypothetical, direct or indirect or exclusive or partial.

5.4.5 *Quantum for Temporary and Permanent Impairment (Disability Rate)*

In Portugal, there are specific barémés, introduced with the Decreto Lei n. 352/2007 of the 23rd of October 2007, which have to be used for quantifying the permanent disability rate.

5.4.6 *Other Pecuniary and Non-pecuniary Losses*

In Portugal, the medicolegal expert ascertains and assesses also some pecuniary damages, such as medical or any other additional expenses, which are related to the trauma/injury (*damnum emergens*) or the loss of earnings and other benefits, which the injured person would have received but for the accident (*lucrum cessans*).

The medicolegal expert must analytically describe the repercussion of the temporary and permanent impairment on the followings.

- Educational and training activities.
- General and specific professional activities.

The Portuguese juridical framework considers *aesthetic damage* as a separate injury in itself.

The medicolegal expert has to analytically describe the location, dimension, orientation, colour and morphology of the aesthetic injury in relation to the age, sex and pre-existing condition of the victim. A *scale* is used by the expert in order to grade the "aesthetic damage", which spans from very slight (1/7) to light (2/7), moderate (3/7), average (4/7), considerable (5/7), important (6/7) and very important (7/7).

Among other non-pecuniary losses, the medicolegal expert has to ascertain also the loss or impairment of the sexual function. Also in this case, a *scale* is used in order to grade the "sexual impairment", which spans from very slight (1/7) to light (2/7), moderate (3/7), average (4/7), considerable (5/7), important (6/7) and very important (7/7).

Below are listed some general bibliographic sources useful to deepen the issue. They are not reported within the text as they are no cited references.

Bibliography

1. Boróbia C (ed) (2006) Informe pericial en la valoración del daño. In: Valoración del Daño Corporal. Legislación, Metodología y Prueba Pericial Médica. Masson, Barcelona, pp 389–430
2. Magalhães T (1998) Estudo Tridimensional do Dano Corporal: Lesão, Função e Situação. Sua aplicação médico-legal. Almedina, Coimbra
3. Magalhães T, Antunes I, Vieira DN (2010) Recommendations to perform clinical forensic medicine reports related with bodily harm assessment in labor law. Revista Portuguesa do Dano Corporal 20:69–78
4. Magalhães T, Vieira DN (2008) A avaliação dos grandes traumatizados e a atribuição de terceira pessoa. In: Vieira DN, Quintero JA (eds) Aspectos Práticos da Avaliação do Dano Corporal em Direito Civil. Caixa Seguros e Imprensa da Universidade de Coimbra, Coimbra, pp 131–147
5. Oliveira C, Santos B, Jardim P, Corte-Real F, Magalhães T (2010) Danger to life' forensic assessment. Revista Portuguesa do Dano Corporal 21:37–48
6. Pérez MG-B (2006) Nuevo Manual de Valoración y Baremación del Daño Corporal, 14th edn. Editorial Comares, Granada
7. Vieira DN (2003) Assessment of bodily damage in civil law: harmonization of an expert protocol. Revista Portuguesa do Dano Corporal 12(13):29–36
8. Vieira DN, Corte-Real F (2008) Nexo de causalidade em avaliação do dano corporal. In: Vieira DN, Quintero JA (eds) Aspectos Práticos da Avaliação do Dano Corporal em Direito Civil. Caixa Seguros e Imprensa da Universidade de Coimbra, Coimbra, pp 61–83
9. WHO (World Health Organization) (2004) International classification of functioning, disability and health. WHO, Geneva

Chapter 6
Methods of Ascertainment of Personal Damage in Spain

Claudio Hernàndez-Cueto

Abstract This chapter illustrates the historical, judicial, and juridical framework of personal injury assessment and compensation in Spain, describing the expert's qualification and competences and detailing the ascertainment methodology and criteria of evaluation utilized for identifying, describing, and estimating any personal injury, its temporary and permanent consequences, and the causal value/link between the event and the injury and between the injury and the impairment/disability.

6.1 Historical, Judicial, and Juridical Overview

Throughout Spanish history, valuation and compensation for damage has not enjoyed particular importance outside the purely criminal sphere. A chapter on Injury from Crimes and Misdemeanors has always existed in our Penal Code, which has generally given prominence to the valuation of output when the judge decides on the penalty to be imposed. Since the partial reform of the Criminal Code of 1983, there has been an introduction of the assessment of the intention (Dolo), but results have continued to be the essential criminal criteria.

The civil law has also considered the consequences of injury by the appropriate valuation for compensation, but viewing them as minor elements that, with exceptions, did not warrant extreme consequences.

Historically, compensation for personal injury, as in other Western Countries with a clear oriental and religious influence (Leviticus, Chapter XXI, verses 16 and following), has been primarily a vengeful view of compensatory damages, only partially modified by the introduction of Roman law and the development of the Law of the Twelve Tables, especially in financial compensation for injury to slaves,

C. Hernàndez-Cueto (✉)
Department of Legal Medicine, Forensic Toxicology and Anthropology, University of Granada, Avda. de la Investigación 11, 18016 Granada, Spain
e-mail: chc@ugr.es

S.D. Ferrara et al. (eds.), *Personal Injury and Damage Ascertainment under Civil Law*, DOI 10.1007/978-3-319-29812-2_6

as was also specified in detail in the work of the jurist ULPIANO (Book XVIII, Ad Sabinum).

Later, with the fall of the Roman Empire and the hegemony of the Visigoths in Spain, the German influence was evident. After the initial legislation of the reigns of monarchs such as Leovigild, Eurico, Gaudenciano, and Alaric II, Fuero Juzgo emerged (VII century), which valued the injuries not for their functional anatomical severity, but their localization. For example, a head injury was compensated with five sueldos if it was not bleeding and one hundred sueldos if it was. Bishops or "Buenos Ommes" ("good men") were in charge of injury compensation, while physicians or surgeons were not mentioned in any way. Inspired by the aforementioned Fuero was the Fuero Viejo de Castilla of 1250, which established the first scale of compensation for injuries in our country.

With the vindictive principle as the guiding element of compensatory damages, the foundations of civil responsibility and economic compensation were laid—in addition to the regular participation of medical experts as advisers to the administration of justice in the laws of many cities, such as the Fuero Viejo (VI century)—which provided financial compensation for blood—or the Fueros of Escalona (1130), Toledo (1118), and Santa María de Cortés (1180). Even the Fuero Real of Alfonso X (1255) distinguished different financial compensation for bloodshed (a wound which is hemorrhaging or not, which affects the bone or not, etc.).

In the thirteenth Century, there were also historical references, especially in the documentation generated by the Kingdom of Aragon, concerning the existence of doctors who cared for the wounded and assessed their injuries. Thirteenth-century records already mentioned the charge of "doctor of wounded and tormented by justice." King James I "The Conqueror" nominated doctors to those charges in 1259 and 1272. Later in 1418, he had already acquired rights to exercise those. Records show requests sent to Fernando I of Aragon so that a specific person or somebody delegated by him could declare the end of hospital care in Mallorca and that the injured party was out of danger (and to be judged). That is, the creation of a body of doctors specialized in this type of assessment to practice before the courts of justice is sought, which unfortunately has not been achieved in our country. It is worth mentioning here that the "Laws of Style" (1310) were also derived from the law of Alfonso X (XIII century) with references to injury.

The enactment in 1532 of the Constitutio Criminalis Carolina by the Emperor Charles V (King Charles I of Spain) in the Diet of Regensburg, based on the Ordinances of the Bishop of Bamberg the same year, marked the final settlement of medical expert evidence in a Court of Justice when they had to rule on issues of medical biological basis. Formerly, this principle had been recognized at times and with different rulers, such as Charlemagne, the Assises of Jerusalem, or the Organization Chatelet with Prince Felipe, but at the same time a principle was established that has not changed in Spanish law since today: personal injury cases before Justice must always be evaluated by doctors as advisors to the judges.

Shortly before, King Juan of Castilla (1406–1454) issued a Royal Decree by which the Protomedicato was organized in Spain. This institution, very important in american territories next centhuries, was defined at the time by the Royal Academy as "the Tribunal constituted by protomedicos (doctors of the king) and examiners (teachers) who recognized the sufficiency of those who aspired to be doctors, granting licenses for such activity, assessed the professional liability cases, et cetera."

After 1492, the institution of Protomedicato reached the New World and new Royal Decrees related to the organization of medicine in new colonies began to be issued. They especially aimed to protect the figure of the chief physician, and the need for professional doctors was previously evaluated by these courts. The most important activity in this sense was developed by King Felipe II, who ruled the Protomedicato in "Las Indias" (spanish colonies in America) in 1555, stating that his Court had three essential functions: teaching, criminal (to examine the faults committed by the physicians in the practice of their profession and pursuing quackery), and economic (setting fines for offenses or violations in the practice of medicine).

As Bonnet pointed out (1980), the Collection of the New Laws of the Indies includes the Royal Decree of 11 January 1570 also issued by Felipe II and consisting of a detailed provision regarding the performance of the protomedicos sent to the New World. It especially rules on requirements for professional practice and training and evaluation of new professionals, but there are likewise references to protomedicos' relations with the Administration of Justice:

"It is our will that are required to reside in one of the cities in which any Court and Chancery, a protomedicos chosen by them and who has to hold the office in that city, about five leagues and not outside..."

And in cases where medical intervention was necessary to the aid of justice, doctors:

"(...) have to make a judgment to accompany one of the judges of the Court.. The Judge is not in a position to arrive at an official verdict without the aforementioned technical opinion (...)"

The main Protomedicatos in America corresponded to the most important administrative areas. Thus, a Royal Edict of June 9, 1646, issued by King Philip IV determined the creation of Protomedicatos of New Spain (now Mexico and part of Central American countries) and Peru. In 1776, Carlos III created the Vice-Kingdom of the Río de la Plata, which included the regions of Rio de la Plata, Paraguay, Tucuman, and Cuyo. In 1798, King Charles IV instituted the Protomedicato of Rio de la Plata. Among his duties as a Court, there were a wide range of functions on the regulation of professional activity and public health control, of which we selected the following.

- To inform about medical problems linked to the ecclesiastical, military, naval, and administrative staff.
- To inform the authority concerning soldiers and sailors on sick leave.
- To control the exercise of the medical profession.
- To advise about measures to be taken for sick prisoners.
- The medical examination of imported or sold slaves.
- To advise Justice in forensic setting.

The damage assessment, firmly framed within Legal Medicine, begins to develop conceptually and scientifically throughout Europe in the sixteenth century when physicians often act as experts in law courts. Medicine begins to see differently and highlights what could be of interest to the judge and the law.

In Spain, the figure of Juan Fragoso is worth mentioning, the personal physician of King Philip II and who analyzed the forensic prognosis in his Declaraciones from 1601. Really, these statements correspond to the second part of his "Universal Surgery," with a complementary text entitled: "Tratado de las declaraciones que han de hacer los cirujanos acerca de diversas enfermedades y muchas maneras de muerte que suceden." ("Handbook abour interventions of doctors at the Court in case of illness and deaths") He would be particularly proud of this:

"(...) A brief statement in order to ensure that surgeons may assist judges and ministers of justice, in cases of death, sickness, weakness and depravity of any member"

He studied the injures according to the organ or region where they relapse, the patient's disposition, and the weapon that caused the injuries, in order to better illustrate the legal medical prognosis. Juan Fragoso should undoubtedly be regarded as the father of Spanish Legal Medicine.

During the eighteenth century, French enlightenment and revolutionary influences were essential to the development of concepts such as the economic value of the person and principles such as the need for compensation to all individuals. In my opinion, two figures dominate this period: Jean Jacques Rousseau and his Social Contract published in 1762 and Cesare Bonasena, Marquis of Beccaria, and his "About Crimes and Punishment" (1763). Both emphasized the importance of Science in order to achieve a more equitable and modern Justice. These ideas influenced the legislative and expert development in Spain as well.

During the Naturalist Positivism, several works need to be mentioned, but especially renowned in Spain was Pedro Mata and Fontanet, Full Professor of Legal Medicine at the Central University of Madrid (Complutense University of Madrid, today) who developed the National Forensic Medical Corps from the beginning of the nineteenth century. This led to the introduction of a group of medical officers who depended on the Ministry of Justice as permanent advisors to the Spanish criminal courts. Currently, these official experts advise all judges and courts in medico-biological expert reports in both the Criminal Law and the Civil, Labor, and legal citizen's claims against the State.

Since the promulgation of the Organic Law of Judicial Power of 1985 and the regulation in the Autonomous Communities from the year 2000 (in Andalusia, for example, from the decree of 2002), official experts have been reorganized as a collegiate body in the Institutes of Legal Medicine (one per province), dependent on the governments of the Autonomous Communities, with Services of Forensic Pathology, Forensic Medical Clinic, a Laboratory, and a Unit of Evaluation of Gender Violence. Some of them also have specific training agreements with the University Departments of Legal and Forensic Medicine, but not expert activities.

The Institutes of Legal Medicine (IML) were created as technical bodies to aid judges, courts, offices of the Civil Registry, and prosecutors in those areas belonging to medicine and human biology that fall within the sphere of forensic medical knowledge.

The continuous increase in the rate of events in which the forensic medical intervention was necessary and the high number of them meant that the work became more specialized, and in this way the mere finding of certain features or elements was replaced, in certain circumstances, by assessment and scientific interpretation. All this was accompanied by a remarkable and significant scientific and technical development through research and publications. The process culminated in our country in the late nineteenth century, particularly with the creation of the National Forensic Medical Corps as a result of the work done by Professor Pedro Mata. The creation began with the Health Act of 1855 and was put into practice by Royal Decree of 13 May 1862, by which those with a certain medical forensic training were assigned to the judicial bodies in order to intervene in relation to any such matters.

Unlike the quick evolution of the scientific knowledge and the complexity of the cases that arise in practice, the functional model has remained relatively rigid under the forensic scheme assigned to a Coroner Court or group of courts, and based on individual and unskilled participation, in which one professional had to respond to any question formulated by a court or tribunal. General scientific expertise and Legal Medicine in particular, linked to technological development which requires knowledge and mastery of a range of instruments in order to study and evaluate the cases arising in practice, have led to a new legal medical model more adapted to the characteristics of the present situation, such as is being developed in most neighboring countries.

The Organic Law of the Judiciary (LO 6/1985) already evaluated the creation of the Institute of Legal Medicine, a process that was completed with the new Organic Regulation of the National Forensic Medical Corps by the Real Decreto (RD) 296/1996 of 23 February) and later Regulation of the Institutes of Legal Medicine (RD 386/1996 of 1 March). A Real Decreto is a Law made by the Government that takes effect 30 days after the promulgation (period for the participation of Parliament to approve or eliminate it). Regulations where the new functional organization and structure of Forensic Medicine around the IML were established, according to the criteria of specialization and rationalization of the human and material resources in order to provide a public service of higher quality.

In Andalusia, the Decree of the Concierge of Justice and Public Administration 176/2002 of 18 June constitutes and regulates the Institutes of Legal Medicine of the region, bringing together the philosophy of the above regulations and reflecting the desire to improve the public medical forensic service and make it a mainstay of knowledge in order to shed light on the shadowy circumstances which have always surrounded crime and court cases. The process culminated with Decree 176/2002 of 18 June, which constitutes and regulates the Institutes of Legal Medicine of the Autonomous Community of Andalusia, and the resolution of the Deputy Minister of Justice and Public Administration, who set 15 July 2003 as the date of entry into operation of IMLs Almería, Cordoba, Granada, Malaga, and Seville. Subsequently, by Resolution of the Secretary General for Relations with the Administration of

Justice of 8 June 2004, he set the date of entry of IMLs of Huelva and Jaen (20 and 26 July), and finally through a similar resolution of January 20, 2005, the date of entry of the IML of Cadiz on 25 January of that year was established.

The creation of eight Institutes of Forensic Medicine in Andalusia and the need to establish guidelines and homogeneous criteria throughout led to the creation of the Coordination Committee of the Institutes of Legal Medicine by Decree 95/2004 of 9 March. This rule also creates the Andalusia Council of Forensic Medicine conceived as a representative college of all institutions involved in the training and medicolegal research, where major research initiatives in these areas are proposed and discussed.

From the above regulations and their spirit there are three basic functions developed by IML. Their development will come tempered by the functional organization of the Institute itself in particular and the existence of other institutions that establish specific projects—we refer mainly to universities in general and in particular medical schools—but also to other Departments and agencies we develop functions related to Legal Medicine, such as the Andalusia School of Public Health (Department of Health) or the Andalusia Women's Institute (Ministry for Equality and Social Welfare).

At the same time, within the MIR test (Internist Resident), which is a national examination plus a term of 4 to 5 years (depending on the type of Specialty) of hospital active attendance, capturing the new generations of doctors for the national health network, the Ministry of Health opens every year a call for posts, in order to train specialists in Forensic Medicine in professional Schools at the Universities of Granada and Complutense of Madrid. In the case of Granada, the call includes an agreement for specific training in forensic pathology at the Institute of Legal Medicine of Granada. These specialists are trained in the extra-hospital setting, and, after obtaining their degree, they do not find a job in the Health Network (not including Medico-Legal hospital jobs) or in the Institutes of Legal Medicine (where only graduates who pass the tests for Forensic Medical convened by the Ministry of Justice are accepted). As a consequence, they end up working for Insurance Companies, as temporary employees or in private practice as Forensic Medical experts.

Finally, to work as an expert for a private practice a specialization is required, so many different specialists in Legal and Forensic Medicine, Orthopedics, Psychiatry, Gynecology, Neurology, Rehabilitation, etc., participate in the valuation and compensation process depending on the case. Sometimes that private practice is official, i.e., requested by a judge or court, what especially happens in criminal matters and to teachers and University departments.

The possible participation of all stakeholders in assessment of injury is particularly widespread in the Civil Law, Labor, and Litigation.

Previously, in Civil law only a weak relationship existed of possible permanent pathologies that the injured could suffer, organized into twelve economic categories that ranged between 1–1000 pesetas (1st category) (1 cent—6.00 €) and 200,000–250,000 pesetas (12th level) (ca. € 1,200.00—€ 1,500.00) in known as "Spanish Scale." Each category contained a minimal set of conditions included in the same, indicating that, if not included on that relationship pathology rating, it would be included in the more related category.

6.2 Identification and Description of Medicolegal Expert's Qualifications

As previously indicated, the medical expert evidence does not require any specialization except a degree in Medicine, as established in the Laws of Spain Procedure (Criminal and Civil). The expertise is understood as a useful judicial tool for both the court and the parties.

The Official experts (Médicos Forenses) do not receive specific training in damage assessment. Some items on the subject are included in the agenda of the test they have to pass. Then, during the brief period before they start to work, they share those tasks that "Medico Forense" exercises, including the review of injured people in Clinics/ Institutes of Legal Medicine.

In the private sphere Medical Specialists and teachers in Forensic and Legal Medicine (who, in turn, tend to be specialists and, in many cases, "Medico Forense" on leave) have indeed been specifically instructed by university professors during a period of at least six months, attending trials, reviewing cases (including participation in scans of patients), and writing appraisal reports of damage, as well as the corresponding theoretical training.

Medical Specialists accede to University Professional Schools of Legal Medicine (only in Granada and Madrid) in order to follow a training program in Legal Medicine during three years and, within it, a specific training in theoretical and practical damage assessment of about six months, other than Forensic Pathology, Toxicology, Psychiatry, and so on. However, these professionals normally go to work in the private sector because there is no space in the Public Health System or the Institutes of Legal Medicine.

Although they are not obliged, the rest of the professionals conduct additional training in damage assessment offered by many universities as postgraduate training, which is a significant economic benefit for them. For example, at the University of Granada I coordinate a Master of more than 500 hours of training in rating Bodily Injury Assessment (including assessment of oral damage psychic, damage, splash damage, damage to the elderly, Orthopedics, Radiology, etc., Practical training with Forensic Medicine, Insurance Companies, Rehabilitation Services, etc). These graduates are generally preferred by lawyers and citizens when they have to go to a doctor for injury report before the judge. Similar courses are held at the Universities of Madrid, Granada, Barcelona, Deusto (Bilbao), Santiago de Compostela, Murcia, etc. Such courses, although with a much more reduced content, are also offered for attorneys and other healthcare professionals, such as physiotherapists.

These options are present both in the judiciary and in the extra-legal field. In the case of Insurance Companies and Mutual of Labor, physicians receive specific training, sometimes through the companies they work for, but usually through Masters and Courses offered by the universities.

In conclusion, with respect to expert evidence (in bodily damage or other area), the following unfortunate absurdity occurs in Spain: while no one would go to a non-specialist to be operated on for a heart problem or for a serious fracture—these being professional territories reserved only for specialists—it is possible to go to any type of medical expert, without specialized previous formation in medicolegal materials, to obtain information on matters of such gravity and personal and economic impact as we are analyzing.

6.3 Ascertainment Methodology

Logically, damage assessment and its methodology vary in each case. These variations permit access to patient records or not, the examination of the same patient on more than one occasion or on only one occasion, access to additional diagnostic tests (laboratory tests, images, etc.) in order to understand the circumstances of the damage caused, and the previous condition of the patient before suffering the injuries that we should now quantify, in addition to many other elements. It is also different based on the patient's characteristics, taking into consideration very different cases requiring different methodologies. Thus, whether the patient is independent or not, if he/she is an adult, a child, or an elderly person in a coma or with severe neurological disturbances, or if he/she is affected by pathologies or psychiatric trauma. Like the classic and successful citation of "there are no diseases, only the sick," we should add here: there are no expert reports, only cases of people to inform.

There is no official valuation guide in Spain, and the optional ones are part of the most modern texts on the subject in the form of suggested methodology that in no case bind the work of the expert.

However, there is a quite common element which determines the working methodology significantly in Spain: a scale or "barème."

As I pointed out before, the reform of the Penal Code in 1983, in terms of injuries, had several objectives. One of these was to reduce the number of cases of damage to people demanding penal treatment and, therefore, not saturate the Courts of Justice. To that end, a mandatory scale in the assessment of all injuries resultant from traffic accidents was drafted and came into force, which should be compensated by civil responsibility motor-vehicle insurances. It was a "barème" of mandatory application by medical experts but, of course, not binding on the court's decision, but very approximate and influential in establishing that decision and, above all, as a tool of uniformity in the treatment of cases and to facilitate as much as possible the attainment of amicable agreements in the private sector that do not require court, or even civil, intervention. It was a good system structured and conducted by the association of insurance companies (Unión Española de Aseguradoras: UNESPA) that became a reference document to be considerate in many cases out of the own injured in traffic incidents. In fact, it has so much influence that often we the experts have it in mind when doing data collection, focusing from the beginning on those aspects that the scale contemplates and, therefore, determining what, how, and with which tools we are going to analyze it.

6.3.1 Collection of Circumstantial and Clinical Data

Data collection is primarily achieved through two pathways: the medical history and patient interview and examination.

In most cases, the expert's work is remote with respect to the trauma suffered by the patient. After the accident and the damage, the patient is treated at the hospital and then in care outside, so that when he/she is recovered or arrives to the final status of his process, he/she goes to a lawyer or to a private medical expert.

Criminal, traffic, and other cases are periodically reviewed by the Médico Forense in the Service of Clinical Forensic Medicine into the corresponding Institute of Legal Medicine, but, usually, when the patient is already out of the hospital and is able to visit the Institute, where he/she is generally reviewed each week or month until the Médico Forense thinks that the process is complete, issuing the final Declaración de Sanidad, which includes the total period of disease, the causal link, and the relationship of consequences, if any. Only in exceptional cases, because of their special importance, social significance, etc., will the Médico Forense visit the patient to the hospital before they are discharged from the medical center. Nor does the Médico Forense usually consult the clinical history as a reference document (except, again, in exceptional cases), but the Informe de Alta, summary document that every hospital must give to the patient at the time of leaving the hospital.

6.3.2 Medical Case History

Any source document is valid, but more often it is the complete medical history, especially in the conduct of private valuations to request from the patient represented by counsel. Patients, through the lawyer, can obtain the medical history documents and the hospital sends a copy to the corresponding Court. Citizens have a summary document of his story from the hospital at the end of the hospital treatment.

Médicos Forenses, in the Institutes of Legal Medicine, tend to work with only the discharge report that the patient provides. In particularly complex cases, full medical history is also requested.

For Mutual Insurance Companies or Labor in which the patient has been treated and reviewed regularly by doctors for these companies, Médicos Forenses use the history made by the medical service itself.

In the case of working with the clinical history as a key source it includes not only documents issued by the various doctors who have attended the patient in different departments and units of one or more hospitals but also the corresponding sheets of nursing, laboratory results, X-rays, or other imaging tests, as well as specialized reports (Eco, Electromyography tests, etc.).

The personal and family history must be taken into consideration. Personal history is crucial in order to know those aspects of the patient's health previous to the injury, whose consequences are especially important for us: other traumatic events, previous hospital stays, previous surgery, longer stay in bed at home, and subjection to previous treatment. But also familiar pathologies could be inherited, conditioning the previous health status of the patient. Clarifying this Previous State is essential to establish further appropriate causal links between each of the effects that the patient may have and the trauma or pathology that could give rise to them or influence their evolution until the final status that we are assessing.

Moreover, on a personal level it is considered to be particularly important to know the family situation of the patient (if he/she is married or permanent partner, if he/she has children and their age) as well as social and leisure situation (sports, hobbies, if he/she drives a motor vehicle, if he/she could treat itself in daily basic activities, if he/she was able to meet its social environment, home, participate in household chores, care of the children, etc.).

In this last section, the patient's psycho-emotional conditions have a big influence. Therefore, the existence of pre-trauma psychological or psychiatric disorders will be very important, including the existence of these disorders in the aftermath of the assessment we are performing. Although, as discussed below, a large battery of tests for the assessment can be used, experts usually go to a specialist psychologist or psychiatrist to obtain the most accurate assessment of the patient's situation in this area and the origin of it.

6.3.3 Systematic Clinical and Medicolegal Visit

As I mentioned above, the expert performance of damage assessment in Spain is usually done later in most cases. If the patient is hospitalized, he usually will not be visited nor assessed by the doctor. Moreover, doctors of insurances companies visit regularly the patients at home every week until the final process. When it is a case interested by Médico Forense, patient must present every week in the Institute of Legal Medicine to be revised. In the first case, the information obtained will be in the Assurance Company Documentation and to read it you need a Court authorization. In the second case, Médico Forense writes a short document with information about the evolution of case (Parte de Estado). At the end, the document (Declaración de Sanidad) contained original diagnosis, time of evolution (hospitality and extra-hospitalary), sequels, and its valoration by the berème. The documents after these work produced by the Médico Forense are publics.

When the patient gets the discharge and returns home, although he continues receiving complementary treatments (rehabilitation, periodic reviews in ambulatory situation, drug treatments, etc.), he is also assisted by professional medical services or Insurance Companies and Professionals Mutual (usually at the state level and as a complement to the Public Health Care System). Both types of entities will have taken charge of the patient from the outset if he did not require hospital treatment.

The Médico Forense, who has the option and privilege of going to the hospital at any time and meeting with the patient or their doctors, or to browse the documentation of clinical history, however, does not usually contact him before discharge, but after, when he reviews periodically (ranging from weekly or monthly, as appropriate) and usually reproduces in his progress reports the essential elements already contained in the Informe de Alta or reports derived from queries facilitated to the patient.

In the cases of private experts, the contact does not occur in most cases until the end of both the previous medical intervention (hospital and extra-hospital) and the Médico Forense one, who usually sets the date when the damage is healing, which will serve to set the period of illness which—counted in days—could be compensable.

Of course, we will conduct a thorough internal review, including the classic stages of the same: inspection, palpation, percussion, and auscultation (cardiac and respiratory), with pulse checking and blood pressure assessment. We will evaluate and ask the patient about his or her eating habits, sleep, sexual relationship, and any possible symptoms of apparatus and system, but especially those involved in the traumatic event to be rated and in relation to the sequels observed.

In many cases, the neurological evaluation acquires special significance, assessing progress, position, balance, reflexes status, sensitivity, etc.

The osteoarticular situation will be evaluated both at rest and with activity, either by active and passive movements. This allows us to know the degree of mobility limitations of the patient and which are true articular disorders produced by pain and which are not.

6.3.4 Additional Investigations

In those necessary situations, it will be possible to do clinical studies and complementary-instrumental studies especially when their complexity and/or significance require specialist involvement, as for the followings.

- Eye Disorders.
- Disorders of the ear.
- Complementary imaging tests (X-rays, MRI, CT scans, contrast evaluations…).
- Other physical diagnostic tests: ECG, EEG, EMG, ultrasound, etc.

– Psychological and psychiatric diagnostic tests, going to the most appropriate test battery at the discretion of the specialist who performs them.

Generally, these elements are especially important in Spain: when a complementary test is necessary for medicolegal reasons only (i.e., not for clinical aims), because it has not been done before, or because a lot of time has elapsed since it was made and some changes are expected. No differences based on the presence/absence of invasiveness or X-ray involvement are done.

In this case, the Medical Specialist will perform the test and write a report in order to complete the expert report.

6.4 Evaluation Criteria

The assessment criteria vary depending on the legal consequences of the damage. Although the common element of the assessment will include a proper anamnesis and a complete physical exam, including additional diagnostic tests if needed, the aspects of interest to be evaluated by the court change depending on cases with criminal, civil, labor, or administrative consequences. The expert, in sight of what aspects should be emphasized, will decide what information becomes more important and what could be considered as complementary. Other factors to consider may lead to subtle changes in the assessment, including age, gender, family circumstances, habits and hobbies, usual type of work, etc.

In the area of criminal law, in view of the provisions of Article 147 et seq. of the current Penal Code (Law 1995), the medical assessment of the outcome is particularly important, because any damage requiring, in addition to an initial medical assistance, additional assistance with medical or surgical not considering the attentions linked to the first service as a second medical act (e.g., removal of stitches, antibiotic prevention, tetanus prevention, etc.). Medical assessment is even more important in the territory of the offense as an additional burden will be imposed to the imprisonment depending on those medical data which reveal a particularly harmful intent by the perpetrator in view of the result, used weapons (weapons capable of causing serious injuries, even though they do not), or weakness of the victim (e.g., mental incapable or a child under twelve) or given the particular outcome in a series of sequels which are particularly important to the criminal text: sterility, severe deformity, severe somatic or mental illness, complete loss of a sense, etc. Then imprisonment could be up to twelve years.

For the Spanish Civil Law, compensation for damage must have an integral consideration and all damage and all the consequences in all spheres of the victim's life must be compensated. This also requires a comprehensive evaluation, including all possible elements which vary from case to case depending on the personal circumstances of the patient, but possible to be summarized as illness period, final state (sequels), consequences in the workplace, in the family life, leisure, life in relationship with others and prejudice of relief, old prejudice, kid or youth prejudice, aesthetic damage, need for assistance from a third person, adequacy home environment (including removal architectural barriers), and special means of transport, etc.

In Labor Law the General Social Security Act of 1974 is the reference text. It establishes the basic concepts of Occupational Disease, Work Accident, Sickness and Common Accident, as well as the consequences either as Temporary Disability (with sequels or not that should be compensated, which is set by the scale or barème, as we see below) or as Permanent Disability in different degrees: Partial for routine work, Total for routine work, Absolute for all types of work, and Severe Disability (Gran Invalidez) where the employee will also require the assistance of a third person to develop the basic activities of daily living. For that, the analysis of the charges of the job position in each case and the compliance with the final state of the patient are not inessential.

Law 41 /2004 Patient Autonomy includes the relationship of rights and duties of users of the Spanish Public Health System and considers the possibility of a claim for damages resulting from the malfunctioning of such services, either as a result of equipment malfunction and/or poor professional performance or the wrong organization and intervention health service itself. This will lead to very similar assessments to those reported for the Civil Law, but it is essential to demonstrate that the negative final results for the patient were disproportionate, arising from malfunction or working method, not attributable to a single professional (because, then, we would be talking about malpractice and a claim for criminal or civil medical responsibility) and demanding an unacceptable degree of sacrifice to the user.

6.4.1 *Psychic and Somatic State Prior to the Event/Injury*

Previous knowledge of the state of the patient is essential. The cause of trauma must face the consequences produced by him/herself or of which he/she is responsible for, but not those others which his/her action did not affect. As a classical concept of Spanish law (common to other Countries): “It will be valued and compensated the damage, all damage, but only damage.” That is, the preexisting disease or that produced in other circumstances and causes unrelated to the initial trauma cannot be considered in the assessment, because they should not have any legal consequences.

That will be very easy in those cases where there are no previous pathologies or these have no connection with the trauma and its consequences, so that they can be established without any doubt. At other times, the relationship between the previous state and consequences of injury is clear, being possible to assert that the previous state is not the responsibility of the person who caused the injury, but the relationship between them (for worsening of prior state or worsening of the consequences of the wound). However, there are some few cases where such limits are not possible to establish, it being very difficult to estimate the responsibility for cause of the injury in the final result (for example, in the classical case of Parodi). The way to establish causal links between trauma and injury outcome, with or without participation of a previous medical condition, will be discussed below in the corresponding section. I can anticipate that the Spanish courts in cases of reasonable doubt question the experts, not being able to identify a clear causal link, in order to establish the more likely causes of damage so as to be able to declare about the legal responsibilities and consequences.

6.4.2 Detailed Reconstruction of the Event/Injury

The study of the traumatic event and its characteristics, the circumstances in which it occurred, and the personal experience of the injured party is usually performed during the anamnesis by a personal interview with the people involved. As noted, this is a remote action subsequent to the post regarding the timing of events. The interview with the expert is usually carried out when the patient has already recovered from the damage—subtracting or not sequels—and claims the compensation through the attorney. It is very uncommon for the expert to have technical information available from the police (in a traffic accident, in aggression, etc.) but he has the initial data contained in health records (report of transfer to hospital by service emergency assistance, first report of emergency department of the hospital). Therefore, the patient's story is essential to clarify and to assess critical aspects such as the followings.

- Circumstances in which the injury occurred (location, time, activity that developed the victim.).
- Immediate symptoms experienced by the patient (loss of consciousness, submission to extraordinary forces, initial attention by the police, witnesses, etc.).
- Circumstances of the transfer to the hospital (immediate or not, by road, helicopter, ambulance).
- Care and initial health status on arrival to the hospital.
- Earliest diagnostic tests and treatments applied.
- Preliminary information provided by the medical staff to the patient or relatives.

Since that first period usually corresponds to phases of unconsciousness or shock states, the additional information at the time of the assessment is particularly important. The closest relatives who accompanied the wounded from the first time of the incident can provide it, especially if the patient has sequels which make it difficult to communicate or remember facts, is a child, or an old man with psychological, memory, or relationship disorders.

From there the medical record, in addition to the statements of the patient and their close family members, will be added as the main source of information pointed out in the medical record.

6.4.3 Personal Injury

From this moment, personal injuries are analyzed carefully, one by one, to study the mechanisms of production, initial symptoms, results of diagnostic tests, treatments applied (with description of surgical techniques applied, placement of osteosynthesis material...), prescribed medication, evolving process, including important issues that required treatment changes or additional actions not provided in principle, evolution during their stays in special service (with particular reference to intensive care units, etc.), studying all developments over the period of hospital stay and, later, outside the hospital: care at home, specialist revisions (Orthopedics, Neurology, etc.) and its evolution, complementary therapies, including periods of rehabilitation (exercises and techniques, application time, frequency of application, total period of treatment, and final progress report after rehabilitation).

6.4.4 Temporary Impairment

In Spain, the assessment of Temporary Disability varies among the different areas of Law. In some of them, as in criminal law, there is no legal interest, but in other areas it acquires an extreme importance.

In labor law the Temporary Disability (TD) ("Baja" or "Invalidez Temporal" = Inactivity) is considered to be the period during which the worker is prevented from addressing the fundamental tasks of their regular work. During this period, the employee receives medical and pharmaceutical cares, in addition to the temporary economic board that allows their subsistence, and is reviewed by his doctor weekly, who reports the course and treatment applied with copies to the worker, the Social Security System, and the worker's company. This period will last a maximum of twelve months, after which the worker will be in one of the following situations: healing and return to his professional activity or assessment of a possible situation of permanent disability. Only in exceptional circumstances can the TD be extended for six months provided that healing is considered very likely to be achieved during this additional period. TD period may also end by the death of the worker or his arrival at the age of retirement. Medical Inspectors (medical corps of the Health National System who have to review disease processes of workers) also may at any time decide to end the situation of TD ("Alta" = Activity) if they agree with the doctor. The disagreement with this decision by the patient could be studied in the Administration of Justice as long as he denounces through his respective attorney (Social Courts).

In civil and administrative cases, TD period or Baja will be counted in days from the date of the accident or the traumatic event to the date when the healing is considered to be produced (with or without sequences). The establishment of the healing time is often the subject of discussion, since it is difficult to define it and there are special situations in which healing is really never achieved. Instead, we must now speak of stabilization with squeals when the patient requires later treatment and care, but without new medical events of interest.

Periods of TD do not allow distinction between full or partial considerations in TD or percentages (100% or 50% of TD, etc.), making distinction of different levels of TD only in cases of damage from traffic accidents which, as I pointed above and I discuss below, should be evaluated by a specific scale (barème) that considers three different levels of TD.

- Hospital.
- Non-hospital.
- Impeditive.
- Non-impeditive.

"Impeditive day" is when the patient cannot develop both his normal duties and professional ones.

The days of hospital TD are compensated at a rate of an amount of money per day, the outpatient impeditive about 50 % of the above, and non-impeditive around 20 %.

6.4.5 Permanent Impairment

The establishment of the moment to evaluate the Permanent Impairment (PI) is usually done using classical and medicolegal criteria as follows: There is the maximum possible evolution of this disease, the maximum possible treatment for healing has been applied, and the patient can return to full independent living, partially or minimally. There are special situations where the latter condition is not satisfied (for example, in a persistent vegetative state after head trauma leading to a coma of long evolution that requires specialized care hospital for many years), but clinical criteria are accepted to set the time of stabilization (e.g., in the previous case after a year of evolution without serious incidents in hospital) to set the compensation of damages.

After setting the "date of cure," it is possible to calculate the healing period for further compensation and to establish the existing sequels, if any, and to know if they have produced a permanent disability in the patient, which is evaluated in Spanish law with labor law criteria.

The General Law of Social Security recognizes the following PI ratings.

- Partial PI: The worker cannot attend all the functions of his regular work duties, but the essential ones.
- Total PI: Worker cannot handle the burden of their regular work, even the vital ones.
- Absolute PI: Worker cannot face the burden of any work.

- Large Disability: In addition to being unable to work, the worker needs the help of a third party to do the basic tasks of daily living (dressing, grooming, moving, etc.).

In labor law each of these situations deserves the major attention of the social security service when severity increases (greater economic pension, assistance at home, etc.). Normally, when the worker recovers or consumes the maximum of TD, he/she is evaluated by medical and technical committee that decides his/her rating in one degree or another. If the patient does not agree with the qualification, he could lodge a legal complaint.

In the case of damage caused by traffic accidents, the corresponding scale provides a number of criteria to increase the compensation correction. One of these criteria is the partial or total disability for working, considering similar levels to those set for the labor law which deserve a different percentage of increasing, but the judge will always be the one who ultimately decides, if there is no previous agreement, whether to accept it and the amount of increase.

6.4.6 *Causal Value/Link*

The establishment of the causal link is essential to admit the existence of liability, so the report of the expert is devoted to investigate two conditions.

- The assessment of the relevant causal links between the traumatic event and the initial injuries.
- The assessment of the relevant causal links among the injuries, their consequences, and the consequences produced in all spheres of the victim's life.

Accepting as valid the most common causal theories, the Spanish Law prefers to apply the principle of the appropriate causality and in many cases by an objective criterion in order to establish the leading cause of the injury to the agent of the damage and determine if it is an unlawful case.

In case of damage, the basic reference focuses on article 1902 of the Civil Code ("The person who by act or omission causes damage to another, by fault or negligence, is obliged to repair the damage."). Useful in the courts of law, in the case of the medical assessment of causality, the concept of "most probable cause" in cases when the medicine is not able to specify a particular cause, which usually happens due to the limitations of medical science and the characteristics of harmful actions, as well by multi-causal origin.

6.4.7 *Personal Damage Quantification*

We need to distinguish the following.

- Quantum for Temporary Impairment: Usually the quantification of TD period is made in Spain by simply counting the days between the date of the event and the date of recovery or stabilization of injuries. Later, in the civil law on TD are compensated at a rate of a monetary amount per day. The great influence that has represented for damage compensation the appearance of scale for compensation for damage caused by road accidents (barème) in Spain, it is used as a reference text in many cases, including those not resulting from traffic accidents. That includes accepting the differences of Table V scale set for the days of TD (hospital and non-hospital days, non-impeditive, and impeditive days).
- Quantum for Permanent Impairment: For PI, the quantification of the consequences is essential and in Spain is carried out with the use of scales of mandatory application, as appropriate.
  - Labor Law: Quantification of anatomical-functional damage suffered by a worker and after healing (including the possible existence of sequels) does not prevent the implementation of the fundamental tasks of their regular work, i.e., does not produce a situation Total PI and becomes totally recovered or in a possible situation Partial IP for their regular work ("no disabling sequels"). He/she is offered reinstatement to his/her regular work or one very similar and in the same company, but with a unique economic compensation (e.g., osteosynthesis material, postsurgical scars, mild loss of mobility, etc.). To do that, Spanish law joined by "Decree of April 15, 1974 as a compensation 'barème' for not disabling sequels in the field of Social Security," the translated version of the Guide for the Evaluation of Permanent Impairment of the American Medical Association.
- This same American scale was also included as a reference by the Ministerial Order of 8 March 1984, which developed the Law 13/1982 on the social integration of disabled people, such as a mandatory tool to quantify deficiencies (genetic or after trauma) that justify the recognition of the situation of disabled people with all the privileges and economic and social benefits that entails. Since it is a well-known document, I do not find it necessary to comment further here.
  - Civil law: It is mandatory in cases of damage resulting from the application traffic accidents popularly known as the "barème of points" or "traffic scale," which emerged in 1984 through the national consortium of insurers (UNESPA) and it has had different versions, being currently in force by the Royal Decree 8/2004, of 29 October, "Law for Civil Responsibility and Assurance of motor vehicles circulation" which contains an appendix entitled "System for assessing damages to people in traffic accidents" It is structured into six sections or tables. The last one (Table VI) contains the "barème," that is, the sequels ordered by organ systems with their corresponding numeric valuation. This tool is also provided for compensation not only for the TD and IP, but also for cases of death, which justifies the appellation: system.

The structure of this document, the latest version of which is appended to this text, is as follows.

Table I: Compensation for death.
Table II: Correction factors for death benefits.
Table III: Compensation for permanent injury (economic value of Points).
Table IV: Correction factors for compensation for Permanent Damage.
Table V: Compensation for Temporary Disability.
Table VI: Classification and Measurement of sequels.

This last table contains the true scale: the ratio of possible consequences, ordered by organs and systems, with an assessment in points (0 points: no damage, 100 points: maximum damage). Normally each sequel is valued in a range, with a maximum and a minimum, within which the expert must explain the reason for the points assigned for each sequel.

The Aesthetic Prejudice receives similar treatment but independent from the rest of the sequels. Considered in five different categories (mild, moderate, medium, large and very important, with a score interval for each), it is assigned the corresponding score, which is studied separately.

Table III transforms the value of each point in an economic value based on two criteria: patient age (point value is higher in younger patients) and the total of damages or point earned (so a patient with many points, with many sequels, receive more value for each point). The value of the points is updated every year by the Ministry of Finance in relation to the minimum wage set by the Government. So, the Table and the system are constantly updated.

Finally, Table IV lists the Corrector Factors, generally to increase economic compensation under judicial decision. The factors to be considered are pecuniary loss, IP (partial, total, absolute, or severe disability), need of home adequacy (barriers elimination), need for adapted vehicle, permanent assistance from other person, etc. Only one factor will be considered for compensation reduction: the co-responsibility of victim producing the trauma event.

A copy of the "Spanish barème of traffic" accompanying this report (Real Decreto Legislativo 8/2004).

6.4.8 Non-Pecuniary Losses

Among the non-pecuniary losses, plus the factors considered into Table IV of Real Decreto legislativo (RDL) 8/2004, the Spanish damage valuation reports usually consider the following losses.

Loss of Welfare: loss of ability to enjoy the pleasures of life. Usually include limitations to practicing sports and leisure activities (dancing, relationship with friends, activities in cultural societies, etc.).

Aging Prejudice: in the case of elderly patients, especially valuing the loss of life expectancy and decrease of quality of life. Frequently, we use scales to quantify the ability to develop basic activities (bathing, dressing, moving independently, etc.) and the instrumental activities (opening and closing doors and windows, dial a phone number, read a newspaper, shopping at the supermarket, make small tasks at bank, pharmacy).

Youth Prejudice: Valuing separation from family during the hospital stay, impaired growth, decreasing of overall capabilities to develop different activities (loss of potential ability), negative effects on school, limitations to sport and plays.

In our judicial and juridical context the "loss of chances doctrine" (i.e., a heightened risk of death or injury) is contemplated and eventually reported into the report if it is necessary, but no quantification is provided.

These prejudices are generally reported by the expert but the judge or the Court who admits their existence and their economic value in each case.

6.4.9 Pecuniary Losses

The economic consequences of injury and illness (professional income reduction, costs incurred, etc.) are elements beyond medical competence, so that they are evaluated by the Courts, but never by medical experts.

Below are listed some general bibliographic sources useful to deepen the issue. They are not reported within the text as they are no cited references.

Bibliography

1. De Ángel R. La experiencia española en materia de Valoración del Daño Corporal. CDC 89, Madrid, 1989; 21–22 de junio
2. Girela E, Hernández-Cueto C (2001) El Informe Médico de los Daños a las personas. In: Hernández Cueto C (ed) Valoración médica del daño corporal. Guía práctica para la exploración y evaluación de lesionados, 2nd edn. Masson, Barcelona
3. Gisbert JA (1991) Medicina Legal y Toxicología. Barcelona, Salvat-Masson
4. Hernández Cueto C (1994) Imputabilidad Médica. Revista Portuguesa do Danno Corporal 2 (4):33–54
5. Hernández Cueto C (1995) Breve revisión crítica del actual sistema de valoración de daños corporales en España. Derecho y Salud 3(2):184–199
6. Hernández Cueto C (1997) La valoración del daño corporal en niños y ancianos. Revista Portuguesa do Dano Corporal 6(7):37–62
7. Hernández Cueto C (1998) La Valoración Médica del Daño Corporal. In: Villanueva E (ed) Medicina Legal y Toxicología. Masson, Barcelona, pp 455–464
8. Hernández Cueto C (2001) La Valoración Médica del Daño Corporal. Guía Práctica para la exploración y evaluación de lesionados, 2nd edn. Masson, Barcelona, 495 pages
9. Hernández Cueto C (2004) La Valoración Médica del Daño Corporal. In: Gisbert JA, Villanueva E (eds) Medicina Legal y Toxicología, 6th edn. Masson, Barcelona, pp 505–515
10. Vieira DN, Corte-Real F (2008) Nexo de Causalidade em Avaliação do Dano Corporal. In: Vieira DN, Álvarez J (eds) Aspectos práticos da avaliação do dano corporal em Direito Civil. Coimbra, Biblioteca Seguros, Caixa Seguros, pp 61–84

Chapter 7
Methods of Ascertainment of Personal Damage in France

Eric Baccino and Jean Sebastien Raul

Abstract The chapter illustrates the historical, judicial and juridical framework of personal injury assessment and compensation in France, describing the expert's qualification and competences and detailing the ascertainment methodology and criteria of evaluation utilized for identifying, describing and estimating any personal injury, its temporary and permanent consequences and the causal value/link between the event and the injury and between the injury and the impairment/disability.

7.1 Historical, Judicial and Juridical Overview

In France the evaluation of permanent incapacity ratios (in percentage of 100 %) has been used for compensation of occupational hazards and accidents since 1898. The Mayet-Rey-Mathieu-Padovani Scale for occupational hazards was the first to be published in 1925 and was actualized many times until 1983.

The first official scale ('barème') for bodily damage assessment due to occupational hazards was issued on May 24, 1939, with a 2nd edition in 1982 and a third in 1996. In the introduction of this scale, the authors made a clear separation between permanent incapacity evaluation in common law and in occupational hazards (or other private laws). For the same anatomical damage, the percentage of incapacity will often be different (usually higher in occupational related incapacity).

Therefore, a much-needed scale for common law was published in November 1959 in a French journal called *Concours Medical*. After five more editions (1980,

E. Baccino (✉)
Service de Médecine Légale, University of Montpellier, Hôpital Lapeyronie, 191 Av. du Doyen Gaston Giraud, 34295 Montpellier Cedex, France
e-mail: e-baccino@chu-montpellier.fr

J.S. Raul
Institut de Médecine Légale, Faculté de Médecine, Université de Strasbourg, 11 Rue Humann, 67085 Strasbourg, France
e-mail: jeanseb.raul@gmail.com

S.D. Ferrara et al. (eds.), *Personal Injury and Damage Ascertainment under Civil Law*, DOI 10.1007/978-3-319-29812-2_7

1982, 1993, 2002 and 2005), it is still known as *barème du Concours Médical* and is by far the most popular used in bodily damage evaluation, since it is of exclusive and mandatory use in all medical assessments or appraisals ordered by French insurance companies. It is written by a body of experts under the umbrella of *Association pour l'Étude de la Réparation du Dommage Corporel* (AREDOC), directly under the control of insurance companies.

This scale is also legally mandatory in medical responsibility appraisals for *Commission Regionale de Conciliation et d'Indemnisation des accidents medicaux, affections iatrogenes et infections nosocomiales* (CRCI or CCI) procedure, which is a specialized commission for medical liability unique to France as it compensates medical *alea* (medical accident without fault or malpractice). The French Society of Legal Medicine (SFML) issued in 2000 a common law scale, more comprehensive than the *Concours Medical* and including scales for suffering assessment (quantum doloris), aesthetic and sexual damages.

Recently, AREDOC and SFML collaborated in producing an actualized scale (0–7) for suffering assessment, including the psychological impact of accidents and diseases.

Due to a recent change (2005) in the number and definition of various bodily damages (nomenclature Dintilhac or listing) originating from a financial decision for the victim's sake, AREDOC recently produced a scale for personal temporary damage evaluation (leaving aside the impact of working capacity).

During the past decades, and especially since Dintilhac in 2005, there has been a clear tendency towards a unification of valuation criteria (i.e. scales) in appraisals ordered by insurance companies as well as by the courts.

As a result, the differences between medical experts working for the courts and medical advisors for insurance companies are diminishing, providing at least fairer, and probably better, valuation for all victims.

This is good news, in times where a shortage of French physicians and thus medical experts is noticeable.

7.2 Identification and Description of Medicolegal Expert's Qualifications

In France, the expert in charge of assessing the damage may be a medicolegal expert trained in one of the French universities during his internship (after 6 years of medicine) and during his fellowship. Usually this training lasts a minimum of 3 years.

Another way to obtain the qualification is to validate a university diploma on assessing damage, which may last 1–2 years and during which the student follows a theoretical course (100 h), in addition to following a senior expert during his/her work.

After this training the student will be a rookie for the court and will finally be a medical expert in the field of damage assessment when he has followed a sufficient number of cases as a rookie. He may then be a judicial expert.

With one of these two qualifications, the physician may also become an extra-judicial expert.

The majority of bodily damage assessments are made by doctors working for insurance companies, who are often called 'experts' but who are actually medical insurance advisors.

There is no good expertise without good experts. This is why the Mediator of the French Republic has recommended reinforcing the procedures for selecting experts, by reviewing, among others, the methods of drawing up the national list of legal experts, currently under the responsibility of the office of the appeal court.

A separate list of experts exists for damage due to medical care and is controlled by the national commission of medical care accidents. When postulating, the expert must send five reports which will be reviewed by this commission. The expert may be an expert in a medical specialty and/or an expert for assessing personal injury. In the latter case, he/she must have one of the two former university degrees.

There is a distinction between the medical assessment of the injury and the legal assessment. The function of the medical expert is only to give indications about factual matters and not to evaluate the injury. The role of the expert is limited by the document issued by the judge (*mission d'expertise*). There have been different model forms of this document, which suggested ways of assessing different injuries. The most recent is the *mission* Dintilhac, which replaced in 2006 the form from the *Association pour l'Étude de la Réparation du Dommage Corporel*, and the *mission d'expertise judicaire handicapés graves troubles locomoteurs*, which was drawn up by a commission of insurers (*Fédération française des societies d'assurance*) and judges. Such documents are not compulsory, but the medical expert must follow any instructions given to him by the judge.

7.3 Ascertainment Methodology

The technique of expertise is contradictory, involving the convocation and presence of all parties, with a shared access to documents also considering a full and unlimited access of patients to their own medical records, as they are responsible for providing medical evidence.

The assistance of a lawyer, an insurance and physician (maybe nominated by defence associations) are guaranteed. A public discussion and consequent conclusion are drawn and a public dictation follows. A preliminary report is sent to the parties with 1-month delay for any remarks.

7.3.1 Collection of Circumstantial and Clinical Data

This information is collected during the victim's examination. Sometimes court files are given to the expert such as accident drawings, photographs of the vehicles or of the objects and police investigation.

7.3.2 Medical Case History

The work of the expert is to collect much information concerning the victim's history. This is done by questioning the victim and/or his family.

The expert focuses on the living (married, lives in a house, an apartment, how difficult can it be to enter the home?), the work (actual and past professional experience, diplomas, etc.), the usual sports performed, the hobbies and so on.

7.3.3 Systematic Clinical and Medicolegal Visit

A global medical examination is done not focusing only (but mainly) on the site of injury; hence general, localized and comparative measures are taken into account. Specifically, internistic (inspection, palpation, percussion and auscultation of cardiovascular, respiratory, digestive, excretory, reproductive, immune and endocrine system), neurological, osteoarticular and musculoskeletal evaluations are performed. An interview is crucial for detecting simulators.

7.3.4 Additional Investigations

Instrumental (i.e. radiological exams) may be wanted by the expert as well as specific tests using specialized instruments and devices like neuropsychic tests. The expert cannot ask for these additional investigations. The judge must validate them or they can be prescribed by the personal physician of the victim for clinical reasons.

7.4 Evaluation Criteria

The different components of the damages are categorized either according to a traditional listing or a more recent listing entitled 'Dintilhac', named after the magistrate who presided over the commission which submitted a report in October 2005 to the Minister of Justice.

This takes into account psychic and somatic state prior to the event/injury, detailed reconstruction of the event/injury circumstances and mechanism of the trauma/injury. The victim is asked for his symptoms in the immediate period after the event/injury, his/her symptoms in the interval between the event/injury and the ascertainment, his/her treatment(s) and/or medication(s) administered in the interval between the event/injury and the ascertainment. Each time the outcomes of treatments already performed are evaluated, and the expert may question the relevancy of continuous treatment (such as physiotherapy).

7.4.1 Personal Injury

The term 'consolidation' is central to the assessment of different injuries. A person is deemed to be consolidated when the injury has stabilized and is not expected to either improve or deteriorate thereafter. A distinction is drawn between the period of temporary impairment and permanent impairment. The noneconomic loss suffered as a result of the temporary impairment was often neglected before 2006 and only the economic aspect of the loss was considered.

Temporary impairment is either total (any period during which the victim is permanently in a hospital or rehabilitation centre) or partial. When partial, it is given with a percentage. Insurance companies have separated into four categories these temporary partial impairments (see below).

Permanent impairment is possible when the victim is consolidated. A clinical description of the impairment is performed and the evaluation is given with a percentage based on barèmes.

7.4.2 Causal Value/Link

To assess the causal value of injury/damage, the medical facts (certificates to ascertain the reality of injury, CT scans, radiography, etc.) and the clinical examination are the basics. The underlying principle for causality is that the claimed damage needs to be the result of a 'direct, certain and exclusive' of one cause.

The type and severity of the injuries sustained during the event/trauma are discussed especially concerning the link with the possible mechanism of injury. Some criteria are necessary, such as the scientific relevance between injury and the mechanism of injury, the possible link between the anatomical site of the damage and the initial anatomical site of the injury, the delay between the injury and the onset of symptoms and the possible clinical evolution. Finally, the medical history of the victim is questioned, especially seeking for anterior impairment or injuries on the site of the damage. When this global evaluation ends, the expert may assess the certainty of the link between the accident and the injury/damage. Moreover, special conditions need to be contemplated, such as pre-existent conditions, predestination (i.e. haemophilia), the presence of aggravating factors of a pre-existing condition and acceleration of the disease.

7.4.3 Quantum for Temporary Impairment

In France no barèmes accepted by the courts exist for the quantification of the temporary impairment (disability rate). Nevertheless, quantifying the temporary impairment may be based on the barème used for permanent impairment. There exists a distinction between what is called total temporary impairment and partial temporary impairment. Total temporary impairment is usually considered when someone is at the hospital or taken in charge day and night in a rehabilitation centre. Insurance companies have classified into four categories (I = 10 %, II = 25 %, III = 50 %, IV = 75 %) partial temporary impairment, based mainly on the use of a wheelchair, the use of crutches and so forth.

7.4.4 Quantum for Permanent Impairment

In France, barèmes are used to quantify the permanent impairment (disability rate) depending on the situation. For classic motor vehicle accidents, two barèmes are used: one from the *Concours Medical*, a French medical journal and also the official barème of insurance companies, and the other from the French Society of Legal Medicine. Other barèmes also exist for accidents and pathologies due to work, for specific insurance contracts.

7.4.5 Other Non-pecuniary Losses

7.4.5.1 Possible Damage to Sexual Function

Loss of sexual function is a factor in the assessment of non-pecuniary damage. Impairment of sexual function and enjoyment and of the ability to have children gives rise to an entitlement to compensation. The loss is distinguished from loss of amenity. It is also distinct from the degree of incapacity. The loss can be only temporary. According to some authors, this can lead to the victim being compensated twice: the first time through compensation for loss of amenity and the second through compensation for loss of sexual function. The victim cannot be forced to undergo any operation. Insurance companies still oppose the individualization of this damage, which was, however, defined in the Dintilhac listing and whose evaluation is required by most of the courts.

7.4.5.2 Aesthetic Damage

This element of loss is called *prejudice esthétique*. Permanent aesthetic damage may in effect constitute a separate injury in itself of some importance (leading to loss of career or causing the victim to avoid social occasions), or it can be a trivial mark left after a minor accident. In order to assess such damage, the medical expert applies a scale graduated from 0 to 7, which does not take into consideration the age and the sex of the plaintiff. However, courts do take these elements into account for financial compensation, as well as the occupation of the victim and whether the victim is unmarried. The *Cour de cassation* has ruled that compensation for aesthetic damage is due even where the victim was in a coma (and the coma was likely to last until the death of the victim). Whenever aesthetic damage affects the ability to continue to carry on an occupation, the personal loss arising from the aesthetic damage resulting from the injury is distinguished from the economic loss. The latter will be compensated under the head of pecuniary losses (and included in the assessment of the degree of permanent incapacity).

Temporary aesthetic damage is also proposed in the Dintilhac list, but due to the lack of barème, most experts only describe the alleged prejudice without quantification. It will be up to the payer to figure out the financial value of it.

7.4.5.3 Pain and Suffering

The element of physical pain is placed within the category of *pretium doloris*. It is recognized as an element of non-pecuniary loss. Both pain suffered in the past and any symptoms which are likely to continue into the foreseeable future are taken into account. However, it is often difficult for medical experts to assess future pain which is neither ‘chronic’ nor ‘functional’. Hence, this item of compensation will normally cover the pain suffered during the period of temporary ‘traumatic’ impairment. This element may also include mental suffering, such as fright and any nervous reaction, the fear of future incapacity, mental anxiety and neurosis. Here too, a scale is used, which specifies differing degrees of pain (very light, light, moderate, medium, quite severe, severe and very severe). It shall be noted that pain and suffering is protected from the recoupment of benefits by social security. The sums awarded under this heading are rather modest (from 1000 € to 15,000 €).

7.4.5.4 Loss of Amenity (*Préjudice d'Agrément*)

The item of loss called *prejudice d'agrément* represents loss of amenity. This type of claim applies even where the victim is in a vegetative state. The courts have devised numerous subcategories of loss of amenity within the scope of the head of *prejudice d'agrément*. According to the *Cour de cassation*, loss of amenity results from the 'loss of quality of life', which concerns not only the future impossibility of doing a particular activity or sport and does not require specific proof that the victim had in fact carried out the sport or other activities prior to sustaining the injury. Loss of amenity can incorporate a loss of sense of smell, an unconsummated marriage and the inability to go for a walk or carry heavy objects. This injury is included within the heading of damage known as *dommage moral* and is different from mere physical injury. The medicolegal expert provides no quantification but a detailed description based on the subject's declarations.

7.4.6 *Damnum Emergens*

French law provides compensation for medical expenses incurred by the injured person in treating his condition and restoring him to health. This includes payments for a prosthesis, wheelchair and housework.

Social security provisions enable the victim to obtain all of his/her medical needs without the need to make any payment whatsoever. There is a general principle of freedom of choice of doctor and hospital. Therefore, the plaintiff is not bound to make use of free medical and hospital treatment, and if he/she receives treatment as a private patient at his own cost, the cost is recoverable and will be paid by the Social Security (up to 80 %). Plaintiff's damages cannot be increased if the size of his medical bill is dictated by his personal situation. The items which may be claimed as medical expenses are many and diverse. The costs of nursing care at home can also be claimed. A plaintiff is equally entitled to recover future expenses as well as those already incurred at the time the court makes its award.

7.4.7 *Loss of Earnings*

The victim may be awarded compensation for temporary loss of earnings. Where the victim used to work, he/she will be compensated for any loss of earnings as a result of having to give up work. The calculation of loss will be carried out by comparing the previous level of earnings and the level of earnings during the temporary incapacity (after deductions of medical payments and social security benefits). Damages can be awarded for the victim's loss of opportunity to gain a promotion in his/her career. Even if the victim did not work at the time of the injury, compensation may not be precluded.

The evaluation of permanent work incapacity relates to the specific work function performed by the subject. If after 'consolidation' the victim cannot resume his/her work for medical reason, his/her scholarship is taken into account to assess the possibility of working in another field. Therefore, a victim may have a permanent working impairment for his/her usual work but not for all types of work.

Below are listed some general bibliographic sources useful to deepen the issue. They are not reported within the text as they are no cited references.

Bibliography

1. Black D (1998a) The limitations of evidence. J R Coll Physicians Lond 32:23
2. Brennan TA, Leape LL, Laird NM, Hebert L, Localio AR, Lawthers AG, Newhouse JP, Weiler PC, Hiatt HH (1991a) Incidence of adverse events and negligence in hospitalized patients—results of the Harvard Medical Practice Study I. N Engl J Med 324:370–376
3. Fischer G, Fetters MD, Munro AP, Goldman EB (1997a) Adverse events in primary care identified from a risk-management database. J Fam Pract 45:40–46
4. Hofer T, Herr E, Hayward R (2000a) What is an error? Eff Clin Pract 6:261–269
5. Hughes G (2009a) Litigation, redress and making amends. Emerg Med J 26:844
6. Hurwitz B (2004) How does evidence based guidance influence determinations of medical negligence? J R Coll Physicians Lond (BMJ 329:1024)
7. O'Neil AC, Petersen LA, Cook EF, Bates DW, Lee TH, Brennan TA (1993a) Physician reporting compared with medical-record review to identify adverse medical events. Ann Intern Med 119:370–376
8. Scobie S, Thomson R, McNeil JJ, Phillips PA (2006a) Measurements of the safety and quality of health care. Med J Aust 184:S51–55

Chapter 8
Methods of Ascertainment of Personal Damage in Italy

Ranieri Domenici

Abstract The chapter illustrates the historical, judicial and juridical framework of personal injury assessment and compensation in Italy, describing the expert's qualification and competences and detailing the ascertainment methodology and criteria of evaluation utilized for identifying, describing and estimating any personal injury, its temporary and permanent consequences and the causal value/link between the event and the injury and between the injury and the impairment/disability.

8.1 Historical, Judicial and Juridical Overview

The Italian legal system is part of the family of the Roman law systems (or civil law). The compensation for the damage to the individual is therefore disciplined by the rules of the Civil Code. However in the last few decades, the most radical changes of the compensation rules have been the result of the evolution of the doctrine and jurisprudence (the so-called living law).

"In the beginning was the income, and the injured was worth what he earned": this was the core of the rule which (almost) by itself for a long time was sufficient to satisfy, in Italy, the demands of compensation for the damage to the individual. The damage may have a negative incidence on property of the injured party, both reducing his earnings (loss of income) and forcing him to incur costs (consequential damage). The economical situation of the injured party thus would be modified to an even worse state. According to this traditional vision, compensable damage turned out to be the difference between the value of the property of the injured party after the damage and the value that the property itself would have had, if the damage had not taken place. Such a conception is effectively demonstrated by the

R. Domenici (✉)
Department of Clinical, Surgical, and Molecular Pathology, Unit of Legal Medicine, University of Pisa, Via Roma 55, 56126 Pisa, Italy
e-mail: ranieri.domenici@med.unipi.it

S.D. Ferrara et al. (eds.), *Personal Injury and Damage Ascertainment under Civil Law*, DOI 10.1007/978-3-319-29812-2_8

well-known "cobbler's case", suggested by Melchiorre Gioia in 1821, where the (productive) value of the individual is compared to that of a machine.[1]

> Let us suppose that the remaining duration left to a ten year old machine [and] ... [its] annual product are 1200 liras. You will have damaged this machine so that, despite reparations, it will only yield 900 liras each year. The yearly loss that you cause to the owner is therefore 300 liras. The compensation you owe him for 10 years is of 3000 liras... A cobbler ... manufactures two shoes and a quarter a day: you have weakened his hand so that he is able to make only one shoe. You owe him the value of the making of one shoe and a quarter, multiplied for the number of days left in his life, minus the non-business days.

The limitation of the compensation only to the patrimonial consequences of the injured party did not appear satisfying to Melchiorre Gioia himself, who observed how the "real value" of a loss should have also included the negative repercussions of the non-economical nature on the life of the injured party ("By impairing the right arm or hand of someone, you take away from the musician the instrument with which he earns his food, that is, by entertaining others; you take away from the proprietor the instrument by which he escapes boredom, entertaining himself; you take away from the woman the manner by which she conducts herself with grace; and you take away from everyone the instrument by which he protects himself from possible accidents, defending himself").

It was Antonio Cazzaniga[2], over one century after Melchiorre Gioia, who elaborated a doctrine capable of widening the area of the compensable damage, albeit within the limits imposed by the persisting juridical conception of the exclusively patrimonial nature of the damage. His work marked the passage from a reimbursement procedure substantially entrusted to the judge's discretion to a more rigorous methodology of evaluation based on the technical and forensic investigation, following parameters that resisted in court for decades.

In Antonio Cazzaniga's view, the principle according to which a pejorative modification of the individual may be compensated only if it causes a pejorative modification of economical nature required an extensive interpretation. The *coefficients of value of the individual* whose impairment entails monetarily commensurable effects appeared to him to be multiple. Next to the current productive capability, actually used for income acquisition (*specific working capability*: the one allowing the cobbler to manufacture "two shoes and a quarter a day", in Melchiorre Gioia's example), one should take into consideration also the potential productive capability, with which every individual is endowed and that he could always make use of in order to make an economical profit (*generic working capability*). Still susceptible of compensation are those *indirect productive coefficients*, which confer value to the

---

[1] M. Gioia: "Dell'ingiuria dei danni, del soddisfacimento e delle relative basi di stima". Lugano, 1821. Melchiorre Gioia (1767–1829) was a political writer and author of works of economics and statistics.

[2] Antonio Cazzaniga (1885–1973) was a full professor of Forensic Medicine, first in Messina and then in Milan, where he founded the Institute of Forensic Medicine. His doctrine about the compensation for the damage to the injured party in civil courts was developed in his treatise "Le basi medico-legali per la stima del danno alla persona da delitto o quasidelitto". IES, Milano 1928.

individual not because they are directly lucrative, but because they are "favourable to the influence that the generic expansion of the personality in the world of relations ends by having on the exploitation of one's energies". The attitude of participating to the collective life in its various forms (*social capacity* or efficiency, later defined "social life"), the *esthetical efficiency* and *sexual ability* all refer to such a category.

The specific working capacity might have been evaluated in percentage terms, according to the specific descriptions, based on the peculiarities of the case under examination. The generic working capability, as a common attribute of the average individual, on the contrary lent itself to a percentage evaluation through a *barème* applicable in every case. The percentage tables of reduction of generic working capability elaborated by Antonio Cazzaniga in 1928 were the result of "a study of integration and comparison" produced using the better exploited elements of pre-existing *barème* in effect in several European countries in the field of studies of work-related injuries and private accidents, as well as in veterans' pensions. In the author's opinion, the "generality of the work should be intended in a very loose way, comprehensive of every sort of productive activity": for this reason the most appropriate references were formed by the tables of the insurance agencies as well as those related to veterans' pensions affairs, rather than the on-the-job injuries, calibrated on the working capability of the blue-collar class.

Antonio Cazzaniga's percentages, thus conceived, were subjected in the following decades to a sort of slow evolution process—the product of the most important experiences of the forensic practitioners and academic reflections—that in 1968 led to the formulation of the so-called table of Como-Perugia by a joint commission of medicolegal experts and jurists. The invalidity percentages of the table always referred to "generic working capability, intended as attribute of the average individual", according to the principle, that every impairment, as long as it has an appreciable influence on the psychophysical of the individual, represents by itself a "biological damage of patrimonial relevance".

In order to complete the picture, it is necessary to add that the Civil Code of 1942 (still in effect) also allowed the compensation for the non-patrimonial damage, but only "in the cases determined by the law" (article 2059).[3]

For a very long time, this article has been interpreted in a limiting sense, and the extra-patrimonial damage has been identified with only the *moral damage*, that is, with the *transitory unsettling of the soul* of those who have been victims of a damage, caused by a fact susceptible to integrate a criminal act (see infra).

The evaluative system founded on the specific working capability/generic working capability pair (with the assimilation of esthetical and sexual damage and social life)—that until the 1980s in Italy constituted the basis for the compensation to the individual in civil law—did not, however, appear satisfying. One primary reason of

[3] Article 2059 of the Civil Code (non-patrimonial damage): "the non-patrimonial damage must be compensated only in those case contemplated by law".

dissatisfaction was represented by the very necessity to find some patrimonial reflection even for those damages that often had none. But there were also other inconveniences, including the necessity that the generic working capability was tied to an income of reference, in theory equal for everybody, but in legal practice often coinciding with the effective one of the injured party: thus imbalances, with different compensations for the same injuries, even more serious when the injured party was a minor and the referred income that of his or her parents.

As a matter of fact, around the middle of the twentieth century, Cesare Gerin[4] had proposed a new and advanced conception of the damage to the individual, based on the notion of *validity*. He observed that it is not only work that gives worth to an individual: the integrity of the individual has itself economical value, independently from its (potential or actual) translation into income. *Validity* is psychosomatic efficiency relating to the implementation of every human activity. Every anatomical-functional loss reducing validity is to be considered compensable damage, independently from its possible income repercussions, which should be restored separately. In the elaboration of the percentages of invalidity, one must consider particularly the physiological value of the various functions with reference to the "more or less significant importance … in the implementation of *the social and vegetative life*", which also include the efficiency of the individual in his or her "*family and social environment*", because "the person cannot but be conceived in function of the community and therefore the relations with the likes of him or her". Even aesthetic damage is included in the concept of validity, in as much it influences the physiognomic function, which in Cesare Gerin's view "is fulfilled by all the exterior attributes of the person and they concur to characterize him or her within his or her social life". Unfortunately, such indications have never translated into the elaboration of a complete *barème*.

But Cesare Gerin's innovative conception did not find, at the beginning, a favourable acceptance by jurists, because—so they stated—the legal system does not protect other damages other than those negatively affecting the patrimony of the injured party (with the exception, it is understood, of the subjective moral damage, through which, however, the sustained impairment is not restored, but only the unsettling of the soul of the injured party is compensated).

The scenario started to change in the 1970s. As it was said before, the category of the "to be" imposed itself on the attention of scholars and judges, who had previously focused on the category of the "to have". The first sentences of the judges of Genoa and later of Pisa, interpreters of a new doctrine developed in those seats, acknowledged the compensation for a new type of damage—legitimate child of the Gerin validity, as acknowledged by the same professionals that were proposing it—the *biological damage* (*danno biologico*) or, according to another

[4] Cesare Gerin (1906–1996) is a professor of Forensic Medicine in Bari and then full professor of the same discipline in Rome. He exposed the theory of validity (originally his own) in "La valutazione medico-legale del danno alla persona in responsabilità civile". Atti Giornate Medico-Legali Triestine, 1952. After his death the Institute of Forensic Medicine and Insurances of the Rome University was named after him.

diction, *damage to health* (*danno alla salute*). In its original setting, the first diction referred to the *impairment of the psychophysical integrity considered per se* and the second to the *negative personal consequences deriving from the reduction of the psychophysical integrity*—both with no reference to any reflection on the patrimony. Now, the somatic-psychic impairment ("biological") lends itself to being compensated in equal terms in every individual, age, gender and precedent state being equal. But the negative consequences of the same impairment may affect in a different measure the life (or, as it is commonly said, the "lifestyle") of different people. Therefore, in this vision, equity implies a careful fine-tuning between the exigency of a basic monetary unit for the compensation of a given impairment and flexibility so as to conform the compensation to the actual peculiarities ("biographical") of the concrete case. In order to stress this difference, the biological damage, in its original meaning, has also been defined as "static" (equal for everyone), so as to compare it to the damage to health, which is defined, on the contrary, as "dynamic".

It is peculiar that, with the passing of time, the content coherent with the conception of the damage to health ended by prevailing, albeit under the *nomen* of biological damage.

The notion of biological to health damage in the 1970s progressively imposed itself in the trial jurisprudence, until the Constitutional Court, in the sentence 88/1979, for the first time stated the exigency to configure the *right to health*, reaffirmed by article 32 of the Constitution[5] "as primary and absolute right, fully operating also in the relations among private citizens", and thus to allow the full compensation for "all the effects of the injury to [such] right".

A subsequent fundamental step, within the systematic framing of the figure of the biological damage (for the sake of simplicity, we will exclusively use such *nomen*) and more in general of the category of the personal injury damages, is the sentence 184/1986 of the Constitutional Court. Very briefly, according to the sentence, there are only three categories of personal injury damages susceptible of compensation:

1. The *biological damage*, subsisting if an impairment of the psychophysical integrity can be proven, compensated for the combination decided by the article 2043 of the Civil Code[6] and the article 32 of the Constitution.
2. The *patrimonial damage* (article 2043 of the Civil Code), subsisting if the concrete case an economical loss is proven.
3. The *non-patrimonial damage* (article 2059 of the Civil Code), essentially defined as a moral damage, that is, as an unfair and transitory upheaval of the

[5] Article 32 of the Constitution: "The Republic protects health as a fundamental right of the individual and collective interest, and guarantees free care to the destitute...".

[6] Article 2043 of the Civil Code (Compensation for an offence): "Any fraud or negligence causing an unjust damage to others forces the individual that has perpetrated the damage to compensate the damage".

normal state of mind of the injured party (and it is therefore different from the biological damage).

If the biological damage is missing, there cannot be compensation even for the patrimonial or moral damage. If patrimonial and biological damage coexist, both must be compensated autonomously.

Just because it was born from the doctrinal and jurisprudential evolution (the so-called living law), the biological damage has not had until now a general definition of law. In anticipation of such a definition, the D Lgs (Legislative Decree) 23/02/00 no. 38 has come up with one, on an experimental basis, to the lone purpose of the tutelage of the mandatory insurance against work-related injuries and occupational diseases (article 13).[7]

Another definition, operating in the field of compensation for the damage in a civil court for traffic accidents, can be found in the Legislative Decree 7/09/05 no. 209 ("*Code of private insurances*"), reiterated in the articles 138 and 139: "…biological damage means *the temporary or permanent injury of the psycho-physical of the individual susceptible of medico-legal ascertainment, which exerts a negative influence on the daily activities and the dynamic-relational aspects of the injured party's life,* independently from possible repercussions on his capability to produce income".

Although such a definition was conceived for a specific sector of personal injury, in reality it ends by extending itself to the compensations in general. It must also be said that it refers to the one approved by the SIMLA (*Società Italiana di Medicina Legale e delle Assicurazioni*—Italian Society of Legal Medicine and Insurances) in 2001.[8]

If ultimately the *nomen* of biological damage includes the content of what the doctrine and jurisprudence in Pisa had denominated damage to health, then it is necessary to define such content. The word health, it is well known, has multiple meanings. The medical meaning, according to which health is the absence of illnesses, is infirmity of physical or psychical defects. The "idealistic" meaning of the World Health Organization (WHO) is that health is identified with a state of

[7] Waiting for the definition of general character of biological damage and the criteria for the determination of the relative compensation, the current article defines, on an experimental basis, for the purposes of the protection of the mandatory insurance against the injuries on the job and occupational diseases, the biological damage as the "lesion to the psycho-physical integrity, susceptible of medico-legal ascertainment, of the individual … the impairments caused by the lesions of the psycho-physical integrity … are evaluated according to a specific impairment table, comprehensive of the dynamic-relational aspects".

[8] The biological damage consists in the permanence of temporary impairment of the psychophysical integrity of the individual, comprehensive of the dynamic-relational aspects, susceptible of the medicolegal ascertainment and evaluation and independent from any reference to the capability to earn income. "The evaluation of the biological damage is expressed in terms of percentage of the impairment of the psychophysical integrity, comprehensive of the incidence on the activities common to everyone. If the impairment itself appreciably affects particular dynamic-relational and personal aspects, the evaluation is completed by further indications, to express in an exclusively descriptive form".

complete physical, psychical and social wellness. The "social" meaning is that health is the condition that allows an individual to fulfil his or her social role. The juridical doctrine has been considering for a long time that healthcare, guaranteed by the article 32 of the Constitution, does not have an exclusive health purpose, but that it should be considered as instrumental to the protection and development of the personality of the individual. But if, on one hand, the medical meaning is too limited, on the other hand, an excessively extensive interpretation does not find support in a legal system that does not guarantee "the right to be happy". By health one should intend the substantial absence of significant illnesses or diseases and consequently the ability of the individual to pursue his or her vital objectives and to function within common social contexts.

The impairment of the psycho-physical integrity, negatively affecting the functions of the organism, can jeopardize health in various manners. First of all, by limiting the actions of the daily life of the injured party, such as those pertaining to personal care and hygiene, the ordinary physical activity, the manual abilities unrelated to one's job, communication, sensorial perception, the ability to move and travel, sleep, etc. Then, by impoverishing the relational life of the injured party, his relating himself or herself as a social being to the other members of the community (or better of the various communities: family, friend, co-students . . .) of which he or she is a member: this is what the slightly cryptic enunciation of "dynamic-relational aspects of life" hints at (articles 138 and 139 legislative decree 209/2005). Lastly, forcing the injured party to life choices different from those he or she would have otherwise carried out (as it was said, "changing his or her life schedule"). In other words, the biological damage includes all the disutilities deriving from the impairment of health asset, with the lone exception of those pertaining to patrimony. And therefore the notion of biological damage is all inclusive, because it gathers under a single heading the multiple figures of damage that the preceding doctrine had created. In this way the *sexual damage, the aesthetic damage and the damage to the social life* (all expressions of the prejudice that the impairment brings to the so-called dynamic-relational aspects of the life of the injured party), as well as *the damage to the generic—no longer work related—capability* (or psychosomatic efficiency to the development of any human activity not finalized, not even potentially, to income production), all merge into the biological damage.

Even the biological damage—just because it pertains to health meant as an attribute of the average person—lends itself to a standardized table-type evaluation, as well as the generic working capability.

Of course, the *barème* used for the evaluation of the latter could not be employed for the biological damage, because one thing is the effect of an impairment on the ability to carry out an "average work" and one thing is the incidence of the same impairment of the health of the injured party. More useful turns out to be the comparison with the guidelines of other countries, such as the French ones turning towards the evaluation of the *incapacité physiologique permanente* as well as those of AMA (American Medical Association) for the evaluation of the permanent impairment: figures more or less strictly related with the biological damage.

Under initiative of the Directive Council of SIMLA, in 1992, a commission coordinated by Marino Bargagna was given the task to set up suggestive guidelines for the evaluation of biological damage, with the discretion of availing themselves of collaborators and all the specialized experts deemed necessary. The three subsequent editions of the guide came to light between 1996 and 2001.

For the monetary translation of the percentages of permanent biological damage, the method of "calculation by points" has become predominant; according to it the economical value of the invalidity point grows in a more than proportional manner compared to the percentage of biological damage.[9] An undesired effect was the heterogeneity of the monetary tables amongst the various tribunals, with a consequent compensation disparity from one court to the next.[10] A further element of subjectivity is represented by the "damage personalization", in observance of the principle of the adaptation between exigency of basic monetary uniformity and flexibility, so as to adjust the compensation to the effective peculiarities of the concrete case. If the ascertained impairment affects specific aspects of the life of the injured party (or as said before "particular dynamic-relational and personal aspects") in a measure bigger than the average, the judge will arrange for a compensation increase.

The legislator—also with the urging of insurance companies—has however arranged to level out the compensation for light entity impairments (invalidity inferior to 10 %) derived from accidents caused by motor vehicles and boats, through a forensic *barème* and a monetary table of laws ("Table of impairments to the psycho-physical integrity included between 1 and 9 invalidity points, DM (Ministerial Decree) 3/07/2003"). With the subsequent DM of 26/05/2004, an inter-ministerial commission was set up for the preparation of a forensic *barème* relating to the 10–100 % range of biological damage, which has been completed, but to this day has still not become a law[11], particularly because of the difficulties of preparing a common monetary table.

A further *barème* ("impairment table" of INAIL, the *Istituto Nazionale Assicurazioni Infortuni sul Lavoro*—National Institute for the Insurance against Work-related Injuries), promulgated with the DM 12/07/00, concerns the evaluation of the damage in the work environment, but is not applied in civil responsibility.

[9] For instance, the 2013 table of the Court of Milan calls for—in the case of a 30-year-old—a basic compensation of about 23,000 € for a 10 % damage (point value about 2300 €) and about 73,000 € for a 20 % damage (point value about 3650 €).

[10] To remedy such disparity, the Civil Court of Appeal, section III, with sentence 12408 of 7 June 2011 had adopted as a standard the tables elaborated by the Observatory of Civil Justice of the Tribunal of Milan.

[11] A commentary is in any case available a guide with comments to the tables referenced in the DM 3 July 2003 (1–9 %) as well to the work of the Commissione ex DM 26 May 2004 (10–100 %), which is commonly used in the forensic evaluation of the biological damage, even for accidents non deriving from road traffic.

A side effect of such legislative production is the fragmentation of the forensic table of damage measure: on one side the law of insured workers, on the other side that of road accident victims and yet on another side those conceived for the total population.

Next to the abovementioned legislative activity, in the last decade that of jurisprudence has acquired prominence. The Supreme Court of Cassation, with five sentences of May 2003, and the Constitutional Court, with the sentence no. 223 of July 2003[12], have wholly accepted the instances of the doctrine for a constitutional interpretation of the article 2059 of the Civil Code, so that it will extend the compensation for the non-patrimonial damage even out of the "cases set by the law", that is, completing the criminal action. As far as legal medicine is concerned, such constitutional interpretation has not modified the content of the biological damage, which has remained unchanged. However the tripartition—designed by the sentence 184/1986 of the Constitutional Court—amongst patrimonial damage, biological damage and moral damage has been definitely discarded in favour of a bipolar system between patrimonial damage and non-patrimonial damage. The latter, in turn, in the sentences of 2003 was articulated in biological damage, moral damage and *existential damage*, a new figure of damage elaborated by the Trieste school. The existential damage differs from the biological damage, because it does not necessarily presume an impairment of the psychophysical integrity, and from the moral damage because it does not consist in a suffering of the soul, but in a "no longer being able to do", in a "being able to do it differently" or in a "have to do" as a consequence of the endured offence, leading to the negative modification of one's characteristics.[13] This has created the problem of the relation between the moral damage, in this new positioning, and the two other figures of non-patrimonial damage.

One (temporarily) unchanged point has been secured by the United States Court of Appeals in its four sentences of November 2008[14]. According to what was established by the United States, *the non-patrimonial damage is a category not susceptible to subdivision into subcategories*. Through this *reductio ad unum*, the Supreme Court of Cassation has also aimed to avoid a situation in which the same damage, under two different *nomina*, would find double compensation ("the compensation must be complete, meaning that it must entirely restore the prejudice, but not beyond it"). The moral damage and those damages "that, inasmuch as they concern the life of a person, may moreover be labelled, if preferred, as existential" can derive from the injury to goods other than health, such as the moral suffering, the mental state of pain and suffering of whoever had been defamed or the

---

[12] Cass. Civ nn 7281/2003, 7282/2003, 7283/2003, 8827/2003, 8828/2003; Corte Cost 233/2003.

[13] Thus Cass. Sez Unite no. 6572/2006: "each prejudice of not merely and interior nature, but objectively ascertainable, that alters the customs and the relational assets, inducing different choices of life as well as the expression and realization of one's personality in the outside world".

[14] Cass. Sez. Unite nn. 26972/2008-26973/2008-26974-26975/2008.

unsettling of the life of those who have suffered unjust imprisonment: they will then enjoy autonomous compensation. But *all* of the negative consequences deriving from the impairment of the health asset (including the *moral* and *existential* ones) must be compensated under the species of *the biological damage*.

Compared to the well-established notion of biological damage, which asserted itself in forensic medicine and is supported by the normative definition mentioned in the articles 139 and 139 Legislative Decree no. 209/2005, the sentences of the United Sections generate a confirmation and an innovation. The confirmation is the perturbations of one's "life schedule" (existential damage) determined by the health impairment included in those personal dynamic-relational aspects. Compensating these very same consequences under two different *nomina* would certainly require a duplication. The innovation is the disappearance of the distinction between moral damage, meant as a transitory upsetting of the soul, not classifiable in a clinical sense amongst psychic perturbations, and the biological damage, founded on psychophysical impairments corresponding to clinical categories. Not only, but the moral damage (or "subjective pain") loses its character of transient alteration, since it can be temporary as well as permanent.

Our discipline had to face the question of whether the moral damage may be ascertained and evaluated by forensic doctors. The opinions are not unanimous and will be discussed in the section devoted to the evaluation criteria.

8.2 Identification and Description of Medicolegal Expert's Qualifications

In civil actions, the role of a court-appointed expert is governed by the Code of Civil Procedure (c.c.p.). In particular, article 61 states that "when necessary, judges can avail themselves of the assistance . . .. of one or more consultants with particular technical expertise. The choice of the expert must *normally* be made from among professionals enrolled in special registers. . .", according to the provisions of article 13 of the application provisions of the c.c.p.: "Each court is to maintain a register of expert consultants. Such register is divided into categories, which must always include: (1) medical-surgical; (2) industrial; (3) commercial; (4) agricultural; (5) banking; (6) insurance". In order to enrol in the first (medical) category of the register, it is sufficient to have a degree in medicine and surgery or dentistry. Enrolment in the register is not, however, compulsory for an appointment as expert by a court. As can be inferred from the caveat "normally" in the above-cited article of law, judges can appoint an expert enrolled in the register of a different court or not enrolled in any register at all. Article 191 of the c.c.p. establishes that "more than one expert can be named only in cases of dire need or in cases for which the law expressly provides". It should be noted that the 2014 Code of Medical Ethics, article 62, instead states that ". . .in cases of medical liability, medico-legal consultants are to avail themselves of a well-established expert colleague specialized in the discipline in question; in analogous circumstances, clinical physicians avail themselves of a medico-legal expert". Thus, the law affords the judge a wide degree of discretion, both in the choice of consultant, who does not necessarily have to be an expert in forensic medicine, and in the decision to appoint two or more experts.[15]

The title of a medical forensic specialist is granted upon completion of a 4-year course of study, which includes amongst its medical training objectives the "acquisition of the theoretical-practical tools for verifying and evaluating injuries and disabilities of criminal or civil legal interest". Graduates of a school of specialization in forensic medicine must present documentation attesting to their having participated in at least 100 medicolegal clinical verifications involving evaluation of injuries and disabilities of interest to criminal proceedings, civil actions or private insurance claims.

8.3 Ascertainment Methodology

The methodology applied in forensic medicine for verifying injuries and disabilities is based on some of the same tools used in clinical medicine (medical history, physical examination, laboratory and instrumental diagnostic procedures, etc.), though modified for its own ends. In particular, with regard to the need to prove a causal link between a tortious act and an injury, as well as between the injury and any disability, the evidence provided of the psychophysical alterations suffered by the victim must be as objective as possible and include any and all elements necessary for appraising the impact of such disability on the victim's health and patrimony.

The report drawn up by the medicolegal expert for the court includes the mission given to him by the judge and a list of relevant documents to be attached to the case files. The first stage of assessment consists of scrutinizing the documentation regarding the events surrounding the tort and the medical treatment received by the injured party. Usually, if the documents produced by the parties involved are incomplete, the judge will authorize the expert consultant to acquire any and all documentation necessary to reconstruct the clinical course and prior state of the injured party. The medical history (familial, physiological, work-related and pathological) aims, above and beyond the usual clinical purposes, to furnish a reliable

[15] The so-called Balduzzi Law (no. 189, November 8, 2012) seems to represent a step in the right direction, as its article 3/comma 4 stipulates that "the expert consultant registers ... must be updated at least every 5 years in order to guarantee a suitably qualified, representative pool of experts, not only in forensic medicine, but also in other specialized fields of healthcare, including the involvement of scientific associations from which to choose appointments, bearing in mind the specific field in question".

picture of the complainant's day-to-day activities, including description of the particular/specific daily recreational activities and social relationships, as well as work duties.

The overall physical exam can be more or less thorough, depending on the specifics of the case. Focalized physical examination and characterization of the areas involved in the injuries should be particularly thorough, accompanied as needed by measurements and photographs. Diagnostic manoeuvres aimed at uncovering and documenting possible simulation are particularly crucial.

Particular cases call for the involvement of specialists (ophthalmologist, otorhinolaryngologist, psychiatrist, etc.), and the expert consultant can moreover prescribe supplementary laboratory and/or instrumental diagnostic procedures, with the exception of invasive ones or those involving exposure to ionizing radiation.

8.4 Evaluation Criteria

The aims and methods of forensic medicine involve not only *verifying* and describing the objective facts of any alterations to a person's psychophysical well-being, but also *evaluating* the damages consequent to such alterations with reference to the specific legal framework of the event. Thus, the consulting medicolegal expert should possess adequate knowledge of the laws applicable to the case at hand: in the present context, those governing civil actions. Forensic medical evaluations should moreover be expressed in language that is "native" to judges, yet modest enough not to venture into making judgments that remain the exclusive competence of the adjudicator.

In the language of forensic medicine, the term *determinants of damage* is used to indicate three fundamental factors: the cause of the injury, the injury itself and the consequent disability or impairment. The *cause of injury* is an external fact that constitutes the *primum movens* of the injury: for example, trauma to the femur. The *injury* (also called *initial injury*) is the alteration to the psychophysical state consequent to the cause of injury: for example, fracture of the femur resulting from the trauma. The impairment is the (temporary or permanent) compromising effects on the victim's physical and psychic well-being due to the injury. The *damage* is thus the result of the degree that the impairment affects the personal rights protected by law: in the present context, to both health (so-called biological damage[16]) and patrimony (a reduction in a person's financial position).

In many cases, the nature and degree of injury and consequent impairment can be ascertained either from the objective or instrumental clinical data contained in the medical documentation at the disposal of the medicolegal expert or by direct

[16] Translator's note: The term "biological damages" (danno biologico) is unique to Italian jurisprudence and includes any and all damages consequent to the compromised health of the victim, independently from possible repercussions on his capability to produce income.

medical examination of the injured party. At other times, instead, complaints of the aggrieved party are primarily or exclusively subjective in nature. Such situations come up frequently in claims of whiplash injuries from road accidents. It was precisely with the aim of avoiding the "abnormal speculation surrounding whiplash injuries" that the legislation was passed (law no. 27 of 2012) to modify the laws governing compensation for disabilities of "modest degree" (physical injury of less than 9 %) consequent to road accidents (art 139 of the Legislative Decree no. 209/2005). Although framed in a rather non-technical language, the provision allows for compensation of injuries or impairments only when they are ascertainable through "objective" (improperly used as a synonym for "visual") and/or instrumental examination.[17] In fact, *solely in this one sphere of civil liability* does the provision recognize only *two distinct ways of evaluating and classifying personal injury according to degree:* "modest" or "not modest". Moreover, although the regulation was conceived specifically for whiplash injuries, it is regularly applied to all types of disabilities, both physical and psychic in the range of 1–9 %. It is obvious that literal interpretation of the law would preclude compensation for any psychic impairment, unless psychodiagnostic tests are considered to be on a par with instrumental examinations. Furthermore, such an interpretation would exclude not only psychiatric disorders from compensation, but also various other afflictions, such as, to cite only one example, complex regional syndromes characterized by neuropathic pain. On the other hand, the borderline between objective sign and subjective symptom is not always so clear: the study of physical signs is also influenced by the subjective perspective of the examiners, who describe what they perceive and interpret it according to their own cognitive schemes. In the field of law, there is currently a trend towards "constitutional interpretation" of the provision, which foresees the possibility of evaluating injury and impairment, not only through objective or instrumental examination but also "by means of recourse to *relevant scientific evidence*, with adequate motivation and indications of the most accredited medical-legal doctrine and scientific literature regarding the specific case at hand".[18] Actually, this is little more than an appeal to apply already well-established methods of forensic medicine, based, as always, on scrutinizing and critically evaluating all the available evidence for the purposes and requisites of the law.

Most matters referred by the courts to forensic medicine experts involve the demonstration of a *causal link*. Actually in most cases, the medicolegal expert should be called upon to verify the existence of *two* such causal links: the first

[17] Law 27/102, article 32 /par. 3, subparagraphs 3 and 4, states: 3-Subpar. 3—The following is to be added to paragraph 2 of article 139 of the Civil Code regarding private insurance: "In any case, injuries of modest entity that are not verifiable by objective instrumental clinical exam cannot be cause for compensation for permanent biological damage". 3-Subpar. 4: "Personal damages for injuries of modest entity, per article 139 of the legislative decree no. 209 of September 7, 2005, are to be indemnified solely subsequent to medico-legal checks that furnish visual or instrumental verification of the existence of the injury".

[18] The legal issue posed by the Milan Court after passage of law 27/2012.

between the traumatic event and the initial injury and the second between the injury and any permanent impairment. As a consequence, the traumatic event needs to be fully understood and described to allow further consideration on the existence of the first ring of the causal chain, as mentioned above. Hence, the medicolegal expert has to reckon the more details and objective data he can, even by the help of other types of experts, such as mechanical or biomedical engineers and so on.

Sometimes such links are self-evident; others, to the contrary, call for exacting study to demonstrate them. In our legal system, in both the penal and civil spheres, the rule sine qua non (the so-called but for rule) holds, though in some sentences it is mitigated by the principle of "adequate causality". The presence of any pre-existing pathological condition (see prior status in the following), even if it had a predominant role in leading to the injury, does not negate the causal link ("the defendant must take their victims as they find them"). The standard of proof required in civil cases is instead different from that in the penal sphere. In a criminal trial, the criterion applied is "beyond any reasonable doubt", whilst civil cases are judged based on the "*preponderance of evidence*", which has been described as just enough evidence to make it *more likely than not* that the fact the claimant seeks to prove is true.

Causal links must be proven according to scientific law, which jurists, faithful to the terminology of Carl G. Hempel, adore classifying into two distinct types: "*universal law*" and "*statistical law*". The former enables concluding that a given antecedent *invariably* leads to a given event, whilst the latter, simply that a given antecedent will, *in a certain percentage of cases*, leads to a given event. Applying exact science would instead call for recourse to deterministic and probabilistic models. However, in the field of civil medical liability (which, coupled with road accidents, most frequently occupy medicolegal experts), such models are rarely applied, since the plaintiffs in medical cases are rarely completely aware of all the consequences of their own choices. Moreover, in such cases, often the malpractice of which physicians are accused results from omission, rather than commission, which further increases the degree of uncertainty involved. According to the Italian Court of Cassation en banc[19], "the rule [of inference]... cannot be based exclusively on a quantitative-statistical determination of the frequencies of a class of events (so-called quantitative probability), but must be verified by referring it to the degree of well-foundedness within the context of the corroborative elements available in the specific case (so-called logical probability)". In other words, faced with two alternative hypotheses (the antecedent has caused the event, or the antecedent has not caused the event), statistics on other events of the same type are only one of the elements that can be used to weigh the probabilities. From time to time, in a specific case, greater weight may be attributed to the "relevant evidence", that is, those elements that can make a hypothesis more or less probable than it would be without such evidence. A number of criteria have been formulated and widely applied in forensic medicine to such evidence, mainly with regard to trauma from

[19] Sezioni Unite della Corte di Cassazione no. 581 Jan. 11, 2008

mechanical agents: topographic criterion, chronological criterion, criterion of event continuity, criterion of quali-quantitative adequacy and exclusion of other causes.

In civil trials, compensation can also be awarded for the *loss of chances*, in the sense of being deprived of the possibility to avoid the consequences of the injurious event. The importance of this approach lies in the fact that it may support damages for lost opportunities or reduced prospects when it is not possible to prove that it was more likely than not that, but for the defendant's tortious conduct, the ultimate injury would have been averted or that some more favourable outcome would have been achieved. This approach has gained support during the past 15 years, especially in medical malpractice actions. Thus, a plaintiff may receive damages if he can prove that the defendant caused the loss of a chance of avoiding the ultimate injury, despite the fact that the chance or likelihood of achieving a better outcome was not better than even. The evidence that enables the formulation of an estimate of the loss of chances is based mainly upon statistical-epidemiological data, which are not always available to an adequate degree. As a rule, the expert's answer should be formulated in terms of a reasonable range of probabilities, at times requiring the use of expressions such as "fundamentally presumable loss of *chance*, though to an indeterminable degree".

After having described the nature and severity of the injuries suffered, along with the causal relation with the events determining the legal action, and the consequent temporary and/or permanent disabilities, medical experts are generally called upon to give an account of the injured party's state prior to the causal event "to the ends of subsequent evaluation" of the *quantum* of compensable damages. The party's *prior state* may in fact play a concausal role, in either the injury (such as the case of a modest trauma producing a fracture in an osteoporotic femur) or the impairment (e.g. the case of someone already blind in one eye who loses sight in the other). By virtue of the sine qua non rule[20], in the first example, the role of the prior state is immaterial to the goals of determining the *quantum* of damages, whilst in the second it must instead be taken into account. In traditional forensic medicine doctrine governing work-related injuries, with regard to prior state, it is customary to distinguish between *coexisting* impairments, which affect different organs or functional systems, and *concurrent impairments*, which affect the same organ or system. A worker who at the time of hiring was already impaired by the loss of the little finger of his right hand and who then suffers an auditory deficit due to an industrial accident (*coexisting impairments*) would receive the same indemnification that he would have if he had never lost the finger. However, if the same worker were to lose the index finger of his right hand in an accident (*concurrent impairments*), he would receive greater indemnification than he would have if his hand had

[20] Actually, a proportional liability approach has been proposed for evaluating biological damage of a psychic nature. Such approach calls for establishing the quantum by multiplying the ascertained percentage of biological damage by a numerical coefficient that measures the injurious effects of the psychic trauma that caused the damage.

not been missing the little finger prior to the accident. In such cases, the law provides for application of an arithmetic formula to calculate the *quantum of damages* (the so-called Gabrielli formula). However, such regulations cannot be transferred en bloc from the sphere of work-related injuries to that of civil liability. The generally accepted guiding principle is to refer to the indications provided in *barèmes* (i.e. tables indicating the percentage of biological damage associated to different injuries) and adjust them *in plus* or *in minus* depending on whether the interactions between the impairment in question and any pre-existing condition either increase or decrease the damage with respect to the mean table values (or apply them "as is" if there is no interaction). There is, however, no agreement, either in doctrine or professional practice, on how to apply this principle. In the simplest cases, the rule generally adopted by common accord is one of "differential damage": for instance, the one-eyed man rendered blind should be awarded a 57 % compensation, which is simply the difference between the biological damage table value for the loss of one eye (28 %) and that for total blindness (85 %).[21] If, as in most cases, the overall biological damage has not yet been established in such tables, an estimate must be made on which to perform the subtraction, which is not always a simple matter when the pre-existing condition involves severe permanent impairment. For instance, the table value of ankylosis of the ankle (12 %) in a paraplegic subject (85 %) would most certainly have to be lowered[22]: most experts would prefer to indemnify such a condition as a very modest permanent impairment, rather than differential damage.[23] Moreover, differential damage calculations become impracticable if both the pre-existing impairment and the acquired one are especially serious, as in the case of a blind person rendered deaf as well. By virtue of the consideration that in the living health has unlimited value, it seems impossible to attribute a biological damage value of 85–100 % to the residual health of a blind person, because doing so would limit the evaluation of any further disability to within this narrow range of percentages.[24] Even in those impairments that most

[21] It is worth noting that according to the view by which the economic value of the percentage invalidity grows in a more-than-proportional manner with respect to the percentage biological damage, a differential damage of 85–28 % would command greater compensation than a 57 % damage with no pre-existing disability. Considering, for instance, a 40-year-old male, according to the monetary tables used at the Court of Milan, biological damage of 57 % would call for compensation of about 476,000 €, whilst a differential biological damage of 85–28 % would be compensated with about 681,000 € (810,000–129,000 €).

[22] This example has been drawn from the "application criteria" of the table of disabilities from 10 to 100 % prepared by the Ministerial Committee per the Ministerial decree of May 26, 2004 (which has yet to be put into effect).

[23] The consequences of the choice are not negligible in economic terms. Using the same monetary tables, modest biological damage of 4 % would lead to indemnification of about 5500 €, whilst differential damage of a single percentage point (86–85 %) would call for compensation of 11,000 €.

[24] Still using the same monetary tables, the difference between 100 and 85 % would correspond to about 154,000 €. Total bilateral complete (50 %) with no pre-existing condition would be indemnified with about 373,000 €, Thus, the sighted person that would receive more than double than what the blind one would clearly highlights the unfairness of the method. In fact, the

severely compromise a person's psychophysical integrity, there remain other abilities that permit a meaningful, high-quality life. It has thus been proposed that such biological conditions represent "another 100 % of personal validity" on which to equitably adjust compensation in the event of any further impairment.

As stated, a disability consists of a temporary or possibly permanent reduction in psychic and bodily efficacy: by encroaching upon the interests protected by law, it leads to damage that may in turn be only temporary or permanent. The borderline between the temporary and permanent stages of impairment is obviously conventional and established on the basis of clinical criteria. The temporary stage is deemed to be over when the impairment subsides without sequela. Vice versa, a temporary disability can be considered as having been transformed into a permanent one when the clinical condition appears "sufficiently stabilized". Moreover, it sometimes happens that, in the transition from the acute stage to a chronic one, an impairment takes on a progressive, rather than a stable nature, as in the case of someone infected with hepatitis C or the HIV virus. In conclusion, there is considerable margin for discretion in the expert's assessment of damages.

Temporary biological damage (TBD) expresses the detriment to good health caused by a temporary impairment. It manifests first and foremost as a disturbance to the normal existence of the injured party due to obstacles to accomplishing deeds that would ordinarily be quite simple. It is in this stage that the most serious physiopathological disturbances and the most intense subjective suffering are commonly manifested. The variability in the negative consequences of such conditions makes it necessary to gauge the severity of TBD. Adopting terminology borrowed from insurance practice, we in fact distinguish absolute TBD (or *total temporary disability*) from partial TBD (or *partial temporary disability*), the latter being expressed in terms of fractions or percentages.[25] Although some authors have proposed formulas for grading TBD, no commonly accepted scales can be said to exist. Clearly, the percentages drawn from the *baréme* in use for permanent biological damages cannot be transferred en bloc to quantify TBD. For example, a patient held in traction for treatment of a fracture of the femur should obviously be recognized as suffering a total, rather than partial, temporary disability, equal to the table value of amputation of the leg (45–60 %). It is in fact believed that absolute temporary disability should be acknowledged not only when the illness completely impedes the carrying out of life's ordinary activities (as in the case of coma), but also when its actual effects are to severely compromise such activities. In practice, the criteria used for grading TBD seem to be quite subjective and highly influenced by local habits and customs.

---

interaction between blindness and deafness increases the damage with respect to the average table values.

[25] Consider art 138, par. 2/2 of the previously cited Legislative Decree 209/2005: "temporary biological damage of less than 100 % is determined in a measure corresponding to the percentage inability per each day".

Permanent biological damage includes *all* of the negative consequences deriving from the compromised health engendered by the persistence of the impairment. As discussed in the foregoing, such consequences can affect the physical and psychic ability to carry out any and all human activities and hence regard the daily life of the injured party, including aesthetic and sexual aspects, and more in general life relationships and choices. The *quantum* of permanent biological damage is expressed by the medicolegal expert in terms of percentages. To such end, *barème* can be used. As stated in the introductory section, a special legally-binding table has been drawn up for impairments of modest entity caused by road accidents: "Table of impairments to psycho-physical integrity of between 1 and 9 % disability" (Ministerial Decree of July 3, 2003). An analogous "Table of impairments to psycho-physical integrity of between 10 and 100 % disability" has also been formulated by a committee of experts appointed by the Ministry of Health, but has never been put into effect.[26] Other *barème*, or rather "guidelines", developed in academic circles, are also available for evaluating biological damage. Authoritative scholars have declared that such guidelines can only be used by those who, by virtue of specific preparation in forensic medicine, are able to fully comprehend and critically evaluate the purposes of and inevitable limits to their application. The percentages reported in such guidelines must, however, always be regarded as merely indicative, as they refer to "ordinary" cases, and hence require adjustments in particular cases with especially harsh consequences. In the event that the disability to be appraised has no suitable corresponding item in the guide, judgments must be made based on a criterion of analogy. In cases where more than one damage item apply (for example, when a single event compromises more than one organ or system), there are no arithmetic formulas to apply (including the simple summation of the individual percentages), but appraisal should be made of the overall effect of the impairments on the injured party's "functioning". In general, using such percentage indications, though essential, does not fulfil the task of the expert, who should always begin the appraisal with an accurate analytical description of the sequelae and their functional consequences. Such a description also takes on even greater importance in cases of particularly severe impairments, for which raw percentage points must play a far less significant role.

In any event, such table percentages are to be read as measures of "standard biological damage", that is, referring to the health of the average person. In some cases, however, the impairment in question significantly affects what have been defined as "particular personal dynamic-relational aspects", such as particular leisure time activities (hobbies, sports, etc.) or life choices (volunteer and cultural activities). The category (*nomen*) conceived as "existential damage" is included in

[26] Article 3, paragraph 3 of the Balduzzi law (see below) stipulates that biological damage consequent to the activities of health professionals be indemnified on the basis of these same tables.

such dynamic-relational aspects. In such cases, the injured party must provide proof of the existence of such "particular personal dynamic-relational aspects". It is then up to the medical expert to illustrate the effects of the demonstrated impairments on the claimed limitations.

One rather controversial issue regards the role of the medicolegal expert in reparation for that which in Italy is termed "*danno morale*" (moral damages, roughly equivalent to "pain and suffering" in other legal systems). As stated above, according to the 2008 sentence of the Court of Cassation (*see above*), pain and suffering are not necessarily transient by nature; the damage suffered may be permanent as well as temporary. More importantly, the Court ruled that such "moral damages" are no longer to be considered as distinct from biological damage. Indeed, until the ruling, the separation of moral and biological damages was based on a distinction between mental anguish, which cannot be classified amongst psychic disorders, at least clinically, and biological damage, which does include those alterations of the psyche classified by medical science as true "mental disorders".[27] One first crucial aspect thus regards the characteristics of the pain and suffering: "inner pain", "moral suffering", "interior suffering", "emotional component of non-patrimonial damage", "emotional reaction to injurious impact", on the one hand, and "psychophysical suffering" on the other. The latter definition has been widely accepted in the relevant jurisprudence. Such a situation moreover involves the risk of duplicate compensation for pain and suffering: physical pain resulting from injuries is already rated through medical forensic *barème*, and further indications of the degree of psychophysical suffering could lead to a second assessment of the same damage, already included in the *barème* percentage. In other words, separating the bodily-perceptive component of physical pain from the experiential-cognitive one seems to pose some rather challenging issues.

In this regard, there are two different schools of thought that are currently in contrast. The first holds that the task of the medicolegal expert includes *quantification* of the degree of the temporary and/or permanent "suffering" through rating scales based on objective parameters, modelled after the "*souffrances*" scales adopted in France.[28] The second, instead, maintains that the medicolegal expert's contribution to compensation for pain and suffering lies solely in providing an accurate *description* of the various components of the biological damage (functional deficit, limitations to daily activities, effects on life relationships and so forth). This serves solely to highlight those elements commonly associated with inner suffering—the actual quantification is to be left up to the judge.

The task of forensic medical consultants does not however end with quantification of the biological damages. Their responsibilities also include performing technical evaluations aimed at fixing the degree of compensation for the so-called

---

[27] The commonly accepted reference (albeit not free of criticisms) is the "Diagnostic and Statistical Manual of Mental Disorders", Fifth ed, abbreviated as DSM5.

[28] The Milan School, for example, has proposed a scale of 1–5 based on five different parameters.

patrimonial damages (including loss of earnings and *damnum emergens*) consequent to any temporary and/or permanent disability. Evaluating the temporary component of patrimonial damage substantially requires making judgments regarding compatibility. It is up to the injured party to prove the economic losses suffered during the period of temporary disability. The medicolegal expert, on the other hand, must establish whether the temporary impairment affected the physical and psychological ability of the injured party to carry out those activities required by his job (*specific work capacity*) and hence led to loss of earnings.

The technical evaluations that medicolegal experts are called upon to perform regarding permanent patrimonial damages suffer from a wide margin of uncertainty, as they involve, amongst other variables, estimates of future earnings. If the injured party already has a job, an estimate must be made of the permanent reduction in his ability to carry out that specific work, which is a separate category with no correlation in terms of percentage quantifications to that of permanent biological damage. There are, in brief, three possible scenarios: (1) the impairment prevents the injured party from carrying out his job; (2) the impairment interferes with the injured party's ability to carry out his job, thereby reducing his productivity; and (3) the impairment has no affect on the injured party's work. The first case calls for specifying whether the disability would permit the performance of other jobs and, if so, what type (clerical, manual, and so on). In the second case, indications must be furnished regarding the degree of impairment of the *specific work capacity*, that is, to what degree the injured party's ability to perform the work required by that particular job has been compromised. Such indications should preferably be expressed in descriptive terms, through specification of the nature and entity of the deficit in functions necessary for productive activity. Usually, assessment of the degree of deficit is requested in percentages terms, which should be expressed cautiously through a suitably wide range of values. In the event that the injured party does not perform any work activity at the time of the tort, but it can nevertheless be concluded according to common experience that the permanent disability represents a significant obstacle to the chances of finding gainful employment, the expert can express an opinion on the loss of *fitness to work*, which in general refers to the ability to perform manual work or conceptual-clerical tasks. The expert's indications, together with the evidence produced by the plaintiff, can be used by the judge to ascribe an economic value to the permanent disability.

Lastly, with regard to the *damnum emergens* (i.e. incurred loss), it is the task of the medicolegal expert to appraise the congruence of the medical expenses already sustained by the injured party and estimate those foreseeable for the future. according to the principle of appropriateness.[29]

[29] Appropriateness may be qualified as the appraisal of a clear proportionality between the injury/impairment and the type and scheduling of the clinical investigation performed and the treatments prescribed.

Below are listed some general bibliographic sources useful to deepen the issue. They are not reported within the text as they are no cited references.

Bibliography

1. Cazzaniga A (1928) Le basi medico-legali per la stima del danno alla persona da delitto o quasi delitto. IES, Milano
2. Gerin C (1952) La valutazione medico-legale del danno alla persona in responsabilità civile. Atti Giornate Medico-Legali Triestine
3. Giolla P (1957) La valutazione del danno alla persona in responsabilità civile. Giuffrè, Milano
4. Bargagna M, Busnelli FD (a cura di) (1986) La valutazione del danno alla salute—Profili giuridici, medico-legali ed assicurativi. CEDAM, Padova
5. Gerin C (1987) La valutazione medico-legale del danno alla persona in responsabilità civile. Giuffrè, Milano
6. Canale M, Gianelli Castiglione A (a cura di) (1990) La valutazione del danno alla persona da invalidità permanente. Giuffrè, Milano
7. Introna F, Rodriguez D (a cura di) (1994) Le piccole invalidità permanenti in responsabilità civile, 2nd edn. Giuffrè, Milano, 1994.
8. Brondolo W, Farneti A, Mangili F, Secchi E, Giannini G, Loi U, Marigliano A, Morini O, Pogliani M, Ronchi E, Toscano G (1995) Il danno biologico, patrimoniale, morale, 2nd edn. Giuffrè, Milano
9. Bargagna M, Busnelli FD (a cura di) (2001) La valutazione del danno alla salute—Profili giuridici, medico-legali ed assicurativi, 4th edn. CEDAM, Padova
10. AAVV (2009) Il danno non patrimoniale—Guida commentata alle decisioni delle S.U. 11 novembre 2008, nn 26972/3/4/5 Giuffrè, Milano
11. Atti delle Giornate Medico-Legali di Como, 30 giugno—2 luglio 1967", Giuffré, Milano 1968. "Atti del IX Convegno per la Trattazione dei Temi Assicurativi. Perugia, 4–6 ottobre 1968 Giuffré, Milano 1968
12. Bargagna M, Canale M, Consigliere F, Palmieri L, Umani-Ronchi G "Guida orientativa per la valutazione del danno biologico permanente" (Giuffré, Milano—prima edizione 1996; seconda edizione 1998)
13. Bargagna M, Canale M, Consigliere F, Palmieri L, Umani-Ronchi G "Guida orientativa per la valutazione del danno biologico" (terza edizione—Giuffré 2001)
14. Palmieri L, Umani- Ronchi G, Fedeli P (2006) La valutazione medico-legale del danno biologico in responsabilità civile. Giuffre, Milan
15. Spera D (ed) (2013) Tabelle milanesi 2013 e danno non patrimoniale. Giuffrè, Milan, pp 53–54
16. Buzzi F, Vanini M (2014) Guida alla valutazione psichiatrica e medico-legale del danno biologico di natura psichica. Seconda edizione aggiornata a DSM-5 e PDM. Giuffrè, Milan
17. Bargagna M, Canale M, Consigliere F, Palmieri L, Umani-Ronchi G (2001) Guida orientativa per la valutazione del danno biologico, 3rd edn. Giuffrè, Milan
18. Palmieri L, Umani-Ronchi G, Bolino G, Fedeli P (2006) La valutazione del danno biologico in responsabilità civile. Giuffrè, Milan
19. Ronchi E, Mastroroberto L, Genovese U (2015) Guida alla valutazione medico-legale dell'invalidità permanente. 2nd edn. Giuffrè, Milan
20. Buzzi F, Domenici R (eds) (2016) SIMLA—Linee guida per la valutazione medico-legale del danno alla persona in ambito civilistico. Giuffrè, Milan

Chapter 9
Methods of Ascertainment of Personal Damage in Belgium

Yvo Vermylen and Katja De Munnynck

Abstract This chapter illustrates the historical, judicial, and juridical framework of personal injury assessment and compensation in Belgium, describing the expert's qualification and competences and detailing the ascertainment methodology and criteria of evaluation utilized for identifying, describing, and estimating any personal injury, its temporary and permanent consequences, and the causal value/link between the event and the injury and between the injury and the impairment/disability.

9.1 Historical, Judicial, and Juridical Overview

9.1.1 History

The first known laws to compensate for damage were issued by Hammurabi in 1725 BC. They were comprised of very cruel punishments such as "an eye for an eye and a tooth for a tooth" and also pecuniary punishments.

In the Middle Ages the Kings made the Laws and different Courts were established to Judge the wrongdoers. Torture was a common method to prove whether somebody was innocent or not.

Modern times began with the Code of Napoleon in 1804. This was adopted in several Countries, including Belgium, which was ruled by the French from 1794 to 1815, when Napoleon lost his last battle in Waterloo.

Y. Vermylen (✉)
Department of Dentistry, Faculty of Medicine, The Catholic University Leuven, Capucijnenvoer 7, 3000 Leuven, Belgium
e-mail: yvovermylen@skynet.be

K. De Munnynck
MedLEx, Rotselaar, Belgium
e-mail: katja,demunnynk@gmail.com

S.D. Ferrara et al. (eds.), *Personal Injury and Damage Ascertainment under Civil Law*, DOI 10.1007/978-3-319-29812-2_9

This Napoleonic code, despite having been amended over time, is the basis of our Civil legislation. The articles (1382–1386) about the necessity for the compensation of human damage are still the same as in 1804.

The Industrial Revolution of the nineteenth century resulted in a shift from agriculture to industry and those employed in the factories had none or limited rights. Accidents at work were not compensated and drove workers and their families into big financial problems. A major accident in the mining industry in 1813 led to an Imperial decree financed by the employers and the miners, who could forthwith benefit from pensions and pecuniary compensation for disability. More and more trade unions were established and in 1903 the First Law for accidents at work was issued. By 1945 all employees were included.

The Belgian Social Security System was built up and included health care (through sick Funds), pensions, financial provisions for disabled and unemployed persons, and compensation for diseases caused by working in a particular profession. This guaranteed at least a minimum income for those who were damaged by health problems.

In 1971 a law was issued making insurance for accidents at work compulsory and included also accidents occurring to and from work in the same Law.

In 1975 the Official Scale of Disability was issued by Royal decree based on the Laws of October 1948 where the reparation of physical damage of soldiers, political prisoners, and members of the resistance was laid down in percentages of impairment. This Scale is *still* used in Belgium for the evaluation of physical disability.

The popularity of insurance has led to a better legal protection for the individual person, providing the assistance of lawyers and medical experts if claims for compensation of physical damage are made. We see an essential increase of claims for sustained physical damage. Many of them are settled out of court, but the number of Court cases is still growing.

In 2004 the First Indicative Table (IT) with a list of all possible damages was assembled by the police courts. That Table was adapted and changed over the years. The latest is the IT of 2012.[1] The aim of the IT is to make sure that the victim will get a more precise and equitable compensation for the damages sustained.

9.1.2 Legal Basis of Liability

The main articles relating to Civil liability are the articles 1382–1386 of the Belgian Civil Code.

Every human being who commits a tortious act causing damage to another person has the obligation to compensate this damage (1382), not only because of his/her actions, but also because he/she was negligent or imprudent (1383).

Persons who are responsible for others (parents for their minor children, teachers for their pupils, principals for their subordinates or servants) can be held liable for

[1] http://www.fcgb-bgwf.be/documents/Tabl_Ind_2012_Fr.pdf.

errors of those under their authority, unless they can demonstrate that they could not have prevented the act (1384).

Additionally, the owners of animals and buildings will be liable if some damage results from it (1385).

Finally, there is a specific article for the liability of persons in a state of insanity (1386).

To be liable evidence must be supplied that a fault, causing damage, has been committed and that there is a causal link between the fault and the damage. This evidence must be provided by the victim.

9.2 The Fault Principle

What is a fault? The criterion is the "*culpa levis in abstracto*" principle. In civil liability the lightest error and in contractual liability the light error is sufficient, but the distinction between light and lightest is difficult to make. It is the task of the court to consider that an error has been made based on the evidence and documents of the case. The Judge will compare the behavior of the perpetrator with the "careful and prudent person under the same circumstances of time and place" [1]. This standard of care is measured through objective and external and impersonal criteria. It does not take into account subjective data such as age, sex, intelligence, and character.

9.3 Causal Link and Equivalence Theory

A causal connection exists when it can be proved that, in the absence of the error, the damage would not have occurred as it happened in reality [2]. The damage must not necessarily be a direct consequence of the fault. It is sufficient that there is a relationship between the error and the injury. The burden of proof of the existence of a causal link is on the victim. The absence of a causal link between fault and damage can be disclosed from the fact that the damage would have appeared even without the fault of the perpetrator.

That burden of proof can be relieved and based on common knowledge (prima facie evidence—on first sight). It is almost the same as the "*res ipsa loquitur*" (the case speaks for itself) rule in Common Law jurisdictions.

The fault of a third party or the victim can lead to a split liability, because there is a combination of errors.

Belgian Law uses the "Equivalence theory." This theory argues that each conduct, which is a condition for the occurrence of the concrete reprehensible event, is considered a cause. If that cause is ignored, then the accident would not have occurred in the same way. The cause must be the "conditio sine qua non." There is no distinction made between the different causes; each cause is equivalent, no matter how slight that cause may be (*culpa levis*).

9.4 Damage and Compensation for Damage

Damage is the most essential element of the trilogy of fault, injury, and causation.

Without damage there will be no liability, while it is possible that there is liability without fault (no-fault liability). The Civil Code (Articles 1382–1386 of the Civil Code) gives no definition of what damage really is. The exact meaning of damage is established by case law.

Damage is a static concept, while compensation is a dynamic concept [3].

The most classical legal definition of damage is the negative outcome of a comparison between two conditions: the current status of the victim after the tort and the hypothetical situation in which he/she would have stayed if the unlawful act or omission did not exist. Damage is, in fact, the disadvantage or loss that is suffered by the victim of an unlawful act.

The compensation for damages is a dynamic concept, namely the restoration of the victim to the situation in which he/she would have remained if the tort was not committed. That can be done by medical/dental treatments or by pecuniary compensation. Restoration of the damage has a priority over pecuniary compensation.

Damage must be certain, personal, and legitimate.

The legal literature [4] and jurisprudence [5] agree that a breach of the law is not absolutely necessary; a breach of interests is sufficient, if that interest is legitimate and that both the existence and the size of the damage are certain.

To correctly evaluate the physical damage, the victim must necessarily find the assistance of a medical practitioner.

Both parties in a dispute must contribute to the proof. The burden of proof should be distributed on the basis of good faith in carrying out agreements [6].

The role of the Judge is neutral; he must adhere to the evidence, documents, and facts submitted by the parties and he must ascertain the equality of the parties in court. The judge can request that certain supporting documents be submitted, even if these documents are in the possession of a third party. The evidence of the damage can be delivered by all legal means. He decides what the content is of the mission given to the expert-witness.

If the existence of the damage is established, the Judge must budget it. Only the existence must be sure, not its size. If the extent of the damage cannot be budgeted correctly, the Judge will do it "*ex aequo et bono*" (to equity). In that event, the Judge must motivate his decision.

Hypothetical damage may not be reimbursed. The liable party will only have to pay damages if it is certain that the assets or the moral condition of the victim are affected. It does not have to be an absolute certainty. A legal or moral certainty is sufficient.

Damage can also occur at a later time and if a causal link can be established it has to be taken into account.

Besides the damage for the degradation of the physical integrity, there is also moral and aesthetic damage, travel costs, temporary and permanent impairment (invalidity), and temporary or permanent incapacity to work. The compensation for damages is integral and all types of damages will be taken into account.

9.4.1 *Loss of a Chance*

The victim loses the possibility to acquire a benefit or to avoid a loss because of the tort.

The damage must be compensated, provided that the opportunity is real and that the loss of a chance is established. The compensation should be in proportion to the degree of probability.

In some recent judgments of the Court of Cassation [7], the application of the loss of a chance is apparently undermined. It must be certain that the loss of a chance (and the injury suffered as a result of that) is due to a mistake and a causal connection between the fault and the damage must be demonstrated. If the injury is not related to the error or would have happened anyway, even in the absence of the error, there is no reason for compensation of damages.

9.4.2 *Reservations for the Future*

It is often impossible to predict the future evolution of an injury. The condition can sometimes seem stabilized, but experience has shown that in some cases an aggravation can occur after a lapse of time (even years). It is then of the utmost importance that a reservation is made for the future evolution. Only in this way can we be certain that the possibility to assess the aggravation later is safeguarded. The expert and also the Court must take up in its report/decision; otherwise, it will be impossible to claim it later.

9.4.3 *Budgeting the Damage*

The Judge will budget the damage at the actual price at the time of his decision. It must be an integral compensation for damages. The damage must be calculated in "*concreto*." In *concreto* means that the calculation of the compensation for damage must be done by invoices or prescriptions for medical treatments and take into account the concrete salary. It has to be the exact price paid for the treatment and not an average price suggested by the expert.

He will take into account increases in the price of the treatments, monetary inflation, increased life expectancy, and all the other circumstances specific for the person of the victim.

The courts do not take into account facts happening after the unlawful act or omission, which have led to an increase of the damage, if there is no causal relationship with the tort.

The compensation is integral, correct, and objective, all the damage, not more, but also not less. Only the error of the victim may reduce the amount of the compensation.

9.4.4 Compensation or Reparation

Reparation is the first choice. The Court of Cassation [8] ruled that the injured party is entitled to seek recovery if it is possible or requested by the injured and/or offered by the liable party.

In many cases, however, reparation does not cover all the damage. The placement of a crown or implant will never be as good as a natural tooth. The victim is doomed to live with an Ersatz. Additional damages on top of the reparation are sometimes awarded to the victim.

9.4.5 The Duty to Limit the Sustained Damage

The insured person must take all reasonable steps to reduce the damage. There is not a general obligation to do so, but he shall take all reasonable and necessary measures to avoid that the damage will grow [9]. The Court of Cassation [10] says in the following way: "Whereas the injured person is in principle entitled to full compensation for his injury, he is not required to limit the damage as much as possible, but he only has to take reasonable measures to limit the damage, and he is only required to do so if that is consistent with the attitude of a reasonable and prudent person." If he doesn't do so, he will not receive full compensation.

On the other end, a victim taking measures that are excessive, extravagant, and overshooting the target will also not get full compensation. He will only receive a compensation which corresponds to the full compensation applicable to his damage.

9.4.6 Preexisting Conditions

The preexisting condition is a concept that can in fact be divided into three assumptions: the predisposition to damage, the aggravation of the preexisting condition, and the advancing of the damage.

In case of a "*Predestination of damage*," there is an existence of negative characteristics with a potential to cause greater damage than one would expect in a normal person: classical examples of this are the man with the egg skull or the patient with hemophilia.

In that case, the preexisting condition is not taken into account and all damage sustained must be entirely reimbursed. Cassation [11] argues that the fact that a pathological predisposition of a person has contributed to the injury does not relieve the obligation of the contributor to reimburse the full damage, except when it comes to effects that, even without the tort, would have occurred. "*The tortfeasor must take the victim as he/she finds him/her*."

The second assumption is about the "*advancing of the damage*." Acceleration of the injury is a dynamic process. An existing eye disease will in the event of an accident lead to quicker blindness or a dormant cancer may result in earlier death of the victim than normal. In these cases, there is no obligation to provide full compensation for the injury because the damage would have occurred even without the error of the contributor. The only thing that must be determined is the exact moment when the injury resulting from the accident would be overtaken by the evolving situation. From that moment on all compensations for damages come to an end.

"Aggravation of a Preexisting Condition" We have a health condition, which is not perfect, but the condition is static and not evolving. The earlier damage is stopped by a treatment. The Court of Cassation stated that: "In case of an injury caused by a wrongful act or omission, all effects contributing to the damage will be taken into account including those related to the already existing weaknesses."

9.5 How to Get Compensation for Physical Damage

The first thing that has to be established is to find out if a third party is involved.

If not, the victim receives compensation from the basic Health insurance or from the Accident at work Insurance. *Recognition* of the accident at work is necessary in the case of an accident at work. Also, special personal insurance against physical damage is a possibility. This is also the case when the third party cannot be identified.

If the third party is identified, liability must be established by a Court decision or by recognition of the liability by the perpetrator or his insurance.

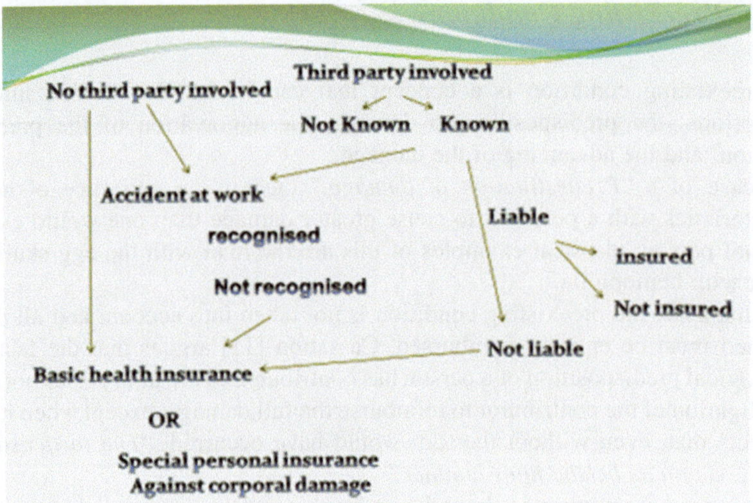

Fig. 9.1 Pathway to get compensation for physical damage

If the third party is liable and has insurance, the insurance company will pay the compensation for damages sustained. If he has no insurance, the third party will have to pay the compensation for damages itself.

If the third party is not liable, compensation only comes from health insurance or personal insurance (Fig. 9.1).

9.6 The Investigation of the Damage

9.6.1 The Immediate Treatment

The first treatment will often take place in the emergency department of a hospital. The staff creates a conclusive report about the injuries sustained and the accomplished treatment. From there on the healthcare treatments will be followed up by the general practitioner.

The victim has a duty to make a file containing all the evidence such as reports, X-ray examinations, photographic evidence, costs of the treatment, and reimbursement of medical costs via the sick funds.

9.6.2 Investigation by the Medical Advisor of the Insurance Company

If the third party is insured, the victim will be asked to undergo a medical examination by the medical advisor of the insurance company. If the victim has a Legal expenses insurance, he will undergo a second examination by the medical advisor of this insurance company.

These medical advisors must defend in an objective way the interests of the insurance company: Is the report of the treating medical practitioner correct? Is there a causal connection between the accident and the claimed damage and how can the treatment be done in the most fair, accurate, and appropriate way?

There is no contradiction between objective advice and defending the interests of the insurer. It is not in the interest of the insurer if the medical advisor should minimize or maximize the budgeting of the sustained damage. When he does so and when the insurer refuses to settle the case based on the report of his medical advisor, the victim may start a judicial procedure. If it then becomes clear that minimizing or maximizing the damage was not correct, the judicial procedure could have been avoided. The insurer will have a lot of extra costs such as the costs of the expert-witness, his own lawyer and the lawyer of the victim, the costs of his dental advisor, and the costs of the procedure.

A medical advisor of an insurance company is a qualified doctor in medicine with a specialization in insurance medicine. That is a 2-year course and there are regularly symposia that they can attend with topics in the field of insurance medicine and insurance law. This is a Master of 2-year jointly organized by the Universities of Ghent, Antwerp, and Leuven.

9.7 Out of Court Settlements and Legal Procedures

9.7.1 Settlement Between Parties

Many cases will be solved out of Court by a settlement between the parties. That does not mean that mutual concessions must be made in relation to the extent of the damage. That would not be fair. It excludes the costs of a judicial procedure and it is faster.

9.7.2 Medical Amicable Expertise

It is a contractual investigation, but it has the same value as a judicial expertise. It is less formal than a judicial expertise and it is in general faster. The two parties are represented by medical advisors (a medical advisor of the insurance company and a medical advisor who represents the victim).

This form of settlement of disputes can be very interesting, on condition that both parties agree on the nomination of a third, jointly chosen, expert. If they do not agree about the third expert, then the third expert will be nominated by the Courts. It is the task of this third expert to decide all points of disagreement and to make a final report. The cost of the medical amicably expertise is spread over the insurance companies. Each party pays the cost of their medical advisor and the cost of the third party will be split into half. All parties are invited to be present at each step of the procedure and all information is made available to each party.

9.7.3 *Judicial Procedure in Civil Courts*

The Judge can appoint an expert-witness, but before doing so he must be sure that such an investigation is necessary and appropriate and cannot be solved through other less expensive means [12].

The judge can appoint any expert with the necessary qualifications in order to accomplish the mission. There are no official lists of experts, although officious lists exist in the Courts of Law. The ambition of the actual Minister of Justice is to establish a national database of legal experts. A recent Law is issued on 10.04.2014. Everyone who wants to be appointed as a legal expert must prove 5 years of professional expertise, the necessary knowledge of his professional field and the law. Implementation is foreseen in December 2016.

Medical experts investigate the available evidence and give technical advice based on their findings. The judge decides the value of the evidence, but has to recognize the strength of the evidence. This means that parts of the report may not be used outside of the context of the report, nor can the judge add anything to the report that is not mentioned, or dispute the existence of the facts of the case. The advice is not binding, so the judge can decide whether to follow or not the report of the expert.

Medical experts can be challenged if they have too close relations with one of the parties. An expert who has any knowledge of a possible challenge will warn the parties or refuse his mission. In that case another expert will be assigned.

The Judge describes the exact mission of the expert, the name and address of the expert, and the monetary provision of the expert. The judge will be kept informed at regular times about the evolution of the proceedings of the expertise.

The expert will convoke all parties to be present at the first meeting. Each party has to present all pieces of evidence at that meeting. All parties have the duty to cooperate with the expert. All parties are invited to be present at each step of the procedure and all information is made available to each party.

The expert will discuss the clauses of his mission with the parties. If both parties agree, some extra investigations can be added to the mission. The expert will hear and question the parties. If some specific further investigations are necessary, the expert will supervise these investigations and make sure that all parties can be present at these investigations, unless they agree that these investigations can be carried out without their assistance. These investigations are carried out by other professionals, specialists in their field of medicine. These investigations are just for medicolegal purposes.

Risky invasive diagnosis or treatments are not allowed. The victim must be informed and has a right to refuse.

X-rays, CTs, or Cone Beam CTs are possible if a correct diagnosis of the injuries cannot be reached with other means or deducted from already existing material.

The expert will decide if further meetings are necessary and will also give an estimation of the cost of the proceedings.

The expert has to finish his/her investigation in a reasonable period and the Judge shall only give permission for a prolongation if it is absolutely necessary and if all of the parties agree.

When the dossier is complete, he/she will write a provisional report (which contains already an advice) and send it to all parties, who have the possibility to make their remarks within a certain time. The expert must answer these remarks in a motivated way and if necessary change his/her conclusions.

He/she will then make a conclusive final report, which is sent to the Judge with all of the evidence. At the same time a copy of the final report is also sent to the parties. At the end of the report, the expert takes an oath and signs the document. If that is not done the entire report is null and void.

If the Judge decides that it is necessary, the expert-witness will be convoked to give evidence in Court and will testify under oath (the oath of expert-witness). The expert can give an opinion concerning any issues that may arise. It is also possible to hear the medical advisor of the liable person, but that is not often the case. That technical advisor does not take the oath of the expert-witness but the oath of a witness.

Appeal is possible by the Courts of Appeal and a new expert can be nominated. That expert may consult all the evidence and also the report of the first expert.

9.7.4 *Procedure Before the Fund of Medical Accidents*

It is a two-way system: The patient has the choice between a court procedure or a procedure according to this law [13]. The initiative to investigate the case comes from the FUND of Medical Accidents (FMA). The procedure is in theory free for the patient and the practitioner. It is also rapid. The aim is that the procedure should be concluded within 6 months.

The FMA investigates the case and establishes liability or its lack and will provide compensation for damages in some cases without any fault, but only under some very specific conditions: it has to be abnormal, unforeseeable damage, taking into account the current position of science, the actual condition of the patient, and the objective predictable evolution of their condition.

The patient has to request an investigation by the FMA by sending a registered letter, describing what happened, the name of the practitioner, and a description of the damage. The FMA will investigate the case if receivable and give an advice within 6 months. If the claim is not receivable the patient can bring their case to a court of Law.

The FMA collects all the information from all parties and shall, if necessary (complicated case), organize a medicolegal investigation by an impartial medical expert. Parties can be assisted by lawyers and medical advisors and the cost of investigation is advanced by the FMA. The advice of the FMA is not binding, but it can be used later in a Court of Law. The costs for the assistance in the procedure (lawyers, medical/dental advisors) are not yet regulated by the law.

That advice should be given within 6 months. It is sent to all parties. If liability is not withheld the patient can bring the case to Court. If liability is withheld, the FMA will ask the insurer to do a proposal.

The compensation for damages is complete and integral, including also moral, aesthetic damage and incapacitation, and also the loss of a chance on a better outcome is covered.

The FMA pays the patient in case of:

- A medical accident with no liability but under certain conditions, which are at least 25 % invalidity, 6 months unable to work, great loss of quality of life, and when the patient dies.
- Further conditions are that the accident is not a normal evolution of the existing condition of the patient, that it is abnormal, not foreseeable, or not predictable, or if the damage could have been avoided taking into account the highest level of actual science and if it was not an accident caused by a defective product. In case of a medical accident with liability and no or insufficient insurance, the Fund starts a procedure against the practitioner.
- If insurer makes a proposal that is obviously insufficient, the Fund starts a procedure against the insurer and/or practitioner.

The advice is sent to all parties and the insurer should make a proposal if the FMA withholds liability. In that case:

- The insurer can immediately dispute the liability of the practitioner.
- If the insurer does not react within 90 days, he/she will receive a registered letter from the FMA. If there is no reaction within a month it is accepted that the insurer does not accept the liability advice of the FMA.
- In both instances the patient can bring the case before a Civil Court of Law.

When the insurer accepts the liability, they will send a proposal to the patient (also to all other parties).

- In that case the patient has 90 days to accept that proposal. If the patient does not react within 90 days, he/she will receive a registered letter from the FMA, and if there is still no reaction, the case will be closed.
- The patient can ask the FMA if the compensation is sufficiently reasonable. If not, the FMA will pay the compensation to the patient and start a procedure against the insurer in a Court of Law.
- The patient accepts the proposal: he/she will be paid within a month.

9.7.5 Procedures by Accidents at Work and on the Way to and from Work

Most of these accidents are dealt with by the medical advisor and the general practitioner.

The victim can also go to the Court of Social Affairs, if no agreement can be reached. This Court works in the same way as the Civil Courts. But they can only decide the pure physical damage and the monetary compensation of the economic disability. All other matters like aesthetic and moral damage and damage to goods (clothes, car) must be obtained by a procedure before the Civil Courts.

The costs of a procedure before the Court of Social Affairs are covered by the Insurance Company that covers the compensation for accidents at Work.

9.8 Qualifications of the Medicolegal Experts

9.8.1 Forensic Pathologists

These medical practitioners are mostly linked to a University Unit of Forensic Medicine. They all have a specialty in Forensic Pathology and a good knowledge of the legislation in relation to the investigation of crime. Forensic Medicine has been recognized since 2002. Training involves a 5-year specialization in Forensic Medicine, including 1.5 years of Clinical Pathology. They also have the specialty in Insurance Medicine and can be nominated in Civil Cases.

9.8.2 The Medicolegal Experts in Civil Cases and the Medical Advisors of Insurance Companies

These medical practitioners mostly followed a 2-year specialty in insurance medicine and are familiar with the different court procedures and the evaluation of human damage. Since 2007, this specialty has been officially recognized.

There are three important medicolegal societies in Belgium:

- Koninklijk Belgisch Genootschap voor gerechtelijke Geneeskunde (Royal Belgian Society of Forensic medicine).
- Nationaal college van gerechtsdeskundigen van België (National College of Legal Experts in Belgium).
- Belgische vereniging van geneesheren-specialisten in de verzekerings- en expertise geneeskunde (Belgian Society of medical doctors, specialists in Insurance and Expertise Medicine).

9.9 Ascertainment Methodology

The medicolegal expert will include the mission given to him/her by the Judge (Court procedure) or the contractual mission in case of an Amicable Medical Expertise.

He/she will compose a complete file, including all medical reports and invoices related to the medical treatments and he/she can ask the parties to produce all the information needed to accomplish the mission.

He/she will examine the victim and describe the injuries sustained in great detail, the cause of the accident, the nature and the possible consequences, and the medical treatments that were necessary until the date of consolidation and give a prognosis for further treatments and medication after the date of consolidation. All these items will be taken up in his/her final report, also called "the consolidation report."

9.9.1 The Report

In accidents at work cases, The Law foresees the following description: the social and economic antecedents of the victim, a possible preexisting condition, the first injuries, the evolution of these injuries, the permanent injuries [disability rate according to the Official Belgian Scale of Invalidity (OBSI), the temporary and permanent economic disability, provided prostheses and ortheses, the date of consolidation, and elements that must be taken into consideration to determine the need for domestic aid.

This is more or less the same in Civil Cases.

It starts with the *text of the mission* of the medicolegal expert, followed by the *list of relevant documents* received from the parties.

The personal anamnesis: this consists not only in a description of the medical findings, but also in describing the probable consequences for the social, professional, and familial role of the victim in the community at large.

This *social anamnesis* contains his/her *personal data*: name, address, nationality, date of birth, marital status, telephone, and E-mail. This identifies the victim and gives them a specific place in the community.

Also *socioeconomic data* such as education, professions, driver's license, domestic activities, sport activities, and hobbies must be described in detail, because it may help in defining what his/her possibilities will be on the job market after the accident.

Medical information (sicknesses, operations, previous accidents, previous prostheses/ortheses) is important for the determination of possible preexisting conditions and the influence they might have on the evolution of the sustained damage of the actual injuries.

A detailed interview of the parties in the procedure will give the medicolegal expert more information about the facts of the accident (causal relation) and the exact sustained damage. The provided documents consist of reports from all those who have given treatment to the victim in great detail. It allows the medicolegal expert to reconstruct the complete treatment and the evolution of the injuries in a chronological way. It will give a good idea of necessary treatments and medication in the future. Also, temporary economic disability can be deduced from this information as well as the temporary need for domestic aid and the possibilities for the victim to continue their hobbies and sports activities.

9.9.2 The Date of Consolidation

This can be the date that the injuries of the victim are more or less healed/stabilized and will not change tremendously in the future. It is the date that a compensation for damages can be calculated. In this context, healing means that the victim has no permanent economic disability or physical/psychic disability anymore.

If the patient suffers from persisting injuries, these must be described in detail. The patterns of complaints include the functional and social aspects of the actual condition of the victim.

The clinical examination of the medicolegal expert must be complete and if specialized examinations are necessary, the victim will be referred. The medicolegal expert cannot conclude or order that invasive examinations should be performed.

The determination of the temporary and permanent disability is also a task of the medicolegal expert. Personal disability is not the same as economic disability, although the disability can have influence in the professional, personal, domestic and social life of the victim. All these disabilities must be separately determined.

The medicolegal expert must evaluate the economic disability by answering some particular questions: what possibilities on the job market are left for the victim, will instrumental/technical aid or domestic aid be needed, and what are the problems in his/her social and cultural life.

Reservations, which make a revision possible in the future, must be explicitly mentioned in the final report and in the judicial decision of the Court.

A consolidation report is a very important document containing the complete history of the sustained damage including the antecedents, the exact description of all damages, and the objective and subjective consequences.

9.10 Evaluation Criteria

The Table is indicative in nature and will only be used if the exact costs cannot be proven. Even then there is a possibility to deviate from the proposed costs of the IT. It is the Judge who will decide. The IT is a kind of instructional booklet for the medicolegal expert.

The medicolegal expert will examine the victim and describe the physical and psychic damage caused by the accident. These findings will lead to the determination of the disability rate and the negative implications on private, domestic, and professional/economic life. Each of these implications can lead to a disability.

Other more specific consequences must be taken into account if they cannot be included in the private, domestic, or economic field, such as pain, aesthetic, sexual, social, and cultural damage.

A special item is the preexisting condition and its consequences on the determination of the damage. One of the most important things to determine is the date of consolidation. Before that date we deal with temporary damage, but after that date with permanent damage.

9.10.1 Temporary Damage

The necessity of *prostheses, ortheses, technical aids, and adaptations on the house or car* are determined and serve to ease the life of the victim in their private, family, and professional activities. In some of these cases, the medicolegal expert will need/ask the assistance of a technical advisor. The medicolegal expert will then determine the costs and these must be proven by the victim through invoices or specifications.

The aid of a third person is sometimes a necessity (expressed in hours/day). A description of the domestic aid, the qualifications of the social workers, and the number of hours is done on a scale of 0–100 for domestic disability. That is important to determine the exact cost per hour of each social worker. These rates are normally fixed by labor contracts between employers and employees for the different groups. The IT foresees a forfeit of 10 € per hour for non-qualified third persons. That is applicable if the third person is a family member.

Personal temporary disability, taking into account the nature of hospital treatments, is estimated on a scale from 0 to 100 and states that the physical or psychic temporary disability is complete or partial. The IT foresees a monetary compensation of 31 € for each day of hospitalization and 25 € for each other day of temporary disability at 100 % and then in proportion to the degressive disabilities.

The temporary domestic and economic disability (on a scale from 0 to 100) is described separately from the physical or psychic disability.

The *temporary domestic disability* is estimated by the IT at 20 € per day at 100 % for a single person and raised by 5 € for each child that is part of the family.

The *economic disability* takes into account the net loss of income. The compensation should always attain the same net income that the victim would have had without the damaging facts. If the victim starts working again with their handicap and if the exact costs of these extra efforts cannot be calculated, the IT foresees 20 € per day at 100 % from the day that the work was resumed.

Temporary aesthetic damage is normally not envisaged, unless in specific circumstances (for example, very serious burns or disfiguration).

The *temporary sexual damage* will be decided by the Judge—the expert will describe the negative consequences and its influence on the sexual life of the victim.

The personal suffering (*quantum doloris*) is on a scale from 1 to 7. If the rate is from 1 to 3, the quantum doloris will be integrated in the personal disability rate. From 4 to 7 they are considered to be an extra damage. The IT foresees a daily compensation: 35 € for 4, 40 € for 5, 46 € for 6, and 53 € for 7.

Loss of a school year. This damage consists of a material damage, a moral damage, and a loss of income in the future. In the case of a lump sum compensation the IT foresees 390 € for primary school, 1000 € for secondary education, 4000 € for the loss of a year at University if the student resides at the University, and 2000 € if he/she resides at home. A further 3750 € is foreseen as moral damage, and a sum that equals the net income of the first professional year (to be proven).

9.10.2 Permanent Damage

The *permanent disability* starts at the moment of consolidation.

The expert will give a detailed opinion as to the date of recovery from the injuries or their consolidation and will describe with precision the remaining complaints as well as the persistent injuries. In addition, the expert will indicate to what extent these attacks on the physical and mental integrity are attributable to the accident.

This refers to costs for future medication, surgery, renewals of prostheses/ortheses, and costs for maintenance. The costs are calculated on the basis of the price at the time of the completion of the report and capitalized. Only treatments that will certainly be needed in the future and in relation to the injuries will be taken into account. A possible worsening of the situation will be included in the form of a reservation.

9.10.3 Methods of Compensation

There are *three different methods*: the reviewable and indexed annuity, the capitalization, and the lump sum compensation.

The reviewable and indexed annuity is the method of choice because the amount granted corresponds more precisely to the reality of the damage sustained. The lump sum compensation will only be used if none of the two other compensation methods is possible.

Specific *mortality tables* [15] are used to calculate the longevity of the compensation.

The *costs of technical aids and prostheses/ortheses* will be paid according to the real costs at the moment of the completion of the report and capitalized.

The *aid of a third person* will be calculated at the exact cost taking into account their qualification and included in the annuity or capitalized.

The *permanent personal, domestic, and economic incapacities* are calculated separately. If the disability rate is lower than 15 % the calculation will be done in a flat-rate way. If it is higher than 15 % the disability rate will be capitalized. Each incapacity (personal, domestic, and economic) will be divided by 3 and multiplied with the disability rate. See the following example for a better understanding (Table 9.1).

In the first two examples the calculation is done in a flat-rate way according to the estimated incapacity rate (Table 9.2).

In the third example there is a choice between flat rate and capitalization. It is obvious that the compensation is higher with the capitalization method.

The flat rates lower than 6 % differ from those from 6 % on and decrease with age.

The *economic permanent disability* is also estimated on a scale of 0–100, taking into account the profession at the moment of the accident and the possibility that the victim can continue to do the same job partially or completely, eventually with extra efforts on his part.

If a return to his previous job is impossible, the expert will, together with an ergonomist, see if another type of work can be found that is possible with his disabilities. If not, the permanent economic disability is a fact.

Table 9.1 Permanent personal, domestic, and economic incapacities

Man 30 years			
Personal incapacity	2 %	850 €	1275/3 × 2
Domestic incapacity	4 %	1700 €	1275/3 × 4
Economic incapacity	0 %	0 €	
Woman 30 years			
Personal incapacity	12 %	11,700 €	2925/3 × 12
Domestic incapacity	10 %	9750 €	2925/3 × 10
Economic incapacity	14 %	13,650 €	2925/3 × 14
Man 30 years			
Personal incapacity	25 % lump sum	24,375 €	2925/3 × 25
Personal incapacity	25 % Cap 1	90,109 €	(25 × 365 days) 25 % × 39,500
Domestic incapacity	10 % lump sum	9750 €	2925/3 × 10
Domestic incapacity	10 % Cap 2	29,170 €	(20 × 365 days) × 10 % × 39,959
Economic incapacity	40 % IE—3	55,029 €	(20 × 240) × 40 % × 28,661
Economic incapacity	40 % LE—4	247,631 €	(1800 × 12) × 40 % × 28,661

Cap 1—365 days at 25 €/day and an interest of 1 % annuity (according to the annual tables); Cap 2—365 days at 25 €/day and an interest of 1 % annuity (according to the annual tables); IE—means increased efforts 240 Working days at 20 € per day and an interest of 1 % annuity monthly and until 65 years; LE—means loss of employment with a net monthly salary of 1800 € and an interest of 1 % annuity monthly and until 65 years

The expert will also evaluate in a motivated way the *permanent esthetic damage* on a scale [16] from 1 to 7, explaining the criteria used. If the aesthetic damage could be surgically ameliorated, the expert will determine the costs and the risks involved, probably leading to periods of incapacity and a persisting disability rate. These criteria are the visibility of the scars, age, gender, profession, marital status, and social activities of the victim (Table 9.3).

The expert will describe in a motivated way the *sexual, social, and cultural damage*. It will be the Judge who decides the monetary compensation.

Sexual Damage is every loss of sexual activity, but also the loss of the possibility of reproduction. The partner can also install a claim for compensation.

Social and Cultural Damages are the deprivation of enjoying cultural events and socializing, but also the impossibility to practice hobbies and sports.

Reciprocal Damage Relatives also have a right to a moral compensation, because they are confronted with the suffering of a beloved one.

Reservations should be made for the future if there is a possibility that the physical or psychic condition may get worse.

Death–Costs of the Funeral In the event that a victim dies as a consequence of the tort, the costs of the funeral will be taken into account. When the duration of survival probability of the one who bears the cost is lower than that of the victim, this one would probably never had to expose them and can accordingly claim full

Table 9.2 Flat-rate way according to the estimated incapacity rate

Age class	Incapacity	
	<6 %	≥6 %
Up to 15 years	1500 €	3600 €
16 years	1485 €	3555 €
17 years	1470 €	3510 €
18 years	1455 €	3465 €
19 years	1440 €	3420 €
20 years	1425 €	3375 €
21 years	1410 €	3330 €
22 years	1395 €	3285 €
23 years	1380 €	3240 €
24 years	1365 €	3195 €
25 years	1350 €	3150 €
26 years	1335 €	3105 €
27 years	1320 €	3060 €
28 years	1305 €	3015 €
29 years	1290 €	2970 €
30 years	1275 €	2925 €
31 years	1260 €	2880 €
32 years	1245 €	2835 €
33 years	1230 €	2790 €
34 years	1215 €	2745 €
35 years	1200 €	2700 €
36 years	1185 €	2655 €
37 years	1170 €	2610 €
38 years	1155 €	2565 €
39 years	1140 €	2520 €
40 years	1125 €	2475 €
41 years	1110 €	2430 €
42 years	1095 €	2385 €
43 years	1080 €	2340 €
44 years	1065 €	2295 €
45 years	1050 €	2250 €
46 years	1035 €	2205 €
47 years	1020 €	2160 €
48 years	1005 €	2115 €
49 years	990 €	2070 €
50 years	975 €	2025 €
51 years	960 €	1980 €
52 years	945 €	1935 €
53 years	930 €	1890 €
54 years	915 €	1845 €
55 years	900 €	1800 €

(continued)

Table 9.2 (continued)

Age class	Incapacity <6 %	≥6 %
56 years	885 €	1755 €
57 years	870 €	1710 €
58 years	855 €	1665 €
59 years	840 €	1620 €
60 years	825 €	1575 €
61 years	810 €	1530 €
62 years	795 €	1485 €
63 years	780 €	1440 €
64 years	765 €	1395 €
65 years	750 €	1350 €
66 years	735 €	1305 €
67 years	720 €	1260 €
68 years	705 €	1212 €
69 years	690 €	1170 €
70 years	675 €	1125 €
71 years	660 €	1080 €
72 years	645 €	1035 €
73 years	630 €	990 €
74 years	615 €	945 €
75 years	600 €	900 €
76 years	585 €	855 €
77 years	570 €	810 €
78 years	555 €	765 €
79 years	540 €	720 €
80 years	525 €	675 €
81 years	510 €	630 €
82 years	495 €	585 €
83 years	480 €	540 €
84 years	465 €	495 €
85 years	450 €	450 €

reimbursement (for example, a parent for her child). If the victim's life expectancy is lower than that of the one entitled to it, the latter would have had to bear in the future and his compensation consists in the advance payment of these costs. The compensation is then formed by the difference between the current expenditure and the constant value of this sum payable to the presumed date of death in the assumption that the accident would not have happened

Death–Damage of the Relatives This suffering of the relatives cannot be expressed in exact monetary terms and must be done with a lump sum (Table 9.4).

Table 9.3 Scale for the permanent aesthetic damage

Age	01/07 Minimal	02/07 Very light	03/07 Light	04/07 Medium	05/07 Serious	06/07 Very serious	07/07 Repugnant
0–10	540 €	2150 €	4850 €	8625 €	10,000 €[a]	15,000 €[a]	25,000 €[a]
11–20	520 €	2075 €	4700 €	8300 €			
21–30	490 €	2000 €	4400 €	7850 €			
31–40	450 €	1800 €	4100 €	7250 €			
41–50	400 €	1600 €	3600 €	6500 €			
51–60	350 €	1400 €	3100 €	5550 €			
61–70	275 €	1100 €	2600 €	4400 €			
71–80	200 €	800 €	1750 €	3100 €			
81 and above	115 €	450 €	1050 €	1850 €			

[a]At least (no maximum)

Table 9.4 Death and damage of the relatives

Deceased victim	Recipient of the allowance	Indemnity
Spouse/cohabitant/civil partnership	Spouse/cohabitant/civil partnership	12,500 €
Parent cohabitee	Child cohabiting	12,500 €
Parent cohabitee	Child cohabiting already orphan	20,000 €
Parent non-cohabitant	Enfant non-cohabitant	5000 €
Child cohabitee	Parent	12,500 €
Child living in autonomy	Parent	5000 €
Miscarriage	Parent	2500 €
Brother/sister cohabiting	Brother/sister cohabiting	2500 €
Brother/sister non-cohabiting	Brother/sister non-cohabiting	1500 €
Grandparents cohabitants	Grandchildren cohabitants	2500 €
Grandparents non-cohabitants	Grandchildren non-cohabitants	1250 €
Grandchildren cohabitants	Grandparents cohabitants	2500 €
Grandchildren non cohabitants	Grandparents non-cohabitants	1250 €

Other parents or relatives of the victim must prove that there is an affective specific link that justifies a compensation of 1500–5000 €

9.10.4 The Ascertainment of the Physical/Psychic Disability: OBSI

This OBSI was issued by Royal decree based on the Laws of October 1948 where the reparation of physical damage of soldiers, political prisoners, and members of the resistance was laid down in percentages of impairment. This Scale is mainly used in Belgium for the evaluation of physical disability.

The OBSI gives a complete overview of all possible disability rates for the entire body. It also gives directives on how to calculate the different disabilities. It is a booklet of 115 pages.

There are 15 chapters: *Bones and joints* including the head, the spine, upper and lower limbs, chest, pelvis, protheses, and ortheses; *Muscles*; *Blood circulation* including the heart, blood vessels, and lymphatic vessels; *Respiratory system* including trachea, bronchi, and lungs; *Digestive tract* including the mouth, pharynx, esophagus, ductus thoracicus, stomach and diaphragm, small intestine, colon, rectum, peritoneum, liver and bile, pancreas and spleen; *Blood diseases; Urine and genital organs; Neuropsychiatry* including brains and spinal marrow, peripheral nerves, mental disorders; *Diseases of nose, throat, and ears; Ophthalmology*; *Skin diseases; General diseases* including septicemia, tuberculosis, endocrinology, rheumatic diseases; *Tropical diseases; Acute intoxications; Concentration Camp pathology.*

9.10.5 The General Principles of the Calculation of the Disability Rate

Besides the OBSI, Belgian medicolegal experts also use the European Medical Scale for the ascertainment of physical and psychic damage.

Another interesting Scale is the ELIDA scale (Estimation of Loss of Independence in Daily Activities) for the determination of the need of third-person aid in case of disability.

References

1. Cass., 10 November 1981, Arr. Cass., 1981-82, 361; Cass., 21 September 1983, R.W., 1984–85, 270; Cass., 24 September 1986, Arr. Cass., 1986–87, 109
2. Simoens D Schade en schadeloosstelling in Beginselen van privaatrecht, Kluwer, Antwerpen, 1999, p 14
3. Simoens D, o.c.; Ronse J, “Schade en schadeloosstelling”, APR, Story-Scientia, Gent, 1984, 10–23; Dirix E, “Het begrip schade”, Maklu, 1998, 22–27
4. Cass., 16 January1939, Pas.1939, I, 25; R.G.A.R., 1939, nr.3002
5. Art 1315 Civil Code en 870 Judicial Code
6. Cass. (1e k.) AR C.09.0190.N, 17 December 2009 (Belgische Staat/Belmagri)
7. Cass. 26 juni 1980, arr. Cass., 1979–80, 1365; R.W. 1980–81, 1661, noot
8. Law on the insurance contract 25 June 1992, article 20
9. Cass. AR 9336, 14 mei 1992 (Arcq/Pussemier)
10. Cass., 06.01.1993, Arr.Cass., 1993, 11
11. Law of May, 15 changing the procedure of the medico-legal expertise in the Judicial Code and art 509, quarter of the Penal Code, B.S. 22 August 2007
12. Law of 31 March 2010 on Compensation for accidents during medical treatment. The Fund of medical accidents is an Institute with an independent administration and financed by the State, the Institute of Health and Invalidity Insurance and financial income from the Fund
13. http://www.fcgb-bgwf.be/documents/Tabl_Ind_2012_Fr.pdf
14. http://www.tafelsschryvers.be/tables?language=fr

15. The scale of Julin: from 1 to 7: minimal, very light, light, medium, serious, very serious, repugnant
16. KB 20 March 1975, 2 July 1975 and 6 January 1976; KB 10 February 1977; KB 29 September 1978; Kb 23 June 1980. http://www.expertisemedicale.be/upload/documents/documentation/bobi.pdf

15. The scale of Julin: from 1 to 7: minimal, very light, light, medium, serious, very serious, repugnant
16. KB 20 March 1975, 2 July 1975 and 6 January 1976; KB 10 February 1977; KB 29 September 1978; Kb 23 June 1980. http://www.expertisemedicale.be/upload/documents/documentation/bobi.pdf

Chapter 10
Methods of Ascertainment of Personal Damage in the Netherlands

Jan Buitenhuis and Wout E.L. De Boer

Abstract This chapter illustrates the historical, judicial, and juridical framework of personal injury assessment and compensation in The Netherlands, describing the expert's qualification and competences and detailing the ascertainment methodology and criteria of evaluation utilised for identifying, describing, and estimating any personal injury, its temporary and permanent consequences, and the causal value/link between the event and the injury and between the injury and the impairment/disability.

10.1 Historical, Judicial, and Juridical Overview

Personal injury can occur in first- and third-party insurances.

In first-party insurances, the victim has an insurance policy which states that sustained impairments can lead to a financial benefit, under certain conditions and with exclusions. The maximum benefit varies with the policy. Policies can include a normalisation clause stating that only impairments that would arise in a person with normal health are covered, thereby excluding individual vulnerabilities.

In third-party insurances, damage is caused by someone who is liable. For instance, all cars in the Netherlands are legally obliged to have liability insurance. Traffic victims can claim from the insurance policy of the liable driver and this liability insurance covers all damages. This includes payment for sustained grief and physical damage, but also disability in all possible domains (e.g. work,

J. Buitenhuis (✉)
Dutch Academic Center for Insurance Medicine (DACIM), University Medical Center Groningen, Afdeling Gezondheidswetenschappen, Sectie Sociale Geneeskunde/secretariaat K623, Sector F/FA10, Ant. Deusinglaan 1, 9713 AV Groningen, The Netherlands
e-mail: j.buitenhuis@dacim.nl

W.E.L. De Boer
Asim Research & Education I Department Clinical Research, University Hospital Basel, Spitalstrasse 12, CH-4031 Basel, Switzerland
e-mail: wout.deboer@usb.ch

S.D. Ferrara et al. (eds.), *Personal Injury and Damage Ascertainment under Civil Law*, DOI 10.1007/978-3-319-29812-2_10

including missed career opportunities, house and garden maintenance) and resulting loss of income, and other extra costs and so forth. The insurer has to take the victim as he finds him/her, thus including individual vulnerabilities. This means that unexpected serious consequences, attributable to individual vulnerability, must be paid for by the insurer.

10.2 Identification and Description of the Medicolegal Expert's Qualifications

Insurance claims are primarily handled by legally trained administrative staff. These claim handlers are in charge of the administrative process. They ask the medical officer for advice regarding medical issues.

In all insurance claims involving medical issues a medical expert of the insurance company, the medical officer, is the first to medically assess the claim. The insured, or victim, can always ask someone, often with a legal background, to help with the claim, or go to Court when there is a dispute, in which case a lawyer is required. Often the lawyer has his own medical expert to assist in the medical assessment of the consequences of the injury.

During the extra-judicial trajectory or during a court case, a clinical examination of the consequences of the injury can be asked for, a so-called independent medical assessment, to be carried out by a clinical specialist.

Medical doctors have completed the University medical education programme which takes 6 years. After this, they can specialise as a medical specialist, such as a neurologist, surgeon, general physician, occupational health physician, or insurance physician. The medical specialty insurance medicine requires a 4-year postgraduate medical education leading to registration as an official medical specialist. This education is open to medical doctors and is provided by the Netherlands School of Public and Occupational Health.

The current qualifications for the medical insurance expert in private insurance, the medical officer, are a specialisation as an insurance physician and, on top of that, a private insurance qualification as a registered medical advisor.

This extra private insurance education consists of two courses: the American Medical Association (AMA) guide to permanent impairment course and the American Academy of Insurance Medicine (AAIM) Mortality course. Both take 2 days. This leads to registration as a registered medical advisor.

This medical advisor assesses life insurance and work disability insurance applications, as well as work disability and personal injury claims. In public insurance claim assessment, the medical expert is an insurance physician. In private insurance medicine, there is no legislation regarding the education of medical officers. However, the de facto standard followed by most insurance companies is that a medical officer should be an insurance physician and a registered medical advisor.

The clinical specialist performing an independent medical assessment needs no official training to perform a medical assessment. There has been, however, a recent initiative to educate clinical specialists in medical assessments and provide a register of educated clinical specialists. An association has been founded and the government has provided financial means to set up the register and build an educational programme. More than 100 medical specialists have taken this 4-day course and followed the programme, where assessment reports are evaluated in small groups, leading to registration in this list of certified clinical experts. The association has formulated guidelines for independent medical assessments [1].

Apart from this medical initiative, there is also a more legal-oriented, 10-day education programme for medical experts involved in criminal court cases at the University of Leiden. After this training, the expert can be registered in a registry of legal specialists [2].

10.3 Ascertainment Methodology

The process of claim assessment is essentially a legal process. The applicability of the insurance policies or the liability has to be settled first. This legal process can lead to medical questions for the medical officer. Sometimes, for instance, it is not clear whether a certain injury is covered by the insurance policies or whether there is a causal relationship between the insured event and the claimed consequences. The medical officer works mostly on the basis of written material. He seldom sees a claimant or victim personally.

10.3.1 Collection of Circumstantial and Clinical Data

The medical officer has to ask the victim for permission in order to request medical information regarding the injury and treatment from the treating physicians. If the victim has asked a lawyer to handle his/her claim, usually the lawyer (or other representative) collects the medical information and sends this to the medical officer of the insurance company. A claim cannot usually be assessed without information from the treating physicians. In case of a traffic accident and when deemed necessary, a technical examination of the physical aspects of the accident can be conducted, usually to determine aspects of legal liability. In rare cases, this information can also be useful when causality of a specific injury is uncertain (see Sect. 10.4.2).

10.3.2 Medical Case History

The recent medical history, after the accident, usually becomes clear through the information from the treating physicians. In some cases, the situation at the moment of the accident or further back has to be made clear. In that case, usually the general practitioner is asked to provide (part of) the medical files. In the Netherlands, everybody has a personal general practitioner. This medical doctor has the medical files of the patient and is informed of all medical procedures, including the findings of the clinical doctors.

10.3.3 Systematic Clinical and Medicolegal Visit

In personal injury, whether in first- or third-party insurances, no routine visits are performed by the medical officer or a clinical specialist. The insurance company usually has specialised personnel to make house calls and talk to victims and/or lawyers. In rare cases, the medical officer can ask a victim to visit the office or makes a house call. There is no such thing as a "systematic clinical-medicolegal visit".

10.3.4 Additional Investigations

In a minority of cases, an examination by a clinical medical specialist is called for, that is, an independent medical assessment. For these cases, a standard list of questions is developed by the VU University Amsterdam [3]. The victim is invited by the clinical specialist to visit his/her office and a complete medical examination is performed. It may be necessary to make (new) X-rays or a CT scan, or whatever medical examination is needed. Before these kinds of extra examinations are performed, the medical adviser usually is consulted because of the costs, and the victim has to agree as well. Especially, invasive or X-ray investigations can lead to discussion and are usually kept to a minimum. Each medical doctor involved has his own responsibilities In case the victim refuses, the insurer will decide on the evidence at hand, possibly not in favour of the victim. As far as we know, this has not led to any legal cases.

10.4 Evaluation Criteria

The assessment of personal injuries roughly consists of two parts. The first is the evaluation of physical and mental impairment caused by the injury. The second is the assessment of disability (for work and other domains of life) caused by the impairments that result from the injury. In both cases, causality plays a major role. Impairment or disability, already present before the accident, or which had most probably also developed in the event the accident had not occurred, has to be determined and subtracted from the current consequences to determine the true consequences of the accident.

In first-party injury insurances usually only the impairment is needed to assess the claim. The insurance policy at hand provides the first and main source of information on which kinds of injuries are covered and to what extent. Many different insurance policies exist. Most insurance policies contain some kind of impairment scale (barème).

In third-party liability cases, the impairment is only of minor importance. It is often only used as one of the relevant factors for determining the amount of indemnity or injury-award. This is part of the payment only partially related to the actual physical damage, but also based on the amount of suffering or grief.

Disability for work is usually far more important since it is related to working capacity now and in the future. Disability for work makes for the major part of the damages.

10.4.1 Psychic and Somatic State Prior to the Event/Injury

As mentioned earlier, in some cases—mainly third-party liability cases—the medical history has to be determined. In those cases, usually the general practitioner is asked to provide (part) of the medical files. The victim has to give the general practitioner permission to do so. The medical history is of special importance when the disability is not readily explained by the injury caused by the accident and a pre-existing disability is suspected.

10.4.2 Detailed Reconstruction of the Event/Injury

In some cases, the relationship between the injury and the accident is not readily clear. The medical officer then tries to a get a good view of the accident using the patient history and information from treating physicians. In rare cases, an accident reconstruction is possible, but this is a technical process which usually aims at clarifying who or what caused the traffic accident, and which was the dynamical sequence of events.

10.4.3 *Personal Injury*

The actual injury usually becomes clear from the information of the treating physicians. When the injury or the consequences are not clear, then the medical officer can call for an independent medical assessment by a clinical specialist.

10.4.3.1 Temporary Impairment

The definition of permanent impairment, which refers to conditions for which no change in impairment is expected within 1 year, leaves room for temporary aspects, such as disability during recovery from the accident injuries is assessed and monitored, in third-party liability. These latter, in a dynamic evolution of the pathophysiological process, identify the temporary impairment.

10.4.3.2 Permanent Impairment

Other than temporary impairment, whenever a condition is expected not to improve within 1 year, it is defined as permanent and subsequently evaluated in this light. Here we need to introduce a distinction between first-party insurances and third-party liability.

In first-party insurances the insurance policies are the first and most important source for information regarding impairment. Most policies contain an impairment scheme. In case of injuries or physical areas not explicitly mentioned in the insurance policies, depending on the other rules of the policies, the AMA Guides to the Evaluation of Permanent Impairment (short: AMA guide) can be used (AMA Guides to Evaluation of Permanent Impairment. American Medical Association). The version of the AMA guides used depends on the insurance policies. Many different insurance policies exist.

In third-party liability claims, the AMA guidelines (currently at the sixth edition) are used to determine a percentage impairment. The scientific associations of the orthopaedic surgeons and neurologists, the two most used clinical specialities for independent assessments, have made supplements to the AMA guides, which are usually used on top of the AMA guides.

As mentioned, the definition of permanent impairment from AMA guides is used, which states that no change in impairment is to be expected within 10.4.6 Causal value/link

Causality is of major importance. Viaene developed a model of human damage which is often used. In that model the line of (for instance) functioning declines right after the accident and then rises again, as the victim recovers, but may never reach the extrapolated situation had the accident not occurred. The difference between the two is the loss from the accident, hence introducing the concept of differential damage with respect to a pre-existing health status (Fig. 10.1).

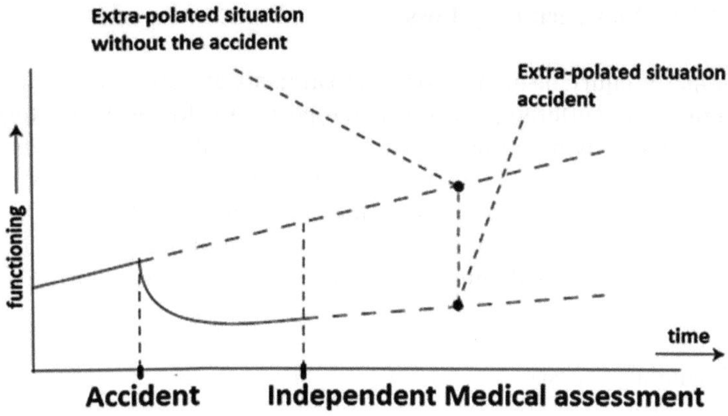

Fig. 10.1 Viaene model of human damage

In real life, the lines may be different, e.g., if one includes the effect of ageing on functioning.

As a consequence, to assess the causality of post-traumatic consequences the factors already existing before the accident, relating to impairment or disability, have to be determined first. Secondly, impairment or disability that has developed after the accident, but which was not caused by the accident, has to be determined. These two aspects have to be subtracted from the current situation to attain the true consequences of the accident, i.e. the differential damage.

The precise injury caused by the accident has to be investigated. Usually, this is clear. In some cases, detailed knowledge of the medical history is needed to determine which injury was caused by this accident, or what consequences occurring later, such as osteoarthritis, for example, are caused by injuries sustained by the accident. For special cases, some guidelines exist, for instance, in case of suspected post-traumatic discus herniation.

An injury can lead to impairment or disability. As mentioned, in case of third-party liability disability is the most important in determining the financial consequences, but not readily derivable from the clinical injury. Assessing the causality of disability can be very challenging, yet is of paramount importance.

10.4.3.3 Personal Damage Quantification: Impairments

As mentioned, the medical assessment process leads to two major results: the impairment and the disability. In first-party insurances, the impairment is determined using the insurance policies. This impairment is then used to calculate the insurance benefit related to the policies. In third-party liability the AMA Guides to the Evaluation of Permanent Impairment are used. The percentage impairment is only used as one of the relevant factors for determining the injury award.

10.4.3.4 Other, Non-pecuniary Losses

In most first-party injury insurances only impairments are covered. In third-party liability claims pain, suffering, and other non-pecuniary losses such as aesthetic damage or a temporarily or permanent inability to enjoy the pleasure of life in the broadest sense are incorporated into a special indemnity, the injury award. Heightened risk of future death or injury—so-called good and bad chances—is usually agreed upon when the total claim is settled. The amount of this payment is usually determined in accordance with other cases and/or based on earlier jurisprudence.

10.4.3.5 Pecuniary Losses

As mentioned, especially in third-party liability, the accident that caused disability is very important. Disability is related to social activities, sports, working in and around the house, and work. Clinical medical specialists are not trained to assess disability; independent medical assessments for attaining the disability are best performed by an insurance physician. In many injury cases with work disability, the victim also claims from the public work disability insurances and is examined there. This information can also be used to assess the consequences of the accident.

In third-party liability, work incapacity for the victim's actual work is used as a starting point. Although the accident victims are obliged to not make the damages bigger than they should be, and cooperate to keep the damage low, they cannot be forced to take any other job. Most accident victims who become work-incapacitated want to be helped, for instance by re-education, to get other work. Insurers propose and finance this support.

In case the victim was used to working in and around the house, disability may prevent this, which would lead to the need for domestic help. In case of lifelong disability, this damage can also be considerable. Since in the Netherlands medical costs are paid for by obligatory health-care insurance, this is usually no aspect in the personal damage claim except for those instances where insurance premiums increase. The health-care insurance company, however, will claim their damages with the liability insurer.

References

1. 'Richtlijn: Medisch Specialistische Rapportage, in bestuursen civielrechtelijk verband. Werkgroep Medisch Specialistische Rapportage (WMSR), in samenwerking met de Koninklijke Nederlandsche Maatschappij tot bevordering der Geneeskunst (KNMG) Utrecht, 31 januari 2008', Dutch only
2. Specialisten opleiding Gerechtelijke Deskundige. Universiteit Leiden Stichting Landelijk Register van Gerechtelijke Deskundigen (LRGD)
3. Vraagstelling causaal verband bij ongeval VU University, Amsterdam

Chapter 11
Methods of Ascertainment of Personal Damage in the United Kingdom

Peter Vanezis

Abstract This chapter illustrates the historical, judicial and juridical framework of personal injury assessment and compensation in the United Kingdom, describing the expert's qualification and competences and detailing the ascertainment methodology and criteria of evaluation utilised for identifying, describing and estimating any personal injury, its temporary and permanent consequences and the causal value/link between the event and the injury and between the injury and the impairment/disability.

11.1 Historical, Judicial and Juridical Overview

11.1.1 Introduction

From the legal perspective, personal injury refers to physical or psychological injury or both, suffered by an individual. It is a type of tort lawsuit alleging that the claimant's injury has been caused by the negligence of another. Damages awarded include for bodily injury and emotional distress either caused intentionally or negligently. A landmark case in personal injury (Donoghue v Stevenson) [1] has come to be known as 'The Paisley Snail Case'.

11.1.1.1 The 'Paisley Snail' Case

The case of Donoghue v Stevenson, a landmark case in Scots delict law and English tort law by the House of Lords, created the modern concept of negligence, by

P. Vanezis (✉)
Department of Clinical Pharmacology, Cameron Forensic Medical Sciences,
William Harvey Research Institute, Barts and the London, Queen Mary
University of London, Charterhouse Square, London EC1M 6BQ, UK
e-mail: p.vanezis@qmul.ac.uk

S.D. Ferrara et al. (eds.), *Personal Injury and Damage Ascertainment under Civil Law*, DOI 10.1007/978-3-319-29812-2_11

setting out general principles whereby one person would owe another person a duty of care.

Also known as the 'Paisley snail' or 'snail in the bottle' case, the facts involved Mrs Donoghue drinking a bottle of ginger beer in a café in Paisley, Renfrewshire. The beer had been purchased by Mrs Donoghue's friend. A dead snail was in the bottle. She fell ill, and she sued the ginger beer manufacturer, Mr Stevenson. The House of Lords held that the manufacturer owed a duty of care to her which was breached because it was reasonably foreseeable that failure to ensure the product's safety would lead to harm of consumers.

11.1.2 Recent Developments

11.1.2.1 Pearson Commission

In the United Kingdom, a Royal Commission on Civil Liability and Compensation for Personal Injury was established in 1973 in the wake of the thalidomide tragedy, under the chairmanship of Lord Pearson (Pearson commission) [2]. The commission reported in 1978 and made radical recommendations for tort reform; Pearson believed that the traditional role of compensation had become outdated with the rise of the welfare state since the end of World War II. He envisaged that the primary role was of a benefit system rather than providing compensation and security following an accident and litigation as being secondary. As a result, the commission recommended a no-fault insurance scheme for road traffic and industrial accidents and a scheme of strict liability for consumer protection. However, the government's response was cool and the recommendations were not followed up.

11.1.2.2 Lord Wolf's Report and the Civil Procedure Rules

In 1994, the Lord Chancellor instructed the Master of the Rolls, Lord Woolf, to report on options to consolidate the existing rules of civil procedure. On 26 July 1996, Lord Woolf published his 'Access to Justice' Report 1996 [3] in which he identified a number of principles the civil justice system should meet to ensure access to justice:

- Be *just* in the results it delivers.
- Be *fair* in the way it treats litigants.
- Offer appropriate procedures at a reasonable *cost*.
- Deal with cases with reasonable *speed*.
- Be *understandable* to those who use it.
- Be *responsive* to the needs of those who use it.
- Provide as much *certainty* as the nature of particular cases allows.
- Be *effective*: Adequately resourced and organised.

Lord Woolf listed two of the requirements of case management as:

- Fixing timetables for the parties to take particular steps in the case
- Limiting disclosure and expert evidence

The second thread of the report was to control the cost of litigation, both in time and money, by focusing on key issues and limiting the amount of work that has to be done on the case.

As a result, The Civil Procedure Act 1997 (c. 12) [4] was enacted on 27 February 1997, and it conferred the power to make civil procedure rules. It also established the Civil Justice Council, a body composed of members of the judiciary, members of the legal professions and civil servants, and charged with reviewing the civil justice system. The Civil Procedure Rules (CPR) 1998 [5] were made on 10 December 1998 and came into force on 26 April 1999. They are the rules of civil procedure used by the Court of Appeal, High Court of Justice and County Courts in civil cases in England and Wales. They apply to all cases and largely replace the Rules of the Supreme Court and the County Court Rules. The 78th edition of the Civil Procedure Rules came into force in January and April 2015.

The CPR were designed to improve access to justice by making legal proceedings cheaper, quicker and easier to understand for nonlawyers. Unlike the previous rules of civil procedure, the CPR commence with a statement of their 'overriding objective', both to aid in the application of specific provisions and to guide behaviour where no specific rule applies.

11.1.2.3 The Overriding Objective

Section 1.1

(1) These Rules are a new procedural code with the overriding objective of enabling the court to deal with cases justly and at proportionate cost.

(2) Dealing with a case justly and at proportionate cost includes, so far as is practicable:

  (a) Ensuring that the parties are on an equal footing
  (b) Saving expense
  (c) Dealing with the case in ways which are proportionate:

    (i) To the amount of money involved
    (ii) To the importance of the case
    (iii) To the complexity of the issues
    (iv) To the financial position of each party

  (d) Ensuring that it is dealt with expeditiously and fairly
  (e) Allotting to it an appropriate share of the court's resources, whilst taking into account the need to allot resources to other cases
  (f) Enforcing compliance with rules, practice directions and orders

Section 1.2
The court must seek to give effect to the overriding objective when it

(a) Exercises any power given to it by the Rules
(b) Interprets any rule

The rules are written to be intelligible not just to lawyers but also to litigants in person.

11.1.2.4 Conditional Fee Agreements

Conditional fee agreements (CFAs) are a type of 'no win no fee' agreement under which lawyers do not receive a fee from their client if they lose a case but can charge an uplift (a 'success fee') on top of their base costs if they win. When the lawyer wins a case, these costs including the success fee are 'recoverable', i.e. paid by the losing party and the client. Under the arrangements prior to recent reforms, success fees of up to 100 % of base costs and after the event (ATE) insurance premiums were recoverable from the losing party. ATE insurance could be taken out by parties in a CFA-funded case to insure against the risk of having to pay their opponent's costs and their own disbursements if they lost. This means that defendants could be liable for almost twice the costs they would normally have to pay if the case was not on a CFA.

CFAs became enforceable under section 58 of the Courts and Legal Services Act 1990 [6], which was brought into effect in 1995. The first HistoricalOrder made it possible for CFAs to be enforced in personal injury claims, insolvency proceedings and applications before the European Court of Human Rights. The initial introduction of CFAs was intended to plug the access to justice gap for those who did not qualify for legal aid but had insufficient funds to afford to pay for legal services. In 1998, the category of case in which CFAs were permitted was extended to all civil proceedings, but not to family and criminal cases.

11.1.2.5 Recent Civil Justice Reforms

Lord Justice Jackson, a Court of Appeal judge, carried out a year-long review of the civil litigations costs and published his final report, Review of Civil Litigation Costs in January 2010 [7].

Lord Justice Jackson found that the costs of civil litigation were too high and were fuelled by the way in which no win no fee CFAs operated. Under the provisions at the time, the claimant was effectively at no financial risk, the risk being borne by the claimant's lawyer and the defendant. On the other hand, a losing defendant had to pay not only the claimant's base legal costs (as is normal in litigation) but also the CFA success fee and the claimant's ATE insurance premium and insurance premium tax both of which are recoverable from the losing side and which can add substantially to costs.

The Government carried out a full consultation between November 2010 and February 2011 on implementing Lord Justice Jackson's main recommendations for the reform of funding arrangements and published its response in March 2011. The Government confirmed that the CFA reforms and other related measures would be implemented.

The Government's proposals were taken forward under Part 2 of the Legal Aid, Sentencing and Punishment of Offenders Act 2012 [8] (the LASPO Act) which received Royal assent in May 2012. The relevant provisions in Part 2 of the LASPO Act came into effect on 1 April 2013, and reforms to civil litigation funding and costs in England and Wales were implemented.

The reforms apply across civil litigation but have a particular impact in personal injury cases, where no win no fee CFAs are used significantly. The main changes are summarised below:

- No win no fee CFAs remain available in civil cases, but the additional costs involved (success fee and insurance premiums) are no longer payable by the losing side.
- No win no fee damage-based agreements (DBAs) are available in civil litigation for the first time.
- Referral fees are banned in personal injury cases.
- The introduction of new protocols extending the Road Traffic Act personal injury scheme to £25,000.
- A new fixed recoverable costs regime.
- Claimants' damages are protected: The fee that a successful claimant has to pay the lawyer—the lawyer's 'success fee' in CFAs or 'payment' in DBAs—is capped to a maximum of 25 % of the damages recovered, excluding damages for future care and loss.
- General damages for non-pecuniary loss such as pain, suffering and loss of amenity (PSLA) are increased by 10 %.
- A new regime of 'qualified one-way cost shifting' is introduced in personal injury cases which caps the amount that claimants may have to pay to defendants. Claimants who lose, but whose claims are conducted in accordance with the rules, are protected from having to pay the defendants costs.
- A new sanction on defendants to encourage earlier settlement of claims.

11.1.2.6 Notes on Damages, Claims and Victims of Crime

Damages

Damages for personal injury are categorised as special or general, and both types can be awarded in a case.

(a) *Special damages* (economic damages) are costs which can be measured and itemised and include:

Past losses: Medical expenses, cost of items purchased because of disability, loss of earnings and damage to property. Interest on past losses is at the appropriate rate from the date of injury to the date of the trial.

Future losses: Future care, medical expenses, loss of earnings, future aids, appliances, and housing needs. There is no interest on future losses.

(b) *General damages* (noneconomic damages) include less measurable costs such as loss of amenity and emotional distress. Damages for loss of consortium were abolished in English Law by the Administration of Justice Act 1982 [9]. Interest on general damages is set at 2 % from the date of service of legal proceedings.

The amount of compensation for a personal injury will primarily depend on the severity of the injury (see Judicial College Guidelines). Serious injuries (such as broken bones, severed limbs, brain damage) that cause intense physical pain and suffering receive the highest injury settlements. Aside from compensation for injuries, the injured person may be compensated for the lifetime effect of the injuries suffered, over and above the award for the injury itself. This is called loss of amenity and is part of the claim for PSLA.

Types of Claims

The most common types of personal injury claims are road traffic accidents, accidents at work, accidents caused by tripping, assault claims, accidents in the home, product defect accidents and holiday accidents. Personal injury also involves medical and dental accidents resulting in a large number of negligence claims every year and conditions that are often classified as occupational disease cases, including exposure to asbestos causing asbestosis and peritoneal mesothelioma, chest diseases (such as chronic obstructive pulmonary disease, pneumoconiosis, silicosis), hand-arm vibration syndrome caused by handheld vibrating machinery, occupational deafness, occupational stress, contact dermatitis and repetitive strain injury cases.

Depending upon the intent or negligence of a responsible party, the injured party may be entitled to monetary compensation from that party through a settlement or a judgement.

Legal aid from the government was largely abolished in England in the late 1990s and replaced with arrangements whereby the client would be charged no fee if his/her case was unsuccessful.

Time Limitation on Claims

In England and Wales, under the limitation rules, where an individual is bringing a claim for compensation, court proceedings must be commenced within 3 years of the date of the accident, failing which the claimant will lose the right to bring his or her claim. However, injured parties who were under the age of 18 at the time of their accidents have until the day prior to their 21st birthdays to commence proceedings. A court has the discretion to extend or waive the limitation period if it is considered equitable to do so. Another exception is if the accident caused an injury, as an example industrial deafness, then the 3-year period will start from when injured party knew or ought to have known that he or she had that injury and a claim (Limitation Act 1980, s.2) [10].

Victims of Crime

The Criminal Injuries Compensation Authority was set up as a result of the enactment of the Criminal Injuries Compensation Act 1995 [11] to provide a scheme for dealing with compensation claims from people who had been physically or mentally injured because they were the blameless victim of a violent crime in England, Scotland or Wales. An application for compensation must be made within 2 years of the crime being committed unless there are mitigating circumstances, and in some cases the limitation period is then waived.

They currently handle up to 40,000 applications for compensation each year, paying out up to £200 million to victims of violent crime. Any compensation claim is entirely dependent on the offender being convicted. Further, if the applicant has a previous criminal record then this is also taken into consideration and could potentially affect the application made.

Claims can also be made through the civil courts for injury, property damage or theft as a result of a crime, even if the perpetrator is acquitted of all criminal charges.

11.2 Identification and Description of Medicolegal Expert's Qualifications

A medical expert who assesses personal injury damages is an experienced doctor or other relevant healthcare professional who has an extensive knowledge within their particular area.

Medical and other healthcare experts are used broadly from all branches of medicine in relation to their own area of specialisation. There is no specific compulsory requirement to undergo medicolegal training to carry out personal injury work, and indeed the vast majority have no specific training in legal medicine.

There are, however, many expert witness training programmes in the United Kingdom which are aimed at doctors who wish to specialise in, or are already participating in, personal injury work. These courses play an important part in the familiarisation of doctors with the requirements for medicolegal work. Many of the medical experts who carry out personal injury work are found in voluntary expert witness registers and/or are well known to lawyers. Those practitioners who are trained in forensic medicine or forensic pathology as their main career path in the

United Kingdom from time to time may deal with personal injury cases, although most of their work involves criminal litigation.

The qualification and knowledge of the expert doctor must be established in court before evidence is accepted either in documentary or oral form. A consultant physician who is in good standing with the General Medical Council and on their specialist register usually will only require in the UK courts submission of his/her CV to demonstrate experience and knowledge in a particular area of specialisation. Although it may be sufficient merely to state academic and professional qualifications, the details of experts' qualifications to be given in reports should be commensurate with the nature and complexity of the case. However, where highly specialised expertise is called for, experts should include the detail of particular training and/or experience that qualifies them to provide that highly specialised evidence.

The British Medical Association produced expert witness guidance for doctors in the United Kingdom in 2007, and the relevant important issues are summarised below:

- *Expert witnesses, however skilled or eminent, cannot usurp the functions of the jury or Judge sitting as a jury, any more than a technical assessor can substitute his advice for the judgment of the court.*
- *Their duty is to furnish the Judge or jury with the necessary criteria for testing the accuracy of their conclusions, so as to enable the Judge or jury to form their own independent judgment by the application of these criteria to the facts proved in evidence.*
- *The opinion evidence, if intelligible, convincing and tested, becomes a factor (and often an important factor) for consideration along with the whole other evidence in the case, but the decision is for the Judge or jury.*
- *The expert witness provides an opinion on the facts of the case, either as provided in written form, or based on the expert doctor's own examination of the patient. This is at the request of one or other party to a claim.*
- *The report, however, is for the benefit of the court, and is entirely independent of that party. Whilst a party can make a request for an opinion on certain specified questions, and it is legitimate to comment upon the answers given and to ask for matters to be considered further, or reconsidered, the opinion must both be and be seen to be independent, objective and unbiased. It is liable to be tested in cross examination.*
- *The independence of thought of an expert witness must be jealously guarded.*
- *The expert doctor's role is to assist the court by providing independent opinion, and his or her opinion may be used to diminish the other side's case. Often, but not always, there is a competing opinion prepared on behalf of the opponents of those who instructed that doctor.*

In some cases, the witness will provide evidence solely upon the basis of documentation. An expert is entitled to ascertain facts by hearsay. For example, in many cases of alleged professional negligence by a doctor, an opinion is provided solely upon the basis of case notes, case histories and other documentation. On other occasions, particularly when considering issues of causation, the extent of an injury that has been caused and a prognosis for the future, the documentation requires to be supplemented by an examination of the claimant by the expert witness and a further medical report.

It is always important for the medical professional to ensure when giving an opinion that they are properly qualified and experienced to do so. If an opinion is sought on a subject in respect of which the expert does not consider that he or she has adequate experience or expertise, it may be appropriate to decline the instruction. It is vital therefore that the correct person is instructed to provide expert evidence in a case. To this end, many legal firms have their own in-house directory of experts that they use. If an in-house directory is not available or inappropriate, then other sources can be used. In the United Kingdom, these include a number of reputable organisations which can provide recognised experts. These include:

- The Association of Personal Injury Lawyers. This organisation provides information to its members of appropriate experts (www.apil.org.uk/).
- Action Against Medical Accidents (AvMA: www.avma.org.uk/).
- The UK Register of Expert Witnesses (www.jspubs.com).
- The Society of Expert Witnesses (www.sew.org.uk/).
- Expert Witness Institute (www.ewi.org.uk/).
- The New Law Journal and Solicitors Journal regularly issue expert witness supplements.
- Professional Institutes which carry a directory of expert witnesses.
- The Medico-Legal Society publishes reports which may reveal names of experts.

11.3 Ascertainment Methodology

11.3.1 Letter of Instruction from the Claimant's Lawyer

If we take the example of injuries sustained in a road traffic accident, in the first instance, the client's lawyers will send a letter of instruction to the medical expert. The doctor is requested to examine their client with a view to providing a full and detailed report dealing with any relevant pre-accident medical history, the injuries sustained, treatment received and present condition, dealing in particular with the capacity for work and giving a prognosis. Prior to instructions being confirmed, the expert is also requested to give an estimate as to the likely time scale for the provision of the report and also an indication as to the fee.

The medical expert in assessment of their client's injuries is required to establish the extent and duration of any continuing disability. With regard to prognosis, the expert is required to specifically comment on any areas of continuing complaint or disability or impact on daily living. If there is such continuing disability, the expert is required to comment upon the level of suffering or inconvenience caused and, if able to do so, give their view as to when or if the complaint or disability is likely to resolve and if necessary comment on impact of injury on life expectancy.

The claimant's lawyers will also obtain notes and records from the claimant's GP and hospitals attended, and they will be forwarded to the medical expert at the time of formal instruction by way of letter of instruction. Once the expert has been instructed and has received the medical records, he/she should be cognisant of the need for strict confidentiality when having access to this data and would be required to give such an assurance to those holding the records and also obtain express permission to view them from the claimant through their lawyers.

It is also incumbent upon the claimant to ensure that the legal team and medical expert are provided with any documentation in relation to the incident which they may have and might include:

- Photographs of the accident location
- Photographs of his/her injuries
- All written reports from where the accident took place or if the police attended, police report
- Documentation from any witnesses

These types of documents will also be required later in the claim if liability is an issue (i.e. if the other party is denying responsibility for the accident). Under such circumstances it will be necessary to provide the other party's insurance company with further documentation and evidence.

Depending on the type of accident, this can include:

- Road traffic accident—Sketch plan of position of vehicles and photographs of road markings
- Trip or slip—Photographs of a raised paving slab or other tripping hazard that caused the claimant to fall
- Accident in the workplace—Specifications of damaged machinery which caused the accident in the workplace
- Industrial disease—Medical evidence to show the cause of the industrial disease links with the company responsible

11.3.2 Documentary Assessment and Medical Examination

The type of expert that an injured person needs to be examined by is usually the same type of doctor who has been providing the care. So if an injured client has been treated by a consultant hand surgeon, then a report from an independent consultant hand surgeon is required. In injuries involving fractures, the client is usually examined by a consultant orthopaedic surgeon.

The medical examination and report can often prove very useful to an injured person because the expert will be dedicating some time to the client's injuries and may often spot issues which the client's own doctors have not seen.

In high value claims, the medical experts may wish to see the client's occupational health and personnel records. Such records may indicate whether a client has had relevant health problems before the accident.

Although, in most accident and injury cases only one medical report is necessary, in more complex personal injury claims or cases involving serious injury, further medical reports may be necessary from medical experts in other fields of medicine or to deal with related care issues. This ensures that the most complete and accurate picture is available before attempting to value the injury claim. It also minimises the risk of under-settling the claim, which is a common problem where inexperienced or unqualified people attempt to deal with personal injury law.

11.3.3 Historical Assessment, Including General and Medical Information

The expert in conjunction with the medical records will ascertain the history from the client to include:

- *Past medical history.* It is important that the medical expert identifies from the records the subject's state of health and fitness as well as any past or more recent conditions that might have a bearing on the injury that is being claimed for:
    - Enquiry should be made of significant illness or conditions, both as a result of natural disease and from unnatural conditions such as trauma which occurred a number of years ago.
    - More recent illnesses: These would include conditions which may be still ongoing or have resolved.
    - Current illnesses: Conditions from which the subject is currently suffering. Illnesses may be acute or chronic and the treatment given, including drug medication and possible side effects.
- *Family history.* A detailed family history should be obtained including marital status, number of siblings, children of other close relatives and particularly in relation to any medical conditions within the family.
- *Recreational activities.* Description of the particular/specific daily recreational activities and an assessment of the intensity and physical impact of these.
- *Social relationships.* Social interaction with friends and frequency of interaction.
- *Work-related activities.* Type of work undertaken and specification of skills required to carry out tasks in relation to the subject's general and specific aptitudes.

11.3.4 Clinical Examination

The extent and type of clinical examination will be governed to a great extent by the type of injury for which the claim is being made.

This examination will include a thorough assessment of the specific injured area or areas to assess the degree of damage and extent of temporary or permanent impairment, both physical and psychological.

In many cases, in order to establish the general condition of the subject, it is important to carry out a full general examination of all the systems, including a detailed psychiatric/psychological assessment where appropriate.

11.3.5 Further Investigations

There may be a requirement for further clinical assessment and/or investigations involving the use of various instrumentation both for imaging and recording purposes which could include radiological examination and specific tests using specialised instruments and devices.

With regard to neuropsychological assessment, there are a number of tests which can be helpful, particularly in an acquired brain trauma such as stroke or head injury, to provide a measure of the cognitive impairment and to consider an individual's strengths and weakness as a result of such trauma, as well as various psychiatric sequelae arising from personal injury including post-traumatic stress disorder (PTSD), anxiety and depression and also to assess whether the subject is exaggerating symptoms or malingering.

Tests which may be employed include:

- Beck Depression Inventory and the Hamilton Rating Scale for Depression are both used for assessing the severity of depression.
- State-Trait Anxiety Inventory is used to assess trait anxiety.
- PTSD Symptom Scale measures the frequency of PTSD symptoms. The PSS is composed of three subscales: re-experiencing, avoidance and arousal.
- Connor-Davidson Resilience Scale assesses resilience, as a measure of stress-coping ability.
- Minnesota Multiphasic Personality Inventory-2 (MMPI-2) is used as a standardised psychometric test of adult personality and psychopathology and may assist in checking for malingering.
- Wechsler Adult Intelligence Scale-IV (WAIS-IV) is a widely used measure of intellectual/cognitive ability.

11.4 Rules for the Use of Experts and Their Conduct

11.4.1 The Civil Procedure Rules and Practice Direction Part 35

The instruction, use and conduct required of experts for carrying out assessment of cases and providing a medicolegal report are subject to the Civil Procedure Rules.

April 1999 saw the introduction of Civil Procedural Rules (CPR 35) which embodied the so-called Woolf Reforms. The Practice Direction for Experts and Assessors (PD35) outlines the instructions and the use of experts by the parties and the powers of the court to order their use.

The Practice Direction Supplement of CPR, Part 35 [12] (updated in 2014), gives guidance on the general requirements of expert evidence, the form and content of an expert's report, the information that should be provided and details relating to instructions, the questions to experts, the single joint expert, the orders and the function of an assessor.

11.4.2 Form and Content of an Expert's Report

- *An expert's report should be addressed to the court and not to the party from whom the expert has received instructions.*
- *An expert's report must:*
    - *give details of the expert's qualifications;*
    - *give details of any literature or other material which has been relied on in making the report;*
    - *contain a statement setting out the substance of all facts and instructions which are material to the opinions expressed in the report or upon which those opinions are based;*
    - *make clear which of the facts stated in the report are within the expert's own knowledge;*
    - *say who carried out any examination, measurement, test or experiment which the expert has used for the report, give the qualifications of that person, and say whether or not the test or experiment has been carried out under the expert's supervision;*
    - *in the event that the expert wished further investigation to be undertaken but for whatever reason could not be attended to, it is normally appropriate to include reference to this;*
    - *where there is a range of opinion on the matters dealt with in the report—summarise the range of opinions; and give reasons for the expert's own opinion;*
    - *contain a summary of the conclusions reached;*

- *if the expert is not able to give an opinion without qualification, state the qualification;*
- *contain a statement that confirms the expert understands their duty to the court, and has complied with that duty; and is aware of the requirements of Part 35, practice direction and the Guidance for the Instruction of Experts in Civil Claims 2014.*

– *An expert's report must be verified by a statement of truth in the following form.*

I confirm that I have made clear which facts and matters referred to in this report are within my own knowledge and which are not. Those that are within my own knowledge I confirm to be true. The opinions I have expressed represent my true and complete professional opinions on the matters to which they refer.

Model forms of experts' reports are available from bodies such as The Academy of Experts and The Expert Witness Institute, and a template for medical reports has been created by the Ministry of Justice

11.4.3 Experts and the Pre-action Protocol

Lord Woolf in his final Access to Justice Report of July 1996 recommended the development of pre-action protocols: Their purpose was to build on and increase the benefits of an early but well-informed settlement, which genuinely satisfies both parties to the dispute. Their aims are:

- More pre-action contact between the parties
- Better and earlier exchange of information
- Better pre-action investigation by both sides
- To put the parties in a position where they may be able to settle a case fairly and early without litigation
- To enable proceedings to run to the court's timetable and efficiently, if litigation does become necessary
- To promote the provision of medical or rehabilitation treatment (not just in high value cases) to address the needs of the claimant

The protocol encourages joint selection of, and access to, experts. The report produced is not a joint report for the purposes of CPR Part 35. Most frequently, this will apply to the medical expert but on occasions also to liability experts, e.g. engineers. The protocol promotes the practice of the claimant obtaining a medical report, disclosing it to the defendant who then asks questions and/or agrees with it and does not obtain his own report. The protocol provides for nomination of the expert by the claimant in personal injury claims because of the early stage of the proceedings and the particular nature of such claims. If proceedings have to be issued, a medical report must be attached to these proceedings. However, if necessary after proceedings have commenced and with the permission of the court, the parties may obtain further expert reports. It would be for the court to decide whether the costs of more than one expert's report should be recoverable.

It is common for the instructing solicitor to ask the expert to prepare a draft of the report so that they can check that the report complies with all of the above requirements and is accurate. Amendments can be made to an expert report in relation to factual accuracy and procedural compliance. However, an expert should not be asked to amend a report in a way that changes or clouds their opinion. On this basis, it is advisable to keep records of all drafts of the expert report along with a note of why any changes were made.

Expert reports are often exchanged simultaneously at the court's request during the case management conference. However, in certain circumstances sequential exchange may be more appropriate. Most importantly, the expert's report must be served by the deadline given by the court.

Occasionally, it may be necessary to make changes to a report or produce a supplementary report. This often happens when new evidence comes to light after the expert report was served, where the expert missed an important point in their original report or if the opposition's expert raises questions. Where a supplemental report is required for new evidence or missed points, the expert is restricted to dealing with those points and as a result can only amend their report rather the rewrite it entirely. The amended report should set out the reasons for the changes and the amendments should be clearly marked. On the other hand, if a supplemental report is required for any other reason, such as to deal with points raised by the opposition's expert, the expert whose report is being questioned should include a short statement confirming the issues that have been agreed by the experts and then deal with the disputed points raised in turn in a supplementary report.

11.4.4 Discussions Between Experts

The court has the power to direct discussions between experts for the purposes set out in the Rules (CPR 35.12). Parties may also agree that discussions take place between their experts at any stage. Discussions are not mandatory unless ordered by the court. The purpose of discussions between experts should be, wherever possible, identified, and discuss the expert issues in the proceedings and attempt to reach agreed opinions on those issues. If that is not possible, then try to see if they can narrow the issues, identifying where they agree and disagree, summarise their reasons for disagreement on any issue and identify what action, if any, may be taken to resolve any of the outstanding issues between the parties. They are not to seek to settle the proceedings.

Where single joint experts have been instructed but parties have, with the permission of the court, instructed their own additional Part 35 experts, there may, if the court so orders or the parties agree, be discussions between the single joint experts and the additional Part 35 experts. Such discussions should be confined to those matters within the remit of the additional Part 35 experts or as ordered by the court.

Where there is sequential exchange of expert reports, with the defendant's expert's report prepared in accordance with the guidance, the joint statement should focus upon the areas of disagreement, save for the need for the claimant's expert to consider and respond to material, information and commentary included within the defendant's expert's report.

At the conclusion of any discussion between experts, a joint statement should be prepared setting out:

- *issues that have been agreed and the basis of that agreement;*
- *issues that have not been agreed and the basis of the disagreement;*
- *any further issues that have arisen that were not included in the original agenda for discussion;*
- *a record of further action, if any, to be taken or recommended, including if appropriate a further discussion between experts.*

Agreements between experts during discussions do not bind the parties unless the parties expressly agree to be bound (CPR 35.12(5)). However, parties should give careful consideration before refusing to be bound by such an agreement and be able to explain their refusal should it become relevant to the issue of costs.

Since April 2013 the court has had the power to order at any stage that experts of like disciplines give their evidence at trial concurrently, not sequentially with their party's evidence as has been the norm hitherto: The experts will then be questioned together, firstly by the judge based upon disagreements in the joint statement and then by the parties' advocates. Concurrent evidence can save time and costs and assist the judge in assessing the difference of views between experts. Experts need to be told in advance of the trial if the court has made an order for concurrent evidence.

11.4.5 Compliance

The CPR enable the court to take into account the extent of the parties' compliance with this practice direction or a relevant pre-action protocol when giving directions for the management of claims and when making orders about who should pay costs. The court will expect the parties to have complied with this practice direction or any relevant pre-action protocol. The court may ask the parties to explain what steps were taken to comply prior to the start of the claim. Where there has been a failure of compliance by a party, the court may ask that party to provide an explanation.

11.4.5.1 Assessment of Compliance

When considering compliance the court will:

- 'be concerned about whether the parties have complied in substance with the relevant principles and requirements and is not likely to be concerned with minor or technical shortcomings;
- consider the proportionality of the steps taken compared to the size and importance of the matter;
- take account of the urgency of the matter. Where a matter is urgent (for example, an application for an injunction) the court will expect the parties to comply only to the extent that it is reasonable to do so'.

11.4.5.2 Examples of Non-compliance

The court may decide that there has been a failure of compliance by a party because, for example, that party has:

- 'not provided sufficient information to enable the other party to understand the issues;
- not acted within a time limit set out in a relevant pre-action protocol, or, where no specific time limit applies, within a reasonable period;
- unreasonably refused to consider alternative dispute resolution (ADR); or
- without good reason, not disclosed documents requested to be disclosed'.

11.4.5.3 Sanctions for Non-compliance

The court will look at the overall effect of non-compliance on the other party when deciding whether to impose sanctions. If, in the opinion of the court, there has been non-compliance, the sanctions which the court may impose include:

- Staying (suspending) the proceedings until steps which ought to have been taken have been taken
- An order that the party at fault pays the costs, or part of the costs, of the other party or parties
- An order that the party at fault pays those costs on an indemnity basis
- If the party at fault is the claimant in whose favour an order for the payment of a sum of money is subsequently made, an order that the claimant is deprived of interest on all or part of that sum, and/or that interest is awarded at a lower rate than would otherwise have been awarded
- If the party at fault is a defendant, and an order for the payment of a sum of money is subsequently made in favour of the claimant, an order that the defendant pay interest on all or part of that sum at a higher rate, not exceeding 10 % above base rate, than would otherwise have been awarded

11.5 Evaluation Criteria

11.5.1 Terminology Relating to Injury and Its Possible Outcomes

- *Injury* is physical or psychological trauma which may lead to impairment and/or disability.
- *Disability* is the loss or limitation of opportunities to take part in society on an equal level with others due to social and environmental barriers. A disabled person is a person with an impairment who experiences disability.
- *Impairment* results from an injury, illness or congenital condition that causes or is likely to cause a loss or difference of physiological or psychological function.
- *Loss amenity* is the negative impact which an injury has had on a claimant's enjoyment of life.

11.5.2 Physical and Psychological Condition Prior to the Event/Injury

It stands to reason that any assessment for the effect of a particular event causing personal injury requires a thorough assessment of the person's life before the event. This will include the state of health both physical and psychological and whether the subject had any disability or impairment. Medical, social and work history are all important. Much of this information will be available from records of the subject's general practitioner, hospital records, employers and other relevant agencies. It will also be particularly important, where there had been significant previous injury, e.g. the type of injury in a vehicular collision, what treatment and rehabilitation was required and how long off work. The solicitor will apply for a copy of the medical records and send a copy to the medical expert who will receive instructions to examine the subject and prepare a report detailing the injuries.

As stated above the claimant's medical records will need to identify any entries which are relevant to the injury for which compensation is being claimed. For example, if claiming compensation for a neck injury, it is likely that any previous entries in GP notes relating to other previous neck injuries will be relevant for the purpose of compiling the comprehensive medical report. It may be that a previous neck injury has left the claimant more vulnerable to subsequent injuries and, whilst this may not affect the amount of compensation received, it would be classed as a material factor as far as the medical evidence is concerned and so would need to be referred to in the expert's report.

11.5.3 Detailed Reconstruction of the Event/Injury

Detailed reconstruction of the event/injury is comprehensive of the following:

- *Circumstances and mechanism of the trauma/injury.* The circumstances in which the injury occurred need to be documented in detail and to reconstruct wherever possible the events and other conditions leading up to the incident causing injury. One of the most common situations involving claims involves injuries received in road traffic incidents. The investigation of the circumstances in such cases, and indeed all road traffic incidents, is carried out by police officers trained in accident reconstruction work and where appropriate, using also civilian accident investigators. The reports they produce are made available to experts acting on behalf of a claimant or defendant. Indeed, the expert may well carry out their own reconstruction of the incident. This will also be the situation for workplace incidents where relevant equipment will need to be examined to assess whether there are any faults which may be relevant to the incident causing injury. In such situations it would be inspectors who are specialist in a particular area who will reconstruct events leading to injury.
- *Description of type and severity of the injuries sustained during the event/trauma.* Description of the type and severity of injuries will clearly depend on the type of injury, its location and body system. However, assessing the recovery of an extremely heterogeneous group of injured persons is challenging to say the least. No two injuries are exactly alike, and when patients have multiple injuries, the difficulties of comparing patients and thus assessing functional recovery are magnified. There are many scales and scoring systems that have been developed to measure the severity of an injury or indeed a combination of injuries such as in road traffic collisions including the Abbreviated Injury Scale which is combined with an Injury Severity Score to assess the full extent of injury. There have been a number of improvements on these scales. Widely used scales for assessing health outcomes include the SF-36v2, EQ-5D developed by the EuroQol Group to provide a generic measure of health and economic appraisal and the CES-D scale for assessing depression.
- *Symptoms in the immediate period after the event/injury.* Evaluating a claimant's symptoms immediately after an event/injury may be extremely difficult or impossible to ascertain from the claimant. It is useful to question any witnesses that were present at the incident as to what symptoms the claimant may have complained of at that time. In a road traffic incident particularly with any concussion, it may be impossible to remember the initial symptoms experienced. In particular, symptoms referable to an incident could be quite varied and overlapping such as nausea, pain, fear, drowsiness and so on. They must be distinguished from clinical signs which are phenomena such as swelling, bruising, heat, impaired or loss of movement generally or of one or more limbs, agitation, tremor and other signs which can be assessed objectively by thorough examination with the use of equipment where necessary the of the various bodily systems by the medical attendant.

- *Symptoms in the interval between the event/injury and the ascertainment.* It is vital to establish a causal link between the effect of an incident for which compensation has been sought and the presenting signs and symptoms as well as other effects as discussed elsewhere, at the time at which the claim is made. The interval between the incident and the start of the action may be widely variable.
- *Treatment/s and/or medication/s administered in the interval between the event/injury and the ascertainment.* The medical treatment received by the patient will be documented from the medical notes and directly from the patient, in terms of its adequacy and appropriateness for the type of injury/injuries sustained.
- *Outcomes of treatments already performed.* The outcomes to the patient's injuries (both physical and psychological) will be evaluated from the medical notes and by questioning and examination of the patient using direct clinical examination for example to assess range of movement in limbs, as well as the use of instruments to investigate for imaging and measurement of different body systems.

Such an assessment will have to take into consideration whether the injury has caused temporary or permanent impairment, the extent of disability, loss of amenity and so on. Careful assessment is made on the effect of other life events within the post incident interval and of any other factors which may have had an effect on the initial incident or not.

11.5.4 Causation, Causal link and the 'But For' Test

The injured person has to not only prove that a third party was responsible for their injury but also that it was caused by that particular event. In practice, in most cases, establishing a causal link can be fairly straightforward. In catastrophic injury claims, for instance, the severity of the injuries may leave little room for doubt. In other not-so-serious cases, medical records will often help confirm 'causation'. However, difficulties arise when the onset of signs or symptoms are not immediate or do not appear serious at the first medical examination. Furthermore, one of the important issues in proving a causal link is that the chain of causation may have been broken as a result of other pre-existing or degenerative conditions.

Problems can also arise in cases where injured people seek treatment abroad. Medical records may not be retained by hospitals or doctors in the same way as in the United Kingdom, and this can have a real impact on the value of the claim.

To demonstrate **causation**, the claimant must establish that the loss they have suffered was **caused** by the defendant. In most cases, a simple application of the 'but for' test will resolve the question. That is, 'but for' the defendant's actions, would the claimant have suffered the loss? If yes, the defendant is not liable. If no, the defendant is liable. The 'but for' test for tortuous liability was introduced in Barnett v Chelsea & Kensington Hospital [1969] 1 QB 428 [13]:

Mr Barnett went to hospital complaining of severe stomach pains and vomiting. He was seen by a nurse who telephoned the doctor on duty. The doctor told her to send him home and contact his GP in the morning. Mr Barnett died five hours later from arsenic poisoning. Had the doctor examined Mr Barnett at the time there would have been nothing the doctor could have done to save him. Held: The hospital was not liable, as the doctor's failure to examine the patient did not cause his death i.e. would the result (death, in this case) have occurred ***"but for"*** *the act or omission of the defendant? If yes, the defendant is not liable.*

In other words, if the claimant would have died in any event, even if seen by a doctor, the fact that the doctor may have acted negligently by failing to provide treatment meant that causation could not be established.

Causation may be problematic where there exists more than one possible cause and various formulations have evolved to ease the burden of proving **causation** in such situations.

In relation to medical negligence, for example, we also need to consider and distinguish in English Law the concept of **factual causation** and **legal causation.**

The most important element in clinical negligence cases is **factual causation** which is determined by the standard 'but for' test, that is, 'but for' the defendant's negligence, would the claimant's loss have occurred. If the answer is yes, there is no factual causation (see Barnett v Chelsea and Kensington Hospital above).

Legal causation is the means of approaching whether the defendant should be held liable, even where the 'but for' test may be met. The rules (remoteness, novus actus interveniens, etc.) apply in general, as they apply in other tort claims (though are often not so relevant). As to novus actus interveniens, for subsequent (negligent) medical treatment to break the chain of causation, it would have to be grossly negligent. However, where the act is by the claimant him or herself, it may be more readily held to be an intervening act (Sabri-Tabrizi v Lothian Health Board) [14].

Background: Pregnant after failed sterilization. The negligence resulted in the pursuer still being fertile, as if the operation had not taken place. The pursuer knew this the second time, and of the risks inherent in having sexual intercourse with her husband. The court held that it was unreasonable for the pursuer to have exposed herself to the risk. The decision to have sexual intercourse in the knowledge that she was not sterile was a novus actus interveniens, thereby breaking the chain of causation. The defenders could, thus, not be held liable.

Further, the acceptance of risk necessary for the application of the maxim volenti non fit injuria must occur either before or at the same time as the negligent act or omission that was clearly not so in the instant case.

11.5.5 Personal Damage Quantification

The English Barema used for the quantification of permanent impairment includes:

1. Head
   Severe disfigurement 100 %
2. Vertebral column
3. Upper limbs
   Amputation at the level of the shoulder joint 90 %. Amputation under the shoulder with a stump less than 20.5 cm in length 80 %. Loss of both hands or amputation located higher up the arm 100 %. Loss of a foot and a hand 100 %. Loss of a hand or a thumb and four fingers of one hand 60 %. Loss of the thumb and its metacarpal 40 %.
4. Pelvis
5. Lower limbs
   Amputation at the level of the hip 90 %. Amputation at the level of the knee or under the knee with a stump less than 9 cm in length 60 %. Amputation of a foot with a functional stump 30 %. Loss of a foot and a hand 100 %.
6. Heart
7. Vessels
8. Respiratory system
9. Digestive system and adnexa
10. Diseases of the blood and blood-forming organs
11. Disorders of the genito-urinary system
12. Neuropsychiatric disorders
13. Diabetes
14. Eye disorders
    Loss of sight to the point where the person is incapable of carrying out any work in which vision is vital 100 %. Loss of one eye without complications, the other being normal 40 %.
15. Auditory system
    Complete deafness 100 %.

11.5.5.1 Assessment of General Damages

In the United Kingdom, the Judicial Studies Board (England) and the Judicial Studies Board for Northern Ireland publish guidelines for the assessment of general damages in personal injury cases. These guidelines identify the scale of general damages being awarded for injuries, divided into types of injury and severity of injury.

11.5.5.2 Other Non-pecuniary Losses: Criteria for Award Evaluation

Pain, Suffering and Loss of Amenity

The injuries sustained not only determine the level of PSLA award but also impact the drafting of the Schedule of Special Damages and Future Losses and Expenses. The award is designed to cover:

- Physical pain caused by the injury.
- Suffering is the rather nebulous anxiety, embarrassment and fear arising from the incident.

The level of award for pain and suffering will take into account the intensity and duration. This should be highlighted in the documentation of inpatient care and the nature of any surgical treatment.

It is rare for a judge to make an award by distinguishing pain and suffering, even when the claimant has sustained a plethora of injuries. Furthermore, the courts do not tend to deal with loss of amenity any differently, even though it is that element which impacts most under the level of damages in this area. Loss of amenity will, to a limited extent (and depending on the discipline of the medical expert), be covered by the consultant in their report. However, to maximise the level of the award, it is essential that interference with amenity is covered elsewhere, either in a schedule of special damages or preferably in the claimant's statement and that of his witnesses. The statement must cover the disability caused by the injury. The statement should make reference to hobbies, pastimes and loss of a skill. Life before the incident should be contrasted with the current position.

The loss of amenity covers the claimant's loss of enjoyment of life or impairment of his senses. There is an important subjective element, in that loss of sex life or enjoyment of eating will matter more to some claimants than others. The award will be influenced by the duration of the loss of amenity and expectation of life in the more serious cases.

An award for pain and suffering depends upon the claimant's personal awareness of pain and his/her capacity for suffering. Consequently, there can be no award for pain and suffering if the claimant is immediately thrown into a state of unconsciousness. However, even in those cases, perhaps when the claimant is in a permanent vegetative state, an award can still be made for the loss of amenity. This arises even when the claimant has no appreciation of the pain and suffering. An award can be made for loss of amenity where the claimant dies after the accident.

The award can be substantial. However, if the claimant dies shortly after the incident, the court may not make any award for pain and suffering as highlighted in Hicks v Chief Constable of the South Yorkshire police [1992] PIQR [15]. Sarah and Victoria Hicks were sisters aged 19 and 15 when they were crushed to death in the Hillsborough football stadium disaster. Their parents brought a claim against the defendants seeking damages in respect of the fear and terror that the sisters would have suffered prior to death over a period of 30 min. Apprehension and fear are themselves not compensable, nor in the judge's view are discomfort or shortness of breath by themselves. The trial judge held that the claimants had failed to prove that either girl suffered before death any injury for which damages failed to be awarded. This decision was affirmed by the Court of Appeal. The parents appealed to the House of Lords. Hicks v Chief Constable of South Yorkshire [1992] All ER 65 House of Lords [16]. Lord Bridges stated:

Anyone who regularly travels on the London Underground frequently suffers discomfort and shortage of breath from the press of bodies in overcrowded trains. There remains in my judgement for consideration only, such pain as occurred in the few seconds between the onset of asphyxia and unconsciousness and the knowledge and fear of impending death which may have occurred in those few seconds. In my view, however, when unconsciousness and death occur in such a short period after the injury, no damages are recoverable.

The fear of impending death itself does not give rise to a call for damages according to Lord Bridges. Indeed from other case rulings, it is evident that there can be no damages for shock, being 'shaken up' and other similar unpleasant emotions.

Where the claimant suffers multiple injuries, the approach to valuation is to assess an appropriate award for the individual injuries and then discount that figure to reflect the overall PSLA. There is no formula; it is impressionistic.

When it comes to negotiating awards for PSLA, practitioners invariably turn to the Judicial College for the assessment of general damages in personal injury cases. They are, however, guidelines and not legally binding as pointed out in the case of Arafa v Potter [1994] PIQR Q73 [17] by Staughton LJ:

They (JSC Guidelines) are not themselves law: they form a slim and handy volume which anyone can slip into their briefcase on the way to the County Court or when travelling on Circuit. But the law is to be found elsewhere in rather greater bulk. In this court we ought to look at the sources rather than the summary produced by the Judicial Studies Board.

However, practitioners will know that judges are now much more inclined to turn to the JSC than perhaps 15 years ago and thus Reed v Sunderland Health Authority (1998) [18] may now be a more balanced judicial view:

As such they (Guidelines) are to be regarded with the respect which we would accord to the writings of any specialist legal author.

Following the decision Heil v Rankin [2001] PIQR Q3 [19], the JSC Guidelines will be the first port of call for practitioners and judges alike.

Relationship Breakdown

An item of damages, relationship breakdown or loss of marriage can form an additional head of claim, for general and special damages. Although claims for relationship breakdown are normally found in existing marriages, there can be no reason why claims cannot also be founded on any relationship where there is good evidence of long-standing association.

Single Claimant

For loss of marriage or perhaps any relationship prospect, damages can be awarded to the single claimant when they can prove that the injury will probably prevent or substantially reduce their prospects in the future. If successful, a separate general damages award can be made or wrapped up in the award of PSLA.

The second element is damages for economic loss which the claimant may be deprived of due to lack of marriage prospects. Historically, awards have been made in favour of women, but again there can be no logic behind depriving men of a similar award.

The majority of women now work and are financially independent, but there will be some women, particularly from specific religious groups, that successfully argue they would not have worked at all and would have been supported by their husband throughout their marriage. In those cases, the claimant will seek an award for the economic loss throughout the marriage.

Women Who Work

At the other end of the scale are working women. If the claimant is a high-earning female who would have worked up to the date of marriage and beyond, before taking time out to care for her child(ren), but returning to work soon after the birth, or each birth, then the claim for economic loss will be at the lower end of the scale. This is even more likely to be the case where the partner is on a low income, or the woman is the sole breadwinner.

Engaged Claimant

The prospects of an award will be enhanced if there is evidence of either a long-standing and/or stable relationship. Therefore, if the claimant was engaged, their prospects will be increased.

Further, a claimant who never intended to work will receive a full award for loss of economic benefit. In Aloni v National Westminster Bank (unreported, May 20 1982) [20], the claimant, aged 32 at trial, had been engaged to a wealthy man. She suffered injuries resulting in paraplegia and the engagement was broken off. The judge awarded £75,000 at 1982 values, for loss of marriage prospects, but made no award for loss of future earnings as she had planned to give up work after they married.

Married Claimant

It is not uncommon in cases of serious injury for previously happy marriage to breakdown and separation and divorce to follow.

As with unmarried claimants, married claimants can claim damages for loss of joy, comfort and companionship and the pain of divorce. As with all awards under this broad heading, it is difficult to specify sums identified in judgements, as the recognition is wrapped up in the award for PSLA, for example, in Tame v Professional Cycle Marketing [2006] EWHC 3751 [21].

Awards for Disability, Physical, Psychological and Scarring

Often accidents cause injuries that can cause permanent disability or partial disability for the claimant, if the claimant sustains a permanent brain or spinal injury as a consequence of the accident, this can have an extraordinarily life-changing impact on day-to-day life. The claimant may require around the clock nursing care, be unable to work, support their family, unable to take part in sporting and other leisure activities, unable to care of their children and may suffer marital difficulties or marriage breakdown.

The claimant may have bowel and bladder impairment and require colostomy and catheter bag assistance. In addition, the claimant may have acute or chronic pain which prevents them from interacting with others and working and caring for themselves and their family. Quality of life may also be affected by such issues as scarring, prosthetics, sexual dysfunction, poor mobility, restriction of dietary requirements, depression and PTSD.

Loss of Leisure Opportunities

Two typical situations where there may be a measurable negative impact on the claimant's ability to enjoy a quality of leisure commensurate with that prior to the accident include:

- *The need for additional hours of working*. Some claimants may have to work longer hours due to the injuries sustained to earn at the same level. In those circumstances the claimant is entitled to an award of damages for loss of leisure time. This may be included as part of the award for general damages for PSLA, or it may be considered separately by the judge, depending on the facts of the case. In reality, it is very difficult to value as a financial loss, and thus, in practice, it is recommended that the facts be used to boost the PSLA award. There is a dearth of case law relating to such claims, but if a claimant does seek a separate award then the starting point must be the hourly rate he is currently paid, to form a baseline.
- *Loss of holiday*. Evidence to establish the cost of the holiday will be required and makes a claim on his holiday insurance or inquiries of the holiday company to establish if he is entitled to a refund. However, it is questionable as to whether an additional award should be made for missing the holiday; since the claimant will have recovered the expense of the holiday, what more has he lost? Further, the defendant may argue that if any additional award is sought, the claimant must give credit for the extra expense on holiday, e.g. purchase of ski hire and alcohol. The authors of Kemp and Kemp consider the award should not be the cost of the holiday but a separate head for general damages. In Jackson v Horizon Holidays [1975] 3 ALL ER 92 [22], the claimant was awarded £1100 for loss of enjoyment of a 4-week holiday in Ceylon. This case established that the claimant could recover not only for his inconvenience and stress but for those members of the family who were taking the holiday with him.

11.5.5.3 Pecuniary Losses

These are losses that can be measured in monetary terms such as loss of earnings, travel expenses, medical expenses, the cost of aids and appliances and the cost of moving home or having the home adapted as a consequence of the injury.

Loss of earnings will form a large part of the claim if the injured person is unable to return to work because of their injury; they will be able to claim past and future loss of earnings. If they were employed at the time of the accident, then payslips for the preceding 3 months will be required to form the evidence to support a loss of earning's claim.

If a person is self-employed at the time of the accident, the claim may be slightly more complex if the accounts of the injured person are not up to date or they have not paid their income tax payments as they should have done. It is sensible to obtain the injured persons business accounts for 3 years prior to the accident to assist in calculating the loss of earnings claim.

Consideration should also be made for those who were temporarily employed at the time of their accident or those who would only have worked for a specific period of time in the future in any event, i.e. close to retirement/early retirement at the time of the accident.

It is necessary to assess if the claimant is able to return to work in the future. If so, would this be on a temporary or permanent basis and will early retirement be required. Often the claimant is unable to return to the job that they are employed/employer at the time. The future loss of earnings claim will include the difference in earnings in the future, to the claimant as a consequence of the accident. This head of claim can be a significant part of the claim, if it can be shown that the claimant has little or no earning capacity post-accident and until retirement. If a city worker aged 35 is unable to continue to work as a business manager but is able to work as a part-time general officer assistant because of the accident and subsequent injury, then the loss of earnings claim will be significant and all benefits in addition to the annual salary should be included in the claim such as car expenses, private medical insurance, gym membership, bonuses, free or discounted travel, discounted goods etc. if they are no longer available due to change in occupation.

Other additional elements to the claim are the Smith v Manchester [23] award which is a lump sum payment to reflect the claimant's disability on the labour market. There may be a claim for loss of chance if it can be shown that the claimant has lost the chance to pursue a career; it is usually the difference in lost gain and actual gain.

Pension loss is also claimed if the claimant was aged 45 at the date of the accident. If early retirement has occurred or is likely to retire, there will be a difference in the level of pension paid at the time of state retirement age. Pension calculations can be complex, and expert evidence may be required to support this head of damage, which can significantly increase the potential value of future losses. The claimant may have retired early in any event or may well have worked past retirement age. Each case is based on the specific facts of the employment issues presented to the claimant.

All other tangible losses that are likely to incur in the future, if supported by evidence, can be claimed such as future therapy, future medical care, future nursing care, future childcare, future aids and appliances, future costs of DIY, maintenance, gardening, car maintenance, mobility needs and care and case management costs, amongst other heads of damage.

Acknowledgements I am grateful to Mrs Stephanie Prior, Solicitor, **Head of Medical Negligence at Osbornes Solicitors LLP** for her invaluable assistance in the preparation and contribution to this chapter.

Cases, Legislation and Government Reports

1. Donoghue v Stevenson [1932] UKHL 100.
2. Royal Commission on Civil Liability and Compensation for Personal Injury, (1978). Stationery Office, Cmnd. 7054.
3. Access to Justice Report (1996) London: HMSO.
4. The Civil Procedure Act 1997 (c. 12).
5. The Civil Procedure Rules, Ministry of Justice (SI 1998/3132).
6. Courts and Legal Services Act 1990.
7. Review of Civil Litigation Costs: Final Report. Ministry of Justice (2010) TSO.
8. Legal Aid, Sentencing and Punishment of Offenders Act 2012.
9. Administration of Justice Act 1982.
10. Limitation Act 1980 s.2.
11. Criminal Injuries Compensation Act 1995.
12. The Practice Direction (2014 with updates) Supplement of Criminal Practice Rules, (Part 35).
13. Barnett v Chelsea & Kensington Hospital [1969] 1 QB 428.
14. Sabri-Tabrizi v Lothian Health Board (1998) SC 373.
15. Hicks v Chief Constable of the South Yorkshire police [1992] PIQR.
16. Hicks v Chief Constable of South Yorkshire [1992] All ER 65 House of Lords.
17. Arafa v Potter [1994] PIQR Q73.
18. Reed v Sunderland Health Authority [1998] All ER (D) 447.
19. Heil v Rankin [2001] PIQR Q3.
20. Aloni v National Westminster Bank (unreported, May 20 1982).
21. Tame v Professional Cycle Marketing [2006] EWHC 3751.
22. Jackson v Horizon Holidays [1975] 3 ALL ER 92.
23. Smith v Manchester Corporation [1974] 17 KLR.

Further Readings

Aronoff GM, Mandel S, Genovese E, Maitz EA, Dorto AJ, Klimek EH, Staats TE (2007) Evaluating malingering in contested injury or illness. Pain Pract 7:178–204

Council of Europe (2002) Assessing disability in Europe: similarities and differences. Report drawn up by the Working Group on the assessment of person-related criteria for allowances and personal assistance for people with disabilities. Council of Europe Publishing, Strasbourg, France

British Medical Association (2007) Expert witness guidance. www.bma.org.uk/-/media/Files/PDFs/. . ./expert%20witness%20guidance.pdf

Chawda MN, Hildebrand F, Pape HC, Giannoudis PV (2004) Predicting outcome after multiple trauma: which scoring system? Injury 35:347–358

Civil Justice Council (2009) Protocol for the instruction of experts to give evidence in civil claims. www.judiciary.gov.uk/about-the-judiciary/advisory-bodies/cjc

Civil Justice Council (2014) Guidance for the instruction of experts in civil claims. www.judiciary.gov.uk/about-the-judiciary/advisory-bodies/cjc

Cornes P, Aitken RCB (1992) Medical reports on persons claiming compensation for personal injury. J R Soc Med 85:329–333

Ghisi M, Novara C, Buodo G, Kimble MO, Scozzari S, Di Natale A, Sanavio E, Palomba D (2013) Psychological distress and post-traumatic symptoms following occupational accidents. Behav Sci 3:587–600

Gill D (2008) Proving and disproving psychiatric injury. Med Leg J 76:143–155

The Judicial Studies Board for Northern Ireland (2013) Guidelines for the assessment of general damages in personal injury cases in northern Ireland (Fourth edition)

WHO (1999) ICDH-2: international classification of functioning, disability and health. WHO, Geneva, Switzerland

Judicial College (2013) Guidelines for the assessment of general damages in personal injury cases, 12th edn. Oxford University Press, Oxford

Kemp and Kemp: quantum of damages. 1975 Editors various. Sweet and Maxwell

Main CJ, Spanswick CC (1995) 'Functional overlay', and illness behaviour in chronic pain: distress or malingering? Conceptual difficulties in medico-legal assessment of personal injury claims. J Psychosom Res 39:737–753

Ministry of Justice. Civil justice reforms. Personal injury claims. www.justice.gov.uk/civil-justice-reforms/personal-injury-claims

Sutherland AG, Johnston AT, Hutchison JD (2006) The new injury severity score: better prediction of functional recovery after musculoskeletal injury. Value Health 9:24–27

Tsushima WT, Geling O, Fabrigas J (2011) Comparison of MMPI-2 validity scale scores of personal injury litigants and disability claimants. Clin Neuropsychol 25:1403–1414

Walton DA, MacDermid JC, Pulickal M, Rollack A, Veitch J (2014) Development and initial validation of the Satisfaction and Recovery Index (SRI) for measurement of recovery from musculoskeletal trauma. Open Orthop J 8:316–325

Chapter 12
Methods of Ascertainment of Personal Damage in Germany

Vera Sterzik, Axel Muttray, Peter Weiß, and Elisabeth Mützel

Abstract The chapter illustrates the historical, judicial and juridical framework of personal injury assessment and compensation in Germany, describing the expert's qualification and competences and detailing the ascertainment methodology and criteria of evaluation utilised for identifying, describing and estimating any personal injury, its temporary and permanent consequences and the causal value/link between the event and the injury and between the injury and the impairment/ disability.

12.1 Historical, Judicial and Juridical Overview

Regarding the different forms of violence, there are three that it is necessary to distinguish: physical violence, sexual violence and emotional violence. In German legal medicine, physical and sexual violence are surveyed. Classifying emotional violence is the purpose of the forensic psychiatrist.

V. Sterzik (✉)
Institute of Forensic Medicine, Kantonsspital St. Gallen, Rorschacher Str. 95, 9007 St. Gallen, Switzerland
e-mail: vera.sterzik@kssg.ch

A. Muttray
Institute of Occupational, Community and Environmental Medicine, Johannes-Gutenberg-University Mainz, Obere Zahlbacher Str. 67, 55131 Mainz, Germany
e-mail: amuttray@uni-mainz.de

P. Weiß
Department of Public Prosecution, Ottostraße 5, 97070 Würzburg, Germany

E. Mützel
Institute of Forensic Medicine, Ludwig-Maximilians-University of München, Nußbaumstraße 26, 80336 München, Germany
e-mail: elisabeth.muetzel@med.uni-muenchen.de

S.D. Ferrara et al. (eds.), *Personal Injury and Damage Ascertainment under Civil Law*, DOI 10.1007/978-3-319-29812-2_12

In Germany, forensic medicine experts mainly work on behalf of the public prosecution department or on behalf of the criminal investigation department. This implies that a victim has to have contact with the police first. However, victims frequently decide to contact the police only weeks or months after the assault. But when injuries are healed completely, the evaluation becomes difficult. For that reason the Institutes of Legal Medicine started opening up more and more walk-in departments, where victims of physical and sexual violence can be surveyed without having to pass by the police first. Offering a low-threshold assessment of the victim's injuries, the aim is to enable more victims to have their injuries recorded shortly after the assault. The walk-in departments were established in order to prevent such difficulties, especially for victims of interpersonal violence in social proximity. Some walk-in departments have been around for years already, but only recently has political support been noticeable due to the increased interest of the media.

Including the examination of a living victim, clinical forensic medicine has always existed. However, during the last 10 years, something has changed fundamentally. Nowadays, the examination of a living victim has established as a more significant role within forensic medicine. It is regarded as an interface between clinical and forensic medicine. Examinations of victims now appertain to the core competences of forensic medicine. For the examination and assessment of a victim, an interdisciplinary network is important.

The definition of criminal acts and how to proceed juristically is determined in the German Criminal Code (StGB), which is based on legal codes dating back to the 1870s. It contains the chapters "Offences against sexual self-determination" (§§ 174–184g) and "Offences against the person" (§§ 223–231). Until 1997 rape between married people (married with each other) was juridically not classified as a criminal act. If anything, it was categorised as bodily injury. Only in 1997 was it admitted to § 177 StGB and thereby became a criminal act. Generally, "sexualized violence" means violence including the genital area. The main reason for sexualized violence is to humiliate the victim rather than to attain sexual enjoyment. § 177 StGB defines the meaning of the terms "Sexual assault by use of force or threats" and "rape". Since 1997, a forced penetration into the body (oral, vaginal or anal) is characteristically called "rape", while other sexual actions without penetration are called "sexual assault".

In § 223 StGB "bodily harm" is defined as "Whosoever physically assaults or damages the health of another person...", whereas it becomes "bodily harm by dangerous means" (§ 224 StGB) when the perpetrator causes bodily harm by:

- Administering poison or other noxious substances
- Using a weapon or other dangerous instrument
- Acting by stealth
- Acting jointly with another
- Methods that pose danger to life

A victim can also, for instance, be injured without intent in a traffic accident or by negligence.

12.2 Identification and Description of Medicolegal Expert's Qualifications

The basic education for becoming a doctor of medicine proceeds according to the EU Directive 2005/36/EG of the European Parliament and Council. Afterwards, a time of further education and training follows for those who want to become an expert in medicolegal medicine. For this period of time, the medical chambers as public corporations bear responsibility. The period lasts at least 60 months and includes 6 months of pathology and 6 months of (forensic) psychiatry and psychotherapy. Furthermore, another 6 months of the following professions can be accepted: pathology, anatomy, public health system, pharmacology and toxicology, psychiatry and psychotherapy, as well as forensic psychiatry. During this period, the following examinations, activities and methods are to be completed:

- 400 inspections of the corpse
- 25 crime scenes
- 300 autopsies
- 2000 histological studies
- 10 evaluations of DNA traces and their storage
- 200 expert opinions for the court (written and verbally communicated)
- 25 forensic osteological and odontological studies

This data is required by the medical chamber of Bavaria, for example. The data required by the medical chambers of other German federal states can differ slightly.

Furthermore, the doctor has to acquire experiences and skills concerning forensic traumatology, biomechanics and forensic anthropology. He also has to study the basics of forensic molecular biology and toxicology. Finally, the examination of living persons is part of the education, including cases of child maltreatment and sexual abuse. When all the skills have been acquired, an oral examination has to be passed.

During the time of education and after some experiences, the trainee can examine a victim for himself. But at the first few times, the examination takes place in the presence of a professional doctor. The trainee is authorised to perform examinations after demonstrating his competences.

12.3 Ascertainment Methodology

There are four different ways to initiate an ascertainment method:

- Appraisal by order of the investigation authority
- Consultative examination by order of the hospital
- Examination and documentation by order of private persons

- Examination by an accident insurance consultant (automatically initiated in case of a commuting accident or an accident at work)

If victims want to complain to the police, they have to report to the criminal police and the public prosecutor. Depending on the interval between the time of the crime and criminal complaint as well as the kind of violence, an investigation in an institute of legal medicine is possible. In case of an appraisal in the order of the investigation authority, the order includes both the physical examination with securing of evidence and a written expert opinion including explanation of the causal links. Injuries should be documented in two ways: by description in words and by photography. Evidence should be secured. Both victims and offenders should be examined after physical violence and/or rape. Some German institutes cooperate with gynaecologists, especially in cases of rape. The investigation, documentation and interpretation of the injuries occur impartially, objectively and with precision.

Consultative examinations in the order of hospitals include standardised injury documentation as well as a verbal discussion concerning the initiation of the injuries. If, in a particular case, a criminal investigation proceeding results, the documentation permits a complete examination report to be written.

Furthermore, private persons can consult a medicolegal expert for the documentation of their injuries without involving the police. Some forensic departments offer this proceeding in the context of officially supported walk-in departments for victims of violence, adults and children. Other forensic departments offer this proceeding without being supported, too, as long as the department can afford this "service" in terms of personnel and finance. In the same way as for the consultative examination, the standardised documentation of the injuries in words and photography is included as well as a verbal discussion. A written examination report is not included, which can be caught up on in case of a criminal investigation proceeding. The aim is to document injuries and save evidence close to the event. If a victim decides to involve the police only long after the event, injuries can be completely healed. Thereby, it can be impossible to come to a diagnosis. By contrast, the walk-in departments guarantee documentation within a narrow time frame. They also serve as a contact point in cases of child abuse—for private persons as well as for other doctors (especially paediatricians) with questions on obscure cases.

If it comes to an examination of a person or to an assessment of medical reports for any reason, the procedure is always the same. There is no difference between a later civil liability and a criminal trial. In general, civil liabilities without criminal trials are rare in Germany (except whiplash claims). In cases of seriously harmed persons, there is a criminal trial first and after that it comes to civil liability. The latter often takes place without a forensic expert, as the forensic expert has already given his report during the criminal trial.

12.3.1 Collection of Circumstantial and Clinical Data

Forensic and clinical examinations should compile a complete record of injuries and all available evidence while being cognizant of the victim's physical and emotional needs. When interviewing or examining the victim, the examiner should be patient and open but also objective and neutral. Especially with regard to victims of sexual violence, the top priority of an examination should be to protect the victim from further trauma. In case of traffic injury, the physical aspects of the accident are analysed by specialised companies. The medicolegal experts pay attention to these results when reconstructing the event and cause of injuries.

12.3.2 Medical Case History

Before examining the victim's body, the examiner must know the victim's account of the crime in detail. The account, injuries and the result of the evidence should offer a single coherent image. The victim can also be asked questions by the examiner. If an offender is examined, it is important to point out that none of the examiner's questions have to be answered. Questions could, for example, relate to when, how and where the incident occurred. Generally, obtaining a report of the crime is important, but the younger a child, the more difficult is the questioning. A toddler can be suggestively influenced through questions. Therefore, it is often best to allow specially trained persons to conduct the questioning.

In 1953, Mueller reported on the assessment of examinations of living persons [1]. He emphasised that the otherwise important anamnesis is to be included only with caution, if at all. He stated that it was frequently the aim of an assessment to determine the anamnesis based on the detected injuries. The structure of a medical report was recommended to be the following:

- Repetition of the question to be answered
- Rendition of the documents important for answering the question
- Own investigations
- Diagnosis and detailed reply to the question asked at the beginning

The evaluation must be plain and objective. The questions are to be answered without legal connotations. Subjective health problems are also to be documented. It is important, however, to particularly denote those as subjective statements of the person examined. To enforce a demand, symptoms are frequently aggravated or simulated.

12.3.3 Systematic Clinical and Medicolegal Visit

In Germany a systematic medicolegal visit includes an examination of the complete and undressed body and the outer genitals. The well-being and health of a victim is the main priority during an examination. The examination should be conducted in a gentle manner and with patience. A victim should never be forced to undergo an examination. When examining a child or adolescent, the presence of a parent or guardian is necessary. The younger the child, the more important the attendance of a parent or guardian becomes. However, the examiner should be aware that the person accompanying the child could be involved in the maltreatment.

Generally, the physical examination should involve all parts of the body. In order to make the victim feel as comfortable as possible, the examination should be done by a person of the same sex [2]. If this is not possible, the examiner should have an assistant of the same sex nearby. Care must be taken that the victim does not undress completely, but only partially, to enable examination of one naked part of the body at a time. The injuries are to be documented in words and pictures.

In case of sexual violence, after the extra-genital examination, a genital examination should occur [3]. Ideally, the genital examination should be performed by a medicolegal expert in cooperation with a gynaecologist. The investigative technique depends on the age of the patient and also on the hormonal influence of girls [4]. A toddler (who is free of hormones) can be examined while sitting on the lap of a parent or guardian, who can hold and spread the legs of the toddler. In this position, the labia majora and minora, the introitus, the hymen and the anus can be inspected. The examination of an older girl in the hormone-free period can take place on the examination table, first in the supine position and after that in the so-called frog-leg position. A girl in the prepubertal or pubertal period as well as a woman can be examined in the gynaecological chair. A boy is to be examined on the examination bed, in a lateral position while bending the hip joint and knee joint. In this position, the buttocks can be spread and the anus inspected. The buttocks should be spread as long as possible to cause a reflexive dilatation of the anal sphincter. The penis is to be examined with regard to bleeding or other injuries. The preputium should preferably be withdrawn by the boy himself.

For inspection of the external genitalia, the labia majora and minora will be spread and then pulled forward and down with the fingers (separation and traction). The inspection of the hymen occurs in this position. Normally, the hymen can be brushed from the inside to the outside with a cotton swab. An investigation with a speculum is necessary only if there is a haemorrhage of the vaginal canal [5] or if there are foreign objects inside. Use of a speculum may create difficulties, because the speculum blocks the view of the hymen, preventing an existing injury from being seen. The speculum itself may injure the hymen, making it impossible to distinguish between an injury caused by sexual intercourse and an injury caused by the speculum.

Independent of a report to the police, the anamnesis and all injuries should be documented in a standardised way. Generally, a documentation form can be used to simplify the process. This can also serve as an aid to memory at a legal proceeding later. The following points are guidelines for filling out a documentation form:

- Descriptions of all injuries are to be written down exactly. That is, characterise the colour, form, margin, dimension and exact localization of the injuries. All injuries must be included.
- The injuries should also be photographed. One overview picture should be taken and a second one showing the injury in detail with a scale. The photo should be taken at a right angle to the injury. If the photo is taken in an oblique projection to the injury, the injury itself may not be sufficiently visible.
- The report of the victim is to be documented exactly and in depth. Sometimes it is important to quote verbatim the words or sentences of the victim. Some victims do not understand technical words. The examiner should speak clearly and should explain these words when necessary.
- Securing traces requires the correct procedure. The examiner may find an explanation of how to secure the traces in the documentation form. Generally, the traces should be dry and clean.
- The injuries and the result of the traces should be interpreted carefully.

12.3.4 Additional Investigations

The medicolegal expert is allowed to collect all information needed for evaluation of the present injuries. He/she is not allowed to ask questions that are not necessarily important for the present issue.

If necessary, blood and urine should be collected both from the victim and, when possible, the perpetrator and tested for alcohol and drugs. DNA swabs should be collected. In case of a sexual assault, vaginal, oral and/or anal swabs should be taken as well as swabs of the penis of the perpetrator. For securing sperm and seminal fluid, several sterile cotton swabs (ideally three or four) should be used at once.

An additional tool is infrared photography. It can be used to visualise bloodstains on dark surfaces, especially clothes. In the infrared wavelength, many dark materials reflect the light so that they seem pale. Blood, however, absorbs the infrared light by which it appears dark-coloured. Using this difference in contrast, bloodstains become visible and interpretable.

There is also the possibility of taking MR/CT pictures and X-rays of the victim. Especially in cases of strangulation, hematomas of the throat can be visualised very well using the MR. When it comes to tests with radiation exposure, risk and benefit have to be weighed carefully. Sometimes, tests are important despite radiation exposure (e.g. in some cases of child maltreatment). But the use of tests with radiation exposure has to be a decision made on a case-by-case basis. The victim must agree to make a radiological investigation.

12.4 Evaluation Criteria

12.4.1 Psychiatric and Somatic State Prior to the Event/Injury

As a basis, the victim should be interviewed about diseases and intake of drugs or alcohol. To evaluate the somatic state prior to the event, the victim and the family physician can be interviewed. The victim has to be in agreement with the latter. To assess the psychiatric state before, during or after the event is not part of legal medicine in Germany. Instead, this lies within the competence of the forensic psychiatrist. Nevertheless, it has to be clarified whether the victim has psychiatric problems, was in psychiatric counselling or needs psychiatric help (e.g. victims with borderline personality disorder).

12.4.2 Detailed Reconstruction of the Event/Injury

The reconstruction of a whole event does not fall within the remit of German legal medicine. Instead, the task of legal medicine is to collect information necessary for the police. Therefore, it is also important to concentrate on the statements of the persons involved. For example, do the story and the injuries fit together? If so, what is the amount of violence necessary to cause their injuries? To reconstruct the mechanism of an injury sometimes requires an interdisciplinary collaboration. Specialists of biomechanics, physics, ballistics or scientific computing can assist in answering questions. In some cases experiments (under similar conditions) are indispensable to ascertain whether a story and an injury fit together or not. Especially when it concerns answering questions about velocity, force, inertia and so on, an interdisciplinary collaboration can be enlightening. Some German forensic departments employ interdisciplinary specialists; others do not. Besides, there is always the possibility to collaborate with the State Office of Criminal Investigations.

12.4.3 Personal Injury

The injury is to be described in words and photographed. In doing so, there are several points of supreme importance:

- Overview picture (making sure to visualise the localisation of the injury)
- Detailed picture
- Usage of a scale
- Standardised illumination and colour management

In order to achieve a faithful colour rendition of the picture, the use of a standardised illumination, e.g. with a daylight lamp, is recommended. The knowledge of the colour temperature is a prerequisite for the correct adjustment of the white balance. The colour management should include the calibration and profiling of the monitor and the profiling of the printer. It is also recommended to shoot the detailed photograph out of a position rectangular to the injury. This way, perspective distortion can be prevented. Describing an injury, it is important to document precisely the localisation, size and appearance of the injury. A person reading the description of an injury should be able to visualise a picture without having seen the photograph of the injury.

Questions about outcome and success of clinical treatments should preferably be answered by a doctor of the appropriate discipline.

12.4.4 Permanent and Temporary Impairment

In Germany, evaluating temporary or permanent impairment is not the task of a legal medicine expert. These topics are evaluated by doctors of medico-actuarial science, community medicine or labour and occupational health. Additionally, a doctor of the appropriate discipline can also be interviewed.

The duration of an impairment due to violence is relevant in various fields of law. According to the seventh volume of the German Social Code (SGB VII), the statutory accident insurance provides services in case of a commuting accident or a work-related accident. Services such as medical care, rehabilitation, injury benefit ("Verletztengeld") and transitional allowance ("Übergangsgeld") are provided independently from the prognosis of an injury. From the viewpoint of statutory accident insurance, permanent impairment means a duration exceeding 26 weeks. This time period is a necessary prerequisite for a pension claim.

The Federal War Victims Relief Act ("Bundesversorgungsgesetz", BVG), which was originally enacted to provide for World War II victims and their surviving dependents, has also been applied for several decades to other groups of people who are entitled to claim under certain secondary legislation (e.g. victims of violent crime, people with vaccine damage, people injured during military or civilian service, people who were imprisoned on the basis of an unlawful sentence under the regime of the Socialist Unity Party of the former German Democratic Republic) [6]. According to § 18a BVG, an impairment becomes "permanent" if the incapacity to work is to be expected to last for at least 78 weeks. The Federal War Victims Relief Act is completed by a particular regulation ("Versorgungsmedizin-verordnung"). The annex to this regulation ("Versorgungsmedizinische Grundsätze") specifies the degree of injury consequences ("Grad der Schädigungsfolgen", GdS). In this regulation, "chronic" is defined as a relevant functional impairment exceeding a period of 6 months with a high degree of probability [7].

The accident insurance covering for civil servants is regulated by the Civil Service Benefits Act (Beamtenversorgungsgesetz). A special compensation after an accident ("Unfallausgleich") can be claimed if a relevant impairment lasts longer than 26 weeks.

Impairment due to violence can be recognised according to the Disabilities Act (Social Code IX, SGB IX), if a relevant functional impairment exceeds a period of 6 months with a high degree of probability [7].

However, there is no uniform definition of "chronic" in the various areas of law. The statutory accident insurance and the authorities, respectively, have to decide whether the criterion of chronicity is fulfilled. Their decisions are often based on medical reports. Physicians of various fields may be assigned to render an expert opinion, depending on the particular question.

12.4.5 *Causal Value of the Event and Causal Link*

"Conditio sine qua non" in German criminal law means "every event or action that is causal for an issue". The issue would not occur if the event had never happened. So it is up to the legal medicine expert to clarify whether an accused action is indeed the causal reason for the injury. In some cases this might be less complicated. In other cases some interdisciplinary reconstructive investigations might be necessary. Special guidelines about when to affirm or deny causation do not exist.

Once causation between event and injury is affirmed by a legal medicine expert, the relation between injury and impairment has to be considered, too. If this does not fit together, a doctor of the appropriate discipline has to be consulted.

The criteria for evaluating the causal link are different in the statutory accident insurance. The impact and the impairment of health must be ensured, and the causal relationship must be "probable". If there are different causes, the occupational impact must be a relevant causal factor [8]. In such cases, the medical expert has to consider the pathogenesis of the disease in detail with regard to all single causes. According to the particular regulation ("Versorgungsmedizinische Grundsätze"), the examination of the causal relationship is analogous to the principles of the statutory accident insurance [7]. In contrast, the recognition of impairment according to the Disabilities Act does not depend on a particular cause. Rather, the extent of the functional impairment is to be assessed [7].

12.4.6 *Personal Damage Quantification*

12.4.6.1 Quantum for Temporary Impairment

As stated above, German social legislation lays down that a disability can be recognised in case of a chronic impairment.

12.4.6.2 Quantum for Permanent Impairment

There are differences between the various areas of law. According to the seventh volume of the German Social Code (SGB VII), the reduction in earning capacity (Minderung der Erwerbsfähigkeit, MdE) depends on the reduction of the percentage of job opportunities due to the impairment. This is to be evaluated in relation to the individual job opportunities before the injury in the entire labour market [9]. In case of a permanent total disability, the reduction in earning capacity is 100 %. If the impairment is less, i.e. the person is not able to work at a certain number of workplaces to a lesser or greater degree, expert opinion may be difficult. In this case, it is impossible to quantify the number of the respective workplaces, which would be the prerequisite for calculating the degree of the reduction of earning capacity. Therefore, textbooks on expert opinion and court decisions are usually the basis for the estimation of the degree of impairment. An impairment of at least 20 % is a prerequisite for a pension. Different insurance cases for the same individual (including recognised occupational diseases) can be considered cumulatively, provided that the reduction in earning capacity is at least 10 % in each case. For example, if a work-related accident and an occupational disease result in a reduction in earning capacity of 10 % each, the total reduction in earning capacity is 20 %. In this case, the person would receive a pension. The seventh volume of the German Social Code § 56 provides that insurance cases under the Civil Service Benefits Act and other laws have to be dealt with accordingly.

The annex to the particular regulation provides that the degree of injury consequences (GdS, according to the social compensation law) and the degree of disability (GdB, according to the Disabilities Act) are related to possible impairments in all areas of life [7], but not to the general labour market. The degree of injury consequences and the degree of disability are expressed as mere numbers and outlined in the annex. The administrations choose experts from the appropriate medical specialities for an expert opinion.

The different fields of law may seem confusing. The application of the various legal provisions shall be explained in an example. A professional violinist has lost one hand due to a violent act. In case of a work-related accident, the seventh volume of the German Social Code applies. However, the experts disagree, whether a possible prosthetic restoration has to be considered or not. The reduction in earning capacity (MdE) may vary between 50 and 80 % depending on the condition of the amputation stump and on the legal position with regard to a possibly successful prosthetic restoration [10]. As the violinist cannot practise his profession any longer, the statutory accident insurance provides an increment, which is usually 10 % [11]. If the violinist is a professional musician employed by the army, the annex to the BVG [7] has to be applied. The degree of injury consequences (GdS) is 50. The competent authority fixes an increment, too. However, the level of the increment is not specified in the annex. A degree of disability can be recognised in addition to the recognition of a work-related accident according to seventh volume of the German Social Code or the Federal War Victims Relief Act, respectively. The degree of disability amounts to 50, there being no increment [7].

To determine a disability rate is not the purpose of forensic medicine.

12.4.6.3 Other Non-pecuniary Losses

Of course, the medicolegal expert can give an overview of losses concerning, for example, daily activities, sports and sexual function. To give a detailed description of how affected a person is based on his or her injuries should be done by a doctor of the appropriate discipline. To investigate how far these influences lead to an existential damage is a task of the court.

When assessing the value of pain and suffering, (civil) courts have to award an adequate compensation to the injured person. Key aspects for determining the compensation are the extent, severity and duration of pain, suffering and disfigurement. However, the victim's personal situation, such as age, sex, occupation and personal inclinations, also has to be taken into account. Within the scope of compensation, the injuring party is also liable for any emotional distress directly caused by and related to the damaging incident. In this respect, a potential uncertainty as to the future healing process or a potentially increased risk of injury or death can also be of importance for the assessment. The same applies to social burdens such as reduced career chances in the present occupation or prevention of career ambitions and objectives. As experience shows, it is often difficult for the victim to demonstrate and prove such emotional consequences of the injuring incident in a plausible way.

Another important aspect is that the victim is entitled to receive just and fair compensation from the injuring party for the wrong suffered. In this context, the degree of guilt plays an important role, although it is not decisive if the competent criminal courts have instituted criminal proceedings against the injuring party. Consequently, damages for pain and suffering are always determined on a case-by-case basis. Accordingly, the number of individual decisions is immense. Certain guidelines are given by Beck's Schmerzensgeldtabelle (Table of compensation for pain and suffering, 2013) [12] or the ADAC Table, published by Hacks/Wellner/Häcker (Amounts of damages for pain and suffering, "Schmerzensgeldbeträge", 2012).

Traditionally, German judges have always been rather cautious when assessing concrete amounts of damages for pain and suffering. For example, 40,000–60,000 € were awarded in the past for the amputation of an arm required after medical malpractice. In most cases, a single payment is awarded, whereas a pension for pain and suffering is to be considered where an important limb was lost or in cases where the victim may suffer detrimental effects in the future. In such cases—i.e. if recovery is uncertain and the long-term medical effects cannot be predicted—the victim can also sue for a declaratory judgement, which would enable him or her to claim damages also in the future.

12.4.6.4 Pecuniary Losses

The costs of medical treatment are an important part of the rehabilitation costs to be compensated to an injured person. If these costs are paid by a social insurance carrier or an insurance company, statutory subrogation is carried out, which means that the insurer is entitled to recover the amount of the claim paid to the victim from the injuring party.

As a general principle, the expenses to be compensated by the injuring party have to be reasonable. Again, this has led to a multitude of judicial case-by-case decisions. For example, the costs for an unconventional medical treatment method have been recognised if it offers a realistic chance of therapeutic success or relief of pain under scientific aspects. Thus, the injured statutory health insurance patient can also claim compensation for therapeutic treatment costs normally not paid by the statutory health insurance as far as these are not disproportionately high. In specific cases, the costs for a rented TV were recognised as reimbursable, whereas the costs for additional reading material were not. Travel costs of close relatives or a domestic partner for visits to the hospital are generally regarded as part of the treatment costs and are thus reimbursable as far as they cannot be avoided. On the other hand, lost leisure time of the family cannot be compensated.

Material damage also includes indirect damage, such as lost profit or lost earnings. The assessment of the amount of the damage caused is subject to the simplified burden of proof as defined in Section 287 of the German Code of Civil Procedure. Generally, damage that may occur in the future is not taken into account. Thus, a musician who lost a hand and can no longer practise his profession cannot make a claim for a concrete amount of money for the presumable loss of earnings in the future, although he has the option to bring an action to establish the liability of the injuring party for any future damage, in addition to the action for compensation of the damage suffered up to the court hearing.

References

1. Mueller B (1953) Gerichtliche Medizin. Springer, Heidelberg
2. Graß H, Rothschild MA (2004) Klinische Rechtsmedizin – Aufgaben und Herausforderungen im Rahmen der medizinischen Betreuung von Opfern häuslicher Gewalt. Rechtsmedizin 14:188–192
3. Banaschak S, Gerlach K, Seifert D, Bockholdt B, Graß H (2011) Forensisch-medizinische Untersuchung von Gewaltopfern. Rechtsmedizin 21:483–488
4. Debertin AS, Seifert D, Mützel E (2011) Forensisch-medizinische Untersuchung von Mädchen und Jungen bei Verdacht auf Misshandlung und Missbrauch. Rechtsmedizin 21:479–482
5. Banaschak S, Debertin AS, Klemm P, Mützel E (2013) Sexualisierte Gewalt. In: Grassberger M, Türk E, Yen K (eds) Klinisch-forensische Medizin. Springer, Berlin Heidelberg, pp 317–325
6. Federal Ministry of Labour and Social Affairs (2011) Compensation and assistance for war victims. http://www.bmas.de/EN/Our-Topics/Social-Security/compensation-and-assistance-for-war-victims.html
7. Federal Ministry of Labour and Social Affairs (2008) Anlage zu § 2 der Versorgungsmedizin-Verordnung vom 2008 "Versorgungsmedizinische Grundsätze". http://www.bmas.de/

SharedDocs/Downloads/DE/PDF-Publikationen/k710-versorgundsmed-verordnung.pdf?__blob=publicationFile
8. Schönberger A, Mehrtens G, Valentin H (2010a) Arbeitsunfall und Berufskrankheit. In: Rechtliche und medizinische Grundlagen für Gutachter, Sozialverwaltung, Berater und Gerichte. Erich Schmidt Verlag, Berlin, pp 46–51
9. Schönberger A, Mehrtens G, Valentin H (2010b) Arbeitsunfall und Berufskrankheit. In: Rechtliche und medizinische Grundlagen für Gutachter, Sozialverwaltung, Berater und Gerichte. Berater und Gerichte, Berlin, pp 97–98
10. Schönberger A, Mehrtens G, Valentin H (2010c) Arbeitsunfall und Berufskrankheit. In: Rechtliche und medizinische Grundlagen für Gutachter, Sozialverwaltung, Berater und Gerichte. Erich Schmidt Verlag, Berlin, pp 689–698
11. Schönberger A, Mehrtens G, Valentin H (2010d) Arbeitsunfall und Berufskrankheit. In: Rechtliche und medizinische Grundlagen für Gutachter, Sozialverwaltung, Berater und Gerichte. Erich Schmidt Verlag, Berlin, pp 539–540
12. Slizyk A (2013) Beck´sche Schmerzensgeldtabelle. Verlag C. H. Beck, München
13. Herrmann B, Banaschak S, Thyen U, Dettmeyer R (2010) Kindesmisshandlung. Springer, Berlin
14. Mützel E (2013) Sexual violence. In: Siegel JA, Saukko PJ (eds) Encyclopedia of forensic sciences, 2nd edn. Academic/Elsevier, Waltham, pp 96–100

Chapter 13
Methods of Ascertainment of Personal Damage in Hungary

Eva Keller, Agnes Dósa, Andras Sarvary, Krisztian Csapó, and Peter Banczerowski

Abstract The chapter illustrates the historical, judicial, and juridical framework of personal injury assessment and compensation in Hungary, describing the expert's qualification and competences and detailing the ascertainment methodology and criteria of evaluation utilized for identifying, describing, and estimating any personal injury, its temporary and permanent consequences, and the causal value/link between the event and the injury and between the injury and the impairment/disability.

13.1 Historical, Judicial, and Juridical Overview

As the system of the law of damages and its fundamental premises in jurisprudence are similar all over Europe on the Continent, the presentation of the Hungarian part will highlight primarily the differences. To limit its length, the chapter can provide a brief presentation of Hungarian law of damages related mainly to accidents.

13.1.1 Historical Outline of Hungarian Law of Damages

Both in terms of its roots, history, and evaluation criteria, the Hungarian law of damages is similar to the legal systems of compensation of other European countries.

E. Keller (✉) • A. Dósa • A. Sarvary
Department of Forensic and Insurance Medicine, Semmelweis University, Üllői út 93, 1091 Budapest, IX, Hungary
e-mail: evakeller690@yahoo.com; dosaagi@yahoo.com; sarvary.andras@gmail.com

K. Csapó • P. Banczerowski
Department of Neurosurgery, Semmelweis University, Amerikai út 57, 1145 Budapest, XIV, Hungary
e-mail: csapokrisztian@gmail.com; idegsebeszet@med.semmelweis-univ.hu

S.D. Ferrara et al. (eds.), *Personal Injury and Damage Ascertainment under Civil Law*, DOI 10.1007/978-3-319-29812-2_13

Precedents can be traced back to Roman law codices, which can be stated regarding other countries as well. The need for compensation of damages appeared at the level of the state very soon: the laws of our first king, St Stephen, contained such provisions already. The chapter of the second book of the decrees on voluntary homicide provides that the perpetrator shall pay the relatives 50 gold coins.

After that, development of the law of damages was tied to criminal law. Compensation was due in an extremely narrow scope, typically to noted persons, if they became the injured party of a crime. It was not before the nineteenth century in the development of law that the terms and institutions of compensation as they are generally known and accepted appeared today.

In addition to pecuniary losses, there was an increasing need for regulation of nonpecuniary damages. The Pain Award can be considered its forerunner; it appeared in the middle of the nineteenth century when the Austrian Civil Code was introduced in Hungary. At that time, it was applied in a narrow scope, mainly in relation to pecuniary loss, and only in the twentieth century did the institution fulfill its purpose.

In the first half of the twentieth century, the need for extension of nonpecuniary damages was constantly a point at issue, but attempts at regulation were able to reach the level of effective law only in a narrow scope; the press law of 1914 was an example for these efforts. On the whole, it can be stated that in the first half of the 1900s, nonpecuniary damages were due in a narrow scope, mainly in cases of personality rights violations.

The slow development was cut short by the Communist regime after 1945: by its Ruling no. III of 1953, the Supreme Court qualified exchange of moral values to money incompatible with the Communist ideology. After that, Act IV of 1959 on civil laws was enacted. This 1959 Code, albeit with major amendments, survived the change of regime, was adjusted to the market economy, and was replaced by the new Civil Code only on 15 March 2014.

In terms of lawmaking, the issue of regulation of pecuniary damages is simpler, since it is easier to stipulate an obligation to pay pecuniary losses that can be measured in money than abstract nonpecuniary losses. For this reason, in the period following 1959, no serious issues were raised concerning causes of pecuniary damages, only nonpecuniary damages remained unsolved, and only the 1977 Amendment introduced nonpecuniary damages, which now—owing to the change of regime—could fully develop. The amendment made nonpecuniary damages conditional upon the aggrieved party being able to prove that—as the legislative text sets it out—"it makes his participation in social life or otherwise his life permanently and seriously difficult, and detrimentally influences the legal person's participation in economic circulation." Judicial practice made efforts to extend the lawmaker's stipulation; in 1981 Directive 16 of the Supreme Court somewhat widened the scope of disadvantages deserving of nonpecuniary damages. Somewhat in the guise of ideology, it declared the importance of nonpecuniary damages: "Protection of pecuniary and nonpecuniary values is the common interest of the members of socialist society." This direction determined compensation practices up to the change of regime.

As the Constitutional Court decision to annul the 1977 Amendment points out, it is not possible to draw a distinction. It can be expected that "civil law should protect persons' personality rights in the same line (with the same weight) as private ownership and other pecuniary rights." Therefore, first, the Supreme Court—right after the change of regime—repealed Directive 16 having represented increasing limitation by then, and after that provisions of the 1977 Amendment to the Civil Code were annulled partly by the Constitutional Court and completely by an amendment to the law.

Pursuant to the Constitutional Court decision 34/1992. (VI. 1.) AB, the provision set out in the part of the text "...if causing damage makes participation of the aggrieved party in social life or otherwise permanently and seriously difficult, and detrimentally influences the legal person's participation in economic circulation" is anti-constitutional, and therefore it abrogates it. The same way, regarding occupational accidents, it annulled a similar provision of the Labor Code. Simultaneously, it simplified the regulation that set out that "the party causing damage shall compensate for the non-pecuniary loss of the aggrieved party."

This Constitutional Court decision has been producing its effect up to now since it provides an interpretation of the term of nonpecuniary damages more adjusted to today's reality and expectations. Up to the present, the interpretation of nonpecuniary damages expounded here is a basis of reference in legal practice. The decision underlines that personality rights are inseparable from constitutional civil liberties.

Liability for nonpecuniary losses is the pecuniary sanction of personality rights. "Non-pecuniary loss has actually no equivalent in money. The function of non-pecuniary damages is to arrange for the rough balancing of the injury suffered by providing a pecuniary service that gives another kind of approximately equivalent advantage for the harm incurred."

13.1.2 The Current Regulation

Following the 1992 Constitutional Court decision and the basically simultaneous 1993 Amendment to the Civil Code, in the past 20 years, there have been no fundamental changes in the practice and regulation of the Hungarian law of damages. On the other hand, in the assessment of compensation regarding specific damage events or accidents, other laws regulating the relevant area must be taken into account. For example, in case of compensation related to traffic accidents and occupational accidents, in addition to other legal rules, the effective provisions of the act on obligatory automobile liability insurance and of the Labor Code must be applied, respectively—in each particular case, as a matter of fact, other legal rules are to be considered to clarify the legal basis.

When writing this chapter, we are living in a transitory period. As from 15 March 2014, Act V of 2013 of the new Civil Code entered into effect. Pursuant to the temporal scope of the legal rule, it shall be applicable only to cases that occur after its entry into effect; so, until former cases have been concluded—owing to actions at law lasting for many years in specific cases—the formerly effective law will apply.

The new system is so recent that until completion of the manuscript, it is not possible to talk about any judicial practice yet. The former and the new system correspond in numerous respects, but also differ fundamentally; it is basically in terms of the new regulation that we present the Hungarian system.

The most important and the most fundamental change is that the new regulation terminates the term of nonpecuniary damages and introduces the term of exemplary damages. At first the two terms seem quite similar; actually, the legislative text enables one to deduce numerous differences.

In terms of its function, the domestic law of damages—corresponding to the legal systems of countries on the Continent—contains preventive and reparative elements. The point of the former is that persons should refrain from causing damage and of the latter that in case they have caused damage, they should compensate it. The punitive element—similarly to the laws of countries on the Continent—does not appear powerfully in the Hungarian system either, although, as a matter of fact, the party causing damage might experience payment of any damages in a given case as punishment.

In the Hungarian system, gaining from damage is prohibited both in case of pecuniary and nonpecuniary loss. It is, of course, an unending problem that providing equivalent pecuniary gain does not imply the same compensation for every person. For example, in practice, loss of a parent means nonpecuniary damages to the amount of approximately HUF 3–5 million (10,000–15,000 euros) to a child aged 18–20, which, in the author's personal view, cannot be equivalent to the harm to everybody.

Pursuant to the Hungarian Civil Code, anyone who causes damage to others shall be obliged to provide reimbursement. So, basically, the party causing damage will be liable when damage occurs that can be attributed and is in casual relation to the chargeable and unlawful impact of the party causing damage, which complies with the requirements of predictability as well. The tort-feasor shall be relieved of liability if they can prove that their conduct was not chargeable. The Hungarian regulation supports the main rule that "all torts shall be unlawful"; the law allows certain exceptions to that, such as specific cases of the aggrieved party's agreement, preventing any wrongful attack, emergency situation, and conduct permitted in a legal regulation. The requirement of predictability means, as set out in the law, that no causality may be established in connection with any damage the tort-feasor did not anticipate or could have not anticipated.

The Hungarian law of damages declares the principle of compensation for damages in full. It is obligatory to recompense any depreciation that occurred in the aggrieved party's property, lost pecuniary advantage, and any costs required to eliminate pecuniary disadvantages that the aggrieved party incurred. Consequently, the damage must be proved: the extent of the amount in pecuniary loss and the effects of the injury suffered in case of exemplary damages and nonpecuniary damages. The Hungarian system does not allocate predetermined amounts to predetermined damages; in theory it is freer than that. Compensation can be claimed under various titles; in accident-related damages, pecuniary titles are, for example, nursing, homework, extra cultural costs, costs of medicine, and extra cost of transport. At the same time, practice has worked out approximate compensation rates belonging to specific nonpecuniary losses, which will be discussed later.

In terms of compensation, first, it might seem a peculiar solution in the new Civil Code that, given the omission of nonpecuniary damages and the introduction of exemplary damages, the rules of the latter are set out in part three on personality rights rather than in part four on liabilities for tort.

In accordance with Sections 2:52-2:53-2:54 (1) of Act V of 2013, the new Civil Code, if an individual is offended in his/her personality rights, he/she shall be entitled to claim for exemplary damages for any nonpecuniary loss caused to him/her. To the terms of the obligation to pay exemplary damages—especially for the determination of the person obliged to pay the damages and the method of apology—the rules on compensation for damages shall be applied with the exception that in order to be considered eligible for exemplary damages, it is not necessary to prove that further disadvantages have occurred over and above the fact of the legal offense. The extent of any exemplary damages shall be determined by the court in consideration of the circumstances of the case—with special regard to the weight of the legal offense, its recurring manner, the extent of the imputation, and the influence of the legal offense on the offended party and his/her surroundings—in a lump sum.

A person, who as a result of the infringement of his/her personality rights suffers a loss, may request compensation for his/her damages in compliance with the rules on liability for damages caused by illegal actions. Personality rights can be asserted personally.

What the legal rule makes clear in the first place is that exemplary damages are not formally compensation, but an institution similar to it. The most important practical novelty of exemplary damages contrary to nonpecuniary damages is that in case of the latter, the aggrieved party had to prove the extent of injury, whereas the new regulation does not require that; the occurrence of the injury is sufficient and disadvantage is presumed by the lawmaker. In given cases this might result in a dramatic increase in the number of loss adjustment proceedings and actions for damages, since in the former system, for example, the majority of insurance companies paid nonpecuniary damages for accident-related injuries only in the event that the injury was permanent. Although it is not necessary to prove the rate of disadvantage suffered, it will play a part in determining the amount, for the rate of exemplary damages can be deliberated by the court already—in this respect with highly extensive discretionary powers—on the basis of the weight of the legal offense, its recurring manner, the extent of the imputation, and the influence of the legal offense on the offended party and his/her surroundings. It is a natural expectation on the side of aggrieved parties, on the grounds of injuries, reduction of way of life, and pains of various extents that they should be granted exemplary damages in proportion to them. This, however, is similar to the determination of the amount of nonpecuniary damages, where similar aspects serve as the basis of the deliberation of the court proceeding in the case.

The punitive function referred to above does not appear in the new regulation either. It can be expected from judicial practice to evaluate aspects other than the above in particular situations of life; for example, whether one or several personality rights have been infringed, whether unlawful business utilization has been implemented through the legal offense, or whether the aggrieved party was also instrumental in the damage, what the financial standing of the aggrieved party and the party infringing rights is?

Exemplary damages are tied to the person; for example, if the aggrieved party dies in the meantime, his/her inheritors cannot lay claim to exemplary damages by virtue of his/her right. If the aggrieved party instituted action in court while still alive, his/her inheritors may step into the claimant's position.

Exemplary damages can be in a lump sum. Maturity will be incurred on the date of the injury, i.e., for example, the accident; and from that time, default interest can be claimed. On the other hand, Hungarian regulations tie default interest to the prime rate, which is currently 2.10 %. In case of compensation proceedings often lasting for years, the present interest rate might in a negligible manner mitigate the stress that the aggrieved client suffers owing to delayed performance. For accidents resulting in tremendous costs, quite often during recovery, wages might be lost. What is more, pursuant to effective regulation, the employer can also terminate the employment relation during the period of being on the sick list. For this reason, it definitely counts when the aggrieved party is given access to his/her money, and the fact that many people are in dire straits is apparent at the time of entering into an arrangement on compensation.

The effects produced by the appearance of exemplary damages are still unknown. The number of lawsuits of low value might rise; yet, the amount of compensation that can be attained in cases of larger personal injuries will probably not increase; the extent of the amount will be presumably adjusted to the rates of the amounts worked out by practice in case of nonpecuniary damages. This is implied by the following statutory provisions: Section 3/A of Act LXII of 2009 on Insurance Against Civil Liability in Respect of the Use of Motor Vehicles, which sets forth that "damage and compensation for damage shall be interpreted also as personality rights violation serving the basis of the claim for exemplary damages and the exemplary damages." Furthermore, Section 55 (2) of Act CLXXVII of 2013 provides that "In case of liability insurance contracts concluded prior to entry into effect of the Civil Code, the aggrieved party can also claim reimbursement of exemplary damages on the basis of the insured event that occurred after entry into effect of the Civil Code, however, the insurance company shall take responsibility instead of the party causing damage only to the extent and under the conditions to the extent and under what conditions it should have been obliged to compensate for non-pecuniary loss before entry into effect of the Civil Code."

In accordance with the rules of common tort by multiple parties, if multiple parties are joint tort-feasors, their liability toward the aggrieved party shall be joint and several; he/she can claim compensation in full from any of the tort-feasors.

Another important and frequently occurring problem is the issue of the instrumentality of the aggrieved party. As its basic case, the act stipulates, first of all, damage prevention, damage elimination, and damage mitigation obligations, and chargeable breach of these obligations might result in the exemption of the party causing damage. The damage caused must be compensated for primarily in proportion to chargeability and secondarily in proportion to instrumentality, and if this cannot be determined either, then it must be split between the tort-feasor and the aggrieved party equally. On the other hand, special rules apply to cases of liability for hazardous operations, as detailed below.

Splitting damage can be regulated by the law in general, and it was fine-tuned by judicial practice. As exemplary damages protect personality rights, which are indivisible (just as in the case of nonpecuniary damages), according to uniform judicial practice, no splitting of damages exists on this basis; yet, the extent of the amount of damages can be reduced in proportion to instrumentality. The situation is different in cases of fatal accidents where the full compensation amount is payable: "in the evaluation of the aggrieved party's claim for damages asserted on his/her own behalf, connected with the death of a relative, application of splitting damages does not lie on the basis that the deceased relative was instrumental in the occurrence of the damage by chargeable conduct" (Pursuant to ÍH 2012/4/168 of the Metropolitan High Court of Justice). So, for various reasons, in case of death, practice works toward damages in full to be provided for relatives. In the same way, splitting of damages will be different from the general rule when the person partly liable for the damage is a person doli incapax, e.g., a minor. In this case, he/she will be liable only in exceptional cases; yet, his/her career or the person supervising him/her can be liable instead of him/her, if he/she cannot prove exculpation. Another frequent case of splitting damages is when a passenger in a car does not use a safety belt and suffers injury. In case of damages owing to accident-related injuries so incurred, in legal practice, 80–20 % splitting of damages have become generally accepted, encumbering the insurance company to a greater extent. The reason for that is that it is also the driver's responsibility not to set out with a passenger without a fastened safety belt; on the other hand, the passenger can be expected to be aware of the consequences of failure to use the belt (Supreme Court BH2008.61).

Similarly to solutions generally accepted in other countries, liability for hazardous operations means a special scope of responsibility, both in the former and the currently effective regulation. The law does not define hazardous operations; according to judicial practice, "only such activities can be made subject to the scope of liability for hazardous operations where in the course of pursuing them occurrence of a relatively low rate of irregularity or low rate of culpability of the person carrying out the activity might result in serious damage or the development of an emergency situation that threatens the life, body and health and property of a larger number of people at the same time" (Metropolitan High Court of Justice ÍH 2012/2/76).

In accordance with the general rule of liability for hazardous operations in the Civil Code, irrespective of culpability, damage shall be reimbursed by the party that engages in an activity involving a particular hazard. This party must prove his/her exemption, which can occur when the damage was induced by circumstances beyond their control and outside the scope of activity involving a critical hazard. In these cases, splitting of damage will be different as well: on the one hand, he/she shall not recompense damage as long as it is derived from the aggrieved party's chargeable conduct. On the other hand, however, when deliberating splitting of damage, the particularly hazardous nature of any activity must be taken into account and charged to the operator. In case of a person doli incapax being instrumental in the damage, splitting damage will not be allowed; yet, the operator of the hazardous operation will have the right to counterclaim toward the carer; in other words, they can claim reimbursement of the damage as defined in accordance with chargeability of the person doli incapax. In case of coincidence of hazardous plants, operators shall be obliged to reimburse damage in proportion to chargeability, and in the absence thereof, compensation shall be the obligation of the party in whose activity involving a particular hazard the irregularity of which leads to the occurrence of the damage. In practice, liability for hazardous operations results in compensation proceedings that are much more favorable to the aggrieved party; yet, the period of limitation is only 3 years, contrary to the general 5-year limitation period.

In addition to substantive law rules, we intend to refer also to certain procedural law solutions, which can be used by the aggrieved parties of accidents. Act XCIII of 1990 on Duties ensures the right to claim expenses in cases of compensation of damage caused to the person's life, body, and health or damage to his property where the person's life, body, and health were in danger as well. This means that it is not obligatory to discharge the cost of institution of action at law in advance; it will be paid at the conclusion of the lawsuit by the party losing the case. Furthermore, the aggrieved parties can seek partial or full exemption from expenses on a social basis. This is a great relief because in accident-related compensation actions, the court uses experts as well, and advancing or paying their fees might constitute an excessive burden to lots of aggrieved parties under the conditions prevailing in Hungary.

Finally, a few words should be said about the issue of a matter judged, *res iudicata*. The fact that damage is due upon its occurrence also means that thereby the assertion of further compensation claims even after a final decision is not ruled out. It might occur, for example, that the court passes a sentence with respect to certain titles, but a later deterioration in conditions (e.g., amputation of an injured leg carried out after a few years) generates new compensation claims. In such cases, as a matter of fact—in the absence of any arrangement—new court action can lie as well. Also, the damage of the aggrieved party's relatives asserted on their own behalf in a given concluded compensation case will not be considered a matter judged—if it was not touched by the sentence of the concluded case or the parties' arrangement.

Furthermore, it is necessary to mention the weight of forensic experts' opinions in accident-related compensation actions. In accident-related compensation actions, the court can pass proper sentence when the opinion of the medicolegal experts or psychologist experts also supports the extent of the injury. General judgment of experts in practice is good; there is no doubt about their independence. The parties to the action at law are entitled to make comments on specific statements of the expert opinion, and it is on this basis that the court can decide in favor of requesting specification, in addition to the expert opinion, to which call the experts must respond within the deadline. The parties themselves can submit an expert opinion; its weight can be different in the relevant case, but in general private expert opinions, only the party's plea will be considered; yet it might be suitable for attaining that the appointed expert withdraw, specify, or supplement their opinion unfavorable to the party.

13.2 Identification and Description of Medicolegal Expert's Qualifications

Evaluation of accident-related injuries is carried out in various, administrative, criminal, and civil proceedings.

Accidents involving personal injury (traffic accidents, occupational accidents) are examined by the police in the first step and the seriousness of the injury suffered (which is an indispensable condition of criminal accountability) by medicolegal experts. The initial expert opinion is made within a short time, a few months after the accident, mostly on the basis of medical documents. The final expert opinion—provided that the initial opinion holds that permanent disability or serious deterioration of health might develop in the person having suffered the accident—is made on the basis of personal examination of the injured/aggrieved party half/one year after the end condition has fully developed. Determination of the seriousness of the injury and declaration of permanent disability and serious deterioration of health are subject to special qualification (in forensic medicine or health insurance); however, often specialists possessing a certificate of clinical examination (e.g., traumatologists) must be involved. In later stages of criminal proceedings, in general, expert opinions made in the investigation phase are used.

In the loss adjustment procedure carried out by the insurance company proceedings and civil law actions, again medicolegal experts proceed, who most often hold qualifications in forensic medicine or health insurance.

The legal regulation applicable to medicolegal experts is highly composite since, in addition to special legal rules applying to experts, the three major procedural law codices also contain provisions pertaining to experts, in accordance with peculiar features of specific procedures.

Act XLVII of 2005 on Forensic Expert Activity entered into effect on 1 January 2006; prior to that statute level regulation regarding expert activity was set out only in the procedural law codices. Enactment of the Expert Act was followed by numerous implementation decrees at the level of both government decrees and ministerial decrees; so, today an extensive body of legal rules covers this area.

The regulation extends to the conditions of becoming a medicolegal expert, the types of expert institutes, experts' rights and obligations, appointment of experts, content elements of expert opinions, expert's fee, experts' mandatory membership in chambers, and, what is more, the minimum physical conditions for the medicolegal expert's activity.

Nevertheless, the basic pillar of expert activity is constituted primarily by procedural law codices (Code of Civil Procedure, Act on Criminal Procedural Law, Act on Rules of Administrative Procedure) since it is they who determine in what cases experts must be used and who can and who cannot proceed as an expert (rules of exclusion). It is somewhat at variance from each other how procedural law codices regulate the issues regarding appointment of experts in criminal proceedings, in civil law actions, and in administrative procedures. Furthermore, the court can appoint medicolegal experts in so-called out-of-court procedures; what is more, experts can be appointed in notarial procedures and during preliminary production of evidence before the notary public. The point of the latter is that it is possible to appoint an expert, even when no proceedings are yet in progress; this expert opinion will operate in later court proceedings in terms of procedural law as if the expert had been appointed by the court. This has significance in two respects: in the cases where the client wants an expert to record their condition before the proceedings and in the cases where the client is uncertain whether it is worth instituting court proceedings and will undertake its costs only if the preliminary expert opinion supports his/her standpoint.

The duty of the medicolegal expert is to help the work of administration of justice, to determine the state of facts in court and authority proceedings, and to decide the professional issue by their expert opinion made by using the results of the development of science and technology. Experts can be used upon appointment by the court, the public prosecutor's office, the police, and other authority determined in legal rule or on the basis of assignment (invitation) by a private party.

Both in criminal proceedings and civil law court and out-of-court proceedings, experts can be used if special expertise is required for determining or judging the fact to be proved.

Experts are used by appointment. In the resolution on appointment of an expert, it is necessary to specify the subject of the expert examination and the questions to be answered by the expert, the documents, and objects to be handed over to the expert and the deadline for submitting the expert opinion. In accordance with both civil and criminal proceedings, as a general rule, one expert must be used; appointment of several experts is usually required only when this is made necessary by the character and complexity of the examination; what is more, in civil law actions, the procedural law act expressly sets forth that several experts can be appointed only in the event that different professional issues arise.

13.2.1 Organization System of Experts

Primarily the following can be appointed as experts—either in criminal proceedings or in civil law actions:

- Medicolegal expert included in the list of experts
- Business association authorized to issue expert opinion
- Expert institute
- Public body, institute, and organization determined in legal rule, with respect to certain professional issues set out in legal rule
- Exceptionally, ad hoc expert

The list of experts is kept by the Ministry of Justice; it includes natural person experts, expert institutes, and expert companies (business associations).

A person can be a medicolegal expert if he/she:

- Is capable of proceeding under the law and is not barred from public affairs
- Has no criminal record and is not barred from practicing any occupation that excludes medicolegal expert's activity or an activity in line with their special area
- Holds a qualification determined for specific special areas, complying with the relevant area and—in the absence of any provisions in legal rules to the contrary—has at least 5-year experience in the special area from acquisition of the qualification
- Assumes the obligation to fulfill appointments by authorities, except for cases set out in legal rule
- Has passed the law examination necessary for becoming a medicolegal expert, organized by the Ministry of Public Administration and Justice
- Is a member of the chamber of medicolegal experts of their domicile, and—if membership in a chamber is required by legal rule for pursuing the activity—is a member of the professional chamber operating in their special area

The inclusion of medicolegal experts against whom criminal proceedings are in progress is prohibited, except for cases of private prosecution or subsidiary private prosecution.

The relevant special areas where classification can be applied for and the conditions of qualifications required for that are set out in legal rule.

Classification of special areas within the scope of medicolegal experts is adjusted primarily to the system of board examination, more specifically, to basic specialist's qualifications (inclusion in the list of experts cannot be applied for in the special areas, e.g., nephrology and plastic surgery, because they can be acquired only as a specialist's qualification secondary to other qualifications).

The determination of the rate of health damage is carried out with the participation, in the first place, of forensic medicine specialists and health insurance specialists as well as those holding a certificate of examination in forensic psychiatry.

Specialization in forensic medicine takes 60 months. The requirement at the end of curriculum is to have performed at least 300 autopsies with histology and to have given expert opinion in at least 200 different clinical forensic cases.

Specialization in forensic psychiatry takes 36 months for certified psychiatrists who have at least 3 years of experience. The training consists of mandatory courses and practical training.

There is a relatively new specialization called insurance medicine, which was introduced approximately 10 years ago. Training is provided by the forensic medicine departments of the universities. Physicians specialized in all clinical disciplines can fulfill the course requirements and sit for the board exams, which consist of an oral and a practical exam. The training period is 24 months. As a result of the training, experts having interdisciplinary knowledge in the area of social insurance and business insurance will be available who:

- Hold specialist qualifications and have clinical experience in a field of medicine
- Know the systems of social insurance and business insurance and have work experience in these fields
- Have general legal and special legal knowledge in health care, social insurance, business insurance, and social allowances

The experts of the new area having appeared within medicolegal expert activity are used by courts primarily in compensation cases.

Like every physician, specialists in legal medicine are required to maintain their knowledge through continuing education. Compulsory courses organized or accredited by the universities have to be fulfilled (attendance and exams), while scientific achievements and publications are awarded extra credits. Compliance with continuing education requirements is rigorously controlled—lack of compliance results in losing the right to exercise the profession.

Knowledge of forensic medicine, health insurance, and law constitutes an important part of the graduate training of medical students, under a 1-year, mandatory course to be closed by sitting for an exam. The syllabus is identical in all of the four universities.

13.2.2 Expert Institutes

Forensic expert institutes can be established and terminated by the minister of justice or in agreement with him/her by another minister; this system is the Network of Forensic Science Institutes. Currently, the network has 12 members nationwide. All of them include experts specialized in various areas, such as medicolegal experts and health insurance experts.

Forensic medicine departments of the universities also qualify as expert institutes. All of the four medical universities have their own independent forensic medicine institute; the largest one is the Forensic and Insurance Medicine Institute of the Semmelweis University in Budapest.

An expert institute operates as a budgetary body, with the main activity to fulfill appointments by courts and authorities. Expert institutes shall fulfill appointments falling within their main activity prior to carrying out any other activity.

The head of the expert institute designates the expert to proceed in the relevant case. The proceeding medicolegal expert cannot be given instructions concerning the content of the expert opinion.

Medicolegal experts employed by the expert institute issue the expert opinion under their own professional responsibility, however, on behalf of the institute and use the stamp of the institute. By his/her countersigning, the head of the institute certifies that the expert opinion was made within the scope of activity of the institute and in compliance with procedural law rules. The expert opinion is signed by the expert; the expert opinion must indicate the name and special area of the forensic expert who made the opinion. Only employees of the expert institute entered in the list of experts can carry out forensic expert activity.

If the court or authority appoints an expert institute as expert, then reasons for exclusion applicable both to the expert and the head of the expert institute shall be taken into consideration. If any reason for exclusion against the head of the institute exists, none of the forensic experts operating at the institute can issue an expert opinion.

13.2.3 Board of Forensic Medicine Experts of the Health Scientific Council

The Board of Forensic Medicine Experts of the Health Scientific Council fulfills a determining role within the medical expert activity; its history goes back to the period of the Habsburg Monarchy (*Constitution Criminalis Theresiana*, 1768). Originally, its duty was to issue an opinion in cases where the opinions of the experts appointed by the court were fundamentally different from each other, and for this reason, the court could not decide the case; in these cases, it was basically the opinion of the Board that was decisive. The institute has survived up to now; however, its role has significantly changed; its opinion is an expert opinion, just like the opinion of any other expert or expert institute appointed by the court (it does not have priority in relation to a procedural law position); since 2005, the structure has also been transformed and the body proceeds in 3–5 member commissions.

13.2.4 Expert Business Associations

As from 2006 forensic expert activity can also be carried out in Hungary by business associations, where more than 50 % of the members are forensic experts and who were entered into the list of experts. In addition to having forensic expert members, the company can also employ forensic experts. The member or employee of the company issues the expert opinion under their own professional responsibility, on behalf of the company. However, the member or employee can issue an expert opinion on behalf of the company only in the special areas regarding which they are included in the list of experts registered for such an area. The expert opinion is signed by the expert; it must indicate the name and special area of the forensic expert who makes the expert opinion. The expert proceeding in the case is designated by the chief executive officer of the company.

13.2.5 *Ad Hoc Expert*

An expert who does not belong to any of the above categories can be appointed only exceptionally, solely when experts or institutes registered in the list of experts are not available. They are called ad hoc experts. It is a special difficulty for the entity appointing the ad hoc expert that the list of experts does not help them in selecting the expert or judging their expertise. Furthermore, an ad hoc expert, as a matter of fact, does not have the special legal knowledge or expertise that is absolutely necessary for submitting an expert opinion complying both in form and content with the requirements.

13.3 Ascertainment Methodology

13.3.1 *Collection of Circumstantial and Clinical Data*

During appointments by authorities or out-of-court proceedings, it is the obligation of the entity appointing/assigning the expert to provide full documentation on the precedents of the incident and medical documents. When the documentation necessary for making the expert opinion is not available or further documents are needed, the expert can request them from the entity appointing them, except when the entity appointing/assigning the expert consents to the acquisition of the documents directly from the aggrieved party. (In cases under criminal proceedings, as a matter of fact, it is the authority that obtains all the necessary documents and medical documents; the appointed forensic expert requests them from the health institute that provides service to the injured party.)

Before the expert examination, the proceeding expert shall inform the examined person of the matter regarding which the expert examination is carried out and the aim and process of the examination and introduces the proceeding experts by name. The expert asks for oral consent in criminal cases and written consent in civil law actions for the examination. In the event that the person examined refuses the examination, the expert will record this fact and the examination terminates.

13.3.2 Medical Case History

In the expert examination, a detailed medical case history must be taken with respect to both the person examined and his/her family.

Concerning brothers and sisters, it is necessary to ask questions about the following:

- What illnesses did they have, and if deceased, what was the cause of death?
- Is there any genetic or chronic disease in the family?
- Have there been any neurological, psychiatric diseases in the family?

Concerning the person examined, it is necessary to ask questions about the following:

- Marital status
- When did he/she conclude marriage; do they have children; how old are they; are they alive or not; what is their occupation; what is their relation to the family; do they live together or separately?
- What diseases are present in the family?

Environmental and social case history

- Does he live together with his wife or live separately; has he divorced?
- What are the housing conditions like; is there a garden; does he carry out gardening alone or with help?

Personality development of the person examined

- Circumstances at birth and development in childhood
- School progress

Occupational case history in the period before the accident:

- Places of work

  Did he take on a job in his elected vocation?
  When did he start working?
  What places of work did he have?
  Did he like his work or choose that vocation only under coercion?

- Impacts at place of work

  Did his disease arise in relation to his work?
  If yes, physical or psychic?
  Were there regular medical control examinations at his place of work or not?
  Were safety-at-work instruments available?

Diseases of the person examined

- Diseases from birth, in childhood and in adulthood
- In-patient periods in hospitals, date, and duration
- Accident-related injuries and occupational accidents, detailed per parts of body

Exact date
Injuries suffered
Residual state
Compensation

- Former operations

Exact date
Character of intervention

Regarding former injuries, we specifically state injuries of the skull and describe them in detail, e.g., faint and duration, if psychic damage has evolved, including residual state.

- Person examined

Use of medicine: regular or ad hoc.
Detailing the relevant diseases.
Stating the starting date of taking the relevant medicine.
We state use of medicine before and after the damage event.

- Hobbies, free-time activities

How frequently and approximately for how long do they engage in leisure activity at home?
What kind of relaxation do they pursue?

- Sports activity

Do they practice sports regularly, in a sports club or only as a hobby?
Approximately how much time do they spend in this activity?
Which frequency: daily, weekly, or monthly?
What sports they practice?

Other questions regard the following:

- Use of consumer goods: Alcohol, drugs, and cigarettes—consumed daily or occasionally.
- Allergy: Stating the date of evolution of possible allergy, we enumerate the types of allergy he has. In this respect, do they use any medicine regularly or occasionally, and what effect do they produce, such as pollen allergy, dust allergy, and animal hair allergy? More specifically, we ask them about medicine allergy.
- Changes in body weight: Have they maintained their body weight, and if it has changed, has it occurred gradually or within a relatively short time and what do they attribute it to?
- Sleeping: In problematic cases, we describe its quality: difficulties in falling asleep (initial insomnia), waking up often, waking in a tired state, etc. And we indicate the efficiency or inefficiency of possible sleep-improving medicines.

We indicate the dominant side of the person in relation to limbs (right handed, right footed or left handed, left footed).

13.3.3 Examination of the Damaging Event

In connection with the relevant event, taking a detailed case history, in which the injured party tells how, in his/her view, the injury happened, during what activity the injury happened, what he/she remembers, and what attendance was he/she given, we record the use of medicine of related present treatments, in addition to every happening related to the damaging event as it is told in the injured party's own words.

We record changes in job features, demands, and skills in detail compared to the period before the injury. First of all, we describe the statements set out in the job description and, compared to them, the eligibility or incapability of the injured party as told by him/her.

Currently existing complaints: we ask questions about and record the complaints of the person examined per organ system. Each time we record the series of events that led to the evolved state.

13.3.4 Systematic Clinical and Medicolegal Visit

Internistic In Hungary medicolegal experts carry out the internal medicine examination, which is for information purposes only. If any disease arises in connection with the damaging event that might influence the evaluation of the damage, then the proceeding expert will refer the examined person to the forensic expert or specialist in the relevant area of internal medicine and will develop his opinion together with such a specialist.

Neurological If there is no alteration implying neurological disease among the documents, then the examination will be carried out by a medicolegal expert, otherwise by a forensic neurologist expert.

In case of damage to the nervous system, the examination must explore the process of disease on the basis of symptoms and complaints. It is necessary to examine the character and outcome of the damage, the extent of the failure of the function that determines the extent of health damage, as well as chances for rehabilitation and the end state.

The process of the examination contains the following:

- Cranial nerves
- Volitional locomotor system, including decrease in muscular strength, distribution of paralysis, tone, trophic disturbances, contractures, superficial and deep reflexes, and pathological reflexes
- Examination of sensory circle

Psychic It is carried out by the forensic psychiatrist, if necessary, by involving a psychologist.

The form of forensic psychiatric expert examination usually corresponds with that of standard psychiatric examinations, but owing to the peculiar aim of the examination, a certain number of its components must be handled more emphatically and must be supplemented by special questions.

The form of recording the data with regard to previous history is basically identical with the form of recording the case history in clinical psychiatric examinations; however, the character of the pathography and the legal issues requires, in certain cases, the highlighting and extension of items.

During exploration, psychopathological alterations are explored again in the form identical with that of clinical examinations. In addition to analysis of the symptoms of the pathography, also in expert examinations, it is very important to get to know the dynamics of the process of disease.

During exploration, it is always necessary to state how the person examined approaches their own disease, whether they correct or maintain their pathological contents during the examination or if dissimulation can be recorded (lack of admission of the disease can make the sufficient cooperation with the patient doubtful).

The analysis of conduct of life (biographical data), which aims at obtaining knowledge of the personality—changes in the human relations of the person examined, their problems, circumstances of life, turning points of their life, etc.—cannot be left out of any expert opinion and is indispensable in certain forms of diseases and their state.

We describe the psychic state (psychopathological analysis) in the usual didactic grouping, underlining psychopathological symptoms by their characterization and valuation. It is desirous to mention the normal findings (e.g., clear conscience, orientation is maintained, etc.), and it is necessary to state in detail the irregularities of conduct as well as cooperation with the examination.

It is absolutely necessary to state the level of the intellect, which can be characterized by the conduct engaged, the terms used, combinations, etc., applied during the exploration. The expert can obtain information on lack of intellectual functions or in case of suspicion of their reduction by causing patients to carry out certain tasks of the thinking examination (Kleist) pattern—through questions focusing on a body of knowledge. And to certify the above, especially in doubtful cases, we carry out the MAVI (Wechsler) test. It is necessary to obtain medical documents on possible former complaints and previous diseases, because knowledge of them might make performance of certain tests unnecessary. Obtaining medical documents in order to avoid "diagnostic errors" is desirous even in cases where in the previous history the examined person reports "serious" symptoms, "lasting diseases," or "hereditary diseases," clearly with the intention to deceive the physician. So, a proper expert opinion includes the documentation of both positive and negative aspects. Obtaining former findings is the duty of the entity ordering or requesting the examination.

It is the expert's task to deliberate what supplementary examinations they consider necessary to support their opinion. The party requesting the examination can also indicate or order the performance of certain supplementary examinations, e.g., EEG and psychological test.

The psychological test can become necessary depending on the expert's tasks. The psychologist expert takes part in examinations with the forensic medicine officer, forensic psychiatrist, or under independent appointment. Their task is to examine psychological components that arise in insurance or nonpecuniary compensation cases.

The questions raised can focus on two groups. They cover actual, direct damages, losses, consequences, and psychologically graspable disadvantages connected with the damaging event (group 1) and those observed on the basis of their experience and appearing in their conduct of life (group 2). In the latter group, the consequences of the damaging event extend to persons who maintain close relations or live in the surroundings of the aggrieved person. The task of the psychological expert is to certify the psychic changes influencing conduct of life, behavior, and efficiency and establish whether these alterations can be connected directly or indirectly with the accident or not. In the evaluation of the data of test examinations, the expert must rely on connections generally accepted and used in clinical practice. Especially important is to compare conduct of life, behavior, and performance data that can be related to cause(s) and can be obtained from the questions put with psychodiagnostic (clinical psychodiagnostic indicators, constellations) results item by item. The psychological expert cannot formulate a diagnosis (diagnoses) in this activity either—only psychopathological syndromes, fundamental psychopathological phenomena, and their consequences in terms of behavior and conduct of life. The expert is allowed to integrate the results of their examination to the diagnoses setup and those contained in the documents.

The dual form of the relevant damages reflected in complaints and their combination will constitute the focal point of examinations and relevant opinions:

- This is a case of psychic alteration that arises in circumscribed or diffuse anatomical injury of the central nervous system during which various forms of mental irregularities (BNO code) can develop. In organically substantiated pathographies, the process might affect various psychic functions to various extents. When putting special questions, the expert should make use of cooperation with the clinical neuropsychologist.
- The experienced event results in permanent or temporary damage that is manifested in psychogenic injuries, which are presumably in direct or indirect causal relation with the damage or loss. These include post-traumatic psychogenic damage, lasting mourning responses, object losses damaging psychic functions and states, and personality reactions generated through conversional or dissociative mechanisms and developed with pathologically elevated awareness of illness.

The expert examination commences by studying the documents, reports, and findings generated in the case and is continued by designing diagnostic procedures applied in clinical psychology in the examination of such cases adapted to the individual case.

Evaluation of the data obtained in the expert examination is carried out in accordance with best practices of clinical psychology but, compared to it, the expert's task can be modified to the extent that, in addition to making psychodiagnostic statements, they must express their opinion on the effects produced by the damage on conduct of life and possibly on their duration. In the evaluation of the data, it is necessary to take account of presumable deviations that might have characterized the state prior to the trauma and compared to which the present state has brought about deterioration in quality of life.

Variables that can be proposed in estimates of durations:

- Length of time passed between the date of the trauma and the examination
- Extent of improvement that can be reconstructed from test data during this period
- Nature of the interventions used in the past period
- Gravity of the alterations of the image obtained in the examination

In the evaluation of data, the duration of estimated change is in proportion to the length of time passed between the date of the trauma and the examination. As an addition, it is possible to make a proposal on the date of the following control examination.

In the examination of children, it can be a separate task to make the inhibiting or compensating development effects of the damage probable. This possible task is individual to such an extent that it is not possible to formulate general guidelines for it and the expert, in addition to thorough knowledge of the case, can rely on his complex developmental psychology expertise.

During examinations, experts often face weaker forms of mental deficiency, rarely their more serious forms. In the pathography of more serious mental deficiency—if no test examination is carried out—difference of opinion rarely occurs. However, some consider weaker forms of mental deficiency debility, while others state in their opinions that the intelligence is at the lower border of the normal domain.

Special considerations are deserved to the forensic experts' opinion on psychic pathographies related to traumas. Injuries of varied seriousness, especially injuries to the skull and brain, are often followed by psychic alterations that might require an expert opinion. With the increase in the number of accidents and relevant injuries, expert opinions on these diseases with outcome are requested more and more often.

We apply the above-described general psychiatric and psychological examination procedures in the cases set out below:

- Acute stress reaction
- Post-traumatic stress disturbance
- Psychogenic blurred state
- Post-traumatic psychosis
- Other psychiatric diseases that can be connected with trauma

Osteoarticular and Musculoskeletal Specific (Local Examination of the Injured Area/Areas)
There are some general rules:

- In injuries to limbs, except for special cases (amputation, stiffening of the joints), we examine the healthy part on the opposite side as well and examine and describe the functional results of the injured limb in comparison with the healthy limb.
- We examine articular functions on lower limbs by loading and without loading.
- We examine measures of the circumference of extremities in identical distances measured from fixed anatomical points.
- We can determine differences in length of extremities objectively only at identical distance from fixed anatomical points—usually on the basis of measuring carried out several times.
- We examine articular motion limits both by active and passive methods. (Aggravation is an important criterion, in order to screen simulation.)
- We control function disturbances complained about by the injured party by a minimum of one but possibly several examination methods in order to be able to check their confirmation/exclusion safely.
- In case of narrowing of movement, we must by all means examine possibilities of para-coordination that can be implemented by bordering joints, by which the extent of functional damages can be reasonably reduced.
- We repeat examinations that cannot be made objectively (sensory disturbances, pressing power examination) several times during the examination and thereby approximate real values that can be considered as objective as possible.

Locomotor Surgery Examinations Cover the Following Parts of Body
It includes the following:

- Face and skull
- Neck, back, and loin spine
- Extremities, lower and upper
- Chest and pelvis/abdomen
- Genitals

Locomotor surgery examinations include radiological (RTG, CT, MR, UH) picture examination and analysis of the injured party, which is a requirement of sitting for an exam in the Hungarian and European International Board Examinations (identification of injuries, evaluation of surgical treatments, evaluation of residual symptoms, etc.).

If necessary, involvement of a radiologist consultant doctor can be reasonable.

13.3.5 Additional Investigations

In Hungary, clinical examinations (additional X-ray, CT, etc.) cannot be carried out by medicolegal experts. They can make proposals on additional clinical examinations, which can be carried out solely with the examined person's consent, even noninvasive examinations (however, if the person declining the examination bears the burden of proof, he might fail in its claim). In view of the fact that examinations exclusively for medicolegal purposes are not covered by social security, the expert must give reasons for the necessity of the examinations and must identify the organization or individual that will reimburse the costs of the examinations to be carried out.

In addition to special areas not mentioned above, the specialist examination of sight and hearing has a great significance, which is carried out by involvement of a specialist or consultant doctor specialized in the relevant area.

Evaluation of damages is based on objective measuring, although it is often difficult to eliminate aggravation, but experience and some maneuvers help to make values objective.

13.4 Evaluation Criteria

The evaluation criteria for damages have been worked out in recent years and now we are in the phase of improving the system. In the presentation of evaluation criteria, reference will be often made to the table, which is attached in full.

Health damage means a state of the components (anatomical structures), physiological functions of the organism different from the standards of the average population, i.e., lack, reduction, or distortion thereof. The degree of damage is determined by the rate of deviation from population standards. Deviation from norms of population can be slight, medium, or serious.

In the evaluation of the damage, efforts should be made to achieve *objectivity*. Evaluation is based on various *health documents.*

Determination of the degree of damage in percentage represents a comparative rather than absolute value and serves to supply information on changes in the person's competence and activity.

In order to differentiate medical treatments, services and legal rules require that impairments, activity limitations, and participation restrictions should be ranked into *categories* that can be characterized in numbers, by proportional numbers. On the scale, value 0 % represents the state free from damages and 100 % the state of being fully damaged. The damage and loss of function can be complete or partial. *Partial damage* and *alterations* require expression as a percentage:

1. No problem, if any, not significant 0–4 %
2. Slight (small, of low extent) problem 5–24 %
3. Moderate (average, tolerable) problem 25–49 %

4. Serious (of great extent, significant) problem 50–95 %
5. Full problem 96–100 %

By proportional numbers, on the basis of damages to specific parts of the body, organs, and organ systems, it is possible to determine the degree of **health damage to the total organism**:

0. No considerable health damage to total organism 0–4 %
1. Slight (small) health damage to total organism 5–9 %
2. Low extent health damage to total organism 10–24 %
3. Average (tolerable) health damage to total organism 25–49 %
4. Great extent (significant) health damage to total organism 50–79 %
5. Full or almost full health damage to total organism 80–99 %

Disability is limitation of a person's activity.

It applies to the activity in the performance of which the person damaged in his/her health is limited.

The WHO definition of disability "is any restriction or lack of ability to perform an activity within the range considered normal for a human being."

Disability can be temporary, permanent, *partial*, or *complete*, when determined in terms of quality. In relation to quantity, it is expressed as *slight*, *moderate*, *average*, or *serious*.

Disabilities can be differentiated on the basis of activity limitations as well: self-sufficiency limitation (self-sufficiency disability), place change limitation (movement disability), sight limitation (sight disability), hearing limitation (hearing disability), etc.

Disability is usually interpreted as a limitation of basic activities. This restriction can be eliminated in a great number of cases by aids and/or proper transformation of the environment. If this cannot be achieved, disability might be realized in participation restriction (handicap).

A damaged and disabled person who is able to perform his/her task without or through transformation of the (work) environment does not belong to persons with participation restriction (handicap).

Handicap is restriction of participation in society, a disadvantage for a given individual resulting from an impairment or disability that limits the fulfillment of a role (determined by age, gender, and economic, social, and cultural factors) that is normal for that individual.

Restriction of participation in one of the most fundamental activities of society. *Performance of work* is defined most appropriately by the term *change in ability to work*:

Consequently, handicap is not the direct outcome of damage and disability, but the result of interaction between the disabled person and their narrower or wider (natural and social) environment.

Opinion on and categorization of the degree of the damage and disability and reduction of ability to work cannot be made in a fully objective form.

The aim is to make the evaluation as *objective* as practically possible and use comparable *standard* data.

The *aim is that judgment should be based on identical procedural and judgment methods and comparable, identical content and concept systems*. At the same time, the aim is to prevent abuses and unfounded decisions.

As generally accepted in practice, when judging the degree of the damage, we record the pre-accident psychic and physical status on the basis of data of precedents. We describe what former hereditary/acquired, degenerative alterations of it can be certified. Accurate separation of the former accident/medical intervention and the damage in the action at law and their distinct evaluation constitute an important part of the opinion. Furthermore, description of former acute or chronic psychiatric diseases and evaluation of possible administration of medicine can be necessary in the opinion.

In addition to the account given by the examined person, we determine the degree of health damage by using the relevant documents and findings of the expert's examinations. Regarding the quantification of temporary and permanent damages, the Barèmes are not used; however, evaluation is helped by a table system. This has been made primarily for establishing social security services related to health damages; 104 evaluation tables in great details regarding 15 disease groups are available. It is on the basis of them that it is necessary to determine the degree of partial health damages in accordance with the client's organism, which should be then added up by the degressive method defined in legal rules, and this will produce the degree of health damage to the total organism. The degree of health damage to the total organism—in addition to other criteria, e.g., eligibility for rehabilitation—considerably determines what type and what amount of social security services the client will be provided with (health damage to total organism below 40 %, i.e., health condition over 60 %, gives title to no service).

It is disputed whether this table evaluation system could or should be used in accident-related compensation proceedings. Some hold the position that with minor modifications, the system should be used as a professional rule, while others argue that the tables have significance merely in terms of social security services and that percentage values related to specific health damages cannot be used in liability proceedings (e.g., accident-related compensation). This professional dispute has not been decided yet.

In the establishment of health damage, special attention must be paid to diseases of natural origin that called for medical intervention in the relevant part of body (e.g., exposing the abdomen owing to ileus 1–2 years before the accident that caused rupture of the spleen), or the limb had already been injured in a former accident (conservatively treated distal-third leg fracture incurred 5 years prior to open leg fracture).

Detailed description of the damaging event and the injury, that is, the description of accident mechanism and circumstances of injury, is required:

- For unconscious clients or injured parties with commotion, the place, date, and circumstances of the accident must be stated on the basis of the account given by the staff transporting the patient and accompanying witnesses or by quoting from accident minutes taken on the spot or documents of hospital treatment (discharge slip). Data can be specified during personal examination of the injured party.

- A detailed survey of the specialist's diagnostic descriptions (X-ray, CT, MR, sonography) is required because sometimes there might be discrepancies between summary pathographies and listed diagnoses. Presumed diagnoses are stated at the time of recording, which are not confirmed later on by instrumental investigations, but remain in the list, and then the uncertified diagnoses will continue to be set out in later repeated recordings and control examinations. Another type of error, injuries recognized subsequently, following the recording, and during treatment, will not be indicated among diagnoses of the treatment. It is absolutely necessary to redress them when compiling the forensic expert's documentation.
- It is fully proposed to check imager diagnostic expert opinions on the basis of the images in order to eliminate possible errors. In doubtful cases, it is necessary to involve a radiologist consultant doctor for proving or eliminating presumed but unproven fractures, other alterations, etc.
- In case of treatment at an intensive care unit, diagnostic and therapeutic activity will be carefully analyzed. In doubtful cases consultant doctors should be involved.
- Comparison of the description of surgical operations and findings of imagers helps to explore the origin of possible therapeutic complications (e.g., owing to improper reposition in surgical stabilization of fracture, stabilization is of decreased value; later on pseudarthrosis will develop). For lack of surgical knowledge, postoperative X-ray descriptions often fail to describe surgery-related deficiencies, and therefore causal relations of later-appearing disturbances in recovery, infectious complications, etc., will not be stated in the expert opinion.
- The findings of control examinations, the patient's subjective complaints, and the results of the expert opinion often differ. (In the description of the control examination, the therapist records more favorable results about the degree of real function, the rate of recovery is slower, and less favorable results can be noticed during the specialist's examination. To clarify these contradictions is clearly the expert's responsibility.)
- Examination documents of rehabilitation institutes (discharge slip, notes of outpatient treatments, functional results measurable in initial and end state). They contain valuable data on the objective results of the treatment, time proportionate residual states, and estimated date of the development of the end state.
- Poly-trauma, after poly-traumatization preliminary examination, was carried out 2–6 months following the injury, and expert examination performed after development of the end state 1 or 2 years later has special significance. Comparison of results makes it easier to judge partial damages more realistically, determine the rate of allowances, evaluate the condition of health and the reduction of ability to work.

Upon development of the end state, we must specify the degree of damage, the developed structural change, and to what extent the latter influences operation of the person's organism and must declare what functions the person has lost, partially or wholly.

Furthermore, it is necessary to determine the possibilities for the person's participation in transport and movement in life in general, including his/her movement limitation. It is necessary to declare to what extent he/she is able to support him/herself or the minor under his/her supervision and in what activities he/she needs help.

Furthermore, it is necessary to declare to what extent the person's life before the damage differs and what quality change has occurred at the time of the examination.

In the evaluation of damages, the expert must take account of the criteria set out below, i.e., regular questions put concerning residual symptoms in court and out-of-court proceedings:

- Has the diagnostic and therapeutic treatment been right or, owing to default, has the end state become worse than the possible outcome?
- Can ability to work and quality of life be improved in the future and to what extent and by what method and aids?
- In what category and duration and to what extent is it reasonable to grant allowance?

The items below are categories used for evaluating residual symptoms of damages, where temporary or permanent mitigation of damages is reasonable: care; full-scope nursing; partial nursing; all kinds of household work; average and hard household work; average and hard agricultural work; straining every nerve; moving with escort, without escort; improving food; medicine costs; therapeutic aids, auxiliary materials; medical gymnastics, physiotherapy treatments; cultural extra costs; cost of washing; cost of heating, lighting; and telephone costs.

In accordance with the degree of the damage, the expert must evaluate the health damage to the total organism arising from the accident or injury, the reduction of ability to work arising from the accident or injury, and the percentage rate of change in condition of health and also provide bases for the judge to determine the amount of nonpecuniary damages and exemplary damages.

Furthermore, it is necessary to make a statement on medical and occupational rehabilitation, concerning whether it is possible or not; if it is, how long it takes and under what conditions it can be carried out and what results can be expected?

The Hungarian law of damages declares the principle of compensation for damages in full—no less and no more. This means that the aggrieved party is entitled to compensation for his/her damages in full, and so-called gaining from damage—pecuniary advantage acquired through compensation—is prohibited. It also follows from this that for reimbursement of losses arising from accident-related injuries that cannot be defined in money, there is no cogent evaluation system at the level of a norm to be followed by every insurance company. While in contract-based policies the parties can stipulate such terms, i.e., how much the insurance company should pay for specific items in case of accident, with regard to compensation for damages regulated under the law, no evaluation criteria are determined for the amounts to be paid. In other words, a spine injury, a permanent ankle injury, and a pelvis bone fracture in terms of nonpecuniary loss/exemplary damages might result in compensation of different amounts for relevant aggrieved parties according to different human fates or situations of life.

Nevertheless, to make the compensation system predictable and consistent, judicial practice and insurers' arrangement practice connect compensation with the degree of health damage suffered through the accident. This is, of course, not automatic because, e.g., mental injury incurred in addition to bodily injury or a more significant than usual decrease in quality of life might increase the amount of compensation, while it works toward reduction of the amount when the relevant person's approach to the given damage is less tragic. For example, concerning loss of a relative, the quality of the relation also counts; in case of a deceased brother or sister, an adult brother or sister who lived with him/her in the same household and those who live in another country, far away, with whom they rarely speak and only by phone will not receive the same amount.

In most of the cases, generally accepted practice in compensation for damages sets the rate of nonpecuniary damages or exemplary damages to the rate of health damage to total organism—reduction of ability to work arising from accident. The two values do not exactly overlap, but this connection means that 1 % of health damage to total organism/reduction of ability to work arising from accident suffered as a result of accident calculated by approximately HUF 100,000–200,000 (equivalent to 320–640 euros). Multiplier produces the amount of compensation that can be expected from the given case by virtue of exemplary damages or nonpecuniary damages depending on whether the arrangement is made in court or out of court. As a matter of fact, this is a kind of brute force rule but it is true for most of the cases. On the other hand, the higher we go, the more this rate is upset; e.g., in case of vigilant coma or complete paralysis, the attainable amount can be even higher. That is why that in actions at law, appointed medical experts have to make a statement on the percentage value of health damage to total organism/reduction of ability to work arising from accident as well. Yet, further difficulties have been caused in the system by the fact that the bases of evaluation in terms of health damage to total organism/reduction of ability to work arising from accident are regulated in law, and therefore various medical experts can define almost identical values; the legal background of evaluation is, nevertheless, tied to the social allowance system. So, when in 2013 the system was reregulated and percentage values were cut, this led to problems in loss adjustment. For example, although loss of smell and sense of gustation represented 10 % value in the old and 0 % in the new system, it does not mean that no compensation is due. These contradictions will be presumably solved by practice; however, differences between the old and new evaluation criteria are causing problems.

In addition to the above system of tort, the evaluation system of medicolegal experts can be determined by specific insurance contracts as well. If the insurance company's payment obligation is incurred under the contract concluded between the insurance company and the client, then the evaluation criteria, the amount allocated to specific injuries or health damages, can, as a matter of fact, vary from contract to contract.

Below are listed some general bibliographic sources useful to deepen the issue. They are not reported within the text as they are no cited references.

Bibliography

1. Dósa Á, Hanti P (2012) Egészségkárosodáshoz kapcsolódó ellátások (Benefits related to health demages). Complex Kiadó, Budapest
2. Dósa Á (2010) Az egészségügyi szolgáltatók kártérítési felelőssége. (Civil liability of health care providers.) Complex Kiadó, Budapest
3. Juhász F (ed) (2004) Irányelvek a funkcióképesség, a fogyatékosság és megváltozott munkaképesség véleményezéséhez (Guidelines of determining disability and reduction of ability to work). Medicina Könyvkiadó Zrt., Budapest
4. Second book of the Decrees of King St Stephen. http://www.1000ev.hu/index.php?a=3&param=274
5. Fézer T (2011) Judgement of non-pecuniary (moral) injuries in civil law. HVG-Orac
6. Bleier J, Certain issues of judgement of claims for compensation of non-pecuniary loss in civil law actions
7. http://fovarosiitelotabla.birosag.hu/sites/fovarosiitelotabla.birosag.hu/files/field_attachment/1_2013._pk_velemeny_-_vitaindito_anyag.doc
8. Division opinion of the Civil Division of the Metropolitan High Court of Justice adopted by its resolution no. 1/2013. (VI. 17.) on certain issues of judgement of claims for compensation of non-pecuniary damages/exemplary damages arising in civil law actions
9. Directive 16 of the Supreme Court on liability for non-pecuniary damages (1981)

Chapter 14
Methods of Ascertainment of Personal Damage in Lithuania

Romas Raudys

Abstract The chapter illustrates the historical, judicial, and juridical framework of personal injury assessment and compensation in Lithuania, describing the expert's qualification and competences and detailing the ascertainment methodology and criteria of evaluation utilized for identifying, describing, and estimating any personal injury, its temporary and permanent consequences, and the causal value/link between the event and the injury and between the injury and the impairment/disability.

14.1 Historical and Juridical Overview

After the restoration of independence of the Republic of Lithuania on 11 March 1990, 16 January 1992 may be considered the beginning of the reform of Lithuania's court system, when the Supreme Council—Restoration Seimas adopted the Law "On Amending and Supplementing Some Articles of the Provisional Basic Law." At the constitutional level, a four-level court system, previously existing in the interwar Lithuania, was restored. Article 113, paragraph 2, of the Provisional Basic Law provides that the courts of the Republic of Lithuania shall be comprised of the Supreme Court of Lithuania, the Court of Appeal of Lithuania, and regional and local courts.

Essential changes within the judicial system are associated with the adoption of our country's new Constitution in the referendum held on 25 October 1992. It is in the Constitution that the principles related to the judicial power and recognized in the Universal Declaration of Human Rights, the European Convention for the Protection of Human Rights and Fundamental Freedoms, and the Council of Europe Committee of Ministers' recommendations, including the crucial importance of the independence of judges, courts, and the overall judicial system, are enshrined.

R. Raudys (✉)
State Forensic Medicine Service of Lithuania, Mykolas Romeris University,
Didlaukio str. 86E, Vilnius 08303, Lithuania
e-mail: romas.raudys@vtmt.lt

S.D. Ferrara et al. (eds.), *Personal Injury and Damage Ascertainment under Civil Law*, DOI 10.1007/978-3-319-29812-2_14

The Constitution enshrines a four-level court system which previously existed in interwar Lithuania and was reestablished in the Provisional Basic Law. Herewith, the judicial system, reestablished at the constitutional level, partially superseded organizational forms of the supreme judicial court units: instead of the Supreme Tribunal, the establishment of the Supreme Court was envisaged and instead of the Appeals Chamber the Court of Appeal of Lithuania. On 31 May 1994, the Seimas adopted a new Law on Courts of the Republic of Lithuania which, with many effective supplements and amendments, was in force until 1 May 2002, when a new edition of the Law on Courts, adopted on 24 January 2002, came into force. Established in accordance with provisions of the Law "On the Establishment of the Supreme Court of Lithuania, the Court of Appeal of Lithuania, and Regional Courts, on the Determination of the Territories of Activity for Regional and Local Courts, and also on the Reformation of the Prosecutor's Office of the Republic of Lithuania" adopted on 15 June 1994, all the courts provided for in the Constitution actually started functioning on 1 January 1995. This judicial system has remained unchanged to the present, although the distribution of judicial competences between individual units within the judicial system has significantly changed. A fundamental reform in the sphere of the judicial competence distribution was conducted on 8 April 1998 by the Law on Amending and Supplementing the Law on Courts, when the cassation hearings function from the Supreme Court of Lithuania, Lithuanian Court of Appeal and the five regional courts was transferred to the Supreme Court of Lithuania alone. Thus, the instance court system was finally arranged and an actual basis to ensure uniformity of case law across the country was established.

14.1.1 Prosecutor's Office

The Prosecutor's Office is a state institution performing the functions provided for in the Constitution of the Republic of Lithuania, the Law on Prosecutor's Office, or other laws. The Prosecutor's Office helps to ensure lawfulness and assists courts in the administration of justice.

Based on the grounds and according to the procedure prescribed by law, the Prosecutor's Office:

- Organizes and directs pretrial investigation
- Conducts pretrial investigation or individual actions of pretrial investigation
- Controls the activities of pretrial investigation officers in criminal proceedings
- Upholds charges on behalf of the state in criminal cases
- Supervises the submission of the judgments for enforcement and the enforcement thereof
- Coordinates actions of the pretrial investigation authorities pertaining to investigation of criminal offenses
- Defends the public interest

- Examines, within its competence, petitions, applications, and complaints submitted by individuals
- Takes part in the drawing up and implementation of national and international crime prevention programs
- Takes part in the legislative process
- Fulfills other functions prescribed by law

The Prosecutor's Office is headed by the Prosecutor General of the Republic of Lithuania (hereinafter—the Prosecutor General) and his deputies, in accordance with the competence set by the Prosecutor General.

The Prosecutor General (his authorized prosecutors or civil servants) is responsible for the economic and financial activities of the Prosecutor's Office.

The Prosecutor's Office consists of the Office of the Prosecutor General and territorial-regional prosecutor's offices.

14.1.2 Police

The main tasks of the Lithuanian Police are the following:

- Protect human rights and freedoms
- Ensure public order and safety
- Render emergency assistance to people, when it is required due to their physical or mental helplessness, as well as to people who have suffered from criminal offenses, other violations of law, natural disasters, or similar factors
- Prevent criminal offenses and other violations of law
- Detect and investigate criminal offenses and other violations of law
- Supervise traffic safety

The Police system is comprised of the following institutions:

- The Police Department under the Ministry of the Interior of the Republic of Lithuania (hereinafter, the Police Department)—central institution of internal affairs
- Territorial police units
- Police professional training institution
- Specialized police units

14.1.3 Pretrial Investigation

The aim of pretrial investigation is to collect evidence related to the crime and to determine whether the suspected individual or individuals have committed the crime. The public prosecutor starts the preliminary investigation which is commissioned to the police—the police interview the perpetrators of the crime, collect evidence, and describe the case in the report. After the investigation is completed, the public prosecutor makes a decision to dismiss the case or refer it to the court where the accused individual undergoes the trial.

If a serious crime is committed or the investigation involves complex cases of minor criminal offenses, the public prosecutor appoints a judge who conducts a pretrial investigation, collects and verifies the evidence, as well as specifies and verifies the circumstances supporting the accused individual's guilt or innocence. The judge submits charges to all the accused, who are suspected of involvement in the offense referred to in the case, and he himself can carry out a search, impose arrest or perform other actions, or appoint the police to do this. The judge can make a decision to imprison any of the accused.

If a pretrial investigation is conducted (at least in criminal cases), the judge shall provide the state prosecutor with a case report. The public prosecutor can order to terminate the accused individual's case or refer it to the court where he would undergo a trial. Closed Chambers of the regional court shall make a decision regarding the compliance or noncompliance with the public prosecutor's requirements.

14.1.4 *Criminal Liability for Crimes Against Human Health*

Chapter XVIII of the Criminal Code of the Republic of Lithuania criminalizes various degrees of health impairment.

Premeditated Crimes

- Severe health impairment (Article 135 of the Criminal Code)
- Severe health impairment caused in a state of passion (Article 136 of the Criminal Code)
- Non-severe health impairment (Article 138 of the Criminal Code)
- Negligible health impairment (Article 140 of the Criminal Code)
- Causing physical pain (Article 140 of the Criminal Code)

Crimes Through Negligence

- Severe health impairment caused through negligence (Article 137 of the Criminal Code)
- Non-severe health impairment through negligence (Article 139 of the Criminal Code)
- Human health is a value protected by law
- The victim—a person of any age
- Offense—unlawful harmful physical impact on another person's body (mechanical, thermal, biological, chemical, etc.)
- Effects/consequences—health impairment or, as a minimum, the physical pain. Causal link between the offense and consequences

- A person liable under the Criminal Code has to be no less than 16 years of age and in the case of premeditated crimes no less than 14 years of age.

14.1.5 Nonpecuniary Damage

Before the entry of the Civil Code of the Republic of Lithuania (hereinafter—the Civil Code) into force in 2000, the concept of nonpecuniary damage was not clearly defined in Lithuania, and in the law practice, it was called moral damage. The current version of the Civil Code specifies both the concept of nonpecuniary damage and its salary-related provisions. Thus, nonpecuniary damage involves a person's suffering, emotional experiences, inconveniences, mental shock, emotional depression, humiliation, deterioration of reputation, diminution of possibilities to associate with others, and so forth and is evaluated by the court in terms of money [Article 6.250 (1) of the Civil Code]. The European Court of Human Rights recognizes that nonpecuniary damage includes trauma, anxiety, the feelings of injustice and helplessness, frustration, inconveniences, anxiety, and grief.

Nonpecuniary damage covers a wide range of different experiences and is very different from pecuniary damage—it is not material and cannot be accounted for in some way. Therefore, the principle of full compensation for damage established in civil law (restitutio in integrum), occurring in the case of compensation for pecuniary damages, is hardly realizable in the cases of nonpecuniary damage. The latter involves the spiritual harm that can only be relatively possible to estimate and compensate materially. The purpose of such compensation is to establish material preconditions to recreate anew something that cannot be returned, as fairly as possible to compensate a person for what often cannot be compensated in general and cannot be replaced by any money or tangible assets (the Constitutional Court decision of 19 August 2006). Referring to the fact that human values are the most important object of nonpecuniary damage, laws are intended to protect them; therefore, it is prohibited to restrict or eliminate civil liability for personal injury, death, or nonpecuniary damage.

It should be noted that the experiences, such as concerns about future consequences, can be attributed to nonpecuniary damage. For example, in the case of physical injury—how the injury will affect health in the future, whether it will be possible to completely eliminate the consequences by undergoing other operations, etc. Concerns about the need and success of the removal of the effects of injury in the future are real and understandable.

Nevertheless, any concern or anxiety cannot be treated as the reason for occurrence of nonpecuniary damage. Concern arising from defending your own rights is a normal and inevitable necessity. The Supreme Court of Lithuania in civil case No. 3K-3-469 (decision of 6 November 2007) argued that the basis for nonpecuniary damage occurs only when such concerns exceed the limits of normal efforts and the fact of mental shock, emotional depression, and infringement of personal honor and dignity is established.

In practice, there are cases when a breach of a person's pecuniary values causes additional nonpecuniary damage to another person, usually to the one emotionally related to the victim. As an example, we can remember the case of injury caused to Laurynas and Martynas Zdaniai (thermal body burns were caused to the newborns through negligence), when the compensation for nonpecuniary damages was adjudged not only to the newborns but to the parents as well. As noted by the Supreme Court of Lithuania, the persons related to the injured individual can suffer a serious nonpecuniary damage (parents, children, spouse), characterized by a serious negative impact.

Nonpecuniary damage is compensated in all cases where it occurs due to the crime against human health or deprivation of life, as well as in other cases prescribed by law.

The Supreme Court of Lithuania has repeatedly noted that violation of moral rights ex facto does not mean that nonpecuniary damage is incurred, and the compensation of nonpecuniary damage for the infringement of moral rights requests conditions for the overall civil liability. The fact that nonpecuniary damage is incurred, as well as the fact that this is the case when the compensation for damage is prescribed by law, must be proved by the plaintiff, who can be a person believing that his moral value has been violated.

The Civil Code provides the cases when the victims, alongside with their other rights specified by these provisions, also have a right to request compensation for nonpecuniary damage. The following articles of the law are associated with personal injury:

- Right to the inviolability and integrity of the person (Article 2.25)
- Personal physical mutilation or other bodily injuries (Article 6.283)

In addition to the Civil Code, the compensation for nonpecuniary damage is also regulated by other laws of the Republic of Lithuania, including the following laws:

- Law on Compensation for Damage Caused by Violent Crime of the Republic of Lithuania adopted on 30 June 2005
- Law on the Rights of Patients and Compensation for the Damage to Their Health of the Republic of Lithuania adopted on 3 October 1996
- Law on Compulsory Insurance Against Civil Liability in Respect of the Use of Motor Vehicles of the Republic of Lithuania adopted on 14 June 2001
- Labour Code of the Republic of Lithuania

In the cases associated with compensation for nonpecuniary damages, the defendants can be either natural or legal persons, including the state. The Supreme Court of Lithuania notes that the state, like any other person, is subject to a general duty of care, enshrined in Article 6.263 (1) of the Civil Code.

It is important to note that not in all cases, in order to defend an infringed moral right, is the compensation for nonpecuniary damages adjudged. The European Court of Human Rights has stated that the recognition of the offense itself is often a sufficient and fair satisfaction for the grievances suffered.

Although the provisions of the Civil Code do not restrict the amount of nonpecuniary damage, certain laws still specify the upper limits. For example, in accordance with the provisions of Article 11(1) of the Law on Compulsory Insurance Against Civil Liability in Respect of the Use of Motor Vehicles of the Republic of Lithuania, the current limit of compensation for nonpecuniary damage incurred per one accident, regardless of the number of victims, amounts to 2500 euros (since 11 June 2012—5000 euros). Certainly, in the case where the victim believes that the insurer has not fully rewarded him for nonpecuniary damage incurred, he has a right to apply directly to the perpetrator regarding compensation of the difference.

Since there is no fixed amount of a particular nonpecuniary damage and the amount of nonpecuniary damage requested by an individual cannot be evaluated as predictable, the court has to determine it in each individual case. It is the determination of fair compensation for grievances suffered that is one of the essential functions of the court when dealing with the cases of compensation for nonpecuniary damages. Due to its specific object and a peculiar expression of the presence of nonpecuniary damage, this process is very complicated.

In determining the amount of nonpecuniary damage, the court shall take into account:

- *Its consequences.* The Supreme Court of Lithuania has stated that when determining the amount of nonpecuniary damage, it is necessary to take into account the severity of injury and its impact on the victim's future life (the Supreme Court of Lithuania decision of 5 November 2003 in civil case No. 3K-3-1049). In this case it was established that during an accident at work, the applicant lost two fingers of her left hand which were later replanted. This injury has caused physical pain, mental suffering, and a reduction of communication possibilities to the applicant; she had to undergo three operations and a thumb replant, the wounds did not heal for a long time, she lost 60 % of her capacity for work, and the consequences of the trauma incurred will persist for the rest of her life.
- *The offender's guilt.* Taking into account the compensatory purpose of compensation for nonpecuniary damage, the offender's fault should be treated as a criterion for determining the amount of nonpecuniary damage only in cases where the degree of guilt basically increases the victim's personal experiences, i.e., the damage was caused deliberately and the outcomes of violation of law are not obvious.
- *The offender's financial situation.* The Supreme Court of Lithuania has repeatedly stated that the offender's financial situation in the case of personal injury or loss of life cannot be a decisive factor for determining the amount of nonpecuniary damage. The essential criterion of compensation for nonpecuniary damages, if damage was caused to health, is the consequences of injury and emotional experiences suffered due to this. In each case, while analyzing the offender's financial status, the Supreme Court of Lithuania requires to assess who is responsible for the damage—a natural or legal person. The court judgment must be implemented in reality and must not lead the individual who

awards the damage to bankruptcy or to the verge of extreme poverty. Thus, it would not be very appropriate and reasonable, for example, to adjudge recovery of a million from an individual whose earnings are minimal. So, the real possibility of recovery of the adjudged amount of compensation awarded from the defendant must be assessed, and such a monetary compensation for nonpecuniary damage must be fixed which would reach the victim within a reasonable time, be relevant to him, and provide a real opportunity to benefit from it. This means that, regardless of the damage caused by a person and his obligation to compensate for nonpecuniary damage, it is important to ensure that the person who has caused the damage shall actually be able to pay the victim the adjudged amount for nonpecuniary damage and shall be concerned to do this as quickly as possible and the injured person will actually receive the amount adjudged to him.

- *The amount of pecuniary damage.* Although the Supreme Court of Lithuania in civil case No. 3K-7-688/2001 argues that the law does not provide an additional basis essential for civil liability for causing moral (nonpecuniary) damage to occur, i.e., including the fact of causing pecuniary damage, we can see that in some laws, albeit indirectly, the interface exists. For example, in the already mentioned Law on Compulsory Insurance Against Civil Liability in Respect of the Use of Motor Vehicles of the Republic of Lithuania, the "ceiling" of the amount of recoverable damage, applicable to the insurer per one event, is a fixed amount, which also includes nonpecuniary damage. Thus, the bigger the part of the claim containing the requirement regarding compensation for pecuniary damage, the smaller is the amount claimable for compensation for nonpecuniary damage.
- *The criterion of justice and reasonableness.*
- *Other circumstances relevant to the case.*

14.2 Description of Medicolegal Expert's Qualifications

In Lithuania the training of medicolegal doctors and doctors of other professional fields is regulated by the Government of the Republic of Lithuania Resolution No. 1359 of 31 October 2003, prepared in accordance with the Law on Medical Practice of the Republic of Lithuania and implementing the provisions of Directive 2005/36/EC of the European Parliament and of the Council of 7 September 2005 on the recognition of professional qualifications (OL 2005 L 255, p. 22), last amended on 13 May 2013 by the Directive 2013/25/EU (OJ 2013 L 158, p. 368) of the Council. According to this Resolution, basic medical studies are integrated university studies of the medicine study field of a duration of at least 6 years and of at least 240 credits, and after the completion of studies, the student is awarded with a higher education diploma stating the medical doctor's qualifications. Residency in medicine is a third cycle university study in medicine, designed for the physicians seeking to acquire or to change the specialization of the professional qualification in medical practice. Residency is full-time training, composed of theoretical courses and the doctor-resident's professional traineeships/practical placements, divided into cycles (modules, practicums). Residency admits persons with the medical doctor's professional qualification and having a higher education diploma and a certificate of internship issued in the Republic of Lithuania or abroad and recognized in Lithuania in accordance with the laws. Having the certificate of internship is not required for a doctor who has been awarded with the doctor pediatrician's professional qualifications in Lithuania and applies for residency studies in child diseases, pediatric surgery, or child and adolescent psychiatry, as well as from a doctor-citizen of other member states of the European Union, Switzerland, or a country having signed the Agreement on the European Economic Area (EEA), who acquired their professional education in medicine outside the Republic of Lithuania, in Switzerland, or in a country having signed the EEA Agreement, if such a document, certifying the completion of general medical practice, is not issued in their country. The right to arrange residency studies is granted to Vilnius University and Lithuanian University of Health Sciences in Kaunas. Duration of residency studies in forensic medicine—4 years.

During the years of forensic medicine residency studies, physicians are taught and acquire practical skills on the following themes:

- Introduction to forensic medicine
- Legal knowledge
- Research methodology and methods
- Introduction to the deontological ethics
- Deontological ethics and expertise (medical malpractice)
- Forensic toxicology
- Clinical toxicology (medicolegal aspects)
- Clinical traumatology (medicolegal aspects)
- Medical examination of the living persons
- DNA and serological examinations
- Forensic thanatology
- Forensic criminalistics
- Pathology

The injured person (e.g., injured in the traffic accident or, possibly, improperly treated) usually applies to the police or the prosecutor's office, and they start pretrial investigation; so, almost in all cases, the performance of medical examination is commissioned to SFMS experts. In separate cases, the injured person applies to independent medicolegal experts. Other doctors (clinicians) usually neither determine the effects of injury nor evaluate the quality of the treatment applied.

14.3 Ascertainment Methodology

In Lithuania the fact of personal injury and health impairment scale is determined by medicolegal doctors (experts) working in the State Forensic Medicine Service (hereinafter—SFMS), as well as by private forensic experts. Hereinafter we will refer exclusively to the methods applicable for the examination of injured persons in SFMS. There are several ways to verify the fact of injury and determine the health impairment scale: through examination of injured persons or reviewing their medical records and if after trauma or other health impairments the person was treated in a health-care facility (in outpatient settings, hospital). In many cases you have to examine the injured person and then proceed with analysis of their medical records. Personal examination is important in cases where injuries were caused recently and, based on their nature and healing characteristics, it is possible to determine the time and mechanism of injury, the injuring tool, etc. Personal examination is also very important in cases when one needs to determine the loss of general capacity for work level incurred due to injury (measured in percentage), because very often the consequences of injury are obvious only after the treatment and rehabilitation have been completed, i.e., after a longer period of time following injury—such examinations involve the assessment of the persisting physical (anatomical) defects, dysfunction, etc.

Personal examination is not purposeful if much time has passed after injury, and the traces of injury are missing and residual effects (consequences) did not develop—in this case, the primary role is focused on medical documentation, which includes records on injuries and other personal data about the state of health immediately after trauma.

The time during which the clinical or medicolegal examination of an injured person must be conducted is not regulated. Clinical examination is usually associated with the victim's feeling after the injury (except in cases where, due to more serious injuries, he is taken to the clinic immediately after the injury). The time of performing medicolegal examination also depends on the victim himself or, more often, on the timeliness of the police actions, who have to notify the victim on the necessity of such an examination.

If the expertise (examination) is performed immediately after the event, it is appropriate to examine the injured person and, if the person has applied to a medical institution, to assess his medical records, as very often personal health-care institutions perform additional instrumental diagnostic tests (radiological) and with their help an externally unnoticeable injury (bone fractures, traumatic brain injuries, etc.) is identified. Medicolegal examination (expertise) of living (injured) persons is performed in the following cases:

– In cases of personal injury (for determining the injuring tool, manner, and time of injury, estimating the residual scars after injury, other consequences of injury, health impairment scale, the loss of general capacity for work level due to injuries)

- In criminal offense cases aimed to satisfy sexual lust and in other cases of sexual offenses [rape, sexual abuse, molestation of minors, when assessing virginity, (former) pregnancy, a former childbirth, abortion, the fetus development time, sex]

  Reference for performing the examination of living persons:

- A written order of a pretrial investigation officer (investigator, prosecutor)
- A request of other legal entities, individuals, or their legal representatives
- Order of the Court

Place and Procedures for the Examination of Living Persons Place of examination—a room (consulting room) of an SFMS structural unit, suitable for examination. In the absence of a possibility to perform the examination at SFMS and in the case of procedural necessity, the examination may be performed in other places as well—health-care institutions, pretrial investigation facilities, detention centers, prisons, etc.—if the quality of examination and (or) sampling can be assured or if the examination cannot be postponed. For the review of the case (civil, criminal, or other), material and medical documents and medicolegal examination (expertise) of living persons can also be conducted in other expertise, pretrial investigation, health-care institutions, etc., related to the expertise. Measurement instruments (a ruler, measuring tape) are used for taking measures of injuries and body parts. Sterile instruments are used for sampling in cases of additional tests.

Objects of examination (expertise) of living (injured) persons:

- Injured person
- Documents and digital media containing medical information (medical records, X-rays, computed tomography, findings of additional tests, conclusions of consultations, etc.)

Personal Identification The person who applies for examination must provide a valid identity proof—a document including a photograph (identity card, passport, driving license, etc.). The examination cannot be started if the identity document is missing, except in cases when the person comes for examination accompanied by a pretrial investigation officer who verifies the individual's identity, or this is indicated in the order. Persons under 18 years of age are examined only in the presence of at least one of his parents or his legal representative, or an officer, after they provide their identity verifying documents. The officer's data (workplace, position, first name, last name) is recorded in the examination protocol. The identity of a person examined in a health-care institution (if the identity documents are not provided) is verified by comparing the data of records in medical documents with those indicated in the pretrial investigation officer's order for performing the personal examination. When examining a person in a health-care institution, the investigative part of the specialist's conclusion shall include the name and department of the institution where the person is examined.

Recording of Examination and Documentation of Data In cases when a medicolegal professional (expert) performs the personal examination in SFMS premises, with a medicolegal registrar or technician (technical employee) present during the examination, the medicolegal professional (expert) dictates the data of the investigative part, i.e., circumstances of the event, as provided by the examined individual, and description of injuries, i.e., their nature, dimensions, data of the submitted medical documents, etc., and the medicolegal registrar prints the text on the computer. If the data of external examination is sufficient, the conclusion shall be written immediately. In cases when the data is not sufficient enough for arranging the conclusion, the client is requested to submit additional medical documents.

Circumstances of the Event In the part of the examination protocol (specialist's conclusion, expert act) named "circumstances of the event," circumstances specified by the client (the police), as well as other circumstances learned from the injured person, are recorded, in order to find out:

- Date and time of personal injury
- Place where personal injury occurred
- Who injured the person (information on the person(s) who caused injury, if known)
- Injuring tools and mode of injury, the number of hitting (traumatic effects)
- Which body parts are injured
- How the person was feeling, his complaints after injury, and if he was unconscious for some time
- If the person applied for medical assistance, where and what kind of assistance was provided
- Where and how much time he was treated, if he is currently being treated, whether, due to injury, he was going to apply to medical institutions later
- The injured person's complaints during the examination

Examination and the Data of Medical Records In cases of examination of living persons, personal examination must be performed very carefully and consistently; it is recommended—from the top downward and from the left to the right—examining not only the areas indicated by the victim but also other areas of the body, which may contain injuries helping to specify the injury-causing mechanism. If the injured person denies examination of the entire body (does not show all parts of the body naked, denies the existence of injuries in other areas of the body, etc.), this shall be recorded in the examination protocol. In the case of examining a person who is suspected of committing a crime (arrested person), accompanied by the police officers, it is necessary to examine the entire body. Injuries can be visualized in the contoured human body schemes or their parts and (or) photographed. The decision on purposefulness of taking photographs or visualizing injuries on the scheme is made by the medicolegal professional (expert). When injuries are photographed, this fact and the storage area of the digital photocopy must be specified in the examination protocol. It is appropriate to take pictures of injuries, which clearly reflect the shape and dimensions of the injuring object or tool, in cases where irreparable rough body defects persist after injury, also in cases of multiple injuries, when their description cannot adequately reflect the overall image of injuries. Photographs and schemes are presented as annexes to the examination protocol.

When describing each injury, it is necessary to specificate the following:

- Specify localization of injuries (indicating the injured part of the body and the distance from the nearest anatomical points and landmarks), if necessary—their mutual distribution
- Indicate the shape and color of injury, its environment and additional components (redness, swelling, if these components are present), and other characteristics of injury, enabling to identify the injury occurrence time, manner, and tools
- Indicate dimensions of injury (length, width, and when possible depth, direction, etc.). When describing two-dimensional injuries (e.g., 2×1 cm subcutaneous hematoma), first the longitudinal dimension is indicated and then the cross dimension

When describing pedestrian injuries incurred during the traffic accident, especially when the motor vehicle is not known, it is appropriate to measure the height of injuries to the legs, pelvis, or other places, starting from the foot. In cases of asphyxia (strangulation), it is appropriate to examine eye conjunctiva, the mucosa of the oral cavity, and other places in search of petechiae. In cases of nasal trauma, by palpation, check the nasal bone fracture crepitation, if there are no contraindications. Medicolegal examination (expertise) of scars which remained after injuries can be performed in order to determine the origin and mechanism of the scar occurrence, scar age, what medical procedures are needed to remove the scar, if the scars can be removed (corrected) by applying cosmetic procedures, etc. For determining the origin and nature of the scar, not only is examination important but the data of medical records as well, if any are available. If necessary (for determining the size, nature of the scar, the scar-causing tools, and manner), it is appropriate to measure the scars and describe their texture, color, origin, mobility, and other important characteristics.

In cases of the loss of *general capacity for work*, examination (expertise) is conducted through reviewing medical documentation, if necessary, and also performing personal examination and additional tests. The scope of examination is determined by a medicolegal professional (expert) together with professionals of other spheres involved in the examination (expertise). The examination (expertise) on the loss of general capacity for work is carried out in accordance with the Rules for Determining the Health Impairment Scale (hereinafter—the Rules) and the Commentary on the Rules for Determining the Health Impairment Scale (hereinafter—the Commentary), specifying the cases where examination can be performed by one medicolegal professional (expert) or together with other medicolegal professionals (experts) or medical doctors of other professional spheres, as well as the principles for determining the loss of general capacity for work. In cases where the treatment for injuries is incomplete and, due to the ongoing treatment, the health impairment scale is still unclear—the client who has requested the examination is asked in writing to submit the requested documents after the treatment is completed.

In such cases, the effects of injuries are assessed in compliance with the locoregional principle, and all the possible effects of injuries are divided into the relevant sections:

Consequences of the central nervous system injuries

- Consequences of the peripheral nervous system injuries
- Visual organs
- Hearing organs
- Respiratory system
- Cardiovascular system
- Digestive system
- Urogenital system
- Soft tissue injuries
- Skeletal injuries of the trunk and extremities (spine, scapula-clavicle, shoulder joint, upper arm, elbow joint, forearm, wrist joint, hand, hand fingers, pelvis, hip joint, femur, knee joint, shin, ankle joint, foot, foot toes)

The consequences of injuries in these regions can be assessed independently by one medicolegal expert, if the information recorded in medical documents is comprehensive and there is no doubt concerning the reliability of this information. If the information is insufficient, an additional examination of the injured person is conducted, together with other specialists.

In cases where another medical professional's (neurosurgeon, neurologist, radiologist, etc.) consultation is needed for the performance of expertise, the medicolegal professional (expert) informs the client, who has ordered the expertise or a person concerned, about the need for such a consultation. The provided written professionals' consultations or other additional data are included in the examination protocol and evaluated when preparing the conclusion. In cases of failure to read (or unreadable) the professional's records in the medical documents, and if these latter are relevant for preparing the specialist's conclusion, the medicolegal specialist (expert) notifies the client who has requested the examination about it in writing, with a request to provide readable records; otherwise (in the case of failure to provide readable records), the medicolegal professional (expert) shall have a right to refuse to provide a conclusion or will answer only part of the questions asked.

Submission of the Results (Findings) If examination for injuries is performed at the injured person's request, the conclusion must include the following:

- Medical characteristic of injury—medicolegal diagnosis
- Injury-making instruments and manner (mechanism)
- Injury occurrence time
- Health impairment scale

In other cases—when personal examination is performed by the order of law enforcement authorities—the conclusion shall include answers to the questions submitted for the expert's opinion.

14.4 Evaluation Criteria

The severity of injury (level) is determined in accordance with the "Rules for Determining Health Impairment Scale" approved by the Minister of Health, Minister of Justice, and Minister of Social Security and Labour of the Republic of Lithuania Order No. V-298/158/A1-86 of 23 May 2003. The Rules specify the concepts of health impairment, injury, and causing a disease. For the determination of health impairment scale, SFMS experts must also follow the provisions of the Commentary on the Rules for Determining Health Impairment Scale, approved by the SFMS Director's order.

Health impairment means causing a personal injury or disease by disturbing the integrity of his body tissues (organs) or disrupting their functions.

Injury implies a disturbance of anatomical integrity of the human body tissues or organs or their functions caused by mechanical, physical, or chemical impact. Mechanical injury involves subcutaneous bruising, skin abrasions, wounds, fractures, etc.: they are made by blunt and sharp objects. Physical factors (usually the impact of high and seldom low temperature) cause burns and frostbite. Chemical factors include various chemical substances, affecting externally (usually causing chemical burns) or inside the body (cause poisoning).

Causing a disease implies impairment of the body's biological functions by a physical, chemical, or psychological impact or when an urgent medical assistance is not provided. Biological factors may involve various infectious factors (e.g., bacteria, viruses), as well as the amount of food and fluids or their components inadequate to the body's needs. Natural factors involve high and low temperatures and ionizing radiation. Chemical factors involve various chemical substances that get into a human body or affect the body from outside.

Consequences of injuries that do not disappear (persist forever) are evaluated as a permanent loss of *general capacity for work level* (percentage). *General capacity for work* is an individual's ability and possibility to perform the work that does not require special knowledge, qualifications, and skills. To put it simply, it is an individual's ability to take care of himself/herself, i.e., to move, dress, and carry out the essential domestic actions.

The basic criteria for determining the health impairment scale are as follows:

- Threat of injury to life
- Duration of health impairment (disorder)
- Outcomes of injury (consequences)

For the determination of health impairment scale due to injury, it is appropriate to assess whether the injury was life-threatening. Life-threatening injuries involve such injuries that cause danger to the victim's life, as well as those that, if medical assistance is not provided, are usually fatal. Such injuries are categorized as *severe health impairment*, regardless of the consequences. If the injury is not life-threatening, then it should be assessed if the victim's health was impaired temporarily (temporal incapacity for work) or permanently (permanent loss of general capacity for work). Referring to the duration of health impairment or the percentage of the loss of general capacity for work, health impairment may be evaluated as non-severe or slight (if there is no evidence of the symptoms of severe health impairment).

Slight health impairment is determined when there is at least one of the following characteristics present:

- Injury or a disease impairs health for no longer than 10 days period.
- Due to injury or a disease, the victim loses 5 % of a general capacity for work.

Non-severe health impairment is determined when there is at least one of the following characteristics present:

- Injury or a disease impairs health for longer than 10 days period.
- Due to injury or a disease, the individual loses more than 5 % but less than 30 % of the general capacity for work.

As mentioned previously, *severe health impairment* is determined based on one of the following factors:

- Threat to life
- Consequences of injury

The Rules include a list of the following major injuries that pose a threat to life and, in its turn, are evaluated as *severe health impairment* (this is the description of injuries as provided for in the Rules and Commentary):

- Open and depressed cranial vault fractures and the skull basal fractures (Rules); closed linear fractures of cranial vault bones and open fractures exclusively of the outer cortical plate are evaluated in accordance with the duration of health impairment (Commentary).
- Cerebral contusions with expressed focal neurological symptoms, verified by special radiological imaging investigations or during surgery (Rules); cerebral contusions must be verified by at least one of the following specific instrumental tests: (a) CT scan and (b) nuclear magnetic resonance. Cerebral contusions, verified by at least one of the above special instrumental tests, are evaluated as severe health impairment only when focal neurological symptoms or neurological symptoms of a focal nature persisting after the treatment are expressed (Commentary).
- Severe diffuse axonal injury (Rules); injury due to severe diffuse axonal injury is evaluated as severe when the injured person was unconscious due to trauma for at least 6 h, unless there are other reasons for the loss of consciousness, e.g., intoxication with alcohol or other substances (Commentary).

- Epidural and subdural hematoma or hygroma liquor (cerebrospinal fluid), causing cerebral compression (Rules); acute epidural and subdural hematoma or hygroma can be classified as severe injury when the clinically identified brain compression requires surgical treatment. Subdural hygroma of traumatic origin can be considered as severe injury only after their direct link to the recent injury is established (Commentary).
- Dislocation (subluxation) or fracture of cervical vertebra with the spinal cord or spinal nerve root lesion (Rules); dislocation of the intervertebral disk with the spinal cord or spinal nerve root lesion is considered as severe (Commentary).
- Spinal cord injury (transverse myelitis) with expressed focal symptoms, verified by specific tests (Rules); spinal cord injury in the absence of expressed symptoms of neurological nature must be verified by the same specific instrumental tests as in the case of cerebral contusion; in the case of partial spinal cord injury (incomplete transverse myelitis), the focal neurological symptoms (dysfunction of pelvic organs) shall have to persist for at least a week (Commentary).
- Perforating injuries of the pharynx, esophagus, larynx, and trachea (Rules).
- The larynx or trachea injury, causing the respiratory disorder, which was eliminated by applying intubation or tracheostomy to the injured person (Rules).
- Perforating injury of thoracic cavity or abdominal cavity with/without the internal organ damage (Rules); perforating injury of pleura (pleural) and perforating injury of the peritoneal cavity must be determined during the surgical wound treatment or radiological investigation. Subcutaneous emphysema, identified in the case of thoracic injuries, cannot be considered as the characteristic of perforating injury of thoracic cavity if there is no pneumothorax or (and) hemothorax present (Commentary).
- Open kidney, ureters, adrenal gland, pancreas, urinary bladder, urethra, prostate, or rectum injury (Rules); only the open membranous urethra injury shall be considered as severe health impairment; rectal injury is considered as severe health impairment only if all three layers of the intestinal wall in intraperitoneal or mesoperitoneal region are injured (Commentary).
- Closed chest or abdominal organs injury identified during surgery (Rules); closed chest or abdominal organ injury is visually determined during surgery by indicating a particular specific localization of the injury and its nature. Closed injuries of abdominal cavity organ [superficial (capsular) lacerations, e.g., capsular laceration of spleen] identified by the radiological imaging investigation and treated conservatively, pleural cavity puncture, or unilateral pneumothorax identified during drainage, in the absence of acute respiratory failure symptoms, are categorized based on the duration of health impairment (Commentary).
- Aortic, common, internal, or external carotid, subclavian, axillary, brachial, common, internal, or external iliac, femoral or popliteal arteries or their corresponding vein injury (Rules).
- Open fractures of the humerus, femur, or tibia bodies (shafts, diaphysis), or closed fractures of any two of the specified bone bodies, or humeral or femoral neck fractures (Rules); closed fractures of at least two of the specified bones (their bodies or necks) are evaluated as severe health impairment (Commentary).

- Bilateral pelvic bone fractures, disrupting the integrity of the pelvic ring (Rules); disruption of the integrity of the pelvic ring is evaluated as severe health impairment if any two of the following pelvic fractures and (or) joint dislocations (unilateral or bilateral): (a) the two branches of the pubis fracture, (b) full dislocation of pubic symphysis, (c) longitudinal acetabular hipbone fracture, (d) longitudinal fracture of the sacrum, (e) complete dislocation of the sacroiliac joint (Commentary).
- Severe shock, fat or air embolism, acute renal failure, or other life-threatening conditions caused by the injury (Rules); (a) shock is considered severe, when systolic blood pressure falls below 80 mmHg, pulse rate reaches 140b/min, and the shock index (the heart rate and systolic blood pressure ratio) reaches 2.0. Sometimes severe shock can also be determined at higher than 80 mmHg systolic blood pressure values, if there are clinical signs of significant organ perfusion disorder present, the skin is covered with cold and sticky sweat, and there are changes in the mental status (from a mild disturbance of consciousness to coma), oliguria or anuria, and insufficient capillary filling; (b) oliguria or anuria is characteristic of acute renal failure, increased blood urea nitrogen and serum creatinine concentration levels in the blood serum, increased arterial blood pressure, and seizures; (c) another group of life-threatening conditions may include (1) coma of different etiologies; (2) clinical death of different etiologies, when asystole is recorded in the monitor or electrocardiogram; (3) acute heart failure of different origins; (4) acute liver failure; (5) severe septic conditions; and (6) acute respiratory failure; this condition is considered as severe health impairment when endotracheal intubation and mechanical ventilation (DPV) is needed. DPV is usually needed in cases of hypoxemia, refractory oxygen therapy (Pa O $2 < 60$ mmHg), hypoventilation (Pa $CO_2 > 50$ mmHg), when the respiratory rate >35 breaths/min, hypoperfusion, and shock (Commentary).
- Burns of different origins, where the total area of 2 A (II) burn degree covers 30 % or more of the body surface, where the burn area of 2 B (III) burn degree covers 20 % or more of the body surface, and where the burn area of 3 (III–IV) burn degree covers 10 % or more of the body surface. Respiratory tract burns (Rules); respiratory tract burn is life-threatening when the congested mucous membranes and glottis narrowing pose a real threat to life due to severe inspiratory dyspnea or the state of shock (Commentary).
- Frostbites of the III–IV degree, covering 10 % or more of the body surface (Rules).
- Ionizing radiation-induced severe radiation sickness (Rules).
- Compression of the neck or other mechanical asphyxias accompanied by cerebrovascular disorder verified by objective data (Rules); the supportive objective data of cerebrovascular disorder due to compression of the neck may include loss of consciousness, objectively confirmed in medical records, spontaneous urination or defecation, retrograde amnesia, and morphological characteristics of compression of the neck: petechiae on the face, eye conjunctiva, and oral mucosa. Only the presence of petechiae does not verify the loss of

consciousness; this characteristic only confirms the neck compression or other respiratory disturbance facts (Commentary).

- Irretrievable mutilation of the body when the law enforcement authority comes to such a conclusion, based on the forensic expert's report regarding the possibility of elimination of the consequences of the injury (Rules); forensic doctors determine that the skin scars, deformities, mimic disorders, or functional limitations of limb movements cannot subside naturally or by applying cosmetic procedures and then evaluate the injury as incurable; the body disfigurement fact is determined by the law enforcement institutions (Commentary).
- Other serious life-threatening conditions, having developed after the injury, and which do not fall under any of the above criteria specified in the Rules, are attributed to the severe mutilation of different character categories. These may include acute respiratory distress syndrome, shaken baby syndrome, post-traumatic cardiac rhythm and (or) conduction disorders (e.g., cardiac shock), skull bone fractures with the craniofacial dissociation (Le Fort III type fractures), and others.

The Commentary also specifies other instructions for the expert, performing personal injury examination, to follow:

- For the determination of the health impairment scale, at least one qualifying characteristic is sufficient. If more of such characteristics are determined, health impairment scale is evaluated based on the characteristic corresponding to a more severe health impairment scale level; when injuries are caused by multiple traumatic impacts, the health impairment scale can be determined for each injury (impact) separately. In cases where multiple injuries aggravate each other, the injuries are assessed as a whole.
- The duration of health impairment is determined referring to the duration of treatment and the sick leave recorded in medical documents. The adequacy of the treatment duration (too long or too short) against the nature of the injury or ailment must be evaluated by the forensic doctor critically, based on the injured person's condition and objective medical records, as well as on the facts regarding the duration of injury healing known in medicine. Nasal or other bone fractures, regardless of the dysfunction, deformation, and treatment applied, or the number and duration of the patient's visits to medical institutions, shall always be evaluated as non-severe health impairment, because broken bones do not heal within 10 days and the damaged anatomical bone integrity persists for longer than a 10-day period. Hematomas and skin abrasions shall be evaluated as slight health impairment, although after 10 days the signs of healing of such injuries may still be visible (except the cases where massive bruising or deep abrasions cause dysfunction or complications due to such injuries occur, such as the soft tissue bruising suppuration).
- For the determination of the duration of health impairment, the injured person's actions can be assessed as well, such as delayed referral to medical institutions without medically justified reasons or other objective reasons, nonadherence to

the prescribed treatment and regime, independent and inadequate medical self-treatment, or other actions which prolong the duration of health impairment.

- Deterioration of the injured person's health status due to deficiencies in provision of medical assistance cannot be the basis for determining a more serious health impairment scale. In such cases, the conclusion must include an indication on the character of the existing worsening of health status or complications and their causal relationship with the identified injuries and deficiencies of medical care. Complications occurring during medical procedures, surgery, or the application of complex modern diagnostic methods are evaluated, in accordance with the Rules, as health impairment only after proving their being the consequence of deficiencies in the conducted medical manipulations; if complications occur during medical procedures at vital indications, the health impairment scale, with regard to such complications, is not determined. If, during surgery or procedures of complex modern diagnostic techniques, complications occur not due to deficiencies in provision of medical care, but due to other reasons (a serious condition of the patient, unforeseen response of the patient's organism, etc.), such complications do not affect the determination of health impairment scale.
- For the determination of health impairment scale of a person who suffers from any disease or other (related) pathologies, only the consequences of the incurred injury or ailment shall be evaluated; also it is necessary to indicate the impact of the injury incurred on a previous disease: worsened, acquired a more severe form, etc. If preexisting diseases aggravate the course of injury or ailment (healing), this shall be recorded in the conclusion.

An inseparable attachment to the Rules is the "Table on the Loss of General Capacity for Work Due to Injury." It includes a description of residual post-traumatic effects of all organ systems and body parts—functional impairment (loss) and anatomical defects. Each position in the table is measured in percentage, and, depending on its size, injuries are evaluated as slight (5 %), non-severe (10–25 %), or severe (more than 30 %) health impairment. If the loss of general capacity for work is determined against the consequences (effects), which are evident immediately after trauma, e.g., an amputated limb or organ removed, this can be determined by one forensic doctor. If the loss of capacity for work level is determined against post-traumatic effects which occur later, and when the examination requires to evaluate the dysfunction level of the body part or organ, this shall be done by a forensic doctor together with a medical doctor of a relevant professional area or another forensic doctor. The loss of general capacity for work is determined when:

- A direct causal link is established between the injury or ailment incurred and the aggravation of the injured person's health status
- The consequences of injury or ailment are evident immediately after trauma (amputated limb or its parts, knocked out teeth, internal organ, or part of it removed)

- The treatment is completed and all rehabilitation measures are utilized; however, the symptoms of the loss of capacity for work persist, but no earlier than after 120 days following the trauma or ailment. When the general capacity for work is lost due to several injuries made at the same time, the percentage is summed arithmetically, but the total amount cannot exceed 100 %. When the general capacity for work is lost due to several injuries simultaneously made in one limb or its segment, the total percentage cannot exceed the amount of percentage lost due to the limb or its segment amputation. For the evaluation of hearing impairment, hearing-enhancing tools (artificial hearing aid) shall not have any effect on the assessment

In Lithuania one more the capacity for work-level (at the same time—the lost capacity for work) assessment system is used. This is the "Description of Criteria for the Capacity For Work-Level Assessment" approved by the Minister of Social Security and Labour and the Minister of Health of the Republic of Lithuania Order No. A1-78/V-179 of 21 March 2005. The description of criteria for determining the capacity for work level (hereinafter—the Description of Criteria) defines the criteria to be referred to for determining the capacity for work level for individuals under 18 years of age, who are (were) insured by the state social insurance, and individuals over 18 years until they reach the age of eligibility for the old-age pension, and their application. The Description of Criteria is the basic document referred to by **the Disability and Working Capacity Assessment Office at the Ministry of Social Security and Labour** of the Republic of Lithuania (hereinafter—DWCAO) for the assessment of the individual's capacity for work level and by personal health-care institutions for sending people to DWCAO for the assessment of the capacity for work level.

The individual's capacity for work level is assessed based on the following criteria:

- Medical, i.e., the individual's basic capacity to work
- Functional
- Professional and other criteria that affect the individual's working capacity and his employability

Causes of the capacity for work level:

- Diseases or conditions
- Diseases or conditions that occurred before 24 years of age
- Accident (mutilation) at work
- Occupational disease
- Disease (mutilation) incurred in military service or military training
- Disease (mutilation) caused by the aggression of 11–13 January 1991 and by subsequent events
- Disease (mutilation) incurred due to the impact of the Chernobyl accident leading to loss of work
- Disease (mutilation) incurred in the course of resistance activities against the occupation of 1940–1990

- Disease (mutilation) caused by unlawful imprisonment and exile
- Disease (mutilation) incurred in the Second World War while serving in the active armies of anti-Hitler coalition states, partisan squads, and units
- Disease (mutilation) incurred in the ghettos and concentration camps or in other different forced-type camps
- Disease (mutilation) incurred in forced labor in Lithuania or outside its borders
- Disease (mutilation) incurred while carrying out the citizen's duty

However, medicolegal experts do not utilize these criteria in forensic practice. Besides, medicolegal experts usually have to determine a permanent loss of general capacity for work caused by events under investigation following the provisions of the Criminal Procedure Code or the Civil Procedure Code, i.e., health impairment incurred due to criminal offenses or settlement of issues of claims in civil cases (when adjudging financial compensation for the damage caused to individual's health).

Chapter 15
Methods of Ascertainment of Personal Damage in Estonia

Marika Väli

Abstract This chapter illustrates the historical, judicial and juridical framework of personal injury assessment and compensation in Estonia, describing the expert's qualification and competences and detailing the ascertainment methodology and criteria of evaluation utilised for identifying, describing and estimating any personal injury, its temporary and permanent consequences and the causal value/link between the event and the injury and between the injury and the impairment/disability.

15.1 Historical, Judicial and Juridical Overview

Disability is an abnormality in an anatomical, physiological or mental structure or function of a person which, in conjunction with different relational and environmental restrictions, prevents participation in social life on equal bases with the others.

Until the year 2000, disability was estimated on the basis of disability categories but now disability is determined by the percentages. The percentage of loss of capacity may be 10–100, but it always ends with the number zero. A pension is paid if the percentage of incapacity for work is more than 40.

In 2000 a new law came into force, the "Social Benefits for Disabled Persons Act". This act determines payment of social grants to people whose disability does not allow them to fully cope with daily life and who require personal assistance [1].

The state pays social benefits to disabled persons if they have additional expenses because of their disability, e.g. they are in need of assistance, care or medical rehabilitation, or the additional expenses are related to transport, employment or studies.

M. Väli (✉)
Estonian Forensic Science Institute, University of Tartu, Ülikooli 18, 50090 Tartu, Estonia
e-mail: Marika.Vali@ekei.ee

S.D. Ferrara et al. (eds.), *Personal Injury and Damage Ascertainment under Civil Law*, DOI 10.1007/978-3-319-29812-2_15

The aim of granting social benefits to disabled persons is to support the ability of disabled persons to cope independently, social integration and equal opportunities through partial compensation for the additional expenses caused by the disability.

Permanent incapacity for work is an injury or illness in relation to work, profession and service or the result of a nuclear disaster, traffic accident or violent crime.

Permanent incapacity for work is divided into total incapacity for work (due to an injury or illness, the person is not able to work in order to support themselves) (100 % loss of capacity for work) and partial incapacity for work (due to an injury or illness, the person is not able to perform the work suitable for them in the amount corresponding to the general national standard for working time) (10–90 % loss of capacity for work). In case of temporary incapacity for work (illness, injury, etc.), the attending physician (family physician or medical specialist) will draw up a certificate of temporary incapacity for work for the person.

On a legal basis, only permanent incapacity for work is determined.

15.2 Identification and Description of Medicolegal Expert's Qualifications

Permanent incapacity for work is certified by the expert commission or expert doctor of the Social Insurance Board. Its members have been trained in the field of loss of capacity determination and they are recognised experts in their field.

The forensic medical doctor determines permanent incapacity for work if determination of health damage severity is necessary.

The competence of forensic medical doctors is regulated by the professional standards approved by the Law and National Defence Council on 11 December 2006. Professional standards III, IV and V have been established for forensic pathologists. The purpose of the system of professional standards is to motivate experts to participate in in-service training, in order to ensure the consistency of their qualifications.

Professional standards are evaluated once every 4 years and the basis for the evaluation is the in-service score system as well as a report on practical activities.

The requirements of the ISO 17025 and ISO 9001 standards are the in-service curriculum of the Faculty of Medicine of the University of Tartu, the 4-year training curriculum of the experts of the Institute and the annual expert training plan of the Institute.

15.3 Ascertainment Methodology

Permanent incapacity for work is established on the basis of the state of health of the person by assessing the impact of the health disorder on their capacity for work. Until 2009, persons visited their attending physicians with an application for examination; the physicians would then submit the application to the Pension Board along with a description of the state of health of the applicant.

The Social Insurance Board will conduct the examination for permanent incapacity for work, engaging medical experts [2, 3].

The examination for permanent incapacity for work may be applied for:

1. By persons of working age, i.e. from 16 years of age until the pensionable age provided in the State Pension Insurance Act
2. By way of exception after attaining the pensionable age or at a younger age than 16 years of age, if the health of the person has been harmed as the result of an occupational disease, work injury, performing the duties of police service, border guard service, rescue service or other such duties of employment, a nuclear disaster, traffic accident or violent crime

In Estonia, occupational diseases are diagnosed in the Centre of Occupational Diseases and Health where physicians with the respective training work. If the patient disagrees with the decision, they are able to request by judicial process that a forensic medical examination be conducted. The forensic medical doctor must verify whether the illness in question constitutes an occupational disease and at which employer the disease was contracted. An occupational disease can serve as a basis for permanent incapacity for work if a connection is established between the occupational disease and the complications, after-effects, illness or the intensification or aggravation of the illness arising therefrom and the permanent incapacity for work.

A forensic medical examination is prescribed first in case of injuries, occupational accidents or illnesses that have been caused as the result of violent crime, sexual offences or traffic accidents. The forensic physician will identify the mechanism of formation of the injuries, the time at which the injuries were inflicted and the severity of the injuries. If an incapacity for work has been caused as a result thereof, the patient may demand that their percentage of loss of capacity for work be established by means of filing a civil action.

Illnesses not caused by accidents or regular employment are established by the attending physician who will submit any documents to the Social Insurance Board. The Social Insurance Board will determine the cause-and-effect relationship between the illness or the later intensification, aggravation, complications or after-effects thereof and the permanent incapacity for work.

The person must fill in a standard format application for the examination for the establishment of permanent incapacity for work. In the application, the person will fill in the data of their family physician or the medical specialist treating them who have the data concerning their state of health that are required in order to establish permanent incapacity for work. The person must have visited the aforesaid doctor within the 3 months preceding the submission of the application.

If required, the person will submit additional documents for the establishment of the reason for permanent incapacity for work along with the application for examination.

The Social Insurance Board will make an inquiry in the Health Information System in order to receive a description of the state of health of the person.

The examination for permanent incapacity for work will be made on the basis of the documents; the applicant will not need to meet the persons conducting the examination.

The Social Insurance Board will formalise a decision concerning the results of the examination for permanent incapacity for work of which the applicant and the physician indicated in the application for examination who submitted the description of the person's state of health will be notified.

Permanent incapacity for work to the extent of 40–100 % grants a person the right to apply for a pension for incapacity for work.

The percentage of loss of capacity for work may be established for a period of 6 months, 1 year, 2 years, 3 years, 5 years or until attaining the pensionable age (but for no longer than 5 years).

15.3.1 Collection of Circumstantial and Clinical Data

The Social Insurance Board shall ask for information on the applicant's state of health from the doctor whose particulars are provided in the application for examination.

If necessary, the applicant provides additional documentation for the application for the examination for establishing permanent incapacity for work:

1. In the case of work injury—work injury report
2. In the case of occupational disease—occupational diseases report
3. In the case of injury sustained while performing the duties of employment of the police force or of illness related to the performance of duties—documentation certifying illness or physical harm (work injury report, occupational diseases report, findings of health check or health certificate, etc.)
4. In the case of injury sustained while performing the duties of employment of the border guard or of illness related to the performance of duties—documentation certifying illness or physical harm (work injury report, occupational diseases report, findings of health check or health certificate, etc.)
5. In the case of injury sustained while performing the duties of employment of the rescue service or of illness related to the performance of duties—documentation certifying illness or physical harm (work injury report, occupational diseases report, findings of health check or health certificate, etc.)

6. In the case of injury sustained while performing the duties of employment or of illness related to the performance of duties—documentation certifying illness or physical harm (work injury report, occupational diseases report, findings of health check or health certificate, etc.)
7. In the case of injury or illness as a result of nuclear disaster, nuclear test or an accident in a nuclear power station—medical documentation to show the cause-and-effect relationship between the nuclear disaster, nuclear test or an accident in a nuclear power station and the injury or illness
8. In the case of injury or illness as a result of a traffic accident—police certificate on said traffic accident
9. In the case of injury or illness as a result of a crime of violence—court judgement or preliminary investigation and authority's certificate of criminal matter

The person conducting the proceedings have to describe the circumstances in which the injuries were inflicted, including traffic accidents, in the part pertaining to preliminary data in the examination ruling. If this is not sufficient for identifying the mechanism of formation of the injuries, the time at which the injuries were inflicted or any other matters, it is always possible to request for additional data from the person conducting the proceedings. The forensic physician will attempt to find the answers to the aforesaid questions, above all on the basis of medical records. There are also a few cases per year where the forensic physician conducts the examination with road traffic experts, i.e. we attempt to identify the mechanism of formation of the injuries by comparing the damage to the vehicle and to the person.

15.3.2 Medical Case History

The physician must indicate the purpose of the description of the state of health.

If the purpose of the examination is the establishment of permanent incapacity for work, the physician will fill in the form of the description of the state of health if the person has visited the physician within the last 3 months before the submission of the application for examination.

The data of the last examination of the person will be described by organ systems. For every organ system, the description of the functional condition thereof without compensations (without using technical aids or medicinal products) and with compensations (using technical aids or medicinal products) will be provided. After that, the prognosis concerning recovery and life will be provided.

The person's diagnoses will be indicated in order of importance, whereas only the diagnoses in relation to health disorders that may be expected to cause permanent incapacity for work or disability will be indicated.

When indicating the diagnoses, the clinical diagnosis will be used as the basis, also indicating the code thereof in the International Classification of Diseases. The course of the illness/illnesses and the prognosis concerning any changes in the functional capacity will be indicated. If possible, the severity of the functional impairment corresponding to the diagnosis will be marked with every clinical diagnosis and the frequency of chronic pain and balance disorders will be assessed. Any examinations and consultation decisions that verify the current functional condition of the person will also be indicated.

The physician will submit the form of the description of the state of health along with the required documents describing the state of health to the Social Insurance Board.

If the data presented in the description of the state of health or the appended documents are insufficient for the examination, the Social Insurance Board will request a supplemented description of the state of health or further data or documents from the physician.

15.3.3 Systematic Clinical and Medicolegal Visit

Examination for establishing permanent incapacity for work shall be carried out on the basis of documents and the applicant does not have to meet the persons carrying out the examination. Medicolegal examination is made usually in the Forensic Science Institute.

Systemic clinical visits and medicolegal visits are different by nature. In case of both visits, the medical history is recorded and the objective examination of the patient is conducted. As forensic physicians cannot conduct further examinations of the patient or draw up a referral to have the patient undergo further examinations (laboratory analyses, radiologic examinations, etc.), the examination conducted by the forensic physician consists, above all, in recording the general condition and objective status of the patient. The forensic physician uses the data of the further examinations conducted by the attending physicians and consults the physicians who conducted the examinations, if required.

15.3.4 Additional Investigations

Additional instrumental investigation will be made if necessary.

If a forensic medical doctor considers that additional investigations are necessary, then he/she needs to send the patient to the hospital (by law in Estonia, a forensic medical doctor does not have the right to refer the patient to another clinical doctor).

The forensic physician uses the data of the further examinations conducted by the attending physicians and consults the physicians who conducted the examinations, if required.

Forensic medical examination is usually made in the Estonian Forensic Science Institute. If necessary, the forensic medical doctor visits the patient at home. In this case the medical history is recorded and the objective examination of the patient is conducted. Local examination of the injured area and determination of the connection between an injury and incapacity for work is the responsibility of a forensic medical doctor.

15.4 Evaluation Criteria

Until 2009, persons visited their attending physicians with an application for examination; the physicians would then submit the application to the Pension Board along with a description of the state of health of the applicant.

The percentage of loss of capacity for work may be established for a period of 6 months, 1 year, 2 years, 3 years, 5 years or until attaining the pensionable age (but for no longer than 5 years).

The examination for permanent incapacity for work may be applied for:

1. By persons of working age, i.e. from 16 years of age until the pensionable age provided in the State Pension Insurance Act;
2. By way of exception after attaining the pensionable age or at a younger age than 16 years of age if the health of the person has been harmed as the result of an occupational disease, work injury, performing the duties of police service, border guard service, rescue service or other such duties of employment, a nuclear disaster, traffic accident or violent crime, or if the person is applying for a pension on the basis of an agreement entered into between the Republic of Estonia and another state.

The examination for permanent incapacity for work will be made on the basis of the documents; the applicant will not need to meet the persons conducting the examination.

The Social Insurance Board will formalise a decision concerning the results of the examination for permanent incapacity for work of which the applicant and the physician indicated in the application for examination who submitted the description of the person's state of health will be notified.

Permanent incapacity for work to the extent of 40–100 % grants a person the right to apply for a pension for incapacity for work.

15.4.1 Temporary Impairment

In case of temporary incapacity for work (illness, injury, etc.), the attending physician (family physician or medical specialist) will draw up a certificate of temporary incapacity for work for the person. The certificate of temporary incapacity for work releases the person from the obligation of performing their duties of employment. The types of certificate of temporary incapacity for work are the following: certificate for sick leave, certificate for maternity leave, certificate for adoption leave and certificate for care leave.

The certificate of temporary incapacity for work must be submitted to the employer who will submit it to the Estonian Health Insurance Fund along with a referral and any required appendices [5].

Benefit for temporary incapacity for work is a monetary benefit paid by the Health Insurance Fund to the insured person on the basis of a certificate of temporary incapacity for work.

15.4.2 Permanent Impairment

Permanent incapacity for work is injury or illness pertaining to work, profession, service, nuclear accident, traffic accident or as a result of violent crime. Permanent incapacity for work is divided into:

- Complete incapacity for work—as a consequence of illness or injury, the person is not capable to earn subsistence through work (loss of capacity for work 100 %).
- Partial incapacity for work—as a consequence of illness or injury, the person is not able to perform suitable work in the scope corresponding to the general national norms of working time (loss of capacity for work 10–90 %).

15.4.3 Other Non-pecuniary Losses

Based on the age of the person, i.e. children (children up to 16 years of age), persons aged 16 years until attaining pensionable age and persons of pensionable age, the degree of severity of disability and the additional expenses arising from the disability will be determined on different grounds.

For children (children up to 16 years of age) and persons of pensionable age, the degree of severity of disability will be determined as follows, proceeding from the need for personal assistance, guidance or supervision:

- Profound, if the person requires constant personal assistance, guidance or supervision 24 h a day
- Severe, if the person requires personal assistance, guidance or supervision in every 24 h period
- Moderate, if the person requires regular personal assistance or guidance outside of their place of residence at least once a week

For persons of working age (persons aged 16 years until attaining pensionable age), the degree of severity of disability will be determined as follows, proceeding from restrictions on participation in daily activity and social life:

- Profound, if the person's daily activity or participation in social life is wholly restricted
- Severe, if the person's daily activity or participation in social life is restricted
- Moderate, if the person has difficulties in their daily activity or participation in social life

The additional expenses arising from the disability of a person of working age constitute expenses on medicinal products, transport, maintenance of medical devices, self-care and household, use of the means of communication, clothing and footwear not financed from the health insurance and other state budget funds, to be made at least once a month in order to reduce the restrictions caused by the disability [6].

Social benefits for disabled persons are paid to persons for whom moderate, severe or profound disability has been established in order to partially compensate for the additional expenses caused by the disability. The degree of severity of the disability may change as the result of rehabilitation, usage of medical devices, adjusting the living environment or other circumstances.

The state pays social benefits to a disabled person if the person incurs additional expenses due to their disability, e.g. if they require medical devices, care, rehabilitation, or if the additional expenses are related to transport, employment or studying.

The additional expenses arising from the disability of a person of working age are established, taking into consideration their needs (medicinal products, transport, medical devices, special needs concerning clothing and footwear, increased self-care and household expenses, means of communication) and the degree of their uncompensated functional impairment.

The state compensates for the expenses on psychological care incurred by victims of an offence and their family members, if required. In 2007, the Victim Support Act entered into force. One of the objectives of the Act is compensating for the expenses on psychological care incurred by victims of an offence and their family members, if required.

The legislation for compensating for the expenses on psychological care was above all created in order to aid the faster psychological rehabilitation of persons who have fallen victim to less severe criminal offences and misdemeanours (e.g. cases of domestic violence) and for improving the social coping of the family members of victims of violent crime and other criminal offences.

The commencement of misdemeanour or criminal proceedings concerning the offence is the prerequisite for receiving the compensation for the expenses on psychological care. For the purposes of the Act, psychological care services are psychological counselling, psychotherapy or support group services. The expenses on psychological care are paid by the Social Insurance Board.

References

1. Social benefits for disabled persons act [RT I 2000, 71, 437]
2. Töövõime kaotuse protsendi määramise juhend 03.01.2002 nr 3 [RT I 2001, 100, 648]
3. Töövõime kaotuse protsendi määramise juhend. 03.01.2002 nr 3. https://www.riigiteataja.ee/akt/163243
4. Püsiva töövõimetuse ekspertiis. http://www.sotsiaalkindlustusamet.ee/ekspertiis-ja-rehabilitatsioon/
5. Determination of degree of severity of disability [RT I 2007, 71, 437]
6. Puude raskusastme ja lisakulude tuvastamine. http://www.sotsiaalkindlustusamet.ee/puude-raskusastme-ja-lisakulude-tuvastamine-3/

Part III
Medico-legal Ascertainment of Personal Injury and Damage Under Civil-Tort Law: Continental Overview – America

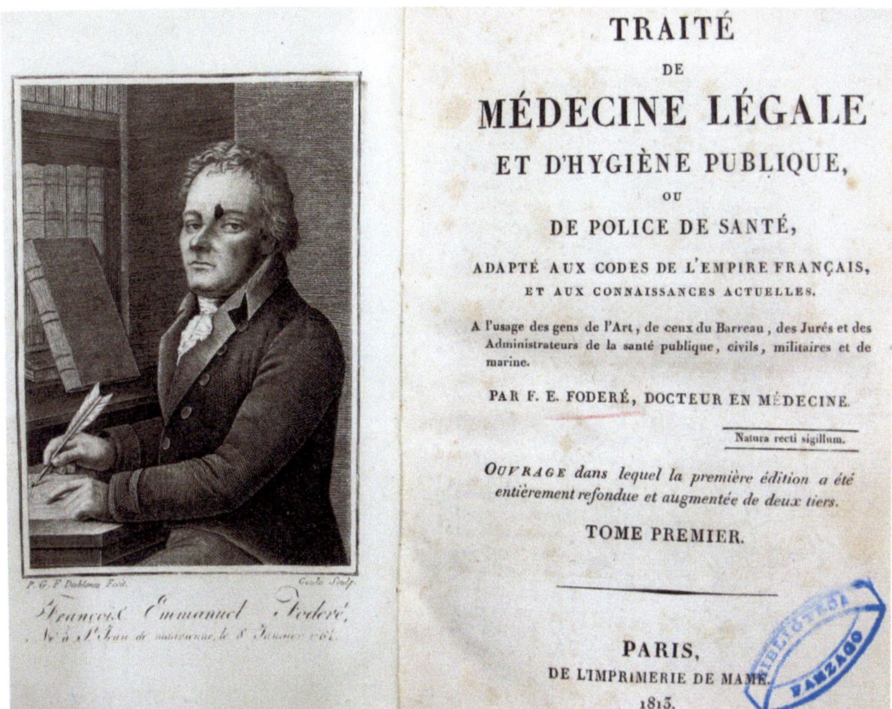
TRAITÉ
DE
MÉDECINE LÉGALE
ET D'HYGIÈNE PUBLIQUE,
OU
DE POLICE DE SANTÉ,
ADAPTÉ AUX CODES DE L'EMPIRE FRANÇAIS,
ET AUX CONNAISSANCES ACTUELLES.
A l'usage des gens de l'Art, de ceux du Barreau, des Jurés et des Administrateurs de la santé publique, civils, militaires et de marine.
PAR F. E. FODERÉ, DOCTEUR EN MÉDECINE.
Natura recti sigillum.
OUVRAGE dans lequel la première édition a été entièrement refondue et augmentée de deux tiers.
TOME PREMIER.
PARIS,
DE L'IMPRIMERIE DE MAME.
1813.

Fodéré, François Emanuel. Traite de medecine legale et d'hygiene publique ou de police de santé Adapté aux codes de l'Empire Francais et aux connaissances actuelles. A l'usage des gens de l'art, de ceux du barreau, des jurés et des administrateurs de la santé publique, civils militaires et de marine. Paris, 1813. Courtesy of historical section of the "Vincenzo Pinali" Medical Library of the University of Padova

Chapter 16
Methods of Ascertainment of Personal Damage in the USA

Mohammed Ranavaya

Abstract The chapter illustrates the historical, judicial, and juridical framework of personal injury assessment and compensation in the USA, describing the expert's qualification and competences and detailing the ascertainment methodology and criteria of evaluation utilized for identifying, describing, and estimating any personal injury, its temporary and permanent consequences, and the causal value/link between the event and the injury and between the injury and the impairment/disability.

16.1 Historical, Judicial, and Juridical Overview

It is written in the Bible that "if any would not work, neither should he eat" [1]. Hence, there has been a long-standing expectation among individuals within any society that members must contribute individually to benefit and share collectively. It appears equally true that individual members who cannot contribute because of disability may be exempt from such expectation and yet still enjoy benefits to which other group members are entitled. It is also possible for an individual to exploit society through unfair and exaggerated claims of disability which becomes an issue of social justice.

Although social justice systems compensate in some way for bodily illness or injury, they must also afford protection against benefits being paid to those who choose not to be productive and fake or exaggerate their disability. Thus, disability assessment and compensation systems provide rules defining disability and entitlement, as well as procedures for determining who qualifies as disabled. These rules are intended to provide fair and equitable distribution of limited system resources to those whose needs are greatest and whose disabilities are most compelling. These systems' rules and laws have been around since the beginning of history and are

M. Ranavaya (✉)
Division of Disability Medicine, Joan C. Edwards School of Medicine, Marshall University, 1600 Medical Center Drive, Huntington 25701, WV, USA
e-mail: mranavayamd@abime.org

S.D. Ferrara et al. (eds.), *Personal Injury and Damage Ascertainment under Civil Law*, DOI 10.1007/978-3-319-29812-2_16

elemental components of our social fabric, rooted in the very origins of human society.

16.2 Global Historical Overview of Personal Injury Evaluation and Compensation

Historical evidence suggests that social justice and systems of compensation have existed globally and have been linked since ancient times [2]. Records exist from ancient Persian societies detailing compensation for injuries suffered in relation to the social order of that time. As far back as 4000 years ago, Babylon compensated for loss of life or limb while in service of the state. For example, the Code of Hammurabi (1750 BC) was an ancient Babylonian legal code, written in cuneiform and containing laws purportedly given to King Hammurabi by Shamash, the Babylonian god of justice [2]. The code represents an advanced attempt to legislate justice in moral, social, and economic spheres, with provisions that decreed punitive action to be taken against a person causing bodily injury, and it bears a striking resemblance to the Mosaic laws. Among these was the principle of Lex Talionis, the "law of retaliation" or "principle of equivalence," which existed to compensate for wrongful bodily injury but dictated that societal retribution should be the same in kind as the offense, as in an "eye for an eye and a tooth for a tooth" [3].

The Babylonian Laws of Eshnunna were a more enlightened yet contemporary approach, as evidenced from the cuneiform text of the old Babylonian kingdom of Eshnunna. The laws were a compilation of rules and ordinances recommending monetary compensation for bodily harm, as the writing attests: "If a man bit and severed the nose of a man, 1 mina silver he shall weigh out. An eye, 1 mina; a tooth, ½ mina; an ear, ½ mina. A slap in the face, 10 shekels silver he shall weigh out" [4].

Among the ancient Egyptians, similar laws provided compensation for wrongful acts resulting in injury. Punitive actions, often severe, could be taken against doctors for acts of malpractice, such as amputating a doctor's hands for causing blindness to a patient after removal of cataracts [5].

Evidence of social compensation exists for other Western societies, including the ancient Greeks, who provided compensation for injured parties. The soldiers or survivors of Alexander the Great's army were compensated for losses of life and limb incurred during the course of military service. In Roman society, compensation was available for both free men and slaves, yet social status dictated that slaves received less compensation than free men [6]. Furthermore; Roman masters were obligated to care for their injured slaves. The concept of *Respondeat Superior* ("let the master answer") was also introduced, which created the legal obligation of a master to answer for the wrongful doings of his servants. These concepts still exist in common law and in military doctrine in which subordinate members who are bound to obey legal orders from their superiors in turn derive legal protection and immunity for actions taken and consequences of following orders.

Around the birth of Christ, the Germanic and Nordic tribes (Lombards) were establishing themselves on the western edge of the Roman Empire as civilized members of the empire. Consequently, the blood feud formerly used as a means of securing justice was formally prohibited, and the state assumed the role of administering justice between the injured and the accused. The compensation for injuries was based on a "whole person" concept. Each tribesman was considered to have an intrinsic monetary value—his wergild or "man value"—which varied according to social status and was typically worth 200 Roman solidi. This was the value of his life, or 100 % whole body impairment. There was a schedule for all sorts of injuries, from as trivial as injury to a toe to loss of limbs, eyes, and life itself. An even greater compensation was awarded for cosmetic loss; thus, if one knocked out one's molar tooth, the compensation was eight solidi (4 % of the wergild), but loss of a tooth that showed on a smile was equal to 16 solidi (8 % of the wergild) [7]. The impairment values are extraordinarily similar to those used today.

State-sponsored care for the poor and disabled without a responsible party (the contemporary concept of social security) has a tradition in history as well. The first state-sponsored social security system was established by Muslims in 640 AD during the reign of the second Caliph Umar. The state treasury provided monthly benefits to those afflicted with blindness and to widows and orphans [8].

During the Middle Ages, a paternalistic system existed in which feudal lords were obligated to care for subjects within their serfdom who became ill or injured. Various craft guilds were formed and developed an early form of disability insurance whereby healthy members of the guild contributed regularly to a fund that was made available to members in the event of injury or illness [9].

Social compensation systems were not unique to civil society. During the sixteenth and seventeenth centuries, the buccaneers of America were engaged in acts of maritime piracy against vessels of trade between Europe and the colonies. Their system of laws was embodied in the ship's "articles of association" and was agreed to by signature of each crew member at the outset of any voyage. The articles specified sums of salary to be paid to the captain and various crew members, the source being the common stock of illegally acquired goods from that particular expedition. Furthermore, they contained an early form of workers' compensation agreement to recompense crew members for serious bodily harm suffered during the voyage. An example follows:

> "...they order for the loss of a right arm 600 pieces of 8 or 6 slaves; for the loss of a left arm 500 pieces of 8 or 5 slaves; for a right leg 500 pieces of 8 or 5 slaves; for a left leg 400 pieces of 8 or 4 slaves; for an eye 100 pieces of 8 or 1 slave; for a finger of the hand the same reward as for the eye" [10].

Among the changes brought about as nineteenth-century society became increasingly industrialized was the increase in the proportion of society members working for low wages. Fear of injury or death in the workplace was a significant concern. Local governments became increasingly concerned with strategies for provision of medical service to the poor and destitute, the systematic and equitable spreading of costs of indigent care, and compensating for lost wages among the working and middle class.

The following overview examines the historical origins of the major US laws and disability assessment and compensation systems, highlighting the fundamental similarities and contrasts between them.

The US legal system is complex due to its large territory (50 state jurisdictions plus 2 commonwealth territories); however, it is essentially based on four basic types of law: constitutional, statutory (legislative), common law (judicial precedent), and administrative law. These basic types are found in all 50 states and in the federal and other administrative systems but with different interpretations resulting sometimes in conflict with other sister jurisdictions; the same factual controversy may be decided in favor of the defendant in New York, but against the same defendant a couple hundred miles south in Virginia. Additionally, in some cases, the plaintiff could win in New York under New York state law but lose in the same state under federal law.

Generally, the US Federal Constitution is the final arbiter of any controversy as it relates to constitutionally guaranteed rights and federal law. This creates predictability and uniformity in the US federal law with the US Supreme Court being the final authority in deciding what the federal law across the USA is [11]. This still leaves various individual state laws at conflict with other states, even those that share a common border. The judicial branch of the government is mainly responsible to interpret the federal and state laws, including the language of constitutions. Unlike the constitutions of many other nations, the US Constitution is the supreme law of the land and, along with the individual constitutions of each state, outlines the powers of the federal and state government and the executive, legislative, and judicial authority.

Moreover, the federal and individual state constitutions guarantee certain legal protection for individuals against governmental action, thereby placing limitations upon governmental powers and creating individual liberties that guarantee individual rights. These fundamental inalienable rights of individual citizens include the right to procreation, the right to marry, the right to privacy, the right to travel, and the right to vote, as well as prohibition against governmental taking of private property without just compensation. Individual freedoms constitutionally protected also include the freedoms of speech, press, religion, association, and bearing arms.

The US statutory (legislative) laws, both federal and state laws created by elected legislative bodies, supersede all other types of law except constitutional law. US federal statutory laws preempt the state laws. These laws can be changed by repeal or modified by further legislation; however, they are all subject to judicial interpretation which sometimes results in varying interpretation of the same law in different jurisdictions. As mentioned earlier, all laws in the USA are subject to the ultimate authority of the US Constitution and its interpretation by the US Supreme Court, resulting in final resolution of a certain case or controversy or dispute.

It is noteworthy that in the USA, the majority of the individual state's legal systems (contract law, property law and tort law/law of delict, etc.) are based on common law (judge-made law) which was inherited from England dating back to colonial times. The common law has its roots dating back to twelfth-century England in the reign of King Henry II when he delegated his judicial powers to various magistrates and judges. The country was divided into a number of circuits, and the king appointed judges for each circuit who were charged with deciding civil cases based on *precedent* (prior decisions and the common customs of society), hence the term *common* law. Common law relies on the legal doctrine of *stare decisis*, which means "let the decision stand." The idea is to have certain predictability in the law for those cases with circumstances similar to cases from the past. Thus common law is a body of law that is based on the precedent value of past decisions of the court, decisions of other courts within the same judicial system, public policy, and/or legal reasoning. Prior decisions of the court are interpreted as having precedent value, furnishing examples or authority when considering an identical or similar case. If the same question of law is raised in another case, the court would attempt to adhere to its prior decision(s).

Common law interpretations can vary between various jurisdictions, but it is subordinate to statutory law as well as state and federal constitutions. Therefore, the elements of common law that offend the prevailing contemporary political and economic ideology can be countered by legislative action, resulting in the statutes that override the common law. However, the judges ultimately interpret these statutes and determine whether the Constitution or certain statutes are applicable or even relevant to the particular facts of a case before the court, hence giving the judiciary ultimate and wide discretion in many cases.

Administrative law is the body of law that covers complex technical and specialized areas often considered to be procedurally unwieldy for the legislature to deal with on a continuing basis. Administrative law is therefore administered under the jurisdiction of an administrative agency that is specifically created by statute for the purpose of promulgating rules and regulations to govern in a specialized area of public interest. Several examples of such administrative agencies include the Environmental Protection Agency and the Department of Labor, with its various injured workers' compensation programs. These agencies, even though quasi-independent, must create rules and regulations that are consistent with the original legislative action, i.e., enabling acts that created the particular administrative agency and are subject to other hierarchies of laws including statutory and/or constitutional law.

Within the USA, under the framework of the complex legal system as described above, various disability and compensation systems arose to ensure that members of society with a medically determinable impairment that may lead to disability have recourse to compensation from various avenues, including tort action in common law against wrongdoers for personal injuries, state and federal workers' compensation laws, veterans benefits, and social welfare programs where appropriate. These systems have diverse historical origins and statutory requirements; consequently, there remains considerable variability between them with respect to the definitions of disability, entitlement, benefits, claims application procedures, adjudication, and the role and relative weight given to medical versus administrative deliberations. In most cases, a medical determination of physical or psychological impairment is necessary, and in some cases the doctor is empowered to render an opinion regarding the nature and extent of medically determined impairment resulting in disability. It is imperative that doctors entrusted with assisting the legal system be familiar with precise meanings and definitions of the terms *impairment* and *disability*, as well as the fundamental requirements, nuances, and jurisdictional variations of the particular disability system within which they are working.

16.3 Contemporary Disability Compensation Systems in the USA

In addition to the tort claims that may arise out of a personal injury caused by motor vehicle accidents, toxic exposure, medical malpractice, or defective products and adjudicated in the individual state court system, the following are other contemporary disability compensation systems in the USA.

16.4 State Workers' Compensation Laws

Because of inadequacies of recovery for industrial injuries under common law, various workers' compensation statutes were enacted around the turn of the twentieth century in the USA with the goal to provide expeditious resolution of industrial injury claims [12]. The need for workers' compensation laws at the individual state level arose in response to many factors, including the societal change from an agrarian society to an industrial age, resulting in catastrophic injuries causing several hundred deaths in single incidents, such as a mine explosion in West Virginia in 1907 as well as a New York sewing factory fire in 1911. The rise of labor unions and increasing awareness of workers' rights were other major factors in the enactment of various workers' compensation legislation. In addition, the only alternative legal remedy available to these injured workers, the common law of torts, was inefficient and ineffective in most cases due to its very lengthy and often expensive process with several unique defenses available to the defendant. The workers' compensation legislation sought to reduce this burden on the injured worker by providing all parties with a more expedited and responsive process and a no-fault system.

Under workers' compensation laws, a "no-fault" system was adopted to resolve the dilemmas of the tort claims process by providing automatic coverage to employees whose claims of injury arise "out of and in the course of employment." In exchange, covered employees forego the right to sue the employer in most instances, except in cases of wanton neglect.

Workers' compensation systems in the USA are mandated by both state and federal legislation to provide economic protection for workers who sustain personal injuries resulting out of and in the course of employment. Generally, this is accomplished through private insurance schemes underwriting the risks of occupational injuries and diseases in return for a premium paid by the employer under the law. Few states serve as the insurer themselves.

The individual workers' compensation legislation in each state has some variation, but common features among all include injured workers' entitlement to benefits if his or her injury is determined to be compensable and can be shown to have arisen "out of and in the course of employment." Historically, workers' compensation statutes are intended to cover injuries that occurred by "accident" (a chance, unexpected, and unintended event) in the workplace at a specific point in time, as opposed to a "disease" entity or condition that arose gradually over time. In reality, this distinction often cannot clearly be made, and coverage is now typically extended to occupational "illness" or disease as well as impairment resulting from "aggravation" of a preexisting and underlying condition [13].

An injured worker is entitled to three types of benefits: survivor benefits in the event of injury or illness resulting in death, medical and rehabilitation expenses, and wage-loss benefits. In the event of death, the surviving spouse and/or children are entitled to funeral expenses and a monthly pension (generally 2/3 of the average monthly wage at time of death up to a maximum cap) which terminates if the spouse remarries or, in the case of children, when they reach the age of 18 (or 22 if they remain a full-time student) or upon marriage. Coverage for medical and rehabilitative expenses is 100 % for authorized services. Wage-loss benefits are paid according to four separate levels of work disability. Temporary disability occurs for the duration of the treatment period and may be total (employee is incapable of any work) or partial (employee is allowed to resume "modified duty" with restrictions) [14].

Upon completion of treatment phase, at the point of maximum medical improvement (MMI) and case closure, the employee may receive compensation for permanent total or partial disability, generally as a lump sum payout calculated according to a predetermined formula specific to each jurisdiction, which takes into account the value of the "whole person" as a number of weeks' pay multiplied by the average weekly wage up to a cap and then multiplied by the impairment percentage of the "whole person."

16.4.1 Medical Evaluation and Reporting Requirements

Within the workers' compensation (WC) system, physicians may be asked to determine causality of a given impairment within medical probability. They may be asked to complete a work status report during various stages of treatment indicating whether or not the employee is ready to return to full or modified duty and to identify activity and material handling restrictions where applicable. They will be asked to address when MMI has occurred or is expected to occur and to issue an impairment rating for work-related condition(s) if MMI has occurred.

16.5 US Federal Social Security Compensation Laws

A loosely structured welfare system existed within the USA as far back as colonial times [15]. Initial programs were informal, voluntary, and operated at the community level. By the early 1900s, social and state-funded programs were in place. The Social Security Act of 1935 was the first federally mandated program and was implemented during the administration of Franklin D. Roosevelt as an attempt to create a federal social welfare system after the Great Depression. Initially, the program was intended to address the needs of individuals disadvantaged by means of old age, unemployment, disability, or death of a spouse. Under Title II of the Act, an old age insurance pension was established for workers when they reached age 65.

The Social Security Administration (SSA) is the largest disability program in the USA, assisting between 33 and 50 % of all persons qualified as disabled [6]. It includes two separate disability benefits programs. The first is Social Security Disability Insurance (SSDI), a program established in 1956 to create a separate fund for workers over age 50 who were totally and permanently disabled. SSDI is federally administered through the SSA and funded through a payroll tax that combines deductions for old age and disability (OASDI). The application process is initiated at the state level with the Bureau of Disability Determination. To be eligible, an individual must have worked in a job covered by SSDI for a minimum period (in general, 5 of the 10 years preceding the onset of disability). Pension benefits are provided to disabled individuals who have contributed through payroll taxes (FICA) during the requisite period and whose disability involves total incapacitation [16].

Supplemental Security Income (SSI) is a second disability benefits program within the SSA, which operates as a federal-state partnership. SSI provides benefits to disabled individuals whose income and assets meet minimum criteria according to a "means test." It is funded through general revenue (i.e., income tax revenues) and does not require work history for eligibility.

16.5.1 Federal Workers' Compensation Laws

The various workers' compensation schemes at the US federal level are distinct and distinguishable from the state workers' compensation legislation and include the Federal Employers Liability Act (FELA) which is the sole remedy for the injured railroad worker against the railroad; the Federal Employees Compensation Act (FECA) which is the sole remedy for job-related injuries and diseases sustained by federal employees including postal workers as well as Peace Corps members against the federal government. Physicians seeking further information as well as opportunities to provide services to these programs should review the Federal Office of Workers' Compensation Programs (OWCP) website at http://www.dol.gov/owcp/. The OWCP also manages the Long Shore and Harbor Workers Act, Federal Black Lung Program, and the Division of Energy Employees Occupational Illness Program.

16.5.2 Federal Employer's Liability Act

The Federal Employers Liability Act (FELA) was enacted in 1908 to provide disability benefits to employees of the interstate railroad industry for job-related injuries. At that time, railroads were the largest employer and rail work was exceptionally hazardous. Before passage of the act, injured employees would seek redress under tort claims as previously described. FELA limited employer defenses to only contributory negligence (now modified to comparative negligence for which an award is apportioned according to percentage of employer versus employee culpability) and increased employers' awareness for liability and incentive for prevention of workplace injuries.

FELA remains a potentially adversarial system in which the injured employee may negotiate an out-of-court settlement. Alternatively, a claimant may file suit for personal losses against the railroad in either a state civil court or federal court. Under FELA, a claimant must prove negligence on the part of the railroad. In turn, the railroad may assert a defense of comparative negligence, whereby recovery for damages can be proportionately reduced. FELA enables a claimant to recover economic damages as well as compensation for pain and suffering. Additional benefits might include retirement and sickness and disability annuities.

16.5.3 Jones Act (Merchant Marine Act)

The Jones Act (Merchant Marine Act) of 1920 is similar to FELA but covers civilian sailors for permanent injury suffered while in the service of a ship in navigable water. To collect, the claimant must bring suit against the master or owner of the ship. Cases are typically settled out of court because seamen are regarded as wards of the state and thereby enjoy liberal treatment by the court system in general.

16.5.4 Federal Employees Compensation Act

The Federal Employees Compensation Act (FECA) was enacted to provide compensation benefits to civilian employees of the federal government for work-related disability. Presently, it covers more than three million civilian employees of the US Government, Postal Service, and Peace Corps, as well as such nonfederal employees as state and local law enforcement personnel and employees of the Civil Air Patrol. FECA is a no-fault system and, consequently, a federal employee cannot sue the federal government or recover damages under any other statute for work-related injuries. Changes in the law in 1974, whereby continued pay was offered to workers injured on the job, resulted in a dramatic increase in the incidence of claims. There is no time limit on wage loss or medical benefits and no cap on medical benefits. FECA is federally administered under the Office of Workers' Compensation Program (OWCP) in Washington, DC.

16.5.5 Longshore and Harbor Worker's Act

The Longshore and Harbor Workers' Compensation Act (LHWCA) was enacted in 1927 to provide compensation benefits to shoreside maritime employees for occupational disabilities received while engaged in longshore work, ship building and repair, and other maritime activities. It is a no-fault system federally administered under the US Department of Labor.

16.5.6 Federal Mine Workers Compensation Act (Federal Black Lung Program)

The Federal Black Lung Program was created by the Federal Mine Safety & Health Act of 1977 to provide coverage for coal miners engaged in surface or underground activity. The act provides monthly pension and medical benefits for total disability caused by pneumoconiosis (Black Lung) arising from employment in and around coal mines [16]. It is administered through the US Department of Labor.

The diagnosis of pneumoconiosis under the act may be ascertained through findings on a chest x-ray according to the International Labor Office (ILO) Classification system. Chest x-rays of claimants are read by "B-readers" who are medical specialists with certification by the National Institute of Occupational Health and Safety (NIOSH) to read chest x-rays of dust-exposed individuals according to the ILO classification. The miner must also show total disability from pulmonary causes as documented by pulmonary function testing. The US Department of Labor has published predetermined disability standards for spirometric values and arterial blood gas values against which a disability claim is referenced. It is estimated that the average cost per miner found eligible for disability benefits under the program is from $350,000 to 500,000 over their remaining life span.

16.5.7 Department of Veterans Affairs

The Department of Veterans Affairs (VA) was established in 1930 as the Veterans Administration to "consolidate and coordinate" government activities affecting American veterans of war. The Veterans Benefits Administration (VBA) was originally established as the Department of Veterans Benefits within the VA in 1953 to administer the GI Bill and VA compensation and pension programs. Presently, the Compensation and Pension Service rests within the VBA. Eligibility for compensation and pensioning within the VA is extended to all veterans who receive honorable or general discharge from active military service. Entitlement decisions are administratively handled by the Adjudication Division of the Compensation and Pension Service. Service-connected entitlement refers to conditions determined by adjudication to be related to injury or disease incurred or aggravated while on active duty, whereas non-service-connected entitlement refers to conditions determined to be unrelated to active duty. VA benefits include disability pensions in the form of monthly monetary support to the veteran because of service-connected disability, or to a spouse, child, or parent of the veteran in the event of service-connected death. Additional benefits include hospitalization and medical care, orthotic and prosthetic devices, durable medical equipment, and allowances for adaptive modifications to the veteran's home and/or motor vehicle where necessary.

Title 38 of the Code of Federal Regulations contains both the VA's Schedule for Rating Disabilities (Part 4) and other VA regulations pertaining to compensation and pension (Part 3). Volume I of Title 38 contains Parts 0 to 17. Ten of the 16 body systems in the rating schedule have been recently revised. They are available online through the Library of Congress website.

The process of compensation requires a veteran to apply for compensation for a particular condition. The claim must be well grounded, which means certain legal requirements must be met. If they are, the rater in a regional office may grant the benefit if the medical evidence of record is sufficient on which to rate (e.g., the service medical records may suffice in a recently discharged veteran), and the regulatory and statutory requirements for service connection are met. Some conditions may only be service connected directly; that is, there must be evidence that the condition began while the veteran was in the service. Many chronic conditions may be service connected if they began within a 1-year period after service was completed; some may be service connected much later if linked to service (e.g., because of herbicide or radiation exposure while in service). If a medical examination is needed, the rater will request one from a VA medical facility through a computerized request process. Some of the examinations may be contracted out if, for example, the required specialist is not available at a particular VA facility.

The VA examiner will receive a computer-generated set of worksheets for guidance as to the requirements of the particular examinations requested. If the examination, and any requested opinions about relationships, etc., are sufficient for rating purposes, the rater will apply the medical information to the rating schedule and assign a rating. Disability evaluations are generally performed by doctors at VHA facilities using the Automated Medical Information Exchange (AMIE) data processing system and associated Disability Examination Worksheets and the VA's Schedule of Rating Disabilities (VASR-D) [17].

There is a local appellate process for veterans who have been denied benefits. Beyond that, there is the Board of Veterans Appeals in Washington, DC, and, finally, there is the US Court of Veterans Appeals. Rarely, cases may go to the Federal District Court and have the potential to go the Supreme Court. In the almost 10 years since the Court of Veterans Appeals began, a large body of case law has developed. Private medical evidence is considered as valid as VA medical evidence if it is sufficient for rating purposes, and veterans may apply for benefits with only private medical evidence.

16.5.8 Americans with Disabilities Act

The Americans with Disabilities Act (ADA) was enacted in 1992 to guarantee equal rights for disabled individuals to employment opportunities, public transportation, and public access. The ADA broadly defines disability as "…a physical or mental impairment that substantially limits one or more of the major life activities of the individual; or a record of such an impairment; or being regarded as having such an impairment."

Discrimination against the disabled in the workplace is prevented under Title 1 (Employment), which applies to businesses in the private sector with 25 or more employees. Title 1 compels the employer to afford equal employment opportunities to an "otherwise qualified" individual with a disability, who meets the "essential functions" of an employment position with or without "reasonable accommodation." "Such accommodation can include structural modifications at the work site to improve access, availability of modified duty, adaptive equipment and devices." Accommodation is reasonable if it does not pose an "undue hardship" (logistically or financially) on the employer, or pose a "direct threat" to the health and safety of disabled individuals and their co-workers. The Equal Employment Opportunity Commission (EEOC) oversees compliance with the law and has an excellent technical manual for those who wish to further educate themselves on the topic.

16.5.9 Family Medical Leave Act

The Family Medical Leave Act (FMLA) was enacted in 1994 to provide up to 12 weeks of unpaid leave under circumstances of medical necessity. The law applies to employers of 50 or more persons, and employees become eligible after having worked for the employer for 12 months or at least 1250 h during the period before the requested leave. Leave may be granted to either gender and for purposes of the birth or adoption of a child, care of immediate family members, or an employee's own illness. It provides for unpaid leave, continued hospitalization, and life insurance protection to an employee during the period of absence.

16.6 Private Insurance Disability Systems

It is estimated that 40 million Americans have private, long-term disability insurance, usually through the workplace. Private insurance plans lack statutory provisions in favor of contractual language that stipulates the criteria for disability and entitlement as well as the benefits of coverage under the policy. Employees who become disabled are initially covered by short-term disability for a period typically of 90 days. If the period of disablement must be extended, a long-term disability policy takes effect after 90 days.

Long-term disability policies may be individual or group policies. Group policies are typically sold to companies and are more affordable than individual policies. Group policies provide coverage to disabled employees who are unable to perform the requirements of their usual and customary job over a finite and specified period, typically 2 years; subsequently, the disabled will continue to receive benefits only if they are unable to perform the functions of "any occupation" as provisionally defined by the policy. Individual policies are available at higher premiums but may afford greater duration of protection to the individual who ultimately cannot perform his or her particular job over an extended, and perhaps indefinite, period. Private disability generally pays up to 60 % of the individual's wages, to a maximum allowable cap, and may have built-in cost-of-living allowances with adjustments for future inflation.

16.7 Identification and Description of Medicolegal Expert's Qualifications

Medical expert testimony is required in a variety of disputes before the courts of law in the USA. Claims of medical malpractice resulting in personal injuries to the patients, motor vehicle accidents resulting in bodily injuries, work-related incidents, as well as criminal trial cases, and other similar litigations almost always require some form of medical expert testimony. Legal systems tend to think that medical sciences have clear and definitive answers to certain factual questions. From the time the Roman doctor Antistius testified before the Roman Senate about the cause of death of Julius Caesar, that of the 23 stab wounds to his body the only fatal wound was to his chest resulting in his death [18], the legal system has relied on forensic evidence from scientific expert witness for the fact-finding.

In the USA, the legal system largely relies on medical and scientific technical experts for personal injury assessment and resulting calculation of damages and disability. This is generally done in the form of evaluation and testimony from an independent scientific expert who is usually qualified by appropriate education, training, knowledge, skills, experience, and abilities. The scientific or technical expert through the special training, knowledge, or experience is able to offer opinion(s) on a particular question in a legal dispute, thereby assisting the legal system in determining what the facts are, relevant to a particular case. It is noteworthy that it is not the scientific expert but rather the judicial process that defines the factual question in the litigation for the expert witness to answer. Different cases require different levels of knowledge, skill sets, and expertise, but all parties are allowed to offer some form of independent medical evaluation to support their claim. Today, many trials in the USA, civil or criminal, state or federal, turn on the testimony of one or more of scientific and/or technical experts.

The laws of expert witness in various US legal systems govern the conduct of the expert witness in that system. The assessment by the expert is usually done in the form of independent review of records and other relevant data as well as an examination of the injured party or deceased if so requested. In some cases, the expert may not have access to the injured party and form an independent scientific opinion by solely relying on the available records, data, and scientific literature.

16.7.1 Independent Medical Examinations

Independent Medical Examinations (IMEs) are examinations performed by a doctor who is not involved in the injured person's care for multiple purposes including determination of physical/mental impairment and disability. IMEs provide medicolegal documentation of fact, analysis, and well-reasoned opinion. The evaluations must be independent, impartial, and without bias. The requester may be the lawyer for any party, the insurer, the employer, state authority, or, in some cases, the court.

IMEs are performed to provide information for compensation case management and for evidence in judicial hearings and other legal proceedings. IMEs are a component of most US workers' compensation statutes as well as common law/tort law, although the specifics vary by state. They are performed at several stages during the course of an injury/illness claim, treatment, rehabilitation, and return to work.

An Independent Medical Evaluation (IME) is different from medical/surgical consultation in the due course of a clinician's practice in that it is almost always a single encounter and no medical care is provided, thereby resulting in no doctor–patient relationship. The key issues associated with an IME differ from clinical consultations in role and focus. The US judicial philosophy views independent assessments by an impartial doctor (other than the treating doctor) to help avoid potential conflicts of interest when analyzing disputed issues in a legal claim of causation, prognosis, need for further treatment, degree of impairment/disability, or work capacity.

In the USA, IMEs may be performed any time there is a dispute, concern, or question regarding the medical treatment or condition of the injured party. These issues include such topics as the following:

- Diagnosis/prognosis
- Proximate causation, and in case of workers compensation claims, work relatedness of an illness or injury
- Identification of other nonmedical factors that can have a significant impact on the outcome of the medical condition or treatment
- Appropriateness of current and proposed medical treatment or diagnostic efforts
- Ability to return to work (fitness for duty) and or appropriate work accommodation
- Maximal degree of medical improvement
- Impairment and disability assessment with quantum for compensation

IMEs can help to untangle the complex relationship between pathology (a medical condition or diagnosis), impairment (an anatomic or functional abnormality or loss), functional limitation (a restriction that can be assessed by objective medical assessment), and disability (inability to perform socially defined activities or roles). For example, the Americans with Disabilities Act defines a disability as "a physical or mental impairment that substantially limits one or more major life activities of such individual, a record of such an impairment, or being regarded as having an impairment." Major life activities include seeing, hearing, speaking, walking, breathing, performing manual tasks, learning, caring for one's self, and working. It is essential that IMEs be performed objectively, using reproducible techniques and agreed-upon standards. Several impairment rating systems exist. The "gold standard" for determining a general physical or mental impairment is the *AMA Guides to the Evaluation of Permanent Impairment* [18]. Specialized systems have been created by the Social Security Administration, the Railroad Retirement Board, and other organizations. Recent publications have added disability duration standards.

Regardless of the referring source, the IME by definition should have unbiased objectivity as one of its primary goals, with emphasis placed on reproducible techniques of examination. Furthermore, the opinions given should be based on the most current scientific knowledge, as well as agreed-upon standards of impairment and disability evaluations such as the *AMA Guides*. IMEs are performed by doctors in many different specialties. Specialized IMEs are performed by other health professionals, many of whom are licensed to perform these evaluations.

Previously, users of expert witness services and IMEs had long expressed dissatisfaction with variations in quality IMEs. Challenges to the field included (1) poor quality evaluations, (2) unavailability of qualified examiners, (3) absence of educational performance standards, (4) lack of standardized training, and (5) no system for determining the competence of examiners. Inadequate quality of examinations was reflected in many ways. For example, evaluations were often not responsive to the judicial systems' need for validated and scientifically supportable answers to the questions and legal claims. The examiners often failed to understand the critical issues such as definitions of causation, impairment and disability, etc. Assessments in some cases were perfunctory, with conclusions without scientific support. One other major concern was biased evaluations performed by so-called experts lacking current clinical competence.

To overcome these critical quality issues, the American Board of Independent Medical Examiners (ABIME) was created in the USA in 1993 as a nonprofit independent accreditation body to improve the quality of independent medical and impairment examinations [19]. The primary mission of ABIME was to do public good by enhancing the quality of independent scientific evidence presented to the legal system through well-conducted and valid independent medical examinations by creating a voluntary process of standard setting, definition of competencies, and performance evaluation for independent medical examiners.

The ABIME board of governors' members are representatives from multiple medical specialties that oversee multiple committees comprising of the examination committee, the standards committee, the ethics committee, etc. The exam committee, the most robust of ABIME committees, is comprised of doctors from dozens of medical specialties, assisted by Human Resources Research Organization (HumRRO) from Washington, DC, an independent professional examination organization responsible for producing the psychometrically validated standardized ABIME examination. Human Resources Research Organization (HumRRO) worked with ABIME to define specific competencies, design an examination that is rigorous and fair, prepare and validate a large pool of test items (questions), perform statistical quality control, and insure integrity of the examination.

The ABIME examination was based on an exhaustive analysis of the job tasks of an independent medical examiner and expert witness. From this job task analysis, the examination committee defined an examination blueprint with the knowledge, skills, and abilities of the content areas of an independent medical examiner. Questions for each version of the examination are drawn from a large pool, to which new questions are continually being added. The examination is continuously revised by regular meetings of the examination committee, working closely with our psychometric consultants.

Requirements for certification by ABIME include (1) a current, unrestricted, medical license or registration with appropriate health regulation authority in the jurisdiction where the candidate resides and practices; (2) a clear record with no disciplinary action for unethical or other offense as imposed by a State Board of

Medical Licensure or similar authority within the last 5 years; (3) board certification in a specialty recognized by the American Board of Medical Specialties, or the American Osteopathic Association, or equivalent from a foreign jurisdiction or documentation that an applicant has been involved in the practice of medicine, including residency (postdoctoral training) years, for a period of 5 years prior to their submitting an ABIME application; (4) completion of at least 30 h of ABIME sponsored continuing medical education (CME) in impairment and disability assessment and independent medical examination within the 3 years prior to taking the examination, 50 h of CME in this field is strongly recommended; (5) signed agreement to abide by the ABIME Guidelines of Conduct; and (6) satisfactory completion of a rigorous written examination of approximately 120 multiple-choice questions.

To encourage awareness of ongoing developments in this rapidly changing arena, ABIME certification is valid for a 5-year period. Recertification requirements include passing the current examination or following an alternate pathway consisting of education and completion of an independent study of prescribed journal articles and submission of answers to CME questions.

From September 1994 through December 2014, for a period of over 20 years, 10,875 doctors from19 countries in the world and all 50 states in the USA took the ABIME qualification examination. 7582 successfully passed the qualification exam and were awarded the prestigious ABIME CIME diploma certificate, valid for 5 years, and are known as certified independent medical examiners, CIME. Certified independent medical examiners are also eligible to participate in the ABIME Board of Registry. The Board of Registry publishes an annual international directory of certified independent medical examiners. This directory, which is also available online, is available to all CIMEs, workers' compensation boards, insurers, employers, managed care organizations, lawyers, and others. The Board of Registry also publishes the Disability Medicine Journal and oversees management of the Alternate Pathway Program for recertification. The International Board of Registry Directory is an increasingly valuable resource for those requiring IMEs. CIMEs have also indicated that the directory has led to increased referrals. The directory is also available online at www.abime.org.

The ABIME Board of Advisors, an organizational entity created by ABIME's board of governors, has over 30 members from various countries and multiple specialties, provides advice and consultation, and helps ABIME develop working partnerships with many employers, insurers, state workers' compensation boards, federal agencies, national organizations, and professional societies. These members of the board of advisors serve as the ambassadors for ABIME in their respective regions and specialty.

Response to ABIME has been highly favorable both nationally and internationally and from the communities it serves and the doctors and other scientific experts involved in this field. Many participants in the arena of independent medical examinations have emphasized the need for quality and consistency among examinations and voluntarily support the nonprofit mission of ABIME. As the number of doctors competently performing IMEs grows, demand will grow to enhance the sophistication of state and national benefit systems.

Challenges include difficulty differentiating work and non-work-related events, distinguishing between impairment and disability, defining work ability, clarifying direct threat to one's self and others, interfacing with adversarial and often dysfunctional systems, iatrogenic components to disability, and inappropriate diagnostic testing and treatment.

16.8 Personal Injury Ascertainment Methodology

Generally, an independent medical evaluation methodology involves the review of all of the following elements of a claim:

- History of presenting injury or illness
- Chief complaints
- Detailed inventory of abilities to perform activities of daily living
- Review of systems
- Family and personal history
- Occupational history and exposure history
- Physical examination
- Review and interpretation of any available laboratory data imaging studies
- Review of available relevant records
- Clinical impression (s) diagnosis(es)
- Prognosis
- Appropriateness of current treatment or proposed treatment if not at MMI
- Maximal degree of medical improvement (MMI)
- Future medical care assessment in catastrophic injuries with financial estimate only if expert, in addition to being an IME, has special training, and has a bona fide accreditation in life care planning
- Impairment assessment using the *AMA Guides* (gold standard)
- Disability assessment if practical or task restrictions
- Apportionment (if indicated)
- Fitness for duty/work capacity
- Causation, apportionment if applicable
- Psychosocial barriers to recovery if relevant

An IME history should be sufficiently comprehensive, yet relevant to the inquiry, and must focus on the questions raised in the case by the referring agency usually contained in the initial retainer or referral letter. Sufficient information should be obtained to address the issues raised. This generally includes all of the following:

16.8.1 History of the Present Injury or Illness

The following have to be taken into account:

- Claimant's reported mechanism of acute injury and or onset of illness, causation, and review of all the details surrounding injury, for example, in claims of fall, the height of fall, the body parts involved, onset and chronology of symptoms, all the treatment to date, compliance with the treatment, and the outcome
- If claim of occupational injury or illness, then a detailed review with claimant of all the various job tasks that are perceived to have caused the injury or illness. In the case of claims of musculoskeletal disorders without acute injury, history of frequency of various tasks requiring repetitions, lifting, bending and postural variables, etc. In the case of claims of toxicological injuries/illness, include a review of chemicals used, particularly the names of the specific chemicals, and onset of symptoms, including positive and negative
- Claimant's injury related perception of injustice and expectations for recovery from the condition
- Work and disability status since the injury or onset of the illness
- Claimant's self-reported pre-injury health status and the pre-injury functional status, including review of preexisting conditions, previous injuries, and previous use of medications should be noted (both prescribed and non-prescribed as well as illegal drugs) including any allergies, etc.
- History of related symptoms such as sleep disturbances, anxiety, depression, or symptoms of other mental and behavioral disorder should be explored.
- Family history of illnesses, injury, or disability
- Social history, including alcohol use, tobacco use (described in dose particularity such as pack year of cigarette smoking), and hobbies
- Educational and vocational history
- Review of systems

16.8.2 Current Chief Complaints

Current chief complaints identifying the body parts involved and the specific type and location of the symptoms include the nature, pattern, and quality of pain if any, aggravating and relieving factors, and the effect on activities of daily living. Examiner should review in detail the claimant's current perceived functional status, including the ability to carry out daily living, recreational, and work activities, with consistencies and inconsistencies noted. Obtaining this history requires an oral interview with follow-up questions, paying particular attention to common ADL, both basic such as toileting, bathing, grooming, and feeding, to advanced ADL such as driving, shopping, traveling, and financial and household management, social functioning, etc. Detailed description of activities must be documented.

16.8.3 Physical Examination

After obtaining the consent, a careful physical examination must be performed and should include the examiner's observation of the examinee's general presentation, behavior, affect, mental status, appropriateness, station, gait, posture, and body movements as well as vital signs, etc. Then a detailed examination of the specific body system involved should be carried out and recorded. For example, in musculoskeletal complaints or when nerve or nerve root compression is suspected, a complete neurologic examination of the affected area and related areas is mandatory. However, the examiner must be careful not to do unnecessary body part examination for areas that are not relevant to the claim of injury. For example, for a claim of injury to the shoulder or wrist, a pelvic or rectal exam is clearly unnecessary, but on the other hand, for the claims of myelopathy with bowel or bladder symptoms, rectal exam is appropriate to determine anal sphincter tone.

Non-physiologic findings should be noted. Such findings might include back pain with axial loading, inappropriate responses to stimuli, and other findings that do not correspond to known anatomic or physiologic problems. Behavioral assessment, including the examinee's responses during the physical assessment, should be noted. In some cases, a formal mental status examination may be indicated. Pain and functional status inventories may supplement the evaluation of behavioral and psychological factors and provide information on the perceived level of function and disability. These questionnaires can provide an indication of behavioral overlay and psychological problems that might contribute to delayed recovery or dysfunction at work or at home. The *AMA Guides to the Evaluation of Permanent Impairment, 6th Edition*, endorses a number of functional assessment questionnaires. These tools can provide consistent and standardized self-report data.

Physical examination may be augmented with laboratory and imaging studies. For example, in claims of pulmonary problems, in addition to examination of chest, various respiratory function tests including lung volumes, imaging procedures, challenge testing, and exercise testing may be necessary.

16.8.4 Review of Available Medical and Other Records

A complete review of available records is useful in understanding the facts of the case which may or may not have been described accurately by the claimant to the examiner. Records should be organized chronologically and reviewed, and appropriate excerpts relevant to the issues in the claim should be recorded as part of the report. In some highly disputed cases, where exaggeration or fraud is suspected, the independent medical examiner may be provided with video surveillance recordings and reports. Surveillance is most useful when an individual is observed engaging in activities that cannot be reconciled with the claimed injury or stated inabilities. For example, a person with a claim of injury claiming that they are unable to use the right upper limb in any activities of daily living but then are recorded on surveillance video to be riding motorcycles, taking out garbage, walking dogs, etc., all of these activities performed with the robust use of the right upper limb. However, the examiner must not solely rely on these video surveillance tapes to form the opinion as there are pitfalls including identity issues, duration of the activity, as well as bias that can occur from reviewing these tapes before a full evaluation. It is prudent that the examiner first reviews the entire case including examinee interview and physical examination and review of all the available medical records and uses the video surveillance tape not as a primary source of evidence but rather as adjunct evidence to form the final opinion in the case.

16.9 Evaluation Criteria

The American Medical Association (AMA) Guides to the Evaluation of Permanent Impairment (Guides) are the recognized international standard for assessing impairment and are ultimately used by adjudicators to assign disability benefits. The *Guides* are a tool to translate human pathology resulting from trauma or disease process into a percentage of the whole person impairment [20]. The primary purpose of the *Guides* is to rate impairment to assist adjudicators and others in determining the financial compensation to be awarded to the individuals who, as a result of injury or illness, have suffered measurable, physical, and/or psychological loss.

The *Guides 6th Edition*, published in 2008, introduced new approaches to medical rating of permanent impairment (PI), a key component of determining permanent impairment and partial disability awards (PPD) for workers' compensation (WC) and other benefit programs including numerous international jurisdictions such as Australia, New Zealand, South Africa, etc. using the *Guides*-based impairment rating as a threshold to determine the severity of personal injury to access the general damage (pain and suffering, etc.) award in common law tort claims of personal injuries, e.g., motor vehicle accidents [21].

Several methodologies and schedules have existed since the beginning of recorded history to allow for monetary compensation for the injured, sick, and disabled. Even though the process of the development of the *AMA Guides* started in 1958, the underlying principles of the *Guides* reflect the cumulative experience of mankind over the centuries. The journey of the *Guides* began five decades ago in the USA as a tool for adjudication of workers' compensation claims. However, with accumulating experience and increasing use in other legal systems, the *Guides* spread across the globe. In addition to its use in adjudication of workers' compensation claims across the globe, the *Guides*, in the past two decades, have also been increasingly used outside of the workers' compensation arena in helping adjudicate the claims of personal injuries from areas other than workers' compensation, mainly in claims of personal injuries from automobile accidents.

The disability determination process requires an initial determination of permanent medical impairment according to specific medical criteria. In order to improve consistency with the ratings system so that two doctors assessing the same claimant would have a similar assessment, the American Medical Association (AMA) has produced a rating manual (the *Guides*) as a benchmark to assist doctors in measuring and rating medical impairments [22]. One of the goals is to create a standardized objective reference. The *Guides* are periodically updated and revised to the current 6th edition. These updates are similar to revisions that occur with other texts, replacing outdated information with current data and consensus reflective of current best practices.

The *Guides* define the terms commonly encountered in medical disability evaluation as follows:

Impairment—a significant deviation, loss, or loss of use of any body structure or function in an individual with a health condition, disorder, or disease.

Disability—an umbrella term for activity limitations and/or participation restrictions in an individual with a health condition, disorder, or disease.

Impairment rating—a consensus-derived percentage estimate of loss of activity, and which reflects severity of impairment for a given health condition and the degree of associated limitations in terms of activities of daily living (ADLs).

Independent medical examination (IME)—a usually one-time evaluation performed by a licensed doctor/surgeon who is not treating the patient or claimant in order to answer questions posed by the party requesting the IME.

Maximum medical improvement (MMI)—the point at which a condition has stabilized and is unlikely to change (improve or worsen) substantially in the next 12 months, with or without treatment. While symptoms and signs of the condition may wax and wane over time, further overall recovery or deterioration is not anticipated. However, both the name given to and exact definition of this status somewhat vary depending on the jurisdiction in the USA.

Permanency and MMI—related concepts which simply mean that a person with an injury, after having received adequate medical, surgical, and rehabilitative treatment and having achieved clinical and functional stability, is now as good as they are going to get. Other synonymous terms in use according to jurisdictional preference include fixed and stable, maximum medical recovery, maximum medical stability, medically stationary, etc. These terms are useful to enable the injured person to exit the temporary disablement stage of recovery, thereby facilitating claim settlement and case closure.

Apportionment—an estimate of allocation of contributions among various causes of impairment. The extent to which each of two or more probable causes were responsible for an effect (injury, disease, impairment, etc.). Hence, the first step in apportionment is scientifically based causation analysis. Second, one must allocate responsibility among the probable causes and select apportionment percentages consistent with the medical literature and facts of the case in question. Arbitrary, unscientific apportionment estimates, which are nothing more than speculations, must be avoided.

Combined Values Chart—a method used to combine two or more impairment percentages that takes into account the impact of impairment from one body part on impairment of another body part. Thus, the largest of multiple impairment numbers is deducted from the first 100 % whole person, and the subsequent numbers are deducted from the remaining person value and not the whole person. This concept is based on the mathematical formula $A + B (1 - A) =$ combined values of A and B. Combining, as opposed to adding, ensures that the total value will not exceed 100 % whole person impairment. Combining must be done at the same hierarchal level and follow the rules as prescribed in the *AMA Guides* [22].

Cause—in general, anything that produces an effect. In medicine, cause refers to an identifiable factor (e.g., genetic abnormality, toxic or infectious exposure, trauma) that results in injury or illness. The cause or causes must be scientifically probable following causation analysis.

Causation—one of the many key questions asked of an independent medical examiner or expert witness is the issue of causation due to its significant economic implications to the parties involved in a legal dispute. The term causation may have different contextual meanings in Medicine vs. Law, and the doctor needs to understand this difference [23].

Medical causation—is biological in nature and is established through scientific analysis of sufficient rigor to demonstrate a cause and effect relationship with a high degree of certainty, e.g., with a statistical probability or P-value of 0.05 or less (or the probability of being wrong 5 % or less). For example, a doctor can reasonably conclude, within medical probability, that asbestos can cause mesothelioma in an individual exposed to some based upon a review of the credible medical evidence in the peer-reviewed scientific literature which has established a causal relationship in this case.

Medical causation—Hill's Criteria of Causation is a generally accepted scientific analysis to establish scientifically valid causal connections between disease and the causative agents. Austin Bradford Hill (1897–1991), a British medical statistician, originally presented these as a way of determining the causal link between a specific factor and a disease. These criteria require analysis of following elements in the context of facts in a given case and are minimal conditions necessary to provide adequate evidence of a causal relationship between an incidence and a consequence.

(1) Temporal relationship between cause and effect

    The effect has to occur after the cause (and if there is an expected delay between the cause and expected effect, then the effect must occur after that delay).

(2) Strength of association

    Association does not mean causation and requires the review of validated scientific literature for studies demonstrating strength of association between cause and effect. The larger the association, the more likely that it is causal; however, small association does not mean that there is not a causal effect.

(3) Dose–response relationship or biological gradient

Greater exposure generally leads to greater incidence of the effect. However, in some cases, the mere presence of the factor can trigger the effect. In other cases, an inverse proportion is observed: greater exposure leads to lower incidence.

(4) Consistency

Consistent causal relationship findings observed by different observers with different samples strengthen the probability of a cause and effect.

(5) Biological plausibility

A biological/scientific plausible mechanism between cause and effect is an important link for greater confidence in the conclusion of causation. However, lack of current knowledge of unknown mechanism may limit the use of this criterion.

(6) Specificity

Causation is probable if a very specific population at a specific site and disease with no other likely explanation. The more specific an association between a factor and an effect is, the bigger the probability of a causal relationship.

(7) Coherence

Coherence between epidemiological and laboratory findings increases the probability of an effect. However, lack of such experimental/laboratory evidence cannot nullify the epidemiological effect on associations.

(8) Consideration of alternative explanations and analogy is useful.

(9) Experiment helpful in some circumstances.

Legal causation—as defined in civil litigation generally has two prongs. First, an act (e.g., a tort) must be the cause in fact of a particular injury, which means that an act or omission was a necessary antecedent to the personal injury. Legally, this issue is analyzed by determining whether the injury would have occurred "but for" the act alleged to be the cause. If an injury would have occurred independent of the alleged act or omission, cause in fact has not been established, and no tort has been committed. When multiple acts/factors have led to a particular injury, the alleged act or omission is determined to be the cause in fact only if the evidence demonstrates this to have played a substantial role in causing the injury. Second, it must also be established simultaneously that the alleged act was the proximate cause of an injury before the legal liability will be imposed. The concept of *proximate cause* is very critical as it limits the scope of liability to those injuries that bear some reasonable relationship to the risk created by the wrongdoer. Proximate cause is evaluated in terms of whether a reasonable person should have foreseen the injury resulting from the act. If a given risk could not have been reasonably anticipated, proximate cause has not been established, and no liability will be attached.

In summary, legal causation is mainly a question of "foreseeability." An actor is liable for the foreseeable but not the unforeseeable consequences of his or her act. For example, it is foreseeable that someone who is left alone on a beach in a drunken stupor at low tide may die from drowning in the rising tide rather than from the excessive alcohol or drugs they have ingested. However, it is not foreseeable that such an individual will be struck by lightning and killed by that event. In such case, the liability for drowning could have a proximate cause in law (for causing death) for anyone who is found responsible for contributing directly to someone's drunken stupor and leaving them exposed to the risk of death by drowning, but not to the risk of death from being struck by lightning, due to its remoteness in probability.

Two important concepts and terms pertaining to causation in relation to a preexisting and underlying condition are aggravation and exacerbation. *Aggravation* refers to a permanent worsening of a preexisting condition that occurs when a physical, chemical, biological, or other factor results in an increase in symptoms, signs, and/or impairment that never returns to baseline or what it would have been except for the aggravation. *Exacerbation* refers to a temporary worsening of a preexisting condition after which the individual recovers to his or her baseline functional status or what it would have been had the exacerbation never occurred.

16.10 Summary of the Current *AMA Guides 6th Edition* Core Methodology

The *Guides* is a tool designed to translate human pathology arising from a trauma or disease and manifested as a structural and/or functional loss at an organ system level into a percentage estimate of loss to the whole person. The document comprises of 634 pages with 17 chapters. The first two chapters outline the key concepts and underlying methodology of the *Guides*. The rest of the 15 chapters deal with a specific human body system, providing specific guidance for that particular body organ or system.

The international classification of functioning, ICF, provides the current conceptual framework, classification, and terminology of disablement adopted for the *Guides 6th Edition*, and the terminology is imbedded in the AMA definitions of *impairment, disability*, and *impairment rating* listed above. It also serves to identify five possible functional levels for purposes of impairment class distinctions adopted throughout the *AMA Guides 6th Edition* to promote conceptual congruity and operational uniformity across organ systems and in particular to identify the five possible impairment classes for the "diagnosis-based impairment (DBI)" method for the musculoskeletal organ system and most other organ systems.

The diagnosis-based impairment (DBI) platform places emphasis upon a diagnosis-based approach to impairment rating. This particularly applies to impairment ratings within the musculoskeletal organ system. Diagnosis-based impairment (DBI) grids are provided for each of these anatomical regions as follows:

- Spine—cervical spine, thoracic spine, lumbar spine, and pelvis
- Upper extremity—digits/hand, wrist, elbow, and shoulder
- Lower extremity—foot & ankle, knee and hip for the lower extremity

Each grid has five potential impairment classes (Class 0–4) consistent with the ICF classification system, and each covers a broad and precise array of diagnoses ranging from soft tissue conditions (nonspecific, chronic, or recurrent) to muscle–tendon and/or motion–segment injuries (sprains, strains, tendinopathies) to ligament, bone, and joint injuries (fractures, dislocations, arthrodesis, etc.).

The impairment rating using the DBI approach becomes a two-step process whereby initial assignment to an "impairment class" requires the rating examiner to identify the most appropriate diagnosis, and each diagnostic-based impairment class has an available range of impairment values arranged within five grades labeled A–E with an initial "default" mid-range value at grade C. The impairment rating (value) is then adjusted within range of grades A–E as a second step, using three separate criteria (functional history, examination findings, and clinical test results) to independently validate the diagnosis and severity of the condition. This second step is termed grade modification, which is a simple triangulation method. Using the metrics associated with each of these results enables a final numerical adjustment upward for less favorable outcomes or downward for more optimal outcomes according to the specific result in each case.

To illustrate using the musculoskeletal organ system, the first step in the impairment rating (IR) process is to determine permanency at *maximum medical improvement (MMI)*. Next is to assign the diagnosis and pick the appropriate impairment class within the appropriate DBI grid. Each impairment class (IC) has an available range of five discrete impairment scores (grades labeled A–E), and the "default" position is the middle score value at grade C. This initial fix on impairment value then goes through further refinement through the second step.

The second step follows whereby three separate "grade modifiers" are independently used to score level of severity (i.e., grade on a scale of 0–4) according to functional history (GMFH), physical examination findings (GMPE), and clinical study results (GMCS), respectively. The final step is to calculate the sum of the differences in numerical severity of the impairment grade modifiers minus IC, respectively, to triangulate the final impairment score within the impairment class according to the formula (GMFH − IC) + (GMPE − IC) + (GMCS − IC). If the sum is zero, the final IR remains at the default middle value. If the sum is + 1 or −1, the IR score moves one position to the right or left, respectively; if it is +2 or −2, it moves two positions to the right or left, respectively (Fig. 16.1).

This methodology simultaneously allows the rater to capture important and useful information on clinical severity and functional outcome for any given condition and to modify the final rating according to precise criteria of severity rather than solely on "clinical judgment." It further provides greater precision and resolution of impairment ratings with a broader array of diagnostic choices than was previously available under the DRE methodology and offers a more transparent pathway to the final impairment determination in all cases.

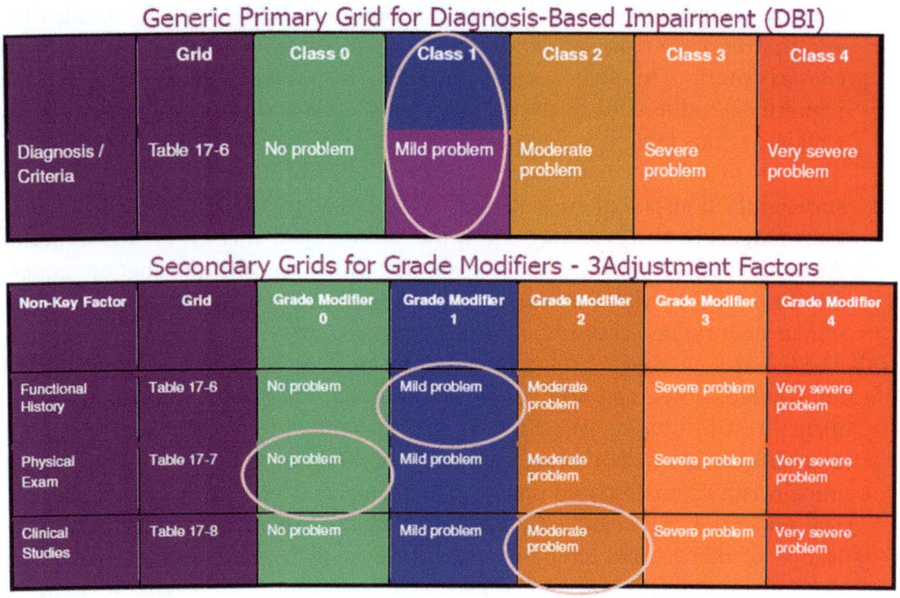

Fig. 16.1 Diagnosis-based impairment methodology summary—*AMA Guides 6th Edition*

16.10.1 The Constitution and Fundamental Principles of the AMA Guides 6th Edition

(1) Concepts and philosophy of Chapter 2 of the *Guides 6th Edition* contains the fundamental principles of the *Guides*.

(2) No impairment of the body may exceed 100 % of the whole person; no impairment arising from a member or organ of the body may exceed the amputation value of that member.

(3) All regional impairments in the same organ or body system shall be combined as prescribed by the existing rule, starting at the same level first and further combined with other regional impairments at the whole person level.

(4) Rating of the impairment must be done in accordance with the relevant organ or system chapter where the injury primarily arose or where the greatest dysfunction consistent with the pathology remains, but not both.

(5) Only permanent medical impairment can be rated and only after maximum medical improvement (MMI) has been certified.

(6) A valid impairment evaluation requires a three-step approach as follows: Step 1 involves *clinical evaluation* which includes a relevant history obtained both from the claimant as well as for the review of medical records and relevant physical examination that includes the alleged injured body parts and the related structures. Step 2 includes *analysis of the findings* which discusses how the specific history and the objective findings of the clinical evaluation

support conclusions as to relevant diagnoses and MMI. Step 3 includes the *description of how the impairment rating was calculated* based on the *AMA Guides* criteria. This step is accomplished by including an explanation of each impairment value with reference to the diagnosis and other rating criteria as well as various table numbers and page numbers referenced from the *Guides*. The aim of this three-step process and report writing is to make the rating sufficiently transparent so that if the first two steps are fully described, any knowledgeable observer may check the finding against *AMA Guides* criteria.

(7) An evaluating doctor must use knowledge, skills, and abilities that are generally expected by the medical scientific community to arrive at the correct impairment rating according to the *Guides*.

(8) The *Guides* is based on objective criteria. The doctor must use clinical knowledge, skills, and abilities in determining whether or not the measurements, test results, or written historical information obtained are consistent and concordant with the pathology being evaluated. If the findings or an impairment estimate based upon such findings conflict with established medical principles, they cannot be used to justify an impairment rating.

(9) Range of motion and strength measurement techniques should be assessed carefully in the presence of apparent self-inhibition secondary to pain or apprehension.

(10) The *Guides* does not permit rating of future impairment.

(11) If the *Guides* provide more than one method to rate a particular impairment, the method producing the highest rating must be used ("law of liberality").

(12) Subjective complaints that are not clinically verifiable are generally not ratable according to the *Guides*.

(13) Round all fractional impairment ratings, whether immediate or final, to the nearest whole number, unless otherwise specified.

16.11 Summary and Conclusions

The medical practitioner who engages in the medicolegal practices of impairment rating and disability determination in the USA can frequently be called upon to perform an independent medical examination (IME). The doctor participating in such evaluation must be familiar with the emerging field of disability medicine, described as a subspecialty of clinical medical practice which encompasses the identification, prediction, prevention, assessment, evaluation, and management of impairment and disability in both human individuals and populations [23].

The IME is typically performed at the request of a party to a disputed claim and is provided by a clinician who is not personally treating the claimant for the purpose of rendering an impartial medical opinion regarding various aspects of the claim. The medical examiner is called upon to review necessary and appropriate records provided in support of the positions being contested and to personally interview and examine the claimant in most cases. The IME examiner must then answer a series of common interrogatives “within medical probability” relating to the following items of interest:

- What is the diagnosis and causal relationship, if any, to work place injury?
- What is the current diagnostic and treatment plan?
- Has necessary and appropriate testing been done and treatment been provided? What additional (if any) testing and/or treatment are indicated beyond this point?
- What other medical or nonmedical factors might be having a significant impact upon the outcome of this particular case?
- Is the claimant at “maximal medical improvement (MMI)” with respect to the condition in question? If so, when did MMI occur? If not, when is MMI expected to occur?
- If claimant is at MMI, what is the medical impairment rating?
- What restrictions and accommodations are medically necessary, feasible, and applicable to the workplace in relation to the claimant’s ability to go to work and be at work, engage in sustained material handling, and to perform certain activities while on the job?

The IME examiner’s opinions are expressed “within medical probability” which means the likelihood exceeds 50 % (more likely than not), as opposed to “medical possibility” (likelihood less than or equal to 50 %).

Since the IME process places the doctor in the role of expert witness, the potential for adversarial relationships exists between the medical examiner and claimant who may find the doctor’s opinion and or testimony unflattering to their position and thereby leading to action which may have legal consequences for the IME examiner. For example, even though the medical examiner is not directly treating the claimant, and the traditional doctor–patient relationship does not exist, he or she is obligated to provide an assessment which conforms to medical standard of care, and in some instances, malpractice liability may apply.

Furthermore, it should be noted that the medical disability evaluator or independent medical examiner acting as an “expert witness” may no longer be shielded from civil liabilities in the manner typically afforded to any other witness in the judicial process. In the past two decades, various state courts have held independent medical examiners and expert witnesses without any doctor–patient relationship accountable to their examinee in terms of ordinary negligence [24, 25], and at least one case found that a doctor owed a patient/claimant a duty of care even though no formal doctor–patient relationship clearly existed [9].

The IME examiner should not only be aware of the legal liabilities in the overall practice of their specialty but also the additional liability exposure from their work as an independent medical examiner. It should be noted, however, that even though the recent case law in some jurisdictions has significantly removed the traditional immunity from medical malpractice claims against IME providers with no doctor–patient relationship with their examinees, there still remains a great need in the US judicial system for IME/expert medical witness services.

Practitioners interested in the practice of Disability Medicine and intending to serve as independent medical examiners are encouraged to attend several of the high-quality training programs offered in the USA to independent medical examiners and expert witnesses with the goal to empower them with the knowledge, skills, and abilities necessary to practice as an independent medical examiner and/or expert witness in the field of Disability Medicine. They must also be familiar with the applicable edition(s) of the *AMA Guides* in order to provide competent and accurate medical impairment ratings appropriate to WC and personal injury claims upon request. Doctors and others wishing to learn more are encouraged to visit the following web sites for available courses and other educational venues and resources of interest:

- American Medical Association. Available at: www.ama-assn.org
- American Board of Independent Medical Examiners. Available at: www.abime.org

References

1. Thessalonians 3:10: "For even when we were with you, we gave you this command: Anyone unwilling to work should not eat"
2. Ranavaya MI, Rondinelli RD (2000) The major US disability and compensation systems: origins and historical overview. In: Rondinelli RD, Katz RT (eds) Impairment rating and disability evaluation. WB Saunders Co, Philadelphia, PA, pp 3–16
3. Ferm V (1945) An encyclopedia of religion. The Philosophical Library, New York, NY, p 320
4. Ranavaya MI, Andersson GB (2001) The impairment and disability evaluations. In: Mayer TG, Gatchel RJ, Polatin PB (eds) Occupational musculoskeletal disorders: function, outcomes & evidence. Lippincott, Williams & Wilkins, Philadelphia, PA
5. Yaron R (1988) The laws of Eshnunna, Section 42. The Magnes Press, The Hebrew University, Jerusalem-Leiden, p 69
6. Papyrus Archives, Cairo Museum, Egypt
7. Ranavaya MI (1996) Impairment, disability and compensation in the United States: an overview. Disability 5:1–20
8. Drew Fischer K (1973) The Lombard laws. University of Pennsylvania Press, Philadelphia, PA, p 62
9. Ranavaya MI (1997) Presidential address. American Academy of Disability Evaluating Physicians
10. Robinson JP, Wolfe CV (2000) Social security disability insurance and supplemental security income. In: Rondinelli RD, Katz RT (eds) Impairment rating and disability evaluation. W.B. Saunders Company, Philadelphia, PA, pp 159–176
11. Esquemeling J (1924) The Buccaneers of America, 1684–5. In: Stallybrass W (ed) Broadway translations. G. Routledge & Sons, London, p 60
12. Marbury v. Madison, 5 U.S. 1 Cranch 137 137 (1803)
13. Rondinelli R, Mohammed Ranavaya R (2013) Disability assessment. In: Benzon HT, Rathmell JP, Wu CL, Turk DC, Argoff CE, Hurley R (eds) Practical management of pain, 5th edn. Elsevier-Mosby, Philadelphia, PA, Chapter 17
14. Novick AK, Rondinelli RD (2000) Impairment and disability under workers' compensation. In: Rondinelli RD, Katz RT (eds) Impairment rating and disability evaluation. W.B. Saunders Company, Philadelphia, PA, pp 141–156
15. Rondinelli R, Ranavaya M (2014) Current American medical association guidelines for evaluating musculoskeletal impairment at maximum medical improvement. In: Gatchel RJ,

Schultz IZ (eds) Handbook of musculoskeletal pain and disability disorders in the workplace. Springer, New York, NY, ISBN-13: 978-1493906116
16. Weaver CL (1982) The crisis in social security. Duke Press Policy Studies, Durham, NC
17. Social Security Administration (1999) Disability evaluation under social security. Office of Disability: SSA Pub. No. 64-039
18. Veterans Benefits Administration. Schedule for rating disabilities. Section 1155, Title 38 CFR, Pensions, Bonuses, and Veterans' Relief
19. Woolf Greg (2006) Et Tu Brute?—The murder of Caesar and political assassination, ISBN 1-86197-741-7
20. Rondinelli RD, Ranavaya MI et al (eds) (2008) American Medical Association: guides to the evaluation of permanent impairment, 6th edn. AMA Press, Chicago, IL
21. American Board of Independent Medical Examiners (1993) Articles of incorporation, constitution, and bylaws. American Board of Independent Medical Examiners, Barrington, IL
22. Ranavaya MI, Brigham C (2011) International use of the AMA Guides to the Evaluation of Permanent Impairment. AMA Guides Newsletter, May/June 2011
23. Rondinelli R, Eskay-Auerbach M, Ranavaya M et al (2012) Commentary on NCCI report. AMA Guides Newsletter Nov–Dec 2012, American Medical Association Press
24. Ranavaya M, Rondinelli R et al (2012) To combine or not to combine—AMA guides rule. AMA Guides Newsletter Nov–Dec 2013, AMA Press
25. Rondinelli RD, Ranavaya MI (2016) Practical aspects of impairment rating and disability determination. In: Cifu DX (ed) Braddom' s physical medicine and rehabilitation, 5th edn. Elsevier, Philadelphia, PA

Chapter 17
Methods of Ascertainment of Dental Damage in Argentina

Marta Beatriz Maldonado

Abstract The chapter illustrates the historical, judicial, and juridical framework of dental injury assessment and compensation in Argentina, describing the expert's qualification and competences and detailing the ascertainment methodology and criteria of evaluation utilized for identifying, describing, and estimating any dental injury, its temporary and permanent consequences, and the causal value/link between the event and the injury and between the injury and the impairment/disability.

17.1 Overview

The study of the valuation of dental injury, together with the total loss of a given piece, based on the allocation percentages in relation to role of the missing piece, is very important for cases of injury judiciables.

The application of these percentages must take into account that the masticatory apparatus, namely, the stomatognathic system, consists of three main components:

- Temporomandibular joint (TMJ) is the link between the fixed part of the system: the skull and mobile jaw.
- Neuromuscular system is the active component, the source, and receiver of motion stimuli acting on the system, consisting of the masticatory muscles (masseter and temporal), mimicry, and suprahyoid.
- Tooth system consists of the teeth, the whole skeletal basis (upper and lower jaws) and the union with the alveolar process (the periodontal ligament, cement, mucosa gold lip, and teeth), which are primary elements in the transmission of force during chewing.

M.B. Maldonado (✉)
Faculty of Odontology, University of Buenos Aires, Viamonte 430, 1053 Buenos Aires, Argentina
e-mail: maldomarta@hotmail.com

S.D. Ferrara et al. (eds.), *Personal Injury and Damage Ascertainment under Civil Law*, DOI 10.1007/978-3-319-29812-2_17

This system is a functional unit that needs all its components to be active and effective. It serves three functions: chewing, phonetics, and aesthetics. According to its location, every tooth in the oral cavity is assigned a value in relation to its role.

Therefore, the masticatory function will have more value than a molar incisor, but if we see it from the perspective of aesthetics, then the incisor will have more value.

The sum of the percentages, according to the three functions and to each lost tooth, should be based on the total value of functional mouthparts, which is assigned 20 %. Reference is then made to the ratio of the working total, depending on the scale of Dr. Bertini, edited by Dr. Pagliera, in 1964, presented and accepted at the Second Conference of Legal Medicine, Córdoba, Argentina.

Most studies that have addressed these issues do so from the point of view of the lost tooth, but it is very common to see in the legal practice of the times pure dental traumatology. There are lesions affecting part of the tooth crown, in its various planes of tissues (enamel, dentin, and pulp or in the root structure), thereby altering the forming tissues and complicating dental integrity, from a simple aesthetic change to the total loss of pulp vitality.

While dental damage is minor compared to other sensory or motor injuries, its exploration, study, and assessment should not be neglected.

Given the increasing number of malpractice claims, accidents, assaults, etc., judges most frequently request specific expertise in relation to dental damage. It is therefore essential to develop a systematic and regulated protocol exploration in order to achieve a correct assessment.

In Argentina, the legal framework for such compensation or disability benefits is within the Civil Jurisdiction. Both a traffic accident and a claim of medical malpractice can be reported in this area, without losing the opportunity to do so in the Criminal Jurisdiction and achieve economic redress from the person or entity that caused the damage. Then there is the Labour Charter which regulates the issue of accidents and occupational illnesses.

The professional to prepare the percentage of disability will be skilled, if the dispute takes place in the Criminal Jurisdiction, appointed by the Supreme Court of National Justice, and may also be convened at the request of the Civil and Labor Chambers. In the field of Civil Jurisdiction, professional specialists appear on lists which are utilized by the courts, and when they are required, they are called to appear in the cases.

17.2 Classification of Dental Trauma

Based on the International Classification of Diseases of the World Health Organization, applied to dentistry in 1985:

- Injuries of hard dental tissues and pulp

  Incomplete fracture of enamel without loss of tooth substance.
  Uncomplicated fracture in the crown.

Limited to enamel and dentin fracture without pulp exposure.
Complicated crown fracture of enamel and dentin with pulp exposure.
Uncomplicated crown and root fracture, affecting enamel, dentin, and cementum without pulp exposure.
Complicated crown and root fracture, affecting enamel, dentin, and cementum with pulp exposure.
Breaking root affects cement, dentin, and pulp.

- Injuries to the periodontal tissues

Concussion: damage to the supporting structures of the tooth does not cause abnormal mobility and displacement, but there is an obvious reaction to percussion.
Subluxation: lesion with abnormal loosening, without dental displacement.
Intrusive luxation: tooth displacement within its socket, comes with comminution or fracture of the alveolar cavity.
Extrusive luxation: partial avulsion of the tooth in its socket.
Lateral luxation: tooth displacement mesial or distal. It comes with comminution or alveolar fracture.
Exarticulation: complete avulsion, displacement of the tooth out of its socket.

- Injuries to the supporting bone

Fracture with minutes of the alveolar cavity, compressing the socket with intrusive or lateral dislocation.
Fracture of the alveolar wall, limited to the buccal or palatal/lingual walls.
Fracture of alveolar process may or may not affect the alveolar cavity.
Fracture of mandible or maxilla affecting or not the alveolar process or socket. Different classifications depend on altered basal level.

- Lesions of the gingiva and oral mucosa

Laceration of the gingiva and/or oral mucosa: superficial or deep wound produced by a tear and caused by acute process.
Contusion of gingiva or oral mucosa: exhibiting no tear due to blunt and not sharp force. It can cause bleeding of the submucosa.
Abrasion of gum or oral mucosa: superficial wound produced by scraping or tearing of tissue, leaving it rough and bloody.

17.3 Calculation of the Percentage of Disability for Loss of Dental Features

As previously mentioned, the dental unit develops three functions: chewing, phonetics, and aesthetics. The assessment of the percentage of disability is made by taking into account the type of teeth affected and the area of the arch in which these pieces are situated, namely, qualification by location and the function they perform.

This study has worked on scales that regulate the percentage of disability for permanent loss of a tooth, in addition to the assessment of disability arising from decreased masticatory function, phonetics, and aesthetics from dental trauma itself, without immediate tooth loss and a dental tissue injury.

Based on the recognized and fair scale of Dr. Bertini, which provides 20 % value for total loss of permanent teeth, the individual percentage of decrease in each function is observed so as to establish the degree of supervening incapacity (Table 17.1).

We should note also the following principles:

- The oral cavity is a complex organ system function, acting in the following components, the maxillary bones, temporomandibular joint, masticatory muscles, nerves, salivary glands, tongue, lips and teeth, each functioning differently and measured in relation to masticatory function, aesthetics, and phonetics
- Dental health status of the individual is described as the number of healthy, restored, diseased, absent, or prosthetic teeth of any kind, maintaining functionality before receiving the trauma
- The total loss of teeth or 20 % of function
- Each tooth has a notation (*Redier*) and a certain value, which will vary according to the chewing function, aesthetics, and/or phonetics considered
- Occlusion is the relationship between the teeth and supporting structures, the TMJ and the neuromuscular system
- The loss of a tooth does not just mean "that" loss but also migration from neighboring parts, extrusion of antagonist, and decreased vertical dimension, i.e., an imbalance of occlusal harmony, negatively altering the whole dental heritage of the injured party
- Chewing is undoubtedly the main function of the dental appliance. To define it, we say that it is the set of biomechanical movements (teeth, jaws, TMJ, masticatory muscles, tongue, and oral soft tissues) whose mission is mechanically to prepare food to be swallowed and digested
- In masticatory function, one must add the value of the counterpart, which has lost its function and has been left without an opponent. Actually, there are two involved components supporting the occlusion lose the occlusal support, since each tooth is related to two of the opposing arch: occlusal triad, the relationship is two-thirds the mesial part and third to distal; to simplify the calculation, total homologous antagonists take part

Table 17.1 Percentage of decrease in each function

Function	Central incisor (Ic) (%)	Lateral incisor (Il) (%)	Canine 1 (C1) (%)	Premolar (Pm) (%)	Premolar 2 (Pm 2) (%)	Molar 1 (M1) (%)	Molar 2 (M2) (%)	Molar 3 (M3) (%)
Masticatory	1	1	2	3	4	6	6	2
Aesthetics (superior)	8	7	7	3	1	1.5	0.5	–
Aesthetics (inferior)	6	5	5	3	1	1.5	0.5	–
Phonetic (superior)	8	7	7	3	1	1.5	0.5	–
Phonetic (inferior)	6	5	5	3	1	1.5	0.5	–

- The amount of the total loss of teeth (20 %) value must be discounted partially, considering the sum of the values of the three functions of every lost tooth
- This value should, in turn, be deducted from the total at the time of the accident, according to the legislation.

17.3.1 Masticatory Function

The function of the incisor tooth is to sever, while the canine tears and the premolars and molars crush the food. The anterior teeth have a minor role in chewing and are thus only given a minimum: 1–2 % of incisors and canines. The premolars act in crushing and the second in projecting, hence the value of 3 % for the former and 4 % for the latter. Masticatory function falls especially on the first molar and then the second, and to each is assigned 6 %, while the third molar is only assigned 2 %, because of lesser participation due to its rear position.

In this function the value will be equal for both the upper arch to the bottom.

The loss of a tooth not only means "this" loss but the migration of adjacent pieces, extrusion of antagonists, decreased vertical dimension, and other disturbances that negatively affect the whole complex dental heritage of the injured party. The teeth are left without their antagonist for the traumatic loss of this latter; they also lose their masticatory function, since the loss physiologically cancels that function. Therefore, the percentage value will double as the antagonist is added to the loss of functional value.

The individual with normal occlusion presents a regulated and coordinated masticatory rhythm, range of motion, and a defined mode of grinding food. This occlusal scheme has some degree of tolerance to certain variations and finds a new neuromuscular balance, but if the variations are medium to extreme, the balance is broken, and parafunctional masticatory movements that are harmful to all elements of the system appear.

In the event that the affected masticatory efficiency up until the time of injury resided in the use of prostheses, artificial parts are considered as natural ones. The severity of the injury is determined by the number of pieces which stop functioning.

If the individual can continue to use their prosthesis as efficiently after injury, then that injury is considered slight. It will be considered as serious in the event that the individual cannot use the same prosthesis, since there has been a weakening or loss of a feature that until then could be exercised.

17.3.2 *Beauty Feature*

The teeth, with the jaws, are the backbone of the soft tissues of the face; their absence causes alterations in the expression and appearance, giving a senescent appearance, affecting the harmony, beauty, and/or estimation of the person.

Aesthetic deficiency means a decrease in the performance of work in certain professions, such as artists, educators, speech, etc.

The aesthetic importance is in descending order from the anterior group of incisors, canine, premolar, and molar to latero-posterior sector. Upper jaw parts have more aesthetic value than lower, so their values will be higher.

In this role antagonistic parts are not taken into account, since their value is not altered.

17.3.3 *Phonetics Function*

The teeth also have a role in articulating words. In studies of articulate sounds, there are letters that are pronounced supporting the tongue against the upper teeth. Those being absent, a hissing sound is produced.

The anterior teeth are the most important in the emission of sounds; hence, the higher values correspond to this sector, as well as for the upper maxillary with respect to the lower. The values of the antagonists are also unaltered parts in this function.

17.4 Application of Factors to Establish the Degree of Disability as a Result of a Tooth Injury

Injury is caused by non-pathological and/or congenital causes of the weakening of the organ of mastication, in its three functions, which could be framed within Articles 89 and 90 of the Argentine Penal Code and included in the International Classification of Tooth Trauma WHO.

In the above table the value of the share allocated to the total loss of each tooth is calculated for each injury, according to the biological weakening caused:

- Coronary fracture that involves enamel: 25 %
- Coronary fracture that involves enamel and dentin: 50 %
- Coronary fracture that involves enamel and dentin with pulp exposure: 100 %
- Root fracture without pulp exposure: 50 %
- Root fracture with pulp exposure: 100 %

17.5 Protocol of Systematic Exploration from Dental Trauma

Classification of dental trauma by WHO will take into account the following steps:

- Clinical Review: exploration of the entire oral cavity, soft tissue, and teeth and creation of an odontogram (Digital DOS system) showing the current state of trauma (healthy and damaged parts)

  On the damaged parts, the following will be effected:

- Test pulp vitality
- Measure displacement (in mm)
- Vertical: intrusive-extrusive
- Horizontal: degrees of mobility (1, 2, 3, 4)
- Periodontium, probing exchanges in mm
- Review of occlusion (online or not)
- Periapical or panoramic radiographs, as needed, fundamental for the diagnosis of internal fractures or dislocations, permanent injury, etc.
- It shall consider whether the timing of the injury is consistent with trauma, as well as the topography of the sequel to the anatomical reception area.

17.6 Valuation of Temporary Replacement

The human species has two dentitions, the temporary or "milk" teeth and the permanent, which is called mixed dentition.

While the acting parts will be replaced by the permanent, often minor injuries are significantly detrimental to temporary teeth and sometimes also affect the permanent teeth. Although not permanent, such injuries could damage the corresponding tooth germ.

It will therefore be important to assess these injuries, which at first glance do not seem to be harmful, but often have an impact on the position of the seed, thereby causing permanent damage. If the traumatic loss of temporary teeth occurs early, before their replacement has formed, its clinical crown may lose space and cause difficulties within the dental arch.

The impact of the trauma on the action of the tooth should also be assessed, since this can impact on the permanent germ causing it to move out of place, preventing its emergence and altering its place in the dental arch or "marking" some of its facets, when it is still in the period of calcification. For these and many other reasons, it will be important to assess the damage to the acting parts.

Apart from the function itself of each temporary piece, keeping space and guiding the emergence of permanent teeth, consideration should be given to the development and evolution that teething contributes to the development of the jaws.

In addition to proper maintenance of occlusal guidance, the newly emerging permanent piece, not having full root process, is very weak and therefore more sensitive to injury.

Losing a permanent piece in a young individual implies greater disability than in an adult.

17.7 Assessment of Tooth Pain

Indicators of posttraumatic abnormality, after a clinical exam, and therefore degrees of pain can be assigned to a scale of values as follows:

Le Roy Scale: 0, null; 1, very light; 2, light; 3, moderate; 4, medium; 5, less important; 6, important; 7, very important.

17.8 Average Healing Period

- Crown fracture without pulp exposure: less than 30 days.
- Crown fracture with pulp exposure: if it is a piece, it will be less than 30 days; if there are four or more pieces, it will be more than 30 days.
- Root fracture without pulp exposure: less than 30 days.
- Root fracture with pulp exposure: if only one piece, it will be less than 30 days; if there are four or more pieces, it will be more than 30 days.

17.9 Time of Disability

It depends on the time of healing treatments necessary to restore function and the aftermath:

- Transitional: possible restoration of function
- Permanent: loss of function, although one could make a prosthesis
- Partial: when only a sector of the oral cavity is affected
- Total: when the damage affects all the teeth

17.10 Reference to the Prosthetic Item

Dentistry and other sciences have developed their knowledge and applied different techniques and materials, giving the patient a restoratory variety of treatments and prosthetics, not only of aesthetic but also of functional quality (masticatory and phonetic).

An example of this is the fixed prosthesis, implant supported, which gives the patient comfort and confidence to engage freely in their life. But we must consider that the best prosthetic restoration achieved can never compete with the natural parts of the individual, since it does not suppress the physiological deficits suffered by a person losing their natural teeth, involving, as it does, a number of undesirable effects such as foreign body sensation, change in eating and speaking, gingival lesions, etc.

Therefore, a percentage deficit of 50 % may be calculated in the case of a removable prosthesis and 25 % in the case of a fixed prosthesis added to a pure percentage allocation failure of each tooth by way of weighting factor or correction of the damage.

It is important to consider factors such as the individual's age, possibility of restoration, prosthetic containment, etc., or apply technical knowledge of dentistry, to relate to the different legal issues arising from injuries produced in the oral cavity.

17.11 Valuation of the Jaw Bone Fractures

17.11.1 Superior Maxilla

They can be classified generally into two groups.

- Intraoral

  The alveolar process, vestibular, or palatal tables
  Tuberosity
  Unilateral palatal portion

- Extraoral

  Le Fort I
  Le Fort II
  Le Fort III

Offers a number of complications, sometimes considerably delayed healing times: average healing time, 130 days; average time of incapacity, 90 days.

Aftermath:

- Anatomical: callus vicious, osteoporosis, osteosynthesis material, associated neurological lesions and vascular structures.
- Functional: it has impact on the masticatory function and therefore feeding disorders. It can affect the respiratory and phonatory function, as well as transient mono- or polyarticular functionality. Neuralgia, even permanent or disobedient to any therapy, can also result.
- Aesthetics: highly variable, sometimes cosmetic sequelae occur due to maxillary surgical fixation. Scars and facial paralysis, which may occur, should also be noted.
- Complications are frequent, including sinusitis-associated infections involving the mouth, loss of teeth, neurovascular injury, facial neuralgia rebels, and facial paralysis.

Degree of disability: with values ranging from 5 to 15 %.

17.11.2 Lower Jaw

It can also be divided into:

- Intraoral, including the dental arch form: partial or complete, single or multiple, comminuted.
- That which does not include the dental arch: located in the angle, coronoid process, or condyle.

Average healing time, 120 days; average time of incapacity, 90 days
Aftermath:

- Anatomical: loss or tooth fractures, strains, dislocations (recurrent or not), osteosynthesis material.
- Functional: affects chewing function, altering food, annulling sometimes for long periods, e.g. 45–60 days. Patient should be fed a special diet. Also, permanent facial neuralgia, lack or limitation of joint mobility.
- Aesthetics: variable, depending on the type of fracture, and can affect facial symmetry. Operative scars often originate.
- Frequent osteomyelitis complications associated with infections of the oral cavity, occlusal disharmony, and digestive disturbances.

Degree of disability: with values ranging from 5 to 15 %

17.12 Assessment of Temporomandibular Joint

One of the most common sequelae in severe facial trauma patients is the limitation of the mandibular movements of opening, closing, and laterality, which may vary from a slight limitation to a complete impossibility (lockjaw).

T.M.J dysfunction may be classified according to their cause.

– Joint injuries

Untreated fracture of one of the mandibular condyles
Comminuted fracture of a condyle
Split-sinking of a condyle in the temporal bone

Keep in mind that the injury to the condyle, if unilateral, causes movement of the chin toward the affected side.

– Extra-articular injuries

Fracture of the zygomatic process that affects the temporal muscle.
Fracture of the coronoid.
Sinking of the malar bone.
Injuries of the masseter and/or temporal muscles as sclerosis, fibrosis, contractures, etc. These lesions are diagnosed clinically and by electromyography.
Flanges buccal mucosa in the back area.

Clinical diagnosis inspection includes the following:

– Aperture range: measuring the distance between points inter-upper and lower incisors, observing whether deviation from the mean inter-incisive line occurs. The distance should be about 45 mm.
– Traps in opening and closing to take into account that the variations that occur in opening, due to disturbances in the articulation and those observed in closure, are the result of occlusal disorders.
– Range lateral movements, which decline, may indicate lack of condylar translation, a difference in the size of the condyle or asymmetry of the skull base.
– Unarticulated sounds always indicate pathology.
– Pain. The intrameatal palpation, performed with the little fingers in the ear canal, using opening and closing movements and pressing forward, should not cause the patient any pain; otherwise, there is evidence of a pathology.
– Evidence of muscle and ligament tone. Simple maneuvers that will provide us, by limiting normal movements, with evidence of limited opening, lateral deviation, or excessive opening due to unilateral or bilateral subluxation.
– Posture. Shoulder height should be observed as it may vary due to a rising or falling injury.
– Other painful symptoms may occur (e.g. headache, etc.).

Alterations in TMJ may be confirmed by clinical examination and different imaging tests. This type of injury tends to evolve over time into ankylosis, which is difficult to treat.

Degree of disability will vary, depending on the damage of 5–20 %, from slight limitation to complete impossibility of mobility: lockjaw.

17.13 Assessment of Dental Occlusion

Dental occlusion involves the relationship of the maxilla with the jaw. It is important to refer to the rarity of an ideal occlusion, which coincides with centric relation (TMJ) and maximum intercuspation (alveolar level).

Therefore, the analysis of this topic should be compared to a good joint where the trajectory between them is free from interference. It should also evaluate the time elapsed between the time of injury and the consolidation of the occurrence of sequelae, since the capacity of occlusal adjustment to new conditions is very large. However, this forced adaptation can cause joint and parafunctional conditions such as bruxism.

Classification of occlusal problems may be divided according to the spatial plane observed:

– Vertical or frontal plane

Premature contacts: produced when closing the joint. It may be due to tooth loss causing movements in other areas and modification of occlusion or after a fracture of the maxilla support plane. The consequences are often pain when occluding, clicking, TMJ pain, subluxation, contracture of the masticatory muscles with episodes of eventual lockjaw, etc.

Anterior open bite: when occluding, no contact between incisor/canine group and their antagonists is present. It may be due to poor craniofacial development, filing habits during development or posttraumatic sequel, after bilateral condylar fracture, and consolidation occurs in anomalous position.

– Horizontal or anteroposterior plane

Exaggeration of overjet: corresponding with Angle Class II division could be due to maxillary prognathism or mandibular retrognathia. This alteration may occur during development or as a result of poorly consolidated condyles and ascending branches of the mandible fracture.

Reversal of the intermaxillary relationship would correspond with Angle Class III division, and they could be for mandibular prognathism or a retrognathia maxilla. It may be due to alterations of development; the mandibular pseudoprognathism can be seen in facial crushing associated with anterior open bite.

– Horizontal or transversal plane

Called iatrogenic or cross bites, these diseases are caused by major trauma, causing significant joint abnormalities.

A particular type of occlusion is called “two times” or pseudoarthrosis, which is the observed occlusion of a dental group and then the others.

17.14 Assessment of Taste Function

Although not part of the stomatognathic system, there is no doubt that taste is closely related with this. The taste, sweet, salty, and sour, stimuli are captured by a number of receptors on the tongue papillae, the soft palate, and surrounding areas. The frequent changes are decreased taste (hypogeusias) and alteration of perception (parageusias).

Factors acting on alterations are the effects of age, smoking, and the use of upper removable prosthesis that blocks receptors.

17.15 Procedure of Dental Trauma Expertise

Usually, the procedure of dental trauma expertise requires a clinical visit and a clinical and radiographic study of the case history so as to gain an accurate perception with regard to the valuation of the resulting disability.

- History
- Origin of injury which will take into account

  Identification of the lesion, for example, coronary fracture angle, cusp, etc.
  Description of injury: size, depth, affecting tissues, recent or longstanding injury
  Location of the lesion: on the tooth surface

- Causal mechanism, has to be defined to assess the causal chain relationship. Most lesions in body chewing are caused by shock or impact mechanism with or against a hard or semihard element.
- Disability. The legal medical disability is defined in terms of time in days, determined by the expert taking into account the duration and severity of the injury. Duration refers to the time in days spent by the tissue to achieve primary biological repair while gravity is determined based on the clinical assessment of the importance of injury to personal integrity. With injury that occurs in the hard tissues of the tooth, there is no biological repair process; the failure is then established based on the severity of the injury, as follows:

  Fractures at the incisal third: 7 days
  Fractures at the middle third: 15 days
  Fractures at the third cervical level: 20 days, if it is a single tooth
  Root fractures: 15–20 days
  Cusp fractures: 10–20 days

Some adjunctive factors may influence the total duration in days.

- Number of teeth involved

  Total exarticulation or one-piece avulsion is equal to 20 days; if there is the loss of two or more pieces: 30 days.

  In the presence of these injuries, medical disability and the definitive legal consequences, if any, can be established in the first survey.

- Supporting bone lesions

  Fracture of tooth socket: between 15 and 20 days, if loss of one or more teeth is homologous to exarticulation or complete avulsion

  Fracture of alveolar process: 20–30 days (depending on its size)

- Dislocations of the temporomandibular joint between 15 and 20 days depending on whether or not bilateral and no sequelae
- Fractures in upper and lower jaw

  Fractures: Le Fort I, 35–45 days; Le Fort II and III merit disability between 45 and 60 days

The finding of injuries not described here, such as osteomyelitis, endocarditis, and meningitis, among others, that may result from injuries of dental origin should be evaluated according to the seriousness of the findings for the specific case.

As is clear from the above, in the Civil Jurisdiction, each type of injury is valued according to the percentage of disability scales, and thus the judge has a vision of the amount of monetary compensation. The Criminal Jurisdiction relies on Articles 89, 90, 91, and 94 of the Criminal Code.

As for dental Praxis, this can be addressed in Criminal Law as framed in Article 94 and in the Civil Law by the scale for financial reward.

The BAREMO is a scale for measuring the impairment caused by the trauma and is endorsed by the legal national scientific society, duly published and accepted by the legal medical advisors.

The procedures referred to determine the damage are based on the scientific literature (see references) and have been officially recognized nationally.

These are all regulations promulgated by our Expert Forensic Department of the Argentina National Justice, Department of Legal Dentistry, based on the existing literature on the criteria of legal medicine and are binding with national criteria and in consultation with other countries of South America, including Peru, Paraguay, Bolivia, and Uruguay, which have not developed scales or percentages for this type of assessment of tooth damage.

Below are listed some general bibliographic sources useful to deepen the issue. They are not reported within the text as they are no cited references.

Bibliography

1. Allan D, Foreman P (1987) Prostodoncia de coronas y puentes. ED. Panamericana, Buenos Aires
2. Andreasen J (1984) Lesiones traumáticas de los dientes. ED. Labor, Barcelona
3. Andreasen J, Andreasen F (1990) Lesiones dentarias traumáticas. ED. Panamericano, Madrid
4. Bakland L (1987) Lesiones traumáticas en endodoncia. ED. Interamericana, México
5. Bertini V (1950) Evaluación legal del aparato dentario. Rev. Del Ateneo de la cátedra de Ortodoncia. Buenos Aires
6. Brignon N (1984) Odontología legal y práctica forense. ED. Purizon, Buenos Aires
7. Clasificación Internacional de deficiencias, discapacidades y minusvalías (O.M.S.) (1983) Madrid
8. Gisbert Calabuig J (1991) Medicina Legal y Toxicología. ED. Salvat, Barcelona
9. Maisto O (1973) Endodoncia. ED. Mundi, Buenos Aires
10. Pagliera J (1962) La pérdida de las piezas dentarias. Rev Asoc Med Arg 76-nov
11. Rojas N (1971) Medicina Legal. ED. El Ateneo, Buenos Aires
12. Pena A (1997) Traumatología muco alvéolo dentario, manual de actualización odontológica. ED. Microsules Bernabo, Buenos Aires
13. Bonnet EFP (1980) Medicina legal. López libreros, Buenos Aires
14. Pérez Perea B, Roldan Garrido B, Sánchez Sánchez JA (1996) Metodología para la valoración del daño buco dental. ED. MAPFRE, s.a. Madrid
15. Blanca Pérez Pineda, Manuel García Blázquez: Manual de la valoración y baremación del daño corporal

Part IV
Medico-legal Ascertainment of Personal Injury and Damage Under Civil-Tort Law: Continental Overview
Africa

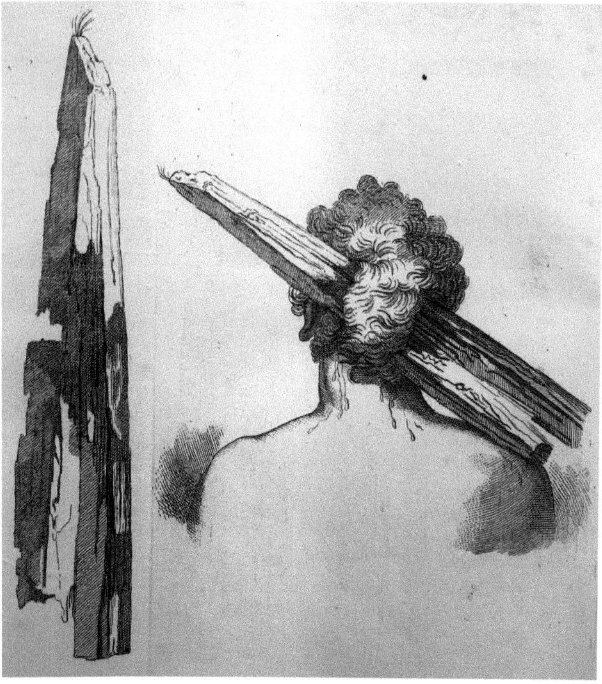

Rima, Tommaso. Tavole con cenni istorici d'alcuni casi chirurgici straordinarj felicemente curati nel Civico ospitale provinciale di Venezia dal chirurgo primario anziano Tommaso dott. Rima...Venezia: G. Antonelli, 1838. Courtesy of historical section of the "Vincenzo Pinali" Medical Library of the University of Padova

Chapter 18
Methods of Ascertainment of Personal Damage in Egypt

Dina A. Shokry

Abstract This chapter illustrates the historical, judicial, and juridical framework of personal injury assessment and compensation in Egypt, describing the expert's qualification and competences and detailing the ascertainment methodology and criteria of evaluation utilized for identifying, describing, and estimating any personal injury, its temporary and permanent consequences, and the causal value/link between the event and the injury and between the injury and the impairment/disability.

18.1 Historical, Judicial, and Juridical Overview

The laws of ancient Egypt were thought to be partially codified. Some of the laws of ancient Egypt were derived from funerary texts, as well as court and other documents (Fig. 18.1).

Essentially, it was believed that Egyptian law was based on a common sense view of right and wrong, following the codes based on the concept of Ma'at that represented truth, order, balance, and justice in the Universe. This concept provided that everyone, with the exception of slaves, should be viewed as equal under the law, regardless of wealth or social position. However, when punishment was meted out, often the entire family of the guilty suffered as well. For example, when individuals were sentenced to exile, their children were automatically outlawed along with them. If a relative deserted the military, or defaulted on the labor demands of the State, the entire family might be imprisoned.

The King, as a living God, was the supreme judge and lawmaker. Of course, much of this power was delegated to others.

It was believed that the title Overseer of the Six Great Mansions refers to our modern equivalent of a magistrate. Mansions is probably a reference to the main

D.A. Shokry (✉)
Department of Forensic Medicine and Clinical Toxicology, Faculty of Medicine, Cairo University, Kasr Al Ainy St. Cairo, 11562 Cairo, Egypt
e-mail: dinashokry_2004@hotmail.com

S.D. Ferrara et al. (eds.), *Personal Injury and Damage Ascertainment under Civil Law*, DOI 10.1007/978-3-319-29812-2_18

Fig. 18.1 Ma'at wearing feather of truth www.ancientegyptonline.co.uk/matt [1]

law court in Thebes. There were, in addition, other major courts in Egypt. Minor cases were tried by a local council of elders, and each town or village had its own local kenet in charge of legal proceedings. Such cases usually involved minor problems, such as default on loans. Still, the most important matters were probably reported to the King, who would then decide the case and the proper sentence.

During the twenty-first Dynasty (1069–1945 BC), law was given through the oracle of Amun. Documentation on prior cases was recorded and retained and, as in our own modern legal systems, were used as precedent for current cases. Some of these documents remain, representing some of our best evidence concerning how the ancient Egyptian legal system functioned [2].

After this era, during the Greek period, Greek law existed alongside that of Egyptian law, but usually these laws favored the Greeks.

When the Romans took control of Egypt, the Roman legal system, which existed throughout the Roman empire, was imposed in Egypt [3].

The modern distinction between civil and criminal law is also hard to transfer to ancient Egyptian practice. There was no state prosecution for actions we would consider criminal, such as theft or assault, but the injured party had to act as plaintiff. Only crimes against the Pharaoh and Gods, like conspiracies or theft from royal tombs or temples, were prosecuted by officials [2].

In many respects, the ancient Egyptian laws remain with us today. Solon, the Greek lawgiver, visited Egypt in the sixth century BC, studied their law, and adapted many aspects of it into the legal system of Athens. During Egypt's Greek period, Egyptian law continued to influence the separate Greek legal system. When the Romans took Egypt, their legal system was affected by both the Greeks and Egyptians and, even today, we continue to implement a number of aspects of Roman law [4].

18.2 The Egyptian Legal System

The Egyptian legal system is built on the combination of Islamic (Shariah) law and the Napoleonic Code, which was first introduced during Napoleon Bonaparte's occupation of Egypt and the subsequent education and training of Egyptian jurists in France.

The Egyptian legal system, being considered as a civil law system, is based upon a well-established system of codified laws. Egypt's supreme law is its written constitution. With respect to transactions between natural persons or legal entities, the most important legislation is the Egyptian Civil Code of 1948 (the "ECC"), which remains the main source of legal rules applicable to contracts. Much of the ECC is based upon the French Civil Code and, to a lesser extent, upon various other European codes and upon Islamic (Shariah) law (especially in the context of personal status) [5].

Despite the nonexistence of an established system of legally (de jure) binding precedents, previous judicial decisions do have persuasive authority. Courts are morally and practically bound (de facto binding effect) by the principles and precedents of the Court of Cassation (for civil, commercial, and criminal matters) and the Supreme Administrative Court (for administrative and other public law matters) [6].

It is worth noting that the classical dichotomy of public and private law has resulted in the crystallization of a separate set of legal rules applicable to transactions involving the State (or any of its institutions, subsidiaries, or state-owned enterprises) acting as a sovereign power. This entailed the establishment of the Egyptian Council of State (Conseil d'Etat), which are administrative courts vested with the power to decide over administrative disputes pertaining to administrative contracts and administrative decrees issued by government officials. These courts apply administrative legal rules, which are not entirely codified, and hence the scope of judicial discretion, insofar as no applicable legislative rule exists, is ample in light of the established precedents laid down by the supreme courts. The judiciary consists of: courts of first instance, all of which hear criminal and civil cases; Judicial Authority Act No. 46 of 1972. Courts of appeal, which hear appeals and have original jurisdiction to hear criminal cases that carry punishments of longer-

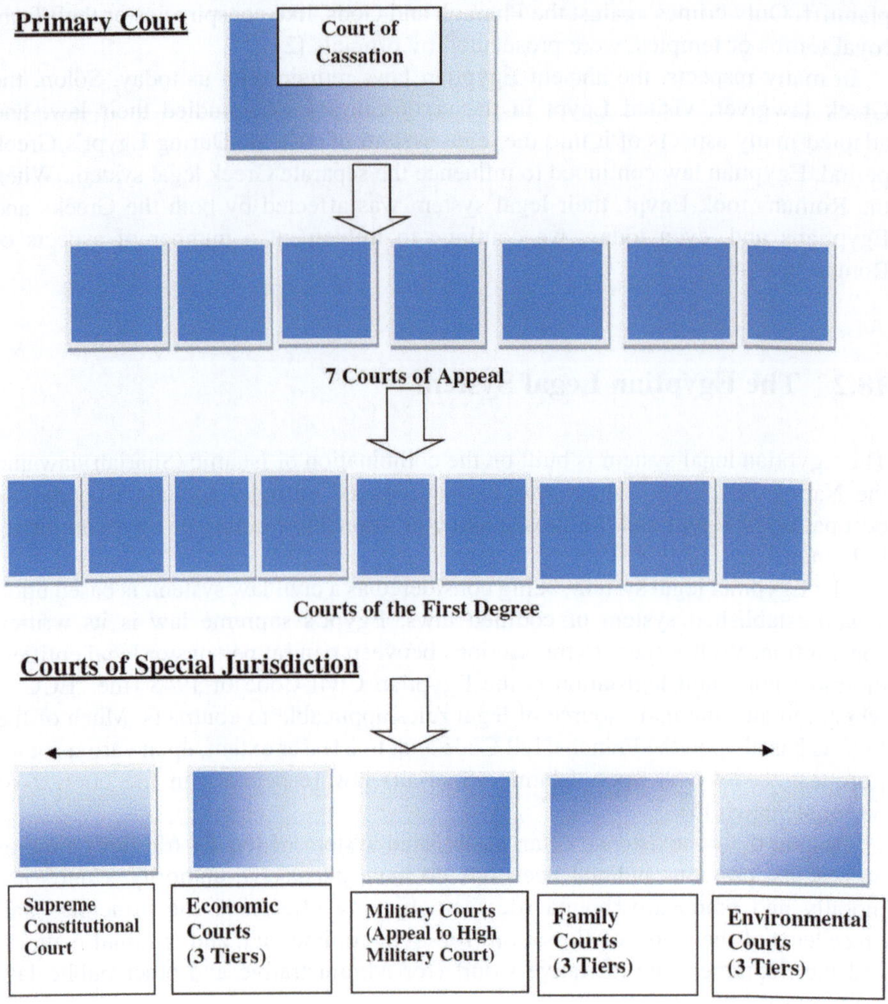

Fig. 18.2 Egyptian court system

term imprisonment or death; the High Supreme Court, which has jurisdiction to hear cases on appeal from the courts of appeal and the Supreme Constitutional Court, which decides on the constitutionality of laws [7] (Fig. 18.2).

18.3 Identification and Description of Medicolegal Expert's Qualifications

In Egypt, any physician may be asked to examine a person who has been wounded, particularly in casualty.

Forensic physicians and pathologists are also asked to examine wounds in a later stage in order to evaluate disability and find out the cause of death in the related cases. He/she is asked also to explore the causal nexus between injuries and death.

The identification and description of wounds may have serious medicolegal implications at a later stage and often after some considerable time has passed since the wounding. It is therefore essential that different types of wounds can be correctly identified and described via the primary wound reports issued in casualty departments or the emergency rooms of various hospitals.

Before describing the qualification of the physicians and medicolegal experts, I would like to mention the journey of the injured case up until the evaluation of disabilities, if any. The following algorithm allows one to understand the healthcare system when it deals with cases of different types of injuries in the Arab Republic of Egypt (Figs. 18.3 and 18.4).

In Egypt, injuries are due either to road traffic accidents, other accidents, violence, or workplace injuries. All acute cases are sent to the emergency rooms of different hospitals to be managed and the primary documentation takes place there. After management of the injury, victims are referred to the Egyptian

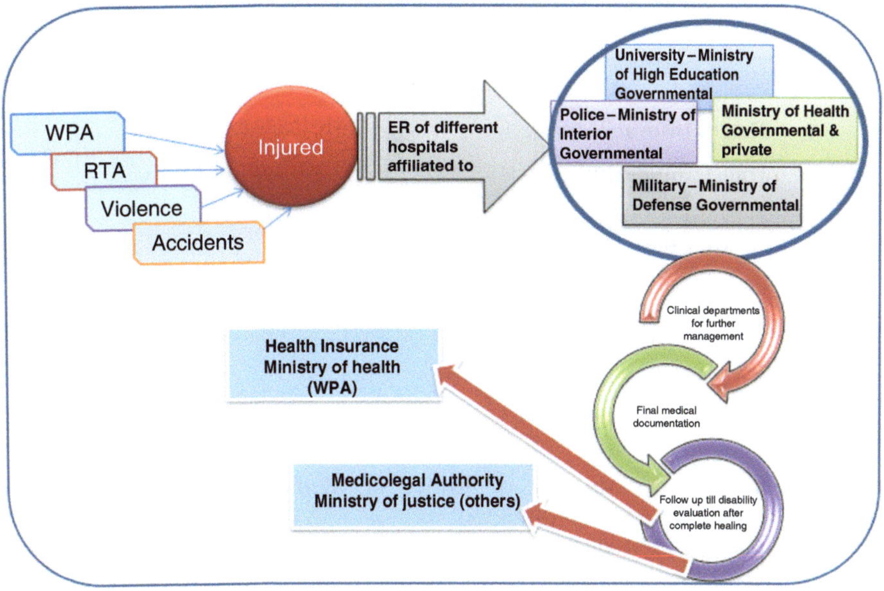

Fig. 18.3 The Egyptian administrative system in dealing with injury cases

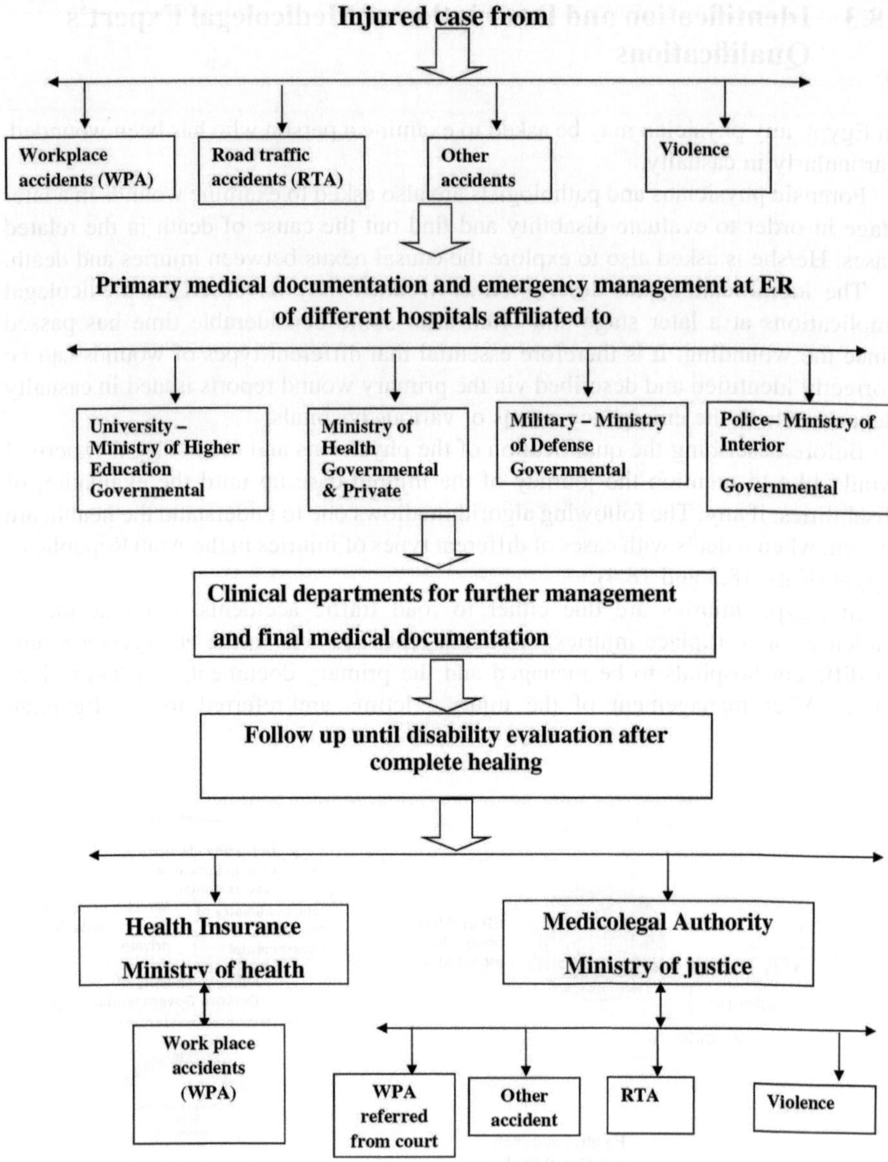

Fig. 18.4 Workflow

Medicolegal Authority-Ministry of Justice or Medical Insurance-Ministry of Health, according to the circumstances.

After being treated, cases of violence, road traffic accidents, and other accidents are followed up by Medicolegal Experts—the Ministry of Justice to trace the healing process until the complete healing takes place and no further changes have been detected to calculate the percentage of disability.

Cases of injury due to work place accidents are referred to the Medical Insurance-Ministry of Health so as to be followed up and to estimate the percentage of disability. Sometimes, the court referred the case to the Medicolegal Authority-Ministry of Justice if the victim complains about the percentage issued or if the court needs the opinion of another expert.

18.3.1 Qualifications

18.3.1.1 For Estimation of Disabilities Due to Violence, Road Traffic Accident Injuries, and Court Referred Cases (Medicolegal Experts)

The new forensic physicians—Medicolegal Authority, Ministry of Justice—are recruited after being selected via a newspaper announcement and after having passed the interview. The training program takes place for 6 months in order for each trainee to begin his professional career as a co-examiner. He/she begins by examining cases of injuries, assaults, sexual crimes, alleged cases of criminal abortion, and injuries due to medical errors as well as performing autopsies for cases of suspected death. They issue the medicolegal reports for such cases with a senior examiner.

The senior forensic physician passes the master degree (M.Sc.) exam in forensic medicine, toxicology, and forensic sciences. It takes him/her a minimum of 30 calendar months to satisfy 35 credit hours of theoretical, practical, and clinical courses, so as to apply for the exam and draft a thesis.

To become a consultant, a forensic physician should pass the medical doctorate degree (M.D.) exam in forensic medicine, toxicology, and forensic sciences. It takes him/her a minimum of 36 calendar months to satisfy 35 credit hours of theoretical, practical, and clinical courses, so as to apply for the exam and draft a thesis. To fulfill the requirements to be a forensic consultant, he/she has to pass through another 3 years of working experience.

According to Egyptian University Law and the guidelines for postgraduate medical education of the Faculty of Medicine at Cairo University in the last amendments in 2014, regarding the registration for the M.Sc., a "Good" grade is necessary for the Bachelor Degree of medicine & surgery and at least a "Good" grade in forensic medicine.

In Egypt, undergraduate medical students should pass an exam in the forensic sciences and toxicology as a core curriculum for 144 teaching hours divided between lectures, practical sessions, and problem-based sessions. This course takes place during the 4th year undergraduate medical study (clinical phase), and each student should pass written, practical, and oral exams. The syllabus includes topics in forensic medicine, forensic & clinical toxicology, and medical ethics & laws.

Moreover, consultants from different medical specialties (surgery, orthopedics, radiology, psychiatry, urology, neurosurgery, anesthesia, cardiology, and cardiac surgery) are giving their scientific opinion to the forensic expert, if needed, in malpractice cases as well as assessment of physical or psychological disabilities. The consultant's opinion is then included in the final medicolegal reports.

For assessment and primary documentation of the injured cases received by University hospitals and casualty departments, the administrator or assistant lecturer of forensic medicine who, possessing the M.Sc. in forensic medicine, is the one who writes the primary wound report.

The primary wound report for the other hospitals, affiliated to the ministry of health and some university hospitals, is the responsibility of the specialist (possessing the M.Sc. in surgery) or assistant specialist (medical graduate with no postgraduate qualification).

18.3.1.2 For Consultant Medicolegal Reports (Professors and Supreme Committees)

In case the injured victim has a complaint concerning the degree of disability issued in the medicolegal report of the Egyptian medicolegal authority, he/she can ask for a consultant report from three or five experts from the medicolegal authority. The victim as well as the court can refer the case for a consultancy report from University Professors, which is considered as a separate medicolegal body for expert reports.

To be a professor of forensic medicine, it is necessary to pass the M.Sc. and M.D. Subsequently, after a doctorate degree, the assistant lecturer becomes a lecturer. To be promoted to the next chair, the staff member should pass the supreme forensic council discussion for the research and scientific activities proposed by him/her. The candidate cannot proceed to the next chair before the lapse of a period of 5 years. After being an Assistant Professor, one can apply to be a Professor after another 5 years. Winning the Professorship chair means your researches, international publication, and your participation in the academic society reach the level of acceptance of the promotion committee of the supreme council of Universities.

18.3.1.3 For the Estimation of Workplace Injuries and Disability Rating (Healthcare Insurance Experts)

The physician should be specialized in occupational and community medicine. The degree of specialization is acquired by passing the M.Sc. examination in community or occupational medicine from any of the Egyptian universities. To be a consultant, as for forensic medicine, the candidate should pass through 3 years of working experience after having his/her Medical Doctorate degree in these specialties.

18.4 Ascertainment Methodology

18.4.1 Collection of Circumstantial Data

The collection of circumstantial data in cases of violence, road traffic, and work place accident is the responsibility of the General Administration for Criminal Evidence Investigations-Ministry of the Interior, which includes two main departments, finger prints and criminal laboratories, which in turn is subdivided into Crime Scene investigation, Counterfeiting and forgery, Crime scene photography, Laboratory investigations (for chemical and drug analysis), and Fire and explosives investigation. The evidence collection and investigation experts who reach the scene first collect data and write the report. The medicolegal expert can use information of this report while investigating his/her case.

18.4.2 Collection of Clinical Data

Clinical data are collected from:

1. Hospital records where the victim takes his/her medical management via primary and final injury reports (hospitals of different affiliation)
2. Medicolegal reports (medicolegal authority-ministry of justice and university professors)
3. Disability rating reports (medicolegal authority-ministry of justice or healthcare insurance)

Hospital records: the first one to examine a case of injury is the casualty physician or the demonstrator of forensic medicine in university hospitals. Wound reports include primary and final wound reports. These reports are issued in accordance with the ministerial decree of minister of health no. 187/2001.

1. For primary medical reports
   (A) The medical examination of the patient should be based on the referral letter issued by the police and includes all of the relevant data.
   (B) The patient is displayed injured, after the ascertainment of his/her identity, and examined by the specialist or assistant specialist to prove his/her injuries and determine the time required for treatment. The report is signed by the specialist or assistant specialist and the casualty manager.
   (C) The duration of treatment is issued, but if disability occurs the period of treatment shall be determined and the percentage of disability caused by it according to the final medical report.

2. For the final medical reports
   (A) This will be issued after the decision to discharge the injured patient permanently from the hospital, and the medical data is taken from his/her medical record.
   (B) The final report should be signed by a specialist or assistant specialist, the head of the department, and the manager of the hospital after reviewing the medical record of the patient and using all the means of diagnosis.
   (C) The final report should be written in clear language and includes a statement of injuries and the final diagnosis and duration of treatment and disability or impairment—if any—and the necessary recommendation, to be the final ruling by the forensic physician. It is sent to the Attorney, upon request, after the authorized representative has received the final report and upon official permission.

The primary injury report includes the following data.

- Physician information (name and affiliation).
- Victim-related data (name, I.D., age, gender, residence, and registry number).
- Accident-related data: (summary, place, date and time, time lapse before reaching hospital).
- General medical examination (conscious state, pulse, blood pressure, respiratory rate, temperature, pupil's size and reactivity, etc.).
- Injuries data (type, number, size, margin, shape, measures, instrument used, etc.).
- Other injuries (cerebral concussion, cerebral compression, coma, shock, bleeding, drug abuse).
- Investigations needed.
- Emergency treatment.
- Anticipated time for recovery (below 20 days or more than 20 days). According to Egyptian criminal law, injuries are legally classified as simple (heals in less than 20 days), dangerous (heals in more than 20 days and/or causing permanent infirmity), and fatal. According to this classification, penalties vary from monetary compensation to a legal sentence including monetary compensation.
- Disabilities—if any—.
- Attached to the report template, a pictogram to shadow the area of injury in an attempt to facilitate.
- The signature of the issuing physician and the manager.
- For cases of road traffic accident, we create a data collection sheet to include items of importance in documentation of such cases.

The final medical report as mentioned above should include details of management and/or complications, disabilities, and the posttreatment as well as follow-up plan.

The medicolegal report includes all medical information about the case issued in the patient's medical records, investigation, and clinical examination during the follow-up and the expert's opinion from consultants of different specialties in the event that the evaluation of the case needs experiences. Rating of disability should be included in the final conclusion.

If there are no documents for the reconstruction of the incident, the mechanism of injuries is judged via the direction and pattern of injuries.

A mechanic issues the only received report for exclusion of intended damage of the car parts.

The disability rating report is issued by the medicolegal physician (Ministry of Justice and Universities) in suspect cases or by the occupational medicine physician (Healthcare Insurance-Ministry of Health) in injuries due to workplace accidents.

During the systemic clinical medicolegal visits, the forensic physician follows the case up and records the progress of healing and the resulting disabilities. This evaluation is done via clinical examination and investigations. The rating of disabilities are not set before final healing. By Egyptian law, the healing is complete and the disability given a rating 6 months after medical stability of the case, i.e., there were no changes in medical status during 2 visits 14 days apart.

18.4.3 Investigations

18.4.3.1 Laboratory Testing

Liver function tests (AST, ALT, albumin, bilirubin, GGT), kidney function tests (blood urea nitrogen, creatinine, and uric acid), complete blood picture (CBC), lipid profile (HDL, LDL, cholesterol, triglyceride), blood sugar (fasting, 2 h postprandial, glycated Hb), erythrocyte sedimentation rate (ESR), creatine kinase (CK) for cases of suspected musculoskeletal injuries, and screening for drugs of abuse. Other tests are included when organ compromise is suspected, e.g., thyroid function in neck trauma, etc.

18.4.3.2 Radiology

X-ray for suspected fractures and follow-up healing, Computerized Tomography (CT), and Magnetic Resonance Imaging (MRI) for head trauma cases and suspected cerebral hemorrhage are included. CT chest, abdomen, and pelvis in suspected internal injuries, Doppler, CT angiography, and multi-slice CT for suspected vascular injuries, ultrasonography and 3D sonar for suspected cases of intrauterine fetal injuries. MRI, CT, EMG, and Nerve Conduction Velocity (NCV) are used for suspected cases of neuropathy.

18.4.3.3 Electro-Diagnostic Testing

Electro-Encephalogram (EEG) for cases of head trauma, Electro Cardiogram (ECG), and Holter for cases of suspected arrhythmias, Electromyography (EMG) combined with nerve conduction tests for suspected cases of nerve injuries are included.

18.4.3.4 Special Tests

Visual acuity, fundus examination for eye trauma cases, auditory brain stem response, subjective hearing test, and Tympanometry for cases of ear trauma.

The above investigations are performed according to the needs of each case as a part of management and to evaluate the injuries sustained, and disabilities encountered are included. In many cases, it cannot be judged whether the medical condition is pre- or postaccident due to a lack of medical information and documentation.

18.5 Evaluation Criteria

Definition of disability and permanent infirmity in Egyptian law: The definition of the Court of Cassation based on the concept of the article (240) of the criminal law is "The loss of function in the organ or permanent loss of function in this organ." The loss of a nonfunctioning organ is considered disfigurement.

Statistics of different injuries in Egypt: Injury-related mortalities due to road traffic accidents comprised a total of 19,731 deaths between 2000 and 2010 (the incidence ranged between 38.3/100,000 and 51.1/100,000). Road traffic accident was the leading cause. Almost 70 % of injury-related deaths occurred in the age group 15–60 years [8].

According to the Statistics and Information Center, General Traffic Administration in Egypt (2008) (9), the number of RTA injured and dead victims in Great Cairo from 2000 to 2007 was 13,374 and 3,607, respectively.

The Egyptian medicolegal authority received three thousand, one hundred, and forty one (3141) cases for autopsy, while the clinical cases accounted for five thousand, two hundred, and fifty two (5252) in Cairo.

During 2007, the number of cases of injury due to work place accidents was 384,172 (Egyptian Central Agency for Public Mobilization and Statistics) [10].

The percentage of disability is calculated according to table no. 2 of social insurance law no. 79/1975 and its amendment by law no. 25/1977. This is applied to all cases of injury whether accidental (due to road traffic or workplace accidents) or criminal. This law allocates a precise percentage for each injury, and the total percentage of disabilities is the sum of the individual disability percentage.

The table covers all disabilities due to musculoskeletal, neurological, eye, ear, nose, neck, jaws, teeth, tongue, pharynx, larynx, esophagus, stomach, intestine, colon, rectum, liver, spleen, abdominal wall, urinary system, thoracic cage, lungs, cardiovascular, and sexual organ injuries.

The neuropsychiatric and psychological impairments are not included in this table. Nevertheless, the estimated psychological disability is only taken into account if the pre-traumatic psychological state was recorded and then the expert can add a percentage for such impairment if it proves to be permanent.

The evaluation of the posttraumatic psychiatric disability is the responsibility of the psychiatric consultant who assesses depression via the Hamilton depression rating scale and Becks depression inventory. The Standardized Mini mental state examination (SMMSE) is used to assess cognitive function.

The Wechsler Adult Intelligence Scale (WAIS) is for measuring IQ (intelligence quotient) & it has to be compared to a previous one or academic achievements to assess the deterioration of IQ.

The Minnesota multiphasic personality inventory (MMPI) is used for measuring personality disorders, which is merely related to Trauma.

For assessment of hearing disability, the audiologist performs both subjective tests (hearing acuity measure) and objective tests (auditory brain stem response), but usually relies on the results of objective testing to eliminate bias and malingering. This test is used to evaluate the degree of hearing loss and identify its type.

The compensation is considered according to the percentage of disability, and the final decision is the court's as the Egyptian law states that the expert's opinion is only of a technical nature.

The items of disabilities that were not included in the tables that list rating of disabilities according to Egyptian law are subject to the assessment of the physician, which should be approved by the court.

The monetary compensation for the healthcare expenses and other pecuniary losses, i.e., loss of properties, sick leave, etc. are subject to the court assessment after applying the necessary documents. The forensic departments are responsible only for the medical evaluation of the injuries sustained and the follow-up of the cases until complete healing so as to calculate and judge the disability rates, if any.

Shortcomings regarding the Egyptian disability estimation table are as follows:

- The skin lesions and disfigurements are not listed
- The psychological and psychiatric disorders or disabilities are not included
- The temporary disabilities are not listed
- Many types of organ losses are not included (ovaries & intestine, etc.)
- Prostheses and transplants are not mentioned
- It is somewhat subjective and dependent upon the expert's experiences

18.5.1 Ascertainment of Causal Relation

In Egypt, the ascertainment of the causal relation in different incidents is a subject of general standards, but our system is lacking the sophisticated and updated tools for reconstruction of the scene, such as imaging and biomechanics.

The causal relation in Egypt is confirmed via:

- Matching between the date of injuries and the date of incident.
- The confirmation that the type of injury could be inflicted by the object used during accidents.
- The mechanism of wound production passes with the scenario of the incident.
- Identification of the driver in case of RTA, which is accomplished by examination of the vehicle and the deceased (examination of finger prints, blood stains, types of injuries matched with being the driver).
- Examination of the scene (finger prints, biological stains, blood pattern, hairs, and fibers).
- Witnesses.

The ever-increasing numbers of people alleging disability and impairment necessitate a professional understanding of the phenomenon, the scope of the problem, and the most effective means to deal with these issues in a medical practice.

Acknowledgement I am deeply indebted to Dr. Hisham A. Farag, the Director of Zenhom Mortuary, for the information concerning the role of medicolegal authority. I would also like to thank Dr. Labib Nancy for her information about rating tools for psychological assessment.

References

1. Hill J (2010) Ma'at image. Available at www.ancientegyptonline.co.uk/maat
2. Harris J (1971) The concept of law in ancient Egypt. In: Theodorides A (ed) The legacy of Egypt, 2nd edn. Clarendon Press, Oxford, pp 291–322
3. Van Blerk NA (2006) Ma'at. In: The concept of law and justice in ancient Egypt with specific reference to the tale of the eloquent peasant. pp. 1–10
4. Lippert S (2012) Law: definitions and codification. In: Frood E, Wendrich W (eds) UCLA Encyclopedia of Egyptology, Los Angeles. http://digital12.library.ucla.edu/viewItem.do?ark=21198/zz002bzzgj
5. Shalakany A (2001) Between identity and redistribution: Shanhuri, genealogy and the will to islamise. Islam Law Soc 8(2):201–244
6. Mohamed SE (2006) An overview of the Egyptian legal system and legal research. http://www.nyulawglobal.org/globalex/Egypt1.htm. Accessed 8-10-2014
7. Supplementary reports of States parties due in 1996: Egypt, UN Doc. CAT/C/34/Add.11, 28 January 1999, para. 140. "As to the military judiciary, article 183 of the Constitution The Egyptian judicial system
8. Wahab MM (2012) Incidence and patterns of injury-related mortality: a register-based follow-up study in Alexandria, Egypt (2000–2010). Egypt Public Health Assoc 87(1–2):8–15
9. Shalaby S, Akeed Y, Fawzy M, Nabil D (2010) Prospective Study of Some Medico-Legal Aspects of Road Traffic Accidents (RTAS) in Great Cairo 2007. Int J Acad Res 2(2):127–137
10. Egyptian Central Agency for Public Mobilization and Statistics. www.capmas.gov.eg

Chapter 19
Methods of Ascertainment of Personal Damage in Nigeria

William O. Odesanmi and Uwom O. Eze

Abstract This chapter illustrates the historical, judicial, and juridical framework of personal injury assessment and compensation in Nigeria, describing the expert's qualification and competences and detailing the ascertainment methodology and criteria of evaluation utilized for identifying, describing, and estimating any personal injury, its temporary and permanent consequences, and the causal value/link between the event and the injury and between the injury and the impairment/disability.

19.1 Historical, Judicial, and Juridical Overview

Understanding of the historical concept of law and adjudication in African societies will help to elucidate the background upon which ascertainment of personal injury and damage rests in Nigeria. Elegido (2007) in his book, *Jurisprudence*, outlined common traits of the historical system of African traditional law as follows [1].

19.1.1 Emphasis on Conciliation and Compromise

The adversarial system is the hallmark of the modern judicial process. The court has to find who has the legal right in a dispute and then the "winner takes all." If the court finds that a piece of land in dispute between A and B belongs to A, then A gets the whole of the land and B gets nothing. If the court had found instead that B had

W.O. Odesanmi (✉)
Forensic Pathology, Ekiti State University, Along Ado-Iworoko Road, Ado-Ekiti, Nigeria
e-mail: odesanmi@yahoo.co.uk

U.O. Eze
Forensic Pathology, University College Hospital Ibadan, Queen Elizabeth Road, Oritamefa, Ibadan, Oyo State, Nigeria
e-mail: uwomeze@gmail.com

S.D. Ferrara et al. (eds.), *Personal Injury and Damage Ascertainment under Civil Law*, DOI 10.1007/978-3-319-29812-2_19

better title to the land, B would have gotten all of it and A would have gone empty-handed. By contrast, traditional African systems laid great emphasis on the need to promote reconciliation and continued fraternity between the parties in dispute.

19.1.2 Emphasis on General Principles

Elegido (2007) in his writing on *Jurisprudence* has referenced a book on the Kikuyu of Kenya, where the author, Lambert, made the following observations: *...the widely held view that Africans have yet to evolve a code of law requires some qualification. Every tribe has a code, but it is a code of general principles, not of detail. Every judgment must conform to it, though the principles are applied with latitude unknown to European law.* Still on the subject, Elegido states, it makes a valid point if it is understood as a general observation, subject to many exceptions, as has been discussed: *...to admit this must not lead to a failure to notice the very many rules of African Laws which are as precise and detailed as any pedantic Chancery lawyer could ask for. Such rules may, for instance, specify in great details the precise compensation to be paid for various kinds of injury; such rules may precisely lay down how one may get married, or divide an estate on death, or acquire entitlement to land, or assert a claim in court* [1].

19.1.3 Group Responsibility

It is very common in African societies for a dispute to involve not only the direct parties to the incident which caused it but also the family or kinship groups of both immediate parties. Thus, for instance, in the case of a killing, it will often be the whole extended family of the party slain that demands compensation and not only the immediate members of the nuclear family. Similarly, it will often be the case that the whole kinship group of the slayer becomes liable to the payment of death money (compensation). And it is also the usual practice that the two families will be immediately involved in the legal proceedings and that, if compensation is not paid, both families will participate in the consequent vendetta or feud. Similar points can be made in respect of marriage, tort claims, etc.

19.1.4 Frequent Use of Informal Enforcement Procedures

In many African societies, it is for the injured party to enforce his own right, sometimes after this right has been vindicated in the proper tribunal. It is very important not to confuse this legally sanctioned self-help with cases of unregulated use of force by the strong to get what they want. In the first place, in cases of legally approved self-help, the group approves of the actions taken and it is a requirement of the legality that the right of the party may have been upheld in legal proceedings or at least be recognized under the norms of the society. A second important point of distinction is that the person exercising his right of self-help will often have the help of his family group or his age group; this help would usually not be forthcoming for an exercise of private or unlawful violence.

19.2 Description of Medicolegal Expert's Qualification

In Nigeria, there is no specific requirement for qualification as a medicolegal expert or a forensic physician to undertake personal injury and damage assessment. In fact, in many jurisdictions in Nigeria where qualifications for a medical practitioner are specified for medicolegal work (especially in Coroner's cases), only a basic medical qualification (e.g., MB, BS) of a doctor is required. A specialist or medicolegal expert qualification is not indicated or required. The background to this circumstance is that Nigerian law is derived from the British law bequeathed to the country from the colonial era. In the course of time after independence, medical training has expanded and expertise in various specialties is now gaining popularity. However, some of these provisions in our law (e.g., Coroner's Law) have remained essentially unchanged since independence. Nonetheless, medicolegal expertise is still grossly underrepresented as only a handful of practitioners are experts in forensic medicine in Nigeria. In a country with a population estimated to be about 170 million, there are no more than ten qualified medicolegal experts. The qualifications include diploma in medical jurisprudence (DMJ); Masters in Forensic Medicine; and other relevant fellowships of the Postgraduate Medical Colleges such as the Royal College of Pathologists (FRCPath) or the Royal College of Physicians of London (FRCP). There are local and regional Postgraduate Fellowships such as the National Postgraduate Medical College of Nigeria (FMCPath) and the West African College of Physicians (FWACP).

In practice, however, the nature of injury and damage suffered by a victim as a result of traffic accidents or medical malpractice will determine the type of medical professional contacted to determine the damage suffered. If the injury is fatal, usually a pathologist is contacted, but in nonfatal injuries, a surgeon or a physician, where available, will be contacted to evaluate injury and determine damage. The medical practitioners who work in government hospitals or health facilities are favored to undertake such task. However, private practitioners may also be called upon to attend to such cases where no government medical practitioner is available for any reason. This is currently what is obtainable in the country, but it is not specified in any legislation or policy document, either at state or national levels.

However, in practice, where a person with insurance coverage is injured, the insurance company requests for injury assessment by a medical practitioner or retains services of a medical practitioner, who undertakes this task of personal injury and damage assessment for the insurance company, for the purpose of payment of compensations. It should be noted that the injured party has the right to institute civil action in a court of law if not satisfied with the assessment of the medical practitioner.

19.3 Present Legislation

The influence of Western culture and colonial heritage has resulted in an adversarial system of governance and justice.

Chapter W6 of the Laws of the Federation of Nigeria 2004 deals on Workmen's Compensation Act [2]. The act defines a workman as a person who has entered into or is working under a contract of service or apprenticeship with an employer, whether by way of manual labor, clerical work or otherwise, and whether the contract is expressed or implied, is oral, or in writing. It is interesting to note that even someone engaged illegally may be covered by this act as indicated in section 1, subsection 3 which states: If in the proceedings for the recovery of compensation under this Act, it appears to the court that the contract of service or apprenticeship under which the injured person was working at the time was illegal at the time when the accident causing the injury occurred, the court may, if having regard to all the circumstances of the case it holds it proper so to do, deal with the matter as if the injured person had been working under a valid contract of service or apprenticeship.

The workmen's compensation Act in Nigeria applies both to workers in the public service as well as those in the private sector.

In Section 3 of Nigerian law, an employer's liability for compensation for death or incapacity resulting from accident is highlighted thus: …if in an employment, personal injury by accident arising out of and in the course of the employment is caused to a workman, his employer shall, subject as hereinafter mentioned, be liable to pay compensation in accordance with the provisions of this Act. However, there is a proviso that an employer shall not be liable to pay compensation under this Act in respect of any injury which does not incapacitate the workman for a period of at least 3 consecutive days from earning full wages at the work at which he was employed and if it is proved that the injury to a workman is attributable to serious and willful misconduct of that workman, and compensation claimed in respect of that injury shall be disallowed. Subsection 5 of section 3 also emphasized another significant disclaimer in respect of any incapacity or death resulting from personal injury, if the workman has at any time represented to the employer that he was not suffering or had not previously suffered from that or a similar injury, knowing that the representation was false.

It is equally important to indicate that provisions of the Nigeria law cover various categories of compensation. The categories are as follows: fatal cases, cases of permanent total incapacity, and permanent partial incapacity.

19.4 Medical Assessment for Injury and Damage in Nigeria

Medical assessment for personal injury and damage in Nigeria by a medical practitioner follows the usual pattern of physical examination by attending doctors. After a general physical examination, the anatomical area involved is examined for any injuries or scars, and the extent of such injuries, scars, or deformities is documented. The doctor also documents the extent of limits to normal/usual activities (if any) and any other damage that may have been a subject for assessment. Presently, there are no specific medical guidelines, standards, or procedures being applied nationally or locally except the provision in the Workman Compensation Act, which is mainly concerned with injuries and damages and strictly stipulates scoring physical outcomes of injuries or damages. It is the responsibility of the medical practitioner to determine the presence of such injury outcomes, and the doctor is at liberty to use any medical procedure in making such determination. The medical practitioner ascertains the damage or injury solely on the basis of the data available at the time of the visit for medical assessment. No further specialized tests are usually requested, except those required by the doctor to come to a logical conclusion of assessment.

Best medical practice requires the review of other organ systems, even when not directly injured or damaged, so as to examine for any functional impairment that may be present and assess if the impairment is related to the injury, mainly for medical assessment purposes. Medical history revolves around circumstances of the injury, which is the presenting complaint, and other aspects of medical history, such as past medical history, review of systems, and relevant social history, in order to exclude any condition that may have impact on the overall health of the subject. The pattern is similar to that of a clinical evaluation of a patient in a typical hospital or health facility.

Unfortunately, any claim for damages is only predicated on the presence of physical injuries and not on other damage that may not necessarily be physical in nature.

The Workman Compensation Act in Nigeria stipulates the appointment of Medical Assessors by the Minister of the Federation on the recommendation of the Minister charged with the responsibility relating to health and with compiling a list of medical practitioners to act as medical assessors for the purpose of fulfilling the requirement of the law in Nigeria. This is where the real problem of ascertainment of personal injury and damage in Nigeria begins. The sheer layers of bureaucracy are involved in the ministerial portfolio that caters for the health of over 170 million people of the federation, which obliges the minister to attend to every case of medical assessment even if such duties are delegated to other officials.

However, a subsequent provision in the Act allows for the discretion of the court to summon to its assistance from the list any medical assessor to act in an advisory capacity in the hearing of any application for compensation in some cases of injuries, but such assessors shall not be employees of or associated with any pecuniary way with the employer by whom the workman is employed. A medical assessor may examine the workman in private, and in making any such examination, he shall also examine as to any allegations which have been made to him in writing either by the workman or by the employer respecting the condition of the workman, and the conclusions arrived at by him on such examination may be taken into consideration in deciding the question in dispute. A medical assessor is disqualified from a particular case of ascertainment if he has a connection with the injury or death out of which the application arises, or has given professional assistance or advice with regard to the accident or question in dispute to either party to the application or to any person with whom an insurance has been effected in respect of the payment of compensation to that workman under Nigerian law.

In order to maintain the objectivity of any medical assessor, payment for services in ascertaining injury and damage to a workman shall be paid out of the Consolidated Revenue Fund of the Federation according to a scale fixed by regulations to be made by the Minister.

Meanwhile, it is important to indicate that there is no statute of limitation of time for any affected party to undergo medical assessment for injury or damage. Nonetheless, the earlier the assessment is carried out, the better the outcome, especially in cases which may end up in civil tort. In effect, medical assessment can be carried out at any time a damaged party calls for it.

19.5 Injury Evaluation

Once there is a complaint of personal injury brought before an employer, a concerned authority, or a court in a civil-tort suit, an appointed medical assessor proceeds to evaluate injuries/damage, as earlier indicated. Criteria for assessing injuries are taken against the background of preemployment medical assessment, which is a mandatory requirement before assumption of any duties in a public institution and private organizations. The medical assessor submits an expert opinion of the causal link between the injury and the damage and also on the degree of impairment. In Nigeria, there is a lot of responsibility and power vested in the medical assessor. However, the opinion of the medical assessor can be challenged in court, and the court could seek other opinions when a civil suit ensues. There is no existing compensation table for impairment or disability in Nigeria. Rather, a table for apportioning percentage of disability exists in the Workman's Compensation Act. This table is not a compensation table and compensation that an injured person is paid is determined by many factors including his earnings prior to injury and damage, percentage of disability, and, in some cases, court pronounced compensation of award of damages. Meanwhile, all cases of medical malpractice go to the court in a civil suit brought on by the plaintiff (the injured party), and malpractice is only determined by the court and the court will also award damages if malpractice is proven.

The second schedule of the Workman's Compensation Act in Nigeria outlined a general guideline on ascertaining the percentage of disability from injuries/accidents in work places or in the course of lawful activities.

The following provision in the Act applies.

- Total permanent loss of the use of a member shall be treated as loss of such member.
- In the case of a right-handed workman, an injury to the left arm or hand and in the case of a left-handed workman, to the right arm or hand, shall be rated at ninety per cent (90%) of the above percentages.
- Where there is loss of two or more parts of the hand, the percentage of incapacity shall not be more than for loss of the whole hand, and any necessary lesser percentage shall be applied accordingly.

The provision of the Workman Compensation Act in Nigeria only allows for evaluation of physical injuries only. There is no provision for disability in terms of its influence upon routine daily activities, relational aspects, social constraints, sports, leisure activities, and quality of life, including possible damage to sexual function, esthetic damage, existential damage, pain, and suffering. Physical injuries must be present as outlined in the table, and various percentages of disability are already assigned.

19.6 Prevailing Practice in Nigeria

A good number of cases for ascertainment of personal injury and damage in Nigeria end up in the court. One of the authors has been involved in court proceeding/arbitration in reviewing a case report for the purpose of the court and consideration of insurance company when such an injured or dead worker is insured at work. A medical doctor would normally be engaged either by the employer or by the injured person (with the approval of the employer) to examine the injured person and render a medical report. Such a medical report is nothing more than evidence that an injury was incurred in the first place. It is entirely different from medical assessment, which is stipulated in the Workman Compensation Act.

Case Report A seaman on a ship in the ocean was discovered to be lying motionless on the deck of the ship the company was using offshore for sea haulage business. He had received a phone call and stepped out to the deck to answer the call on his mobile phone. When his workmates thought it was taking too long for him to return to his post on the ship, one of them went out to check on him and saw him lying face down on the deck and motionless. He was eventually certified dead. The subsequent autopsy indicated that the cause of death was Cardiac Arrest. He was insured under the Workman Compensation Policy and his company filed an insurance claim on behalf of his family. The insurance company responded that cause of employee's death was as a result of "Cardiac Arrest" and not "Bodily injuries sustained during the period of insurance by an employee" described in the schedule of insured employees, caused solely and independently of any other cause by accidental, violent, external, and visible means and resulting in death or disability as provided in the Workman Compensation Policy. Consequently, compensation was denied as the death was ascertained to be outside the scope of cover granted by the Workman Compensation Policy. The ensuing court case between the deceased company and the insurer called for an expert witness. Subsequent review of the case by one of the authors, including a visit to the scene of incident, revealed evidence of accidental fall and head injury in an employee prone to cardiovascular disease. The accident was a trigger to subsequent myocardial infarction. Cardiac arrest as a cause of death was misleading as it is merely a mechanism of death. The review was acceptable to both parties who settled at the court of arbitration. A clause in the workman compensation policy states that now this policy witnesses that if at any time during the period of insurance, any employee in the insured's immediate service shall sustain personal injury by accident or disease arising out of and in the course of his employment by the insured in the business and if the insured shall be liable to pay compensation for such injury either under the Law(s) set out in the schedule or at common law, the company will indemnify the insured against all sums for which the insured shall be liable and will in addition be responsible for all costs and expenses incurred with its written consent in defending and claim for compensation. This is the usual scenario in Nigeria. Ascertaining personal injury and damage in Nigeria usually ends up in court.

However, the picture is different in a neighboring West African country, Senegal, where one of the authors spent some time in 2011 at the Department of Forensic Medicine, University of Dakar (Université Cheikh Anta Diop), as a Fellow of West African Health Organization (WAHO) in Forensic Medicine. During the posting at Dakar, it was observed that ascertainment of Personal Injury and Damage was based in institutions like the department of Forensic Medicine, and forensic practitioners did a complete assessment of injuries and disability following history and examination of the patient and carried out some ancillary investigations, where necessary. This system offers the opportunity to interact with the injured on a broader sense, beyond the mere recording of physical injuries. Each injury/disability was evaluated on a case-by-case basis instead of the "one format fits all" approach by strictly prescribing physical injury assessment in the Workman Compensation Act of Nigeria.

Under Section 8(1) of the Act, the Labor Minister may, on the recommendation of the Minister charged with responsibility for matters relating to health, compile a list of medical assessors for the purposes of the Act. By subsection 2 of that section, the court may, in its discretion, summon to its assistance from the list of medical assessors prepared by the Labor Minister any medical practitioner to act in an advisory capacity in the hearing of any application for compensation in cases of injuries which are not specified in the Second Schedule of the Act. Those cases specified in the Second Schedule of the Act in Nigeria are the injuries listed in the table. It is under this provision that other damages related to sexual function, esthetic damage, etc., may be resolved out of court, since they are not quantified like physical injuries. This is where the court may exercise a lot of the discretion conferred upon it by the Act.

Furthermore, under section 17(2) of the Act, the court also has discretion to invite any public officer or any medical practitioner to give evidence if it is of the opinion that such expert knowledge will be of assistance to it. No special qualification or skill is specified for the public officer or medical practitioner who may be invited by the court. Meanwhile, the effect of the discretionary powers given to the court by these provisions is that medical assessment is not mandatory in all proceedings relating to compensation under the Act. Secondly, it is submitted that in the case of proceedings for compensation in respect of injuries resulting in disability specified in the Second Schedule to the Act (see table of injuries and percentage disability), medical assessment is essentially unnecessary. This is because the Second Schedule to the Act reproduced in this article appears to have facilitated the exercise of computing the percentage disability to applicants whose disabilities come under it without the necessity for a medical assessment. Of course, medical assessment will be required to ascertain other damages outside of the stipulated physical injuries, and the discretion of the court comes into place in deciding the type and skill of medical practitioner to carry out the assessment.

It can be stated, therefore, that in Nigeria compensation in respect of injuries/disabilities specified under the Second Schedule to the Act is not necessarily a medical issue to be determined by a medical doctor, but is a legal issue based on the provisions of the Act and the Schedule on which the trial court can reach a decision as it deems necessary.

19.7 Summary of Medical Assessment Under Workman's Compensation Act in Nigeria

- Where Medical Assessment is relevant under the Act, it must be proved that the maker of the document is in the list of medical assessors compiled by the Minister of Labor for the purposes of the Act pursuant to section 8(1) thereof.
- For a medical assessment to be of any probative value where it is relevant, section 8(2) provides that the assessor must not be the employee of, or associated in any pecuniary way, with the employer of the injured workman.
- The Second Schedule to the Act which has adequately provided for the percentage of disability suffered by workmen makes medical assessment superfluous in cases coming under it. In addition to this, the provision of section 8(2) also renders medical assessment irrelevant in proceedings involving compensation for disability specified under the Schedule. It makes it abundantly clear that medical assessment is only relevant in cases not falling within the injuries specified under the schedule as shown in the table above.

- Medical report may be required to prove the injury sustained by a workman in any proceedings for compensation for injuries, which are specified in the Second Schedule to the Workmen's Compensation Act [3]. The maker of such a report need not be in the list of medical assessors as indicated in section 8(1) of the Act.
- In all matters relating to compensation under this Act the decision of the court is final. Accordingly, the court is not bound to follow a medical report/assessment, but may reach a decision as it deems fit having regard to the provisions of the Act and the evidence before it.

19.8 Definition of Terms

The following terms are given interpretation provided by the Workman Compensation Act in Nigeria.

- "Dependents" includes
  - those members of the family of a workman who were wholly or in part dependent upon his earnings at the time of his death, or would have been, but for the incapacity due to the accident
  - where the workman, being the parent or grandparent of an illegitimate child, leaves that child dependent upon his earnings, but a person shall not be deemed to be a partial dependent of another person unless he was dependent partially on contributions from that other person for the provision of the ordinary necessaries of life suitable for persons in his class and position.
- "Earnings" includes
  - wages paid to the workman by the employer and the value of any food, fuel, or quarters supplied to the workman by the employer if, as a result of the accident, the workman is deprived of such food, fuel, or quarters
  - any overtime payments or other special remuneration for work done, whether by way of bonus or otherwise, if of constant character or for work habitually performed, but shall not include remuneration for intermittent overtime, or causal payments of a nonrecurrent nature, or any ex gratia payment, whether given by the employer or other person, or the value of a travelling allowance, or the value of any travelling concession or a contribution paid by the employer of a workman toward any pension or provident fund, or a sum paid to a workman to cover any special expenses entailed on him by the nature of his employment.
- "Employer" includes
  - the Government of the Federation of Nigeria and of any State
  - a body of corporate or unincorporated persons and the legal personal representative of a deceased employer

  - where the services of a workman are temporarily lent or let on hire to another person by the person with whom the workman has entered into a contract of service or apprenticeship, the latter shall, for the purposes of the Act, be deemed to continue to be the employer of the workman whilst he is working for that person
  - in relation to a person employed for the purposes of any game or recreation and engaged or paid through a club, the manager, or members of the managing committee of the club.

- "Minister" means the Minister charged with the responsibility for matters relating to labor.
- "Partial incapacity" means
  - where the incapacity is of a temporary nature, such incapacity as reduces the earning capacity of a workman in any employment in which he was engaged at the time of the accident resulting in the incapacity
  - where the incapacity is of a permanent nature, such incapacity as reduces his earning capacity in every employment which he was capable of undertaking at the time.
- "Total incapacity" means such incapacity, whether of a temporary or permanent nature, as incapacitates a workman for any employment which he was capable of undertaking at the time of the accident, resulting in such incapacity.

References

1. Elegido JM 2007 (1994) Jurisprudence, Aguda R (ed) Spectrum Books Limited, Ibadan, pp 128–130
2. CAP. W6, Workmen's Compensation Act, The Laws of the Federation of Nigeria 2004
3. The Injured Workman, Medical Evidence and Assessment of Compensationunder the Second Schedule to the Workmen's Compensation Act. http://www.nigerianlawguru.com/articles/labour%20law/THE%20INJURED%20WORKMAN,%20MEDICAL%20EVIDENCE%20AND%20ASSESSMENT.pdf. Accessed 24 Mar 2015

Part V
Medico-legal Ascertainment of Personal Injury and Damage Under Civil-Tort Law: Continental Overview – Asia & Oceania

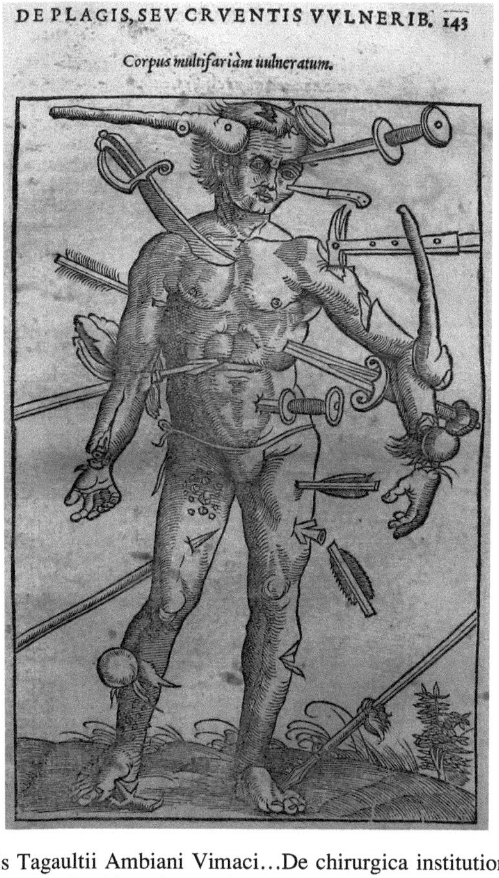

Tagault, Jean. Joannis Tagaultii Ambiani Vimaci...De chirurgica institutione libri quinque. His accessit sextus liber de materia chirurgica, authore Iacobo Hollerio Stempano, medico Parisiensi Parisiis: apud Christianum Wechelum, sub scuto Basiliensi in vico Iacobaeo & sub Pegaso in vico Bellouacensi, 1543. Courtesy of historical section of the "Vincenzo Pinali" Medical Library of the University of Padova

Chapter 20
Methods of Ascertainment of Personal Damage in Turkey

Mete Korkut Gulmen, Haluk Ince, and Ahmet Hilal

Abstract This chapter illustrates the historical, judicial, and juridical framework of personal injury assessment and compensation in Turkey, describing the expert's qualification and competences and detailing the ascertainment methodology and criteria of evaluation utilized for identifying, describing, and estimating any personal injury, its temporary and permanent consequences, and the causal value/link between the event and the injury and between the injury and the impairment/disability.

20.1 Historical, Judicial, and Juridical Overview

To consider the individual as a whole within the context his environment, to evaluate every element that threatens his health in the context of that particular environment so as to prevent hazards, and to provide health services with the aim of eliminating risks are all requirements of the welfare state, which can ensure a healthy life for its citizens. All processes related to working life are regulated by a set of rules to make sure that employees continue operating in a state of complete physical, mental, and social well-being. With those processes called Occupational Health and Safety (OHS) legislation, the State, exercising its role as regulator and

M.K. Gulmen (✉)
Medical Faculty, Department of Forensic Medicine, Cukurova University, Adli Tip Anabilim Dali, 01330 Balcali, Adana, Turkey
e-mail: mete.gulmen@gmail.com

H. Ince
Medical Faculty, Department of Forensic Medicine and Public Health, Istanbul University, Beyazıt, 34452 Fatih/İstanbul, Istanbul, Turkey
e-mail: hince@istanbul.edu.tr

A. Hilal
Medical Faculty, Department of Forensic Medicine, Cukurova University, Çukurova Üniversitesi Rektörlüğü, 01330 Adana, Turkey
e-mail: ahilal@cu.edu.tr

S.D. Ferrara et al. (eds.), *Personal Injury and Damage Ascertainment under Civil Law*, DOI 10.1007/978-3-319-29812-2_20

supervisor, is responsible for the protection of its citizens, both employer and employee [1].

Traffic accidents/occupational accidents/occupational diseases, which represent the majority of injuries, constitute an important part of the processes that result in permanent damage. Incidences of injury constitute a particularly important field of interest for Forensics because of criminal and compensation lawsuits that aim to prevent unjust treatment of individuals. Courts in need of expertise, insurance companies, or individuals requiring incident reports ask for the opinion of committees, which include forensic experts.

The right to a healthy life is the most fundamental human right. According to ILO (International Labor Organization) sources, 1.2 million men and women die each year as a result of occupational accidents and diseases. According to the same sources, each year 250 million people are injured in occupational accidents and 160 million suffer from occupational diseases. A healthier and safer working environment is also a prerequisite for enhanced productivity. Especially in developing countries, occupational health and safety are among the determinants of social development [1].

Studies on occupational health in Turkey can be separated into three groups.

- Before the "Tanzimat" (Reform) Era: It is reported that guild organizations helped those people in case of being "malulin" (disabled) from a "teavün sandığı" (charity fund).
- During the "Tanzimat" (Reform) and "Meşrutiyet" (Constitutional) Era: In 1865, the first legislation for the protection of workers was promulgated. This legislation called "Dilaver Paşa Nizamnamesi" (Dilaver Pasha Regulations) aimed to improve the conditions of coal miners. "Maadin Nizamnamesi" (Mines Regulations), which was promulgated in 1869, has formed the foundation of the workplace health organization and occupational safety [1].
- Republican Period: The most important law in Turkey concerning workers' health was "Umumi Hıfzısıhha Kanunu" (Public Hygiene Law) dated 1930, which also aimed to prevent child labor. By this law, "Regulations on the Protection of Workers' Health and Occupational Safety" were planned, and this has been a great progress in the area of workers' health. In 1945, the Ministry of Labor and in 1946 workers' insurances were established. Firstly, the "Regulations on the Types and Extents of the Disabled on Active Duty" in 1953 and then the Law No: 224 caused ideas about occupational health and safety to rise and as a result, with the Social Insurance Law (SIL) No: 506, the occupational safety entered the state's agenda. The reforms on occupational safety in the Republic of Turkey were attained with the Constitution of 1960. The revision of the Labor Law in 1967 included, for the first time, regulations on workers' health and occupational safety. These regulations are still in effect in accordance with Law No: 1475. With the new Labor Law No: 4857 issued in 2003, the issues previously mentioned in Law No: 1475 as advisory became mandatory. In 2012, Occupational Health and Safety Act No. 6331 was issued, and this was followed by the addition of the Regulations on the Determination of

Disability in 2013. Thus, Turkey has attained the best legal regulations of the Republican Period.

Rate of mortality due to occupational accidents in Turkey was reported to rise from 13.91 in a hundred thousand in the year 2000 to 15.49 in 2005 [2]. According to the statistics of Ministry of Labor and Social Security, 79,027 cases of occupational accident and 574 cases of occupational disease occurred in 2006, 1601 of which resulted in death. In 2006, the number of working days lost as a result of occupational accidents and diseases was 1,895,235. The losses due to occupational accidents and diseases unreported in the Occupational Health and Safety statistics should also be considered [3].

Both economic losses and mental anguish caused by occupational accidents and diseases pose major obstacles for development efforts in developing countries. The economic cost is 4.03 % of the Gross National Income. Those incidences cause people to lose their lives due to avoidable problems. On the other hand, taking into consideration the economic losses the state and the corporations suffer every year and the damage cost methodology of the accidents, a planning approach needs to be adopted [3].

In Turkey, occupational accidents occur mostly in Small and Medium-Sized Enterprises (SME) that constitute 98 % of all enterprises. 50 % of the occupational accidents in SMEs are observed in establishments with 9 or less employees [1, 2]. The highest number of accidents occur in the "metal goods manufacturing" industry, with 14 % of total accidents, secondly in the construction industry, with 8.7 %, and thirdly in the coal mining industry, with 8 %. The three industries which have the highest number of fatal occupational accidents are the construction industry, with 290 fatalities, the transportation industry, with 163 fatalities, and the coal mining industry, with 82 fatalities [4]. Another study have also reported that 31 % of the fatal occupational accidents occurred in construction sites [5].

Other negative outcomes of accidents besides death need redefining. The WHO (World Health Organization) has made definitions of negative conditions that the survivors suffer such as impairment, disability, and handicap. This classification is widely used in many countries around the world. Definitions of the terms are as follows.

Impairment: Any loss or abnormality of psychological or anatomical structure or function. This includes defects on the organ level.

Disability: Any restriction or lack of ability to perform an activity in the manner or within the range considered normal for a human being caused by an impairment resulting from deterioration of health. This refers to disorders at an individual level. Disabilities may be temporary (malnutrition, infectious diseases), permanent (blindness, mental retardation), and progressive (degenerative diseases, heart disease).

Handicap: A disadvantage for a given individual, resulting from an impairment or a disability that limits or prevents the fulfillment of a role that is normal for that individual depending on age, sex, and social and cultural factors [6, 7].

The Welfare state is responsible for solving the problems that arise from the risks with legal regulations and assuring its people a healthy and happy life in all aspects. One of the state's major tasks is to protect the rights of accident victims. A just identification of the deterioration in the individual's health (handicap or disability) is a requirement of the welfare state.

Although the disability evaluation process of every country is specific to its own medicolegal structure, there are some common aspects. Many institutions such as the "American Medical Association (AMA)" have issued guidelines to evaluate the severity of disability [8]. Article 2 of the English Social Security Act defines "disability" and, unlike the private insurance legislations, emphasizes that the dysfunction should be permanent, untreatable, or fatal. The degree of disability is determined by a team that includes a physician and an occupational disease specialist. In the United States the Social Security Act defines being disabled. According to the definition a physical or mental dysfunction that prevents the person to work should exist and this dysfunction should be medically diagnosed and should last for at least 12 months or should result in death. Similarly in Turkey, the Social Security Institution, which is affiliated with the Ministry of Labor, has Health Affairs Terms of References and Disability Board of Health Regulation guides.

In our country, economic life was the first arena where the definitions of disability and victimization were used. The Republic of Turkey took a step forward by adopting Work-related Accidents, Occupational Health and Maternity Insurance Law (Law No: 4772) for the first time on 07.07.1945, which went into effect a year later on 01.07.1946. This law was repealed by the adoption of Law No: 506 on 01.03.1965, which also incorporated other insurance types. This aimed to regulate the consequences experienced by the insured as a result of work-related accidents or occupational diseases while working at a facility defined in Law No: 506. The aim was to compensate for the damages suffered by the insured as a result of work-related accidents or occupational diseases [9].

Law No: 506 Article 11 Subsection A defines occupational accidents as:

"Occupational accident is an incident that occurs in one of the following circumstances and conditions that causes a physical or mental dysfunction immediately or afterwards.

- While the insured is at work
- In connection with work carried out by the employer
- During time spent not doing the main job because of being sent by the employer on duty to an other location
- For the insured nursing woman during time reserved for breastfeeding
- While the insured employees are collectively being transported to and from the work place by a vehicle provided by the employer." [8–10].

Employers are obliged to inform the authorized local constabulary immediately after the incidence and to notify the Ministry of Labor within 2 days. The employer covers the necessary health expenses until the Social Security Institution (SSI) puts the person that had the accident under treatment. Documented expenses and transport costs are paid to the employer by the Institution. However, those expenses will not be paid if the employer does not make notification within the statutory period. The employer is liable for all damages of the Institution resulting from incomplete or incorrect information on the occupational accident notification form. Although the insured is also obliged to report the occupational accident to the employer and the Institution within 2 days, there is no sanction if he/she does not [9].

Contributions made by the Institution to the insured person who has had an occupational accident can be summarized under four headings, as discussed in the following paragraphs.

20.1.1 Health Benefits

After the occupational accident, all treatment costs of the insured and, if needed, all prosthetic devices are covered by the Institution. Health benefits continue as long as the health condition of the insured requires. The main objective is to restore the insured's ability to work and to increase his/her self-sufficiency.

Insureds are obliged to comply with the measures and recommendations of the physician during and after treatment. If the treatment prolongs, a disability develops or the degree of disability increases because of the insured's noncompliance; the Institution may reduce the temporary incapacity allowance or the permanent disability income according to degree of fault but the reduction cannot exceed 50 % of the total amount. Furthermore, if the insured refuses the recommended treatment despite the Institution's written notification, the health benefits and temporary incapacity allowance or the permanent disability income will not be paid until the date the insured applies to the Institution for the treatment.

20.1.2 Temporary Incapacity Allowance

After the occupational accident, the Institution pays the insured a temporary incapacity allowance until the date they restart working, which is half the amount of their daily incomes during inpatient treatment and two-thirds of the incomes during outpatient treatment.

20.1.3 Permanent Disability Income

By the end of a temporary incapacity period following an occupational accident, the loss in the wage earning capacity of the insured is assessed by the examination of the reports on the resulting disorders of the insured, which are filed by the Institute or the health board of the health facility referred, according to the Social Insurances

Health Operations Regulation by the Disability and Occupational Accidents Evaluation Department of SSI General Directorate of Health Affairs Treatment Services and Disability Department [6, 7, 9].

If the loss is 10 % or more, the insured is paid permanent disability income. If the insured needs constant care of another party, the income is increased by 50 % [10, 11].

This is essentially a lifelong income for the insured. But in cases where the wage earning capacity from the given profession is confirmed to have decreased by less than 25 %, and when this condition is not expected to change within 3 years, the income can be paid as capital if the insured demands.

After beginning to receive permanent disability income, the insured may request at any time for an amendment to the income on the grounds that the degree of incapacity to work has raised or that constant care of another party is needed. The Institution may also request an affirmation checkup at any time. In this case, the insured is reexamined in the Institution's healthcare facilities, and if the reports of the medical board reveal any change in the condition of the insured, the income increases, decreases, or stops, starting from the beginning of the month following the report [9–11].

Among the insureds that have lost 60 % or more of their wage earning capacity from a profession due to occupational accidents, those who meet the requirements may additionally receive a disability pension in case they request to be retired due to disability. The Institution pays the insureds monthly the total amount of the higher income and 50 % of the lower income [9–11].

The notion of disability is not sufficiently included or is evaluated differently in Turkish social security systems. This leads to a number of drawbacks and injustices in working life. While SSI evaluates the degree of disability using various parameters (age, line of business, degree of dysfunction severity, etc.), some health institutions consider determining the degree of dysfunction severity (degree of disability) alone to be sufficient. Because of that, the degrees of disability are calculated differently for the same kind of injuries or disabilities of individuals working in the same line of work, having the same age and gender. These differences lead to inequalities in the compensation amounts the individuals receive and cause some individuals to lose their rights [12].

All parties expect an accident and risk-free working life. Another expectation is to suffer less after an accident. The great care shown to the victim immediately after the accident decreases with time. Solving the problems of the victim and to compensate for the rights lost is one of the basic human rights. The cases sent to the Council of Forensic Medicine (CFM), which is the competent authority for final decisions concerning occupational accidents, constitute 1 % of the annual number of occupational accidents. The Council of Forensic Medicine's 3rd Board of Specialty is recognized as the final authority of appeal for cases concerning occupational accidents. Occupational accidents are discussed primarily in the SSI General Directorate of Health Affairs. In the event of dispute, the case goes to Social Security Supreme Board of Health and finally to CFM 3rd Board of Specialty and General Assembly of Forensic Medicine [13].

The number of disability degree arrangement scales is quite high in Turkey.

- The Social Insurances Health Operations Regulation No: 85/9529 dated July the 3rd 1985 and regulations on determination of disability made in the year 2011 are used for occupational accidents.
- "The Regulation on the Method of Determining the Disability Degree of the Employee Who Will Benefit From Disability Discount and Its Application," which is updated in 1998–2006–2008, is used for issues such as tax reduction and determination of degree of disability.
- "Regulations on the Types and Extends of the Disabled on Active Duty," which was issued for public servants in 1953, is still in effect. Most recently "the Regulation on the Determination Process of Disability," which is a part of the OHS Act, was enacted in 2013. Apart from these, a payment is made from a security account opened for traffic accidents to individuals who have become disabled based on the degree of disability. The scale explained above in number 2 is also used for these payments.

In a study conducted in 2002, 1st and 3rd scales, which were used for the evaluation of 164 cases that came to CFM due to work-related accidents, were compared. When the cases were evaluated using both of the disability parameters, the number of employees with complete disability was 17 according to the 1st scale, whereas according to the 3rd scale the number dropped to 15. If the disability calculation of these employees were made using the 3rd scale instead of the 1st scale, there would have been a great loss of rights. When those scales are compared in terms of distribution range and the average, it is observed that the 3rd scale damnifies people. Calculations made using the 2nd scale show similar problems. Of the 164 patients included in this study, 95.1 % were male and 4.9 % were female employees [11]. In a study conducted by Güven, 97 % of the 36 cases with disabilities resulting from occupational accidents were male and 3 % were female. Aşıcıoğlu's and Forst's studies revealed that the 86 % of the cases who had occupational accidents were male and 14 % were female [14–16]. This is because women are less active in economic life in Turkey and all over the world. Additionally, they benefit less from the social security system. In other words, men occupy a larger part within the insured working population [17–21].

When the cases are examined according to the distribution of age groups at the time of the accident, it is observed that occupational accidents are more frequent in the 30–39 age group than in other age groups [21]. The fact that the accident rate drops in the 50 years and over age group can be explained both by the decrease in the working rate and the decrease in the accident rate due to higher level of experience [11]. In Umut's study, 27.4 % of the occupational accidents happened in the 30–39 age group; where as in Ertürk's study the ratio was 25.27 % for the same age group [22, 23]. Similarly, in a study conducted by Ways, most of the cases that had an accident were in the middle age group [24]. On the other hand, Skov's study reports that occupational accidents occur at a young age [25]. In Hunting's study, 45.6 % of the accidents are reported to occur in the 25–34 age group [18]. Suruda found the mean age in occupational accidents to be 29.2 years

[26]. According to SSI statistics in Turkey, the median age in time of accident is 29 years for women and 32 years for men [5]. In Ince's study, the median age for occupational accidents was found to be 31 years for men, 27.5 years for women [11]. The fact that the young populations' high percentage is not reflected in the statistics suggests that these individuals are mostly involved in the unrecorded economy.

The length of trial period is the most important problem in occupational accidents. The cases examined in 2002 have shown trial periods of 24 years at the longest and 2 years at the shortest. This reveals another aspect of damnification. The expression "Justice delayed is justice denied" is unfortunately true, especially for legal cases. One of the reasons for prolonged trial periods is the delay in the correspondence due to missing documents in files sent by the courts to CFM 3rd Board of Specialty. Another reason is the strong tendency to send cases that could be resolved locally to CFM. In the year 2002, 73.2 % (*n*: 120) of cases were sent from Labour courts and 26.8 % ($n = 44$) from Civil Courts. Conflicts concerning occupational accidents and diseases are usually resolved in civil courts due to the insufficient number of labor courts. Being specialized courts, labor courts pay special attention to not having any missing documents in the files whereas the same kind of attention is not paid in civil courts. Compared to civil courts, the cases are resolved more rapidly in labor courts by specialized judges and prosecutors. A prolonged trial process leads to losses in compensations and claims of individuals. Therefore, it is necessary to increase the number and the geographic extent of labor courts, which are currently limited to provinces and large districts [11].

In Turkey, the calculation of disability and degree of disability is the responsibility of the Ministries of Labor, Health and Justice. Giving the responsibility to a single authority and deciding on a single scale for the calculation is of great importance for the solution of the problem. In some state hospitals, the degree of disability is calculated according to undefined criteria, which leads to confusion in courts. That is why the present disability scales should be updated and their shortcomings should be corrected. This update should be the product of a joint study of various institutions and various areas of expertise. It would be appropriate to evaluate all groups of employees according to a single scale. In this regard, a joint disability calculation program should be developed, not on a national level, but internationally. The studies pioneered by Ranavaya beginning in December 2010 in Hatay, Turkey, and continuing with a workshop in the 22nd Congress of the IALM are important. In Turkey, those studies on disability should continue and the use of the directory, which the American Medical Association (AMA) occasionally updates and provides training about, should be encouraged [8]. AMA should be contacted for the training on evaluation of disability in accordance with the directory. The use of the scale prepared by the trained experts in view of the directory should bring a solution to the confusions mentioned above.

Treatment reports should not suffice when calculating the degree of disability; preemployment medical reports should also be investigated in order to assess the suitability for the job. The physician should take into account the physical and mental condition of the employee candidate when ruling him/her healthy, thus ensuring a suitable employee for the job.

Syndicates also have duties concerning occupational accidents and diseases. Syndicates should show in collective agreements that they recognize the importance of OHS institutions in the field of education and collective agreements. Syndicate representatives should be present at OHS committees and should participate in the planning together with the employer. Employing occupational physicians and occupational safety specialists in establishments with more than 50 workers is obligatory. These physicians and specialists should plan together in order to ensure the proper functioning of OHS committees. An occupational physician should keep in mind that his/her duty in the workplace is to exercise preventive medicine. Increasing the number and the quality of labor courts would reduce the length of trial periods, thus preventing right loss of individuals.

In Turkey, about 600 traffic accidents happen every day, 25 every hour, and unfortunately 5–20 people die and 200 people are injured every day. The number rises especially before and after Ramadan and Feast of Sacrifice holidays. Careful driving safety training must be received; active crash safety and passive safety measures must be taken in the car. The legal procedure to follow in case of an injury resulting from a traffic accident that occurs despite those measures is very clear and under state guaranty, but victimizations still happen due to ignorance of the law and its misapplication.

Degree of disability is calculated by measuring the permanent damage to the patient. This measurement is done according to certain procedures. After the accident, as the injured (victim/patient) will not be capable of doing any work he/she is considered 100 % disabled during medical recovery until the treatment process ends and he/she returns to his/her daily life. An examination is made at the end of all medical procedures. It is checked if the damage is permanent or not. If there is no permanent damage, a temporary degree of disability may be calculated. Patients are called to reexamination. The time of this reexamination is determined by physicians committee. If the examination reveals a permanent disability, it must be noted that its degree will not change for life. If the examination that determines the degree and the scale that is used for the calculations are standardized and internationally accepted, then the problem will be solved to a great extent.

20.2 Identification and Description of the Medicolegal Expert's Qualifications in the Ascertainment of Personal Injuries and Damage

During the rehabilitation period following the initial and emergency treatments, the patient is considered 100 % disabled. This period is called medical recovery period. The duration is different for each injury. For example, while the recovery period of a fibula fracture is 3 weeks, it is 18 months for a comminuted fracture of the femur.

During this period, the patient does not work and his/her salary is paid. He/she will undergo the necessary treatment. When the court asks about the disability of the person during the judicial process following the accident, the medical recovery period is particularly specified in the results section. In Turkey, disability (permanent disability) is not calculated according to a single standardized scale that is accepted by all experts. The disability can be calculated according to various legislations mentioned above. However, the Law Courts and the Supreme Court in Turkey accept the results of the Council of Forensic Medicine relying on its reports. The disability calculation method used by the institution is described below.

20.2.1 Points to be Considered when Calculating the Ratio of Disability

According to the mandatory provisions of Law No. 506, in occupational accidents the degree of disability is primarily determined by the General Directorate of Social Security Institution. In case of appeal, the Social Security Supreme Board of Health is responsible for evaluating the appeal. If there is an objection to this result, the Councils of Medical Faculties or the Council of Forensic Medicine are asked for their opinions (in accordance with the decisions no: 1989/6431 E and no: 1989/6178 K dated 09/18/1989 of the 10th Civil Chamber of the Supreme Court).

When determining the degree of disability resulting from occupational accidents, the application of the aforementioned Health Operations Regulations is obligatory. The Supreme Court states in a number of its decisions that lawsuits concerning occupational accidents are filed in accordance with the relevant articles of the Social Security Act No. 506 and that for this reason when evaluating the degree of disability it is a legal obligation to comply with the regulations issued according to article no. 135 of the mentioned act. The degree of disability is evaluated according to the regulations in effect on the date of the occupational accident. The same regulations are applied for the evaluation of disability degree resulting from incidents other than occupational accidents (such as traffic accidents and gunshot wounding). Also for those cases, it is compulsory to apply the regulations in effect on the date of the incident.

20.2.2 Calculating the Degree of Disability

The standard disability formula used for the calculation of disability degree, the criteria that make up this formula and their brief descriptions are given below.

20.2.2.1 Profession, Group Number

The lines of business, the profession groups within those lines and the numbers given to the related profession groups are cited in scale B in the Health Operations Regulation. However, in order to be used in the calculations, this profession group number must be reported to the Council of Forensic Medicine by the court. If the person declares his/her profession and the profession is present in scale B, its group number can be used for the evaluation of disability degree. Profession group numbers are between 1 and 52.

20.2.2.2 Defect List Number

Scale A in the Health Operations Regulation must be referred. In scale A the defects are arranged in lists. For example List I shows defects of the head, List X shows the defects of the spine etc.

20.2.2.3 Defect Serial Number

Each defect present in scale A of the Health Operations Regulation has a serial number.

20.2.2.4 Defect Severity Level

Each defect present in scale A of the Health Operations Regulation has a defect severity level.

20.2.2.5 Permanent Inability to Work Symbol

There is a symbol used for each disability degree evaluation. To determine the symbol, the profession group number and the defect serial number are crossed in scale C of the Health operations Regulation.

20.3 Ascertainment Methodology

This section has two stages. One of them is the calculation of the loss of capability for physical work made by forensic medicine specialists and the other is the actuarial calculations that ensure the calculation and the compensation of the financial losses. The disability calculations are made only by forensic medicine specialists, whereas the actuarial calculations are made by a wide range of professional groups such as forensic medicine specialists or lawyers. Those two calculations are shown below through examples.

Wage earning capacity = roughly as a main heading for calculating disability (Which items will be included in this calculation?)

- The percentage of function loss of the damaged area
- The profession of the employee
- The age of the employee can be used to correct the degree

The present-day disability calculating method required by the Courts of Law in Turkey is explained below.

20.3.1 *Standard Disability Formula*

Profession Group No-Defect List-Defect No-Defect Severity Level-Permanent Inability to Work Symbol-Degree for 38–39 years Gr. 1 II 3 25 A 29, From Scale C: Profession group number × Defect serial number = Permanent inability to work symbol; From Scale D: Defect Severity Level × Permanent inability to work symbol = Degree of disability for 38–39 years of age; From scale E: Degree of disability for 38–39 years of age × the individual's age on day of incident = disability degree for the age on day of accident.

The disability degree of the individual for his/her age on day of accident is calculated by crossing the degree of disability cited for 38–39 years of age in scale E of the Health Operations Regulation with the age of the individual.

The first age group in the Health Operations Regulation is "21 years of age and younger than 22"; the age groups that follow are "22, 23–24, 2 5 ...... 62, 63–64, and older," respectively. As can be seen from the groupings, there is no variance of disability degree for the ages between 0 and 21 (including 21 years) as well as for ages over 64.

20.3.1.1 First Example

The profession group number of an individual who is 35 years old on day of incident is reported by the court to be 41 (HGV driver). Causal link is established between the incident and the defect. If the examination reveals 10/10 vision in the right eye and 0 in the left eye, what is the degree of disability?

Step 1. To put in place the profession group number: reported by the court as 41.

Step 2. To find the defect list number: it is found in scale A, the number of the eye defects list is H.

Step 3. To find the defect serial number: it is found in scale A, the defect serial number of 0 left eye vision is 1.

Step 4. To find the permanent inability to work symbol: it is found in scale C as described below.

From scale C

Profession group number × Defect serial number = Permanent inability to work symbol.

41 × 1 = D

Step 5. To determine the degree of disability for 38–39 years of age: it is found in scale D as described below.

From scale D

Defect severity level × Permanent inability to work symbol = Degree of disability for age 38–39.

35 × D = 46 %

Step 6. To determine the degree of disability for the age on date of incident: it is found in scale E as described below.

From scale E

Degree of disability for 38–39 years of age 46 % × The individual's age on date of incident 35 = Degree of disability for the age on date of incident. 37.2 %.

If the defect does not yet turn into a sequel, although considerable time has passed after the incident and determination of disability degree is requested, the disability is given with a note of "for the current situation." When determining the disability of upper extremities, the disability of the non-preferred side is reduced by 1/5 (the disability of the left hand if the person is right-handed, the disability of the right hand if the person is left-handed is reduced). For this case, no difference exists between right and left eye.

A recovery period is stated for every case with a degree of disability lower than 10 % and for cases with higher degrees if the court requests. This is because SSI does not pay permanent disability income to persons with disabilities lower than 10 %. The degree of disability is the permanent disability degree. During the recovery period, the patient is considered 100 % disabled.

The name of the court that has sent the file, the date and number of the request letter, the identity card information of the patient, and the question asked by the court are written at the beginning of the report. In the first section, all medical reports of the patient should be recorded in order, with the names of the hospitals, dates, and serial numbers of the reports. In the second section, the patient's medical information should be summarized, the sequela should be clearly stated, and then the result should be written.

20.3.1.2 Second Example

The reports by State Hospital A, dated 07.06.1997 and numbered 1200, State Hospital A, dated 11.05.1997 and numbered 2123, State Hospital B, dated 12.05.1998 and numbered 658, State Hospital B, dated 02.03.1999 and numbered 100, and the medical examination report of the Council of Forensic Medicine dated 09.04.1999 are reviewed. A 1/3 upper end femur amputation is detected.

Report results: A.U., born in 1950, is reported to have acquired a defect as a result of the traffic accident that occurred on 07/06/1997. The defect is analyzed utilizing the provisions of The Social Insurances Health Operations Regulation No. 85/9529 accepting that (the appropriate one from the statements cited below should be written here), 1. Since the profession group number is not reported, it is presumed to be group 1 (one), 2. Since the profession is reported to be HGV driver, the profession group number is taken as 41 (forty-one), 3. The profession group number is 4 (four) (if the profession group number has been used in a previous disability degree calculation made by SSI), 4. If the person is under 18 years of age and the profession and rank he/she will exercise (will get, will come up to, will achieve) later on life is not reported, the profession group number is 1 (one)

Gr1 XII (9 Aa - 56) A 65 %

It is the Council's opinion that the person should be considered to have lost 69.0 % (sixty-nine percent) of his wage earning capacity for his age. If severity level of the defect detected during the Council's examination does not correspond to the regulation, for example, although the defect severity level is 30 for fibular paralysis in the regulation, if the defect is detected to be on a paresis level and it is decided that the level of severity for this defect is 10, the fibular paralysis formula is still used, but the disability calculated with the formula is reduced by 1/3, with a "DISCRETION" remark and then this degree is adjusted for the person's age.

20.3.1.3 Third Example

Gr1XII (38B-3 0) A 34 % × 1/3 = 11.3 % (Discretion). The opinion is that the person has lost 12.3 % of wage earning capacity for his age (accepting that he was 50 years old on the date of the incident).

The disability degree for multiple defects and the percentage of wage earning capacity loss in case of multiple defects or in case of an addition of a new defect to an already existing defect are calculated according to Balthazard formula. First, the percentage of wage earning capacity loss is calculated separately for each defect. Those percentages are put in a descending order. The highest percentage is subtracted from 100 %, which shows the total work capacity. The result of the subtraction is multiplied by the second disability degree on the list, and the result of this multiplication is added to the largest disability degree. Thus, the total disability degrees of the 1st and 2nd defects are calculated. If the person has more than two defects, the sum of the 1st and 2nd defects, which is calculated with the Balthazard formula, is subtracted from 100 % and the remainder is multiplied with the 3rd defect. The result of the multiplication is added to the sum of the 1st and 2nd defects.

Step 1. The percentage of wage earning capacity loss is calculated separately for each defect.

Gr1 XII (9C a ------- 45) A 49 % (distal femur amputation)

Gr1 II (3 ------------- 2 5) A 29 % (loss of vision)

Gr1 XII (27A a --------- 15) A 19 % (ankylosis or arthrodesis of the ankle)

Step 2. The highest percentage is subtracted from 100 %, which shows the total work capacity.

$100 - 49 = 51$

Step 3. The result of the subtraction is multiplied by the second disability degree on the list, and the result of this multiplication is added to the largest disability degree.

$0.51 \times 0.29 = 0.1479$

$0.49 + 0.1479 = 0.6379$

If the person has more than two defects,

Step 4. The sum of the 1st and 2nd defects is subtracted from 100 %.

$1.00 - 0.6379 = 0.3621$

Step 5. The remainder is multiplied with the 3rd defect. The result of the multiplication is added to the sum of the 1st and 2nd defects.

$0.3621 \times 0{:}19 = 0.068$

$0.6379 + 0.068 = 0.7060 \div 100 = 70.60\,\%$

The opinion is that the loss of wage earning capacity according to the Balthazard formula is 70.60 % (value for the 38–39 years of age) and is 70.0 % (seventy point zero) for the patient's age. The sum of more than one defect on an extremity cannot exceed the disability degree in case of its amputation. In this case, it is considered like an extremity amputation.

In certain circumstances, the defects detected during the person's examination can be considered equivalent to amputation. For those cases, calculations are made as amputation. The percentage of wage earning capacity loss for multiple nerve paralysis on upper extremities cannot exceed the percentage of wage earning capacity loss for amputation.

The state of losing at least 2/3 of work capability: the loss of at least 2/3 of the work capability requires disability retirement. This is explained in Article 10 of the Health Operations Regulation. The diseases are cited under the lists of head defects, eye defects, abdominal diseases, and defects. The insured who sustains damage from either one of those diseases is considered to have lost 2/3 of work capability if he/she certifies the condition with a Health Committee Report. In that case, the insured is retired due to disability.

Finally, the conditions in which the patient is considered to be in need of constant care of another party are:

- Quadriplegia, paraplegia, diplegia, flaccid hemiplegia that prevents the person to continue with his/her daily life without help, and other disorders and diseases of the nervous system associated with sphincter dysfunction
- Mental disorders that require occasional stays in a mental hospital and that are untreatable
- 100 % loss of vision in both eyes
- Loss of both hands
- Loss of an arm below the shoulder, loss of a leg below the hip
- Loss of both legs below or above the knee

– Patients suffering from severe nutritional disorders and cachexia resulting from an untreatable disease need the care of another party in order to continue with their lives and for their personal care. It is requested whether those conditions exist

20.3.2 Actuarial Calculations

In every situation, where an individual is harmed as a result of another person's fault or negligence, the faulty party causing the harm has an obligation to financially compensate the patient or his/her next of kin. The financial damage is calculated and the sum is given to the beneficiaries in forms such as death indemnity, compensation for destitute of support, etc. In the Turkish legal system the methods used for the calculation of compensation for deceased patients are:

– Amounting method,
– Full increase full discount method
– Capital in advance method
– Arithmetic average method

There are three periods for the calculation of compensation for destitute of support for the next of kin in cases where the patient is deceased;

– The period of occurred damage or income.
– The period of future or unknown damage.
– The passive term damage period.

When calculating the compensation;

– The most important data is the patient's pre-accident income (salary). This income should be proven with legal documents. If he/she did not have an occupation or the occupation is not specified, it is calculated according to the state's official minimum wage.
– Another important data is the age of the accident victim. The calculation for adults is not complicated. However, for children the age of the parents is also a factor and is included in the calculations.
– Fault degree of the person or persons causing the damage is another data. The judge takes this data into consideration when distributing the compensations according to the Law of Obligations.
– Patient's documented healthcare and treatment expenses are included in the calculation. Today every individual in Turkey is under the protection of the social security system. So any extra cost is included in the calculations.
– A judge's right of discretion on the subject of damage is not standardized; it is variable.
– A payment can be asked for the pain, anguish, and suffering caused by the accident. This is not standardized either.

20.3.2.1 Example

Patient L.Y. has a disability of 29.2 % resulting from an accident. The accident scene investigation has revealed that 6/8 of the fault is of the person causing the damage.

- The patient who was 39 years old on the date of calculation would have an active working period until the age of 60. The 21-year period is calculated as the damage period.
- Since the patient's occupation and income were not presented to the court, the minimum wage is used in the calculation.
- The annual increase of income is calculated as 10 %.
- Period calculation is made beginning from the date of the incident until the date of calculation based on minimum wage,
- As the person causing the damage has 6/8 fault, this ratio will be used for the discount.

Year	Basic pay
1	2673
2	2685
3	2779
4	2900
5	3038
6	3190
7	3355
8	3533
9	3724
10	3930
11	4151
12	4388
13	4643
14	4916
15	5209
16	5523
17	5861
18	6224
19	6614
20	7033
21	7484
Total	93,853

$93{,}853 \times 29.2\,\% \times 6/8 = 20{,}553.00$ TL (6800 euros)

The calculation does not include treatment costs as they were not documented and the elements of non-pecuniary damages. Inclusion of all the documents concerning the treatment costs within the file is a legal requirement. On the other hand, non-pecuniary damages are left to the discretion of the judge. In Turkey, it is obligatory that the amount determined by the judge for non-pecuniary damages cannot cause the enrichment of the victim. This is a self-control mechanism of the court.

So far, we have provided information regarding how permanent damages are evaluated by forensic medicine specialists in Turkey regardless of the cause of trauma. As can be understood from the article, Turkey has no established standard on the subject and an issue that can be resolved very easily has become extremely complicated. An increase or decrease in the degree of permanent damage over the years is medically possible but the likelihood is very low. A single scale for the degree of permanent damage has to produce consistent results for every case. What we are aiming at today and the reason for our researches is to put this single scale into use. Therefore, the scale used since 1985 should be replaced by an updated scale that is standardized and internationally accepted. In addition to this, the forensic medicine specialists that will use the new disability scale should receive certification training for the correct application of the scale.

All these operations must be carried out together with the State of Turkish Republic. The first necessity is to put the scale in effect as a legal obligation with the state's support. Secondly, the ones that can calculate disability are forensic medicine specialists, approximately 95 % of whom are civil servants, and their training expenses must be covered. For these reasons cooperating with IALM on a project that will enable the integration with Europe will put us on the right track with regard to disability.

As a result, the Social Security Institution that embodies all social security services should create a new regulation, by taking into consideration the opinions of Institutions of expertise on the subject to replace the Social Insurances Health Operations Regulation dated 1985, which is still in use for the degree of disability calculations. Care should be taken not to repeat any shortcomings present in the previous regulation, to avoid arbitrary practices, and to make sure first and follow-up examinations are done in order to determine disability. Increasing the number and the quality of specialized Labor Courts would reduce the length of trial periods, thus preventing individual loss of rights.

References

1. İnce H (2003) Adli Tıp Açısından İş Kazalarının Değerlendirilmesi. Adli Tıp Bülteni 8(3): 82–87
2. Yardım N, Çipil Z, Vardar C, Mollahaliloğlu S, Hastalıkları İKVM (2007) Türkiye İş Kazaları Ve Meslek Hastalıkları: 2000-2005 Yılları Ölüm Hızları. Dicle Tıp Dergisi 34(4):264–271
3. www.ssk.gov.tr. Accessed 2 Feb 2009
4. 28 Nisan Dünya İş Sağlığı ve Güvenliği Günü "Türkiye Dosyası" 2007, www.sosyalhaklar.org. Accessed 2 Feb 2009
5. Küçük Şantiyelerde İş Sağlığı ve Güvenliği. http://insaat.calisma.gov.tr. Accessed 2 Feb 2009
6. WHO (1981) Disability prevention and rehabilitation. Report of the WHO Expert Committee on Disability Prevention and Rehabilitation. Technical report series 668, Geneva

7. Dünya Sağlık Raporu 1998, 21. Yüzyılda yaşam, Herkes için bir vizyon, DSÖ, Genevre 1998.
8. Rondinelli R, Genovese E, Katz RT, Mayer TG, Mueller K, Ranavaya M, Brigham CR (2008) Guides to the evaluation of permanent impairment, 6th edn. AMA, Chicago
9. Kabakçı M. Sosyal Sigortalar Kurumu Başkanlığı'nın İş Kazaları ve Meslek Hastalıklarındaki Uygulamaları. MESKA 2004 Kongre Kitabı, 26–30 Nisan 2004, İstanbul
10. İnce H (2004) Maluliyet Oranının Zamanla Değişimi. Adli Tıp Bülteni 9(1):19–21
11. İnce H (2005) İş Kazaları ve Meslek hastalıkları Sonucunda Ortaya Çıkan Meslekte Kazanma Gücü Azalma Oranlarının Hesaplanma Yöntemlerinin Farklı Sosyal Güvence Kurumlarına Göre Araştırılması ve Standardizasyonu. İ.Ü. Sağlık Bilimleri Enstitüsü, Bilim Doktora Tezi
12. İnce H, İnce N, Tüzün B (2000) İş kazaları ve Çalışma Gücü Kayıplarının Türkiye deki Yasal Düzenlemeleri. Adli Tıp Bülteni 5(1):12–14
13. Birgen N, Okudan M, İnanıcı MA, Okyay M (1999) İş Kazasına bağlı olgularda maluliyet oranı hesaplanması: Adli tıp açısından değerlendirilmesi. Adli Tıp Bülteni 4(3):101–108
14. Aşıcıoğlu F, Okudan M, Umut S, Suyugül N (1994) Göze yönelik travmalarda maluliyet olgularının değerlendirilmesi. Ulusal Adli Tıp Kongresi (1–4 Kasım/İstanbul) Kongre Kitabı, İstanbul, pp. 171–177.
15. Forst LS, Hryhorczuk D, Jaros M (1999) A state trauma registry as a tool for occupational injury surveillance. J Occup Environ Med 41(6):514–520
16. Güven E (1986) Adli Tıp Açısından Maluliyetin Değerlendirilmesi (Uzmanlık Tezi) T.C. Adalet Bakanlığı Adli Tıp Kurumu Başkanlığı, İstanbul
17. Christoffel KK (1993) Child and Adolescent Injury in the United States: How occupational injuries fit in. Am J Ind Med 24(3):301–311
18. Hunting KL, Nessel-Stephens L, Sanford SM, Shesser R, Welch LS (1994) Surveillance of construction worker injuries through an urban emergency department. J Occup Med 36(3): 356–364
19. Sahli BP, Armstrong CW (1992) Confined space fatalities in Virginia. J Occup Med 34(9): 910–917
20. Suruda A, Floccare D, Smith G (1991) İnjuries from tire and Wheel explosions during servicing. Ann Emerg Med 20(8):848–851
21. WHO (1997) WHO's global healthy work approach. A strategy for the development of a comprehensive approach towards the promotion of health of all working populations. World Health Organization, Geneva
22. Ertürk S, Ege B, Yemişçigil A, Aktaş Ö (1994) Maluliyet oranları saptanan olguların özellikleri. 1. Ulusal Adli Tıp Kongresi (1–4 Kasım/İstanbul) Kongre kitabı İstanbul, pp. 139–142
23. Umut Ş (1984) Adli Tıp Açısından Maluliyetin değerlendirilmesi(Uzmanlık Tezi). T.C. Adalet Bakanlığı Adli tıp Kurumu Başkanlığı, İstanbul
24. Ways and means Committee (1996) Social security: the Old Age, Survivors, and Disability Insurance (OASDI) Programs. U.S. Government Printing Office, pp. 104–114
25. Skov O, Jeune B, Lauritsen JM, Bafred T (1999) Occupational hand injuries. A population-based description of the incidence and referral to casualty departments. Ugeskr Laeger 161 (22):3285–3288
26. Tan O (2001) İş Kazalarında Maliyet Metodolojisi, İ.Ü. Sağlık Bilimleri Enstitüsü Master Tesis

Chapter 21
Methods of Ascertainment of Personal Damage in the Kingdom of Saudi Arabia

Osama Mohammed Al Madani, Manal S. Bamousa, and Magdy A. Kharoshah

Abstract This chapter illustrates the historical, judicial, and juridical framework of personal injury assessment and compensation in the Kingdom of Saudi Arabia, describing the expert's qualification and competences and detailing the ascertainment methodology and criteria of evaluation utilized for identifying, describing, and estimating any personal injury, its temporary and permanent consequences, and the causal value/link between the event and the injury and between the injury and the impairment/disability.

21.1 Historical, Judicial, and Juridical Overview

The Islamic religion is a doctrine and law. It is a religion of beliefs and worship with an integrated law that regulates the different aspects of human life and enacts rules and provisions to help people live in the right way. The Islamic criminal justice system is considered one of the most important aspects that Islam took care of to organize the lives of Muslims, in any place of the world. It also set up an integrated system of punishments to deter the offenders. Islamic law established the interests of Muslims and had them protected by the rules of criminality, thus establishing five interests: religious preservation, self-preservation, mental health preservation, offspring preservation, and, finally, money preservation. Shariah law is not dogmatic and can always be open to further interpretation according to changing circumstances. It shows equality for both the duties and rights of Muslim and non-Muslim alike and to ensure protection of their rights in practicing their faith freely unless these practices are harmful to the community or country [1–3].

O.M. Al Madani (✉) • M.S. Bamousa • M.A. Kharoshah
Forensic Medicine, SCFHS Riyadh, Forensic Medicine Center, King Khaled Street, Dammam, Eastern Province 6668/31176, Saudi Arabia
e-mail: omadani@hotmail.com; manalbamousa@hotmail.com; drmkharoshah@hotmail.com

S.D. Ferrara et al. (eds.), *Personal Injury and Damage Ascertainment under Civil Law*, DOI 10.1007/978-3-319-29812-2_21

21.1.1 The Primary Sources of Islamic Legal Law (Shariah)

- Quran
- Sunna
- Ijtihad which is divided into [Qiyas and Ijma'a]
- Subsidiaries sources.

21.1.2 Definition of Shariah Law

It has two definitions: Specific provisions, rules, and guidance for civil and criminal matters. The other one is the provisions of the Quran, which are meant for all times and all circumstances and not only during the life of the prophet.

Sunna: The model established by the prophet in terms of practice, explanation, and approval matters. Basically, it confirms supplements and interprets and details the Quran's rules and provisions. The Quran, being the word of god (Allah), abrogates Sunna, and Sunna cannot abrogate the Quran because its basic function was to interpret it [4].

Ijtihad: An independent deduction of laws, which is a collective effort or exercise by Muslims or jurists and judges that which they reached from an independent deduction of the rules and laws from recognized sources. These laws are either reached by Juristic consensus of opinions [Ijma'a] or reasoning by analogy [Qiyas] [4, 5].

Ijma'a: Are laws based on the juristic consensus of opinion of all competent juries after the death of the prophet Mohammed (PBUH). And it can be inspired by the decisions of the four successors, "KHALIFS," of the prophet or the prophet's friends (Sahaba). These laws can abrogate the law of Quran or Sunna [4, 6].

Qiyas: Reasoning by analogy and the adoption of principles established by the Quran, Sunna, and Ijma'a to the solution of a problem not expressly regulated for or mentioned there [5, 6].

The last source of Islamic jurisprudence is constituted by the *Subsidiary Sources*, which include Public interest, Prevention of harm, and Customs, "given that they do not contradict Shariah law."

The legitimate punishments established by the Islamic law, though they may seem to be intense and meticulous, do not propose torture as punishment. On the contrary, Islamic law is well known for its compassion towards all people. Islam does not achieve the target of general security of a community by the threat of sanctions; instead, it implements the approach of general deterrence and private deterrence, as well as attaining the satisfaction of the victim and his family. Everyone is in agreement that the embodiment of Islam is distinctively universal [3].

No one disagrees that the universality and comprehensiveness of Islam has required that its rules change with the locations and times. In our day and age, huge changes have occurred in the social, economical, and political aspects of life and these changes have demanded the presence of newer needs and necessities to maintain an adequate style of life. Jurists in Islam should take the new needs and necessities into account and these should be carefully considered when inserting new provisions or sub-provisions, whether for worship or transactions. The holy Quran and the Sunna are considered to be the highest original source of Islamic jurisprudence [7].

Before the birth of Islam, Arabs had a tribal-based society. Written laws did not regulate their lives, but all the different tribes did in fact ban some acts which were considered forbidden and passed out punishments on those who committed them. Nowadays, these acts are considered as "crimes" in the language of the law. And if one individual committed one of these forbidden acts, the whole tribe would bear the responsibility of his actions; this usually sparked the beginning of many long tribal wars [7].

For this situation arose the concept of making amends between the tribes by paying for mistakes in order to achieve overall peace and well-being. This concept is called the "Deya'a." Islamic scholars are all in agreement that a Deya'a is a form of penalty bestowed on an individual who has committed manslaughter. This form of financial sanction is Islam's way of deterring individuals from committing such acts of violence. Several verses from the Holy Quran and the Sunna have discussed and explained this concept in detail. It is important to note a very common misconception among people, namely, that when a Deya's is given to the victim's heirs or family it is not in any way a form of compensation for their loss [8].

Al-Deya'a is literally defined as "the money that is paid to the victim of a felony or his heirs, whether the felony was intentional or accidental." Such money has been called Deya'a by the Holy Quran in one of its verses (and compensation payment presented to the deceased's family "is required" unless they "give up their right to" charity) "Alnisa'a/92."

While for injuries or nonfatal felonies, the money paid to the victim or his heirs is called an Arsh. In Islamic criminal law, sanctions are not limited to, but include, financial sanctions such as Deya'a and Arsh. These two are the most significant forms of financial sanctions. Islamic criminal law defines the Arsh as the financial sanction for an assault that results in injury or damage to the victim's body parts [9].

There are two kinds of Arsh.

Estimated Arsh: this type of Arsh has a specific amount that has been identified by Islamic law, for example, the Arsh for the eye, hand, and the foot is half a Deya'a. In other circumstances, the Arsh may be a quarter of a Deya'a or even a one-tenth of a Deya'a, such as the case for cutting of one finger.

Unrated Arsh: this type of Arsh has not been specified by a specific amount in Islamic law. Instead, it is left to an experienced judge to make an informed decision. This form of Arsh is also called a judgment of justice. A judgment of justice is an un-estimated Arsh in nonfatal crimes.

Decisions regarding any harm or injuries whose penalties, whether a Deya'a or Arsh, were not specified by the prophet Mohammed, peace be upon Him, are left to the discretion of a judge, being based on the latter's experience and knowledge [10].

21.1.3 Financial Penalties in Islamic Jurisprudence

Money in Islamic Shariah has a special quality as it is invested by the state for the sake and the benefit of the individual and for the public treasury. The public treasury is a form of social solidarity among members of the community. The Deya'a fine is a punishment and is concerned with paying money from the public treasury, according to the rules of the Islamic Shariah, but it is paid to the victim or his heirs to achieve the idea of satisfaction and in order to overcome the idea of the ownership of the individual over the idea of state ownership. And this is perhaps what has created confusion for some jurists about the nature of Deya'aweatherit' as a form of compensation for the victim or his heirs. Is it a form of punishment, because it was originally a fine, with equal value in relation to the person who commits manslaughter or unintentional murder? Or is it a compensatory penalty where, instead of having the culprit (who killed another person with purpose) executed when the heirs of the victim offer forgiveness, these latter receive money for such forgiveness instead? [11]

The point here is that the Deya'a is a financial penalty and the money that gets paid by the accused or his family is not to the government. Instead, they pay the money to the victim's family or his heirs. Nothing will change the way it is paid or to whom. Deya'a only compensates for the physical damages that resulted from a crime; it does not include the moral damages that result from the crime [8].

The justice system in the Islamic Shariah has a unique exclusiveness, because it is closely related to the Islamic system, which carries a degree of individuality and differs from the rest of the other legislator regulations. Islamic Shariah is different from the law and they cannot be compared, because the nature of the Islamic Shariah is different from the nature of the law [9–11].

The person who commits manslaughter or homicide is the person obligated to give compensation, as Allah said (every soul, for what it has earned, will be retained) "Almuddaththir 38." There is no doubt that the compensation would be paid by the assailant (the guarantee) to the victim, in accordance with the provisions of the law [12].

The estimated amount of compensation should include the resulting emotional damage (psychological) and it should be calculated by a judge on a case-by-case basis. The compensation or insurance has to be paid immediately after the judge has passed his verdict. The term insurance is used here because it is a broad term that does not denote the compensation of damage alone, but it encompasses many different aspects such as sponsorships, commitment, responsibilities, and fine [13].

21.1.4 Types of Court in Saudi Arabia

There are four main identified types of courts in Saudi Arabia:

- *Summary courts*: examines the civil, matrimonial, and juvenile cases.

- *General Courts*: concerns civil, criminal, family, and matrimonial trials. It involves one judge in small cases and three judges in major cases.
- *Supreme Courts*: examines all verdicts by other courts. It includes three main circuits each chaired by the chief justice and two other judges. In major cases, it includes a chief justice with four judges.
- *High Judicial Board*: involves a president and 10 members. Their roles are to examine all matters referred by local governors, to discuss the controversial legal matters that are referred by the Ministry of Justice, and to make a revision of all convictions examined previously by other courts [5].

After taking a good look at the history and laws pertaining to the issue of financial reimbursement in personal injury cases through an Islamic perspective, it is possible to lay down the exact and correct legal steps and measures needed to take in cases of both civil and criminal personal injuries in need of financial reimbursement.

At the time of the injury, the victim will head straight to the hospital to receive the adequate medical and/or surgical care required. It is the duty of the hospital to inform the police of the injury. Upon the arrival of the police at the hospital, they begin a preliminary investigation and relay the case to the commission of investigation and public prosecution bureau of investigation and public prosecution, whose job is to perform an in-depth investigation of the case. After the proper investigative processes have been complete, the case is sent to the courts. The courts will hand the case over to the medical commission, which is a committee made up of several consultant medical doctors from different specialties and doctors of religious science. This committee takes on the task of reviewing all of the medical paperwork related to the victim's injury that led to their hospital stay, including their relation to the assault/accident that resulted. If the age of the injuries corresponds to the time of the assault/accident, the committee also has the right to perform any medical test they see fit. The purpose of the medical commission's inquires is to reach an informed decision about the degree of disability of the victim as a result of the injuries. The decision is then written up as a report and sent back to the courts, which will then be able to specify the exact amount of reimbursement entitled to the victim in accordance with Islamic Sharia'a Law.

21.2 The Expert's Qualifications to Conduct the Examination and Evaluation

There are four governmental stakeholders that evaluate cases to determine the deficit or damage ratios of car accidents and other causes that may lead to damage or loss of an organ of the body. These five agencies include the Ministry of Health (forensic medicine, the medical corps, the medical committee in case of medical negligence and medical liability), the Ministry of Justice, and finally, in relation to social insurance, the Ministry of Social Affairs, which defines rates of incapacity.

Regarding forensic medicine, when a case is referred to a forensic medical center to determine the percentage of disability as a result of an injury, the proceedings of these issues are handled by one of the qualified forensic doctors who have the necessary credentials and a master's degree or doctorate in clinical forensic medicine, based on the note of the Ministry of Health 549/760/17 dated 12/16/1418 AH.

The medical committee includes consultants in all medical specialties, each of whom possesses a higher degree or fellowship in his specialty. There are also, across the Kingdom of Saudi Arabia, four medical bodies (Riyadh, Jeddah, Dammam, and Medina) located in the main areas of the country.

Medical committee legitimacy, the third participant, includes consultants in various medical specialties. Each of them holds a higher degree or fellowship in different specialties. It should be noted that the forensic medical committee is concerned only with quantifying the deficit in medical negligence cases and the medical liability rates that result from medical error when a patient files a complaint in relation to a doctor.

Social insurance in the Ministry of Social Affairs is concerned with evaluating and assessing the rates of deficit from work injuries. They make their decisions based on medical reports prepared by consultants in various medical specialties after the disclosure of the patient and the performance of necessary tests [14–16].

21.3 Ascertainment Methodology

21.3.1 Hospital Medical Report Description

The medical report should be comprehensive, recent, and relevant to the traumatic incident by all treating hospitals which took part in the patient's medical management. The report must be in the English language and include the following information.

- Personal information: Name, age, address, telephone number, and insurance information.
- Current illnesses: A list of significant illnesses, operations, as well as fixative aiding instruments that had been used.
- Medication Record: A list of medicines prescribed or given to the patient.
- History and Physical examination: A record that describes any major illnesses and surgeries the patient has had, any significant family history, genetic history, health habits, and current medications. It should also state what the physician found during the examination.
- Admission notes: including the clinical status of patient, Glasgow Coma Scale (GCS) and the vital signs upon ER arrival, resuscitation (if done or not), and duration of hospital admission with highlights of the Progress Notes made by the doctors, nurses, therapists, and social workers caring for the patient that reflect

the patient's response to treatment and the doctor's observations and plans for continued treatment during hospital admission.

- The follow-up care that took place after the hospital discharge with clarification of health progression and whether there was any improvement or worsening.
- Consultations—An opinion about certain conditions made by another specialty physician, while staying in the hospital, not by the original treating physician.
- Special Physician's Orders—treating physician's directions to other members of the healthcare team regarding the patient's medications, tests, diets, and treatments.
- Imaging and X-ray Reports—Description of the findings of X-rays, CT scans, MRIs, mammograms, ultrasounds, and other highly specific scans. The actual films are maintained in the radiology or imaging departments or on a computer and a CD copy should be given to the patient.
- Lab Reports—Describing the results of tests conducted on body fluids in a chronological order. It should include chemistry, virology, bacteriology, urinalysis, stool analysis, and blood typing.
- Immunization Record—Documenting immunizations given for diseases such as polio, measles, mumps, rubella, and the flu. Parents should maintain a copy of their children's immunization records with other important papers, if preserved.
- Consent and Authorization Forms—Copies of consents for admission, treatment, surgery, and release of information.
- Operative Report—A document that describes surgeries performed, if ICU has been indicated, and any medical instrumental methods that have been implemented, e.g., "Orthopedics fixative prosthesis" has been used and gives the names of surgeons and assistants.
- Pathology Report—Describes tissue removed during an operation and the diagnosis based on the examination of that tissue.
- Discharge Summary—A concise summary of a hospital stay, including the reason for admission, significant findings from tests, procedures performed, therapies provided, response to treatment, condition at discharge, and instructions for medications, activity, diet, and follow-up care [14, 15].

21.3.2 Medical Committee

Committee doctors/forensic doctors are obligated to provide the board and all parties involved with their best professional opinion based upon certain guidelines of the claimant's medical condition, degree of impairment, and functional abilities.

The Agenda Guidelines provide detailed criteria for determining the severity of a medical impairment, with a greater weight given to objective findings in cases of work-related injuries. It is their responsibility to submit medical evidence that the Board will consider in making a legal determination about a disability.

21.3.3 Medical, General Physical, and Regional Examination

Once the medical report has been prepared, the next step is to compose a report on permanent impairment. This can be achieved by reviewing the Agenda Guidelines, studying the medical report, performing a thorough history and physical examination, as well as examining findings and appropriate test results. It should state the work-related medical diagnosis (i.e.) based upon the relevant medical history, examination, and test results. It should also identify the affected body part or system by referring to the Agenda Guidelines and follow the recommendations for establishing a level of impairment [14].

As a first step, doctors should obtain additional medical information and reevaluate the case at the current time. Like any clinical medical evaluation, doctors should introduce themselves to the patient, let him/her understand what is the exact role for the committee and the reason of this visit, ask the patient about any current symptoms, the patient's overall progression of condition with time, any recent medical illness that have evolved, or physical insults that have happened recently, and recount the relevant medical history. Doctors will obtain more details on any form of negligence that had happened to the patient, such as a delayed hospital presentation for seeking medical care or discharge against medical advice, or even the absence of any relevant follow-up care. Then a full medical examination will take place, beginning with the inspection of each body system to assess normal conditions and deviations. Doctors will assess for color, size, location, movement, texture, symmetry, odors, and sounds, in the same way as any other doctor might assess each body system. Then, palpation would take place by touching the patient in different areas, using varying degrees of pressure. Wearing gloves when palpating mucous membranes or areas in contact with body fluids is mandatory, especially in the presence of some current sporadic diseases. Palpation of tender areas is the final step. Percussion comes later which involves tapping the doctor's fingers or hands quickly and sharply against parts of the patient's body to locate organ borders, identify organ size, shape and position of certain organs such as liver, uterus, etc., and determine if an organ is solid or filled with fluid or gas. Lastly, auscultation, which involves listening for various lung, heart, and bowel sounds with a stethoscope. The neurological assessment would be based on the patient's reaction to the aforementioned, the patient's reactions during the interview, and the level of consciousness. There are many neurological tests that should be made, such as cranial nerve testing, papillary response, motor and sensory functions, tone and cerebellar functions, such as Romberg test, finger to nose test, etc. [14, 15].

Regarding cases of limitation of movement of the victim, a full comprehensive examination of all the limbs is performed to assess the amount of limitation and the level of disability.

It is important to note that before the case is presented to the medical commission for assessment, it must first be established whether the injury has reached its final stage; that is, it will not progress any further for the better or for the worse. In cases when the victim's injury has not yet stabilized, the commission medically reevaluates the victim after a 1-year period has elapsed, depending on the specific circumstances of the case. This time period is given to allow the injury to stabilize in order to allow a just and fair evaluation of the disability. This can be explained as when maximum improvement level has been reached, with no expectation of improvement or significant changes that might happen in the forthcoming 12 months from the date of evaluation.

The medical commission has the right to enlist the help of any consultant in any medical specialty, within reason, to aid in the evaluation of the degree of disability. The commission also has the right to order any further medical investigation in order to help in the review.

Getting to know the client may reveal many hidden subclinical psychotic symptoms that would not be disclosed directly by the patient. In this case, the committee doctors should assess the case carefully and determine the need to engage a consultant psychiatrist in a future appointment.

If the case requires any additional investigative tests, the patient can be directed to the tertiary governmental hospital of that area [14].

21.4 Evaluation Criteria

The evaluation criteria and injury determination, whether a permanent disability or not, will be thoroughly described in this section.

In The Kingdom of Saudi Arabia, the standards for the ascertainment and compensation of personal injury under civil-tort law are enforced through the court judicial system based on unique references to the Islamic Sharia'a Law.

In Saudi Arabia, we have two main categories: (a) work-related injuries or (b) personal injuries. The latter will include any injuries that result from any cause not related to work, such as accident, trauma, insult, disease, etc. In the event that an injury is related to work, the patient must be thoroughly evaluated by a governmental medical committee related to Ministry of Health. Under Agenda Guidelines, which are approved by the Ministry of Labor, the percentage of deficit will be calculated upon the Agenda's table. Later, the court would receive the final percentage level that is approved by the medical committee and sentencing compensation will follow accordingly [14–16].

Many examples have been chosen and discussed while writing this chapter. Different systems with different dimensions and variable perspectives have been searched thoroughly in relation to our target. Those systems are Cardiovascular system, Respiratory system, Central nervous system, and Psychological AND psychiatric system.

On the other hand, the second category that we will discuss is cases of personal injury not due to work. The process of evaluation and determination of the permanent disabilities would have a different pathway through governmental sectors, with different reference. Once fully recovered, the patient will be directed to a regional medicolegal committee, which is also related to the Ministry of Health. There are currently 4 such committees in Saudi Arabia. These committees request a full medical report, including the laboratory investigations that were done for the patient. The specialized committee members can request any further additional tests such as a Computerized Scan, Magnetic Reasoning Images, and Electroencephalogram, etc. Then, a final opinion will be issued based on the whole case, accordingly.

If the patient has not yet fully recovered, and his/her status doesn't reach the maximum medical improvement, which has been described earlier as (Medical Stability State); in this case, the evaluation and examination will be postponed within the forthcoming year.

21.4.1 Causal Link

Enables the determination of the causal link of the traumatic incident and the injuries, and depends on the following.

- A detailed memo from the legal authorities such as court or bureau of investigation and prosecution, which are based on the police report that thoroughly describes the traumatic incident.
- Full, comprehensive medical report, which includes the date of the incidents. It should describe the injuries that resulted from the incidents and should include site, size, base, edge, length, dimensions, color, alignments, healing type, complications ("if presented"), and the relation to other anatomical areas. Moreover, the medical report should assess the nature of the injury and give, if possible, a description of the causative tools, the medical intervention that took place, and the estimated period required for full recovery.

21.4.2 Work-Related Injuries

Based on the Ministry of Labor's decree number 160/insurance on May 2009 [14, 15], which stated: "upon declaration of general council organization for social insurance number 929 which approved the agenda of sustained rates of disabilities according to certain formula and criteria." This will be thoroughly described in the present section, although it is important to highlight some basic terms, as follows.

- *Deficit*: Is defined as partial or total loss of a human's body parts or functions. Once the state of medical stability has been achieved, a permanent disability may be considered.
- *Medical Stability State*: This can be explained as when the maximum improvement level has been reached, with no expectation of improvement or significant

changes that might happen in the forthcoming 12 months from the date of evaluation.

- *Dominant Upper Limb*: The upper limb used for writing purposes.
- *Agenda Guidelines*: A booklet that determines the percentage of permanent disabilities, which was approved by the Ministry of Labor in 2009. It consists of 15 chapters, including chapters on the cardiovascular system, respiratory system, gastrointestinal tract, genitourinary tract, skin diseases and its disfigurement, blood diseases, endocrine system, the ear–nose–throat system with hearing loss, eye diseases, the central nervous system (peripheral and central), the psychological and behavioral system, spine and vertebrae, upper limbs, lower limbs, and pain.

21.4.2.1 Principles and General Considerations

- Patients should complete the medical treatment until the state of full stability is reached. This is based on a medical judgment that the claimant has recovered from the work injury to the greatest extent and no further improvement in his/her condition is reasonably expected. Then the estimation of percentage of personal damage (i.e.) rate of disability would follow.
- If the traumatic injury leads to a total loss of function of an organ, the level of deficit would be equivalent to eradication level. On the other hand, if less extensive damage has been confirmed, the level of deficit would be equal to amputation level.
- The patient's previous condition, which is prior to the traumatic event, must be a reference for evaluation.
- All deficit percentages of the approved Agenda should be applied without any changes, modifications, or adjustments. However, there are certain conditions or "exceptions" for which the degree of deficit could be readjusted and liable for a 25 % addition. These exceptional conditions include the following.
- Nature of work in relation to the deficit: job performance is affected because of the deficit, e.g., for a writer who has lost fingers, a 10 % addition is acceptable.
- Age: less than 40 years of age can have an increase of up to 5 % of the estimated percentage.
- Job experience: for those who have worked 10 years or more at the same job, an increase of up to 5 % of the estimated percentage is envisaged.
- Level of education: patients with a high school education or lower can get an additional 5 % of the estimated percentage.
- If the client has more than one part involved in the injury, the percentage for each should be made independently. Subsequently, a total summation of these parts according to the approved Agenda for the determination of the rate of disabilities (deficit) should be determined.
- Consideration of the upper limb dominance should be made, if it is involved.
- When determining the permanent percentage deficit, all assisting devices should be removed, in a non-harmful manner.

- The medical committee report should be detailed and descriptive for the deficit/ disability. A consideration of its percentage and its causative reasons should be made. Moreover, the committee has the right to phrase recommendations, accordingly, such as the owning of an artificial "prosthesis" or keeping the client away from exposure to any harmful agent.
- If the injurious event affected one of the dual organs, such as the eyes, ears, or lungs, and assuming that the other one was already injured before the traumatic event, the formula would be as follows:
- Permanent disabilities = Total dual percentage of both – Single organ percentage loss.
- When the committee is convinced that there is a new or an additional diagnosis connected to the original injury being assessed by the committee, the case should be referred for medical reevaluation before any final decision is made.
- If the causative agent of the loss has involved both the central and peripheral etiologies, then the percentage would be encountered upon the higher value, not the sum.
- The pain resulting from the injuries has been taken into account when developing the agenda, and thus it should not be included in the deficit. However, chronic pain has been mentioned in the agenda.
- The outcome of the injuries and their consequences (affection) should be the main focus while determining the percentage of deficit, not its causes or its nature. An example of these are daily work activity, personal care, communication, transportation, physical activity, sexual activity, the five senses, sleep ability, and hand functions.
- A thorough description of aiding methods while assessing the case should be made according to that which is set out in the tables of the agenda.

21.4.2.2 CVS: Cardiovascular Impairment Guidelines

This involves three tests: MET'S (metabolism), EF% (Ejection Fraction), and FCCD (Functional Classification of Cardiac Disease).

The FCCD can be subclassified into four degrees.

(i) Heart disease not interfering with physical activity.
(ii) Heart disease which has minor effect on physical activity.
(iii) Heart disease which has marked effect on physical activity.
(iv) Heart disease which is associated with dyspnea during rest.

All of the aforementioned criteria will be collectively analyzed and, according to Table 21.1, the categorization will be determined. If more than one category has been found, the largest ratio will be considered.

The peripheral vascular compartment of both upper and lower limbs has five main categories of disabilities, as follows: 7, 25, 55, 80, and 100 %. These percentages are mainly based on certain variables which include presence or absence of muscular aches in relation to the degree of physical activity, degree of vascular

Table 21.1 Cardiovascular impairment guidelines for classification

	First category 7 %	Second category 20 %	Third category 45 %	Fourth category 80 %
MET'S	7 ≤ OR	7> - 5 OR	5> - 2 OR	2 > OR
EF%	50 ≤ OR	40–49 OR	31–39 OR	30 ≥ OR
FCCD	1st grade	2nd grade	3rd grade	4th grade

injury in relation to the need of amputation, presence of vascular calcification based on a radiology diagnosis, response to treatment of Raynaud's phenomenon, loss of peripheral pulses, amount of tissue loss underneath skin, and degree of peripheral edema and its response to treatment.

21.4.2.3 Respiratory System Impairment Guidelines

There are six categories for determining the permanent respiratory disabilities. It exclusively depends upon the respiratory function tests, which include the following indicators: FVC, FEV1, and FEV1/FVC%; the diffusion capacity [D co]; and oxygen uptake parameter VO^2 max mL/(kg.min). For rating objective pulmonary test results, please refer to Table 21.2.

Regarding work-related injuries, it refers to asthma that is induced (occupational) or exacerbated (work aggravated/exacerbated) by inhalation exposures at work. These provoked types of asthma might be a result of a patient's exposure to irritants, such as animals, birds, sea foods, insects, diisocyanates (e.g., in glues, coatings, paint), plant parts, including wood and grain dusts, vegetable gums, and baking flour, pharmaceuticals and enzyme powders (e.g., detergents and dough additives), anhydrides (in epoxy, resins, plastics), amines (in shellac, lacquer, hairdressing, paint, plastics, resins), solder fluxes, colophony, and metal dusts and salts (e.g., platinum, nickel, cobalt, chromium). Moreover, irritants are extremely important in this respect, since Saudi Arabia is one of the biggest oil and gas producing countries worldwide. Such irritants include chlorine, ammonia, sulfur dioxide, nitrogen oxides, phosgene, smoke, and high level irritant dust. It is very important to remember that one of the committee's recommendations should include the client's avoidance of identified provocative agents.

In order to be rated for asthma, there should be a diagnostic workout that confirms the diagnosis of asthma. The treating physician should establish the diagnosis upon a compatible history of episodic symptoms, which include chest wheeze, cough, sputum, chest tightness, or breathlessness, which is worse at night. Spirometry is used to demonstrate any airflow obstruction by determining the FEV1 and its corresponding changes in response to the treatment of short-acting B agonist and/or a trial of corticosteroids.

Table 21.2 Respiratory system impairment guidelines for classification

Indicator	1st group 0 %	2nd group 10 %	3rd group 20 %	4th group 35 %	5th group 50 %	6th group 80 %
FVC	80 % ≤ and	71–79 % OR	60–70 % OR	56–59 % OR	51–55 % OR	50 % ≥ OR
FEV1	80 % ≤ and	71–79 % OR	60–70 % OR	51–59 % OR	41–50 % OR	40 % ≥ OR
FEV1/FVC%	70 % ≤ and					
D co	70 % ≤ OR	65–69 % OR	60–64 % OR	51–59 % OR	41–50 % OR	40 % ≥ OR
VO^2 max mL/ (kg.min)	25 ≤	24-23	22-20	19-18	17-16	15 ≥

Table 21.3 Bronchial asthma impairment guidelines for classification

Indicator	FV1 after treatment with short-acting B agonist	% Change of FEV1 after treatment of short-acting B agonist	OR	PC_{20} mg/mL Value	AND	Medication and therapy status
0	80 % ≤	10 % >		8 <		Without
1	70–79 %	10–19 %		8-0.6		On bronchodilators, occasionally
2	60–59 %	20–29 %		0.6-0.125		Daily use of bronchodilator + low dose of inhaled cortisone
3	50–559 %	30 % ≤		0.125≥		Bronchodilator (PRN) + high daily dose of inhaled cortisone, or oral tablet of cortisone
4	50 % >	–		–		Regular use of daily cortisone both orally and inhaled + Bronchodilator (PRN)

Airway hyperresponsiveness is measured by PC_{20} (mg/mL) value, which is ultimately used in the rating methods of bronchial asthma.

For detailed information on impairment guidelines of Bronchial asthma, please refer to Table 21.3.

After measuring the percentages of each indicator, the final result will be the total index of bronchial asthma. This value will follow values mentioned in Table 21.4 for eliciting the final deficit ratio mark.

Table 21.4 Total index for bronchial asthma

The total index of bronchial asthma	% Deficit
0	0 %
1	10 %
2	15 %
3	20 %
4	25 %
5	30 %
6	40 %
7	50 %
8	60 %
9	70 %
10 ≤	80 %

21.4.2.4 Psychological and Psychiatric Impairment Guidelines

This involves work-related posttraumatic neurosis, posttraumatic stress disorder, and other causally related psychiatric conditions. Such cases should have psychiatric and psychological evaluations and opinions, as well as psychological and/or neuropsychological testing.

The impairment evaluation should include the impact of the psychiatric impairment on functional ability, consisting of the following components.

- *Activities of daily living*: personal hygiene, communicative abilities, physical activities, five senses, hand functions, transportation, sexual function, and normal sleep pattern.
- *Social activities*: ability to take part in social gatherings and activities.
- *Ability to concentrate*: completion of work responsibilities.
- *Ability to accommodate* in any situation under variable common circumstances.

For more information on the psychiatric and psychological impairment guidelines, please refer to Table 21.5. Note that all of the criteria mentioned in one category should be considered collectively.

21.4.2.5 Nervous System Impairment Guidelines

The nervous system impairment guidelines have been classified into the following parts.

(i) *Cranial nerves impairment guidelines*

Table 21.6 sets out the requirements, as follows.

(ii) *Consciousness*

It has been categorized into five groups. For more information on the consciousness impairment guidelines, please refer to Table 21.7.

Table 21.5 Psychiatric and psychological impairment guidelines for categorization

Category type	%	Case descriptive criteria
1st category	0 %	• Perform normal daily activities • Perform the responsibilities under normal circumstances or coercive condition without difficulties • Although patients may have psychological illness, they still can do the tasks with no impairments
2nd category	5 %	• Perform normal daily activities with mild social and personal impairment • Patient has minor anxiety (feeling uncomfortable) which affects performance • Almost performs the given tasks, which is due to development of secondary symptoms of psychological impairment under minor stresses at work
3rd category	20 %	• Housework is easily performed, which is different from the external environment due to loss of trust and dependency needs • Marked social and personal impairment or having an anxiety attack, unexplained fear of reinjury, or continuous isolation associated with depression • The degree of psychological impairment may need amendment of the given tasks
4th category	40 %	• Complains of marked family relationship deterioration and, to a lesser extent, social relationships • Complains of depressive attacks for long periods of time or abnormal behaviors leading to avoidance of daily activity • Hospital admission might be needed with urgent need of functional task's amendment
5th category	65 %	• Cannot perform any activity whether inside or outside home for chronic period of time • Complains of severe amnesia, loss of concentration, poor self-hygiene, or loss of interest in life and is not able to control mood or has psychotic illnesses which require continuous supervision, admission, and amendment of functional tasks

(iii) *Epileptic fits*: If the epilepsy is episodic, which does not require any medical treatment, the deficit will be 5 %. Another relevant factor while determining the deficit percent of an epilepsy patient is whether the epilepsy is controlled by treatment or not. The deficit will be 10 and 25 %, respectively.

(iv) *Sleep disorders*: When the sleep pattern does not affect the performance of daily activity, then the percentage of deficit is 7 %. On the other hand, mild, moderate, and severe effect on daily activity would result in 15, 30, and 50 %, respectively.

(v) *Mental health impairment guidelines*: The mental health functions include awareness, memory, attention, judgment, and ability to solve problems. The extent of how much daily life activity has been involved is the key element for determining the impairment deficit percent. Moreover, the ultimate needs of supervision by others and the self-care disabilities are important factors. The range of deficit varies from 7 to 60 %.

Table 21.6 Cranial nerves impairment guidelines for classification

Cranial nerve	Presenting illness	Approved percentage
1st cranial nerve	Complete anosmia	3 %
2nd cranial verve	Reference to the visual examination methods previously mentioned	Specific table
3rd, 4th, and 6th nerve	Reference to the visual examination methods previously mentioned	Specific table
5th nerve	Mild trigeminal neuralgia (Douloureux) not responding to treatment	7 %
	Moderate trigeminal neuralgia (Douloureux) not responding to treatment	20 %
	Severe unilateral trigeminal neuralgia (Douloureux) not responding to treatment	25 %
	Severe bilateral trigeminal neuralgia (Douloureux) not responding to treatment	30 %
7th nerve (facial nerve)	Mild unilateral facial weakness or loss of taste on up to 2/3 of the ipsi-lateral tongue	4 %
	(i) Mild-moderate facial weakness bilaterally or unilateral facial palsy	15 %
	(ii) Bilateral facial palsy	35 %
8th nerve	Hearing impairment	Refer to hearing loss tables
	Tinnitus	5 %
	Ataxia: (i) Mild degree with minor precautions	7 %
	(ii) Moderate degree with precautions in most physical activities, not including personal care	20 %
	(iii) Moderate to severe degree in almost all physical activities including personal care	40 %
	(iv) Sever ataxia which needs help and close supervision	60 %
9th, 10th, and 12th nerve	(i) Mild dysphasia or dysphagia while eating fluid or semisolid food	10 %
	(ii) Moderate dysphasia or dysphagia with hoarseness of voice and food aspiration	30 %
	(iii) Severe dysphagia with continuous aspiration of saliva	50 %

(vi) *Ataxia*: Walking impairment is mainly dependent on whether the patient can stand or walk. If a patient can walk, what distance can he/she cover? Finally, whether an aiding or assisting device is needed. For further information, please refer to Table 21.8.

(vii) *Spinal cord dysfunctions*:

Diseases of the spinal cord may have different forms of presentation such as respiratory symptoms, urinary symptoms, fecal incontinence, symptoms

Table 21.7 Consciousness impairment guidelines for categorization

15 % deficit	30 % deficit	50 % deficit	80 % deficit	100 % deficit
Mild frequent attacks with mild limitation of daily activity Or Frequent loss of consciousness	Mild frequent attacks with moderate effect on daily activity	Prolonged conscious impairment with inability to care for self	Semi-comatose state with need for nursing care and therapy	Irreversible comatose patient who needs continuous medical care

Table 21.8 Walking impairment guidelines for categorization

Description	Percentage of deficit
Can stand and walk, but with difficulties in climbing stairs	7 %
Can stand and walk for some distance without need of aiding devices	15 %
Can stand and walk with support	30 %
Cannot stand without support and needs assisting device	50 %

of sexual dysfunction, and palsy. Each of them has its own guidelines and will be clarified and discussed.

- *Respiratory illness*: Spontaneous respirations with difficulties in breathing varying from a 10 to 35 % deficit depending on whether the patient is moving or at rest. If the patient is on a bed, the value will reach 70 %, while no spontaneous breathing implies a 100 % deficit.
- *Urinary symptoms*: Controlled urinary incontinence would encounter 7 % deficit, while an uncontrolled one is equivalent to 15 %. A higher rate of 32 % in case of uncontrolled urinary dripping is confirmed in the agenda of permanent work-related disabilities. A complete loss of urination with the need of a catheter insertion is considered as being a 50 % deficit.
- *Fecal incontinence*: Partial impairment of fecal incontinence would be considered as 10 %. This value might increase to up to 45 % with complete loss of control. Preservation of anal reflex would lower the rate to 30 %.
- *Sexual dysfunctions*: please refer to Table 21.9.

  If patient's age is less than 40 years, a 50 % of calculated deficit value would be added using the previous table, whereas a 50 % of the calculated value will be subtracted when the age of patient exceeds 65 years.
- *Paralysis*: Quadriplegia encounters 100 % deficit; dominant hemiplegia will be equivalent to 80 %, while a nondominant one would be much less (65 %). A unilateral lower limb involvement would be 50 %, while bilateral lower limb paralysis is much higher (85 %).

Table 21.9 Sexual dysfunctions guidelines for classification

Description	Deficit %
Difficulties in erection, ejaculation, or impaired libido function with preserved neurological reflexes	7 %
No libido with preserved neurological reflexes	15 %
Complete loss of sexual function with inabilities to have sexual intercourse	20 %

(viii) *Muscular paresis*:

Involvement of dominant limbs would give rise to a higher level of deficit than a nondominant one. Similarly, paresis of two limbs would be double the value of single limb paresis.

21.4.3 Personal Injuries

21.4.3.1 General Principles and Considerations

These are injuries not related to work, for which the following principles are valid.

- The preemployment full medical examination needs to be conducted on all candidates as well as periodic examinations for the professions which require them. They should be done when considering the nature of the position for the determination of the permanent disability. If there is no medical evidence, then the candidate is considered 100 % healthy.
- The word organ in the table means any organ, part of the body, extremity, nerve, bone, or muscle, and any full resection or removal of it leads to total loss of employment.
- While determining the percentage of the permanent disability the age of the affected person, gender, and nature of the position, the effect of the disability on his/her performance, social and general state, physical and mental abilities, and the fact that he/she is unable to perform daily activities are all taken into consideration. The committee has the right to determine the percentage of the disability and increase it to 40 % of the deserved percentage depending on how much it affects his/her professional performance, on the condition that it does not reach 100 %.
- Permanent disability is determined in cases of organ loss, delimiting its purpose, deformation, or any disability caused by a chronic illness that has settled, after guaranteeing the absence of progression upon its cure in spite of the use of medical care. The committee has the right to recommend any procedures to cure the case including surgeries if they determine that the temporal disability could be cured or helped. They determine the percentage after these procedures, based on the results.

- When losing a dual organ such as the eyes, arms, and legs, if one of them was lost before the accident then the determination of disability percentage is measured as if he/she lost both at once, because this organ was the dependent one.
- If the worker was left-handed, the loss of his left extremities will be determined by the right and vice versa.
- A partial loss of any complete organ which is mentioned in the schedule will be determined according to the professional effects of that loss or by cutting the loss percentage from the total.
- If an injury affects more than one organ or part of the body, the disability percentage will be determined for each and then combined together without reaching 100 % and in all cases not less than 1 %, where the affected person needs the help of others. The deficit will increase by 50 %.
- Disability percentage is determined in an injury as a whole.
- Disability percentage is determined for any damaged nerve by the affected organ according to the results it has on job performance.
- If a person is taking indemnification for an organ injury and had late complications affected by the same injury, the percentage changes according to the complications. Temporary disability is considered permanent after 5 years.
- Defects, illnesses, and deformations since birth, previous illnesses, or injuries do not entitle the affected person to indemnification unless his/her job causes more complications.
- An organ that is not mentioned in the schedule will be determined according to the effect of that loss, in professional terms, and by comparing it to similar injuries mentioned in the schedule.
- Psychological cases caused by professional injuries are dealt with exactly as physical injuries, considering the disability percentage determined by specialized medical committees. Thus, they are not mentioned in the schedule.
- As for noncontagious diseases caused by receptivity, the disability percentage is measured according to the complications arising from the disease, not the disease itself. In case of death, it needs to be precisely proved using a medical examination that death was the result of complications of that disease.
- The remaining part will explain some examples on how to determine personal injuries: pain and upper limb and lower limb disabilities [16].

21.4.3.2 Pain

It is agreed upon that estimating the degree of pain in a neurological disability is a precise situation.

The pain arising from a neurological disability is originally caused by personality disorders affected by different factors: the first factor is the affected person's real feelings, how he/she is expressing and handling them, and his/her psychological state. Most of the time such pain is the symptom of many diseases, such as essential nerve inflammation, nerve contusions, compression of nerves, nerve roots compression by joints or bone diseases, root inflammation, and marrow inflammation.

The percentage of permanent disability in these cases is caused by organic diseases that cause "hip inflammation and the compression of nerves." This kind of pain is considered as a factor for the increase of the percentage of the permanent disability. In most cases, the existence of neurological pain is assured by objective signs which are sometimes clear and sometimes ambiguous. Determining permanent disability is measured by the strength of the pain and its prevalence, including its effect on working and daily life [16].

21.4.3.3 Limbs

General considerations while assessing upper limb.

- Partial amputation of a phalanx, for example, would be considered as a complete loss of that part.
- When a vascular, tendon, muscular atrophy or chronic infection of any parts of the upper limb has been involved, the determination of the impairment deficit would include complications that resulted from that injury. This should not exceed 70 % for the right arm and 60 % for the left arm [16].

References

1. Aowdah A (1978) Islamic criminal legislation comparative with status law. Al-Resala Press, Beirut
2. Ahmed FA, Ghonaim AA (1992) Al-Waseet in the judicial organization of the Islamic Jurisprudence. Al-Esha'a Press, Alexandria
3. Al-Amrawi AG (1986) Judiciary and judges. Al-Farazdak Commercial Press, Riyadh
4. Ghanem I (1981) Islamic medical jurisprudence. Med Sci Law 21:275–287
5. Ghanem I (1983) Outlines of Islamic jurisprudence (Islamic Law in nutshell). Saudi Publishing and Distributing House, Riyadh
6. Murad K (1981) Shari'ah—the way of justice. Islamic Foundation, London
7. General Organization for social Insurance, the corporation board of director's decision number 929, issued on March 2009
8. Al-Amrousi A (1984) Legislation and judiciary in Islam. University Youth Establishment Press, Alexandria
9. Al-Zuhayli M (1995) History of judiciary in Islam. Dar Al-Fikre Al-Mo'asser, Beirut
10. Al-Zuhayli M (1998) Islamic during the region of Prophet Mohammed. Dar Al-Maktabi Press, Damascus
11. Awdah A (1959) Criminal jurisprudence in Islam in comparison with status law. Dar Al-Orouba, Cairo
12. Chairman of the presidium of the council of ministers, decree number 7/7/15007, issued on March 1998
13. Dwairy MA (1998) Cross–cultural counseling. The Arab–Palestinian case. Haworth, New York

14. Ministry of Labour, decision number 160/insurance. Issued on March 2009. Kingdom of Saudi Arabia
15. Ministry of Health, Forensic Medicine (1990) Rules of implementation for regulation of the practice of medicine and dentistry Kingdom of Saudi Arabia, Forensic Medicine. Al-Shorouk Press, Riyadh
16. Ministry of Health, Forensic Medicine General Directorate, Works procedure for forensic physicians legitimates guideline. Kingdom of Saudi Arabia, first edition

Chapter 22
Methods of Ascertainment of Personal Damage in India

Adarsh Kumar

Abstract This chapter illustrates the historical, judicial, and juridical framework of personal injury assessment and compensation in India, describing the expert's qualification and competences and detailing the ascertainment methodology and criteria of evaluation utilized for identifying, describing, and estimating any personal injury, its temporary and permanent consequences, and the causal value/link between the event and the injury and between the injury and the impairment/disability.

22.1 Historical, Judicial, and Juridical Overview

22.1.1 History

We all know that the first known laws to compensate for damage were defined under Hammurabi code around 2200 BC which advocated for "an eye for an eye and a tooth for a tooth," along with monetary punishments. In India, the first legal code was formulated between 3000 and 1000 BC as described under "Manu-smriti" ("*The Dharma Text of Manu*"), which says that the drunk, insane, hungry, thirsty, tired, and those persons with defective sense organs were not permitted to be witnesses in court. Statements of children, old men, diseased persons, and weak minded persons were not to be relied. These were based on various "Dharmashastra" which described punishments for adultery, seduction, incest, and unnatural sexual offences. Around 300 BC, the great Indian Philosopher, teacher, and royal advisor to the Maurya dynasty, Chanakya (also known as Kautilya and Vishnugupta) wrote "Arthashastra" with the purpose of governance, which also described the use of medical knowledge for the purpose of law. In 250 AD—"Charaka Samhitha" contained moral & ethical principles and in

A. Kumar (✉)
Forensic Medicine, Medical Disability Evaluation Board, JPNA Trauma Centre, All India Institute of Medical Sciences, Ansari Nagar East, New Delhi, Delhi 110029, India
e-mail: dradarshk@yahoo.com

S.D. Ferrara et al. (eds.), *Personal Injury and Damage Ascertainment under Civil Law*, DOI 10.1007/978-3-319-29812-2_22

300 AD, Sushrut was the first person to codify various punishments. Afterwards, during the medieval period in India, the criminal laws were further developed under various Hindu and Muslim rulers. During this period "Quasi-I-Mumalik" was the arbiter of civil and criminal litigations and his function was to find out facts and apply the law. The specified penal code, however, was implemented in 1860 during the British regime. The Civil Procedure Code was afterwards founded in 1908 with an aim to provide a litigant a fair trial in accordance with the accepted principles of natural justice. There have been several amendments over the period of time, but the basic structure remains the same and still follows British laws to a great extent. Of particular importance is Sect. 11 which contains the rule of conclusiveness of the judgment based partly on the maxim of Roman jurisprudence "interest reipublicae ut sit finis litium" (it concerns the State that there be an end to law suits) and partly on the maxim "nemo debet bis vexari pro una et eadem causa" (no man should be vexed twice over for the same cause). The section does not affect the jurisdiction of the court, but operates as a bar to the trial of the suit or issue, if the matter in the suit was directly and substantially in issue (and finally decided) in the previous suit between the same parties litigating under the same title in a court, competent to try the subsequent suit in which the issue has been raised. "Res judicata pro veritate accipitur" (a thing adjudged must be taken as truth) is the full maxim which has, over the years, shrunk to mere "res judicata".

The industrial revolution of the 19th century resulted in a shift from agriculture to industry and this led to the introduction of Workmen Compensation Act in 1923 (amended in 2009).

The Workmen's Compensation Act, 1923 provides for payment of compensation to the workmen and their dependents in the case of injury by industrial accidents including certain occupational diseases arising out of and in the course of employment resulting in death or disablement. This Act applies to certain railway servants and persons employed in hazardous employments at locations such as factories, mines, plantations, mechanically propelled vehicles, construction work, etc., specified in Schedule II of the Act. However, the Act is not applicable to the employees who are covered under the Employees' State Insurance Act, 1948. The Second National Commission on Labour set up in the year 2002 made certain recommendations relating to the amendment of the Workmen's Compensation Act, 1923. Ultimately, it was notified in 2009 after consultation with the concerned Ministries/Departments/State Governments and the Union territory Administrations.

Salient points are the following:

- "Workman" was substituted by the term "employee."
- Increase of the minimum rates of compensation payable to a worker from 80,000 rupees (1300$) to 120,000 rupees (2000$) for death and from 90,000 rupees (1500$) to 140,000 rupees (2300$) for permanent disability and empowerment of the Central Government to enhance the minimum rates of said compensation from time to time.

- Increase of the funeral expenses from 2500 rupees (40$) to 5000 rupees (80$) and to empower the Central Government to enhance the same from time to time.
- Provide reimbursement of actual medial expenditure incurred for treatment of injuries caused during the course of employment.
- Speedy disposal of case within 3 months from the date of reference and to intimate the decision in respect thereof within the said period to the employee.
- Increasing coverage by omission of the restrictive clauses in Schedule II of the Act and inclusion of additional hazardous activities.

In 1948, soon after gaining independence, various trade unions demanded for regularization, which led to introduction of *Employees' State Insurance Act, 1948*.

The basic aim of this act was to provide for certain benefits to Employees in case of Sickness, Maternity, and Employment Injury and to make provisions for related matters. The Act is applicable to the "Factories" employing ten or more persons irrespective of whether power is used in the process of manufacturing or not. Under it, the scheme has been extended to shops, hotels, restaurants, and cinemas, including preview theaters, road motor transport undertakings, and newspaper establishments employing 20 or more persons. The scheme has also been extended to Private Medical Institutions and Educational Institutions employing 20 or more persons. It is a self-financing social security and health insurance scheme for Indian workers. For all employees earning Rs.15000/ (US$240) or less per month as wages, the employer contributes 4.75 % and the employee contributes 1.75 %, for a total share of 6.5 %. This fund is managed by the ESI Corporation (ESIC) according to rules and regulations stipulated in the ESI Act 1948, which oversees the provision of medical and cash benefits to the employees and their families through its large network of branch offices, dispensaries, and hospitals throughout India. In the ESI scheme, a worker in insurable employment is called an insured person. Insured persons and their families are entitled to different types of benefits, broadly classified in two ways: (1) Medical benefits and (2) Cash benefits. The employees registered under the scheme are entitled to medical treatment for themselves and their dependents, unemployment cash benefit in certain contingencies, and maternity benefit in case of women employees. In case of employment-related disability or death, there is provision for a disability benefit and a family pension, respectively. Funeral Benefits are provided to dependents of Insured Persons/Insured Women to the amount of Rs.15,000/—(US$250).

22.1.2 *Judicial*

India lacks a social security system scheme. Hence, in cases of bodily injury claims, in addition to above 2 acts (if one is employed as the case may be), one has to depend either on personal insurance or calling for compensation from third party interventions. This situation is frequently encountered in road traffic accident cases.

Increase in the number of motor vehicles, poor maintenance of roads, and negligence by drivers have led to a substantial increase in road accidents, resulting in death or injuries. India ranks 3rd for the number of fatalities due to road accidents, but data concerning persons becoming permanently disabled from such accidents is lacking. Until 1988, when the victim or their heirs approached the civil courts, they were required to prove negligence by the driver of the offending vehicle in order to make the owner liable to pay compensation. This, at times, was a daunting task for the heirs of the deceased, who did not witness the accident. Even in case of the injured victim, he/she could hardly be expected to recall the exact manner in which the accident had occurred. Denial of compensation on the ground that negligence of the driver of the vehicle was not established was highly unfair to the victim, particularly in a democratic country like India. The compensation was provided under Section 140 of the Motor Vehicle Act, which was limited to 50,000 Rs in cases of death and 25,000 Rs in cases of permanent disability.

Becoming aware of this huge lacunae, parliament passed the Motor Vehicles (Amendment) Act, 1994 (54 of 1994) inserting Section 163-A in the Motor Vehicles Act, 1988 with effect from November 14, 1994. The section provides for compensation on a structured-formula basis as indicated in a tabular form in the Second Schedule forming part of the Act. In a claim for compensation under this provision, the claimant is not required to plead or establish that death or permanent disablement was due to "any wrongful act or neglect or default of the owner of the vehicle." In other words, the claimant is entitled to compensation in accordance with the Second Schedule on the principle of no-fault liability. For instance, in the case of death of a person aged 25 years whose annual income was 12,000 Rs, the compensation payable to the heirs as per the Second Schedule would come to approximately 136,000 Rs. Section 163-A is a provision intended to provide for immediate relief to the victims of motor accidents. Surprisingly, however, lawyers and litigants have not come forward to take maximum benefit of this statutory amendment, with the result that the victims have to wait many years for the final adjudication of the claim petition.

The Court's observations were in response to the introduction of Section 92-A in the Motor Vehicles Act, 1939 (Section 140 of the 1988 Act), providing for a lump sum compensation of 15,000 Rs in case of death and 7500 Rs in case of permanent disability, on the principle of no fault. The Supreme Court found the amendments a welcome step and observed thus:

"Where a pedestrian without negligence on his part is injured or killed by a motorist whether negligently or not, he or his legal representatives, as the case may be, should be entitled to recover damages if the principle of social justice should have any meaning at all. In order to meet to some extent the responsibility of the society to the deaths and injuries caused in road accidents there has been a continuous effort throughout the world to make the liability for damages arising out of motor vehicles accidents as a liability without fault."

The issue of evaluation of disability invariably came into question and in September, 1981, an "Expert Group Meeting on Disability Evaluation" comprising of about 50 experts in different fields of the medical sciences was held in New Delhi with the objective to develop simple norms for the evaluation of permanent physical impairment in Indian patients. Guidelines developed at the meeting were given due trial at various centres in the country. It was then followed by the "National Seminar on Disability Evaluation & Dissemination" held in December, 1981. A manual was afterwards developed as an outcome of these seminars to evaluate permanent physical impairment, which was primarily based upon "Disability—Determination and Evaluation" by Dr. Henry H. Kessler, West Orange, New Jersey, USA. The basic aim was that it would facilitate medical practitioners in evaluating the degrees of permanent physical impairment. It would further uniformly standardize the evaluation system in the country. It would facilitate handicapped persons in the rural areas to obtain the benefits existing under various provisions. While developing the criteria of evaluation of physical impairment, due consideration was given to terms like "impairment," "functional limitation," "disability," and "normal."

In 1995, The Persons with Disabilities (Equal Opportunities, protection Of Rights and Full Participation) Act (henceforth PWD Act) came into force. It provided 3 % reservations for disabled people in poverty alleviation programs, government posts, and in state educational facilities, as well as other rights and entitlements. The specific objectives of the Act include Prevention and Early Detection of Disabilities, Education, Employment, Affirmative Action, Non-Discrimination, Research and Manpower Development, as well as some kind of Social Security. This act was further amended in 2009 with the placement of exhaustive guidelines regarding calculation of disability and the clarification of certain terminologies, such as "person with disability" meaning a person suffering from not less than 40 % of any disability as certified by a medical authority and "medical authority" meaning any hospital or institution specified for the purposes of this Act through notification by the appropriate Government. In pursuance of this, State Governments/UT administrations are required to notify the medical authorities to issue a disability certificate. The maximum period of validity of a temporary disability certificate will be 5 years.

22.1.3 *Juridical*

Liability. Tort law defines the conditions under which a person is entitled to damage compensation if his or her claim is not based on contractual obligation, i.e., either covered under the Workmen Compensation Act or the Employee State Insurance Act. Damage results from the loss or impairment of property, health, life, or limb, from the infringement of rights or from pure financial or nonfinancial losses. Economically speaking, every reduction of the individual's utility level caused by a tortious act can be regarded as damage. Tort law rules aim at drawing a just and fair line between those noxious events that should lead to damage compensation and others for which the damage should lie where it falls. In India, it has developed from a large body of formerly unrelated doctrines, such as conversions, trespass, nuisance, defamation, negligence, deceit, and rules from case laws.

Tort Suit A tort suit enables the victim of some injury to make their problem someone else's problem. Unlike a criminal case, which is initiated and managed by the state, a tort suit is prosecuted by the victim or his legal heirs. Moreover, a successful tort suit results not in a sentence of punishment but in a judgment of liability. Such a judgment normally requires the defendant to compensate the plaintiff financially. In principle, an award of compensatory damages shifts all of the plaintiff's legally cognizable costs to the defendant. On rare occasions, a plaintiff may also be awarded punitive damages, defined as damages in excess of compensatory relief. In other cases, a plaintiff may obtain an injection: a court order preventing the defendant from injuring him/her or from violating one of his/her property rights. The law does not recognize just any injury as the basis of a claim in tort.

Types of Duties Tort distinguishes between two general classes of duties.

- Duties not to injure.
- Duties not to injure negligently, recklessly, or intentionally.

When one is engaged in an activity the law regards as extremely hazardous (e.g., blasting with dynamite), it is the duty of the first type but when one is engaged in an activity of ordinary riskiness (e.g., driving), it is covered under the second type, i.e., a duty not to injure negligently, recklessly, or intentionally, and is governed by fault liability.

Scope of Tort Liability This depends to a great extent on two factors, the availability of private insurance against hazards and the capacity of the civil system to obtain and process information. If private insurance is easily obtainable for both victims and tortfeasor, secondary costs are independent from the loss.

In India, there is no concept of social security and therefore insurance markets are grossly underdeveloped. It leads to a tendency to shift the costs of accidents to these large insurance companies by way of third party.

22.2 Identification and Description of Medicolegal Expert's Qualifications in Ascertainment of Personal Injuries and Damage

22.2.1 The Immediate Treatment

In case of any injury suffered, the first treatment point is usually the emergency department of a hospital, whether government or private. In India, a doctor owes two types of duty in such situations. One of them is a primary medical duty, i.e., pertaining to treatment and other medicolegal duty, i.e., pertaining to law. The medicolegal report (MLR) is prepared after the initial first-aid treatment or stabilizing the patient. Preparation of MLR is part and parcel of the duty of the doctor who has attended the victim first. In cases of injuries, the doctor reports the injuries on a specified document in duplicate, the original of which is taken by the law enforcement/police investigative agencies. This information about the occurrence of a medicolegal case has to be either reported to the nearest police station as per jurisdiction of the hospital or, if the victim is accompanied by the police, of the jurisdiction where the alleged accident took place. In the case of the former, it will be the duty of the nearest police station to coordinate further with the jurisdiction in which the alleged accident took place.

22.2.2 *Investigation by the Police/Law Enforcement Agencies and Insurance Companies*

Every case of unnatural/unknown circumstances/accident has to be investigated by police and submitted to the Motor Accident Claim Tribunal (MACT)/Civil Court for information. This information itself is treated as a preliminary application for fixation of the claim, in addition to criminal action later. The victim can request for the copy of all medical treatment papers including all the reports and costs of the treatment. The MLR and original X-ray, however, are the property of the police and are handed over to them. The police act on behalf of the victim in most of the cases. However, the victim is empowered to lodge a separate suit directly by name if the whereabouts of the perpetrator are known. The cost of treatment incurred by a victim is usually verified by insurance agencies that directly approach the relevant hospital. If the patient is being treated in a public hospital the cost of treatment, being heavily subsidized, is exempted from it. There is no need to undergo a further medical examination by any other agency. The concept of medical advisors in the insurance company is nonexistent. Usually, it is surveyor who simply verifies the facts from hospital records. Afterwards, it may be contested in a court of law whether a causal connection existed between the accident and the claimed damage and if there was any gross negligence on part of treating doctor.

There is no such entity as insurance medicine in India, since the whole system runs in a totally different manner. Depending upon the earning capacity and quantum of damage, as well as due consideration of the dependent family members, the court decides an amount to be paid by the opposing party through his insurance company.

22.2.3 *Judicial Procedure in MACT/Civil Courts*

Because of the huge number of cases, a special type of court, i.e., the Motor Accident Claim Tribunal (MACT), has been opened in bigger cities since 1988 after the introduction of the new Motor Vehicle Act, which has now gone to district levels of several states. It has all of the powers of a civil court and was basically established in order for a settlement to be reached at the first instance by mutual agreement.

The presiding judge under whose jurisdiction the case has filed then consults all of the records of the police investigation and examines all of the eyewitnesses and expert witnesses concerned with the case, whereupon the role of the doctor comes into play. Primarily, the first doctor who prepared the MLR gives his opinion about the injuries and then all of the doctors who were primary or expert treatment givers are also called upon in relation to the type of intervention done/operations performed.

Where a claims tribunal has been constituted for any areas, no civil court shall have jurisdiction to entertain any question relating to any claim for compensation which may be adjudicated upon by the Claims Tribunal for that area, and no injunction in respect of any action taken or to be taken by or before the claims tribunal in respect of the claim for compensation shall be granted by the civil court.

The MACT is a civil court, for all intents and purposes of adjudication of claims for compensation in motor accident cases. From the scheme of the Motor vehicles Act and the Rules framed thereunder, it is clear that a Claims tribunal is constituted for a specific area, which is specified in the notification for the adjudication of such claim. The institution of the proceedings is by an application for compensation. The tribunal disposes such an application by giving the parties an opportunity of being heard and holding an inquiry into the claim and it then has to make an award determining the amount of compensation to be paid and the amount which is to be paid by the insurer. The tribunal has been given all the powers of a civil judge for the purpose of taking evidence on oath and enforcing the attendance of witnesses and of compelling the discovery and production of documents, the reception of evidence on affidavits, as well as requisitioning any public record or document or copy of such a record or document from any court or office. The right to appeal to the High Court is also provided.

The victim can file a claim in any of the following MACT.

- The Tribunal within the local limits of whose jurisdiction the accident has occurred.
- The Tribunal within the local limits of whose jurisdiction the claimant resides or carries on business.
- Within the local limits of whose jurisdiction the defendant resides.

22.2.3.1 Who Can File a Claim

In case of damage to property, the application for compensation has to be made by the owner of the property damaged. It is implied that in case of the death of the owner of the property, the legal representatives of the deceased can competently claim compensation.

- People who have been injured in accidents on the road can themselves file for compensation or route the claims through their advocates.
- But accident victims, who are below 18 years of age, cannot file for compensation themselves; they have to go through their advocates.
- Legal heirs of people who have died in accidents can also claim compensation; alternatively, they can route their claims through their advocates.

22.2.3.2 Who Can Report to MACT in Case of Accident

- The victim himself or, through an advocate, in the case of personal injury.
- An advocate in the case of an applicant below the age of 18 years.
- Legal heirs themselves or their advocate, in the case of death.
- The owner of the vehicle in the event of property damage.

22.2.3.3 Essential Documents Required to File Claim

The following documents are required for a compensation claim.

- Copy of the First Information Report registered with police in connection with said accident, if any.
- Panchnama copy (this is a list of damages that is drafted by the police in the presence of witnesses).
- Copy of the MLR/Post Mortem Report/Death Report, as the case may be.
- The documents of the identity of the claimants and of the deceased in a death case.
- Original bills of expenses incurred in relation to the treatment along with the treatment record.
- Documents of the educational qualifications of the deceased, if any.
- Disability Certificate, if already obtained, in an injury case.
- The proof of income of the deceased/injured.
- Documents about the age of the victim.
- The cover note of the third party insurance policy, if any.
- An affidavit detailing the relationship of the claimants with the deceased.
- Road Transport Office Certificate (showing the name and address of owner and insurance particulars of vehicle/s involved in the mishap).
- Passport-Size Photograph.
- Court-Fee Stamp.

22.2.3.4 The Court Fees for Filling an Application for Compensation

A court-fee stamp needs be affixed of 0.25 % of the claim if the amount is between 10,001 Rs and 50,000 Rs; 0.5 % of the claim if the amount is between 50,001 Rs and 100,000 Rs; and 1 % if the amount is more than 100,000 Rs with a maximum amount of 15,000 Rs.

22.2.3.5 Pecuniary Jurisdiction

The pecuniary jurisdiction of the MACT has a double implication, i.e., compensation in case of death or bodily injury and in respect of damage caused to any property. Section 165 of the Act empowers the tribunal to award compensation not only for death and bodily injury but also for damage to property. As regards the former, there are three different provisions in the Motor Vehicles Act, 1988, namely:

- Compensation in certain cases on the principle of no fault, as provided in Section 140 of the Act.
- Compensation on structured formula basis, under section 163-A of the Act
- Compensation which appears to the MACT to be just, under section 168 of the Act.

Compensation can be awarded either in cases of death or in cases of the permanent disablement of any person, and in either case, the different amounts have been fixed, respectively, for death and permanent disablement. The relevant provisions are subsections (1) and (2) of section 140. The injured or the legal representatives of the deceased can file a claim application in a prescribed format making the driver, owner, and insurer a party. The driver is not a necessary party in some states, e.g., in the state of Rajasthan the MACT Rules provide that only the owner and insurer are required to be parties. No limitation has been prescribed for the filing of the claim application. Initially, when the law came into force the limitation was 6 months, which was later increased to 1 year and ultimately, in the garb of welfare legislation, the provision of limitation was deleted. A claim launched by dependents of the deceased but not by his/her legal representatives would be defective unless the legal representatives of the deceased have been joined either as claimants or even as respondents.

The problem arose when an individual is not working, especially married females who constitute about 20 % of the cases. In India the Courts have recognized that the contribution made by the wife to the house is invaluable and cannot be computed in terms of money. The gratuitous services rendered by a wife with true love and affection to the children and her husband, in addition to managing the household affairs, cannot be equated with the services rendered by others. A wife/mother does not work by the clock. She is in the constant attendance of the family throughout the day and night unless she is employed and is required to attend the employer's work during particular hours. She takes care of all the requirements of husband and children, including the cooking of food, washing of clothes, etc. She teaches small children and provides invaluable guidance to them for their future life. A housekeeper or maidservant can do the household work, such as cooking food, washing clothes and utensils, and keeping the house clean, but she can never be a substitute for a wife/mother who renders selfless service to her husband and children. It is not possible to quantify any amount in lieu of the services rendered by the wife/mother to the family, i.e., husband and children.

However, for the purpose of the award of compensation to the dependents, some pecuniary estimate has to be made of the services of the housewife/mother. In that context, the term "services" is required to be given a broad meaning and must be construed by taking into account the loss of personal care and attention given by the deceased to her children as a mother and to her husband as a wife.

They are entitled to adequate compensation in lieu of the loss of gratuitous services rendered by the deceased. The gratuitous services rendered by wife/mother to the husband and children cannot be equated with the services of an employee and no evidence or data can possibly be produced for estimating the value of such services. It is virtually impossible to measure in terms of money the loss of personal care and attention suffered by the husband and children on the demise of the housewife. In its wisdom, the legislature in 1994 fixed the notional income of a nonearning person at Rs.15,000/- per annum and in case of a spouse, 1/3rd income of the earning/surviving spouse for the purpose of computing the compensation. Though Section 163A does not, in terms, apply to the cases in which claim for compensation is filed under Section 166 of the Act, in the absence of any other definite criteria for determination of compensation payable to the dependents of a nonearning housewife/mother, it would be reasonable to rely upon.

The disability however has to be calculated as per provisions of Persons with Disabilities (Equal Opportunities, Protection of Rights, and Full Participation) Act. Since 1999, the guidelines for evaluation of following disabilities and procedure for certification were notified.

- Visual impairment.
- Locomotor/orthopaedic disability.
- Speech and hearing disability.
- Mental retardation.
- Multiple disabilities.

As per the PWD Act, effective from 2009, authorities providing disability certificates were a medical board duly constituted by the central and state governments. The state government may constitute a medical board consisting of at least three members, out of which one shall be a specialist in the particular field. The evaluation of the disability percentage should be done as per the guidelines issued in the notification. The concept of extra-judicial assessment is not applicable in India. Only government authorized institutes and doctors working in the setup are empowered to issue disability certificates after following the guidelines. Usually, the medical superintendent of the hospital acts as chairman of the medical board, being the administrative head of the hospital. Every hospital has a medical board for this purpose. As clarified in the act, one doctor from concerned specialty, e.g., orthopedics, ophthalmology, ENT (ear, nose and throat), surgery, neurosurgery, and psychiatry, is essential. Invariably, forensic medicine practitioner is also either a member of the board or chairman of the board, but practice varies from place to place. The Chairman is free to co-opt any specialist depending upon the type of disability to be evaluated. The board usually meets periodically on prefixed dates or days depending upon the case load. On representation by the applicant, the medical board may review its decision having regard to all the facts and circumstances of the case and pass such an order in the matter it considers fit.

There is no discretion in choosing the expert or appointing the expert. The doctor who has primarily treated and the hospital from where the disability certificate is issued is the only authority who are afterwards called to testify. Recently, however, with a view to extending further help to the victim the government hospitals under whose jurisdiction the victim resides have also been authorized to issue the disability certificate. The disability is calculated in relation to the percentage loss of function of that particular limb and not in relation to the whole body. Medical experts are called to give the evidence and technical advice based on their findings after taking oath. The defense lawyer is free to ask any question to discredit the evidence and argue his case with all witnesses, including the doctor.

The judge, after carefully listening to both parties, decides the value of all evidence, but has the discretion to use it as per his wisdom, mainly in relation to the percentage loss in relation to whole body. An appeal can be made by either of the parties if unsatisfied with the judgment to higher courts, i.e., the High Court of the state and, ultimately, to the Supreme Court situated in New Delhi, the capital of country.

These courts, if they feel consider there has been a gross discrepancy, may refer the whole case to the highest government medical college of the state or the Supreme court to the most prominent medical and research institute of country. In either case, a medical board comprising of various specialties will be constituted to reexamine the victim and give their opinion. This medical board consults all the previous reports, if it is deemed necessary. The compensation for damages is complete and integral, including moral, esthetic damage and incapacitation, and also the loss of a chance on a better outcome is covered.

22.2.3.6 Qualifications of the Medicolegal Experts

As per the Indian legal system, at present a registered medical practitioner is legally competent to handle any medicolegal case. The basic undergraduate medical degree is labeled as MBBS (Bachelor of Medicine and Bachelor of Surgery). In India, currently almost 80–85 % of the total medicolegal workload is handled by these MBBS doctors, including the accident cases. The subject of forensic medicine is a compulsory subject and presently being taught during the second professional of the MBBS. The total duration of MBBS is 4½ years of which the 2nd professional is of

1½ years in duration, starting after completion of the first year to completion of 2½ years. This is one of the main reasons for overall poor medicolegal functioning. The situation in bigger cities is, however, totally different, where both government and private medical colleges are situated. In most of these cities, the medicolegal work is handled by forensic medicine experts.

Forensic Medicine Experts These medical practitioners are mostly attached to a medical college, whether government or private, with a department of Forensic Medicine & Toxicology. They all have a specialty in Forensic medicine and a good knowledge of the legislation in relation to the investigation of crime. Forensic medicine is recognized since 1956 when it was bifurcated from pathology. The postgraduate degree in forensic medicine is of 3-years duration which encompasses traumatology, pathology, legal knowledge, toxicology, ethics, and applied legal aspects of various other branches like anthropology, dentistry, and psychiatry. There is no separate existence of specialty of insurance medicine and that is covered under forensic medicine itself.

The Medicolegal Experts in Civil Cases and the Medical Advisors of Insurance Companies The concept of private medicolegal consultancy is in infancy. Few forensic medicine experts act as advisor to the lawyers and extend their help to them and thus their roles are limited. There are three important medicolegal societies in India.

- Indian Academy of Forensic Medicine.
- Indian Association of Medicolegal Experts.
- National Action Committee for Progress of Forensic Medicine and Toxicology.

As clarified earlier, disability has to be calculated by a designated and authorized medical board and not by any private, single doctor or medicolegal expert.

22.3 Ascertainment Methodology

The assessment of damages to compensate the dependants is beset with difficulties, because from the nature of things it has to take into account many imponderables, e.g., the life expectancy of the deceased and the dependants, the amount that the deceased would have earned during the remainder of his life, the amount that he would have contributed to the dependants during that period, the chances that the deceased may not have lived or the dependants may not live up to the estimated remaining period of their life expectancy, the chances that the deceased might have obtained better employment or income or might have lost his employment or income altogether.

The determination of the temporary and permanent disability is decided by medical board. Physical disability is not the same as economic disability, although physical disability can have its influence on the professional, personal, domestic, and social life of the victim. Other than physical disabilities, the rest is decided by the Court after hearing the parties.

The manner of arriving at the damages is to ascertain the net income of the deceased available for the support of himself and his/her dependants and to deduct there from such part of his/her income as the deceased was accustomed to spend upon him/herself, as regards both self-maintenance and pleasure, and to ascertain what part of his net income the deceased was accustomed to spending for the benefit of dependants. Then that should be capitalized by multiplying it by a figure representing the proper number of the year's purchases.

The multiplier method involves the ascertainment of the loss of dependency or the multiplicand having regard to the circumstances of the case and capitalizing the multiplicand by an appropriate multiplier. The choice of the multiplier is determined by the age of the deceased (or that of the claimants whichever is higher) and by the calculation as to what capital sum, if invested at a rate of interest appropriate to a stable economy, would yield the multiplicand by way of annual interest. In ascertaining this, regard should also be had to the fact that ultimately the capital sum should be consumed over the period for which the dependency is expected to last. The multiplier method is logically sound and legally well established (Table 22.1).

However, a claim for compensation under section 163A and section 166 of the Act can go together, both being independent provisions and awarding of compensation under section 163-A, unlike that under section 140, does not detract or defeat the provisions of section 166. Total reliance cannot be placed on this schedule, since it does not provide any computation chart for the persons having more than Rs.40,000/- annual income. A claim petition can also be filed under Section 166 of Motor Vehicle Act pleading negligence where the claim shall be assessed by the Judge not on the basis of structural formula but on the basis of evidence.

Table 22.1 Multiplier table in claim cases under Section 166

Age of the victim (years)	Multiplier
15–18	20
18–22	18
23–27	17
28–32	16
33–37	15
38–42	14
43–47	13
48–52	12
53–57	11
58–62	10
63–67	9
68–72	8
73–77	7

22.4 Evaluation Criteria

Disability refers to any restriction or lack of ability to perform an activity in the manner considered normal for a human being. Permanent disability refers to the residuary incapacity or loss of use of some part of the body, found existing at the end of the period of treatment and recuperation, after achieving the maximum bodily improvement or recovery, which is likely to remain for the remainder life of the injured. Temporary disability refers to the incapacity or loss of use of some part of the body on account of the injury, which will cease to exist at the end of the period of treatment and recuperation. Permanent disability can be either partial or total. Partial permanent disability refers to a person's inability to perform all the duties and bodily functions that he could perform before the accident, though he is able to perform some of them and is still able to engage in some gainful activity. Total permanent disability refers to a person's inability to perform any avocation or employment-related activities as a result of the accident. The permanent disabilities that may arise from motor accident injuries are of a much wider range when compared to the physical disabilities, which are enumerated in the Persons with Disabilities (Equal Opportunities, Protection of Rights and Full Participation) Act, 1995 ("the Disabilities Act", for short). However, if any of the disabilities enumerated in Section 2(i) of the Disabilities Act are the result of injuries sustained in a motor accident, they can be permanent disabilities for the purpose of claiming compensation.

In India, only death or grievous hurt (few sub-clauses) in issues of compensation are recognized.

Section 142 of MVA defines Permanent Disablement if such a person has suffered by reason of the accident, any injury or injuries involving:

- Permanent privation of the sight of either eye or the hearing of either ear, or privation of any member or joint
- Destruction or permanent impairing of the powers of any member or joint
- Permanent disfiguration of the head or face

The percentage of permanent disability is expressed with reference to a particular limb. When a disability certificate states that the injured has suffered permanent disability to an extent of 45 % of the left lower limb, it is not the same as 45 % permanent disability with reference to the whole body. The extent of disability of a limb (or part of the body) expressed in terms of a percentage of the total functions of that limb obviously cannot be assumed to be the extent of disability of the whole body. If there is a 50 % permanent disability of the right hand and a 70 % permanent disability of right leg, it does not mean that the extent of permanent disability with reference to the whole body is 120 % (that is 70 % plus 50 %). If different parts of the body have suffered different percentages of disabilities, the sum total thereof expressed in terms of the permanent disability with reference to the whole body cannot obviously exceed 100 %.

Where the claimant suffers a permanent disability as a result of injuries, the assessment of compensation under the head of loss of future earnings would depend upon the effect and impact of such permanent disability on his earning capacity. Therefore, it remains a gray area and in most of the cases the percentage of economic loss, that is, the percentage of loss of earning capacity, arising from a permanent disability, will be different from the percentage of permanent disability.

Temporary disability is not compensated. The date of consolidation is not defined and the victim has to be reassessed after a period of 1 or 2 years depending upon the disability of the part to claim for it. Otherwise, also given the duration of lengthy legal procedures, that time has often already passed. All the costs incurred have to be compensated. However, there are a number of cases which deviate from the proposed costs and depend upon the discretion of the judge. It is the lawyer of the party who files the case while filing the claim.

These findings will lead to the determination of the disability rate and the negative implications on his private, domestic, and professional/economic life. Each of these implications can lead to a disability. Other more specific consequences in the private, domestic, or economic field such as pain, esthetic, sexual, as well as social and cultural damage have not been specified. It is usually based on case laws. The economic disability takes into account the net loss of income during the period of disability.

22.4.1 *Type of Disabilities*

For sake of convenience and better understanding, the five types of disabilities as described under PWD Act have been categorized and discussed individually for the purpose of assessment methodology and evaluation criteria, i.e., mental retardation, visual impairment, speech and hearing disability, locomotor/orthopaedic disability, and multiple disabilities.

22.4.1.1 Mental Retardation

Mental retardation is a condition of arrested or incomplete development of the mind, which is especially characterized by impairment of skills manifested during the development period which contributed to the overall level of intelligence, i.e., cognitive, language, motor, and social abilities.

Categories of Mental Retardation are the following.

- Mild Mental Retardation. The range of 50–69 (standardized IQ test) is indicative of mild retardation. Understanding and use of language tend to be delayed to a varying degree and executive speech problems that interfere with the development of independence may persist into adult life.

- Moderate Mental Retardation. The range of 35–49 is indicative of moderate mental retardation. The level of development of language is variable. Some of those affected can take part in simple conversations while others have only enough language to communicate their basic needs.
- Severe Mental Retardation. The IQ is usually in the range of 20–34. In this category, most of the people suffer from a marked degree of motor impairment or other associated deficits indicating the presence of clinically significant damage to or mal-development of the central nervous system.
- Profound Mental Retardation. The IQ in this category is estimated to be under 20. The ability to understand or comply with requests or instructions are severally limited. Most of such individuals are immobile or severally restricted in mobility incontinent and capable at most of only very rudimentary forms of nonverbal communication. They possess little or no ability to care for their own basic needs and require constant help and supervision.

The Process of Certifications consists of two main stages.

- A disability certificate shall be issued by a Medical Board consisting of three members duly constituted by the Central/State Government. At least one shall be a Specialist in the area of mental retardation, namely Psychiatrist, Pediatrician, and clinical Psychologist.
- The examination process will consist of three components, namely clinical assessment, assessment of adaptive behavior, and intellectual functioning.

22.4.1.2 Visual Disability

Blindness refers to a condition where a person suffers from any of the following condition, i.e.,

- Total absence of sight.
- Visual acuity not exceeding 6/60 or 20/200 (Snellen) in the better eye with best correcting lenses.
- Limitation of field of vision subtending an angle of 20 degree or worse.

Low Visions referred to a person with impairment of vision of less than 6/18–6/60 with best correction in the better eye or impairment of field in any one of the following categories:

- Reduction of fields less than 50 degrees.
- Hemianopia with macular involvement.
- Altitudinal defect involving lower fields.

The Process of Certification consists of a disability certificate which shall be issued by a Medical Board duly constituted by the Central/State Government having at least three members. Out of which, at least one member shall be a specialist in ophthalmology.

22.4.1.3 Speech and Hearing Disability

Hearing Disability involves a person with hearing impairment having difficulty in hearing sounds. The type for impairment ranges from various degrees of mild hearing loss to total deafness.

The following have to be considered.

- Pure tone average of hearing in 500, 2000, and 4000 HZ by conduction (AC and DC) should be taken as basis for consideration as per the test recommendations.
- When there is only an island of hearing present in one or two frequencies in better ear, it should be considered as total loss of hearing.
- Wherever there is no response at any of the four frequencies (500, 1000, 2000, and 4000 HZ), it should be considered as equivalent to 100 dbles for the purpose of classification of disability and in arriving at the average.

The Process of Certification includes a disability certificate which shall be issued by a Medical Board duly constituted by the Central and the State Government; out of which at least one member shall be a specialist in the field of ear, nose, and throat.

22.4.1.4 Locomotor Disability

The following definitions are considered.

- Impairment. Impairment is any loss or abnormality of psychological, physiological, or anatomical structure or function in a human being.
- Functional Limitations. Impairment may cause functional limitations which are partial or total inability to perform those nativities necessary for motor, sensory, or mental function within the range or manner of which a human being is normally capable.
- Disability. A disability is any restriction or lack (resulting from an impairment) of ability to perform an activity in the manner or within the range considered normal for a human being.
- Locomotor Disability. Locomotor disability is defined as a person's inability to execute distinctive activities associated with moving both himself and objects, from place to place, and such inability resulting from affection of musculoskeletal and/or nervous system.

22.4.1.5 Multiple Disabilities

Multiple disabilities means a combination of two or more disabilities as defined.

In order to evaluate the multiple disability, the same guidelines shall be used as have been developed by the respective subcommittees of various single disability, i.e., Mental retardation, Locomotor Disability, Visual Disability, and Speech & Hearing disability.

However, in order to arrive at the total percentage of multiple disability, the combining formula **a + b (90−a)/90** as given in the Guidelines shall be used, where "a" will be the higher score and "b" will be the lower score. However, the maximum total percentage of multiple disabilities shall not exceed 100 %. For example, if the percentage of hearing disability is 30 % and visual disability is 20 %, then by applying the combining formula given above, the total percentage of multiple disability will be calculated as follows : **−30 + 20 (90–30)/90 = 43**

The Procedure for Certification of Multiple Disabilities will remain the same as has been developed by the respective subcommittees on various single disabilities. The final disability certificate for multiple disability will be issued by Disability Board which has given higher score of disability by combining the score of different disabilities using the combining format, i.e., **a + b (90 − a)/90.**

In case where two scores of disability are equal, the final certificate of multiple disabilities will be issued by any one of them as decided by local authority.

The Process of Certification consists of a disability certificate which shall be issued by a Medical Board of three members duly constituted by the Central and the State Government, out of which, at least, one member shall be a specialist from either the field of Physical Medicine and Rehabilitation or Orthopedics.

22.4.2 *Methods of Compensation*

The assessment of compensation, however, can be made effectively, but cannot be said to be without flaws. In every such assessment, certain assumptions are to be made and there is a possibility of discrepancies from Judge to Judge in applying the various principles enunciated by the Courts from time to time. The Supreme Court, while dealing with a related matter, evolved a formula. Yearly Income and yearly expenditure of the deceased gives the sum expended on legal representatives. If this amount is capitalized subject to certain deductions, pecuniary loss to the family can be assessed. While improving the above formula, the Supreme Court has stated that there is no exact uniform rule for measuring the value of human life, and the measure of damages cannot be arrived at by a mathematical calculation, but the amount recoverable depends upon the life expectancy of the legal beneficiaries. The Supreme Court of India, with the development of accident claims, has decided to take into consideration the annual income of deceased. This ranges to double the income, depending upon the nature of the job, age, future prospects, etc. The Supreme Court has held that after determining and doubling annual income, 1/3 should be deducted towards the expenses to be incurred of the deceased, and the remaining amount should be multiplied by a multiplier depending on the age of the deceased and the beneficiary. The maximum multiplier approved by the Supreme Court in this case was 16. Later, the Supreme Court's 3 Judges approved the Davis formula along with determination of dependency on a unit basis in which the adults were not considered as 2 units and the minors were considered as 1 unit. In this case, the court did not allow double of the amount except that a premium may be given in consideration of future prospects. But, in a recent Supreme Court judgment, in order to make compensation just and to take consideration of overall factors, the multiplier was reduced from 16 to 12 in the case of a deceased individual of 38 years. In similar circumstances, in another case the Supreme Court stated that the determination of the multiplier depends upon (1) age of deceased, (2) age of claimants, (3) marital status, (4) education and employment of the claimants, and (5) loss of pecuniary benefits. The Supreme Court also held that criteria of awarding compensation includes some guess work, some hypothetical considerations, and some amount of sympathy linked with the nature of the disability caused. But, all such elements are required to be viewed with the objective standard.

In view of the above case law, one can say that the assessment of compensation is to be guided by way of applying precedents on the facts and circumstances of a particular case. It should not be misunderstood that an injured or legal representative of the deceased should be given an exorbitant claim, but the law restricts them to be "just compensation" so as to save the injured or legal representatives of the deceased from possible pecuniary and non-pecuniary losses, guided by the above judgments.

The effect of the permanent disability on the earning capacity of the injured is to be assessed, and after assessing the loss of earning capacity in terms of a percentage of the income, it has to be quantified in terms of money to arrive at the future loss of earnings (by applying the standard multiplier method used to determine loss of dependency). It is to be paid in as a lump sum only.

The following must therefore be taken into consideration:

- Whether the disability is permanent or temporary
- If the disability is permanent, whether it is permanent total disability or permanent partial disability
- If the disability percentage is expressed with reference to any specific limb, then the effect of such a disability of the limb on the functioning of the entire body, that is, the permanent disability suffered by the person

If the Tribunal concludes that there is no permanent disability, then there is no question of proceeding further and determining the loss of future earning capacity. But if the Tribunal concludes that there is permanent disability, then it will proceed to ascertain its extent. After the Tribunal ascertains the actual extent of permanent disability of the claimant based on the medical evidence, it has to determine whether such permanent disability has affected or will affect his earning capacity.

However, the situation varies from case to case and is usually decided on basis of case laws.

The following example is given for illustration.

In Ajay Kumar's case MAC.APP.378/2013, the court clearly held that the assessment of compensation under the heading of future earnings would depend upon the effect and impact of such permanent disability on the earning capacity. This can be assessed only on appreciation of the evidence. The appellant was an accountant and thus was doing a desk job and his disability in relation to the lower limbs had not left him totally incapable of performing his job. In the facts and circumstances, the learned tribunal assessed the percentage of whole body disability of the appellant as 40 %.

The total loss of future earning on account of disability = 215,250 × 17 (multiplier) × 40/100 (permanent disability) = 1,463,700/- Rs.

- Loss of earning capacity due to injuries 1,463,700/- Rs.
- Compensation towards pain and sufferings. 100,000/- Rs.
- Loss of amenities and enjoyment 150,000/- Rs.
- Compensation towards disfiguration 100,000/- Rs.
- Loss of earning of petitioner for 5 months at 8200/- Rs per month, 41,000/- Rs.
- Expenses towards medical bills 311,619/- Rs.
- Compensation towards conveyance and special diet (without bills) 10,000/- Rs.
- Compensation towards prosthetic leg 70,000/- Rs. 224,631/- Rs.
- The appellant shall be entitled for the interest of 7.5 % per MAC.APP.378/2013.

22.4.2.1 Death: Costs of the Funeral

In the event that a victim dies as a consequence of the tort, the costs of the funeral will be taken into account. When the duration of survival probability of the one who bears the cost is lower than that of the victim, this one probably never have had to bear them and can accordingly claim full reimbursement (e.g., a parent for her child). If the victim's life expectancy is lower than that of the one entitled to it, the latter would have had to bear in the future and his compensation consists in the advance payment of these costs. The compensation is then formed by the difference between the current expenditure and the constant value of this sum payable to the presumed date of death in the assumption that the accident would not have happened.

22.4.2.2 Death: Damage of the Relatives

This suffering of the relatives cannot be concretely expressed and must be done with a lump sum.

Below are listed some general bibliographic sources useful to deepen the issue. They are not reported within the text as they are no cited references.

Acknowledgment Help and technical inputs provided by Ms. Versha Singh, Practicing Advocate, Delhi Bar Association at Sessions Court and High Court of Delhi in preparing this manuscript is gratefully acknowledged.

Bibliography

1. Black D (1998b) The limitations of evidence. J R Coll Physicians Lond 32:23
2. Brennan TA, Leape LL, Laird NM, Hebert L, Localio AR, Lawthers AG, Newhouse JP, Weiler PC, Hiatt HH (1991b) Incidence of adverse events and negligence in hospitalized patients—results of the Harvard Medical Practise Study I. N Engl J Med 324:370–376
3. Fischer G, Fetters MD, Munro AP, Goldman EB (1997b) Adverse events in primary care identified from a risk-management database. J Fam Pract 45:40–46
4. Hofer T, Herr E, Hayward R (2000b) What is an error? Eff Clin Pract 6:261–269
5. Hughes G (2009b) Litigation, redress and making amends. Emerg Med J 26:844
6. Hurwitz B (2004) How does evidence based guidance influence determinations of medical negligence? J R Coll Physicians Lond (BMJ 329:1024)
7. O'Neil AC, Petersen LA, Cook EF, Bates DW, Lee TH, Brennan TA (1993b) Physician reporting compared with medical-record review to identify adverse medical events. Ann Intern Med 119:370–376
8. Scobie S, Thomson R, McNeil JJ, Phillips PA (2006b) Measurements of the safety and quality of health care. Med J Aust 184:S51–55

Chapter 23
Methods of Ascertainment of Personal Damage in China

Ping Huang and Ya-hui Wang

Abstract This chapter illustrates the historical, judicial, and juridical framework of personal injury assessment and compensation in China, describing the expert's qualification and competences and detailing the ascertainment methodology and criteria of evaluation utilized for identifying, describing, and estimating any personal injury, its temporary and permanent consequences, and the causal value/link between the event and the injury and between the injury and the impairment/disability.

23.1 History and Outline of Forensic Medical Examination of Human Injury and Damage

China has a long history of forensic science. According to the existing literature, Chinese forensics can be traced back to more than 2200 years ago, and China was one of the first countries in the world to develop forensic medical examinations of human injury. In books dated 262–217 BC, there are descriptions on the examination methods of cadavers and living bodies and detailed field investigations, damage characteristics, and inferences of trauma-causing weapons; thus, it was during that time that forensic damage examinations began to take shape.

During the Han and Tang Dynasties (206 BC–907 AD), the ancient Chinese legal system was developed and improved. The provision made it clear that the forensic medical examination subjects were the sick, the dead, and the injured, which remained true up to the Qing Dynasty (1636–1912 AD). During the Song Dynasty (960–1279 AD), clear provisions were issued concerning the application of the examination, preliminary examination, reexamination, and exemption of examination based on the inherited examination system of the Tang Dynasty. At the time of the Song Dynasty, relevant official autopsy documents were issued,

P. Huang (✉) • Y. Wang (✉)
Shanghai Key Laboratory of Forensic Medicine, Institute of Forensic Science, Ministry of Justice, Shanghai 200063, People's Republic of China
e-mail: huangp@ssfjd.cn; wangyh@ssfjd.cn

S.D. Ferrara et al. (eds.), *Personal Injury and Damage Ascertainment under Civil Law*, DOI 10.1007/978-3-319-29812-2_23

including an examination record form and the conclusion of the cause of death. In the Song Dynasty, injury examinations were taken very seriously, which was an important reason for the publication of "Collected Cases of Injustice Rectified." The Chinese forensic medical examination system during this period was the most advanced and comprehensive system in the medieval world, taking a leading position in world history.

The forensic medical examination systems of the Yuan, Ming, and Qing Dynasties basically inherited the provisions of the Tang and Song Dynasties, without adding any new measures that went beyond the scope of visual examination of cadavers. Due to the long-standing prohibition of doctors performing autopsies, the development of China's forensic medicine after the Song Dynasty was very slow and lagged behind that of the rest of the world in the nineteenth century. During the era of the Republic of China, physicians were allowed to perform examinations of cadavers and autopsies as well. In 1932, the Nationalist government established the "Forensic Institute of Justice and Administration" in Shanghai, the first forensic medical examination entity set up by the government in Chinese history; it is responsible for the forensic medical examination of difficult cases nationwide, the training of graduates from medical schools, and the appointment of medicolegal physicians to provinces and cities. In 1946, forensic offices were established in some police departments, such as the Shanghai City Police Department.

After the founding of the People's Republic of China, forensic institutions were gradually established in some of the medical schools and in the Public Security Organs (PSO), prosecution, and court systems. After 1958, most of these forensic institutions were managed by their respective system. After the Cultural Revolution, the PSO, prosecution, court, justice, public health, and university systems reestablished the forensic institutions based on the demand, in which four levels of examination institutions (central, provincial, municipal, and county levels) were established by the PSO, prosecution, and court systems and formed the present pattern of multilevel, multisystem, and independent institutions. From October 1, 2005 on, provisioned by the "Decisions on the management of justice examinations" issued by the National People's Congress, the court system stopped the forensic medical examination work. The PSO, prosecution department, and justice administration department managed the respective examination institutions and the examiners and conducted the qualification evaluation, annual assessment, and training of the examination institutions and the examiners within their respective departments. Over the last 20 years, there has been a rapid development at the examination level and research level of Chinese forensics examination and the forensic medical examination system, as well as the adoption of international standards.

23.2 Conditions, Qualifications, and Training of Forensic Medical Examiners

23.2.1 Conditions and Qualifications of Forensic Medical Examiners

In China, the forensic medical examiners are mainly classified as follows: (1) the personnel of the internal examination office established by the PSO and prosecution departments, who usually do not engage in external examination work but only service internal examinations within the department and (2) the professionals from the judicial examination institutions (e.g., hospitals, research institutes, and universities) who have been granted the accreditation of judicial forensic medical examination by the Ministry of Justice. Chinese laws and regulations also provide the qualification requirements of the examiners of forensic injuries.

Forensic medical examiner applicants should have a senior professional title that is related to the applied examination matters. For this type of examiner, there is no requirement of specific work experience because the prerequisite of obtaining a senior professional title ensures that the applicant must have significant work experience and solid theoretical knowledge and research ability; furthermore, as the senior expert in a certain field, the applicant's knowledge and prestige already adequately qualify them as an examiner.

Forensic medical examiner applicants should have the professional certified qualification that is related to the applied examination matters or at least a Bachelor's degree for the relevant specialties and must have engaged in related work for more than 5 years.

Those forensic medical examiners who have committed a crime, been criminally punished for a duty negligence crime, or been punished with expulsion from the public service and revocation of their registration are all banned from engaging in judicial forensic medical examination businesses.

23.2.2 Training of Forensic Examiners

23.2.2.1 Job Training

Job training refers to the learning and training activities that purport to enable the trainees to meet the requirements of the post of injury and disability examinations and the certification and to adapt to the demand of the job qualifications. The subjects of the job training are those who apply for the certification of injury and disability examinations and those who have obtained the certificate, but have still not independently practiced. The job training contents include the relevant governmental policies and guidelines, professional knowledge, relevant legal knowledge, professional ethics, professional discipline, and practice rules. The job training is divided into preservice training and training for job transfers. Preservice training refers to the training of those who have not obtained the examiner's certificate and those who have obtained the examiner's certificate but have still not independently practiced. The training for job transfers refers to the training of those who have already obtained the examiner's certificate and have practiced and those who have not independently practiced. The trainees are mostly doctors from related fields or university teachers from the department of forensic medicine. The preservice training programs are formulated and implemented by the PSO, the Procuratorate, and the Ministry of Justice. The preservice training is conducted with the standardized training content, training requirements, training time, examination form, and certificate.

23.2.2.2 Continuing Education

Continuing education refers to academic education and nonacademic education of forensic medical examination practitioners to further improve their knowledge structure and ability to conduct their practice. The purpose of continuing education is to continuously improve the quality of expert services and professional and moral qualities and to achieve sustainable development. Continuing education is primarily aimed at new theories, new knowledge, new technology, and new methods in forensic medical examination. The continuing education implements the annual study hour system, which requires the examiner to participate in the continuing education program for not less than 40 h per year. The examination institution needs to submit the relevant evidence related to participation in the continuing education activities by examiners within the institution to the administrative department within the prescribed time annually; furthermore, they must record the study hours and store the data in the archive.

23.3 Techniques and Methods of Clinical Forensic Judicial Examinations of Human Injury and Damage

The techniques and methods of clinical forensic judicial examinations include the investigation of the case, the investigation of the injury, in vivo inspections, and laboratory tests. The problems to be solved by the clinical forensic judicial examinations are as follows: determination of the presence or absence of injuries, determination of the type of injury, inference of the trauma-causing weapon, determination of the time of the injury, determination of the consequences of the injury, in vivo skin scarring inspections, determination of the causal relationship between the injury and disease, and determination of the nature of personal injury and the formation mechanism.

23.3.1 *Investigation of the Case*

The main contents of the investigation of the case include the time, location, cause, involved people, injury-causing weapon, or substance. The main purpose of the investigation of the case is to clarify the nature of the injury (self-injury or injury by others) and the injury-causing mode (direct violence injury or indirect violence injury), which are critical to the clarification of the examination items and the legitimacy of the purpose of the examination items. In special circumstances, the forensic examiner can apply to authorized agencies, such as the PSO, prosecution, and court departments, to conduct an investigation on issues related to the examination and generate investigative records. Records of onsite investigation and other documents of the case provide important evidence to prove the incident and also the objective basis to indicate the feature exhibits, environment, timeline, and clinical manifestations of the examinee of the investigating case; furthermore, these records can provide valuable information to analyze the case and other specific issues combining the forensic medicinal in vivo inspection results.

23.3.2 *Medical Records Collection*

The injury investigation process is the process of collecting medical records. Medical records are also referred to as medical documents and provide the primary evidence for the clinical forensic medical examination with the following evidentiary values.

First, objective, timely medical records can prove the facts of the case. (1) The involved party seeks timely treatment at the time of the injury, which continuously and completely reflects the human injury case or traumatic incident. Although the nature of the case or the incident cannot be determined, the approximate time of the case (incident), injured body part, injury extent, and severity of injury can be clearly recorded. If, after the injury, medical help is not sought in a timely manner, even several days after the injury, the question of whether the injured party has secondary injuries derived from other circumstances is often raised in trauma cases and is prone to generate controversy. (2) The medical records document the facts of the injury, which is not only a part of the case but also provides an important scientific basis of the description of the facts by third-party professionals who have neutral, impartial legal efficiency; additionally, the records supply standardized, detailed, timely, and long-term storage of the facts.

Second, comprehensive and detailed medical records can indicate the degree of the injury. Medical records document the diagnosis and treatment processes and contain the detailed interrogation records (the family history, medical history, personal history, drug history, allergies, and other social relations of the examinee), physical examination, auxiliary examination, differential diagnosis, and treatment of trauma (e.g., treatment plan and surgical records). Many injuries have contemporariness and non-repeatability and cannot be reproduced afterwards, such as the degree of injury-induced hemorrhagic shock, breathing difficulties, and non-missing injuries of internal tissues and organs. Therefore, the record on the degree of the injury in the medical records is sometimes the only evidence to determine the final result of the examination conclusion. In addition, the medical records of the hospitalization and the medical records from multiple hospitals can be used to determine changes in the degree of the injury in the examinee through dynamic analysis and help analyze the causal relationship between the traumatic incident and the consequences of the injury.

Third, accurate, intact medical records can be used to determine the consequences of the injury. In China, whether it is judicial examination institutes at various levels, forensic medical examination entities sponsored by universities, or privately run forensic medical examination organizations, the vast majority do not have the specialized equipment to complete the relevant tests on the examinees. Thus, when assessing the extent of the injury, especially in grading the disability level, the forensic medical examination organization needs to combine the records in the medical documents and delegate the examinees to qualified, competent physicians to conduct the specialist examination. The inspection report is issued by the hospital, and the current consequences of the injury are drawn by the forensic examiner by comprehensively considering the medical history and the current status of the examinee. Next, the degree of the injury and the level of the disability are evaluated according to the provisions of the relevant standards. Therefore, medical documents are critical to forensic medical examination practice.

23.3.3 Identification Time of Human Injury and Damage

Forensic medical identification should be based on the original damage inspection, and records should be completed as soon as possible in relation to the damage. It should test after clinical medical treatment; forensic medical identification could be applied in 3–6 months after injury in principle. In China, the statute of limitation time of the compensation of personal injury is about 1 year. Therefore, the duration of forensic medical identification is generally not more than 1 year. Of course, special injuries, which have been treated, but still not healed, such as treated limb fractures that do not heal within a 1 year or that are combined with other complications (chronic osteomyelitis, bone nonunion, etc.) should be exempted.

In general, identification time of brain and spinal cord injuries should be completed between 6 and 12 months after injury; identification time of appearance effect or damage should be completed between 3 and 6 months after injury; identification time of spine and pelvis damage should be completed between 3 and 6 months after injury; identification time of eye and ear damage should be completed between 3 and 6 months after injury; identification time of limb fracture should be completed between 4 and 6 months after injury. If the internal fixation is still present in relation to limb fracture and influences the functioning of the limbs, the identification should be completed 1 month after the internal fixation has been removed.

23.3.4 *In Vivo Inspection*

The main purpose of in vivo inspection is to verify the injury of the examinee through the processes of the investigations of the case and the medical history and to assess whether the medical treatment of the injured examinee should be terminated; furthermore, the inspection aims to examine and evaluate the tissue and organ dysfunctions derived from the traumatic incident in the examinee. In contrast to clinical patients, due to the psychology of revenge or compensation claims, the examinee sometimes intentionally exaggerates the injury or fakes dysfunctions in their limbs and organs in the in vivo inspection process. This situation requires the examiner not only to have rich experience to seek the truth and discard the falsehoods but also to identify fraud and malingering through special detection tools or methods when necessary.

23.3.4.1 Requirements of In Vivo Clinical Forensic Inspections

Following the principle of seeking truth from facts, the subjective and objective physical signs derived from the primary injury to the human body and the surface injury, limb deformity, defect or dysfunction and other complications caused by the injury or sequelae are subjected to comprehensive, careful inspection to provide evidence analysis for the examination conclusions; typically, local photographs are taken to fix the evidence. The measurement instruments used in the inspection must be tested and calibrated in accordance with the state standards. When inspecting the body of a female subject, the examination should be performed by a female forensic examiner; if a female forensic examiner is not available, it can be performed by a male forensic examiner, but the procedure must be attended by female staff and a family member of the examinee. Examinations based on the consequences of the injury should be conducted after completing the clinical treatment, in principle, 3–6 months after the injury is inflicted.

23.3.4.2 Clinical Forensic In Vivo Inspection Items

In China, a comprehensive clinical forensic in vivo inspection includes: (1) general aspects, such as height, weight, and secondary sexual characteristics; (2) a surface inspection with descriptions of the location, shape, size, color, and texture and other characteristics of abrasions, contusions, and skin scarring; (3) a brain examination that includes the cranial nerve, sensory function, motor function, reflex, skull fracture, brain injury, and brain injury-derived sequelae; (4) inspections of eye and ear injuries; (5) inspections of neck injuries, such as larynx, trachea, and esophagus injuries; (6) inspections of the chest, such as rib fractures, lung injury, and cardiac insufficiency; (7) closed and open abdominal injuries and injury-derived sequelae; (8) inspections of pelvic and perineal areas for pelvic fracture, pelvic vital organ damage, and reproductive system damage; (9) spinal fracture and dislocation; and (10) fractures, dislocations, damage to important nerves, and vasculature of the limbs and joint dysfunction.

The above described clinical forensic in vivo inspection items can be selectively assessed in focus according to the case, the examination item, and the site and nature of the injury, but items that impact the examination conclusions should not be omitted. When performing the inspection on the examinee, the examiner can invite a specialist physician with a senior professional title to assist, but the examiner must be responsible for the inspection results that serve as the basis for the examination.

23.3.4.3 Forensic Clinical In Vivo Inspection and Record

The human body damage inspection and record is an important process of forensic medical identification. It involves the inspection of damage to patients by a legal medical expert in order to find the nature, the location and degree of damage, the cause and mode of the damage, as well as other important information. An effective record of this valuable information is attained by reviewing the appraisal opinions.

Skin Damage

Skin damage is divided into skin abrasions, contusions, sharp device, and scalp avulsion injury. For the different skin damage, the damage location, shape, color, area, injury, bleeding, blood loss evaluation, local swelling, presence of foreign bodies, and presence of combined fracture should be inspected and recorded. For the formation of damage, the important features of location, shape, length, width, depth, the edge shape, wall, horn, bottom, and cavity of wound should be observed upon inspection and recorded.

Skin Scar

Skin scar includes superficial scar, hyperplasia scar, keloid scar, atrophic scar, and cupped scar. The legal medical expert should pay more attention to the location, length, width, area, shape of scar, subcutaneous tissue adhesion, presence of pigmentation, the effect on adjacent tissues and organs function, etc. during the inspection of the body surface. Meanwhile, during the inspection, it should be ascertained whether the wound has been stitched and whether there is a presence of secondary infection during scar healing. For irregular scar measurement, transparent film records can be utilized and then the irregular skin scar area can be calculated with computer software.

Skin Pigment Change

Skin pigmentation is mainly due to the skin melanin cell activity increase or melanin cell populations. Skin pigment loss is mainly due to the decreased melanin cell activity or melanin cells caused by reducing the number. As for skin pigment changes, both in pigmentation and pigment loss, the position and size of such changes should be inspected and recorded. If necessary, transparent film records can be utilized and then the irregular skin scar area can be calculated with computer software..

Nervous System Inspection and Record

The nervous system inspection and record mainly relate to sensory function, motor function, and nerve reflex.

Sensory function mainly includes light touch, light pain, temperature sense, deep feeling, and the cerebral cortex. The above sensory function evaluation utilizes cotton swabs, pins, a cold and hot water tube, and a tuning fork. The patient undergoes a series of tests and is questioned concerning his/her related reactions and perceptions.

Motor function examination is performed mainly through the test of muscle strength, muscle tension, muscle atrophy, and coordinated movements. According to the range of motion of limbs and gravity resistance, muscle strength is divided into six levels (0–5), according to the paralyzed parts can be recorded as: monoplegia, hemiplegia, paraplegia, quadriparesis, and crossed paralysis.

Nerve reflex examination includes shallow reflex, deep reflex, pathological reflex, and autonomic nervous function. Abdominal wall reflex, testosterone reflex, anus reflex, and plantar reflex belong to light reflex. Biceps reflex, triceps reflex, radial reflex, knee reflex, and the achilles tendon are deep reflex. The inspection results of shallow and deep reflex are recorded as follows: normal, weaken, or disappear. For the central nervous system damage, the legal medical expert should pay special attention to check the Babinski sign, Oppenheim sign, Chaddock sign, Gordon sign, and Hoffmann sign. The inspection results are recorded as follows: negative, positive, or weakly positive.

Autonomic nerve function mainly includes the skin scratch test, the sphincter function test, the starch iodine test, and the ninhydrin test. The skin scratch test evaluates vasomotor reflex and can be used to position the reference of nerve injury. The sphincter function test mainly includes the test of bladder sphincter function and anal sphincter function, mainly used to determine early spinal shock or the degree and scope of horsetail nerve damage. The starch iodine test and ninhydrin test are used to evaluate the sweat function of the skin

Important Parameters of Limb Measurement and Record

After the healing of limb fractures, in the process of forensic medical identification, the legal medical expert should measure and compare limbs' length on both sides, including the length of upper arm, forearm, leg, thigh, and calf, which must be measured using in the same method. The length of corresponding limbs can differ by about 1.0 cm.

Nerve injury patients usually have nerve muscle atrophy and, therefore, it is also necessary to pay attention to the diameter of corresponding limbs.

After extensive damage to the soft tissue, different degrees and ranges of skin scars are usually present. In the process of damage identification or disability rating, it is necessary to measure the surface skin scar as the percentage of total body surface area. At this time, an accurate measurement of surface skin scar area is very important. Usually, the scar area can be calculated using computer software. The Chinese adult body surface area calculation formula is as follows: surface area (m^2) $= 0.0061 \times$ height (cm) $+ 0.0128 \times$ weight (kg) $- 0.1529$. The body surface area calculation formula for Chinese children is as follows: surface area of child's weight 30 kg($m^2 =$ weight(kg) $\times 0.035 + 0.1$, surface area of child's weight ≤ 30 kg(m^2) $= 1.05+$(weight-30) $\times 0.02$.

23.3.4.4 Evaluation Method of Dysfunction After Injury

In China, the evaluation of dysfunction of human body injury or damage mainly focuses on the visual and auditory functions, men's sexual function, and body movement function, and in these research fields, there are several designated laboratories in the Institute of Forensic Science, Ministry of Justice, P.R. China.

Evaluation of Visual Function

In damage identification and disability rating, the degree of visual dysfunction often needs to be evaluated, and according to the visual dysfunction, the degree of damage and level of disability are determined. Therefore, it is necessary to ensure that the results of the visual function test are reliable and give objective, accurate, and reliable results concerning the identification of visual dysfunction.

In China, the evaluation of routine visual function inspection includes central vision, far vision, near vision inspection, diopter inspection, vision detection, and false blind test. Evaluation of visual function via electrophysiological testing mainly includes the electro-retinogram and the visual-evoked cortical potentials. These detection methods are mainly used to evaluate the structure and function of the visual system. In particular, the visual cortex-evoked potential is not only used to evaluate the visual system structure and function but can also be used to check visual acuity test results.

Evaluation of Auditory Function

In damage identification and disability rating, the degree of auditory dysfunction often needs to be evaluated, according to the auditory dysfunction, so as to determine the damage degree and level of disability. Therefore, it is important to ensure that the results of the scientific auditory function test give objective, accurate, and reliable results in relation to the identification of visual dysfunction.

In China, the evaluation of detection methods mainly include pure tone hearing threshold measurement, acoustic immittance test, auditory-evoked potential test, and distortion product otoacoustic emissions. The pure tone hearing threshold measurement requires to pass through more than two times after testing according to the results of comprehensive evaluation; acoustic immittance test, including drumtype immittance testing, acoustic reflex threshold (stapes muscle acoustic reflex threshold) test, and acoustic attenuation measurement test. The test report should include at least tympanum figure type, middle ear function evaluation, and acoustic reflex threshold. The auditory-evoked potential test includes auditory brainstem response, 40 Hz auditory event-related potential, an electrocochleography test, and auditory steady-state response; distortion product otoacoustic emissions due to pure tone hearing threshold changes have forecast the effect of hearing changes and is of great significance for the differential diagnosis of after cochlear deafness.

Evaluation of Male Sexual Function

Penile erectile dysfunction (ED) of males is not uncommon in forensic medical identification. In China, there are forensic medicine appraisal standards in relation to male sexual dysfunction. ED detection methods contain pudendal nerve-evoked potential, corpus cavernosum hemodynamic examination, endocrine function test, and penile erection test. The pudendal nerve-evoked potential test includes sacral reflex latency, spinal pudendal-evoked potential, cortical pudendal-evoked potential, cortical motor-evoked potential, spinal motor-evoked potential, and penile sympathetic skin response. The corpus cavernosum hemodynamic examination includes sponge injected vasoactive drugs test, Doppler Ultrasound examination, after injection of vascular active drugs using doppler ultrasound detection of blood flow to the penis, color Duplex Ultrasonography, and performance (perfusion) sponge imaging. The endocrine function test is mainly used to measure blood testosterone, shortness of follicular hormone and luteinizing hormone, prolactin, and to determine hormone estradiol levels. The penis erection scanning and audiovisual sexual stimulation test determine penis hardness and change in size.

In China, the forensic identification of ED within the knowledge of neurological ED, vascular ED, secretory ED, drugs, sex ED, psychogenic ED, and the differential diagnosis of mixed ED. Neurological ED and vascular ED are mostly types in forensic medical identification.

Evaluation of Body Movement Function

Measurement of neck and waist motion activity is a basic examination in forensic medical identification, because these measurement results correspond to the degree of damage and the specific clauses in the disability grade appraisal standard, and it will directly affect the scientific and objective identification. The angles of neck and waist motion measurement include six directions of movement, respectively: forward bends, after stretching, left and right bend, and the left and right side rotation. Usually, by comparing the measured results with normal results, the loss percentage of neck and waist motion measurement could be calculated.

The measurement of limbs joint movement activity includes shoulder, elbow, wrist, hip, knee, and ankle. By measuring the activities of the damaged joint, divided by the motion of the normal results, then multiplied by the weight coefficient (the weight coefficient of shoulder, elbow, and wrist are 0.7, 0.12, and 0.18, respectively; the weight coefficient of hip, knee, and ankle are 0.6, 0.28, and 0.12, respectively). Finally, the function loss of single limb movement can be calculated. But the degree of limb movement function loss is not completely equal to limb joint function. Peripheral nerve injury can cause body muscle loss, but does not effect the passive joints movement activity. Based on this, joint movement activity and muscle strength are used as indexes to evaluate the joint function. At the same time, they are used in order to make up for reliance on computing loss of mobility of joint function, and the method of scoring according to the calculated results directly is adopted to evaluate joint function loss ratio.

23.3.5 Laboratory Tests

Laboratory tests are part of the in vivo inspection to examine and evaluate the examinee's organ function through special techniques or equipment in the in vivo inspection process. In China, common forensic clinical laboratory test items include radiographic examinations (e.g., X-ray, CT, and MRI), ultrasound imaging tests (e.g., B-mode ultrasound and color ultrasonography), and neuron-evoked electromyograms (e.g., visual-evoked potentials, auditory-evoked potentials, somatosensory-evoked potentials, and motor-evoked potentials), based on which the examiner makes an objective assessment of the visual, hearing, male sexual, and physical functions after the traumatic incident in combination with the primary injury in the examinee.

Because the reliability of the inspection results of visual and hearing functions relies on the technical proficiency of the examiner and the level of cooperativeness of the examinee, the examiner should be very careful to use the inspection report provided by the medical institution; furthermore, it is usually required that the inspection performer, who is specialized in the aforementioned professional field, has the basic proficiency of analyzing the inspection report. In examination practices, in addition to the fact that medical institutions with a high technical level should be selected to perform the test, it is also encouraged to appropriately increase the number of repeated tests when necessary to ensure the accuracy and reliability of the test results.

23.4 Standards of the Clinical Forensic Judicial Examination of Human Injury and Damage

23.4.1 Overview of the Assessment of the Extent of Human Injury and Disability Level

In China, the extent of human injury and disability level assessments are two important components of the clinical forensic judicial examination.

Here, the extent of injury includes major injuries, minor injuries, and slight injuries, the assessment of which provides evidence for the trial of criminal cases. At present, the assessment of the degree of injury in the clinical forensic judicial examination is conducted in accordance with "The appraisal standards of the degree of human injuries" jointly promulgated on January 1, 2014 by the Supreme People's Court, the Supreme People's Procuratorate, the Ministry of Public Security, the National Security Agency, and the Ministry of Justice of the People's Republic of China.

In China, the examination in civil cases of the injury incident is mainly based on the forensic assessment of the level of disability and the work loss period, rehabilitation period, and nutrition period (the "three-period" examination). The disability level examination provides the basis for the court to decide the civil liability and civil compensation. The contents of the examination include the assessment of the disability grade of road traffic accidents, work injuries, medical malpractice, and the "three-period" examination after the injury. At present, the standards of the examination of the disability grade and the "three-period" examination include (1) GB 18667–2002 "Assessment of the disability grade of injuries from road traffic accident" (national standards); (2) GB/T 16180–2014 "Assessment of the work ability—Assessment of the grade of work injuries and occupational diseases" (national standards); (3) "Assessment of the disability grade from medical injury (malpractice)" (ministerial standards); and (4) GA/T 1193–2014 "Provisions of the assessment of the loss of work period, rehabilitation period and nutrition period after personal injury" (the industry standard). In addition to the assessment of the common anatomical structure and physiological dysfunction of the injured party, the examiner also needs to evaluate the causal relationship between the disability grade and the primary injury based on the standard "Provision of forensic medical examination of injuries and diseases" (SJB-C-6-2009, ministerial provision) compiled by the Institute of Forensic Science of the Ministry of Justice.

23.4.2 Assessment of the Grade of Disability of the Injured in Road Traffic Accidents

In China, road traffic accidents refer to injuries that happen to vehicle drivers, pedestrians, passengers, and other persons in the road and road traffic activity-related persons. The standard of the grade of disability assessment of the injured is based on "Assessment of the disability grade of injuries from road traffic accident" (national standard), which consists of five chapters. Chapters 1–3 are mainly about the scope, definition, and general principle of the assessment, Chapter 4 covers specific items of the grade of disability, and Chapter 5 discusses supplementary provisions, which are the supplementary remarks on the relevant issues in the assessment process to facilitate the implementation of the standard.

"Assessment of the disability grade of injuries from road traffic accident" is the standard that is specifically applicable to disability evaluation of the injured from road traffic accidents and divides the degree of the injury into 10 levels, from level 1 (100 %) to level 10 (10 %), based on the condition of the injuries from road traffic accidents. Each of the levels is arranged based on the order of brain, spinal cord, and peripheral nerve injuries, head and facial injuries, spinal injuries, neck injuries, abdominal injuries, pelvic injuries, perineal injuries, and whole body skin injuries. The standard has two appendices, of which Appendix A explains in detail the grading basis of disability in each of the injury levels and Appendix B provisions the comprehensive calculation methods and specific formulas of the compensation for multiple disabilities. The calculation method calculates the actual amount of compensation for the victim based on the total amount of disability compensation, the liability coefficient, and the compensation index. For those who are injured with multiple injuries, the disability level of the most severe injury is used as the basis of the compensation, with each additional disability injury, a certain compensation proportion is also added, but the total compensation proportion of the additional compensation cannot exceed 10 %. Therefore, in the evaluation of the disability derived from road traffic accidents in China, it is necessary to assess the disability level of each of the injuries on the victim's body.

23.4.3 Examination of the Work Ability, Disability Grading of Work-Related Injuries, and Occupational Diseases

In China, the evaluation of disability from work-related accidents requires the forensic medical examiner's judgment of the loss of work ability (disability degree) and the degree of self-care impediment (care level) after the worker suffers from a work-related injury or occupational disease based on the relevant medical examination and the national standards. The assessment of the disability level of work-related accidents is conducted based on the four aspects of organ damage, dysfunction, medical dependency, and care dependency, which are divided into five categories by "Standard for identifying work ability—gradation of disability caused by work-related injuries and occupational diseases" according to the relationship between the clinical specialties and disciplines: (1) neurology, neurosurgery, and psychiatry; (2) orthopedics, plastic surgery, and burn unit; (3) ophthalmology, otolaryngology, and dentistry; (4) general surgery, thoracic surgery, and genitourinary unit; and (5) occupational medicine. According to the above five categories, the disability levels of work-related accidents are divided into 572 terms of the 10 levels based on "organ damage, dysfunction, medical dependency, care dependency, and mental disorder," with level 1 as the most severe and level 10 as the mildest. Victims with disability levels 1–4 have entirely lost the ability to work, those with disability levels 5–6 have lost most of their work ability, and disability levels 7–10 have partially lost their work ability. Work-related disability assessments should be performed after the completion of the medical treatment; in the case of multiple injuries or the coexistence of injury and disability, the injuries and the disabilities should be individually assessed based on the examination standards. When the levels of the multiple disabilities are different, the most severe level of disability is used to grade, and the level can be upgraded when there are more than two disabilities that have the same grade; however, this upgrade is limited to one level above. The assessments of the medical and care dependencies are performed based on the circumstances after the level of disability is determined. The evaluation of the mental disorders needs to be performed by qualified professionals of forensic psychiatrics. When assessing the level of disability, the effect of the original injuries and diseases on the consequences of the new injury and the causation should be taken into account.

23.4.4 Assessment of the Disability Level of Medical Injuries (Malpractice)

In China, assessments of disabilities derived from medical mistakes must first assess the medical malpractice, in which the forensic or medical doctors determine the liability after the investigation of the case, the autopsy (in mortal cases) or physical examination, laboratory equipment inspections, inspection of the medical history documents, and listening to the testimony of witnesses and the statements of the involved parties and family members. The relevant clinical medicine experts in the medical malpractice related field are consulted; combining the opinion of the clinical experts, the forensic doctor (examiner) assesses the facts regarding whether there is medical malpractice and whether a causal relationship between the medical malpractice and the consequence of the damage exists. In some cases, the court may require the forensic doctor to provide the contribution proportion of the medical malpractice-caused damage in the total consequences of the injury.

At present, there is a lack of a nationally unified assessment standard for injuries and disabilities caused by medical malpractice in China; therefore, in civil cases of medical injury, the damage and disability caused by medical malpractice should be assessed according to the standards "Standard for identifying work ability—gradation of disability caused by work-related injuries and occupational diseases" and "Assessment of the disability grade of injuries from road traffic accident."

23.4.5 Assessment of the Work Loss, Rehabilitation, and Nutrition Periods

The rest period refers to the time period that is required for the injured to be cured (clinical symptoms and physical signs disappear), generally recognized by clinical medicine after treatment, also known as the work loss period in China. During the rest period, the injured cannot engage in normal work, study, and other activities. The rest period includes the treatment period and rehabilitation period. The treatment period refers to the time the victim spends in hospital for clinical treatment until being clinically cured, which is generally based on the time of hospitalization. The rehabilitation period refers to the time period for which the injured needs the care of others, as required by the needs of treatment and rehabilitation after the injury, which generally starts from the time of injury to the time the injured acquires self-care capability. The nutrition period refers to the time period after the injury when a normal daily diet cannot fully meet the requirements of the body's recovery, and special diet and proper nutrient supplements must be supplied. After the injured party is clinically stable, the nutrition supplement can be stopped.

23.4.6 Analysis of Causal Relationship Between Injury and Disease

In damage appraisal and disability grade appraisal, the analysis of the causal relationship between injury and disease is usually required. Actually, it is the analysis of the causal force between external injury factors and the consequence of the damage. In accordance with the "classification of the international function and diseases," in the course of forensic clinical identification, the casual force is divided into six kinds of circumstances, namely, no effect, slight effect, secondary effect, same effect, primary effect, and complete effect, and use degree of participation to quantify casual force. The specific methods are: (1) No effect: there is no causal relationship between external injury factors and damage consequence, the degree of participation lies 0–4 %, the average value is 0 %. (2) Slight effect: there is an indirect causal relationship (incentive form) between external injury factors and damage consequence, the degree of participation lies between 5 and 15 %, the average value is 12.5 %. (3) Secondary effect: there is an indirect causal relationship (auxiliary form) between external injury factors and damage consequence, the degree of participation lies between 16 %~44 %, the average value is 25 %. (4) The same effect: there is critical relationship between external injury factors and damage consequence, the degree of participation lies between 45 and 55 %, the average value is 50 %. (5) Primary effect: there is a direct causal relationship between (primary form) external injury factors and damage consequence, the degree of participation lies between 56 and 95 %, the average value is 75 %. (6) Complete effect: there is a direct causal relationship between external injury factors and damage consequence, the degree of participation lies between 96 and 100 % and the average value is 100 %.

This chapter was funded by the Council of the Natural Science Foundation of China (No. 81273339), the Council of the Natural Science Foundation of China (No. 81102305, 81571859), the Key Projects in the National Science & Technology Pillar Program during the Twelfth Five-Year Plan Period (No. 2012BAK16B01-3), and the Shanghai Key Laboratory of Forensic Medicine (No. 14DZ2270800, 14231202500).

Below are listed some general bibliographic sources useful to deepen the issue. They are not reported within the text as they are no cited references.

Bibliography

1. Black D (1998c) The limitations of evidence. J R Coll Physicians Lond 32:23
2. Brennan TA, Leape LL, Laird NM, Hebert L, Localio AR, Lawthers AG, Newhouse JP, Weiler PC, Hiatt HH (1991c) Incidence of adverse events and negligence in hospitalized patients—results of the Harvard Medical Practise Study I. N Engl J Med 324:370–376
3. Fischer G, Fetters MD, Munro AP, Goldman EB (1997c) Adverse events in primary care identified from a risk-management database. J Fam Pract 45:40–46
4. Hofer T, Herr E, Hayward R (2000c) What is an error? Eff Clin Pract 6:261–269
5. Hughes G (2009c) Litigation, redress and making amends. Emerg Med J 26:844
6. Hurwitz B (2004) How does evidence based guidance influence determinations of medical negligence? J R Coll Physicians Lond (BMJ 329:1024)
7. O'Neil AC, Petersen LA, Cook EF, Bates DW, Lee TH, Brennan TA (1993c) Physician reporting compared with medical-record review to identify adverse medical events. Ann Intern Med 119:370–376
8. Scobie S, Thomson R, McNeil JJ, Phillips PA (2006c) Measurements of the safety and quality of health care. Med J Aust 184:S51–55

Chapter 24
Methods of Ascertainment of Personal Damage in Japan

Toshiko Sawaguchi

Abstract The chapter illustrates the historical, judicial, and juridical framework of personal injury assessment and compensation in Japan, describing the expert's qualification and competences and detailing the ascertainment methodology and criteria of evaluation utilized for identifying, describing, and estimating any personal injury, its temporary and permanent consequences, and the causal value/link between the event and the injury and between the injury and the impairment/disability.

24.1 Historical, Judicial, and Juridical Overview

The Japanese Research Association of Compensation Medicine was established in 1982 in Japan. It was renamed as the Japanese Society of Compensation Medicine in 1984 and was further renamed as the Japanese Society of Compensation Science in 1997. It was registered under the Section 2 Social Law of the Science Council of Japan in 2000.

The purpose of the Society is to "academically study various problems in relation to compensation for damage from both the medical and juristic aspects in order to contribute to the certification of personal injury as well as to a justification of civil liability." A fairly substantial number of members of the Society are practitioners, such as professionals of forensic medicine and clinical medicine. This includes emergency medicine as well as healthcare professionals in the area of medicine and attorneys of civil law, insurance law, etc., in the areas of jurisprudence, while many are in teaching and research positions at universities. Both medical and legal professionals have reviewed and discussed the same subject over several years as CS (projects of compensation science) in the Society. It aims, particularly, at scientific contribution in the area of compensation law by

T. Sawaguchi (✉)
Department of Legal Medicine, Tokyo Women's Medical University, 8-1, Kawada-cho, Shinjuku-ku, Tokyo 162-8666, Japan
e-mail: sawaguchitoshiko@gmail.com

S.D. Ferrara et al. (eds.), *Personal Injury and Damage Ascertainment under Civil Law*, DOI 10.1007/978-3-319-29812-2_24

emphasizing practical experience in jurisprudence and medicine, without being biased only by logic.

The Society is considered as targeting knowledge in the field wider than general civil forensic medicine.

The boundary region of medicine and jurisprudence is targeted in order to handle problems mainly on occurrence of compensation for damage, indemnity, etc., to use medical and scientific knowledge for their interpretation and to achieve appropriate civil liability in personal injury.

In particular, the following have been identified as *areas of compensation problems* that require medical knowledge:

- Dispute on malpractice
- Traffic accident
- Occupational injury and illness
- Pollution
- Chemical injury

Furthermore, the following have been identified as *themes common to each of the above problem areas*:

- Etiology
- Aftereffect
- Feigned illness and whiplash
- Method to prepare clinical charts and medical certificates
- Method to prepare expert opinions as well as expert opinions in writing
- Standardization of criteria for treatment and judgment (preparation of soft laws, such as guidelines, EBM, etc.)

24.2 Legal Aspects of Tort Law Under Civil Laws

The legal basis of compensation science is mainly the tort law in Articles 709–724 of the Civil Code of Japan.

Torts are acts that infringe on the rights of others in the relation to personal life and are evaluated as bearing on prohibitive rules and orders established under the law to protect such rights, where such infringement of rights is within the purpose of protection of prohibitive rules and orders. In this case the victim, whose rights are infringed, is given a method to receive relief from the assailant (the person who commits the act of infringement) in regard to the disadvantage that occurs as a result of infringement of rights [1].

In other words, the role of tort law is fair distribution of damage between the victim and assailant to protect the victim. Fair distribution of damage in this case means fair distribution with society as the standard, rather than individual rights as the standard in the case of individualism.

Tort law under the Civil Code of Japan is characterized as follows, in comparison with various countries:

- Article 709: Under a relatively broad concept of rights, benefits worthy for legal protection (legal benefits) are covered, requiring infringement on such broad rights (concept of rights has a wider definition than Germany).
- Article 709: The fault liability principle (Verschuldensprinzip), i.e., "no fault, no liability," was adopted to compensate for free actions by a performer (influenced by the tort law on the European Continent).
- Exceptions to (2) include employer liability in Article 715 of the Civil Code and product liability in Article 3 of the Product Liability Act, which justify reasons of compensation for damage based on the principles of hazard liability and compensation liability.

Contractual obligations may or may not be consistent with due diligence under tort law. The cases are consistent when a contractor is required to take reasonable actions according to the effect of a contract such as obligation of means, obligation of diligence, and obligation of best efforts; however, they are inconsistent when the realization of specific results are not guaranteed by contract as contractual obligations, such as obligation of results.

The principle of relief is monetary compensation based on an actual cost principle or actual loss principle, while restoration to the status quo is only allowed in the case of defamation.

Tort law under Articles 709–724 of the Civil Code of Japan can be classified into:

- Torts in general
- Special torts: the burden to prove fault is converted (Articles 714, 715, and 717: occupiers' liability and Article 718) and no-fault liability (Article 717: owner liability).

Furthermore, related special laws under the Civil Code include the Automobile Accident Compensation Act and the Product Liability Act.

Four conditions need to be met for a tort to come into effect and liability for damage to occur as follows:

- A wrongful act exists. Negligence or deliberation exists in the wrongful act.
- A damage (bodily damage = economic damage + noneconomic damage; property damage) exists.
- Causality exists between the wrongful act and damage (the damage is the result of a wrongful act).
- The scope of damage to be compensated is limited to the case where causality with the wrongful act exists.

Causality under the Civil Code is considered as adequate causality, meaning that the occurrence of such results from a certain act is empirically common. Causality can be explained with its high probability. Highly probable causality means that it can be proven to the extent that it is impossible to interpolate reasonable doubts.

24.3 Extrajudicial Efforts to Resolve Disputes

Here we report specific examples mainly with a Consulting Business such as Counselling Waseda University Legal Clinic. The Legal Clinic is a course for clinical legal education at the Waseda Law School where law school students meet actual clients and learn through cases under the direction and supervision of a teacher qualified as a practicing attorney at the law firm associated with Waseda University. There are two types, including free legal consultation as a course at the Clinic (for education) and request/consultation as a normal law firm for profit. The former offers free legal consultation by a teacher with qualification of a practicing attorney and student of the Waseda Law School as part of courses at the Waseda Law School, established to develop legal professionals. The following include the areas covered:

- Consultation on civil and domestic affairs.
- Consultation for consumers such as consumer damage, consultation on conflicts over an apartment complex, and consultation for foreigners are also available.

Japan Legal Support Center

The Japan Legal Support Center (JLSC) was established as the central organization to provide legal assistance to citizens, based on the goal to "realize a society where legal information and services are accessible anywhere in the country." The JLSC constitutes one of the three pillars of Japan's "judicial reform." The JLSC is a public corporation established according to the frameworks of Incorporated Administrative Agencies under the Comprehensive Legal Support Act. The mission of the JLSC is to promptly and properly implement operations related to comprehensive legal support.

With the aim of creating a society where necessary information and services for legal solutions of disputes on both civil and criminal are universally available throughout Japan, the JLSC facilitates the use of the court and legal system for the legal resolution of disputes and promptly, properly, and effectively manages operations that provide comprehensive assistance for citizens to readily access services offered by attorneys at law, legal professional corporations, and judicial scriveners as well as other related legal experts and specialists (parties or persons who are not attorneys at law or legal professional corporations, but who are authorized to engage in the practice of handling other persons' legal affairs based on laws). The contents of its business are information services, civil legal aid, services for areas with insufficient legal services, crime victim support, services related to court-appointed defense counsel, and entrusted operations.

Briefing Sessions

Briefing sessions are held and may be publicly transmitted, in some cases, as a method for organizations and agencies as parties at fault, such as hospitals, railway companies, airline companies, etc., to communicate with sincerity with victims who have suffered personal injury and damage and in order to make efforts to shed lights on the facts.

Medical Safety Support Centers
Medical safety support centers have been established in each prefecture as well as cities or special wards where health centers were established around 2003. They have been legislated with revision of the Medical Service Act in 2006 and further established in the secondary medical district as well. There are approximately 400 centers nationwide. Medical safety support centers provide consultation on complaints, inquiries, and questions of patients in regard to medical care and at the same time provide information and advice.

Extrajudicial Agencies and Systems to Resolve Disputes for Each Type of Personal Injury and Damage Mediation of Civil Affairs
It is a method to mediate conciliation so as to attempt resolution based on agreement by the parties.

Arbitration and Mediation System by a Bar Association
Arbitration is a method for both parties to entrust dispute resolution to the judgment of an arbitrator to resolve disputes at the discretion of the arbitrator. Each bar association has been implementing a dispute resolution center. ADR (alternative dispute resolution) has also been implemented in accordance with the Act on Promotion of Use of Alternative Dispute Resolution (ADR Act). They are mediation/intermediation centers certified by the Minister of Justice, and one or more attorneys undertake discussions. Examination lasts several months and ends earlier than lawsuits, and the costs are also low, which are advantageous to the victim. This path is frequently used for medical disputes in particular. Even in the case that the dispute does not ultimately reach resolution, it often concludes in a favorable manner by organizing the points in dispute. For example, medical ADR comprised of three bar associations in Tokyo does not address cases in bitter disputes, where the point in dispute is the existence of consideration, but only handles cases where the amount of damage is alone under dispute and quick resolution is the aim.

Ombudsman
Bridge between an assailant and victim; however its limitation has been pointed out.

Dispute Settlement System within an Assailant Organization
Some kind of neutral settlement committee has been established by each prefectural medical association in regard to dispute on malpractice, while disadvantages include difficulties in obtaining consent from the patient (joining a medical association is optional in Japan).

Obstetric Care Compensation System
To tackle the problem of insufficiency in the number of obstetricians and ensure a system that provides basic obstetric care, the obstetric care compensation system was established as part of a drive toward environmental maintenance so as to ensure proper obstetric care. There are three objectives, as follows. Financial burdens due to children with severe brain paralysis, occurring in relation to childbirth, and borne by their families, are promptly compensated. Causes of onset of brain paralysis are

analyzed to provide information to serve as prevention of similar cases. Attempts are made for dispute prevention, early resolution, and quality improvement of obstetric care based on the above.

The Japan Council for Quality Health Care, being the organization in charge of this system, handles the enrolment childbirth facilities in the system, the insurance subscription, the collection of premiums, the certification of eligible compensation, the long-term payment of compensation money (insurance claim procedure), the cause analysis and recurrence prevention, etc. Childbirth facilities enrolled in this system promise compensation for all childbirths they manage after the beginning date of compensation. Childbirth facilities also report the number of childbirths they handle to the management organization and pay the relevant premiums. When eligible compensation is certified by the managing organization, the insurance company pays the insurance to the guardian of the child in the form of monetary compensation. This is a system that childbirth facilities enroll in, and premiums for compensation are paid by childbirth facilities.

Compensation is paid in the case that all of the following standards are met. Applicable standards are as follows, to be claimed when the child reaches 5 years of age.

If the birth weight is 1400 g or more and the gestational age is 32 weeks or longer, or the gestational age is 28 weeks or longer, then (1) or (2) in the following is relevant.

- Metabolic acidosis (acidemia) is recognized in umbilical arterial blood due to sustenance of a hypoxic condition (pH value is <7.1).
- A hypoxic condition is caused due to placental abruption, cord prolapse, uterus rupture, eclampsia, fetal-maternal transfusion syndrome, bleeding from placenta previa, sudden onset of twin-to-twin transfusion syndrome, etc., that subsequently accompany one of the following findings from (i) to (chi):

(i) Idiopathic and persistent bradycardia.
(ro) Late deceleration that appears in 50 % or more of contraction.
(ha) Variable deceleration that appears in 50 % or more of contraction.
(ni) Loss of heart rate—baseline variability.
(ho) Severe bradycardia that accompanies decrease in heart rate—baseline variability.
(he) Sinusoidal pattern.
(to) 1-min Apgar score is 3 or less.
(chi) Blood gas analysis value for a child within one hour after birth (pH value is <7.0).

The following standards are not eligible for compensation:

- Brain paralysis not caused by any one of the following:

Innate factors (such as genetic abnormality)
Factors during the neonatal period (such as infectious disease after childbirth)

Willful or material negligence of a pregnant woman during pregnancy or childbirth

- Natural disasters including earthquake, eruption, and tsunami as well as emergencies, such as war and riot. Death within 6 months after birth is not eligible for compensation.
- In addition, the standard of severity needs to be available, and brain paralysis equivalent to grades 1 or 2 of the disability level, for physically disabled people, needs to be certified, according to the standard of disability level for severe brain paralysis stipulated by the management organization.

Pharmaceuticals and Medical Devices Agency

Pharmaceuticals and Medical Devices Agency (PMDA) is a Japanese regulatory agency, working together with the Ministry of Health, Labour and Welfare. Its obligation is to protect public health by ensuring safety, efficacy, and quality of pharmaceuticals and medical devices.

It conducts scientific reviews of marketing authorization application of pharmaceuticals and medical devices, monitoring their post-marketing safety. It is also responsible for providing relief compensation for sufferers of adverse drug reaction and infections from pharmaceuticals or biological products.

Following the Reorganization and Rationalization Plan for Special Public Corporations that was approved in a Cabinet meeting in 2001, the PMDA was established and came into service on April 1, 2004, under the Law for the Pharmaceuticals and Medical Devices Agency.

Their contents of services are:

- Drug and medical device reviews
- Post-marketing safety
- Relief services for adverse health effects
- International programs
- Promotion of regulatory science

Although utilized very frequently, difficult problems on the patient's part can remain, including the case where a lawsuit and a claim to the Council progress in parallel, beside the response, to a physician in the case of inappropriate use of drugs.

Business to Report Accident Investigation

A business to investigate medical accidents is organized in regard to medical accidents.

When a medical accident/damage occurs, the patient desires a sincere response and explanation from the medical provider to help the decision-making of the patient him-/herself. Investigations of medical accidents are conducted by the medical accident investigation committee within the medical facility where the accident occurs in the form of joint efforts with a third-party agency, external professional, and patient/family, in principle. A business to collect reports on medical accidents began in 2004 under the Enforcement Regulation of Medical Service Act, to examine measures to prevent recurrence discussed by the institutional committee in accordance with investigation results of the accident for effective utilization in the future. National medical institutions, university hospitals, advanced treatment hospitals, etc., report accident information to the Council for Quality Health Care within 2 weeks. Factors of accident occurrence, factors relating to the patient, emergency treatment, causes of the accident, the situation of accident verification, improvement measures, etc., are to be reported. A hospital accredited by the Council must report improvement measures within 45 days after the accident.

Other Third-Party Agencies that Will Be Needed in the Future

Two parties have already been suggested as follows in regard to the subject matter:

- Third-party agency that takes care of prompt and simplified procedures for compensation to victims
- Third-party agency that conducts forensic autopsy as requested by a bereaved family or a medical institution upon consent from a bereaved family in relation to medical care-related death and reports autopsy results to both parties, both the patient and medical provider

Regarding the latter, a model project has been implemented by the Ministry of Health, Labour and Welfare as the foundation of such third-party agency, and a model project for research and analysis of death relating to a medical act has been implemented by the Japanese Society of Internal Medicine as the operating body since September, 2005. Their purpose is to enhance the quality and safety of medical care, ensure transparency of medical care through notification of autopsy results, and ensure reliability. An autopsy is conducted in the presence of each coroner of forensic medicine and pathology as well as a clinician. A case is reviewed after autopsy by a local evaluation committee comprised of a clinical specialist, a planning nurse, and a lawyer; and a report of evaluation results is prepared within approximately 6 months after first acceptance. The determination rate of the actual cause of death is reported to be approximately 10 %.

24.4 Identification and Description of Medicolegal Expert's Qualifications

As a premise, forensic medicine is defined by the Japanese Society of Legal Medicine as follows.

The purpose of forensic medicine is to contribute to the protection of the basic human rights of individuals, to a safe society, and maintenance of welfare by making scientific and fair medical decisions in regard to legal cases and matters that require medical interpretation and advice.

A member of the Japanese Society of Legal Medicine would state an expert opinion in relation to forensic medicine under this definition. However, a system of clinical forensic medicine has not been established in Japan and a considerable number of members of the Japanese Society of Legal Medicine do not have a medical qualification. Each of them states his/her opinion as a professional, or private clinicians suitable for respective cases state their opinions in some cases. There are also cases where professionals who belong to the National Research Institute of Police Science, the Metropolitan Police Department in Tokyo, or crime laboratories at prefectural police stations in each local government retire and open a laboratory to specialize in expert opinions privately provided for profit.

Systems of medical specialists in the Japanese Society of Legal Medicine include the system to certify doctors of forensic medicine and the examination doctor system of forensic medicine.

These systems began from 2009, and supervising doctors of forensic medicine are certified by accredited doctors of forensic medicine when the Society affirms that they have reached the goals of the Society in terms of acquisition and practice of knowledge, skills, and capacity to train and guide certified doctors of forensic medicine (Article 5 of the regulation on the system for certifying doctors by the Japanese Society of Legal Medicine). There is also a system to certify honorable forensic doctors.

The above includes all systems for professionals in the Japanese Society of Legal Medicine, and there is no training of professionals or issuance of specific qualifications for personal damage in particular or depending on specific extrajudicial or judicial objectives.

On-site visits are accepted, and training is provided at the Medical Examiner's Office (Tokyo, Osaka, and Kobe) as necessary in regard to administrative external examination and administrative autopsy, and training is also provided to staff at a forensic class of a medical school at each university.

24.4.1 Association of Medical and Medicolegal Experts in both Extrajudicial and Judicial Contexts

Involvement by Stating Verbal Opinions

Professional members are court personnel with tenure of 2 years whose task is to explain about general matters with professional knowledge. They are different from experts, in the sense that their opinions do not become part of judicial materials or simplified expert opinions.

In the case of attempting conciliation, the professional member system and professional mediator system are often utilized if medical experts are needed in the attempt to proceed to a process of resolution by agreement.

Professional members can be utilized to listen to explanations based on professional knowledge also in the case of reconciliation.

Professional members were essentially implemented in the system in order to provide medical knowledge for the solid organization of points in dispute, the organization of evidence, and the procedure for investigating evidence in general.

Consent from parties in a lawsuit is also required, in the case of lawsuits involving professional members, for them to ask questions for investigation of evidence and to be involved in conciliation. In addition, a court utilizes professional members who are doctors as general advisors or to help representatives of the patient (victim) with extremely poor professional medical knowledge. There are also cases where the representatives of healthcare providers indicate doubts as to the involvement of professional members who are doctors. It is common for professional members who are doctors to respond by answering questions presented by parties in advance, upon organization of the points in dispute.

If the content stated by a professional member in the judicial system as a judicial material is to be made use of, a literature or statement by a cooperating doctor is newly submitted.

A person registered as a professional member often stands in a courtroom as an expert witness by submitting an expert opinion in writing in the role of an expert in the judicial system or otherwise states verbal opinions as a cooperating doctor for similar or related cases in the extrajudicial system.

In the extrajudicial system, a cooperating doctor verbally states professional knowledge, or a person registered as a professional member often gives verbal opinions as a cooperating doctor for similar or related cases in the extrajudicial system.

Involvement as a Preparer of a Private Opinion in Writing

Both sides, namely, the patient (victim) and medical care provider (assailant), are able to submit private opinions in writing by a medical expert, describing professional medical findings.

Private opinions in writing by doctors can be submitted from the early stage in both cases through extrajudicial system and judicial system, while it is effective to submit them when points in dispute regarding liability and causality are clarified to some extent.

Private opinions in writing are often considered, such as documents prepared by a doctor who provides favorable opinions in relation to a fee-paying party, and it is important to consider to what extent materials, etc., are reviewed. It is possible, in the context of the judicial system, to submit private opinions in writing in parallel to expert opinions in writing. However, supplemental opinions by experts are often attached.

24.4.2 Association of Medical and Medicolegal Experts in Extrajudicial Context

Mediators can be doctors or other medical experts in the case of civil mediation.

24.4.3 Association of Medical and Medicolegal Experts in Judicial Contexts

Professional Lay Judge System

When professional knowledge on medicine is supplemented, a system utilizing professionals such as doctors who participate as legal professionals in lawsuits, in addition to judges, is adopted in Japan, instead of appointing a judge with medical qualifications. A department that specializes in cases relating to medical affairs is established in major district courts, to which professionals such as doctors are assigned [2].

Involvement as an Expert

It is considered possible to maintain neutrality of experts in the procedure of expert opinions conducted by a court (Articles 214, 216, and 201-1 of the Code of Civil Procedure). A court stipulates matters for expert opinions (Regulation 129 of the Code of Civil Procedure). An expert opinion is only one of the methods of evidence, and evaluation or adoption of the results of an expert opinion is under free evaluation of evidence by a court [3].

Questioning of an expert currently begins with a statement of verbal opinions by the expert, followed by questioning on the order of the judge, the party requesting the expert opinion, and the other party. The content of questions is limited to clarification of the expert's opinion and confirmation of the grounds only (Regulation 132-4-1 of the Code of Civil Procedure).

Pool of Experts in the Medical Malpractice Litigation Committee

The medical malpractice litigation committee (comprised of doctors and legal professionals) was organized within the Supreme Court in 2001, and candidates of appropriate experts have been recommended by each academic society. Furthermore, an extensive network has been incorporated between the Supreme Court and District Court in order to recommend experts.

Method of Expert Opinions

In the past, an expert opinion was limited to one expert only, and multiple experts were selected only when revising expert opinions.

There is currently a method to select multiple experts from the beginning and order an expert opinion from each of them as well as a method for multiple experts to verbally present expert opinions in a roundtable courtroom.

Even when multiple experts are simultaneously selected in the case of (a), expert opinions can be verbal or in writing.

24.5 Ascertainment Methodology

A medicolegal system of clinical forensic medicine to evaluate personal injury and damage has not been established in Japan. People who are engaged in forensic medicine individually come to ascertainment through their own examination activities as police surgeons or medical examiners, or in the practice of four types of forensic autopsy, including administrative autopsy, forensic consent autopsy, new law autopsy, and judicial autopsy.

Clinical forensic medicine in Japan has usually been handled by police surgeons as well as clinicians requested by the police. The former normally execute a contract with the police to manage people in the custody of police which is also utilized for examination. Although the ascertainment methodology used by clinicians is not always reflected in the calculation of compensation for damage or indemnity in the case of civil lawsuits, it is internationally used, including one of the examples below. Other than protocols commonly used by coroners and clinicians or routine methods to obtain general findings, those which are deeply related to personal injury and damage and are likely to be reflected in compensation for damage, as well as in indemnity and security in the future, are particularly noted.

24.5.1 International Classification of Functioning, Disability, and Health

The "International Classification of Functioning, Disability, and Health" (ICF) was adopted as a revision of ICIDH at the 54th WHO general meeting in 2001 when the existing classification of ICD with etiology → pathology → manifestation (disease) was considered as insufficient and the need to analyze manifestation → impairment → disability → handicap was indicated [4]. With the ICF, positive aspects of disability are emphasized and understood at three levels of "functional and structural impairments," "activity restrictions," and "participation restrictions."

Medical professionals engaging in rehabilitation, such as occupational therapists (OT) and physiological therapists (PT), are not allowed to run independent medical practices in Japan; they therefore practice medical care under the instruction of doctors. Medical accidents in this type of occupation are rare, and ICF used by OT and PT as the index of injury is infrequently reflected in compensation for damage in civil cases of medical accidents in the area involving rehabilitation medicine. ICF as the guidepost of injury is referenced upon creating a treatment menu of rehabilitation, while many doctors seem to consider that it is not fully effective for direct determination of disability level. In the area of rehabilitation medicine, ICF is considered as a concept that is likely to be linked with social security rather than compensation for damage.

ICF relates to compensation for damage in the area of care welfare, welfare for the disabled, etc., and may be applied when compensation is necessary as a result of providing welfare services. In addition, the disability grade in the event that the Automobile Liability Security Act is applied to disability and residual disability resulting from accidents during transport, as well as the disability grade in physical disability, intellectual disability, and mental disability under the public pension system, is not consistent in Japan. In order to avoid unfair opinions due to such inconsistent disability grades, ICF could be used as a standard scale.

24.5.2 Collection of Concrete Data for Personal Injury

In order to determine damage suffered as a result of a traffic accident or medical error, various types of clinicians are involved in each case, most often to collect clinical data. Usually patients with personal damage are carried to hospitals by ambulances, and it is possible that provision is made in Japan for a medical examination for personal injury ascertainment via special medical certificates for aftereffects of the accident made by clinicians. Here, medicolegal doctors are generally not included among these clinicians.

To issue medical certificates concerning possible aftereffects of the accident, the following medical information is required:

- Name, sex, date of birth, age, address, and occupation of patient
- Date and time of the accident
- Date and time without possibility for improvement of symptoms by any medical treatment
- Period under medical treatment with and without hospitalization and/or attending outpatient clinic
- Name of damage and disease, case, or medical history
- Subjective symptoms
- Aftereffects at each area

Neurological and mental symptoms (objective symptoms and results of medical tests) including neurological findings (perception, reflexes, muscular atrophy, etc.); results of mental tests including intelligence test and psychological test; results of X-ray, CT, and EEG; and disturbance of the eye, ear, and limbs

Disturbance of internal organs of the chest, abdomen, and urogenital area including degree of function disorder and concrete symptoms with biochemical test tables and blood test tables

Disturbance of eyes and eyelids including acuity, visual adjustment function, visual field defects with visual field table, diplopia, eye movement (disturbance of eye attention), deficit of eyelid with figures, baldness of eyelashes, disturbance in closing of eyes, and causes of eye symptoms

Disturbance of ears and auricle with audiogram, including hard of hearing, level of auditory capacity, defect of auricle with figures, and tinnitus

Disturbance of nose including deficit of nasal cartilage, difficulty of nasal respiration, and deficit or decrease in sense of smell

Disturbance of chewing and language disorder, including causes and degree

Poor general condition, including appearance, limbs, face, neck, etc., with figures

Disturbance of the vertebra including pressure fracture and dislocation with or without vertebrectomy, laminectomy, spinal fusion, and fixation, disturbance of movement of cervical vertebrae and chest/abdominal vertebrae with angles and directions, and disturbance of load function with or without necessity of corset

Deformation of the body trunk including the clavicle, limbs, face bones, cervical vertebrae, etc.

Disturbance of limbs and fingers including shortening of lower limbs, causes, sites, deformation of long bones including callus and malunion with X-ray film and sites

Deficit of limbs and fingers with site description

Disturbance of joint function including name of joints, kinds of movements, subjective findings, and objective findings

Outlook in terms of worsening and improvement

As general physical examinations, the following are measured and investigated, but are not decided upon officially and depend on each clinician:

- Range of motion (ROM)
- Length of limbs including spinal malleolar distance (SMD)
- Length of circumference of limbs and comparison between right side and left side
- Manual muscle testing (MMT) with five levels
- Perception examination including two-point discrimination
- Test of reflex including deep tendon reflex, superficial reflex, and pathological reflex

As the locoregional examination, the following are performed, but these are not decided officially and depend on each clinician.

For functional disturbance:

- Range of motion (ROM)
- Manual muscle testing (MMT)
- Brunnstrom recovery stages (BS or BRS)
- Modified Ashworth Scale
- Stroke Impairment Assessment Set (SIAS)
- Visual analogue scale (VAS)
- Ratings of Perceived Exertion (RPE)

For functional restriction:

- Functional Reach (FR)
- Functional Balance Scale (FBS)
- Timed "Up and Go" (TUG) test
- Manual Function Test (MFT)
- Simple Test for Evaluating Hand Function (STEF)
- Maximum walking speed (MWS)
- 6-min walking distance (6MD)
- Physiological Cost Index (PCI)
- Incremental shuttle walking test (ISWT)
- Motor Assessment Scale (MAS)

For activities of daily living (ADL):

- Barthel Index (BI)
- Functional Independence Measure (FIM)
- TMIG Index of Competence
- Instrumental activities of daily living (IADL)

These examinations are structured with visual examination, palpation, image diagnosis, laboratory tests, biopsy, and physiological tests.

24.5.3 Clinical Visit and Flow for Authorization of Classified Degree of Physical Impediment

In the process of compensation of damage, the separate claim is needed before and after the date and time without possibility for the improvement of symptoms by any medical treatment.

After the accident has occurred and before the date and time without possibility for improvement of symptoms by any medical treatment, payment for medical treatments, traffic costs, nursery costs, costs for hospitalization, direct business interruption coverage, and mental compensation for hospitalization and admission to outpatients clinic can be paid. After the date and time without possibility for the improvement of symptoms by any medical treatment, compensation for imputed loss of income, mental compensation for physical impediments, care fee, etc., can be paid. Different claims are needed by claimants (sufferers) in relation to both.

In both processes, clinical visits are required prior to the claim.

Claimants (sufferers) must send the aforementioned medical certificate for physical impediments to an insurance company, which sends said information, including a medical certificate, to the Non-Life Insurance Rating Organization of Japan (nonprofit organization). The Non-Life Insurance Rating Organization of Japan sends the result of investigation to the insurance company, which sends the claimants the authorized result regarding the classified degree of physical impediment.

Before and after the date and time when no improvement of the symptoms is possible, clinical visits are required. Also in the case that sufferers cannot obtain an authorized result of a classified degree of physical impediment, clinical visits are also needed.

As for the tables of national references, the following exist:

- Table of degree classifications, containing each of the physical impediments with loss rates of working ability
- Abridged time table
- Table of annuity value with Leibniz's rule and new Hoffman's rule
- Cost sheet with Leibniz's rule and new Hoffman's rule
- Wages Census with annual exempt amount

24.5.4 *Trials of the Japanese Association for the Surgery of Trauma*

The Japanese Association for the Surgery of Trauma is operating for the purpose of "contributing to the progress and development of traumatology and related areas and at the same time to preserving the lives and health of Japanese people, through collection, provision, and exchange of information on traumatology."

The trauma registry handled by the Association was explained in the above, and other categories include the following. (The Japan Society of Neurotraumatology is operating the databank of head injuries as a similar attempt.)

A. *Classification of organ damage*

One of the following is described for the site of each organ, in order to describe organ damage. Each site is stipulated depending on the organ.

- Type I: Subcapsular injury
  - (a) Subcapsular hematoma
  - (b) Intraparenchymal hematoma
- Type II: Superficial injury
- Type III: Deep injury
  - (a) Simple deep injury
  - (b) Complex deep injury

B. *Classification of head injury*

It was developed as a common language in the place of joint treatment for a trauma surgeon in charge of primary care, an emergency doctor, and a neurosurgeon upon visit by emergency patients with head injury. It was prepared mainly with clinical symptoms and findings from image tests such as CT, x-rays, etc., in the acute stage, based on the Gennarelli classification. Minor cases include hospital admission for observation, and moderate cases include admission followed by follow-up observation under strict control, or a condition to consider a preventive surgical procedure and intracranial pressure monitor. Serious cases include a situation on the premise of intensive treatment, such as a surgical procedure and intracranial pressure monitor. Serious cases are promptly examined by a neurosurgeon. For local brain injury, in this classification, external force affecting a specific site of the cranium becomes the basis of neurologic symptoms, including cerebral contusion, acute extradural hematoma, acute subdual hematoma, and intracerebral hematoma. For diffuse brain injury, primary brain injury and secondary brain injury due to rotating external force or acceleration become the basis of neurologic symptoms, including diffuse brain injury, subarachnoid bleeding, and diffuse brain swelling. Diffuse brain injury is mainly due to primary brain injury.

A thickness of at least 1 cm, at least 20 mL on the tentorium, hematoma with at least 3 cm diameter, broad contusion edema, and loss of basal cistern or perimesencephalic cistern are evaluated from CT findings in order to determine need for surgery.

- Psychic
- Osteoarticular and musculoskeletal
- Specific (local examination of the injured area/areas)
- Additional investigations

Trauma Scores: Prediction of Severity and Prognosis in the Case of Trauma

AIS (Abbreviated Injury Scale)

It is designed in the United States for the purpose of utilization as an extensive database on automobile accidents and was published in 1971. The AIS expresses types of trauma and anatomical severity with codes, which is evaluated in six stages (Fig. 24.1).

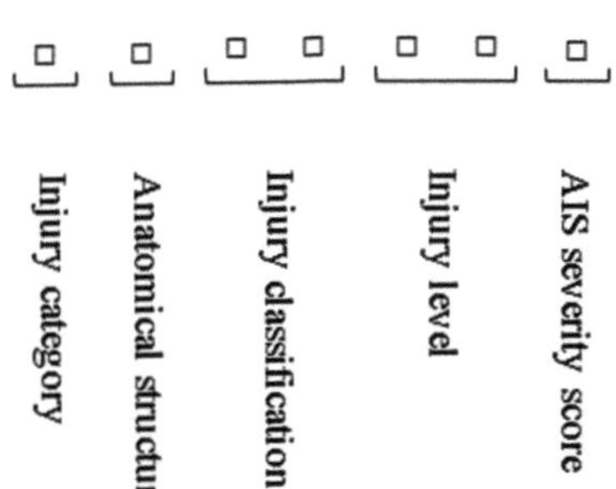

AIS code	Injury level
1	Minor
2	Moderate
3	Serious
4	Severe
5	Critical
6	Maximum (substantia impossible to rescue)

Fig. 24.1 Abbreviated Injury Scale (AIS)

ISS (Injury Severity Score)

Severity of multiple injuries is evaluated on the basis of the AIS, and the injured sites are divided into six categories including the (1) head and neck, (2) face, (3) chest, (4) abdomen and pelvic organ, (5) limbs and pelvis, and (6) body surface. The three highest AIS severity scores for each site are extracted and each of them is squared and added for evaluation. The highest value is 75 points.

- ISS 15 or higher indicates serious or increasing severity, and inpatient treatment and follow-up observation is necessary.
- ISS 25–34 indicates higher than 30 % mortality, and it is reported that mortality exceeds 50 % in the case of ISS > 35.

Only anatomical evaluation is conducted with the ISS, and physiological evaluation such as vital signs is not included; therefore, it cannot be used for severity determination prior to hospitalization. (A patient who is already in a state of shock at the time of the visit cannot be distinguished from a patient whose blood pressure is maintained.)

Physiological Indices
RTS (Revised Trauma Score)

While AIS/ISS are indices based on the anatomical morphology of injury, severity based on physiological indices is evaluated with the RTS. The most critical score is 0 and the best score is 7.84 (Fig. 24.2).

Possibility of Rescue
TRISS (Trauma and Injury Severity Score)

Probability of survival (Ps) is calculated with the TRISS by adding physiological severity, anatomical severity, and age factor. Death with Ps > 0.5 is considered as

Code (score)	Awareness level (GCS)	Systolic blood pressure	Respiratory rate
4	13 – 15	90 or higher	10 – 29
3	9 – 12	76 – 89	30 or higher
2	6 – 8	50 – 75	6 – 9
1	4 – 5	1 – 49	1 - 5
0	3	0	0

RTS = 0.9368 x GCS score + 0.7326 x score of systolic blood pressure + 0.2908 x score of respiratory rate

Fig. 24.2 Revised Trauma Score (RTS)

$$Ps = 1 / (1 + e^{-b})$$

$$b = b0 + b1 \times RTS + b2 \times ISS + b3 \times \text{age score}$$

	b0 (Constant)	b1 (RTS)	b2 (ISS)	b3 (Age)
Blunt trauma	-0.4499	0.8085	-0.0835	-1.7430
Penetrating trauma	-2.5355	0.9934	-0.0651	-1.1360

Fig. 24.3 Trauma and Injury Severity Score (TRISS)

Activity	Action	Score
Eye opening	Spontaneous	E4
	To speech	3
	To pain	2
	Nil	1
Verbal response	Oriented	V1
	Confused	2
	Inappropriate word	3
	Incomprehensible sound	4
	Nil	5
Best motor response	Obeys order	M6
	Localizes the painful site	5
	Bends the limbs	
	Withdraws	4
	Abnormal flexion	3
	Extends the limbs	2
	Nil	1

Fig. 24.4 Glasgow Coma Scale (GCS)

preventable death, $0.25 \leqq Ps \leqq 0.5$ is considered as preventable trauma death (PTD), and $Ps < 0.25$ is considered as non-preventable death (Fig. 24.3).

GCS (Glasgow Coma Scale)

Response is categorized into three factors: eye opening, verbal response, and motor response. Each category is scored and the total sum is called the Glasgow Coma Scale. In the event of severity of head injury, 3–8 points are categorized into serious injury, 9–13 points are categorized into moderate injury, and 14–15 points are categorized into mild injury (Fig. 24.4).

24.6 Evaluation Criteria

24.6.1 Psychic and Somatic State Prior to the Event/Injury

When a victim claims that only an organic mental disorder existed prior to the event/injury and the court has an impression that the cause is a nonorganic mental disorder, possible certification of nonorganic mental disorder is positively interpreted, which is being recognized by more and more courts. It is difficult to determine causality between the event/injury and nonorganic mental disorder in this case; however, comprehensive determination is considered to be important by investigating the relation between the event/injury and onset as an objective factual relationship, including situation of the accident, confirmation of situation of injury and time of onset of mental symptoms, history prior to the visit to the psychiatric specialist, psychiatric diagnosis, stress factors other than the accident, medical history, etc. Furthermore, in the case that symptoms existed prior to the event/injury and still remain after the event/injury, both the influence of event/injury to the course of treatment after onset or to persistent symptoms and the influence of factors other than the event/injury are investigated for comprehensive evaluation, to determine causality with persistent symptoms.

The onset time of mental symptoms can be confirmed with the "certification standards for mental disorder from psychological burdens" [5], announced by the Bureau of Labor Standards, Ministry of Health, Labour and Welfare, on December 26, 2011.

Another issue is at what stage symptoms are considered as fixed (healed) to determine the disability grade in the case of nonorganic mental disorder. It is stipulated in the Rosai (2011) Mental Disorder Certification Standards as follows: "If medical rehabilitation was performed, this period is considered as the treatment period. At the point of completion, symptoms are normally considered as fixed (healed). Furthermore, in the case that remission is diagnosed indicating that symptoms of mental disorder do not appear or are stable under the condition that routine work is possible, it is normally considered as healed (fixed symptoms) even though medication is still continuing."

In addition, the rate/period of losing labor ability is definitively certified in many cases, since nonorganic mental disorder could be healed.

Furthermore, nonorganic mental disorder could be subject to proportional conclusion that offsets reduction in the amount due to predisposition. However, there is room for consideration in the case that involvement or nonorganic mental disorder prior to onset of the event/injury led to occurrence and expansion of the event/injury and there are competing mental factors, such as mental weakness, stress factors, etc., that exceed individual differences. In this case, factors to consider in the case of resolution with proportional offsetting include personality and character, social adequacy, stress resistance, medical history, occurrence of another mental disorder after the accident, psychogenesis, contribution level as the cause of accident, stress factors other than the accident, etc.

Cases where proportional reduction and offsetting is significant are characterized by the following:

- The damage itself is large, but the contribution level as the cause of accident is low.
- Previous mental illness is involved.
- Stress factors after the accident are involved.

The method to certify a specific disability grade includes the following:

1. *Understanding of mental symptoms*

   Disabilities remain, such as depressed state, anxious state, low motivation, chronic hallucination and delusion, disorder of memory and intelligent ability, indefinite complaints, impulsivity, etc.
2. *Evaluation criteria on abilities*

   The disability level in regard to eight abilities including personal daily activities, positive attitude in work and life, compliance with commuting and work hours, sustained work, communication with others, interpersonal relationship and cooperativeness, maintenance of personal safety, and risk avoidance as well as handling of difficulty and failure is reviewed with "unable," "needs frequent advice and assistance," and "appropriate or able in general."

Based on the evaluation results, the disability grade is certified with three stages:

- Grade 9: "Frequent advice and assistance" is required for four or more evaluation items.
- Grade 12: "Occasional advice and assistance" is required for four or more evaluation items.
- Grade 14: "Occasional advice and assistance" is required for one or more evaluation items.

24.6.2 Reconstruction of the Event/Injury

The trauma registry by the Japanese Association for the Surgery of Trauma in the above is a kind of reconstruction of the event/injury, while it is exceptionally used as the evidence data in civil lawsuits for parties. Reconstruction of the event/injury for each patient is handled by a police officer, judicial police personnel, coroner, clinician, or crime lab technician who witnesses the scene. It is essential to clarify the mechanism of injury for reconstruction of the event/injury.

The developmental mechanism of injury can be assumed by clarifying the following: action of kinetic energy to the body (weight and speed, active area, etc.), action of force and damage mode (direct damage or indirect damage, original site of load of stretching, negative or positive action of acceleration, action angle, existence of contrecoup occurrence from cavitation and suction distortion, diffusion of internal pressure, etc.), classification of injury (blunt trauma or penetrating trauma; cause and method such as traffic injury, industrial accident, athletic injury, battle injury, etc.; cause of injury such as an accident caused by a second party, self-inflicted accident, unexpected accident, etc.; open injury or closed injury; single injury or multiple injuries; superficial injury, head injury, facial injury, chest injury, abdominal injury, limb/pelvic injury, or spinal injury; in the case of traffic accident, whether in a vehicle, thrown out of the car, injury from the air bag, motorcycle driver's accident, or pedestrian's accident; head-on collision, offset collision [= head-on collision where the collided part in front of the vehicle is not 100 %], side-on collision, or rear-end collision [= bump from behind]; injury from fall; height of fall, description of point of fall, first contact point with the ground, and existence of structure during fall; and whether puncture wound, bullet wound, impalement injury, explosion injury, or compression injury), fastening or unfastening the seatbelt, etc.

Refer to the Japan Advanced Trauma Evaluation and Care JATEC™ and Japan Prehospital Trauma Evaluation and Care JPTEC™ (http://www.jtcr-jatec.org/index_jatec.html) published by the Japanese Association for the Surgery of Trauma in regard to symptoms and treatment (primary survey, secondary survey, curative treatment, complications to be concerned, and response to preventable trauma death).

24.6.3 Personal Injury and Personal Damage Quantification

Trauma scores as evaluation indices are described in section Ascertainment Methodology, where qualification is also explained. Direct evaluation methods to determine whether the injury is temporary or permanent, or to test separately, were not found in relation to the Japanese Association for the Surgery of Trauma, while ACS COT: Resources for Optimal Care of the Injured Patient 1999 was referenced to indicate cases where transfer to a tertiary emergency medical care facility was determined. This is not an absolute standard, and flexible application is suggested in accordance with medical care capacity of the destination hospital.

Tertiary emergency medical facilities in Japan are equipped with an advanced medical examination system to accept all severe emergency patients (head injury, cardiac infarction, stroke, etc.) who cannot be handled by the secondary emergency system or across multiple clinical departments around the clock, and tertiary emergency medical facilities requested by a prefecture upon approval of the Ministry of Health, Labour and Welfare are called critical care centers. They are required to be equipped with ICU (intensive care unit), CCU (coronary care unit), etc.

Various **evaluation methods** are used in regard to disability in the area of rehabilitation.

- Manual muscle testing (MMT).
- Modified Ashworth Scale: Increased muscle stress is important to predict occurrence of joint contracture in the area of rehabilitation. Contracture can be considered as chronic (permanent) disability.
- Brunnstrom Approach to spastic hemiplegia: Comprehensive evaluation is possible with 12 stages.
- Milani-Comparetti Motor Development Screening Test for evaluation of developmental diagnosis for brain paralysis.
- Glasgow Coma Scale (GCS) and Japan Coma Scale (3-3-9 method) for disturbed consciousness.
- ADL evaluation table, ADL disability evaluation table, revised Barthel Index, and Functional Independence Measure (FIM) by the State University of New York Research Foundation as evaluation methods of daily living.
- Evaluation criteria for the degree of independence in everyday life (degree of the bedridden) for the elderly with disability as a method to evaluate chronic (permanent) disability = activities of daily living evaluation.
- SIAS (Stroke Impairment Assessment Set) for stroke.
- ASIA Impairment Scale (in the international standards booklet for neurological and functional classification of spinal cord injury) for spinal cord injury.

24.6.4 Causal Value/Link

The legal process when civil liability is called into question, with regard to personal injury and damage, includes tort structure and default structure. In the case of medical malpractice, violation against general obligations of due diligence of a doctor as a professional who treats personal injury and damage is called into question in terms of tort structure, and breach of the duty of care (Article 644 of the Civil Code) by a doctor as mandatory of a medical care agreement (quasi-engagement agreement) between the doctor and patient is called into question in terms of default structure.

From the viewpoint of bearing the burden to prove violation against the obligations of due diligence (fault), the claimant has the burden of proving the change of rights as tort liability. The burden to prove the change of rights owed by the claimant in this case is to clarify the reasons as the basis of such change of rights, i.e., fault, since payment of damages is requested. As for default liability, a creditor is in the position to expect the debtor's performance and is certainly able to pursue default liability to the debtor; therefore, the fact of default needs to be proven. In the case of default liability, the medical provider is responsible to prove the nonexistence of fault, and the patient (claimant/creditor) has to prove existence of default.

Liability in the case of default means both the obligation of results (impossibility of performance; presumption of default is acceptable if the results of the performance are not visible) and the obligation of means (specific difficulty in provision as the contractual purpose; incomplete performance; incomplete performance needs to be proven). Lawsuits are often structured by both tort and default in recent cases.

The statute of limitations is 3 years after damage/attack occurs or 20 years after the time of tort in the case of the right to seek compensation due to a tort (Article 724 of the Civil Code) and 10 years after the time when the right can be executed (Article 166 Section 1 of the Civil Code) in the case of the right to seek compensation due to default (Article 167 Section 1 of the Civil Code). There are multiple points of time in the case of tort, such as the time of accident occurrence, time to claim for damage, time of definite diagnosis, and time to deliver a sentence. The "time when damage and attack is known" is not the time when a tort is known, but the time when the causality between the attack and damage is known, which is adjusted with both objective factors and subjective factors based on recognition of the victim. In the case of default, the "time when the right can be executed" is the time when there is no legal barrier against execution of the right, and it does not matter if the creditor is aware of it or not.

The main body of civil liability is the contracting party on the side of the medical provider, i.e., the proprietor of the hospital (national/local government, corporation, etc.), and doctors in private practice in the case of medical malpractice if the lawsuit is structured with default, and hospital doctors and medical assistants are considered as assistants of performance. In the case of structuring a lawsuit with a tort, joint tort by a doctor, medical assistant, proprietor of the hospital, etc. (Article 719 of the Civil Code) or employer's liability (Article 715 of the Civil Code) is called into question.

Theory of the Condition Sine Qua Non

In the above, requirements of tort liability occurrence (Article 709 of the Civil Code) include existence of deliberation or negligence, illegality, or infringement of victim's right or legal benefits, resulting in causality or damage. Requirements of default liability occurrence (Article 415 of the Civil Code) include existence of performance not in compliance with the purpose of liability, fault (deliberation or negligence of a debtor or reasons that should be identified as the same in accordance with the doctrine of good faith), causality, and damage occurrence.

Causality can be sufficiently proven by clarifying high probability in both tort liability and default. It is considered as difficult for the patient to prove causality to the extent of clarifying high probability in the case of medical malpractice; therefore, estimation of causality is considered as sufficient by alleviating the level of proof.

But-for Cause

Causality is necessary between the action of the assailant and the right of the victim as well as between the action by the assailant and the damage of the victim (Article 709 of the Civil Code).

Etiology includes three types: factual causality (sine qua non), adequate causality, and proportional causality. Generally speaking, factual causality is adopted by the Penal Code, adequate causality is adopted by the theory of judicial precedents in the Civil Code, and proportional causality is adopted in the area of forensic medicine and compensation science in Japan. In the case of adequate causality, however, liability for damage and the scope of compensation for damage are determined on the premise of existence of factual causality.

Sine qua non is the premise for both factual causality and adequate causality; therefore, causality does not occur without a cause, and claim for damage cannot be approved.

From a legal standpoint, claim for damage is possible only with existence of adequate causality.

Regarding a tort by omission, the obligation to act takes precedence in order to evaluate the legal value of the tort by omission and determine the extent of omission of not doing certain acts in the case of breach of the obligation to act. Determination of the obligation to act in the case of prioritizing the obligation to act is consistent with the determination on the obligation to avoid risks in the case of fault (Y. Shiomi: Tort Law I, P. 347, Shinzansha, 2011). Thus, when a fault (obligation to act and its breach) is determined and a certain act is ordered as a standard, omission by the assailant is evaluated according to the breach of the standard.

From the viewpoint of legal professionals, it is often considered that filing an action should be avoided in general, if the cause is unknown. When the cause is unknown in the beginning of an investigation, evidence may be preserved in any case. Reasons of an unknown cause and the degree also become the issue and expert opinions may be requested after filing an action; however, development of the lawsuit may not be expected in many cases.

Equivalence Theory of Causes

Table 24.1 Criteria for the contribution level of accidents with Watanabe method (revised in 1984)

Classification/ sign	Degree of determination	Explanation	Contribution level of the accident (%)
A	Stage 0	Judgment on illness or injury that exists irrelevant to the accident and on illness or injury due to the accident coexists, and it is certain that the former consists of the cause of death (or injury/residual disability)	0
B	Stage 1	Illness is induced by the accident, and death is provoked within a short time after the accident	10
C	Stage 2	Death (or injury/residual disability) where the cause of illness or injury could be the accident is inferior to other causes	20
D	Stage 3	Death (or injury/residual disability) where the main cause of illness or injury could be the accident is inferior to other causes	30
E	Stage 4	Death (or injury/residual disability) where the definite cause of illness or injury could be the accident is inferior to other causes	40
F	Stage 5	Illness or injury that exists irrelevant to the accident competes with illness or injury due to the accident, and death (or injury/residual disability) is possibly not provoked only with one of them	50
	Stage 6	Illness or injury that exists irrelevant to the accident competes with illness or injury due to the accident, and death (or injury/residual disability) is probably provoked with either one of them	60
H	Stage 7	Death (or injury/residual disability) where the cause of illness or injury is probably the accident is superior to other causes	70
I	Stage 8	Death (or injury/residual disability) where the main cause of illness or injury is probably the accident is superior to other causes	80
J	Stage 9	Death (or injury/residual disability) where the definite cause of illness or injury is probably the accident is superior to other causes	90
K	Stage 10	Judgment on illness or injury that exists irrelevant to the accident and on illness or injury due to the accident coexists, and it is certain that the latter consists of the cause of death (or injury/residual disability)	100

Table 24.2 Criteria for the involvement level of external factors

Classification		Explanation	Involvement level of external factors	
			Medical judgment	Determination
Normal pattern	A	It is judged as certain that existing physical/mental disorder or death is based on the direct action of the relevant external factor as well as on its secondary illness or complications. Even if "previous illness" exists, it is not necessary to consider their influence at all	Almost overall	100 %
	B	Although existing physical/mental disorder or death is mainly based on the direct action or the relevant external factor as well as on its secondary illness or complications, it is judged as impossible to completely deny involvement of "previous illness, etc.," either. In other words, unless "previous illness, etc.," exists, it is determined that severe disability that currently remains would not occur, that death would not result, or that a long time would have been required before death	Approximately 3/4	75 %
	C	It is judged that existing physical/mental disability or death occurs with the involvement of both the direct action of external factor as well as its secondary illness or complications and "previous illness, etc.," at the same level	Approximately 1/2	50 %
	D	Although existing physical/mental disorder or death is mainly based on the "previous illness, etc.," it is judged as impossible to completely deny involvement of the direct action of the relevant external factor as well as either its secondary illness or complications. In other words, unless the direct action of the external factor as well as its secondary illness or complications exists, it is determined that severe disability that	Approximately 1/4	25 %

(continued)

Table 24.2 (continued)

Classification		Explanation	Involvement level of external factors	
			Medical judgment	Determination
		currently remains would not occur, that death would not result, or that a long time would have been required before death		
	E	It is judged as certain that existing physical/mental disorders or death are based on the "previous illness, etc.," The influence of the direct action of the relevant external factor as well as its secondary illness or complications does not need to be considered at all	Almost none	0 %
Special pattern	F	An external factor occurs due to the existing illness or injury and its secondary illness or complications (previous illness), and it is determined that such an external factor causes the existing physical/mental disorder or death	The cause is previous illness and the relevant external factor is the secondary illness	Separate judgment
	G	Existing illness or injury and its secondary illness or complications (previous illness) cause death, followed by accident occurrence	None	0 %

When multiple causes compete and lead to one result in the case of proportional causality, the level of influence by each of the multiple causes to the result is considered and quantified depending on the level of contribution. Quantification uses the standards in Tables 24.1 and 24.2. The idea of proportional causality is to bear liability for damage according to the level of contribution of each performer or predisposition, in the case that there are multiple performers or competing predispositions, which relates to the idea of compensation science in Japan as well as the idea of medicolegal experts.

Adequate Causality

Requirements of adequate causality include existence of a cause, result, and causality between the cause and result.

If existence of causality cannot be proven in the cases relating to medical care, the theory of infringing the expectancy right, theory of infringing the legal right to the benefit of life extension, and the theory of losing a treatment opportunity are developed. These three theories are explained in the damage theory later. A theory of affirming claim for damage in certain cases (theory of infringing a certain level of possibility) is observed.

In the case of proportional causality, adequate causality is considered as adequate when the level of contribution is high.

Under the laws of Japan, claim for damage is possible only when adequate causality exists. Existence of factual causality becomes the point in dispute as the premise of adequate causality in the courtroom of medical malpractice. In the case of damage with factual causality, adequate causality is recognized and damage can be claimed only when the circumstances of damage occurrence are successfully predicted in regard to the damage that should normally occur or occurred under special circumstances (Study Group of Medical Malpractice Problems: Good Handling of Disputes on Medical Accidents, P. 304, Study Group of Civil Laws, 2010). Requirements of adequate causality include the following.

To adequately prove causality in a courtroom, it is necessary to specifically claim and prove the existence of the above factual (conditional) causality between the fault/accident and damage as well as the facts to substantiate that adequate causality is within the scope of appropriateness. In the case of medical malpractice, adequate causality is proven by comprehensively determining the existence of inefficiency in the medical act, temporal proximity between the medical act and results, general or statistical probability of similar results occurring from the same type of medical acts, quantity and content of the medical act as well as the occurrence rate of the results, biological relevance between the medical act and vital reaction, peculiarity of the patient, existence and level of possible intervention of other causes, force majeure, etc.

Chronology/Continuity of Event and Permanent Event

When a traffic accident and medical accident occur continuously or when one patient visits a previous doctor and subsequent doctor, causality where multiple causes act chronologically is prioritized by the time of occurrence according to the medical viewpoint in WHO's principle of underlying cause of death, and multiple factors are considered to have continuous causality. Legally speaking, a factor with a higher level of contribution or a factor that occurs temporally close to the event/injury is weighed heavily and at the same time causality among multiple factors is considered as separate. Damages are generally established for each factor that is weighed heavily from a legal standpoint. When multiple factors occur temporally, this kind of difference exists between medical causality and legal causality.

In regard to residual disability, the time or situation when the improving effects of treatment can be no longer expected in relation to a symptom occurring due to a certain cause after proper medical treatment for a certain period is called the fixed symptom, and the symptom of the patient in this situation is a fixed symptom. A fixed symptom is not a medical term but can be interpreted as permanent or semipermanent. In Japan, monetary damages are paid to the damage determined as the fixed symptom which cannot return to the original state (mutatis mutandis application of Articles 722 and 417 of the Civil Code). A medical certificate on this fixed symptom is medical but retrospective, and in many cases it is difficult to medically assume the extent of total healing or medical causality between the patient's symptom and event/injury at the time of preparation by a person in charge of diagnosis. In regard to higher brain dysfunction, after injury, for example, neuropsychological testing and behavior observation such as ICF are required every 6 months; therefore, medical causality seems to be replaced with the existence of adequate causality that can be explained with high probability in this case.

24.6.5 Personal Damage Quantification

24.6.5.1 General Matters

Compensation is approved when causality between breach of duty and results is recognized in the case of claim for damage under the Civil Code. This principle is equal to claims in the case of torts, such as traffic accidents as well as claims accompanying damage as a result of death and injury due to medical malpractice. The following should be noted as peculiarities in the damage theory relating to medical malpractice litigation.

A. *Fault on the side of medical providers is evident.*

Causality between the doctor's act and fault on the patient's part is not observed (infringement of the benefit of life extension, infringement of the expectancy right, loss of a treatment opportunity).

Causality is considered in the case that high probability existing at the time of death is recognized, and the subsequent extent of probability is handled as the problem for calculation of damage. If a certain level of possibility to avoid the results can be recognized, claim for compensation is approved in regard to infringement of the possibility, even though there is no high probability. The borderline of the above two is not clear, while the amount of consolation money is evidently in the low trend for the latter.

- A doctor neglected the obligation to explain. Even without causality between a doctor's breach of duty to explain and damage, including death payment of compensation is approved on the basis that the opportunity to choose treatment is deprived = infringement of the right of self-determination.
- Autopsy was not recommended. In the case that a doctor does not give an explanation or recommendation on autopsy to clarify the cause of death, payment of compensation is approved on the basis of infringement of the expectancy right to medical care on the part of the patient.

B. *Comparative fault (Articles 418 and 722 of the Civil Code).*

A patient and doctor are in a relationship of quasi-engagement agreement under the Civil Code of Japan. The system for attempting a reduction in the compensation amount due from the assailant, for the purpose of fairness between contractual parties, is called comparative fault.

The victim (patient) did not communicate or insufficiently explained matters that would influence the medical examination by the doctor, did not obey the doctor's instructions, was late for visits, or did not visit on a continuous basis.

Even when comparative fault is not relevant, the compensation amount is also reduced when there are negative causes of action on the patient's part.

In the case that mental damage (falsification of medical charts by a medical institution, inappropriate explanation, etc.) occurs in addition to economic damage, the compensation amount is increased.

Determination of the adjusted amount of consolation money is at the discretion of the judge.

C. *Fetal death.*

Claim for damage is approved only in the form of consolation money claimed by an expectant mother and her husband in the case of fetal death as well. Loss of profits is not approved in the case of fetus.

D. *Compensation for damage.*

Damage occurrence and the amount of damage need to be proven by the patient. However, certification by a court is possible in the case that providing such proof is extremely difficult under Article 248 of the Code of Civil Procedure. Compensation by regular payment of a fixed amount is also approved, instead of compensation by lump-sum payment.

E. *Problems with this type of damage theory.*

The following issues have arisen in relation to the subject matter.

- Damage exists as a fact; however, monetary evaluation as the compensation amount is too low or monetary evaluation significantly varies depending on cases. Variation in monetary evaluation occurs due to the fact that what is included in the factual damage varies depending on cases.
- If the cases under the extrajudicial relief system are included, variation in the amount of monetary compensation by case is even larger.
- Possibility to comprehensively calculate damages in relation to medical accidents in a uniform manner needs to be considered.
- There is room to consider whether or not to include economic damage in legal benefits, such as infringement of the benefit of life extension, infringement of the expectancy right, loss of a treatment opportunity, etc.

24.6.5.2 Economic Damage

Economic damage means the actual cost paid or to be payable by the victim (patient).

Active damage includes medical examination expense, admission/attendance expense, visit/attendance expense, care expense in the future, miscellaneous hospitalization expense, transportation expense for visits, attorney expense, appliance/apparatus expense, modification expense of house and automobile, funeral-related expense, gratuity to a doctor, etc.

Passive damage includes loss of profits, such as damage due to taking leave of absence from work, death, and residual disability.

There are strong aspects as a subject of legal study in regard to active damage as well as to damage due to absence from work as passive damage. Loss of profits and compensation due to death and residual disability as passive damage are based on ICF described in the above and have strong aspects as a subject of academic study.

24.6.5.3 Noneconomic Damage

Noneconomic damage means mental damage (pain) suffered by a victim, and relevant compensation includes consolation money for death, residual disability, and injury and compensation for close relatives.

Criteria for the contribution level of accidents (Table 24.1) and for the involvement level of external factors (Table 24.2) are briefly summarized.

24.6.5.4 Payment Standards of Automobile Liability Insurance

Payment standards of automobile liability insurance are stipulated by damage. Both injury and residual disability can be claimed in the case of injury resulting in residual disability, and both injury and death can be claimed in the case of injury resulting in death.

Damage Due to Injury
Maximum amount: 1,200,000 yen (Table 24.3).

Damage Due to Residual Disability
Maximum amount: in accordance with the grade (Table 24.4).

Loss of Profits in the Case of Residual Disability

A. **Calculation formula**
   Result = Basic income amount × Loss rate of labor ability × Leibniz coefficient corresponding to the loss rate of labour ability (Table 24.5)
B. **Basic income** (Table 24.6)
   The Wage Census is a basic statistical survey on wage structure by the Ministry of Health, Labour and Welfare and used as a guideline of annual income by gender, age, and academic history.
   Loss rate of labor ability (Table 24.7)

Table 24.3 Damage due to injury

Expense item	Definition/explanation	Payment standard
Treatment expense	First aid, medical examination, hospitalization, medication, surgical procedures, etc.	Necessary and reasonable amount
Care expense	Care during hospitalization A close relative attends a child at age 12 and under	4100 yen per day
	Home care or ambulatory care A close relative attends a child at age 12 and under Need of care is recognized by a doctor	Necessary and reasonable amount; 2050 yen per day in the case of close relative
Transportation expense for visits	Transportation required for visits	Necessary and reasonable amount
Miscellaneous expense	Miscellaneous expense during hospitalization	1100 yen per day of hospitalization
Expense for artificial limbs, etc.	Artificial limbs, dental prosthesis, artificial eyes, hearing aid, crutches, etc.	Actual amount recognized as necessary and reasonable by a doctor
Expense for medical certificates, etc.	Publication of medical certificates, medical fee bills, etc.	Necessary and reasonable amount
Documentation expense	Certificate of traffic accident, seal certificate, etc.	Necessary and reasonable amount
Damage due to taking leave of absence from work	Income decrease due to injury from accident	5700–19,000 yen per day
Consolation money	Indemnity of mental and physical pain	4200 yen per day of hospitalization or visit [to be calculated with the less of actual days of treatment × 2 or treatment period]

Table 24.4 Damage due to residual disability

Damage	Definition/explanation
Loss of profits	Income decrease to occur over the future as a result of residual disability to the body leading to decreased labor ability
Consolation money for residual disability	Indemnity toward mental and physical pain as a result of traffic accident

Table 24.5 Loss of profits in the case of residual disability

Definitions	
Basic income amount	Annual income that becomes the basis of calculation
Loss rate of labor ability	Proportion of labor ability lost due to residual disability; stipulated by grade
Loss period of labor ability	Period of lost labor ability as a result of residual disability; normally calculated up to age 67 In the case of whiplash, the period is limited to 10 years or less for Grade 12 and 5 years or less for Grade 14 in many cases
Leibniz coefficient	The interest portion (statutory interest: 5 %) that arises by receiving the lump-sum amount of compensation including the future portion is deducted using the coefficient

Table 24.6 Basic income

Standard of automobile liability
Employed people Principle: Higher of 1-year income prior to the accident or the average annual income by age based on the Wage Census • Younger than age 35 and can prove 1-year income prior to the accident → Higher of the annual income, the average annual income for all ages on the *Wage Census*, or the annual income by age • Difficult to prove the annual income prior to the accident → In the case of younger than age 35, higher of the average annual income for all ages on the *Wage Census* or the annual income by age → In the case of age 35 or older, the annual income by age on the *Wage Census* • Unemployed people within 1 year after resignation → Mutatis mutandis application of the above standard
Babies, children, pupils, students, and homemakers Average annual income for all ages on the *Wage Census*; however, in the case that the average annual income by age is lower than the average income for all ages for people age 58 or older, average annual income by age
Other people who have the will and ability to work Average annual income by age on the *Wage Census*; limited to the average annual income for all ages

Damage Due to Death

Maximum amount: 30,000,000 yen (Table 24.8).

Loss of Profits in the Case of Death

A. *Calculation formula*

$$\text{Result} = \text{Basic income amount} \times (1 - \text{Living cost of the individual}) \times \text{Leibniz coefficient corresponding to years of possible working duration}$$

Years of possible working duration is the period from the age of death to age 67 (Table 24.9).

B. **Basic income** (Table 24.10)

C. **Standard for deduction of living expense** (Table 24.11)

Table 24.7 Loss rate of labor ability

Grade	Maximum amount of payment	Consolation money	Loss late of labor ability (%)
Care grade 1	40,000,000 yen	16,000,000 yen	100
Care grade 1	30,000,000 yen	11,630,000 yen	100
Grade 1	30,000,000 yen	11,000,000 yen	100
Grade 2	25,900,000 yen	9,580,000 yen	100
Grade 3	22,190,000 yen	8,290,000 yen	100
Grade 4	18,890,000 yen	7,120,000 yen	92
Grade 5	15,740,000 yen	5,990,000 yen	79
Grade 6	12,960,000 yen	4,980,000 yen	67
Grade 7	10,510,000 yen	4,090,000 yen	56
Grade 8	8,190,000 yen	3,240,000 yen	45
Grade 9	6,160,000 yen	2,450,000 yen	35
Grade 10	4,610,000 yen	1,870,000 yen	27
Grade 11	3,310,000 yen	1,350,000 yen	20
Grade 12	2,240,000 yen	930,000 yen	14
Grade 13	1,390,000 yen	570,000 yen	9
Grade 14	750,000 yen	320,000 yen	5

Table 24.8 Damage due to death

Type of damage	Definition	Amount
Funeral expense	Altar, burial, thank-you letters to attendees, etc.	600,000 yen (in principle)
Loss of profits	Calculated by subtracting the living expense of the individual from the income that could have been acquired unless the victim died	Refer to the following figure
Consolation money	Individual	3,500,000 yen
	Consolation money for the bereaved family (father, mother, spouse, and child of the victim)	1 claimant → 5,500,000 yen 2 claimants → 6,500,000 yen 3 claimants → 7,500,000 yen When the victim has dependents → add 2,000,000 yen

Table 24.9 Damage due to death

Definitions	
Basic income amount	Annual income on the basis of calculation
Deduction of living expense	The living expense that ceases to occur due to death is subtracted from the basic income
Years of possible working duration	Period when income could have been earned from working without death; normally calculated up to age 67
Leibniz coefficient	The interest portion (statutory interest: 5 %) that arises by receiving the lump-sum amount of compensation including the future portion is deducted using the coefficient

Table 24.10 Basic income

Standard of automobile liability
Employed people Principle: Higher of 1-year income prior to the accident or the average annual income by age based on the Wage Census at the age of death • *Younger than age 35 and can prove 1-year income prior to the accident* → Higher of the annual income, the average annual income for all ages on the *Wage Census*, or the annual income by age • *Difficult to prove the annual income prior to the accident* → In the case of younger than age 35, higher of the average annual income for all ages on the *Wage Census* or the annual income by age → In the case of age 35 or older, the annual income by age on the *Wage Census* • Unemployed people within 1 year after resignation → Mutatis mutandis application of the above standard
Babies, children, pupils, students, and homemakers Average annual income for all ages on the *Wage Census*; however, in the case that the average annual income by age is lower than the average income for all ages for people age 58 or older, average annual income by age *Recipients of pension* Annual income
Other people who has the will and ability to work Average annual income by age on the *Wage Census*; limited to the average annual income for all ages

Table 24.11 Standard for deduction of living expense

Standard of automobile liability
The living expense for the individual is subtracted
There is a provider → 35 %
There is no dependent → 50 %

References

1. Shiomi Y (2011) Tort Law, P. 2, 2nd edn. Shinzansha
2. Urakawa M, Kanai Y, Yasuhara Y, Miyazawa J (2010) Malpractice Lawsuits, P. 626. Study Group of Civil Laws
3. Urakawa M, Kanai Y, Yasuhara Y, Miyazawa J (2010) Malpractice Lawsuits, P. 633. Study Group of Civil Laws

4. Watanabe T (1985) International Classification of Impairments, Disabilities and Handicaps [ICIDH], Compensation Medicine, P. 1
5. Rosai (2011) Mental Disorder Certification Standards

Chapter 25
Methods of Ascertainment of Personal Damage in Australia

George Mendelson and Danuta Mendelson

Abstract This chapter illustrates the historical, judicial and juridical framework of personal injury assessment and compensation in Australia, illustrating the expert's qualification and competences and the ascertainment methodology for identifying, describing and estimating any personal injury, its temporary and permanent consequences and the causal value/link between the event and the injury and between the injury and the impairment. In particular, the chapter discusses the principles related to the assessment of personal injuries and impairment, both physical and psychiatric, when assessing the extent of damages resulting from traffic accidents and from wrongful injuries sustained in other compensable circumstances, such as medical malpractice, in Australia. The emphasis is on the medical methods of ascertaining the quantum of damages, which in Australia is generally undertaken in accordance with impairment rating instruments prescribed by statute.

25.1 Historical and Juridical Overview

When the Commonwealth of Australia came into existence on 1 January 1901, six Australian colonies (New South Wales, Victoria, Tasmania, Queensland, South Australia and Western Australia), became the original States of the Federation, united under the *Commonwealth of Australia Constitution Act, 1900* (UK). The *Commonwealth Constitution Act* ratified the agreement among the old colonies to give up some of their powers to the new central body—the Commonwealth—while preserving sovereignty over the powers they had retained. The 'residual' powers, which remained with State Parliaments and were subsequently partially vested in the Australian

G. Mendelson (✉)
Faculty of Medicine, Department of Psychiatry, School of Clinical Sciences, Nursing and Health Sciences, Monash University, Clayton, VIC, Australia
e-mail: george.mendelson@monash.edu

D. Mendelson (✉)
Faculty of Business & Law, School of Law, Deakin University, Caulfield Junction, Australia
e-mail: danuta.mendelson@deakin.edu.au

S.D. Ferrara et al. (eds.), *Personal Injury and Damage Ascertainment under Civil Law*, DOI 10.1007/978-3-319-29812-2_25

Capital Territory and the Northern Territory Parliaments, encompassed the legislative power to administer and regulate the common law of torts. Each jurisdiction had created its own legislative framework that provided rehabilitation and compensation benefits for those injured in motor vehicle accidents. Likewise, jurisdiction over personal injury litigation at common law remained with the States and Territories.[1]

Consequently, Australia does not have a uniform nationwide legal framework governing motor vehicle accidents and award of damages for injuries sustained in such accidents. Except for Victoria (*Transport Accident Act 1986*),[2] Tasmania (*Motor Accidents (Liabilities and Compensation) Act 1973*),[3] the Northern Territory (*Motor Accidents (Compensation) Act 1979*)[4] and partly *Motor Accidents Compensation Act 1999* (NSW) s 7A in New South Wales[5], all other schemes are fault based (*Motor Accident Insurance Act 1994* (Qld), *Motor Accident Commission Act 1992* (SA), *Motor Vehicle (Third Party Insurance) Act 1943* (WA), *Road Transport (Third Party Insurance) Act 2008* (A.C.T.)). Under some no-fault schemes, persons wrongfully injured in motor vehicle accidents may have a choice of either claiming benefits under the relevant statutory motor vehicle compensation scheme or suing for damages at common law. For example, in the *Transport Accident Act 1986* (Vic) s 93(4)(b), 'serious injury' is defined as an impairment of 30 % or more, which gives the claimant a right to sue for damages at common law.

---

[1] Mendelson D. Devaluation of a constitutional guarantee: the history of Section 51(xxiiiA) of the Commonwealth Constitution. (1999) 23 *Melbourne University Law Review* 308. For a general introduction to Australian legal history, the reader is referred to Castles, A.C., *An Australian Legal History*, (Sydney, 1982).

[2] *Transport Accident Act 1986* (Vic): benefits in respect of loss of earnings and medical and associated expenses are provided, regardless of fault, to all persons injured in 'transport accidents', defined in s 3(1) as incidents 'directly caused by the driving of' a motor car or motor vehicle, railway train or tram. *Transport Accident Act 1986* (Vic) s 93(17) prescribes that to sue for damages at common law, the claimants have to be assessed as having suffered 'serious injury'—a disability of 30 percent or greater (serious long-term impairment or loss of a body function, or permanent serious disfigurement, or severe long-term mental or severe long-term behavioural disturbance or disorder or loss of a foetus).

[3] *Motor Accidents (Liabilities and Compensation) Act 1973* (Tas): the no-fault compensation scheme provides for scheduled benefits payable in cases where a Tasmanian resident dies or suffers bodily injury as a result of an accident occurring in Tasmania or involving a vehicle registered in Tasmania. The maximum total sum payable for medical and disability (loss of income and the inability to perform housekeeping duties) benefits for persons injured in a motor accident is $400,000 (additional benefits are accessible on the basis of special need).

[4] The *Motor Accidents (Compensation) Act 1979* (NT) provides a no-fault accident compensation scheme, but abrogates common law damages (s 5). The scheme covers everyone injured or killed in a motor vehicle accident in the territory, irrespective of where the motor vehicle is registered (s 6).

[5] *Motor Accidents Compensation Act 1999* (NSW) s 7A provides that road users can claim for a blameless motor accident: i.e. 'a motor accident not caused by the fault of the owner or driver of any motor vehicle involved in the accident in the use or operation of the vehicle and not caused by the fault of any other person'. Excluded from recovery of damages are drivers who by an act or

25.2 Damages for Personal Injury Under Australian Law of Torts

In August 2001, the second largest Australian insurance group, HIH, collapsed. The collapse affected some 30,000 policyholders ranging from home and small-business owners to public authorities and such professionals as medical practitioners, lawyers, engineers, etc. At the end of 2001, three major medical insurance companies (United Medical Protection Ltd, Australasian Medical Insurance Ltd and MDU Australia Insurance Co Pty Ltd) went into provisional liquidation blaming record damages awarded to plaintiffs suing in for medical malpractice [1]. The causes of the 2001 insurance crisis were multifactorial, including a dramatic increase in personal injury litigation payouts over the final two decades of the twentieth century [2].

During September 2002 a special panel, chaired by Hon Justice David Ipp, and appointed by Commonwealth, State and Territory ministers, completed and published the report titled *Review of the Law of Negligence Report* and known as the *Ipp Report* [3]. It recommended partial codification of modified law of negligence and the law of damages that each jurisdiction would enact as a single, nearly identical statute. This did not happen. Instead, during 2002–2003 each parliament enacted its own statutory code of tortious liability based on, but not always replicating, the *Ipp Report*'s model statutory provisions. The new statutory principles are applicable to any claim for damages for personal injury or death resulting from negligence, regardless of whether the claim is brought in tort, contract and equity or under a statute or any other cause of action.

The main thrust of the post-Ipp reforms was to restrict tort liability for personal injuries by introducing statutory thresholds that claimants have to meet before they can obtain damages for noneconomic loss. It should be noted, however, that in some jurisdictions motor vehicle accident compensation schemes incorporated thresholds to claims for benefits prior to the Ipp inquiry.

There are four different statutory models in Australia for determining whether the claimant is entitled to sue for noneconomic loss at common law:

(1) Under the *Competition and Consumer Act 2010* (Cth) ss 87P–87S and the *Civil Liability Act 2002* (NSW) s 16(1), 'the severity of the non-economic loss ...

omission caused motor accident in which they were injured or killed even if (a) the act or omission did not constitute fault by the driver in the use or operation of the vehicle (e.g. the vehicle's brakes failed), (b) the act or omission was involuntary (e.g. heart attack), (c) the act or omission was not the sole or primary cause of the death or injury or (d) the act or omission would have caused the death or injury but for the occurrence of a supervening act or omission of another person or some other supervening event (s 7E). Also, under *Motor Accidents Compensation Act 1999* (NSW) s 7J: children under 16 years of age, who at the time of the accident are residents of NSW, can make a claim for the children's special benefit (hospital, medical, rehabilitation, pharmacy, respite care and attendant care expenses and in the case of death funeral or cremation expenses). However, under s 7K of the Act, special entitlement is not available for a child injured or killed while, or following, engaging in conduct that constitutes an offence punishable by 6 months or more in prison.

[must be] at least 15 per cent of a most extreme case'. A judge's assessment of whether a case is 'a most extreme case' involves:

> Questions of fact and degree and matters of opinion, impression, speculation and estimation, calling for the exercise of common sense and judgement (*Dell v Dalton* (1991) 23 NSWLR 528 at 533–534)

Statutory table in *Civil Liability Act 2002* (NSW) s 16(3), based on the table contained in s 79A of the *Motor Accidents Act 1988* (NSW), sets out percentages of loss relative to a most extreme case and the corresponding statutory percentage of the maximum award. The amount payable is determined by multiplying the maximum amount that may be awarded in a most extreme case by the percentage set out in the table [4].

(2) South Australia's *Civil Liability Act 1936* s 52(1) specifies that to be compensable the injury need not be permanent; however, damages may only be awarded for noneconomic loss if: '(a) the injured person's ability to lead a normal life was significantly impaired by the injury for a period of at least 7 days; or (b) medical expenses of at least the prescribed minimum have been reasonably incurred in connection with the injury.' Once this threshold is reached, the court has to assess (under *Civil Liability Act 1936* (SA), s 52(2)):

   (a) Whether the claimant has established, on the balance of probabilities, that his or her injury resulted in compensable noneconomic loss on the grounds of pain and suffering, loss of amenities of life, loss of expectation of life and/or disfigurement.
   (b) The level of severity, which might be significant, moderate or low.
   (c) Then allocate the value of the claimant's injury by comparing it 'with the most serious and the least serious non-economic loss which anyone could suffer'—on a value scale of 0–60.

In Queensland, under the *Civil Liability Act 2003* (Qld), ss 61 and 62 provide for a similar process, though scale is from 0 to 100. Provisions in both jurisdictions (Queensland and South Australia) assume that the gravest conceivable kind of injury would attract the highest value. Monetary damages for noneconomic loss are calculated by application of a statutory mathematical formula.

(3) In Victoria the *Wrongs Act 1958*, ss 28LB, 28LE and 28LF, and in the Northern Territory the *Personal Injuries (Liabilities and Damages) Act 2003*, Division 4, ss 22–28 require claimants to establish a minimum statutory level of permanent impairment defined as 'significant injury'. In the *Wrongs Act 1958* s 28LB, '*threshold level*' is defined as:

   (a) 'in the case of injury (other than psychiatric injury), impairment of more than 5 per cent'
   (b) 'in the case of psychiatric injury, impairment of more than 10 per cent' of the 'whole person resulting from the injury' as assessed by an approved medical practitioner or a medical panel (*Wrongs Act 1958* (Vic), s 28LF(1) (a) and s 28LF(2))

Secondary psychiatric or psychological impairment cannot be included in the assessment of degree of impairment:

> In assessing a degree of impairment of a person under this Part, regard must not be had to any psychiatric or psychological injury, impairment or symptoms arising as a consequence of, or secondary to, a physical injury. (*Wrongs Act 1958* (Vic), s 28LJ)

There is a provision for binaural loss of hearing of more than 5 % (*Wrongs Act 1958* (Vic), s 28LK). The loss of a foetus, or loss of a breast, and 'psychological or psychiatric injury arising from the loss of a child due to an injury to the mother or the foetus or the child before', during or immediately after the birth, come within the definition of 'serious injury'.

(4) The Tasmanian *Civil Liability Act 2002* s 27(4) and the Western Australian *Civil Liability Act 2002* s 9 and s 10 set minimum indexed monetary thresholds of \$5000 or \$15,500, respectively, for eligibility to claim noneconomic loss. Western Australia has a statutory formula for small claims' payouts. Under the Tasmanian scheme: (1) If the amount of noneconomic loss is assessed to be not more than \$5000 (gazetted for period between 1 July 2013 and 30 June 2014), no damages are to be awarded for noneconomic loss. (2) If the amount of noneconomic loss is assessed to be more than \$5000 but not more than \$25,000 (gazetted for period between 1 July 2013 and 30 June 2014), damages awarded for noneconomic loss are calculated as follows: amount awarded = 1.25 × (amount assessed minus \$5000). (3) If the amount of noneconomic loss is assessed to be more than \$25,000, damages awarded for noneconomic loss are an amount equal to the amount assessed.

The Australian Capital Territory does not impose monetary thresholds on damages; however, the *Civil Law (Wrongs) Act 2002* (A.C.T.) s 181 imposes a statutory maximum on amounts for legal services payable in cases where damages recovered on a claim for personal injury are \$50,000 or less.

The relevant legislation and regulations in the various States and Territories that provide for compensation and determination of the quantum of damages for personal injuries sustained in traffic accidents and injuries negligently caused by another person (as in the case of medical malpractice and other torts) are:

- New South Wales
  - Motor Accidents Compensation Act 1999
  - Civil Liability Act 2002
- Queensland
  - Motor Accident Insurance Act 1994
  - Motor Accident Insurance Regulation 2004
  - Civil Liability Act 2003
  - Civil Liability Regulation 2014
- South Australia
  - Motor Accident Commission Act 1992

- Civil Liability Act 1936
- Civil Liability Regulations 2013
- Civil Liability Variation Regulations 2014

- Tasmania
  - Motor Accidents (Liabilities and Compensation) Act 1973
  - Motor Accidents (Liabilities and Compensation) Regulations 2010
  - Civil Liability Act 2002
- Victoria
  - Transport Accident Act 1986
  - Wrongs Act 1958
- Western Australia
  - Motor Vehicle (Third Party Insurance) Act 1943
  - Civil Liability Act 2002
- Australian Capital Territory
  - Motor Vehicle (Third Party Insurance) Regulations
  - Civil Law (Wrongs) Act 2002
- Northern Territory
  - Motor Accidents (Compensation) Act 1979
  - Motor Accidents (Compensation) Regulations
  - Personal Injuries (Liabilities and Damages Act) 2003

In the assessment of damages for personal injury, one of the questions asked of expert medical witnesses is to quantify the extent of permanent impairment. The assessment of permanent impairment is particularly difficult where the injury is not apparent to the judge, jury or tribunal, for example, in cases of chronic pain or mental illness. As a result, the evaluation of impairment and disability has been an ongoing problem in the psychiatric assessment of plaintiffs in personal injury claims and of applicants for pension and other social security benefits [5].

According to Colledge and Krohm, writing in the journal of the International Association of Industrial Accident Boards and Commissions, 'even primitive workers' compensation schemes had intuitive systems for cash awards for permanent injury, with amputation of extremities being the easiest cases to assess and assign specific benefits' [6]. They wrote that 'Caribbean pirates in the early colonial era had developed written rules for compensating loss of hands, arms, eyes, etc in the course of their nefarious 'trade''.

Lerner referred to 'medically determinable impairment' leading to cessation of work as an important factor in the determination of eligibility for disability benefits. Lerner also noted that 'substantial loss of functional capacity' had to be present, but no specific method of rating psychiatric impairment was given in his article [7].

Many medical writers on the subject of impairment and disability have confused these concepts. Because of this, the concepts of impairment and disability are frequently misused, and the two terms used interchangeably. It is, therefore, important, in discussing the evaluation of impairment and disability, to provide clear definitions of what is meant by these terms.

Impairment, according to the *International Classification of Impairments, Disabilities, and Handicaps* (ICIDH) published by the World Health Organization (WHO), denotes 'any loss or abnormality of psychological, physiological, or anatomical structure or function', whereas a disability is 'any restriction or lack (resulting from an impairment) of ability to perform an activity in the manner or within the range considered normal for a human being' [8].

Additionally, handicap is defined as 'a disadvantage for a given individual, resulting from an impairment or a disability, that limits or prevents the fulfilment of a role that is normal (depending on age, sex, and social and cultural factors) for that individual'.

The ICIDH, in an explanatory note, states that the term 'impairment' is 'more inclusive than disorder in that it covers losses—e.g., the loss of a leg is an impairment, but not a disorder'. It is further noted that

> Impairment is characterized by losses or abnormalities that may be temporary or permanent, and that include the existence of occurrence of an anomaly, defect, or loss in a limb, organ, tissue, or other structure of the body, including the systems of mental function. Impairment represents **exteriorization** of a pathological state, and in principle it reflects disturbances at the level of the organ. (emphasis added)

The ICIDH thus makes it clear, both in the definition of impairment and in describing its characteristics, that impairment is the objective, externalised loss or abnormality of structure or function. Impairment is what can be demonstrated, assessed, evaluated and measured by an external observer, appropriately trained in distinguishing the normal from the pathological in relation to the specific aspect of structure or function that is the subject of the evaluation.

Impairment is therefore not a subjective complaint or symptom; it is not the complaint of inability to move a limb where physical examination reveals a near-normal range of joint movement, and it is not a statement that the person feels 'depressed' where the mental status examination reveals no manifestations of lowered affect, anhedonia, depressive thought content or psychomotor disturbance.

Equally, impairment has to be differentiated from both disability and handicap, both of which might (but not always) be the consequences of an objectively demonstrable impairment. To reiterate, disability is a loss or restriction of the ability to perform an activity, whereas an impairment is an objectively demonstrable loss or abnormality of (psychological, physiological or anatomical) structure or function. Such an impairment must be capable of being described in terms of the specific normal basic function that has been lost or rendered abnormal.

In physical medicine, impairments are often assessed in terms of restrictions of the normal range of joint movements, for example, due to pain, which can be measured. In psychiatry, impairments are abnormalities of the normal mental functions; these are commonly termed intelligence, thinking, perception, judgement, mood (or affect) and behaviour. Impairment of these basic mental functions can give rise to a range of disabilities, that is, inability to perform certain activities in a normal manner. However, such disability must be differentiated from impairment of the basic aspects of mental functioning listed above.

Lasky (1983) specifically noted that, in the final analysis, it is the responsibility of the judge—or of the administrative law tribunal—to make the definitive determination of the percentage of disability, whereas the medical expert witness can only properly determine the extent of the impairment [9].

Thus, while the rating of impairment—as defined in the ICIDH—is the task of the medical practitioner undertaking the assessment, the determination of disability involves legal and administrative factors in accordance with the relevant legislation. This is an important point to emphasise, as frequently conclusory opinions concerning work disability are inappropriately given by the medical practitioner as part of the evaluation and report [10].

Nevertheless, once the rating of impairment has been made, medical practitioners with specialised experience in occupational or rehabilitation medicine might be able to give an opinion as to the specific work disability resulting from the particular impairment in relation to the individual's work demands. However, rating of work disability requires knowledge of the particular work environment and work activities required of the individual and, for this reason, should only be undertaken by appropriately qualified and experienced practitioners.

In Australian jurisprudence, the distinction between subjective symptoms and objectively assessed impairment was emphasised in the judgement of Neilson J, in *Moran v Thomson Adsett & Partners Pty Ltd* [1996] 13 NSWCCR 484 at 491), who held that an asymptomatic constitutional back condition may be a contributory factor causing permanent impairment. This decision also, in effect, established that an impairment may be present in the absence of a diagnosable symptomatic disorder.

This chapter will review the methods specified in Australian legislation for the assessment of physical and psychiatric impairments and will also discuss provisions that specify the qualifications of the medicolegal experts whose independent medical examinations and impairment ratings are accepted by courts in the various jurisdictions that award compensatory damages for injuries caused by traffic accidents and/or other torts.

25.3 The Medicolegal Expert's Qualifications

As noted above, the various Australian jurisdictions that provide compensatory damages for those injured in motor vehicle accidents or as the result of tortious acts have differing statutory mechanisms for the assessment of impairment and determination of damages.

Similarly, there are differing provisions in relation to the qualifications of medicolegal experts whose opinions are admissible in legal proceedings to obtain damages. The considerations and qualifications as set out in the relevant legislation and case law are described in this section.

Statutory definitions of experts and expert witnesses tend to be broad. For example, according to the Uniform Civil Procedure Rules 2005 (NSW) r 31.16, an 'expert', in relation to any issue, means 'a person who has such knowledge or experience of, or in connection with, that issue, or issues of the character of that issue, that his or her opinion on that issue would be admissible in evidence'.

The 'expert witness' is defined as 'an expert engaged or appointed for the purpose of:

(a) providing an expert's report for use as evidence in proceedings or proposed proceedings, or
(b) giving opinion evidence in proceedings or proposed proceedings'.

The *Victorian Civil and Administrative Tribunal Act 1998* (Vic) s 3 defines 'expert witness' as 'a person who has specialised knowledge based on the person's training, study or experience'.

25.3.1 New South Wales

Motor Accidents Compensation Act 1999 (NSW)

Section 3.4 of the *Act* deals with 'Medical Assessment'. It provides that the Motor Accidents Authority, established under the *Act*, which is the statutory body responsible for administration of the *Act*, 'is to establish in association with its operations a unit, to be known as the Motor Accidents Medical Assessment Service (s 57A(i))' and that 'The Service is to consist of medical assessors and such officers of the Authority as the Authority determines' (s 57A(2)).

Section 58 provides that the Service will determine disagreements 'between a claimant and an insurer' concerning, inter alia, 'whether the degree of permanent impairment of the injured person as a result of the injury caused by the motor accident is greater than 10 %'.

Section 59, which deals with the appointment of medical assessors, states that (1) 'The Authority is required to appoint medical practitioners and other suitably qualified persons to be medical assessors for the purposes of this Part' and that (2) 'The terms of any such appointment may restrict a medical assessor to disputes of a specified kind'.

While the legislation does not expressly require the medical practitioners to have any particular training or specified qualifications, in practice appointed medical assessors will have completed a training course in the use of the relevant chapter of the *Permanent Impairment Guidelines* published by the Motor Accidents Authority, and the terms of the appointment will 'restrict' the medical assessor to consider disputes concerning permanent impairment concerning the body part or system relevant to the assessors' specialist qualifications and the training in the application of the *Permanent Impairment Guidelines*.

The power of the Motor Accidents Authority to allocate medical assessors to hear and determine disputes is not subject to judicial review (see *Goodman v The Motor Accidents Authority of New South Wales & Anor* [2009] NSWSC 875).

Civil Liability Act 2002 (NSW)

Compensation for noneconomic loss or general damages is provided under s 16 of the *Act*. Noneconomic loss is defined to mean one or more of (a) pain and suffering, (b) loss of amenities of life, (c) loss of expectation of life and (d) disfigurement.

Damages for noneconomic loss may not be awarded unless the severity of the noneconomic loss is at least 15 % of a most extreme case; the maximum that can be awarded (for a most extreme case) is AU$572,200 (this figure applies from 1 October 2014 and will be reassessed after 12 months). It should be noted, however, that as specified in the table set out in s 16 of the *Act*, the amount of damages is not directly proportional to that of the 'most extreme case' but is scaled so that, for example, an assessment below 33 % of the 'most extreme case' leads to an award lower than the corresponding percentage of the 'most extreme case'. The table, showing the amounts applicable to ratings of noneconomic loss from 15 to 33 %, is set out below.

What constitutes 'a most extreme case' is difficult to determine, and it has been held (*Owners-Strata Plan 156 v Gray* [2004] NSWCA 304) that 'a most extreme case' might include 'cases of quadriplegia, some serious cases of paraplegia, cases of serious brain damage and perhaps some cases of extremely serious scarring and disfigurement may fall into this category'.

It is of particular relevance that in this case the New South Wales Court of Appeal held that the determination of what constitutes '15 % of the most extreme case' involved a legal and not a medical assessment; that is, it was not the same as an assessment of permanent impairment.

Part 3 of the *Civil Liability Act 2002* deals with damages for 'mental harm'. It defines 'mental harm' as 'impairment of a person's mental condition' and distinguishes 'consequential mental harm' ('mental harm that is a consequence of a personal injury of any other kind') from 'pure mental harm' ("mental harm other than consequential mental harm").

Section 29 of the *Act* places some limits on recovery of damages where the injury is solely related to 'mental or nervous shock'. Section 31 of the *Act* provides that there is 'no liability to pay damages for pure mental harm resulting from negligence unless the harm consists of a recognised psychiatric illness'. The *Act* also stipulates that a defendant will only owe a duty of care to a plaintiff in regards to psychiatric illness if the defendant 'ought to have foreseen that a person of normal fortitude might, in the circumstances of the case, suffer a recognised psychiatric illness if reasonable care were not taken' (s 32).

In *Hollier v Sutcliffe* [2010] NSWSC 279, the court held that the determination of what constitutes 'normal fortitude' is one that rests with the court as a determination of fact and that it was therefore not a 'medical question' to be decided by expert opinion.

Unlike the *Motor Accidents Compensation Act 1999*, the *Civil Liability Act 2002* does not provide for permanent psychiatric impairment assessment in relation to plaintiffs who have a compensable 'recognised psychiatric illness', and thus the damages for noneconomic loss to which they might be entitled are to be determined under the general provisions of s 16.

25.3.2 Queensland

Motor Accident Insurance Act 1994 (Qld)

Motor Accident Insurance Regulation 2004 (Qld)

Section 45A of the *Act* states that the Motor Accident Insurance Commission (MAIC), established pursuant to s 6 of the Act, '(a) may establish a panel of experts for reporting on the medical condition of claimants and their prospects of rehabilitation (the 'official panel of medical experts'); and (b) may revise the membership of the panel from time to time by adding to, or removing from, the names of the experts who constitute the panel'.

This section further provides that in deciding on the composition of the panel, the Commission '(a) must consult with the professional bodies with which consultation is required under a regulation; and (b) may only include an expert on the panel if—(i) the expert's inclusion is endorsed by the relevant professional bodies; or (ii) the commission is satisfied there is good reason for inclusion of the expert on the panel despite the absence of endorsement by the relevant professional bodies'.

Section 28 of the *Motor Accident Insurance Regulation 2004* (as at 16 January 2014) states that pursuant to section 45A(2)(a) the prescribed professional bodies are APLA Limited, Insurance Council of Australia, and Queensland Law Society; thus, no professional medical colleges or organisations are required to be consulted as part of establishing the 'official panel of medical experts'. 'APLA' is the abbreviation formerly used by the Australian Plaintiff Lawyers Association, which was established in 1994, and in 2004 'rebranded' itself as the Australian Lawyers Alliance.

The *Motor Accident Insurance Act 1994* also provides (s 46) that an insurer and a claimant may jointly arrange for an expert report but that 'neither an insurer nor a claimant is under any obligation to agree to a proposal to obtain a report under this section'.

Pursuant to s 46A, if the insurer wants to obtain an expert report on the claimant's medical condition or prospects of rehabilitation but fails to obtain the claimant's agreement, the claimant 'must comply with a request by the insurer to undergo, at the insurer's expense—(a) a medical examination by a doctor to be selected by the claimant from a panel of at least 3 doctors nominated in the request; or (b) an assessment of cognitive, functional or vocational capacity by an expert to be selected by the claimant from a panel of at least 3 experts with appropriate qualifications and experience nominated by the insurer in the request' unless such an obligatory examination 'is unreasonable or unnecessarily repetitious' (s 46A(3)).

The legislation does not provide any further guidance as to the method of appointment to the 'official panel of medical experts' and does not contain any specific provisions in relation to the professional qualifications of such 'experts'.

Civil Liability Act 2003 (Qld)

Civil Liability Regulation 2014 (Qld)

Pursuant to the *Civil Liability Act 2003* (Qld) and the *Civil Liability Regulation 2014*, general damages arising from wrongfully inflicted injuries are calculated on the basis of Injury Scale Values (ISV). Schedule 4 of the *Civil Liability Regulation* sets out the Injury Scale Values applicable to a large range of physical injuries, arranged by body systems, as well as mental disorders.

Schedule 3 of the *Regulation* sets out 'Matters to which Court may or must have regard in the application of Schedule 4'. The principal *Act* and the *Regulation* do not provide for a 'medical expert' to determine the applicable Injury Scale Values other than in relation to mental disorders. The *Regulation* specifies, in schedule 5, that the PIRS (Psychiatric Impairment Rating Scale—vide infra) is to be used to determine the extent of psychiatric impairment.

The earlier *Civil Liability Regulation 2003* included a Note, under s 11, stating that 'It is the function of a court, and not a medical report, to assess an ISV for an injury'.

The *Civil Liability Regulation 2014* states, in Notes at s 11, that 'It is not a function of a doctor to identify—(a) the item in schedule 4 to which an injury belongs; or (b) the appropriate ISV for an injury'.

Nevertheless, with respect to psychiatric impairment rating using the PIRS, the *Regulation*, in schedule 8 ('Dictionary'), states that a 'medical expert, for an assessment of a PIRS rating, means a person who—(a) is appropriately qualified to perform the assessment, including a psychologist, neuropsychologist or psychiatrist; and (b) has had appropriate training in the use of the PIRS'.

25.3.3 South Australia

Motor Accident Commission Act 1992 (SA)

The *Act* established the Motor Accident Commission 'to provide policies of compulsory third party insurance under Part 4 of the *Motor Vehicle Act 1959*' (s 14 (1)(a)) and, inter alia, 'to perform the functions of the nominal defendant while the Commission holds that office under Part 4 of the *Motor Vehicle Act 1959*' (s 14(1) (c)).

Claims for noneconomic loss arising from a motor vehicle accident may be made with respect of pain and suffering, loss of amenities of life, loss of expectation of life and/or disfigurement. No claim may be made unless the plaintiff can show that there had been significant impairment for at least 7 days or medical expenses had exceeded the prescribed minimum.

Compensation payable for noneconomic loss is assessed on a numerical scale (the Injury Scale Values or ISV) ranging from 0 to 100 points. Damages for noneconomic loss will only be made if the ISV for the injury exceeds ten.

The ISV is determined by 'an accredited health professional'; such medical assessments might be requested either by the insurer (Allianz), which administers the scheme on behalf of the Motor Accident Commission of South Australia, or by the plaintiff's lawyer.

Any claim for a psychological injury that does not develop from a physical injury ('pure mental harm') is assessed using the *Guides to the Evaluation of Psychiatric Impairment for Clinicians* (GEPIC; see below).

An accreditation scheme for Injury Scale Value assessments, pursuant to s 76 of the *Civil Liability Act 1936*, was established during 2014. An Accreditation Panel, appointed by the responsible minister (the State's Attorney General) and consisting of representatives from the Motor Accident Commission, The Law Society and Australian Medical Association, was appointed to establish the criteria for accreditation of health professionals who will be able to undertake ISV assessments or to perform psychiatric impairment assessments using the GEPIC.

Civil Liability Act 1936 (SA)

Civil Liability Regulations 2013 (SA)

Civil Liability Variation Regulations 2014 (SA)

The *Act* and *Regulations* establish an Accreditation Panel that determines:

- The criteria for accreditation of health professionals to undertake ISV or psychiatric impairment assessments
- The process of accreditation
- which health professionals meet the accreditation criteria for inclusion on the register of accredited health
- professionals
- Performance requirements and to review accredited health professionals
- The process by which accredited health professionals are removed from the register

As indicated above, the accredited health professionals pursuant to s 76(2) of the *Civil Liability Act 1936* (SA) will also be accredited under the *Motor Accident Commission Act 1992* (SA).

With respect to psychiatric impairment assessments using the GEPIC, the *Civil Liability Regulations 2013* provide (s 3) that

medical expert, in relation to an assessment of a GEPIC rating, means a person:

(a) Who is registered under the Health Practitioner Regulation National Law:

    (i) To practise in the medical profession
    (ii) Holding specialist registration as a psychiatrist

(b) Who has successfully completed a course of training in the use of the GEPIC under a scheme determined by the minister for the purposes of these regulations.

25.3.4 Tasmania

Motor Accidents (Liabilities and Compensation) Act 1973 (Tas)

Motor Accidents (Liabilities and Compensation) Regulations 2010 (Tas)

Pursuant to s 4 of the *Act*, the Motor Accident Insurance Board (MAIB) operates a combined common-law/no-fault motor accident scheme in Tasmania. As noted elsewhere in this chapter, this scheme provides medical and income benefits on a no-fault basis to persons injured in motor vehicle accidents while enabling access to common law.

The *Motor Accidents (Liabilities and Compensation) Regulations 2010* (Tas) quantify the benefits payable by the MAIB and specify conditions that may apply.

The total amount payable for medical and disability benefits is subject to a maximum sum ($400,000 for injuries sustained on or after 23 November 2005 or $500,000 from 1 August 2012 if the injured person was hospitalised continually for longer than 4 days commencing on the day of the accident).

The legislation and regulations under the *Act* do not provide for expert assessment of the degree of disability resulting from a motor vehicle accident.

If the person had been injured through the negligence of another, damages at common law can be sought pursuant to the *Civil Liability Act 2002* (Tas).

Civil Liability Act 2002 (Tas)

Section 27 of the *Act* sets out the 'Restrictions on damages for non-economic loss (general damages)'. Pursuant to s 27(1) 'If the amount of non-economic loss is assessed to be not more than Amount A, no damages are to be awarded for non-economic loss'. For the financial year ending on 30 June 2004, Amount A was $4000. The amount is calculated for each financial year based on a formula that takes into consideration the consumer price index (CPI) for Hobart, the capital city of Tasmania. For the period 1 July 2014 to 30 June 2015, the applicable Amount A is $5500.

Section 27(2) provides that 'If the amount of non-economic loss is assessed to be more than Amount A but not more than Amount B, damages awarded for non-economic loss are calculated as follows: amount awarded = 1.25 x (amount assessed minus Amount A)'. Section 27(4)(b) provided that 'Amount B is five times Amount A' ($27,500 for the period 1 July 2014 to 30 June 2015).

Section 27(3) provides that 'If the amount of non-economic loss is assessed to be more than Amount B, damages awarded for non-economic loss are an amount equal to the amount assessed'.

There is no provision for expert health practitioners to quantify the extent of physical or psychiatric impairment under the *Act*. Section 33, however, provides that 'There is no liability to pay damages for pure mental harm resulting from breach of duty unless the harm consists of a recognised psychiatric illness', and similarly s 35 provides that 'A court cannot make an award of damages for economic loss for consequential mental harm resulting from breach of duty unless the harm consists of a recognised psychiatric illness', and therefore in practice an expert witness would be involved in the determination as to whether or not a diagnosable mental disorder is present.

25.3.5 Victoria

Transport Accident Act 1986 (Vic)

Sections 93(2) and 93(3) of the Act specify that to sue for damages at common law, the claimant has to be assessed as having suffered a 'serious injury', defined as an impairment of 30 % or greater when assessed in accordance with the American Medical Association's *Guides to the Evaluation of Permanent Impairment* (4th edition, for physical injuries sustained after 19 May 1998) or if he/she is accepted as having:

(a) Serious long-term impairment or loss of a body function
(b) Permanent serious disfigurement
(c) Severe long-term mental or severe long-term behavioural disturbance or disorder
(d) Loss of a foetus (Transport Accident Act 1986 (Vic) s 93(17)(d))

The *Act* provides that the assessment of psychiatric impairment be undertaken according to the GEPIC (see below).

Under the 'no-fault' provisions of the Act, impairment benefits are payable for an impairment greater than 10 % assessed under the AMA Guides. The maximum amount payable under this provision of the Act was $320,130 (for the 12-month period commencing 1 July 2013).

The impairment assessment can only be undertaken by a registered medical practitioner who has completed a course approved by the responsible minister (s 46A(2)(b)); at the time of writing, such courses are conducted by the Victorian branch of the Australian Medical Association. The course, as currently structured, provides administrative information on the assessment of impairment, as well as theoretical and practical training in assessing impairment in the area relevant to the medical practitioner's specialty.

However, by virtue of the Transport Accident Act 1986 (Vic), s 93(4)(b), even persons whose degree of impairment was assessed at less than 30 % may still bring proceedings for the recovery of damages at common law if either the Transport Accident Commission issues a certificate that it is satisfied that the injury is a serious injury or a court, on the application of the injured person, gives leave to bring the proceedings.

Wrongs Act 1958 (Vic)

Division 3 of the *Wrongs Act 1958* (Vic) deals with 'Assessment of impairment'. Section 28LH provides that 'The assessment of degree of impairment must be made by an approved medical practitioner'.

Section 28LB defines an 'approved medical practitioner' as a medical practitioner who 'has successfully completed' an approved course with reference to the

Accident Compensation Act 1985 (the *Act* that provides for the workers' compensation arrangements in Victoria).

For all practical purposes, an 'approved medical practitioner' under the *Wrongs Act 1958* is the same as an 'independent impairment assessor' under the *Transport Accident Act 1986* (Vic).

25.3.6 Western Australia

Motor Vehicle (Third Party Insurance) Act 1943 (WA)

Section 3C(2) of the Act provides that 'The amount of damages to be awarded for non-pecuniary loss is to be a proportion, determined according to the severity of the non-pecuniary loss, of the maximum amount that may be awarded'. Pursuant to s 3C of the Act, non-pecuniary loss means '(a) pain and suffering; (b) loss of amenities of life; (c) loss of enjoyment of life; and (d) bodily or mental harm'.

Section 3C(3) provides that 'the maximum amount of damages that may be awarded for non-pecuniary loss ... may be awarded only in a most extreme case'. As of 1 July 2014, the maximum amount that can be awarded is $390,000. No damages are awarded if the threshold of $19,500 (as of 1 July 2014) is not met; the legislation provides that from claims awarded below $59,000, the threshold amount is deducted from the entitlement; there is a sliding scale of deductions from awards between $59,000 and $78,500, and there is no deduction from amounts greater than $78,500 (all amounts stated as of 1 July 2014).

The quantum of damages is decided by the Insurance Commission of Western Australia; there is no provision for assessment by a medical expert. In case of a dispute, the injured person is entitled to commence legal proceedings against the commission.

Civil Liability Act 2002 (WA)

The *Act* provides that the ward for general damages (noneconomic loss) must exceed a specified 'threshold' amount before payment can be made. At the time the legislation was enacted that threshold was $12,000; at the time of writing (January 2015), the threshold is $19,500. Plaintiffs whose damages for noneconomic loss fall between $19,500 and $59,000 will receive a percentage calculated according to a statutory formula (s 9(4)).

The legislation does not prescribe any method for the determination of general damages, and the task is undertaken by the court. There is thus no role for a medical expert in determining damages for noneconomic loss pursuant to the *Civil Liability Act 2002* in Western Australia.

25.3.7 Australian Capital Territory

Motor Vehicle (Third Party Insurance) Regulations (ACT)

Civil Law (Wrongs) Act 2002 (ACT)

In the Australian Capital Territory, common law applies to general damages awarded to those injured in motor vehicle accidents as well as those suing for the tortious infliction of personal injury. There is no threshold, and the quantum of damages is decided by the court.

In this jurisdiction there is no statutory provision for medical experts to quantify the extent of impairment suffered by the plaintiff whatever the mechanism of injury.

25.3.8 Northern Territory

Motor Accidents (Compensation) Act 1979 (NT)

Motor Accidents (Compensation) Regulations (NT)

The *Act* established a no-fault accident compensation scheme and pursuant to s 5 (1) abrogated common-law damages. The scheme covers everyone injured or killed in a motor vehicle accident in the territory, irrespective of where the motor vehicle is registered (s 6). The scheme is administered by the Territory Insurance Office (TIO).

Permanent impairment benefits are available under the *Act* provided that the injuries sustained in the motor vehicle accident are permanent and stable, and there is a whole person impairment (s 17(2)). The TIO arranges for the extent of impairment to be assessed by an independent medical specialist in the appropriate field, and the legislation stipulates that the American Medical Association (AMA) *Guides to the Evaluation of Permanent Impairment* be used.

Regulation 4 of the *Motor Accidents (Compensation) Regulations* (NT) (which commenced on 1 July 2007) provides that, pursuant to s 4C(2)(a) of the *Act*, the 6th edition of the AMA *Guides* is prescribed.

Section 4C(2)(b) of the Act states that the determination as to whether an impairment or combination of impairments is permanent and, if so, the extent of the permanent impairment is to be made 'on the advice of a medical practitioner', but it does not specify the specialist or other qualifications that should be held by that medical practitioner.

Personal Injuries (Liabilities and Damages Act) 2003 (NT)

Section 26(1) of the *Act* provides that 'A court, in determining the degree of permanent impairment suffered by an injured person, must do so on the basis of evidence adduced under this section'. Under s 26(3) 'Evidence of permanent impairment is to be given only by a medical practitioner who has assessed the degree of permanent impairment in accordance with the prescribed guides and any applicable regulation'.

Section 26(4) states that "The Regulations may provide for any matters in relation to the assessment of permanent impairment suffered by an injured person, including the following: (a) the content of the prescribed guides, including by modification of the American Medical Association Guides to the Evaluation of

Permanent Impairment; ((b) procedures relating to the assessment of permanent impairment; (c) the qualifications of medical practitioners who may give evidence under this section; (d) the costs in connection with the assessment of impairment".

Personal Injuries (Liabilities and Damages) Regulations *(NT) (accessed 26 January 2015) do not specify which edition of the AMA Guides is to be used pursuant to the* Act, *and they are also silent with respect to any specific 'qualifications of medical practitioners who may give evidence' under s 26(4)(c) of the principal* Act.

25.4 Evaluation Criteria

As discussed above, each of the six Australian States and the two Territories has legislation to provide benefits to those injured in motor vehicle accidents as well as those injured by the tortious acts of other persons. Under some legislation lump sum benefits are provided for persons who have suffered permanent impairment, and the rating method is specified either by statute or regulation made under the relevant act.

This section will describe the permanent impairment rating methods used to quantify the quantum of damages that are prescribed by legislation.

25.4.1 New South Wales

Motor Accidents Compensation Act 1999 (NSW)

Among the objects of this *Act* is 'full compensation for those with severe injuries involving ongoing impairment and disabilities' (s 5). Section 44 provides for the issuing of guidelines (MAA Medical *Guidelines*) with respect to 'the assessment of the degree of permanent impairment of an injured person as a result of an injury caused by a motor accident' (s 44(1)(c)). The *Act* further provides that '[N]o damages may be awarded for non-economic loss unless the degree of permanent impairment of the injured person as a result of the injury caused by the motor accident is greater than 10 per cent' (s131).

Section 133 of the *Act* specifies that '[T]he assessment of the degree of permanent impairment is to be made in accordance with: (a) MAA Medical Guidelines issued for that purpose, or (b) if there are no such guidelines in force the American Medical Association's Guides to the Evaluation of Permanent Impairment, Fourth Edition'.

With respect to the assessment of permanent impairment, the Motor Accidents Authority has issued Permanent Impairment Guidelines (http://www.maa.nsw.gov.au/about-us/guidelines/permanent-impairment) 'developed for the purpose of assessing the degree of permanent impairment arising from the injury caused by a motor accident, in accordance with section 133(2)(a) of the New South Wales Motor Accidents Compensation Act 1999'.

While the MAA Guidelines are based on the American Medical Association's *Guides to the Evaluation of Permanent Impairment* (4th edition, 3rd printing, 1995), the introductory chapter notes that there are 'some very significant departures from that document' and that

> These MAA Guidelines are definitive with regard to the matters they address. Where they are silent on an issue, the AMA 4 Guides should be followed. In particular, Chapters 1 and 2 of the AMA 4 Guides should be read carefully in conjunction with this Chapter of the MAA Guidelines. Some of the examples in AMA 4 are not valid for the assessment of impairment under the Motor Accidents Compensation Act 1999. It may be helpful for assessors to mark their working copy of the AMA 4 Guides with the changes required by these MAA Guidelines (emphasis in original).

The MAA Guidelines provide detailed instructions for the assessment of permanent impairment in relation to the following:

- Upper extremity impairment
- Lower extremity impairment
- Spinal impairment
- Nervous system impairment
- Ear, nose and throat and related structure impairment
- Mental and behavioural disorder impairment
- The respiratory system
- The cardiovascular system
- The haematopoietic system
- The visual system
- The digestive system
- The urinary and reproductive systems
- The endocrine system
- The skin

A detailed discussion of each section is beyond the scope of this chapter. However, because the MAA Guidelines require that impairment due to 'Mental and behavioural disorders' be assessed using a method that had been developed in New South Wales and therefore is likely to be unfamiliar to readers of this book, that method (PIRS, which has been referred to previously) will be described in detail.

The Motor Accidents Authority of NSW (MAA) had initially considered adopting, for the purposes of the Motor Accidents Compensation Act 1999 (NSW), the *Clinical Guidelines to the Rating of Psychiatric Impairment* prepared by the Medical Panel (Psychiatry) in Victoria (see below). These *Clinical Guidelines*, however, were apparently considered to be too generous to prospective claimants. Following initial contacts with the authors of the *Clinical Guidelines* in use in Victoria, the MAA established a Psychiatric Impairment Reference Group, who developed guidelines that have been published as Chap. 7, 'titled Mental and Behavioural Disorders Impairment', of the MAA Impairment Assessment

Guidelines (MAA *Guidelines*). This chapter sets out a Psychiatric Impairment Rating Scale (PIRS).

As stated in subsection 5(1)(e) of the *act*, the aims of the legislation are 'to keep premiums affordable, in particular, by limiting the amount of compensation payable for non-economic loss in cases of relatively minor injuries'. Subsection 5(2)(b) of the *Act* states 'that the law (both the enacted law and the common law) relating to the assessment of damages in claims made under this *Act* should be interpreted and applied in a way that acknowledges the clear legislative intention to restrict non-economic loss compensation in cases of minor injury'. In pursuit of these economic imperatives, the *Act* provides that no damages may be awarded for noneconomic loss unless the degree of permanent impairment is greater than 10 %.

Although titled 'Psychiatric Impairment Rating', Table 7.1 sets out six 'areas of function' to be rated, such as 'self care and personal hygiene'; 'social and recreational activities'; 'travel'; 'social functioning'; 'concentration, persistence and pace' and 'adaptation'. All of these have been taken directly from the relevant chapter of the 4th edition of the AMA *Guides*; the first three items are included within the 'activities of daily living' head of the *Guides*.

Even a cursory glance at the definitions of impairment and disability given above will make it clear that what these 'guidelines' assess is disability and not impairment. Indeed, the authors of these guidelines state '[O]ne of the ways to determine whether psychiatric impairment reaches the 10 % threshold is to examine the level of disability produced by a 10 % impairment caused by physical injuries... The compatibility between psychiatric and physical disability [sic] will minimize discrimination between persons suffering psychiatric injuries and person [sic] suffering physical injuries'.

These 'guidelines' thus rate disability and, by attempting to apply a backward leap from the disability to extrapolate what degree of impairment may have caused it, offer a percentage rating of 'impairment'. The 'guidelines' do not, however, at any stage evaluate 'impairment' in the sense in which that concept is defined by the relevant WHO publication quoted in the introduction to this chapter.

The PIRS, as published within the MAA *Guidelines*, provides five 'classes' of impairment for each of the six aspects of disability. Class 1 corresponds to either 'no deficit, or minor deficit' in the range of 0–3 %; for the other classes the corresponding percentages are as follows: Class 2 'mild impairment' 4–10 %, Class 3 'moderate impairment' 11–30 %, Class 4 'severe impairment' 31–60 % and Class 5 'totally impaired' >60 %.

The whole person psychiatric impairment is to be calculated using the median method. No allowance is made for a skewed distribution of scores, as provided for in the *Clinical Guidelines* in use in Victoria.

Other comments in Chap. 7 of the MAA Impairment Assessment *Guidelines* indicate that the 'mental and behavioural disorders impairment' rating was designed with the specific 10 % threshold in mind; the authors state explicitly that '... the threshold defined by the Act ... must be clarified. The terms 'severe injuries' and 'relatively minor injuries', contained in the Act are of some guidance'. As a result, these 'guidelines' were designed so that mild psychiatric impairment, which could attract an impairment rating of up to 20 % south of the Murray, will at most rate at 10 % in NSW.

A further hurdle for prospective claimants assessed using the PIRS is that 'the impairment must be attributable to a recognised psychiatric condition'. There is no such requirement for the presence of a specific diagnosable mental disorder in any of the scales that assess true psychiatric impairment, because it is recognised that individual aspects of mental functioning may be impaired in the absence of a diagnosable psychiatric illness.

In *Jones Bros Bus Co Pty Ltd v Baker* (1992) 8 NSWCCR 30, the court considered the meaning of note (a) at the end of the Table, which states "[W]here a range of percentages is provided by this Table, the maximum percentage is payable only in a most extreme case and the percentage payable in any other case shall be reasonably proportionate to that maximum percentage having regard to the severity of the matter. The amount payable in any particular case shall, in default of agreement, be determined in accordance with this Act by the Compensation Court".

A subsequent decision by the Court of Appeal, in *Langdon v New South Wales* (1996) 13 NSWCCR 552, held that "[T]he legislative purpose of including 'brain damage' injuries in the Table was to extend the right to lump sum compensation to: (a) those who, by reason of consequential impairment to their higher intellectual function, while still able to engage in some form of work, were no longer able to work in their prior employment; and (b) so as to enable those who had lost, either in whole or in part, some faculty or the efficient use of some bodily part which was controlled by the brain, and the loss of which faculty, or loss of the efficient use of which bodily part was not already provided for in the new Table".

The definition of 'permanent brain damage' was considered in *Skea v Legg & Another* (2000) 19 NSWCCR 644. With respect to 'permanency', authority was cited for the view that "permanent' is a relative term and is not synonymous with 'everlasting". The trial judge then adopted the view expressed by Woodward J. in *McDonald v Director-General of Social Security* (1984) FCR 345 that 'the true test of a permanent, as distinct from a temporary, incapacity is whether in the light of the available evidence, it is more likely than not that the incapacity will persist in the foreseeable future'.

In relation to the definition of 'brain damage', the trial judge, with respect, failed to differentiate between the manifestations of brain damage that might affect motor, sensory and/or cognitive functions (although there was reference to 'extensive testing' by a psychologist that 'did not indicate any pathologically severe disorders associated with intellect, memory or frontal lobe functions') and 'losses in mental functioning from ... psychological injury'. Reference was made to *Federal Broom Co v Semlitch* (1964) 110 CLR 626; that case, however, while holding that 'losses or impairments that flow from psychological injury are compensable', clearly cannot be considered relevant to the determination of the meaning of the phrase 'permanent brain injury' introduced into statute many years later.

With the greatest respect to the trial judge, there is further confusion of what is meant by 'brain damage' in the comment in paragraph 456 of the decision, which reads '[T]he reality in this case is that both Dr Stening and Dr White have found permanent brain damage, although they disagree considerably about whether or not it has an organic component and on the quantum of s 66 assessment'.

It is difficult to know what to make of the learned judge's conclusions 'that the applicant suffers from both organic and psychological permanent brain damage', that 'the applicant [has] both an organic and a psychological injury which have caused permanent brain damage' and that the plaintiff was 'a case involving predominantly psychological brain damage'. In the instant case, Walker J. found that 'Mr Skea's permanent brain damage represents 25 per cent of that extreme case'.

Civil Liability Act 2002 (NSW)

As discussed above, the Act does not specify that a specific impairment rating method be used to determine the damages payable to those injured by the tortious act of another person. Section 16(1) provides that 'No damages may be awarded for non-economic loss unless the severity of the non-economic loss is at least 15 % of a most extreme case'. That determination is made by the court.

The maximum amount of damages is prescribed by legislation and is adjusted annually; at the time of writing (January 2015), it is $572,000.

Section 16(3) states 'If the severity of the non-economic loss is equal to or greater than 15 % of a most extreme case, the damages for non-economic loss are to be determined' in accordance with the Table shown below (Table 25.1).

25.4.2 Queensland

Motor Accident Insurance Act 1994 (Qld)

Among the functions of the Motor Accident Insurance Commission, established under section 6 of the *Motor Accident Insurance Act 1994* (Qld), are to provide a compulsory third-party motor vehicle insurance system in Queensland and to supervise insurers under the statutory scheme. Under s 3, the objectives of the *Act* also include the encouragement of 'speedy resolution of personal injury claims resulting from motor vehicle accidents' and the promotion and encouragement 'as far as practicable, the rehabilitation of claimants who sustain personal injury because of motor vehicle accidents'.

To achieve these aims, s 45A states that the commission 'may establish a panel of experts for reporting on the medical condition of claimants and their prospects of rehabilitation (the 'official panel of medical experts')'. The *Act* also provides that an insurer and a claimant may jointly arrange for an expert report on the claimant's medical condition or prospects for rehabilitation (section 46). Section 46A provides that, in the absence of agreement between the parties, the claimant 'must comply with a request by the insurer to undergo, at the insurer's request' a medical examination by a doctor selected from a panel of at least three doctors nominated in the insurer's request unless 'it is unreasonable or unnecessarily repetitious'.

Table 25.1 Damages for noneconomic loss equal to or greater than 15 %

Severity of the noneconomic loss (as a proportion of a most extreme case) (%)	Damages for noneconomic loss (as a proportion of the maximum amount that may be awarded for noneconomic loss) (%)
15	1
16	1.5
17	2
18	2.5
19	3
20	3.5
21	4
22	4.5
23	5
24	5.5
25	6.5
26	8
27	10
28	14
29	18
30	23
31	26
32	30
33	33
34–100	34–100, respectively

The *Act* does not specify the methodology that should be used by the doctor in assessing the claimant's condition or prospects of rehabilitation or in determining the extent of any permanent impairment.

In *Kalb v Smith & Ors* (2001) QSC 216, a decision given by Wilson J. in the Supreme Court of Queensland on 22 June 2001, a psychiatrist stated that 'from a psychiatric point of view', the plaintiff had an impairment of 20 % 'of his whole body'. There is no indication in the judgement on what basis that conclusion, which was accepted by the learned judge, was reached.

In *Goode v Thompson & Anor* (2001) QSC 287, decided by Ambrose J. on 2 July 2001, a 12-year-old boy had been struck by a motor vehicle and suffered severe head injuries. The judgement refers to resultant permanent 'grave intellectual impairment', but there is no specific mention of expert evidence as to the extent of that impairment or its clinical assessment or the extent of impairment resulting from post-traumatic epilepsy. Damages for the intellectual impairment, epilepsy and other physical injuries were awarded under the head of 'general damages' for 'pain and suffering and loss of amenities' at $150,000.

Civil Liability Act 2003 (Qld)
Civil Liability Regulation 2014 (Qld)

Section 61 of the *Civil Liability Act 2003* (Qld) states that 'if general damages are to be awarded by a court in relation to an injury rising after 1 December 2002, the court must assess an injury scale value' on a scale from 0 to 100.

The *Act* further states that 'the scale reflects 100 equal gradations of general damages, from a case in which an injury is not severe enough to justify any award of general damages to a case in which an injury is of the gravest conceivable kind' (s 61(1)(b)).

Section 61(1)(c) provides that 'in assessing the injury scale value, the court is to consider—(i) the range of injury scale values for similar injuries, prescribed under a regulation; and (ii) the injury scale values attributed to similar injuries in prior proceedings'.

General damages are to be calculated in accordance with a sliding scale, as provided by s 62. Thus, if the scale value of an injury is assessed at five or less, the scale value is to be multiplied by $1000. If the scale value is assessed as ten or less but more than five, the damages are calculated by multiplying the number by which the scale value exceeds five by $1200 and adding $5000. For the most severe injuries, in the range between 90 and 100 on the 'scale value', the damages are set at $215,000 plus the amount calculated by multiplying the number by which the scale value exceeds 90 by $3500 (s 62(n)). (These figures were current at 31 December 2003.)

Schedule 3 of the *Civil Liability Regulation 2003* (Qld) referred to the use of 'AMA 5' (the 5th edition of the American Medical Association's *Guides to the Evaluation of Permanent Impairment*, as set out in schedule 7) in the assessment of 'whole person impairment percentage'. However, 'AMA 5' is not to be used in the 'medical assessment of scarring or of a mental disorder'. In assessing the 'Injury Scale Values' (ISV) of a mental disorder, the prescribed instrument is the Psychiatric Impairment Rating Scale (PIRS). Schedule 3 also provides that 'an ISV assessed by a court must be a whole number' (s 14).

Schedule 3 s 5 deals with what is described as an 'adverse psychological reaction', as follows:

(1) This section applies if a court is assessing an ISV where an injured person has an adverse psychological reaction to a physical injury.
(2) The court must treat the adverse psychological reaction merely as a feature of the injury.

The following section, headed 'Mental Disorder', provides that:

(1) This section applies if:

    (a) A court is assessing an ISV.
    (b) A PIRS rating for a mental disorder of an injured person is relevant under schedule 4.

(2) The PIRS rating for the mental disorder of the injured person is the PIRS rating accepted by the court.
(3) A PIRS rating is capable of being accepted by the court only if it is:

(a) Assessed by a medical expert as required under schedules 5 and 6
(b) Provided to the court in a PIRS report as required under schedule 5, section 12

The 'Dictionary' set out in schedule 7 of the Regulation states that "mental disorder' means a mental disorder recognised under DSM 4' and that "DSM 4' means the 4th edition of the *Diagnostic and Statistical Manual of Mental Disorders, Text Revision (DSM-IV-TR)* published by the American Psychiatric Association in 2000'.

It is not clear why the *Regulation* accepts as mental disorders those described in what is, in essence, a regional classification developed for use in the USA, rather than the classification of mental disorders published by the World Health Organization, currently in its 10th edition (ICD-10), which is the classification officially recognised by, and used for statistical purposes in, Australia [11].

The *Regulation* also provides that a 'medical expert' for the purposes of an assessment of a PIRS rating 'means a person—(a) who is appropriately qualified to perform the assessment, including a psychologist, neuropsychologist or psychiatrist; and (b) who has had appropriate training in the use of the PIRS' (schedule 7).

Again, it is not clear why the *Regulation* includes in its definition of 'medical expert' those who have not undertaken medical studies or obtained a medical qualification and whose professional training does not include the study of the diagnosis, management and treatment of mental disorders. Neuropsychologists have their own field of expertise that differs from the study of mental disorders, while clinical psychologists—let alone psychologists who are not members of the College of Clinical Psychologists within the Australian Psychological Society—similarly do not have specific training in the diagnosis and treatment of patients suffering from psychiatric disorders.

As noted above, the PIRS was initially developed in New South Wales for use by the Motor Accidents Authority, and it was based on the 4th edition of the American Medical Association's *Guides*. The introductory chapters of the AMA *Guides* (Chaps. 1 and 2) repeatedly refer to the use of the *Guides* by 'physicians'. It is clear both from the *Guides*, and from the introduction to the PIRS, that both were designed and intended for use by medical practitioners rather than by any other healthcare practitioners.

Part 2 of schedule 4 of the *Regulation* sets out 'items' that rate the severity of the mental disorder as follows:

- Item 10—extreme mental disorder (corresponding to a PIRS rating between 31 and 100 %)
- Item 11—serious mental disorder (PIRS rating between 11 and 30 %)
- Item 12—moderate mental disorder (PIRS rating between 4 and 10 %)
- Item 13—minor mental disorder (PIRS rating between 0 and 3 %)

Schedule 6 sets out the Psychiatric Impairment Rating Scale to be used for the purposes of the *Civil Liability Act 2003*. The PIRS specified in this legislation is very similar to that set out in the MAA *Guidelines* in NSW, with some changes in the wording of the descriptors. However, whereas the instructions for the calculation of whole person psychiatric impairment under the MAA *Guidelines* simply require the conversion of the median class score into a percentage rating, the method prescribed in the *Civil Liability Regulation 2003* (Qld) requires the calculation of both the median class score **and** the total class score be fore using the 'Conversion table for percentage impairment' to obtain the final PIRS rating (schedule 5).

The PIRS, as noted above, is based on the 4th edition of the American Medical Association's *Guides to the Evaluation of Permanent Impairment*. At p. 6 of the Guides, it is specifically stated that

It must be emphasized and clearly understood that impairment percentages derived according to Guides criteria should not be used to make direct financial awards or direct estimates of disabilities.

Despite this caveat, the Queensland statute directly translates the impairment rating obtained using the PIRS into the amount to be awarded as general damages under the *Civil Liability Act 2003*.

It should also be noted that the PIRS used under the *Civil Liability Act 2003* differs from the two versions used in NSW and from that used in the workers' compensation jurisdiction in Tasmania; at the time of writing, there are thus four different versions of the PIRS in use in Australia.

As noted above, the *Act* states that the injury scale 'reflects 100 equal gradations of general damages, from a case in which an injury is not severe enough to justify any award of general damages to a case in which an injury is of the gravest conceivable kind'. However, it is not possible to assess injuries in terms of 'equal gradations' of severity. At best, injuries can be graded on an ordinal scale (i.e. stating that a particular injury is more severe or less severe than another) [9]. For gradations to be 'equal', it would be necessary for precise measurements to be made, as is the case for interval and ratio scales (e.g. measurements of length or temperature). Clearly, this degree of precision cannot be applied to the assessment of injuries.

25.4.3 South Australia

Motor Accident Commission Act 1992 (SA)

The *Motor Accident Commission Act 1992* provides for the establishment of a Commission to administer the compulsory third-party insurance scheme that covers all users of motor vehicles in South Australia. The statutory provisions that control the award of damages in respect of injuries arising from a motor accident are set out in the *Civil Liability Act 1936* (SA) (formerly known as the *Wrongs Act 1936* (SA)), as amended. Section 35A deals with motor accidents.

Compensation for noneconomic loss under the *Civil Liability Act* is awarded for pain and suffering, loss of amenities of life, loss of expectation of life and disfigurement. It is calculated on a scale of 0–60 points, as assessed by the court on the basis of lay and medical evidence, pursuant to section 35A(b)(i) of the *Civil Liability Act 1936* (SA). The points received are multiplied by a sum that is increased each year according to the CPI.

Section 35A(c) of the *Civil Liability Act 1936* provides that:

No damages shall be awarded for mental or nervous shock except in favour of:

(i) A person who was physically injured in the accident, who was the driver of or a passenger in or on a motor vehicle involved in the accident or who was, when the accident occurred, present at the scene of the accident
(ii) A parent, spouse or child of a person killed, injured or endangered in the accident

The *Act* does not provide for any specific method to be used in the medical assessment of the severity of injury or permanent physical impairment, although as noted above during 2014, an Accreditation Panel was established to develop a format for Injury Scale Value reports pursuant to the *Civil Liability Act 1936* that also will apply to assessment of damages under the *Motor Accident Commission Act 1992*.

Permanent psychiatric impairment is to be assessed using the *Guides to the Evaluation of Psychiatric Impairment* (GEPIC; see below).

Civil Liability Act 1936 (SA)

Civil Liability Regulations 2013 (SA)

Civil Liability Variation Regulations 2014 (SA)

The *Civil Liability Regulations 2013* (SA), which is subordinate legislation under the *Act*, in Part 2 provide for the award of damages for noneconomic loss in accordance with 'Injury scale values' (ISV). Schedule 1 of the *Regulations* sets out the 'Ranges of injury scale values' according to the body system injured. The schedule provides ranges for different types of injuries and provided 'examples of factors affecting ISV scale' to be considered for each injury.

As an example, under the rubric of 'Central nervous system and head injuries', the 'range' of ISV for quadriplegia is given as 80–100, and the factors to be considered are listed as:

- Presence and extent of pain
- Extent of any residual movement
- Consequential mental harm
- Level of function and pre-injury function
- Degree of independence
- Ability to participate in daily activities, including employment
- Presence and extent of secondary medical complications
- Loss of reproductive or sexual function
- Bowel or bladder incontinence

At the other end of the scale, with respect to chest injuries, a 'soft tissue injury, minor fracture or minor internal organ injury' is given an ISV of 0–4, with the comments that 'The injury will involve a soft tissue injury, minor fracture, or minor and non-permanent injury to internal organs' and 'there may be persistent pain from the chest, for example from the chest wall or sternochondral or costochondral joints'. A further 'comment about appropriate level of ISV' states 'An ISV at or near the bottom of the range will be appropriate if there is a soft tissue injury from which the person will fully recover'.

Section 13 of the *Regulations* provides that '(1) This regulation applies if a court is assessing an ISV where an injured person suffers consequential mental harm following a physical injury', and '(2) The court must treat the consequential mental harm merely as a feature of the injury'.

With respect to 'pure mental harm' (i.e. a psychiatric injury that is not secondary to a physical injury), s 14 states:

(1) This regulation applies if:
 (a) A court is assessing an ISV.
 (b) A GEPIC rating for psychiatric impairment of an injured person is relevant under schedule 1.

(2) A GEPIC rating may be accepted by the court only if it is:
 (a) An assessment of pure mental harm
 (b) Assessed by a medical expert
 (c) Provided to the court in a GEPIC report

Whole person impairment due to 'pure mental harm' is to be assessed using the GEPIC.

Pursuant to s 16 of the *Regulations*, if a medical report 'states a whole person impairment percentage', it must state how the percentage is calculated. Section 16 (c) mandates that if the percentage is 'based on criteria provided under AMA 5', then an identification of the relevant provisions of AMA 5' and 'if a range of percentages is available under AMA 5 for an injury of the type being assessed—the reason for assessing the injury at the selected point in the range' must be stated.

The court is required to 'give greater weight to a medical assessment of a whole person impairment percentage' if the assessment is based on AMA 5 criteria 'than to a medical assessment of a whole person impairment percentage not based on the criteria'—this stipulation does not apply to 'assessment of scarring or of mental harm' (s 17).

25.4.4 Tasmania

Motor Accidents (Liabilities and Compensation) Act 1973 (Tas)

Motor Accidents (Liabilities and Compensation) Regulations 2010 (Tas)

The Motor Accidents Insurance Board (MAIB), established under the *Act*, provides no-fault statutory benefits to persons injured in motor accidents in Tasmania.

The MAIB also indemnifies motorists who might have been negligent in motor vehicle accident in which another person was injured.

In addition to the statutory no-fault scheme, Tasmania allows unrestricted access to common law where the fault of another party can be established.

Scheduled benefits are set out in schedule 1 of the *Motor Accidents (Liabilities and Compensation) Regulations 2010* (Tas). Part 5 provides for disability allowance of the lesser amount than 80 % of average weekly earnings if these exceed $400 per week or three times the adult average weekly earnings.

Section 27(1) of the *Act* states that ‘Except as provided by subsection (2), if a liability has been incurred for the payment of damages to a person in respect of a personal injury the payment to that person of a scheduled benefit in respect of that personal injury shall, so far as it extends, be taken to be a payment in or towards the discharge of that liability, and the amount of those damages shall be reduced accordingly’.

Section 27B of the *Act* provides that the MAIB ‘may require an examination of a person to whom this section applies to be carried out if . . . the right to, or amount of any, scheduled benefits or damages payable in respect of an injury referred to in subsection (2) depends on a determination by the Board, a decision of the Tribunal or a judgment by a court’.

The *Act* and the *Regulations* under the *Act* do not specify the method by which the extent of any impairment arising from a personal injury compensable under the *Act* should be determined.

Injured motorists are entitled to sue for common-law damages if they consider that the injury was due to another person’s negligence. The amount of general damages that is recoverable is determined in accordance with the provisions of the *Civil Liability Act 2002* (Tas).

Civil Liability Act 2002 (Tas)

As in other jurisdictions in which comparable legislation was enacted following the Ipp Report (vide supra), the *Act* was intended to limit the quantum of damages for personal injury, including damages for noneconomic loss.

Section 27(1) of the *Act* provides for a threshold and states ‘If the amount of non-economic loss is assessed to be no more than Amount A, no damages are to be awarded for non-economic loss’. The threshold (Amount A) was $4000 at the time the *Act* was proclaimed. This amount is increased annually in line with the CPI (consumer price index), and at the time of writing (January 2015), it was $5500.

The *Act* does not specify any method for the assessment of impairment due to physical or psychiatric injury on which the quantum of damages is to be based; the task of calculating the appropriate damages is left to the court.

Section 28 states:

Tariffs for damages for noneconomic loss (general damages)

(1) In determining damages for noneconomic loss, a court may refer to earlier decisions of that or other courts for the purpose of establishing the appropriate award in the proceedings.

(2) For that purpose the parties to the proceedings or their counsel may bring the court's attention to awards for noneconomic loss in those earlier decisions.
(3) In this section—other courts include a court of any jurisdiction within Australia, including Tasmania.

Part 8 deals with general damages for 'mental harm'. Section 33 provides that 'There is no liability to pay damages for pure mental harm resulting from breach of duty unless the harm consists of a recognized psychiatric illness', and s 35 has a similar provision with respect to "consequential mental harm".

25.4.5 Victoria

Transport Accident Act 1986 (Vic)

In Victoria, the *Transport Accident Act 1986* (Vic) provides that if the Transport Accident Commission 'has determined the degree of impairment of a person who is injured as a result of a transport accident; and the degree so determined is more than 10 per centum the Commission must assess an impairment benefit in respect of the person' (s 47). The lump sum impairment benefit under this section is assessed in accordance with the formula $(A - B)/C \times \$61{,}940$, where A is the degree of impairment assessed, B is 10 % and C is 90 %. The impairment assessment is undertaken 18 months after the accident or when the injury stabilises 'whichever last occurs' (s 46A).

It will be therefore apparent that the injured person must be more than 10 % impaired to be eligible for impairment benefits.

Impairment of 30 % or more is deemed to be a serious injury for the purpose of bringing proceedings for damages (s 93), and those who are less than 50 % impaired are not eligible for no-fault benefits for longer than 3 years (s 53). Persons less than 50 % impaired are eligible for benefits up to a total of $99, 220 (s 53(3)).

Amendments inserted into the workers' compensation and motor accident statutes during 1998 provide that impairment assessment pursuant to the *Transport Accident Act 1986* (Vic) must be undertaken in accordance with the 4th edition of the *Guides to the Evaluation of Permanent Impairment* published by the American Medical Association in 1993, with exceptions in relation to Chapter 14 (psychiatric impairment), Chapter 15 (pain) and hearing loss. Section 46B(1) of the *Act* states that '[I]n determining a degree of impairment of a person, regard must not be had to any psychiatric or psychological injury, impairment or symptoms arising as a consequence of, or secondary to, a physical injury'.

Chapter 14 of the 4th edition of the AMA *Guides*, which provides for the assessment of impairment due to 'mental and behavioural disorders', does not rate aspects of mental functioning and does not provide a method of quantifying impairment in percentage terms; instead, it discusses activities of daily living, social functioning, concentration and adaptation and was therefore considered to be quite unsuitable for the purpose of assessing psychiatric impairment as required under the provisions of both the *Transport Accident Act 1986* (Vic) and the *Accident Compensation Act 1985* (Vic). Section 46A(6) of the *Transport Accident Act 1986* (Vic) provides that '[F]or the purposes of determining the degree of psychiatric impairment, the A.M.A. *Guides* apply as if for Chapter 14 there were substituted the *Clinical Guidelines to the Rating of Psychiatric Impairment* prepared by the Medical Panel (Psychiatry) Melbourne October 1997 and published in the Government Gazette'. (These *Guidelines* are discussed below.)

Finally, s 46A(7) of the Act states '[I]n this section "A.M.A. Guides" means the American Medical Association's Guides to the Evaluation of Permanent Impairment (Fourth Edition) (other than Chapter 15) as modified by this Act'.

Wrongs Act 1958 (Vic)

The *Wrongs and Other Acts (Law of Negligence) Act 2003* (Vic) extensively amended the *Wrongs Act 1958* (Vic), particularly with respect to compensation for negligence and mental harm, and the liability of public authorities.

Section 75 of the *Wrongs Act 1958* (Vic) now provides that 'A court cannot make an award of damages for economic loss for mental harm resulting from negligence unless the harm consists of a recognised psychiatric illness'. Section 43, however, states that 'injury' includes 'psychological or psychiatric injury'. The phrase 'psychological or psychiatric injury' is not specifically defined in the Act and neither is 'recognised psychiatric illness'. There is an obvious inconsistency between the implication that 'psychological injury' is the same as 'recognised psychiatric illness'. It would be generally considered that 'psychological injury' means an emotional reaction that is an understandable psychological response to a physical injury or other stressful event and one that does not amount to a 'recognised psychiatric illness', that is, an emotional reaction that does not lead to, and does not meet the diagnostic criteria for, a mental disorder.

Part VBA sets out the 'thresholds in relation to recovery of damages for non-economic loss'. Under the definitions in s 28LB, a 'threshold level' of 'more than 10 per cent' is set for impairment due to psychiatric injury. Section 28LG provides that 'The assessment of degree of impairment must be made by an approved medical practitioner'. 'Approved medical practitioner' is defined (s 28LB) as '(a) if a training course has been approved under section 91(1)(b) of the Accident Compensation Act 1985, a medical practitioner who has successfully completed the course; or (b) if a training course has not been so approved, a medical practitioner'.

In accordance with s 28LI, psychiatric impairment is to be assessed using the *Clinical Guidelines to the Rating of Psychiatric Impairment.* Section 28LJ provides that 'In assessing a degree of impairment of a person under this Part, regard must not be had to any psychiatric or psychological injury, impairment or symptoms arising as a consequence of, or secondary to, a physical injury'.

As noted above, the *Guide to the Evaluation of Psychiatric Impairment for Clinicians* (GEPIC), published in the *Victoria Government Gazette* on 27 July 2006, is used in Victoria to assess psychiatric impairment, in accordance with the provisions of the *Transport Accident Act 1986* and the *Wrongs Act 1958* when the initial assessment is undertaken after 28 July 2006 or the motor vehicle accident occurred on or after 26 July 2006.

The GEPIC lists six factors that are to be assessed to provide the percentage rating of psychiatric impairment, namely, intelligence, thinking, perception, judgement, mood and behaviour. These six aspects of mental functioning may be briefly described as follows:

(1) *Intelligence*: refers to the level of cognitive (intellectual) function. It includes global orientation (in time, place and person), fund of general information, capacity for abstract thinking, memory functions and aspects of the use of language. Intelligence can be clinically assessed during a psychiatric consultation, and if considered necessary a screening test such as the Mini Mental State Examination can be performed. Significant impairment of intelligence occurs in dementia (e.g. following severe head injury or due to degenerative brain disease) or might be congenital or developmental.

(2) *Thinking*: impairment includes formal thought disorder involving thought processes (loosening of associations, interpenetration, metonymy, thought blocking) and abnormalities of thought content (delusions, overvalued ideas) and abnormalities of the stream of thought (e.g. pressure of speech with flight of ideas or slowed thinking due to psychomotor retardation). Delusions can be primary or secondary and might be persecutory, grandiose, etc. or involve delusions of reference. In patients with schizophrenia, specific delusions of thought broadcasting, delusions of influence, etc. might occur (sometimes termed first-rank symptoms).

(3) *Perception*: disorders of perception which need to be assessed as part of the mental status examination are hallucinations and illusions. Hallucinations are subjective sensory perceptions in the absence of an actual external stimulus; these might occur in any one of the five sensory modalities. Illusions are defined as distorted perceptions of real external stimuli; they are usually visual but might involve misperception of sounds.

(4) *Judgement*: this refers to the ability to evaluate various situations and information and reach an effective conclusion. Impaired judgement might affect the individual's capacity to perform certain complex tasks and to make autonomous decisions at work. Following injuries to the frontal lobes, judgement might be impaired leading to socially inappropriate behaviour.

(5) *Mood*: this refers to the assessment of the person's sustained feeling state, which tends to be persistent and stable, and colours the total experience of the individual. During the consultation mood tends to be manifested by the subject's affect, which is the individual's immediate emotional experience. Mood is generally described along a continuum from the extreme of severe depression with suicidal ideation to that of euphoria. Affective instability (emotional lability) with marked shifts of mood might be apparent during a consultation. Another aspect of emotion that might be present during the consultation is anxiety.

(6) *Behaviour*: impairment of behaviour is present when the individual acts in a manner that is disruptive or aggressive; disruptive behaviour might be due to agitation or argumentativeness. Persons with an obsessional disorder might be impaired by compulsive activity. In psychotic disorders, catatonic posturing or stereotyped movements interfere with goal-directed activity.

Examples are given in the GEPIC for each type of impairment, allowing a rating to be made of the severity of impairment ranging among five classes, similar to those used in the 2nd edition of the AMA Guides. The whole person psychiatric impairment rating is determined using the median method as described in the Guide.

Because a training course in the use of the *Clinical Guidelines* has been approved pursuant to the *Accident Compensation Act 1985* (Vic), in effect medical practitioners who have completed that course are 'approved medical practitioners' for the purposes of s 28LB.

If the impairment assessment is disputed as to whether or not the 'threshold level' has been reached, it can be referred as a 'medical question' to the Medical Panel established under the *Accident Compensation Act 1985* for determination that is binding on the parties and on the court (s 28LZI).

25.4.6 Western Australia

Motor Vehicle (Third Party Insurance) Act 1943 (WA)

Section 30 of the Act provides for the medical examination of injured persons, at the request of either the insured person or of the Commission established under the *Act*.

Subsection 3C(2) provides that an 'amount of damages to be awarded for non-pecuniary loss is to be a proportion, determined according to the severity of the non-pecuniary loss, of the maximum amount that may be awarded'. Subsection 3C(1) states that non-pecuniary loss means 'pain and suffering; loss of amenities of life; loss of enjoyment of life; curtailment of expectation of life; and bodily or mental harm'.

The *Act* does not prescribe a methodology for the assessment of the 'severity' of the 'mental harm' or any of the other types of non-pecuniary loss enumerated in this subsection.

Civil Liability Act 2002 (WA)

Section 9(1) of the *Act* provides that 'If the amount of non-pecuniary loss is assessed to be not more that Amount A, for the year in which the amount is assessed, no damages are to be awarded for non-pecuniary loss'. For the 12 months commencing from 1 July 2014, that threshold amount is $19,500.

With respect to 'mental harm: duty of care', s 5S(1) provides that 'A person (the defendant) does not owe a duty of care to another person (the plaintiff) to take care not to cause the plaintiff mental harm unless the defendant ought to have foreseen that a person of normal fortitude might, in the circumstances of the case, suffer a recognized psychiatric illness if reasonable care were not taken'.

The *Act* is silent on the subject of who will determine 'normal fortitude' (the court or a psychiatric expert witness).

The Act also does not prescribe the methodology to be used to determine the extent of either physical or psychiatric impairment on which the quantum of damages is to be based.

25.4.7 Australian Capital Territory

Road Transport (Third Party Insurance) Act 2008 (ACT)

The ACT, like other Australian States and the Northern Territory, has a compulsory third-party insurance scheme to cover those injured in motor vehicle accidents.

The ACT Compulsory Third Party (CTP) Insurance Regulator is an independent authority established under s 14 of the Act to regulate the CTP scheme in the Territory. The legislation provides that the Director General of the Chief Minister and Treasury Directorate is the CTP Regulator.

Pursuant to s 156C(1) of the *Act*, the CTP Regulator 'may make guidelines (the non-economic loss guidelines) setting out information to assist courts in deciding the appropriate level of damages for non-economic loss in motor accident claims', but at the time of writing (January 2015), no such guidelines had been issued.

Although the Standing Committee on Public Accounts of the ACT Assembly recommended, in its inquiry into the *Road Transport (Third Party Insurance) Amendment Bill 2011*, that the principal *Act* be amended to provide that the AMA Guides be used to determine 'non-economic loss impairment' and introduce thresholds, that recommendation was not adopted.

At the time of writing, the *Act* does not specify any method by which general damages are to be assessed, and these are determined by common-law principles.

Prior to the reform of liability insurance subsequent to the publication of the Ipp Report in September 2002, as stated in *Suffolk v Meere* (2001) ACTSC 24, the principles to be applied in the ACT to determine compensation in personal injury cases arising following motor vehicle accidents in the ACT were those enunciated by the High Court of Australia and summarised by McHugh J. in *Nominal Defendant v Gardikiotis* (1996) 186 CLR 49:

> When a defendant has negligently injured a plaintiff, the common law requires the defendant to pay a money sum to the plaintiff to compensate that person for any damage that is causally connected to the defendant's negligence and that ought to have been reasonably foreseen by the defendant when the negligence occurred. The sum of money to be paid to the plaintiff is that sum which will put the plaintiff, so far as possible, "in the same position as he would have been if he had not sustained the wrong for which he is now getting his compensation".

Subsequent to the 2002 reform, the principles applied are those set out in the *Civil Law (Wrongs) Act 2002* (see below).

Civil Law (Wrongs) Act 2002 (ACT)

The *Act* does not provide any threshold for the recovery of damages for non-economic loss. Section 99(4) provides that in relation to 'Tariffs for non-economic loss' governing awards under this legislation, 'non-economic loss includes the following: (a) pain and suffering; (b) loss of amenities of life; (c) loss of expectation of life; (d) disfigurement'. A note to this section of the *Act* states that 'Damages for non-economic loss for injuries caused by motor accidents are subject to limitations under the *Road Transport (Third Party Insurance) Act 2008*' pursuant to any guidelines issued by the CTP Regulator; no such guidelines have been issued (see above).

Section 35 of the *Civil Law (Wrongs) Act 2002* (ACT) provides that '(1) damages must not be awarded for pure mental harm to a person resulting from negligence unless the harm consists of a recognized psychiatric illness' and '(2) damages must not be awarded for economic loss for consequential mental harm to a person resulting from negligence unless the harm consists of a recognized psychiatric illness'.

Although the *Act* defines 'mental harm' as 'impairment of the person's mental condition' (s 32), it makes no provision for assessment of that impairment by a psychiatrist expert witness utilising any recognised methodology. According to s 99 '(1) In deciding damages for noneconomic loss, a court may refer to earlier decisions of that or other courts for the purpose of establishing the appropriate award in the proceeding' and '(2) For that purpose, the parties to the proceeding or their lawyer may bring the court's attention to awards of damages for non-economic loss in those earlier decisions'.

25.4.8 Northern Territory

Motor Accidents (Compensation) Act 1979 (NT)

Motor Accidents (Compensation) Regulations (NT)

The *Act* establishes a no-fault compensation scheme that, among other benefits, provides 'compensation for loss of limb or other permanent impairment' (s 17). The Northern Territory, Tasmania and Victoria are the only jurisdictions in Australia that have a no-fault statutory compensation scheme, with replacement of earnings, for persons injured in motor vehicle accidents.

Subsection 17(1)(b) states that compensation for permanent impairment is payable if 'the extent of the impairment, as assessed by the Commission, is at least 5 %'.

Section 4C(2) of the *Act* states that determination of permanent impairment is to be made '(a) in accordance with the edition of the American Medical Association Guides to the Evaluation of Permanent Impairment prescribed by regulation as modified by regulation; and (b) on the advice of a medical practitioner'.

Regulation 4(1) of the *Motor Accidents (Compensation) Regulations* (NT) provides that 'For section 4C(2)(a) of the Act, the American Medical Association Guides to the Evaluation of Permanent Impairment, 6th Edition is prescribed'.

Personal Injuries (Liabilities and Damages) Act 2003 (NT)

Section 26 of the *Act* provides that in determining the degree of permanent impairment suffered by an injured person, 'Evidence of permanent impairment is to be given only by a medical practitioner who has assessed the degree of permanent impairment in accordance with the prescribed guides and any applicable regulation' (s 26(3).

Pursuant to s 27(2), 'A court must not award damages for non-pecuniary loss if the court determines the degree of permanent impairment to be less than 5 % of the whole person'.

Section 26(4)(a) states that the degree of permanent impairment is to be assessed in accordance with 'prescribed guides, including by modification of the American Medical Association Guides to the Evaluation of Permanent Impairment' as provided by Regulations made under the *Act*.

The definition of 'prescribed guides' in s 18 of the *Act* states '(a) the guides prescribed by the Regulations; or (b) if no guides are prescribed by the Regulations—the American Medical Association Guides to the Evaluation of Permanent Impairment (s modified by any regulation) as published from time to time'.

There are no guides prescribed by the Regulations at the time of writing.

In *Kampourakis v DCT (NT) Pty Ltd* [2013] NTSC 76, the Supreme Court of the Northern Territory discussed the principles relevant to the assessment of the quantum of damages for noneconomic loss pursuant to the *Personal Injuries (Liabilities and Damages) Act 2003* (NT). With reference to the use of the AMA Guides, the court stated that whereas 'as a matter of practice, the most current of the Guides available is likely to be preferred; however, an assessment made using an earlier Guide is not by virtue of that fact invalid'.

The *Act* does not make any special provisions for the award of damages with respect to mental harm or psychiatric injury.

25.5 Summary

According to Biklen, the exercise of clinical judgement in the rating of impairment and disability is influenced by many factors. Among such factors, of which the rater may be unaware, are service traditions, economics, bureaucratic exigency, politics and societal prejudice. Indeed, Biklen considers these factors to be so pervasive that he describes reliance on clinical judgement to be 'little more than a mythology' [12].

In view of the statutory requirements noted above, which vary to the extent to which they require medical ratings of impairment for the purpose of assessing the quantum of damages for noneconomic loss as against assessments made by the court, there is a clear need for a wider appreciation both of the different and, specifically defined, concepts of impairment and disability and also of the method of impairment rating if this has been stated in the relevant legislation.

The difficulties in the rating of psychiatric impairment and disability were discussed by Heiman and Shanfield, who noted the tendency—with respect to the evaluation to of psychiatric impairment—to 'legitimize subjective distress' that might be overemphasized during the process of psychiatric assessment [13]. In the absence of objective, agreed upon, impairment rating criteria, this at times causes personal values to influence the assessment of impairment due to both physical and psychiatric injuries.

It is to avoid the likelihood of such personal and idiosyncratic factors influencing the rating of psychiatric impairment that detailed and specific evaluation methods are required.

As described above, different methods of assessing physical and psychiatric impairment are in use throughout Australia.

Following the changes, subsequent to the Ipp Report in 2002, to liability for personal injury, there has been a move to introduce specified methods for the assessment of physical and psychiatric impairments as well as both thresholds and caps for damages.

The most objective methods of rating impairment are those that are based on a structure or function, including the basic aspects of mental function, as defined by the WHO assessment of abnormality or loss of anatomical, physiological or psychological indirect methods that purport to evaluate impairment but in reality assess disability, such as the PIRS, and are influenced by the various factors that impact on the examiner as well as those that affect the subject. Factors that influence the examiner were noted by Biklen and have been listed above—they include service traditions, economics, bureaucratic exigency, politics and societal prejudice.

Factors that influence the subject's level of function and disability include motivation, as well as numerous other factors related to premorbid personality, demographics, interpersonal dynamics, cultural and occupational factors as well as societal and economic factors. It is because these various factors impact on the various aspects of functioning that the rating of impairment can only take into consideration that which can be directly observed by the examiner and which represents a departure from normal anatomical, physiological or psychological structure or function.

The adoption of uniform methodology for the assessment of impairment in the various Australian jurisdictions, based on rating instruments for physical and psychiatric injuries that truly assess impairment rather than disability, would be an important step in eliminating the haphazard ways in which entitlements to damages for non-pecuniary loss, as well as other statutory entitlements, are currently assessed, and it would make a significant contribution to the establishment of a more equitable approach to the awarding of benefits and compensation for those who had suffered a personal injury through no fault of their own.

References[6]

1. Mendelson D (2014) The new law of Torts, 3rd edn. Oxford University Press, Melbourne, pp 113–115
2. Mendelson D (2014) The new law of Torts, 3rd edn. Oxford University Press, Melbourne, pp 27–28
3. http://www.amatas.com.au/assets/ipp_report.pdf. Accessed 15 Jan 2015
4. Holman Webb Lawyers (2014) Civil Liability Act 2002 (NSW): Schedule of Non-Economic Loss—2013/14. http://www.holmanwebb.com.au/blog/civil-liability-act-2002-nsw-schedule-of-non-economic-loss-2014/15. Accessed 23 March 2016
5. Mendelson G (1991) The rating of psychiatric impairment in forensic practice: a review. Aust N Z J Psychiatry 25:84–94
6. Colledge A, Krohm G (2003) Improvements to the rating of impairments from injury. IAIABC J 40(2):32
7. Lerner J (1966) Psychiatric disability and the industrial physician. J Occup Med 8:257
8. World Health Organization (1980) International classification of impairments, disabilities, and handicaps. World Health Organization, Geneva
9. Lasky H (1983) The usable psychiatric report: workers' compensation style. In: Chan R, Chan B (eds) Workers' Compensation Psychiatric Evaluation Program syllabus. Southern California Psychiatric Society, Los Angeles, CA
10. Meyerson AT, Fine T (eds) (1987) Psychiatric disability: clinical, legal and administrative dimensions. American Psychiatric Press Inc., Washington, DC
11. World Health Organization (1992) The ICD-10 classification of mental and behavioural disorders. World Health Organization, Geneva
12. Biklen D (1988) The myth of clinical judgment. J Soc Issues 44:127
13. Heiman EM, Shanfield SB (1978) Psychiatric disability assessment: clarification of problems. Compr Psychiatr 19:449–454

[6] Parts of this chapter are based on previous publications by the authors, especially 'Mendelson, G., Survey of methods for the rating of psychiatric impairment in Australia. (2004) 11 Journal of Law and Medicine 446' and 'Mendelson, D., The New Law of Torts. 3rd edition, Oxford University Press 2014 (Chapter 1)'.

Part VI
International Overview and Epicrisis

Della Croce, Giovanni Andrea ca. 1509–1575. Chirurgiae Ioannis Andreae a Cruce, Veneti medici libri septem, quamplurimis instrumentorum imaginibus arti chirurgicae opportunis suis locis exornati, theoricam, practicam, ac uerissimam experientiam continentes. In quibus ea omnia, quae optimo chirurgo in curandis vulneribus conuenire videntur, ordine quodam amplissimo concerni possunt nunc primum in lucem editi … Venetiis : Apud Iordanum Zilettum, 1573. Courtesy of historical section of the "Vincenzo Pinali" Medical Library of the University of Padova

Chapter 26
International Overview on Dental Damage Compensation

Vilma Pinchi

Abstract After a brief international overview on the legislative and juridical frameworks of pecuniary and nonpecuniary losses related to dental injury, this chapter illustrates the methods of ascertainment and criteria of evaluation to be used for assessing these specific kinds of losses. In particular, the chapter describes in detail the medical interview; the physical examination of the claimant; the additional clinical and radiological investigations; the methods and criteria to be used for identifying, describing, and estimating any dental injury/damage; the treatment expenses; the temporary and permanent impairment; and the causal value/link between the event and the dental injury/damage.

26.1 Background

Whereas the medicolegal evaluation of dental and oral damage needs to be more thoroughly investigated in different countries by comparing methodological procedures and the qualifications of the experts who carry out such assessments in various legal frameworks, there is very little literature published on this subject. Occasional information can be obtained from scientific papers which mainly report dental malpractice cases or iatrogenic or traumatic lesions due to road or domestic accidents and crimes, but such seemingly small attention to this medicolegal field is linked to the dual nature of the activity. The dual nature of medicolegal activity implies two levels of reasoning, both "medical" and "legal," moving from collected clinical evidence to providing an evaluation according to specific legal compensation rules such as dentist liability, motor accident, worker compensation, etc. Therefore, the evaluation of damage, meant as the final assessment of ascertained physical or psychological impairment according to legally provided criteria, is intrinsically conventional and not easily subject to scientific experimentation.

V. Pinchi (✉)
Department of Health Sciences, Section of Forensic Medical Sciences, University of Florence, Largo Brambilla 3, 50134 Florence, Italy
e-mail: vilma.pinchi@unifi.it

S.D. Ferrara et al. (eds.), *Personal Injury and Damage Ascertainment under Civil Law*, DOI 10.1007/978-3-319-29812-2_26

Thus, the discipline of damage compensation tends to occupy a significant place in the field of law, with the related medicolegal aspects being generally reported in national contexts, given the national variability of compensation systems and rules. The medicolegal ascertainment of a lesion or impairment relies first and foremost on "medical" assessment of the anatomical or functional loss that negatively influences a subject's ability and has caused suffering. Thus, diagnostic procedures that are clinically and scientifically accredited, including evidence from updated epidemiological studies, contribute to scientific knowledge about the causal link of injury and lesion. In addition to the different compensation rules and legal purposes underlying medicolegal activity, its specific diagnostic approach, along with legal or forensic demands, there is an autonomous, internationally recognizable and comparable discipline, with proper and appropriate procedures and methods and expertise qualification standards. Regardless of whether a dental impairment or lesion is to be assessed, the same medicolegal expertise is required of the dentist or forensic odontologist charged with damage assessment by the court, insurance company, or other interested parties. This chapter will discuss the particular diagnostic and prognostic issues connected with the medicolegal ascertainment of dental and oral impairments and the necessary qualification of the expert who deals with damage evaluation. A comparison of national impairment scoring systems or scales with those of other countries is not possible because of the extremely mixed criteria used to determine the degree of impairment and noneconomic loss due to injuries.

26.2 Ascertainment Methodology

The methodology for the ascertainment of dental or oral impairments requires appropriate and specific attention in order to reconstruct the event, as well as an interview with the individual who is claiming pecuniary or other loss compensation.

26.2.1 Reconstruction of Event and Causal Link

In case of dental or oral injury, an appropriate reconstruction of events through collection of circumstantial and clinical data is necessary to ascertain and evaluate the prior state of the subject, as well as the nature, entity, and plausibility of the causes of injury, by discerning the causal role of an accident or possible substandard care in comparison with preexistent or spontaneous pathological conditions.

Ascertaining the causal link between a possible cause and its consequence requires a complex evaluation, based on access to health records, accident reports, and other evidence. The first issue emerging from a comparison of different legal systems is the identification of the individual who has the burden of proving what damage has occurred and evidence for proving or disproving the causal link. In Italy the injured subject (due to improper dental care or a motor/domestic accident) must prove the impairment, but the burden of proof concerning causal link depends on whether it is a case of dental professional liability (contractual civil liability) or of general civil liability (motor, school, domestic accidents, general tort law). In cases of suspected dental/medical negligence, the patient must allege the damage suffered and prove the contract with the hospital or doctors (a simple receipt is enough); then the hospital or doctors must disprove their liability, so they are not condemned to compensate the damages. In cases of general civil liability, the injured person must prove the damage/injury, the causal link, and the fault that caused the injury/impairment. In Belgium, Poland, and some countries with no-fault compensation schemes (Sweden, Denmark, New Zealand), the burden of proof is on the damaged person/patient. Referring to Sweden, Denmark, and New Zealand's no-fault systems, it is highlighted: "Whatever criteria are chosen, thorny causation issues will remain. Claimants still must establish a causal relationship between their injury and the care rendered (or not rendered)...moving to an avoidability standard, or even of "no-fault" does not change this." However, also in those countries where the patient must prove the fault of the doctors/hospital, there is a trend toward the lightening of this burden, as reported by Kinga Baczyk-Rozwadowska: "medical and dental liability is based on fault... The general rule is that a patient is burdened with proving damages, fault and a causal connection between the faulty conduct and damages. However, in the field of medical malpractice, these strict requirements have been lowered by case law in order to be more convenient for a claimant."

Since the reconstruction of the event is quite relevant both for the individual injured in a motor accident and for the patient who alleges to have been damaged by improper care, the availability of and access to clinical records is always a key point of all medicolegal files. The reconstruction of the event for motor accident relies on the accessibility by the medical/dental assessors to the documentation of the accident (damages to car, reports of police, etc). In Italy, the UK, the USA, Australia, and presumably most countries, the dental consultant charged as medicolegal expert by the motor authority, insurance company, or the court may access all this information. Secondly, some information can be retrieved from health documentation released by rescue services, first-aid facilities, etc. This documentation can be accessed only by the injured individual, who must then provide it in order to prove any injury suffered as a consequence of an accident. Sometimes first-aid records do not accurately register missing or fractured teeth in case of multi-trauma patients who are in a critical condition. Thus, forensic odontologists should consider the possibility of oversight and discuss the compatibility of the dental injuries reported by the subject with his/her trauma and other facial lesions in the medicolegal report. Even if poorly registered, the sequence of events and any urgent treatment provided may be of great importance for reconstruction of the event and evaluation of the traumatic injury, to exclude that improper care was given, and for final assessment of impairment after stabilization of the injury.

The obligation of the claimant to prove the injury suffered is more complicated in cases of litigation, and often this evidence can be provided only by obtaining clinical records or administrative data from dentist's office. The release of such documentation becomes an important issue in patient-dentist disputes.

A complete circumstantial and clinical data collection supports the medicolegal expert by answering the classic questions of an investigation (Who? What? When? Where?), in order to provide evidence about the cause(s) and their causal link with the claimant's pecuniary or nonpecuniary loss.

When investigating what events caused an injury (such as dentist malfeasance, mistreatment, accident, crime), the forensic expert should never exclude that some injuries may have been caused by violence or aggression, and this possibility ought to be explored and considered (such as domestic accident or violence, battered child syndrome, etc.). The intensity, point of application, duration, direction of traumatic force, position of the body, and vehicle damage should all be investigated to explain the traumatic mechanism in case of accident (e.g., road or domestic accident). Ascertaining the causal link of event and injury is sometimes difficult due to multicausality, such as in cases where dentist malpractice is alleged in cases of complex dental treatment carried out in different phases by different practitioners or when a patient claims negligence in posttraumatic care on the part of the intervening physicians or dentists. Dental negligence cases require an evaluation of both the dentist's and the patient's conduct since therapy outcome or duration could be influenced by a patient who is noncompliant to prescriptions, recommendations, or appointments with the dentist. If another practitioner intervenes on the same patient, the actual condition or injury may have been caused by the first, the second, or both dentists. The expert must consider all overlapping causal factors in the evaluation of their role in determining injury or impairment.

The medicolegal evaluation of compatibility of a lesion with a trauma, assault, or improper treatment invariably requires a careful consideration of the time of the occurrence and the time lapse between the alleged cause and the effect, including what happened in the meantime. Moreover, what happened immediately after the traumatic event is also relevant in assessing dental damage and the related impairment. For instance, whether a lost tooth was correctly preserved before reimplantation in the empty socket and how long the tooth remained out of the mouth are critical elements for evaluation of the possible duration of a reimplanted tooth or even of the appropriateness of the decision to proceed with reimplantation. Claims that dental treatment has been inappropriately performed invariably require backup of correct time allocation, since the prosthesis may seem inadequate due to the time which has elapsed and not because of being incorrectly performed.

Through an accurate chronologic reconstruction of events, the forensic odontologist may provide useful and pragmatic information on important issues connected with medicolegal and insurance handling of cases. Insurance policies specify periods of validity, meaning that the time when an event occurred is always relevant. There are also different kinds of professional liability insurance based either on "loss of occurrence" or "claims-made" basis, since the time at which the event occurred and the time the claim was filed, respectively, can infringe on coverage.

26.2.2 Interview and Visit with the Claimant

When examining the claimant, forensic odontologists must respect the same legal and ethical duties and rules of good clinical practice that regulate the dental profession at large. Forensic odontologists should carefully inform the patient about the aims of the visit, which is not intended for diagnostic or therapeutic purposes in a traditional sense. Although the examination for medicolegal purposes requires that only limited information be given to the patient, the process is demanding for medicolegal experts since they have no prior relationship with the individual they are examining, unlike their personal physician/dentist. More attention should be paid than in general dental practice to the protection of privacy and confidence, since medicolegal reports, containing the patient's personal and health data, are often seen by insurers, loss adjusters, and lawyers. Therefore, the claimant must provide appropriate and specific authorization.

In addition to the deontological and legal obligations, which all medical professionals must assume, of reporting incompetent, impaired, or unethical colleagues, forensic odontologists and other medicolegal assessors is requested to review and examine many clinical certificates or reports of other specialists/experts, so that there is more likelihood of disclosing medical misconduct. Therefore, medicolegal experts bear greater responsibility in balancing their duties toward their patients with the respect due to their colleagues and need robust evidence of negligence or unethical behavior before releasing a verbal or written opinion to a patient.

The medicolegal expert's visit with the claimant should include both the familial and personal (physiological and pathological) history of the patient in relation to the subject's age, gender, claimed dental treatment, etc. and the lesion/impairment under investigation and evaluation. For instance, tooth emergence and menarche are factors usually investigated if an orthodontic treatment is questioned or should be performed to amend injuries; pregnancy status is relevant if the patient needs an X-ray. Some malocclusions or periodontal diseases are familial, so their possible occurrence in the patient's family should be inquired about. Past facial and oral traumas should always be reported, especially in growing subjects, in whom they may cause defective development of dentition, malocclusions, or late pulp necrosis, which does not emerge until months or more frequently years after the traumatic event. General health conditions should be carefully investigated (systemic pathologies, surgical interventions, drugs, radiotherapy of skull-neck, etc.) in order to explain oral symptoms (e.g., diabetes, periodontitis, osteonecrosis related to medication/radiotherapy, xerostomia due to drugs). The familial and personal medical history is a mainstay of the prior state of the subject needed to identify the entity of the damage and assess what part of the impairment is due to preexistent or autonomous conditions. The subject's employment or profession should be investigated since his/her ability to work may be impaired after facial/oral/dental traumas or improper therapy.

The medicolegal expert's examination of the patient should report on the general appearance of the patient's face; aesthetic abnormalities; the condition of the teeth, tongue, and gum; temporomandibular joint (TMJ) functionality; etc. The visit should focus on the specific dental/oral impairment or injury: teeth (occlusion, chewing, aesthetic function, etc.), periodontal structures (gum, alveolar, bone, etc.), and maxillaries (deformities, malocclusions, limitations to mouth opening, etc.), TMJ (pain, limitation, etc.), nerve lesions (taste and sensitivity disturbances/loss), speech impairment, suction, and swallowing disturbances. The description should be complete and objective, clearly indicating the adopted teeth numbering system (FDI—World Dental Federation, universal, etc.) and reported according to accredited glossaries and abbreviations for dental treatments conveniently explained in the text. Although official glossaries and coding systems are generally endorsed by national and international dental associations for achieving a standardization of registrations, the medicolegal report is addressed to non-dentists, and an excess of technical codes or abbreviations may be cryptic and hinder rather than facilitate immediate understanding.

26.2.3 Additional Investigations

Radiological exams are a mainstay for clinical diagnosis and medicolegal assessment of dental or bone injuries or impairments. As in routine dental work, bidimensional X-rays usually suffice for investigating oral/dental injuries or impairments (intraoral, bitewing, orthopantomograph, radiography of temporomandibular joint syndrome). Some patients may have to undergo computerized tomography (CT), using multislice CT, dentascan, or cone beam CT, to complete the diagnostic process (bone fracture, impacted teeth, penetration of maxillary sinus, etc.). Magnetic resonance imaging (MRI) is limited to very special cases (e.g., temporomandibular joint syndrome, internal derangement), and ultrasound is mainly used for detecting pathologies affecting salivary glands. Some neurophysiological exams (e.g., blink reflex) can be used to assess lesions of the trigeminal nerve fibers. Generally speaking, the justification of exams performed for medicolegal reasons invariably raises issues connected with the biological risks to the patient and costs of the procedures, especially in cases of repetition of exams or exploratory investigations.

Although X-rays are of vital importance in assessing oral injuries/impairments, legal restrictions and ethical recommendations must be kept in mind by medicolegal experts since this relevant matter has been dealt with by specific laws. Directive 97/43/Euratom defines medicolegal investigations as "radiological procedures performed for insurance or legal purposes without a medical indication." Furthermore, the directive requires that special attention be paid to justification and optimization of such practices and that clear procedures and responsibilities be defined.

The recent Council Directive 2013/59/Euratom, "Laying down basic safety standards for protection against the dangers arising from exposure to ionising radiation, and repealing Directives 89/618/Euratom, 90/641/Euratom, 96/29/ Euratom, 97/43/Euratom and 2003/122/Euratom" has established: "The so-called "medico-legal" exposures introduced in Directive 97/43/Euratom have now been clearly identified as the deliberate exposure of individuals for other than medical purposes, or "non-medical imaging exposures". Such practices need to be placed under appropriate regulatory control and should be justified in a similar way as for medical exposures. However, a different approach is needed on the one hand for procedures using medical radiological equipment and on the other hand for procedures not using such equipment. In general, the annual dose limits and corresponding constraints for public exposure should apply." The IRMER 2000 in the UK provides that "Medico-legal procedures are those which do not have a clinical benefit to the patient, but are carried out to provide legal evidence, e.g. in the case of an allegation of assault. A medico-legal exposure must still be justified in that there is a net benefit to the individual or to society." The medicolegal exposures are widely diverse, possibly including all exposures not directly related to the health of the individual undergoing X-ray examination, mainly, but not exclusively, represented by those performed for insurance or legal proceedings (e.g., security scanners). Although many countries have implemented European Union Directives in their national legislative frameworks, justification of medico-legal exposures and procedures is of constant concern, especially when they imply high-dose radiography, a repetition of X-rays, or radiological exams in multi-exposed subjects or children. These issues have been addressed in some countries by imposing a referral to a practitioner who must evaluate the justification of the X-ray exam, with the consequence that exposures performed at the request of insurers are considered unjustified. Medicolegal experts should appropriately address the collection of radiological exams that patients have already undergone, assisting and motivating requests for radiography copies from hospitals, radiological services, and dental practitioners, thus avoiding exposing the patient to useless and unjustified procedures. Nevertheless, cases can occur in which the radiological exams undertaken for clinical reasons do not suffice for medicolegal diagnosis. For instance, if the healing process is still ongoing from when the last X-rays were taken, serious clinical doubts exist about the complete healing or the gravity of possible residual dental or bone damage. In such cases, a very typical diagnostic aim exists and X-ray exposure can be justified when properly addressed by physicians or dentists.

26.3 Evaluation Criteria

In every country, the individual who is requesting damage compensation must prove to have suffered pecuniary and nonpecuniary loss in order to be eligible for compensation. In case of oral injuries, the medicolegal expert may face very specific demands relating to temporary and permanent impairments and expenses for amending dental damages as well.

26.3.1 *Temporary Impairment*

Injured patients may experience temporary conditions of serious physical pain and limitations of chewing, speech, or aesthetic alterations of the face. Additional treatments, such as root canal, endodontic therapy, and bone fracture synthesis, can result in a prolongation of symptoms affecting stomatognathic function. Pain, bleeding, edema, or trismus, due to oral injury, can lead to dietary restrictions to soft or liquid food for days, difficulty in speaking, and alteration of facial aesthetics and requires specific pharmacological therapy or oral hygiene procedures that are difficult for the subject to comply with away from home. Consequently, the subject may experience a temporary inability to work and to attend school, social, or recreational activities. This type of damage is generally called "temporary impairment or temporary invalidity" and is recognized as a specific kind of loss and suffering entitled to compensation under specific legal conditions in all civil legal systems. In Italy, temporary impairment of 100 % occurs when the subject is hospitalized or largely impaired, while partial temporary impairment (25 % or less) is very common in dental injuries when one or some bodily functions are temporarily limited (speech, dietary restrictions due to chewing limitations, aesthetic facial alterations due to edema or hematoma, etc.). Very low rates of temporary impairment for long periods, even years, may be compensated for when a subject must have an orthodontic appliance inserted to correct posttraumatic malocclusion. In France, the "souffrances endures" (time of suffering and pain) and "prejudice esthetique temporaire" are assessed in addition to the deficit "fonctionnel temporaire." In Belgium, compensation is awarded for temporary economic disability and domestic or school disability, while temporary aesthetic impairment is not normally considered except in the most severe cases (disfigurement). Temporary impairment must generally be proven beyond the absence from work and cannot rely merely on certificates from a general practitioner. In New York State, the court trial of Daviero v. Johnson, 451 N.Y.S.2d 858, held that such a claim does not meet the requirement of a "significant limitation of a use of a body function or system.... The court noted that the mere fact of absence from work, without medical proof indicating a significant limitation of a use of a body function or system is manifest and contrary to the intent of the Legislature."

26.3.2 *Permanent Impairment*

Practically every civil legal system provides compensation for certain permanent impairments, which are generally defined as the assessable condition of permanent detriment of physical or psychological function, when the symptoms due to injury have stabilized. The key points of the related medicolegal activity rely upon two ascertainment phases addressed to disclose the existence of the impairment itself and its degree and whether it is permanent. The medicolegal ascertainment of a body detriment requires a specific approach in comparison with general clinical procedures designed to provide the most appropriate care to patients, according to coincident interests of the various "parties" (doctors/hospitals and patients). On the contrary compensation can be legitimately sought when certain kinds of loss/damage have been assessed and appropriately correlated with an illegal conduct. Inevitably, therefore, at least two parties arise with different interests and biases. For instance, the claimant could be biased toward exaggerating the symptoms, by incorrectly reporting limitations to daily life activities or pain and suffering or by seeking for unjustified clinical consultations and certifications to complete the claim. Conversely, defendants, insurance companies, or institutions burdened to grant compensation under specific circumstances have the opposite interest in wishing to demonstrate that the purported loss is unfounded.

The medicolegal expert must typically and appropriately go through the clinical conditions of the claimant and the documentation comprising the claim, looking beyond the possible bias of the parties, and eventually addressing the question about the existence and degree of the purported physical/psychological impairment, on the basis of the evidence available and at the time when the medicolegal opinion is released.

Thus, medicolegal activity is highly demanding, and experts need to be as acquainted with clinical issues relating to difficulties in reporting subjective symptoms, such as pain, as they are with the legal framework they are operating within, keeping in mind first and foremost who is burdened to prove or at least allege the loss or impairment and what level of evidence is requested by the different compensation rules. The abovementioned issues concerning the existence and proof of impairments eligible for compensation equally affect the ascertainment of permanent physical damage occurring in the oral and facial region. Facial or TMJ pain or sensitivity disturbance of trigeminal nerve fibers can be mentioned as meaningful examples which challenge medicolegal diagnosis due to the high subjectivity of symptoms and the uneven or seldom effective evidence provided by instrumental exams.

Ascertaining the permanency of any given physical or psychological condition is another very specific step of medicolegal expertise, which requires follow-up schedules and timely impairment evaluation when stabilization has occurred. The improper medicolegal evaluation of a given impairment may result in an inconclusive report or, worse, in an incorrect estimation. In the field of oral and dental impairments, some pathological conditions require that the final medicolegal assessment be postponed for months or years after the injury. Most neurological lesions to trigeminal branches (lingual or alveolar nerves) occurring during oral interventions heal spontaneously within about a year from the iatrogenic insult, so that the final ascertainment of whether the nerve lesion is permanent or temporary cannot be made before an appropriate number of months and clinical follow-up.

Possible impairments due to maxillary or dental trauma occurring in little children frequently need to be assessed years after the injury to exclude that a deficit of development has emerged from permanent dentition or skeletal structures. Otherwise, an underestimation of impairment and the compensation due can occur, and the subject could be damaged twice: by trauma and by incorrect medicolegal handling of the case.

Oral/dental injuries can result in more than one impairment due to structural/anatomical and functional loss. Possible impairments to mastication, deglutition, digestion, speech, trigeminal nerve, and facial aesthetics are constantly investigated in cases of oral injury in an ascertaining approach that is similar in all legal systems. Although the need to investigate impairments eligible for compensation is dictated and influenced by different legal systems, the ascertainment of the existence and gravity of a dysfunction/alteration/deformation relies on very similar procedures that invariably precede and support the final medicolegal evaluation of loss/damage. Similarly, in most countries, the medicolegal ascertainment of impairments due to tooth loss takes into consideration the amendment/alleviation capacity of dental treatments (fillings, prosthesis, etc.) and the possible change in treatment or prosthetic appliance compared to the prior state of the subject, thus addressing the related cost in the compensation assessment.

Remarkable differences emerge when medicolegal evaluations of ascertained impairments are compared in different countries. For instance, in Italy, the average detriment due to the loss of an upper central incisor is considered equal to that due for the loss of the first upper molar, while in the UK the loss of a back tooth is generally less compensated than a front one. Dietary restrictions are highly considered, especially in the USA and Australia where they are the prevalent criteria in cases of dental/TMJ injuries (1st grade (diet is limited to semisolid or soft food), 2nd grade (diet is limited to liquid food), 3rd grade (ingestion of food requires tube feeding or gastrostomy)), while damage to the teeth can mainly be compensated when there is a permanent impact on chewing and swallowing. In many countries with Roman law such as Italy, France, and Belgium, permanent impairment is calculated in percentages according to tables which generally provide detailed values for each type of tooth loss (incisor, canine, etc), TMJ or trigeminal disturbances, aesthetic alterations, etc. In some countries, personal injury thresholds are provided by compensation schemes for road accidents so that an injured person can recover certain noneconomic losses (e.g., pain and suffering) through a civil suit unless he/she can demonstrate to have incurred "serious injury," such as dismemberment, disfigurement, permanent impairment, or loss of function of a body organ. Thus, the accurate assessment of functional or structural impairments becomes extremely important in this field, since it can affect the plaintiff's opportunity to demand broader compensation according to a tort lawsuit. For instance, in Australia (State of Victoria—TAC, Transport Accident Commission), in cases of motor accidents, impairment is compensated with a lump sum if the permanent impairment score is over 11 %. This sum is intended to compensate for loss of function and movement, not pain and suffering or loss of enjoyment of life—which are covered under common law payments.

26.3.3 Dental Treatment Expenses

The costs of dental care intended to amend lesions/injuries caused by an injury or malpractice are another mainstay of dental damage evaluation. In most countries, dental treatment costs of alleviating dental injury or impairment are compensated for, and the assessor is charged with evaluating such therapies and their related costs. The expert's opinion on the eligibility for reimbursement of dental care expenses requires several considerations. First it must be verified if the care is intended to amend those impairments eligible for compensation and if the treatment for the clinical condition of the injured patient is appropriate, since some claimants seek compensation for the most expensive treatment (implants, prostheses, e.g.) even if his/her condition could contraindicate it (untreated and severe periodontitis, e.g.). Sometimes the damaged individual seeks compensation before undergoing dental treatments, filing the claim with dental surgeons' certifications and/or plans of treatment with presumptive costs for dental care in a complex and general plan of therapy, so that the medicolegal expert is required to provide detailed differentiation of costs due to additional care.

A second challenging part of the expert's job consists in the evaluation of expenses due to future dental treatments. Practically all dental treatments (fillings, prostheses, implants, etc.) must be renewed during a lifetime or replaced by another treatment (an incisor treated two or three times with large fillings may eventually need root canal treatment and a crown). There are two main approaches for this type of expense compensation: in some countries (Belgium or in Italy for worker compensation), the need of a dental treatment replacement or renewal is assessed by a dental advisor/assessor who evaluates the related expenses time by time, while in others (in Italy, for general civil liability as well as medical/dental malpractice, motor accident compensation, etc.), a lump sum is provided as compensation after the damage assessment so that the dental assessors must be able to predict all treatment renewals or replacements that will be necessary during the lifetime of the individual and calculate all the related costs. Inevitably, the latter compensation system raises issues connected with longevity, the average duration of different types of dental treatments, and the average treatment costs not granted by the national health services (as mostly they are not in Italy). Assessors can experience great difficulty in foreseeing what will happen in future decades of that subject's life, first and foremost, because scientific evidence or statistical data describe the "mean" subject or the "mean" treatment or the average cost of dental treatment, but nothing can predict the future of one single individual, his/her duration of life, or the treatments he or she will need. In Italy the expectation of life is calculated on data provided for male and female subjects by the National Institute of Statistics, but of course if a male is supposed to live up to 85 years, this does not mean that he will really live exactly 85 years. Some scientific evidence supports criteria for calculating the average duration of dental treatments that are assumed to be 6–7 years for fillings; 8 years, dentures; and 10–12, crowns; and a renewal is needed when subject is aged <40 years for implants.

26.4 Qualifications of a Medicolegal Expert

A discussion about the qualifications of an expert who evaluates dental damage requires preliminary considerations about a dentist's activity. The European Union (EU) Directive 78/687 in 1978 recognized the profession of dentist at a European level, reserving to dental practitioners some specific diagnostic and therapeutic activities such as the diagnosis (plus prevention and treatment) of anomalies and diseases of the teeth, mouth, and related tissues. This EU law recognized that medicine and dentistry are two different healthcare professions, limiting both to their specific area of comptence so that a physician cannot perform dentistry and vice versa. In addition to the legally established separation between the two professions in the EU, the traditional differences in terms of formal qualification and training have collocated the diagnosis of dental pathologies into the competence area of the dentist in an undisputed way when clinical activity is considered. Conversely, when the diagnostic ascertainment of dental and oral affections is required for medicolegal purposes, a dentist's opinion is not always requested as it should be. A recent survey of the International Organization for Forensic Odonto-Stomatology (IOFOS—not yet published) reported that in most EU countries as well as Australia, New Zealand, and the USA, the medicolegal evaluation of dental or oral injuries and the severity of impairment and necessary treatments are generally provided by dentists who are specifically trained in the medicolegal field and/or serve as forensic odontologists in different areas (crime, violence, body identification, etc). In some countries, such medicolegal assessment of oral lesions or impairments can alternatively be provided by non-dentist assessors such as specialists in legal medicine or merely physicians. For instance, in Italy, specialists in legal medicine or physicians who practice legal medicine, even without a postgraduate course of specialization, may evaluate dental impairments, especially when a plan for dental treatment has been provided by the treating dental practitioner and when the patient has been injured due to an accident (car, domestic, etc). The position that a non-dentist may perform an oral and dental visit of an individual exhibiting symptoms and provide a diagnosis and prognosis is highly questionable, since this activity is reserved to dentists according to Italian law, and some disciplinary issues have already been raised. According to the Motor Accidents Authority of Australia, minor dental injuries (chipped or cracked teeth, the loss of one tooth) may be handled by a non-dentist assessor. Non-dentist assessors are medically trained MAS (Medical Assessment Service) assessors (excluding psychiatrists) who do not possess formal training in the area of dentistry but have successfully undertaken training offered by the MAS and have passed an examination in relation to the assessment of minor dental injuries. In Canada the Ontario Insurance Act 34/10 provides that at least the request of dental treatments must be filled in by a dentist: "A claim for dental goods or services completed and signed by a dentist and in the form approved by the Ontario Dental Association is deemed to be a treatment and assessment plan that satisfies the requirements …."

In addition to the formal and legally provided limitations to activities of non-dentists but medically trained assessors, although it is generally deemed that oral or dental pathologies should appropriately undergo diagnosis and care provided by a dentist, the diagnostic ascertainment of dental impairments and medicolegal evaluation of related damages eligible for compensation should also involve a dentist. Proceeding in medicolegal assessment of dental impairments without the adequate contribution of a dentist can result in a demanding and frustrating experience for a non-dentist assessor who must face the very specific issues of dental nomenclature, treatment glossary, evaluation about dental treatment alternatives, costs, average duration and diverse amending capacity, difficulties in ascertaining some oral symptoms (pain) or in prognostic evaluations of traumatic injuries and in growing children, etc. However, medicolegal ascertainment and activity generally require specific qualifications and training that can be of legitimate concern for most dental practitioners. In fact, in most countries, there are no specific postgraduate courses to provide specific education in the medicolegal field for dentists. Often those involved as experts in judicial trials or as insurance advisors have mixed qualifications and experience, depending on the specific rules that regulate different fields of the expert's activity (the courts, insurance companies, etc.) in different countries. Hence if dental lesions or impairments should be ascertained and assessed by dentists or forensic odontologists, these are supposed to provide the same medicolegal "performance" requested of a medicolegal expert or specialist, in terms of appropriateness of the ascertainment procedures and well-addressed answers to fulfill the legal or insurance needs. Providing a medicolegal opinion in dental cases can be a highly demanding and challenging activity if done by someone who is not specifically qualified and trained as a dentist or not acquainted with the legal requirements, the medicolegal methodology, and forensic activity at large. In this sense, dentists who serve as court experts or insurance advisors should seek specific education and training and become properly qualified and acquainted with medicolegal issues, the various legal frameworks, insurance contracts, and management of claims. Furthermore, when a dentist is required to serve in cases of dental litigation, the possible composition of a dispute through mixed approaches that are alternative to a court trial often requires that the experts/advisors be familiar with the adjudicative system as well as alternative procedures (mediation, conciliation, e.g.) available for conflict resolution.

Below are listed some general bibliographic sources useful to deepen the issue. They are not reported within the text as they are no cited references.

Bibliography

1. American Medical Association (2008) AMA guides to the evaluation of permanent impairment, 6th edn. American Medical Association, Chicago
2. Baczyk-Rozwadowska K (2011) Medical Malpractice and Compensation in Poland, 86. Chic-Kent Law Rev 1217. http://scholarship.kentlaw.iit.edu/cklawreview/vol86/iss3/9

3. Barsley RE (2010) Odontology as a forensic science, the North American experience. Forensic Sci Int 201:5–7
4. Béry A, Cantaloube D, Delprat L (2010) Expertise dentaire et maxilla-faciale, principes, conduit, indemnisation, EDP Science, France
5. Brauer HU, Walther W, Riesen C, Dick M (2011) Training for legal dental expert witnesses in Germany: an instrument for professional development. J Dent Educ 76:656–660
6. Clement J (2013) Forensic odontology's migration from an occupation with "hobby status" to a recognized, registerable specialty within dentistry. J Forensic Odontostomatol 31:1
7. Comandé G (2014) Italy. In: Nys H (ed) International encyclopaedia of laws: medical law. Kluwer Law International, Alphen aan den Rijn, Netherlands
8. Craig P, Clement J (2012) The Dentist's responsibilities with respect to a nofault motor accident compensation scheme. J Forensic Odontostomatol 30:40–46
9. Directive 2005/36/EC of the European Parliament and of the Council, 7 September 2005 on the recognition of professional qualifications
10. Horton P, Järvinen H, Mayo J, O'reilly G, Picano E, Remedios D, Le Heron J, Rehani M, Holmberg O, Czarwinski R (2012) Justification of diagnostic medical exposures: some practical issues. Report of an International Atomic Energy Agency Consultation. Br J Radiol 85(1013):523–538
11. Hove LD, Nielsen HB, Christoffersen JK (2006) Patient injuries in response to anaesthetic procedures: cases evaluated by the Danish Patient Insurance Association. Acta Anaesthesiol Scand 50:530–535
12. Jones KD (2008) What ethical issues should a dentist consider when providing expert testimony in a judicial or administrative action? JADA 139(3):354–355
13. Jonsson PM, Øvretveit J (2008) Patient claims and complaints data for improving patient safety. Int J Health Care Qual Assur 21:60–74
14. Jerrold L (2003) Benedict Arnold as an expert witness. Am J Orthod Dentofacial Orthop 123:707–708
15. Memento de bonnes pratiques, Recommandations de bonnes pratique en matière de reparation des dommages corporels, Cour d'appel de Lyon. http://www.ca-lyon.justice.fr/fichiers/CONSIGNY/memento.pdf
16. Permanent impairment guidelines, Guidelines for the assessment of permanent impairment of a person injured as a result of motor vehicle accident, Sept 2005, Motor Accidents Authority
17. Proceedings of 8th International Symposium Advances in Legal Medicine (ISALM) combined with the 90th Annual Conference of the German Society of Legal Medicine, Rechtsmedizin 2011 21:341–432
18. Rolland A (2002) The evaluation of permanent labial damage. Annales de Chirurgie Plastique Esthétique 47:615–622
19. Handschel J, Figgener L, Joos U (2001) Die forensische Bewertung von Verletzungen der Nerven und des Kieferknochensnach Weisheitszahnentfernungen im Blickwinkel der aktuellen Rechtsprechung. Mund Kiefer GesichtsChir 5:44–48
20. http://www.acc.co.nz/PRD_EXT_CSMP/groups/external_providers/documents/guide/wcmz002231.pdf
21. Motor Accidents Authority, The assessment of minor dental injuries: an information sheet for stakeholders. http://www.maa.nsw.gov.au/default.aspx?MenuID=284
22. Murray M, IR(ME)R 2000 and IR(ME) Amendment regulations 2006 and 2011. http://www.sor.org/learning/document-library/irmer-2000-and-irme-amendment-regulations-2006-2011
23. Norelli GA, Pinchi V, Scarpelli M, Borioli A, Garatti S, Pradella F, Odontologia Forense II (2011) Guida alla valutazione del danno odontostomatologico. Piccin, Padova
24. O'Reilly G, Malone JF (2008) Ethical issues in medico-legal exposures. Radiat Prot Dosimetry 129:307–310
25. Malone J, Guleria R, Craven C, Pinchi V, Pradella F, Gasparetto L, Norelli GA (2013) Trends in endodontic claims in Italy. Int Dent J 63(1):43–48

26. Pinchi V (2013) Mapping forensic odontology: a research project of I.O.F.O.S. J Forensic Odontostomatol 31:7
27. Pinchi V, Varvara G, Pradella F, Focardi M, Donati MD, Norelli G (2014) Analysis of professional malpractice claims in implant dentistry in Italy from insurance company technical reports, 2006 to 2010. Int J Oral Maxillofac Implants 29:1177–1184
28. Raborn GW (1999) CarterRM, using simulation to evaluate clinical competence after impairment. J Can Dent Assoc 65:384–386
29. Stavrianos C, Papadopoulos L, Vasiliadis A, Pantazis A, Kokkas A (2011) The role of expert witness in the adversarial English and Welsh legal system. Res J Med Sci 5:4–8
30. The ACC User Handbook to the AMA "Guides to the Evaluation of Permanent Impairment" 4th edition, Warren S. Koster, A Guide to New York State No-Fault Law, Koster & Brady New York. http://www.ckbblaw.com/library/nys.pdf
31. Wood EB, Freer TJ (2001) Incidence and aetiology of facial injuries resulting, from motor vehicle accidents in Queensland for a three-year period. Aust Dent J 46(4):284–288

Chapter 27
International Comparative Epicrisis on the Ascertainment and Evaluation of Personal Injury and Damage

Guido Viel, Rafael Boscolo-Berto, and Santo Davide Ferrara

Abstract After a brief historical overview on the role of clinical and forensic medicine in personal injury compensation, the chapter presents a critical comparative epicrisis on the ascertainment and evaluation of personal injury and damage under civil/tort law in Argentina, Australia, Belgium, China, Egypt, Estonia, France, Germany, Hungary, India, Italy, Japan, Kingdom of Saudi Arabia, Lithuania, the Netherlands, Nigeria, Portugal, Spain, Turkey, the UK and the USA. The diverse logical, methodological and criteriological phases of the ascertainment and the medicolegal evaluation of the injury, impairment, disability and any other pecuniary/non-pecuniary loss causally related to the damaging event are critically analysed and discussed. The final part of the chapter summarises the data and evidences discussed in Parts 1 and 6 of the monograph and sheds light on the necessary evolution and investments of bio-medicolegal sciences for keeping in line with postmodernity.

The flowering of modern legal medicine, which can be placed between 1800 and 1850 with the founding of the first university chairs in Strasbourg (1794), Dorpat (1801), Krakow (1804) and Vienna (1805), was characterised by a holistic view of the discipline, substantiated by the systematic methodology and the common aims of ascertainment, or the application of specialised knowledge and expertise to the administration of law in its broadest sense. This period, defined by historians as the "golden age" of legal medicine, saw the birth of university institutes of legal medicine and the development of important satellite disciplines, such as forensic histopathology, toxicology and haematology.

Between 1900 and 1950, there was a further important historical transition, with the introduction of a new issue into the world of legal medicine, the ascertainment and evaluation of personal damage under civil/tort law and the birth of clinical

G. Viel (✉) • R. Boscolo-Berto • S.D. Ferrara
Department of Legal and Occupational Medicine, Toxicology and Public Health, University-Hospital of Padova, Via Falloppio 50, 35128 Padova, Italy
e-mail: guido.viel@unipd.it; rafael.boscoloberto@unipd.it; santodavide.ferrara@unipd.it

S.D. Ferrara et al. (eds.), *Personal Injury and Damage Ascertainment under Civil Law*, DOI 10.1007/978-3-319-29812-2_27

forensic medicine which prospered in the countries of Mediterranean Europe and was exported to Latin America and partly to the Far East.

The diverse historical, political and geographical evolution of legal medicine has created different international professional scenarios, especially with regard to the ascertainment of personal injury and damage, which is often entrusted to specialists in insurance medicine, physiatry, orthopaedics, psychiatry or non-medical figures such as insurers, brokers and loss adjusters.

There is no doubt that the assessment of personal injury and damage is an ascertainment of a purely medical nature, implying the need for diagnosis and an evaluative epicrisis of anamnestic, clinical-objective, test, instrumental and laboratory data. Similarly, there is no doubt that these analyses are medicolegal and not clinical in nature, since the purpose is not diagnostic or therapeutic, but that of ascertainment and evaluation. Indeed, the ascertaining physician has to collect substantiated objective data based on scientific evidence, which must be able to overcome the cross-examination between the plaintiff and defendant and take on the character of scientific proof. Following the pervasive Daubert vs. Merrell Dow Pharmaceuticals, Inc. judgement of the Supreme Court of the USA, it is clear that the cross-examination of postmodern justice is represented by the solidity and scientific nature of the methodology utilised for the collection of evidence and the knowledge of the intrinsic error—systematic, erratic, random, conscious or intentional and very rarely malicious—that inevitably accompanies any kind of measurement or ascertainment [1]. In this posing a tremendous challenge to the medicolegal discipline, which must be able to develop new conceptual paradigms and ascertainment methodologies, taking the perspective of the researcher of the third millennium, constantly chasing errors and aware of the fallibility of the ascertainment, of the contestable nature of the assessment and, therefore, of the need for a scientific and technological renewal aimed at rendering the ascertainment methodology of personal injury, impairment, disability and handicap more objective, reproducible, accurate, precise and robust. Unlike the clinician who can rely on the accuracy of the set of symptoms reported by the patient who consults the physician to resolve, or at least improve, their health condition, the medicolegal expert cannot ignore the existence and effects of response bias, a class of behaviours of the examinee that reflect less than fully truthful, accurate or valid symptom report and presentation, whether deliberate or unconscious. Although the incidence of response bias can only be estimated and not objectively measured, there are several reports showing high rates of exaggeration and malingering in the context of impairment and disability assessment [2, 3].

Following the definitions of the World Health Organization (WHO) and the *International Classification of Functioning, Disability and Health* (ICF), the medicolegal expert must objectively ascertain "any loss or abnormality of psychological or anatomical structure or function" (i.e. impairment) and "any restriction or lack (resulting from an impairment) of ability to perform an activity in the manner or within the range considered normal for a human being" (i.e. disability). The conditions for the ascertainment and assessment of the injury, impairment and disability are, therefore, a perfect knowledge of the anatomy and physiology of the human person and the ability to identify and objectively measure a deviation of the functionality of an organ or apparatus from its normal range. Currently, for many somatic and/or psychic disorders, there exists a lack of biological markers of impairment and disability. The ascertaining physician, while following an evidence-based ascertainment methodology, is often unable to objectify a symptomatology reported by the patient, especially if it pertains to the somatosensory or psychic sphere. The ascertainment of pain, hypogeusia, hyposmia/anosmia, mild neuropsychological impairments and subtle neurological or soft tissue damage, such as those arising from a mild traumatic brain injury or accompanying whiplash injuries, is impossible or inaccurate, imprecise and poorly reproducible [2]. It appears quite evident that the bio-medicolegal sciences need to develop new markers of disease and markers of function/impairment, capable of enhancing diagnostic efficiency in terms of sensitivity and specificity, and to provide objective evidence of the existence of the disorder and its functional implications. In view of the fact that the bio-medicolegal sciences have historically benefited from advances in biomedicine, applying its scientific findings in the forensic field, it is equally clear that many of the current technological platforms of clinical and experimental use could be effectively adopted in clinical forensic and legal medicine for the ascertainment of personal injury and damage. This concerns, in particular, non-invasive or minimally invasive imaging techniques usable in vivo on the examinee, not being dangerous to the health of the same [4–10].

Currently, there is a lack of supranational and/or national guidelines and protocols on personal injury and damage; thus, huge heterogeneity exists not only in the legislative frameworks of compensation but also in the methods and criteria used to verify the existence and extent of the injury/damage.

In the following paragraphs, an international comparative epicrisis on the ascertainment and evaluation of personal injury and damage is given, critically analysing and comparing the overviews on *Europe* (Portugal, Spain, France, Italy, Belgium, the Netherlands, the UK, Germany, Hungary, Lithuania, Estonia), *North and South America* (the USA, Argentina), *Africa* (Egypt, Nigeria) and *Asia and Australia* (Turkey, Kingdom of Saudi Arabia, India, China, Japan, Australia) presented in detail in Parts 2–5, Chaps. 5–25 of the monograph.

27.1 Expert Definition, Qualification and Essential Knowledge

A universal definition of specialist in legal medicine or personal injury and damage evaluator is currently missing, leading to a lack of an international recognition of such an authority.

In all the 21 analysed countries, the expert must possess a medical degree (MD) in order to perform the ascertainment and evaluation of personal injury/damage in both the extrajudicial and judicial settings. In 43 % of the countries considered, a specialisation in legal and/or forensic medicine or a post-lauream training in insurance medicine is required by law for being classified as an expert in personal injury/damage. Being a specialist in legal and/or forensic medicine or in insurance medicine is mandatory in Belgium, China, Estonia, France, Hungary, India, the Netherlands, Saudi Arabia and Turkey. In the remaining countries, there are no specific compulsory requirements to undergo a medicolegal training in order to carry out personal injury/damage casework.

27.2 Methods of Ascertainment

27.2.1 Collection of Circumstantial, Clinico-documental-Instrumental Data

In all the analysed countries, the first step of the ascertainment is the collection of circumstantial, clinico-documental and instrumental data, with the retrieval of the information believed to be useful for a diagnostic framework, for the reconstruction of the injuring event and the characterisation of injuries, impairments and disabilities.

In the extrajudicial framework, the above data are furnished by the examinee (with his/her consent) or by the lawyer prior and/or during the clinical, medicolegal examination. In the judicial framework, medical and healthcare documentation is presented by the plaintiffs and defendants. In the vast majority of the analysed countries, in the private law framework, the examination is limited to the documents presented by the parties. There are some exceptions, particularly in the African countries. In Egypt, the collection of circumstantial data in cases of traffic or workplace accidents is under the responsibility of the General Administration for Criminal Evidence Investigations—Ministry of the Interior—and the expert can ask for any information deemed necessary. On the other hand, in Nigeria, the medical practitioner ascertains the injury and damage solely on the basis of the data available at the time of the visit (i.e. medical history and clinical visit).

27.2.2 Systematic Clinical and Medicolegal Examination

In 95 % of the analysed countries, each extrajudicial or judicial personal injury/damage case implies a systematic clinical and/or medicolegal ascertainment, including case history and psychophysical examination. The only exception is the Netherlands, where the insurance companies use specialised personnel to make house calls for reducing the number of clinical examinations to be performed by the medical officer and/or the clinical specialist.

There are no national guidelines specifically dealing with the methods to be used for conducting the clinical and/or medicolegal examination. In the majority of the national frameworks examined, the case history includes family, physiological, remote and recent disease history, along with the collection of any information deemed useful for reconstructing the damaging event and the mechanism of injury. In all the analysed countries, the psychophysical examination includes a full general examination followed by a local assessment of the specific injured area/areas. Due to the absence of specific supranational and/or national guidelines/protocols, the timing, duration, extension and clinical methodology adopted by the ascertaining physician vary considerably within and across different national jurisdictions.

27.2.3 Additional Exams and/or Specialist Consultation

If after the systematic clinical examination further anatomo-functional data are needed, a specialist can be consulted or instrumental exams can be prescribed.

In about 80 % of the analysed countries, the ascertaining physician can directly prescribe non-invasive exams or radiological exams not based on ionising radiations if the patient agrees to undergo that investigation. Invasive or radiological examinations based on ionising radiations are generally prescribed by a specialist after carefully weighing the risk-benefit ratio, in the presence of a clinical reason. In the majority of the analysed countries, indeed, invasive examinations and/or X-rays cannot be performed for medicolegal reasons only, even if the patient gives his/her consent.

27.3 Criteria of Evaluation

In all the analysed countries, the evaluation phase is performed when the injury/disease has reached its maximal medical improvement, which means that healing or stabilisation to a permanent sequela occurred.

27.3.1 Evaluation of the Psychic and Somatic State Prior to the Event/Injury

In 80 % of the analysed countries, the examining physician reconstructs the psychic and physical condition of the examinee prior to the event/injury, using preceding clinical documentation, remote and recent case history and eventual interviews with the family or personal physician. The pre-existing health status of the examinee can affect the reconstruction of the causal link between the damaging event and the injury/impairment and the estimation of the impairment/disability causally related to the damaging event. If the pre-existing health condition (e.g. egg skull or haemophilia) has caused greater damage than one would expect in a normal person, it is generally not taken into account, and all damages sustained by the examinee are reimbursed. On the other hand, if the event has caused an aggravation of a previous disease in the majority of the analysed countries, only the aggravation is compensated (i.e. differential damage with the pre-existing condition). Only 30 % of the authors, however, have explained in detail the procedure used in their country for calculating the differential damage (i.e. Belgium, France, Italy, Spain, the Netherlands and the USA).

27.3.2 Detailed Reconstruction of the Damaging Event and Mechanism of Injury

In all the analysed countries, the ascertaining physician integrates the available circumstantial data, the recorded medical history and the clinical objective data in order to reconstruct the damaging event and the most probable mechanism of injury. In about 50 % of the countries, the ascertaining physician cooperates with a biomechanical expert or traffic expert for reconstructing the dynamics of the event, comparing the biomechanical data (e.g. velocity, trajectory, energy, etc.) with the clinical and medicolegal data (location, extension, morphology of the injuries).

27.3.3 Identification of Clinico-Pathological Features

In all the analysed countries, the ascertaining physician reconstructs the clinico-pathological features of the injury/disorder in order to reach a clinical diagnosis of the initial, intermediate and final stages and describes the physiopathological pathways, which connect the diverse evolutive phases of the injury/disease. These features and pathways are examined on the basis of scientific sources, such as guidelines, consensus documents, operational procedures, evidence-based publications, treatises and other literature data. In 30 % of the analysed countries, a specific source hierarchy is adopted by the ascertaining physician, who grades the evidence emerging from the literature in the following order: guidelines, consensus documents, procedures, evidence-based literature and finally treatises.

27.3.4 *Identification of Personal Injury and Temporary Impairment*

In all the analysed countries, the ascertaining physician identifies and analytically describes the injury/injuries related to the damaging event. In Australia, Portugal, the Netherlands and the USA, the expert classifies the injury/disorder using the *International Classification of Functioning, Disability and Health* (ICF).

In 95 % of the analysed countries, the ascertaining physician estimates the duration of the temporary impairment, specifying the length of the initial and intermediate stages of the injury/disorder (e.g. treatment and rehabilitation periods) until stabilisation is reached. The only exception is represented by India where temporary impairment is not compensated. In about 60 % of the analysed countries, temporary impairment is classified in absolute and partial. In Belgium, France, Italy and Spain, three categories of partial impairment are used (75, 50 and 25 % of temporary impairment). In 70 % of the countries, the expert differentiates the general temporary impairment (i.e. duration of the treatment and rehabilitation periods) from the work-related temporary impairment.

27.3.5 *Identification of Permanent Impairment*

In all the analysed countries, the ascertaining physician identifies and analytically describes the permanent impairment related to the injury, detailing how the physical or psychological pathology of the examinee affects the functioning of his/her organism. As described in detail in Sect. 27.3.7 in several countries, specific national Barèmes and/or evaluation tables exist for the quantification of the degree of impairment expressed as percentage.

27.3.6 *Causal Value and Link*

In all the analysed countries, the ascertaining physician reconstructs the causal value/link between the event and the injury and between that injury and the temporary/permanent impairment. In the vast majority of the countries considered, the juridical basis of causality is the "conditio sine qua non", and the expert uses the "but-for test" (i.e. counterfactual reasoning) to determine if the condition was necessary to complete the set. Although the standard of proof required in tort/civil cases varies according to the different national juridical systems, it is generally based on the rule of "more probable than not", which means that enough evidence does exist to make the scientific explanation more likely than not that the fact the claimant seeks to prove is true.

27.3.7 Impairment and Disability Description and Estimation

In all the analysed countries, the final step of the clinical and medicolegal assessment is the analytical description of the temporary/permanent impairment, the disability and the pecuniary and/or non-pecuniary losses causally related to the damaging event. The expert describes also the repercussions of the impairment on the work capacity of the examinee, the daily activities and the relational and social life.

27.3.7.1 Barèmes for Impairment Quantification

In 50 % of the analysed countries, specific guidelines or Barèmes or compensation tables exist for quantifying the degree of impairment expressed as percentage of the whole person, with 0 % reflecting a normal function and 100 % a total impairment approaching death.

In *Australia*, *the Netherlands* and *the USA*, the estimation is based on the AMA Guides.

In *Belgium*, the national reference system is the "Official Belgian Scale of Invalidity".

In *China*, permanent impairments are rated according to the "Assessment of the disability grade of injuries from road traffic accident", which consists of five chapters and divides the degree of impairment into ten levels.

In *Egypt*, the percentage of permanent impairment is calculated according to Table n. 2 of the Law 79/1975 on social insurance.

In *France*, permanent impairment rates are estimated using the Barèmes of the Concours Medical or those elaborated by the French Society of Legal Medicine.

In *Italy*, a compensation table by law (Ministerial Decree of the 3 July 2003) has to be used for impairments of less than 10 %, whereas the Barèmes of the Italian Society of Legal Medicine (SIMLA) are utilised for any other kind of impairment including aesthetic prejudice and/or sexual dysfunction.

In *Spain*, permanent impairments caused by traffic accidents are quantified with the "barème of points" or "traffic scale" in force with the Royal Decree 8/2004 (29 October 2004), whereas any other impairment is estimated with the AMA Guides.

In *Portugal*, there are specific Barèmes introduced with the Decreto Lei n. 352/2007 (23 October 2007).

In the *UK*, a national compensation table called "English Barema" is used for the quantification of permanent impairments.

27.3.7.2 Damnum Emergens and Lucrum Cessans

In 65 % of the analysed countries, the clinical or medicolegal expert verifies the appropriateness of the additional expenses incurred as a result of the injury/damage (i.e. medical costs, transportation costs, nursing care expenses, etc.).

Regarding the *lucrum cessans*, in 70 % of the countries, the physician identifies and estimates the temporary work incapacity, and the judge calculates the related loss of earnings. In 85 % of the analysed countries, the physician estimates the permanent work incapacity, describing the general and specific work disability related to the permanent impairment. The economic loss is then quantified by the judge.

27.3.7.3 Other Non-pecuniary Damages

Moral damages (also known as "pain and suffering", or "pretium doloris") are compensated in about 70 % of the analysed countries. Generally, the clinical or medicolegal expert furnishes a description of the physical, psychic and psychological suffering of the examinee during the treatment and rehabilitation phases and after the stabilisation of the injury/disorder. In Belgium, France, Italy, Portugal and the USA, the physician graduates "pain and suffering" using quantitative scales. In Belgium, "a minimum" of 4 points in a 7 degree scale is required for "pain and suffering" be compensated as an extra-damage. In Italy, a 5 degree scale is used, whereas in France and Portugal, a 7 degree scale is adopted.

In 30 % of the analysed countries, "existential damage", defined as loss of amenity, decrease of quality of life or disability to enjoy the pleasure of life, represents a separate category of non-pecuniary damage. In Belgium, the physician describes the repercussion of the impairment and disability on the social and cultural environment of the examinee. In France, Italy and Spain, the medicolegal expert describes the potential effects of the impairment on the quality of life of the damaged individual detailing if the claimed modifications of the lifestyle are compatible with the impairment and disability.

27.4 Conclusions

The assessment of personal injury and damage in the postgenomic era requires a huge investment in human capital, through teaching and education at a university level. The main responsibility of academic institutions, indeed, is to educate towards a critical mentality and a democratic citizenship of the world, safeguarding the transmission of knowledge of the past together with the defence of the idea that it is feasible to innovate such knowledge (Chap. 1).

The role of legal and forensic medicine is to develop a unitary model derived from the characteristics of the datum and the methodology used for acquiring it, along with a "holistic" view of the damaged person, who must be considered a complex ensemble requiring medicolegal representation, and not just a sum of different parts and/or organs (Chap. 2). The medical and medicolegal contribution to compensation for personal damage cannot pursue different directions from that of the scientific approach of general medicine, looking at the deepest component of the person, detailing how the injury, the impairment and the disability influence the existence and quality of life of the damaged individual. The maximum objectivation in the data collection procedure, the highest reproducibility in its utilisation, would ensure the scientific nature of the assessment of personal injury and damage, defining common rules and setting educational standards.

Moreover, it must always be kept in mind that the reconstruction of the causal link between the event and the injury/impairment requires solid and rigorous scientific laws of coverage (Chap. 3), with the final aim of increasing the quality and equity of the system.

The starting point for harmonising personal injury compensation across different juridical systems and improving both vertical justice (among lesser and greater injuries/impairments) and horizontal justice (among similar injuries/impairments) could be the development of a shared clinical and medicolegal methodology for ascertaining and evaluating psychophysical impairments and disabilities (Chap. 4).

The comparative epicrisis conducted on 21 countries (Chaps. 5–25), belonging to five different continents, evidenced that huge heterogeneity still exists not only in the juridical frameworks of personal injury compensation (i.e. liability, burden of proof, causation, categories of compensable pecuniary and non-pecuniary damages) but also in the methods of ascertainment and criteria of evaluation used by the clinical and/or medicolegal expert in order to identify, describe and characterise the injury, the temporary/permanent impairment, the causal value/link between the event and the injury, the work temporary and permanent incapacity, the repercussions of impairments and disabilities on social life and leisure activities and other non-pecuniary losses such as "pain and suffering" and "existential damage" (Chaps. 5–25).

Clinico-medicolegal rigorous and homogenous data, indeed, regardless of the national juridical and judicial framework, offer reproducible parameters to the judge or the jury for evaluating non-pecuniary damages, safeguarding personalization and the equitable power of the judge/jury.

Innovation is absolutely crucial in the field of physical damage and dental damage (Chap. 26) and in the reconstruction of the dynamics of the event by the consultation of a biomechanical expert and the use of finite element modelling (Chap. 28). In the case of suspected simulating or dissimulating behaviours, the ascertaining expert should utilise specific neuropsychological tests in order to detect malingering (Chap. 29), which is of special value when dealing with the psychic-existential damage (Chap. 30), where several disorders and/or impairments are difficult to objectify (e.g. post-traumatic stress disorder, mild brain injuries, etc.).

In light and line with the above, Members of the IALM Working Group on Personal Injury and Damage drafted a methodology to be used for ascertaining psychic-existential damage (Chap. 30). Moreover, during the consensus conference held in Padova in 2014, Members of the IALM Working Group on Personal Injury and Damage comparatively examined the clinical and medicolegal data outlined in the present chapter and elaborated the *Padova Charter* (Chap. 31), the very first international guideline focussing on the methods of ascertainment and criteria of evaluation of personal injury and damage under civil/tort law and a guideline for the ascertainment of whiplash-associated disorders (Chap. 32).

References

1. Ferrara SD, Pfeiffer H (2010) Unitariness, evidence and quality in bio-medicolegal sciences. Int J Legal Med 124(4):343–344
2. Zasler ND, Martelli MF (2003) Mild traumatic brain injury: impairment and disability assessment caveats. Neuropsychol Rehabil 13(1–2):31–41
3. Larrabee GJ (2003) Exaggerated MMPI-2 symptom report in personal injury litigants with malingered neurocognitive deficit. Arch Clin Neuropsychol 18(6):673–686
4. Allen MD, Owens TE, Fong AK, Richards DR (2011) A functional neuroimaging analysis of the Trail Making Test-B: implications for clinical application. Behav Neurol 24(2):159–171
5. Zysk AM, Nguyen FT, Oldenburg AL, Marks DL, Boppart SA (2007) Optical coherence tomography: a review of clinical development from bench to bedside. J Biomed Opt 12(5): 051403
6. Gutiérrez-Chico JL, Alegría-Barrero E, Teijeiro-Mestre R, Chan PH, Tsujioka H, de Silva R, Viceconte N, Lindsay A, Patterson T, Foin N, Akasaka T, di Mario C (2012) Optical coherence tomography: from research to practice. Eur Heart J Cardiovasc Imaging 13(5):370–384
7. Carignan CS, Yagi Y (2012) Optical endomicroscopy and the road to real-time, in vivo pathology: present and future. Diagn Pathol 7:98. doi:10.1186/1746-1596-7-98
8. Wang LV, Hu S (2012) Photoacoustic tomography: in vivo imaging from organelles to organs. Science 335(6075):1458–1462
9. Yang JM, Favazza C, Chen R, Yao J, Cai X, Maslov K, Zhou Q, Shung KK, Wang LV (2012) Simultaneous functional photoacoustic and ultrasonic endoscopy of internal organs in vivo. Nat Med 18(8):1297–1302
10. Walhovd KB, Johansen-Berg H, Káradóttir RT (2014) Unraveling the secrets of white matter—bridging the gap between cellular, animal and human imaging studies. Neuroscience 12(276): 2–13

Part VII
Methodology of Ascertainment and International Guidelines

Tagliacozzo, Gaspare (1545–1599). De curtorum chirurgia per insitionem libri duo. In quibus ea omnia, quae ad huius chirurgiae, narium scilicet, aurium, ac labiorum per insitionem restaurandorum cum theoricen, tum practicen pertinere videbantur, clarissima methodo cumulatissime declarantur. Additis Cutis traducis instrumentorum omnium, atque deligationum iconibus, & tabulis. … Venetiis : apud Gasparem Bindonum iuniorem, 1597. Courtesy of historical section of the "Vincenzo Pinali" Medical Library of the University of Padova

Chapter 28
Physical and Biomechanical Methods of Ascertainment

Luigi Cicinnati

Abstract After a brief introduction on the contributions that basic sciences, such as mathematics, physics and engineering, can furnish to personal injury and damage assessment, this chapter illustrates the methods of ascertainment to be used for the biomechanical reconstruction of any traumatic collisional event. It explores, in particular, the use of special measurement tools (i.e. anthropomorphic and anthropometrical testing devices) in combination with mathematical techniques, such as the finite element modelling (FEM), for reconstructing the acceleration, velocity, trajectory and energy of the collision. These data, interpreted in combination by the biomechanical and biomedical experts, are extremely useful for reconstructing the causal link between the traumatic event and the injuries/damages suffered by the claimant.

28.1 Physical and Biomechanical Aspects

The scope of this part of the work is intended to improve the research with a supplementary contribution to medicine from biomechanics, physics and other sciences.

Any event is ruled by the physical laws. In particular, if the event is characterised by an impact that involves persons and objects, it is necessary to evaluate, from the physical point of view, the history in time of the single phases of what happened and the consequent interaction with the environment.

Synergy with physics and mathematics may be an additional tool in the strategy of the reconstruction of any event, provided that a suitable quantity of information is available.

The aspects of this methodology require, first of all, the data regarding the scenario where the event happened. It is necessary to know the scenario condition

L. Cicinnati (✉)
Research and Development, Cincinnati Engineering - Padova, Via Croce Rossa, 62, 35129 Padova, Italy
e-mail: luigi.cicinnati@libero.it

S.D. Ferrara et al. (eds.), *Personal Injury and Damage Ascertainment under Civil Law*, DOI 10.1007/978-3-319-29812-2_28

before and after the event, too. At a later stage a physical and mathematical model of the whole real scenario will be built using all pertinent data, available and verified.

The theoretical model thus constructed (e.g. FEM) will be processed by the mathematical calculator of a powerful computer, taking into account the aspects of specific interest (acceleration, velocity, trajectory, energy, deformation and so on). This process, composed of a variable number of computational mechanics, as compatible as possible with the precision necessary in the specific case, represents the calibration process of the whole numerical model. It is similar to the tuning of a violin string in order that the desired key be reproduced exactly.

At any tour of the calibration process, an expert analyst examines the copious amount of results and evaluates if they are in agreement with the established precision degree regarding the specific event. If necessary, he applies a corrective factor.

The model is considered suitable to properly describe the event when the results are in conformity with the established degree of precision and the error made is smaller than an established factor of control.

At this stage the model is correct and adequate to describe accurately the specific case reproducing, theoretically, the real or experimental event at any time.

As a consequence of that, the most interesting aspect regards the fact that, modifying lightly a given input parameter, it is possible to use a coherently modified model to predict a similar result or to rebuild, in a different initial hypothesis, a similar well-documented incident. Therefore, the methodology allows the expert to find the correct engineering reconstruction within a group of different solutions.

The medical expert may compare his own evaluation with the additional evaluation of the analyst engineer: if the conclusions are coincident, a new tool may be gainfully added in the ascertainment methodology of events in which a collision involves one or more persons and any kind of object.

The method is suitable to be used in many other cases.

28.2 The Injury Caused by the Collision

The cause which provokes injuries or damage to a person is generally a collision against an object, the object and the person being in relative movement.

The collision of two or more objects distributes in a different way the initial kinetic energy of the system under consideration. The masses and the velocities of the objects have a decisive role in the evolution of the event: the velocity, in particular way, has a substantial influence on the new distribution of the stress and the strain of the colliding parts.

In addition to that, the materials react differently to the impact according to its mechanical properties, and each material has different behaviours depending on its velocity of deformation. Many materials and organic tissues have different behaviours depending on the load direction, too.

It is impossible to leave out this essential aspect regarding a collision: it is often a complex event where many forces interact, in different instants and along various directions, within a specific time interval.

In this context a greater force acting later may have a lower influence if compared with a weaker force acting earlier.

28.3 Accidental Events

The aim of this chapter is to provide support, as efficient and as practical as possible, using mathematical, physical and engineering tools, to medicine in the field of medicolegal ascertainment.

In this chapter the biomechanical, physical and mathematical aspects will be discussed, with reference to traffic injury, in particular, and to all kinds of collision causing personal damages in general. To do that, it is improper to carry out calculations manually due to the large number of variables characterising the problem, but it is essential to use computational mechanics and biomechanics.

Special measurement tools, anthropomorphic and anthropometrical testing devices, ATD, react, during a collision, to the stress and deformation and other loads, transforming the mechanical impact in readable machine data (Fig. 28.1).

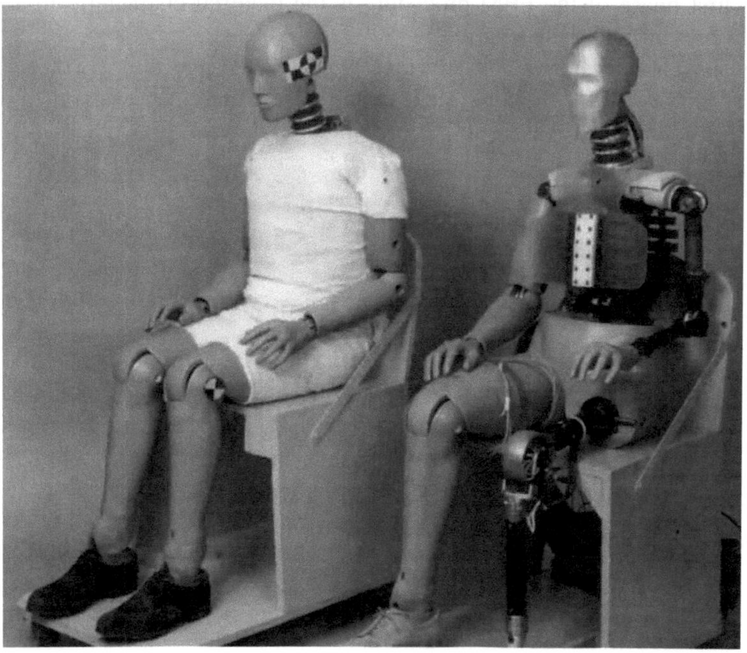

Fig. 28.1 ATD Hybrid III adult male dummy [1]

28.4 Finite Element Modelling

In mathematics, the finite element modelling, FEM, is a numerical technique for finding approximate solutions to boundary value problems for differential equations. It uses variational methods (the calculus of variations to minimise an error function and produce a stable solution), analogous to the idea that connecting many tiny straight lines can approximate a larger circle. FEM encompasses all the methods for connecting many simple element equations over many small subdomains, named finite elements, to approximate a more complex equation over a larger domain.

It foresees three fundamental phases:

1. Modelling phase: building of the physical and mathematical model equivalent to the real system, including the theoretical (FEM) anthropometrical test devices
2. Activation phase of mathematical calculation phase: data processing and output of numerical results
3. Rendering phase: summary of the numerical results by means of a specific software that uses graphic tools

The numerical results include the data relevant to the theoretical anthropometrical testing devices, ATD, readable by the biomechanical engineer and to be interpreted by the medical specialist and by the biomechanical engineer as well (Fig. 28.2).

The first phase of the FEM procedure is the material characterisation of each material present into the scenario.

Any inorganic material and any biological tissue have their own mechanical property expressed by their physical quantity, and it is necessary to utilise the correct value in the FEA code to perform a valid analysis (Figs. 28.3 and 28.4).

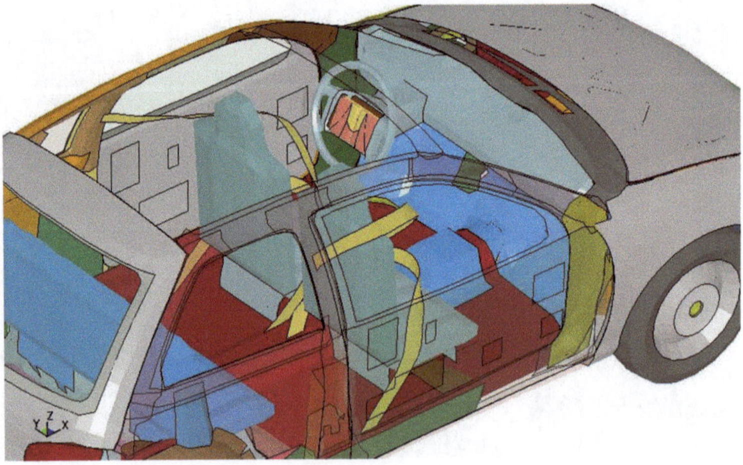

Fig. 28.2 FEM model of a small car

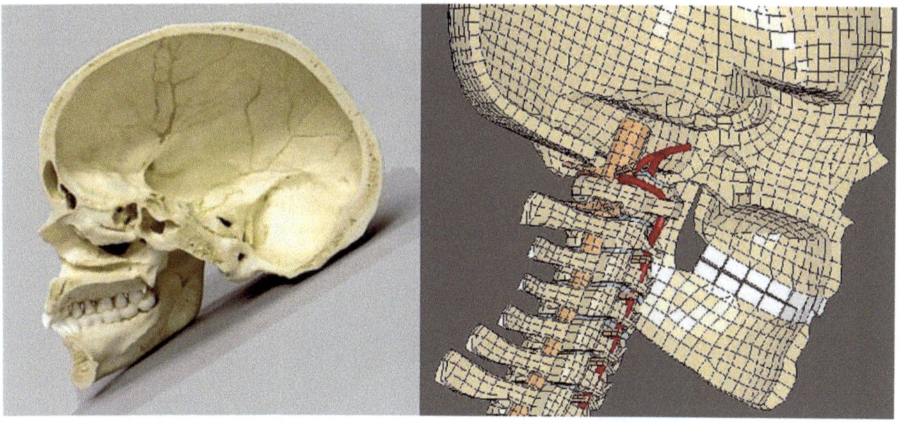

Fig. 28.3 Real skull and theoretical skull FEM model

Bone	Force Range (N)	Force Mean	Sample size	Impactor area (cm^2)
Frontal	2,670–8,850	4,930	18	6.45
Frontal	4,140–9,880	5,780	13	6.45
Frontal	2,200–8,600	4,780	13	20-mm-dia bar
Frontal	5,920–7,340	6,370	4	6.4-mm-dia bar
Frontal	8,760–8,990	8,880	2	25.4-mm-dia bar (sagittal)[a]
Frontal	N/A	6,550	1	50.8-mm-dia bar (90 durometer, sagittal)[a]
Frontal	N/A	6,810	1	203-mm-radius hemisphere
Frontal	4,310–5,070	4,690	2	76-mm-radius hemisphere
Frontal	N/A	5,120	1	50.4-mm-dia bar (sagittal)[a]
Left frontal boss	2,670–4,450	3,560	2	25.4-mm-dia bar
Temporoparietal	2,215–5,930	3,490	18	6.45
Temporoparietal	2,110–5,200	3,630	14	6.45
Temporoparietal	2,500–10,000	5,200	20	5.07
Parietal	5,800–17,000	12,500	11	50
Zygomatic arch	930–1,930	1,450	11	6.45

[a]Major axis of bar parallel to sagittal plane.

Fig. 28.4 Skull fracture force [1]

The interaction between inorganic objects and anatomical parts and tissues is the cause of the injury or damage if its value is greater than the specific collapse threshold.

The ultimate threshold depends on the material properties, material behaviour, speed impact, load direction and other conditions. Mainly it depends on time (and, consequently, on speed impact and the sequence of events) (Fig. 28.5).

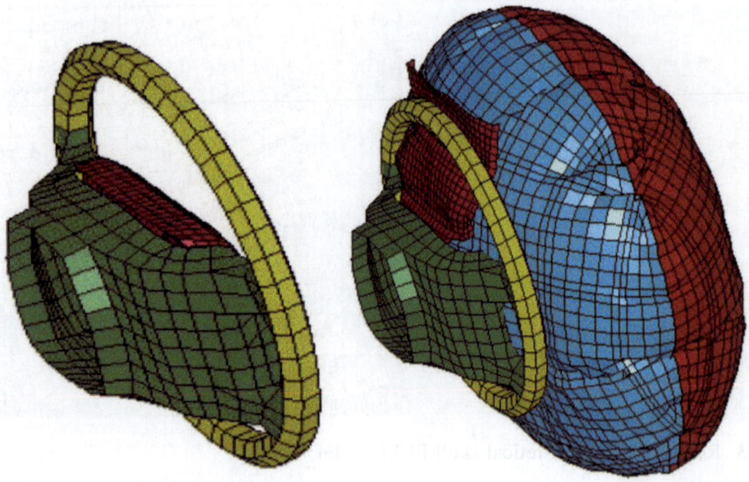

Fig. 28.5 Car steering wheel and exploded air bag

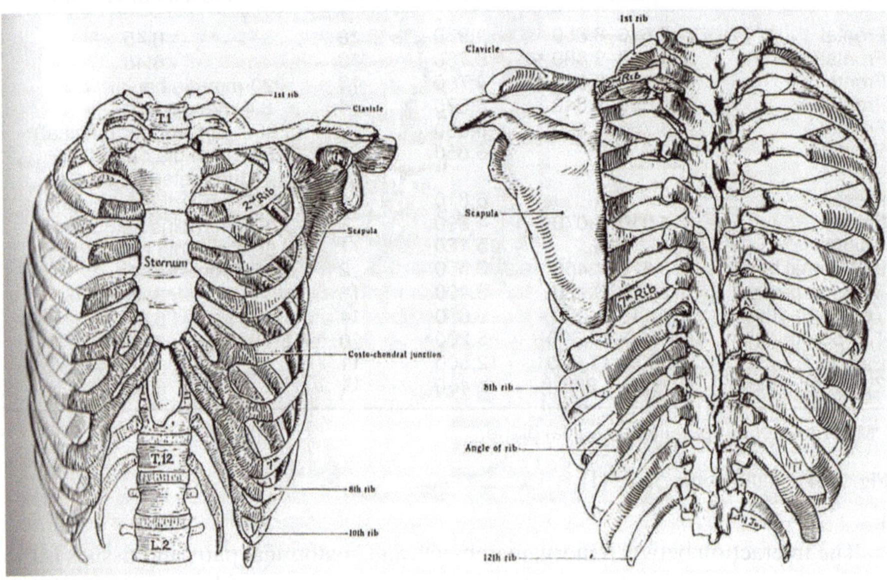

Fig. 28.6 Thorax bones mainly exposed to collisions [1]

So, the force, due to the shoulder belt and due to the air bag, acting on the thorax bones, depends on the relative impact acceleration (in this due to the velocity of the car). In the case of high value of the velocity of the collision, the thorax bones react with fragile fractures of the ribs, whereas in the case of low speed the interaction affects a larger area of the thorax and assumes the behaviour of a light diffused compression, sometimes without any fracture (Figs. 28.6 and 28.7).

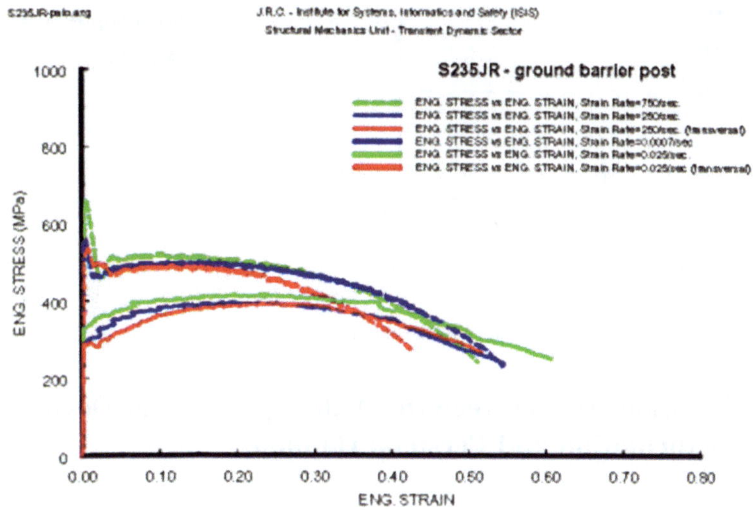

Fig. 28.7 Relationship between stress and strain in the case of different speed

28.5 Time History of Variables and Causality

To evaluate if a relationship of cause and effect exists, it is necessary to reconsider the concept according to which, within a time interval, the events that occur before the others in the domain of reference are more important in determining causality than the compatible effects that it is possible to observe.

If the compatibility with the specific injury or damage exists, in fact, the previous event is the effective cause of the visible harmful effects, since the following event occurs when the scenario has been modified completely and irreversibly.

Consequently, during the accident phases, the events that occur after the first compatible event cannot be considered the cause of the damage, even if they are compatible with the specific damage and more harmful than the preceding event (Fig. 28.8).

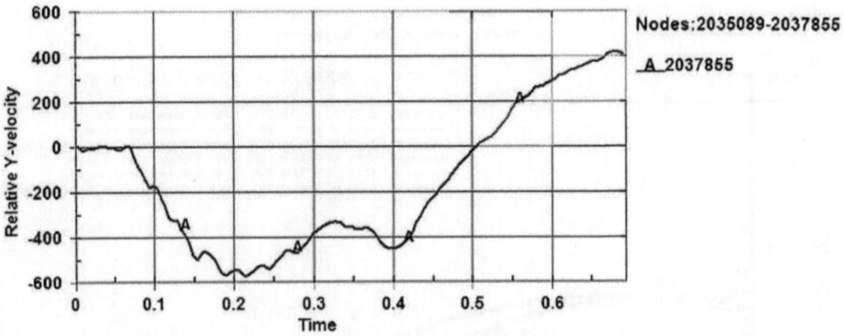

Fig. 28.8 Example of the time history of the relative y velocity

28.6 Relationship Between the Anthropometrical Device Deformation and Personal Damage

The ATD Hybrid III was designed and realised by the General Motors Company in many versions and editions with the aim of studying the safety of its cars in traffic.

Thus, the resistance of the parts of the device is compatible with the resistance of the corresponding parts of the human body.

During the phases of a major road collision, an ATD may crash time after time and receive innumerable stresses and deformations compatible with a specific damage threshold.

The events that occur after the first compatible event cannot be considered the cause of the mechanical damage, even if they are compatible with the specific threshold or more harmful than it.

It is necessary to consider the combined effect of all the crashes and—first of all—to determine which event occurred previously (Fig. 28.9).

The medical specialist in traumatology has many abilities available for evaluating the correct sequence of particular events.

In addition to that, the supplementary contributions of a FEA permit the analyst to correlate any variable pertinent value with the collision time interval, setting the time of any event and the instant value of any variable.

This brief consideration regarding the supplementary contributions to the medicolegal ascertainment methodology from other sciences, such as biomechanics, physics, mathematics and engineering, mainly pointed out the following aspects:

- It is essential to evaluate the scenario's geometry and the mechanical properties of the materials, including its own behaviour in dynamics.
- One of the most effective supplementary tools regarding the medicolegal ascertainment methodology appears to be the finite element analysis, FEA method. Its codes show the values of any variable in time and, consequently, allow one to understand, at any time since the beginning of the collision, the behaviour assumed by any object and its variables, ATD included.

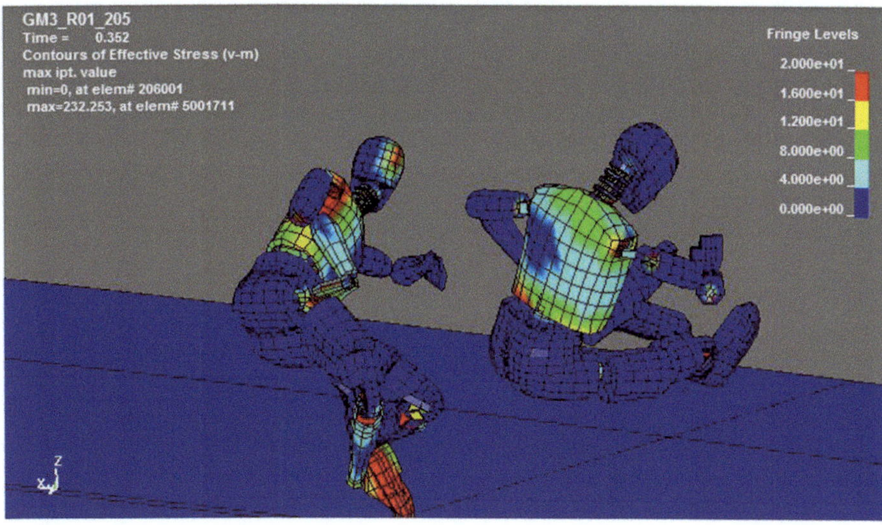

Fig. 28.9 Stress render of ATD during a collision

- The most probable cause of the damage or injury seems to be the first event compatible with the peculiar threshold of reference. In fact, during the accident phases, the events that occur after the first one compatible with a significant injury or damage cannot be considered the cause of the accident, even if they are compatible with the first damaging event and are more harmful.
- This peculiarity of the FEA method is fundamental to determine causality with the effects of the compatible harmful event that are possible to observe. That is the reason why the FEA method is one of the most useful supplementary tools in medicolegal ascertainment procedures.

Many aspects have to be further examined, and the detailed study of the impacts appears strictly necessary from several further points of view.

Reference

1. Nahum AM, Melvin JW (eds) (1993) Accidental injury biomechanics and prevention. Springer, New York, pp 292–310

Chapter 29
Detection of Malingering in Personal Injury and Damage Ascertainment

Giuseppe Sartori, Graziella Orrù, and Andrea Zangrossi

Abstract One of the most important challenges encountered by forensic and medicolegal professionals is the evaluation of simulating and dissimulating behaviors exhibited by litigants. The main feature of malingering is represented by the intentional production of false or exaggerated symptoms, motivated by external incentives. Assessment of malingering is often inadequate when exclusively based on the clinical interview, sometimes also grounded solely on the clinician's negative opinion. For this reason, the misclassification rate in the detection of malingerers can be considered alarmingly high (over 80 %). Malingering is not an all-or-nothing phenomenon, but it can be realized on several levels. Moreover, an examinee may attempt to malinger in a number of different ways, including fabricating or exaggerating psychiatric symptoms or presenting various types of cognitive deficits. Thus, several strategies have been identified for malingering detection (e.g., discrepancy method, symptoms analysis, and symptom validity testing).

Moreover, some of these strategies may be applied for the interpretation of a number of tests that have been developed for the identification of malingering.

Therefore, multiple sources of independent data (e.g., clinical data, test scores, etc.) should be considered and compared in order to accurately confirm or disconfirm cases of malingering. This chapter presents a non-exhaustive review of strategies and tests used for the detection of malingering of both psychopathological and cognitive symptoms/diseases.

29.1 Malingering in Litigation

One of the most important challenges encountered by forensic scientists and medicolegal professionals is the evaluation of simulating and dissimulating behaviors exhibited by litigants.

G. Sartori (✉) • G. Orrù • A. Zangrossi
Department of Psychology, University of Padova, Via Venezia 8, 35131 Padova, Italy
e-mail: giuseppe.sartori@unipd.it; graziella.orru@unipd.it; andrea.zangrossi@gmail.com

S.D. Ferrara et al. (eds.), *Personal Injury and Damage Ascertainment under Civil Law*, DOI 10.1007/978-3-319-29812-2_29

In 1866, Erichsen published results concerning patients (workers for the Prussian railroad) who developed persistent complaints after sustaining mild head trauma. Some years later, with regard to this concept, Rigler (1879) coined the term "compensation neurosis" in order to describe the origin of these injuries (or as the causative effect of these injuries). He strongly believed that the boost of long-term disabilities was due to a policy for compensating injured workers, introduced by the Prussian railroad. Another important contribution was made by Charcot, at a later stage. He supported the idea that the long-term symptoms resulting from "mild head injury" were ascribable to "hysteria and neurasthenia." By 1934, the diagnostic entities mentioned above ("compensation neurosis" and "hysteria") have contributed to the current diagnosis of "post-concussion syndrome" [1].

Recent approaches to malingering have been systematized in the DSM-5 [2]. The Diagnostic and Statistical Manual of Mental Disorders, Fifth Edition (DSM-5) classifies malingering with a V-code (V65.2), thus indicating that it is not a mental disorder but rather one of the "additional conditions that may be a focus of clinical attention" (Ref. 3, p. 739).

According to the DSM-5 (pp. 726–727) "[t]he essential feature of malingering is the intentional production of false or grossly exaggerated physical or psychological symptoms, motivated by external incentives." These incentives may be referred to gaining an advantage (e.g., economic/financial compensations) or avoiding a loss (e.g., imprisonment). In the clinical practice, malingering should always be suspected if at least one of the following circumstances is observed: (1) medicolegal context of presentation, (2) marked discrepancy between the individual's claimed stress or disability and the objective findings and observations, (3) lack of cooperation during the diagnostic assessment and poor adherence to prescribed therapies, and (4) the presence of antisocial personality disorder.

Despite the number of available strategies, the assessment of malingering in the forensic context presents a number of difficulties: problems in truthfulness evaluation or in estimating malingering base-rate in different contexts and the influence of variables related to the clinical interaction that can affect the forensic psychological assessment. For these reasons, assessments often show inadequate conclusions derived from subjective impressions, sometimes also grounded solely on the clinician's negative opinion of the examinee [3]. According to Rogers and Vitacco (2002), using the DSM-IV as criteria for the detection of malingerers, the misclassification rate can be considered as over 80 % [4].

The expansion of clinical evaluations into the legal arena, coupled with the fact that symptom report and effort on testing are under the direct control of the examinee, has led to an explosion in research on malingering in the past 10 years. For example, in 1980 only a few papers per year were published on malingering, whereas in 2009, there were more than 90 publications on this topic. In the 20 years between 1989 and 2009, over 1200 papers (ISI Web of Science) and volumes (e.g., [5]) on malingering were published. This growing number of publications has led to the development of several standardized tools that can be used in clinical and forensic practice for detecting malingering of both psychopathological and cognitive symptoms.

Plaintiffs may attempt to malinger in a number of different ways, including fabricating or exaggerating psychiatric symptoms or presenting various types of cognitive deficits. Thus, malingering is not an all-or-nothing phenomenon, but it can be realized on several levels. An examinee who exaggerates genuine psychopathological symptoms could represent one such level [6].

The voluntary component is not always present when feigned symptoms are detected. Indeed, it allows the differentiation between malingering and the factitious disorder which, in contrast, requires the absence of reward. In this case the aim behind the patient's fabricated symptoms is the need to assume the role of the sick person (without any form of external incentive). With the same criterion (presence of will and conscious deliberation in symptom fabrication), malingering could also be differentiated from conversion disorder and somatic symptom-related mental disorders.

A reliable sign of feigning, such as the presence of an obvious loss of function during the examination, but not at home, strongly suggests:

(a) a diagnosis of **factitious disorder** if the aim of the individual is to assume the role of a sick subject;
(b) a diagnosis of **malingering** if the aim is related to the achievement of an incentive (i.e., money).

Despite the oddities in malingering criteria, researchers have tried to estimate the incidence of malingering in a medicolegal setting. The base-rate of malingering and symptom exaggeration has been estimated in a large sample of personal injury cases ($N = 33{,}531$) by Mittenberg, Patton, Canvock, and Condit (2002) [7]. Twenty-nine percent of personal injury cases have been estimated to involve malingering or exaggeration of symptoms.

Furthermore, using a variety of methodological approaches, studies reported a prevalence of about 40 % of malingering in forensic settings [7]. By contrast, in a survey of 221 forensic psychologists, the prevalence of malingering was estimated at 17.4 % [8]. Additionally, depending on diagnoses and referral circumstances, base-rates of malingering and exaggeration may vary.

Although malingering may be easy to define, its detection and diagnosis in clinical practice are not so simple. Moreover, the detection of malingered symptoms becomes more difficult when referred to psychopathological disease, as a great part of the psychological assessment is grounded mainly on the evaluation of what is verbally reported by the examinee. In fact, psychopathological evaluation depends upon an accurate symptom report by the examinee. In order to help examiners, some strategies have been studied, such as those introduced by Slick, Sherman, and Iverson (1999) concerning malingered neurocognitive dysfunction (MND) [9].

29.2 Strategies for Detecting Malingering of Psychiatric and Cognitive Symptoms

Several strategies have been identified to be adopted for detection of malingering, both in clinical and forensic settings. Here we present a non-exhaustive review of strategies used for the detection of malingering of both psychopathological and cognitive symptoms/diseases.

29.2.1 Qualitative Analysis of Symptom Characteristics

From a clinical point of view, some typical characteristics of malingering can be identified [6].

- Simulators become increasingly normal as time goes by, so it could be useful to protract interviews if malingering is suspected.
- Delusions and hallucinations can be artificially produced, but catatonic behavior or inappropriate affect is rarely simulated, as malingerers are more likely to call attention to their delusions.
- Disorganized speech, lack of associations, and flight of ideas (that characterize thought disorders) are really difficult to fake throughout the interview.
- Unclear, vague answers.
- Positive answers are given in order to confirm symptoms. Usually, malingerers display this kind of behavior because of their belief that endorsing a symptom will increase the appearance of psychopathology.
- Symptoms not related and/or consistent with any mental disorders. Malingerers have the tendency to report many symptoms, indiscriminately; particularly, this is due to the belief that by reporting a larger number of symptoms the disorder will be perceived as more serious and severe.

29.2.2 Discrepancy Method

The above listed criteria have to do with the evaluation of isolated psychiatric symptoms, while the discrepancy method discussed below consists in evaluating the syndromic associations of symptoms that in the malingerer does not correspond to known syndromic entities.

One of the first and most adopted strategies in medicine and in psychology is called *discrepancy method* and refers in general to the clinical evaluation of the difference between observed findings and typical findings expected in a claimed disease. According to Larrabee (1990), five forms of discrepancy can be distinguished, as reported below.

- *Internal consistency of neurobehavioral domains*: divergent performance on tests that should be highly correlated
- *Disease-deficit compatibility*: production of symptoms not considered as primary manifestations of a reported disorder
- *Inconsistency with severity of injury*: divergence between the magnitude of the disease and the impairment with related symptoms
- *Ecological validity discrepancy*: inconsistency between performances in tests investigating a certain domain and the observed behaviors from the same domain
- *Violations of performance curves*: if a range of items from relatively easy to very difficult is presented, honest responders should correctly answer the easy items and possibly make errors in answering more difficult items. Malingerers, however, may perform poorly on easy items (intentionally choosing the wrong answer) and paradoxically improve their performance as the items increase in difficulty [10].

Consider, for example, the assessment conducted by A. Coppola in the case of the "*Smemorato di Collegno*" [11]: Coppola administered the Collegno amnesic, a short memory test consisting of the recall of a list of random digits. The amnesic recalled a string of eight digits but failed to recall a list of three digits. This is equivalent to lifting 100 kg, but failing to lift 10 kg. It is extremely unlikely, Coppola, for a genuine amnesic to recall eight digits but fail to recall three digits.

29.2.3 Rare Symptoms and Unrelated Symptoms

Another important general method is focused on the qualitative and quantitative analysis of symptoms. For instance, the presence of *rare symptoms* could be analyzed, that is, if the examinee reports symptoms that are infrequently seen in a clinical population. The *indiscriminant symptom endorsement* is also considered: when given the opportunity, malingerers may report a wide variety of symptoms, trying to feign an unspecified psychopathology without having in mind specific symptoms of a particular diagnosis. *Obvious symptoms* are also an important source of information: symptoms that are considered clearly indicative of mental illness are more often endorsed than those less obviously associated with psychopathology. An examinee should be suspected of malingering also if he/she shows *improbable symptoms* characterized by an extremely bad or fantastic quality or by an *extreme or unusual severity*. Indeed, malingerers are often not able to estimate how severe the symptoms should be in order to be credible nor how many of them there should be. Sometimes, an examinee can also interpret a stereotypical role related to *erroneous stereotypes*, thus reporting mixed symptoms of different diseases (e.g., describing a schizophrenic condition as "having two personalities" [6]). Moreover, sometimes an examinee reports *symptoms not congruent with his/her behavior*.

Some psychometric tests such as SIMS [12] are the standardization of the rare symptom approach described above.

29.2.4 Neuropsychological Tests in the Detection of Malingering

A third kind of method for detecting malingering is focused on the use of specific types of testing techniques. The *symptom validity testing* (*SVT*), for example, applies to two alternative, forced-choice testing. This strategy is simple and efficient. A patient with a genuine impairment (not able to choose the correct answer between the two stimuli) over many trials should give a performance at chance level. On the contrary, malingerers usually select the wrong response deliberately and thus perform significantly below chance. The most likely explanation for this performance is that the examinee knows the correct answer but decides not to choose it. This strategy can be considered similar to the abovementioned analysis of the performance curve.

The *floor effect strategy* is another method for detecting malingering. It is based on the assumption that even severe brain trauma patients are able to answer simple questions about themselves (i.e., "How old are you?") or make easy comparisons (i.e., "Which is more expensive, diamond or platinum?"). Starting from the assumption that even severely impaired subjects are successful in answering them, a failure on these simple questions is an important indicator of malingering.

In order to distinguish cognitive malingerers from genuine organic patients, empirical research highlights how Rey's 15-Item Test is an effective tool that utilizes the *floor effect*. Rey's 15-Item Test is a visual memory task and is presented to a potential malingerer as a difficult task (by stressing the number of items to be recalled). In the study [13], the items to be recollected were selected specifically, for the easy way that they can be grouped and/or remembered. Floor effect data should be used cautiously, since coaching can increase a malingerer's ability to foil this detection strategy.

Professionals almost always need to consider outside data in addition to the basic clinical interview in order to reliably detect and diagnose malingering. In fact, Rogers et al. (2002) warn against solely using the additional factors of "strongly suspected" malingering laid out by the DSM-IV-TR as a detection strategy, as doing so can result in a misclassification rate of over 80 % [4]. For instance, Resnick and Zuchowski (2007) note that in a criminal justice setting, an individual may begin the assessment with three out of four of the aforementioned factors simply because of the setting itself [14]. Therefore, it is imperative that one or more of the valid, structured measurement techniques designed specifically for malingering detection, as well as multiple sources of independent data, be used in order to more accurately confirm or disconfirm cases of malingering [15].

29.2.5 Tests for Detecting Malingering

Since the 1920s, there has been the need to design specific tools able to accurately detect malingering. The first malingering detection strategies were applied in 1926 in a notorious judicial and media affair concerning the alleged reappearance (in 1926) of a man who had gone missing in World War I. The Bruneri-Canella case, called in Italian the case of the "*smemorato di Collegno*," is probably the most famous case of malingered retrograde amnesia ever known in Italy. In brief, a man who appeared to have lost all his autobiographical memories and identity spent nearly a year in the Collegno asylum of Turin without a name. At first, the man was identified as Giulio Canella, the director of the "*Scuola Normale di Verona*" who disappeared during the war in 1916. Later, the man was identified as being Mario Bruneri, a petty crook from Turin who played the part of an amnesic whose retrograde memory gradually returned [11]. A long investigation was necessary, and, subsequent to an inquiry and several trials and appeals, the court found that he was indeed Bruneri. Despite the fact that several clinicians and academics evaluated the case, only Coppola diagnosed him with a "malingered retrograde amnesia," using a method that was extremely innovative for that period.

The question of his identity was thoroughly discussed worldwide, in newspapers and courtrooms. The debate endured for almost 40 years. Due to nationwide interest in the case, the term *smemorato di Collegno* became a common saying since the 1930s, meaning a person who forgets everything of his past life.

29.2.6 Tests for Detecting Malingered Psychiatric Symptoms

Several tests, for supporting psychiatric diagnosis, incorporate a quantitative approach in the identification of malingering and are described below.

- Minnesota Multiphasic Personality Inventory-2 (MMPI-2; [16]): this is the most widely used and researched multi-scale measure of psychopathology. In order to generate hypotheses of dissimulation, trained professionals can use the validity indicators, in particular the F scales (F, Fb, Fp). Furthermore, consistency scales (VRIN and TRIN) can be particularly useful to distinguish random responding and reading problems from other types of invalid profiles.
- Personality Assessment Inventory (PAI; [17]): this is a psychometrically sound multi-scale inventory very helpful in both clinical and forensic contexts.
- Negative Impression Management scale of the PAI (NIM; [17]): this is used to identify exaggeration of psychopathology and possible malingering.
- Structured Interview of Reported Symptoms (SIRS; [18]): this is a 172-item tool designed to assess a wide range of psychopathology and symptomatology. It consists of eight primary scales and five supplementary scales. Scores from the primary scales are classified into one of the four following categories: honest responding, indeterminate, probable feigning, and definite feigning.

- M-Test (M-Test; [19]): this test assesses the possibility of feigning or exaggeration of psychiatric symptoms. The M-Test was developed as a screening measure to specifically detect the malingering of schizophrenic symptoms.
- Structured Inventory of Malingered Symptomatology (SIMS; [12]): is a self-report measure designed to detect malingering of psychiatric symptoms and/or cognitive impairments. It consists of 75 dichotomous items (i.e., true-false) that focus on the following domains: low intelligence (LI), affective disorders (AF), neurological impairment (N), psychosis (P), and amnestic disorders (AM). Strategies used to detect deviant or malingered response patterns include endorsement of bizarre experiences and highly atypical symptoms.

29.2.7 Tests for Detecting Malingered Cognitive Symptoms

A variety of tests for detecting malingered cognitive symptoms are mainly focused on the detection of feigned memory impairment as this is one of the most frequent malingered cognitive symptoms. Here we present those most frequently used in clinical and forensic practice as they address symptoms which are frequently feigned.

- Test of Memory Malingering (TOMM; [20]): this is a recognition test composed of two trials of 50 items designed for adults to discriminate between true memory-impaired patients and malingerers. This tool is a particularly useful test to detect exaggerated or malingered memory impairment. A cutoff score of 45 on Trial 2 (i.e., 90 % correct responding) and Tombaugh's investigations [20] revealed a correct classification of 95 % of all non-demented patients as not malingering.
- Rey's 15-Item Visual Memory Test (MFIT; [21]): this test is used as a screening measure for malingered memory impairment. It consists of 15 items, arranged in three rows and five columns. The traditional scoring method involves simply counting the total number of items correctly recalled, with scores of less than nine items for raising the suspicion of malingering.
- Word Memory Test (WMT; [22]): this is a computer-administered memory task in which a 20-item word list is presented. Then, words appear in pairs: one word is presented, followed by the next, 1 s later. The pair disappears and another set is presented 2 s later. The list is presented twice, and then the subjects are asked to recall as many of the word pairs as possible.
- Dot Counting Test (DCT; [13]): this is another screening measure for malingering developed by Andre Rey. It consists of 12 cards on which are printed a series of dots. Respondents are presented with the cards in a fixed nonsequential order and are instructed to count the number of dots as quickly as possible. It is expected that the non-malingering patient will take longer to count the ungrouped dots than the grouped dots, with increases in counting time proportional to increases in the number of dots.

As mentioned above, in this context several neuropsychological tests have been applied, and in what follows we report some other helpful instruments.

- 48-Pictures Test
- Digit Memory Test (DMT)
- Portland Digit Recognition Test (PDRT)
- Computerized Assessment of Response Bias (CARB)
- 21-Item Test
- Coin-in-the-hand test
- The b Test

All the above tests are designed to investigate trait characteristics, while they are not able to be tailored to the specific symptomatology of a particular case. To overcome this problem, in recent years some techniques have been introduced, such as those described in the next paragraph.

29.3 New Techniques for Detecting Malingering

The techniques described above aim at detecting malingering behaviors of the respondent rather than a specific malingered datum. In some instances the plaintiff may overreport specific symptoms (e.g., shoulder pain, amnesia for the crime, etc.); in these cases, the above reported techniques may be of scarce utility. Recently, a number of procedures have been developed that may efficiently detect very specific malingered symptoms. These techniques include aIAT and TARA.

The aIAT [23] is a novel variant of the Implicit Association Test [24] that can be used to establish whether an autobiographical memory trace is encoded within the respondent's mind. More specifically, with the aIAT, it is possible to evaluate which one of two autobiographical events is true [23]. Nevertheless, aIAT has been tested in different domains and on different constructs such as future-, medium-, and long-term intentions, white lies and underlying intentions, mock crime, holidays, cocaine/heroine consumption, driving license, flashbulb memories (see [25] for a review), and whiplash malingering [26]. Thus, the aIAT has been applied in both forensic and clinical settings. It has been demonstrated that this tool can determine which of two autobiographical events is true with 91 % accuracy [23]. Despite the different kinds of investigations and constructs on which aIAT has been applied [25], the structure of the method is always maintained.

The aIAT includes stimuli belonging to four categories: two of them are logical categories represented by sentences that are certainly true (e.g., "I am in front of a computer") or certainly false (e.g., "I am climbing a mountain") for the respondent and relate to the moment of testing. The other two categories are represented by alternative versions of the construct under investigation (e.g., "I went to Paris for Christmas" vs. "I went to London for Christmas"), only one of the two being true. The aIAT is structured in five classification blocks: three simple categorization blocks (1, 2, 4), and two combined categorization blocks (3 and 5). In simple blocks, each response button is used to classify sentences related to only one category. In double blocks, each response button is used to classify sentences related to two different categories. In Block 1, participants have to classify true and false sentences (e.g., I am in front of a computer vs. I am in front of a television) using two response keys, one on the left and one on the right of the keyboard. In Block 2, participants have to classify autobiographical sentences (e.g., I went to Paris for Christmas vs. I went to New York for Christmas) with the same two response keys. In Block 3 (double categorization block), true sentences and sentences related to the first autobiographical event (e.g., Christmas in Paris) are paired on the same response key, and false sentences and sentences related to the second autobiographical event (e.g., Christmas in New York) are classified with the other response key. In Block 4, only autobiographical events are reverse classified with the two response keys. Finally, in Block 5, participants have to classify both true sentences and sentences related to the second autobiographical event (Christmas in New York) with the same response key and false sentences and the first autobiographical event (Christmas in Paris) with the other key.

The basic principle of aIAT (and original IAT) is that the pairing of a truly autobiographical event with certainly true sentences should facilitate faster responses, so that the specific pattern of RTs for the double categorization blocks indicates which autobiographical event is either true or false. The true autobiographical event is identified because it determines faster RTs in the block in which it shares the same motor response with true sentences. Validation studies of the aIAT have been carried out on over 500 subjects, on an array of conditions, and the validity of the technique has been confirmed in a number of different labs, on different languages (see [25] for a review).

Evidence-based investigations of aIAT to efficiently detect faked whiplash symptoms or faked depression. Single case studies have been carried out to assess phantom limb pain and psychogenic amnesia.

In terms of layout and logic, another technique has much in common with the IAT/aIAT, as it is a timed, multi-block classification task: the Timed Antagonistic Response Alethiometer (TARA; [27]). This technique refers to a computer-based classification task in which honest respondents are able to complete a series of compatible classifications, but in which dishonest respondents are obliged to complete a series of incompatible ones. Doing the latter is harder than doing the former. Consequently, dishonest respondents must go more slowly than honest respondents to achieve equivalent levels of accuracy. Thus, longer average RTs suggest dishonesty and shorter ones honesty.

The TARA, like the IAT, is also a timed, multi-block classification task in which two types of statement are presented: target and control. Target statements express true and false propositions about respondents themselves. Control statements express true and false propositions about an irrelevant topic. In Block 1 control statements (false/true) are presented. The subject has to respond honestly. As in aIAT, the TARA discriminates the true statement from the false statement by detecting long reaction times to false statements (as compared to true statements). Block 2 would be identical to Block 1 except that the stimuli would be made of target statements. Block 3 would combine Blocks 1 and 2. Thus, respondents would press the left key for false target and control statements and the right key for true ones. Block 4 would be identical to Block 2 except that responding would now be dishonest. Thus, respondents would press the right key for false target statements and the left key for true target statements. Finally, Block 5 would combine Blocks 1 and 4. Responding would be honest for control statements but dishonest for target statements. Thus, respondents would press the left key for false control or true target statements and the right key for true control or false target statements. In consequence, respondents would have to go slower when lying (Block 5) than when telling the truth (Block 3), to achieve equivalent levels of accuracy. The difference in their average RT between these blocks could therefore be used as a basis of distinguishing lying from truth telling [27].

Note that the principle proposed to underlie the TARA, unlike that proposed to underlie many traditional lie detectors, is simple, general, and uncontroversial: holding the error rate constant, incompatible tasks take longer to complete than compatible ones.

29.4 Conclusions and Future Directions

The recognition of probable malingering or symptom exaggeration in individual cases requires several inferential methods. The diagnosis typically involves consideration of the medical record, the patient's self-report, the observed behavior, and the results of a comprehensive neuropsychological examination [9].

The evaluation of malingering and other types of deception is a cornerstone issue in forensic practice and litigation evaluations especially when psychiatric and cognitive symptoms are under investigation. There is increasing interest in the application of reliable methods for the detection of deception to aid accurate diagnosis and prognosis in the legal arena. The key advantage of the new technique (aIAT) over traditional techniques is that it permits accurate and reliable inferences to be made at the level of the individual. While there are significant theoretical and practical challenges related to this approach, the results of the studies published so far are encouraging and may provide the first steps toward the development of a computer-based diagnostics in forensic psychiatry.

References

1. Hall RCW, Hall RCW, Chapman MJ (2005) Definition, diagnosis, and forensic implications of postconcussional syndrome. Psychosomatics 46(3):195–202
2. American Psychiatric Association (2013) Diagnostic and statistical manual of mental disorders, 5th edn. American Psychiatric Association, Washington, DC
3. Drob SL, Meehan KB, Waxman SE (2009) Clinical and conceptual problems in the attribution of malingering in forensic evaluations. J Am Acad Psychiatry Law 37(1):98–106

4. Rogers R, Vitacco MJ (2002) Forensic assessment of malingering and related response styles. In: Van Dorsten B (ed) Forensic psychology: from classroom to courtroom. Kluwer Publishers, Boston, MA
5. Larrabee GJ (ed) (2007) Assessment of malingered neuropsychological deficits. Oxford University Press, New York
6. Conroy MA, Kwartner PP (2006) Malingering. Appl Psychol Crim Just 2(3):29–51
7. Mittenberg W, Patton C, Canyock EM, Condit DC (2002) Base rates of malingering and symptom exaggeration. J Clin Exp Neuropsychol 24(8):1094–1102
8. Rogers R, Salekin RT, Sewell KW, Goldstein A, Leonard K (1998) A comparison of forensic and nonforensic malingerers: a prototypical analysis of explanatory models. Law Hum Behav 22:353–367
9. Slick DJ, Sherman EM, Iverson GL (1999) Diagnostic criteria for malingered neurocognitive dysfunction: proposed standards for clinical practice and research. Clin Neuropsychol 13:545–561
10. Larrabee GJ (1990) Cautions in the use of neuropsychological evaluation in legal settings. Neuropsychology 4:239–247
11. Zago S, Sartori G, Scarlato G (2002) Malingering and retrograde amnesia: the historic case of the Collegno amnesic. Cortex 3:519–532
12. Smith GP, Burger GK (1997) Detection of malingering: validation of the Structured Inventory of Malingered Symptomatology (SIMS). J Am Acad Psychiatry Law 25:183–189
13. Lezak MD (1995) Neuropsychological assessment. Oxford University Press, New York
14. Resnick PJ, Zuchowski SJ (2007) Malingering and psychopathic disorders. In: Felthous A, Sass H (eds) The international handbook of psychopathic disorders and the law: laws and policies. Wiley, Indianapolis, IN
15. Vitacco MJ, Jackson RL, Rogers R, Neumann CS, Miller HA, Gabel J (2008) Detection strategies for malingering with the Miller Forensic Assessment of Symptoms Test—a confirmatory factor analysis of its underlying dimensions. Assessment 15(1):97–103
16. Butcher JN, Dahlstrom WG, Graham JR, Tallagen A, Kaemmer B (1989) MMPI-2: manual for administration and scoring. University of Minnesota Press, Minneapolis, MN
17. Morey LC (1991) Personality assessment inventory: professional manual. Psychological Assessment Resources, Odessa, FL
18. Rogers R, Bagby RM, Dickens SE (1992) Structured Interview of Reported Symptoms professional manual. Psychological Assessment Resources, Odessa, FL
19. Beaber RJ, Marston A, Michelli J, Mills MJ (1985) A brief test for measuring malingering in schizophrenic individuals. Am J Psychiatry 142:1478–1481
20. Tombaugh TN (1996) Test of memory malingering. Multi-Health Systems, Toronto, ON
21. Rey A (1964) L'examen clinique en psychologie. Presses Universitaires de France, Paris
22. Green P, Allen L, Astner K (1997) The word memory test: a manual for the oral and computerized forms. CogniSyst, Durham
23. Sartori G, Agosta S, Zogmaister C, Ferrara SD, Castiello U (2008) How to accurately assess autobiographical events. Psychol Sci 18:772–780
24. Greenwald AG, McGhee DE, Schwartz JLK (1998) Measuring individual differences in implicit cognition: the implicit association test. J Pers Soc Psychol 74:1464–1480
25. Agosta S, Sartori G (2013) The autobiographical IAT: a review. Front Psychol 4:Article 519
26. Sartori G, Agosta S, Gnoato F (2007) High accuracy detection of malingered whiplash syndrome. Paper presented at the international whiplash trauma congress, Miami
27. Gregg AP (2007) When vying reveals lying: the timed antagonistic response alethiometer. Appl Cogn Psychol 21:621–647

Chapter 30
A Novel Methodology for the Objective Ascertainment of Psychic and Existential Damage

Santo Davide Ferrara, Viviana Ananian, Eric Baccino, Ranieri Domenici, Claudio Hernàndez-Cueto, George Mendelson, Gian Aristide Norelli, Mohammed Ranavaya, Claudio Terranova, Duarte Nuno Vieira, Guido Viel, Enrique Villanueva, Anna Chiara Zanuzzi, Riccardo Zoia, and Giuseppe Sartori

Abstract The process of ascertaining impairments and/or disabilities which pertain to the "personal sphere" of the individual, such as pain and suffering, loss of amenity, and/or psychological-existential damage, poses particular difficulties in relation to the obtainment of scientific evidence. The "immateriality" and the subjective connotation of the "personal sphere" are, in themselves, critical issues.

Electronic supplementary material: The online version of this chapter (doi:10.1007/978-3-319-29812-2_30) contains supplementary material, which is available to authorized users.

S.D. Ferrara (✉) • V. Ananian • C. Terranova • G. Viel
Department of Legal and Occupational Medicine, Toxicology and Public Health, University-Hospital of Padova, Via Falloppio 50, 35128 Padova, Italy
e-mail: santodavide.ferrara@unipd.it; ananian.viviana@gmail.com; claudio.terranova@gmail.com; guido.viel@unipd.it

E. Baccino
Service de Médecine Légale, University of Montpellier, Hôpital Lapeyronie, 191 Av. du Doyen Gaston Giraud, 34295 Montpellier Cedex, France
e-mail: e-baccino@chu-montpellier.fr

R. Domenici
Department of Clinical, Surgical, and Molecular Pathology, Unit of Legal Medicine, University of Pisa, Via Roma 55, 56126 Pisa, Italy
e-mail: ranieri.domenici@med.unipi.it

C. Hernàndez-Cueto
Department of Legal Medicine, Forensic Toxicology and Anthropology, University of Granada, Avda. de Madrid 11, 18071 Granada, Spain
e-mail: chc@ugr.es

G. Mendelson
Faculty of Medicine, Department of Psychiatry, School of Clinical Sciences, Nursing and Health Sciences, Monash University, 2499, 3161 Caulfield, VIC, Australia
e-mail: george.mendelson@monash.edu

S.D. Ferrara et al. (eds.), *Personal Injury and Damage Ascertainment under Civil Law*, DOI 10.1007/978-3-319-29812-2_30

This chapter presents a novel methodology for the objective ascertainment of psychic and existential damage under civil-tort law, already illustrated by the "IALM Medico-Legal Guidelines" (IALM Working Group on Personal Injury and Damage) [1]. This chapter represents a slightly modified version of an article published in the International Journal of Legal Medicine.

30.1 Introduction

Personal injury is a legal term for a physical or psychic injury suffered by the plaintiff under civil and/or tort law. Damages related to the injury can be pecuniary or non-pecuniary in nature. With reference to non-pecuniary damages, the evidence itself of physical and/or psychic injury is not sufficient for damage compensation, as it is essential to provide scientific proof of the causal value/link between the harmful event and the "injury," as well as between the latter and the temporary/permanent "impairment" and/or "disability." Following the definitions of the World Health Organization (WHO) and the International Classification of Impairments, Disabilities, and

G.A. Norelli
Department of Health Sciences, Forensic Sciences Section, Institute of Legal Medicine, University of Florence, Largo Brambilla 3, 50134 Florence, Italy
e-mail: ganorelli@unifi.it

M. Ranavaya
Division of Disability Medicine, Joan C. Edwards School of Medicine, Marshall University, 1600 Medical Center Drive, Huntington 25701, WV, USA
e-mail: mranavayamd@abime.org

D.N. Vieira
Department of Forensic Medicine, Ethics and Medical Law, Faculty of Medicine, University of Coimbra, Pólo das Ciências da Saúde—Unidade Central, Azinhaga, de Santa Comba, Celas, 3000-354 Coimbra, Portugal
e-mail: dnvieira.pt@gmail.com; dnvieira@fmed.uc.pt

E. Villanueva
Department of Legal Medicine, Toxicology and Physical Anthropology, University of Granada, Avda Madrid 11, 18071 Granada, Spain
e-mail: guadalfeo40@telefonica.net

A.C. Zanuzzi
Department of Private Law and Critique of Law, University of Padova, Via 8 Febbraio 1848 n.2, 35122 Padova, Italy

R. Zoia
Department of Health and Biomedical Sciences, Section of Legal Medicine, University of Milan, Via Luigi Mangiagalli 37, 20133 Milan, Italy
e-mail: riccardo.zoia@unimi.it

G. Sartori
Department of Psychology, University of Padova, Via Venezia 8, 35131 Padova, Italy
e-mail: giuseppe.sartori@unipd.it

Handicaps (ICF), the medico-legal expert must objectively ascertain "any loss or abnormality of psychic or anatomical structure or function" (i.e., impairment) and "any restriction or lack (resulting from an impairment) of ability to perform an activity in the manner or within the range considered normal for a human being" (i.e., disability).

Impairments and disabilities pertaining to the somatosensory or psychic sphere which imply coenesthesic alterations and substantial loss of personal fulfillment and/or reduction of the quality of life pose significant difficulties in relation to the achievement of Scientific "Evidence."

In particular, the "immateriality" and the subjective connotation of the "personal sphere" are, in themselves, *critical issues*. The clinical data obtained from the neuropsychological ascertainment find their essential prerequisite in the active participation of the Examinee who, in legally relevant contexts (criminal law, civil law, insurance), may be "affected" by personal interests.

In the absence of a defined Systematic Methodology, the ascertainment of "intangible" pain and suffering, loss of amenity, and/or psycho-existential damage is often characterized by a lack of diagnostic power in relation to malingering, the identification of which remains assigned to the clinical judgment and subjective experience of the individual Professional, from which derive a high probability of inaccuracy.

This chapter presents further analysis on the subject of personal injury and damage ascertainment, issuing from the "International Guidelines on Medico-Legal Methods of Ascertainment and Criteria of Evaluation of Personal Injury and Damage Under Civil-Tort Law" produced by the "IALM Working Group on Personal Injury and Damage" [1].

By means of the specialist review process of the clinical-instrumental and psychological testing for the objectification of psycho-somatic impairments conducted by the International Clinical and Medico-Legal Experts, a systematic interdisciplinary Ascertainment Methodology was defined with the aim of attaining greater precision, accuracy, and reproducibility in relation to pain and suffering, loss of amenity, and/or psycho-existential damage.

30.2 Methods of Ascertainment

The Ascertainment Methodology, structured in a complex Flow-Chart, is outlined in the following sections, as well as in Figs. 30.1–30.6 and in Table 30.1.

In particular, it consists of four logical Steps, respectively entitled:

- Step 1—Pre-Existing Social—Psycho—Somatic State.
- Step 2—Injuring Event.
- Step 3—Current Social—Psycho—Somatic State.
- Step 4—Detection of Examinee's Level of Cooperation.

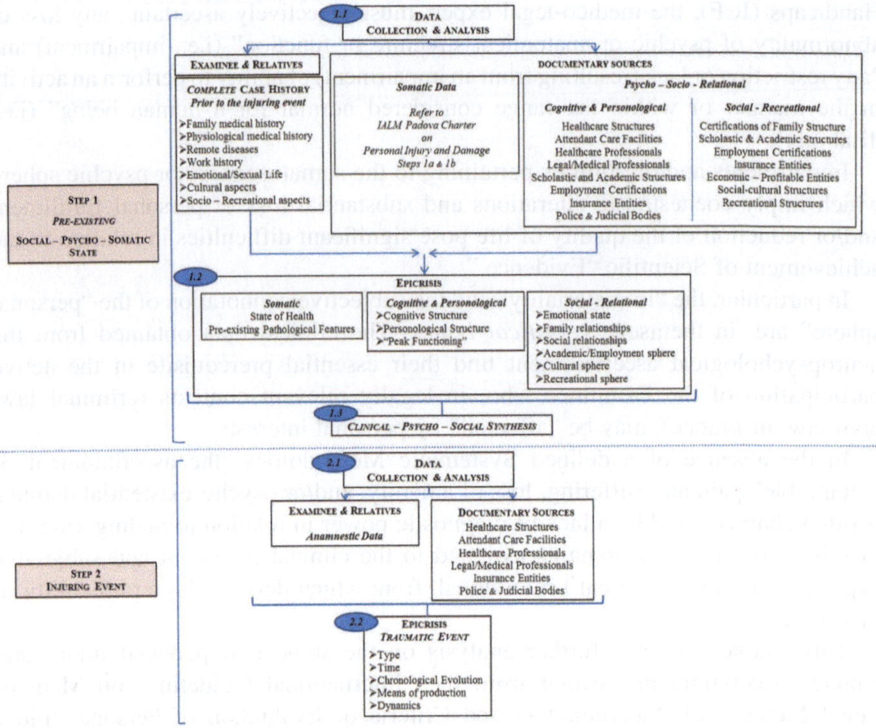

Fig. 30.1 Step 1—Pre-existing social-psycho-somatic state. Step 2—Injuring event

30.2.1 Step 1. Preexisting Social-Psycho-Somatic State

The first Methodological Ascertainment Step, aimed at the complete definition of the "Pre-existing Social-Psycho-Somatic State" prior to the injuring event, comprises the collection and analysis of medical records and documents, the epicrisis, and clinical-psycho-social synthesis, as set out below.

30.2.1.1 Step 1.1: Data Collection and Analysis

The collection and related analysis of data with probative value, derived from specific "documentary sources," aim at the objective demonstration of the Pre-existing Social—Psycho—Somatic State prior to the injuring event (Fig. 30.3).

A. *Case History*

The complete case history aims at the exclusive survey of data regarding the period prior to the injuring event, as described below. Data can be collected directly from the Examinee and/or from close relatives.

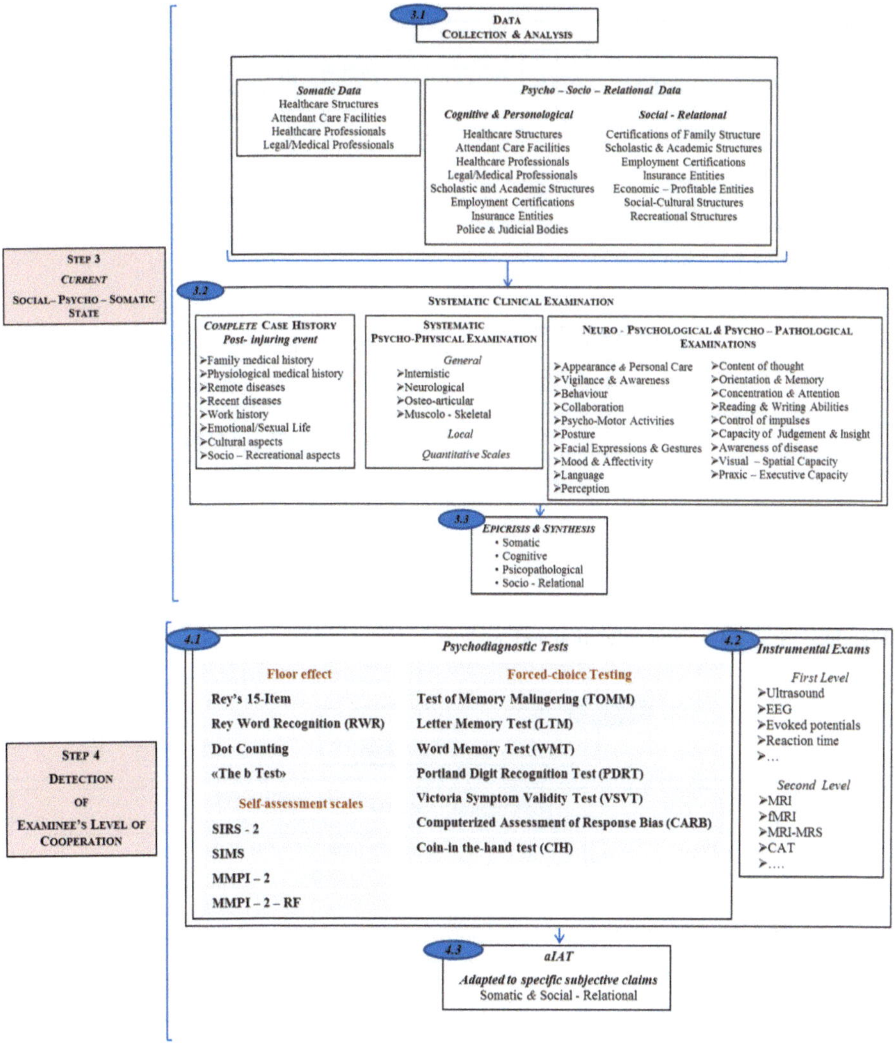

Fig. 30.2 Step 3—Current social-psycho-somatic state. Step 4—Detection of examinee's level of cooperation

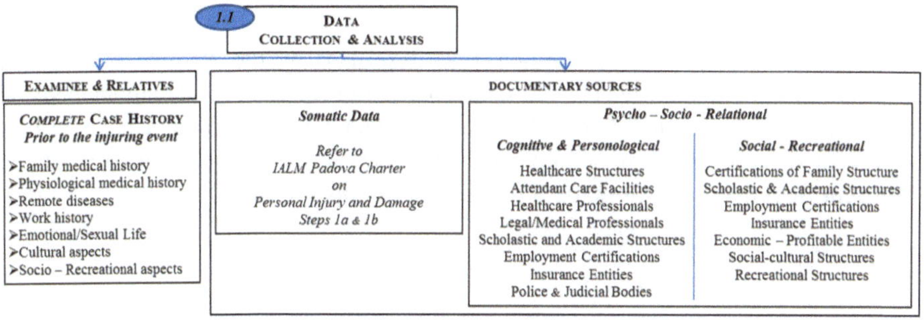

Fig. 30.3 Step 1.1—Data collection and analysis

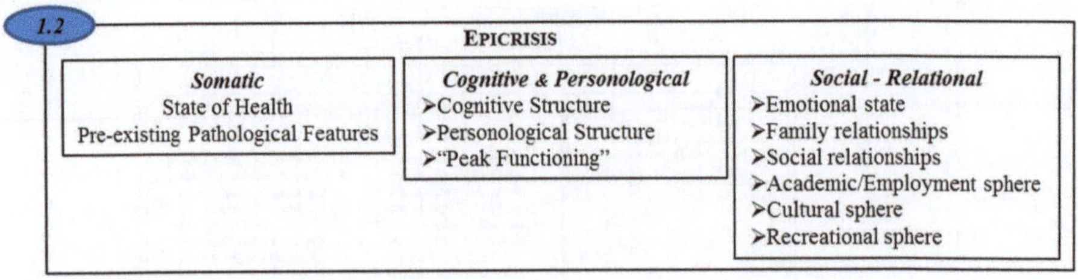

Fig. 30.4 Step 1.2—Epicrisis

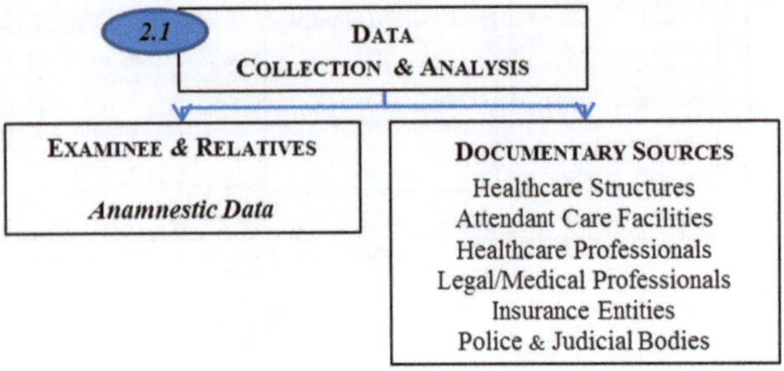

Fig. 30.5 Step 2.1—Data collection and analysis

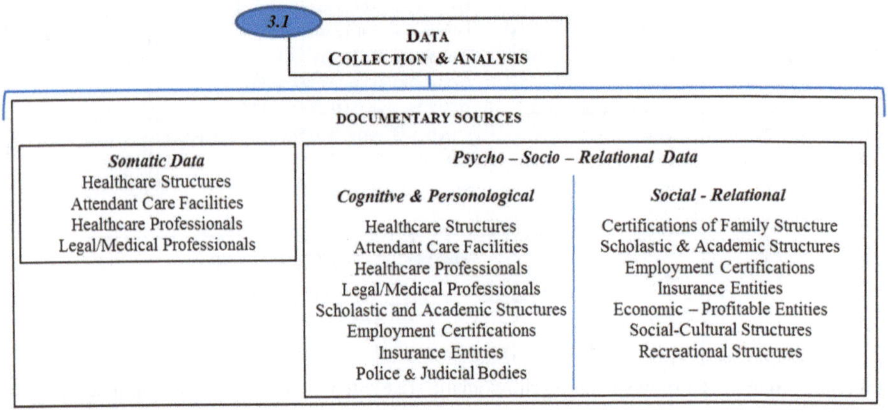

Fig. 30.6 Step 3.1—Data collection and analysis

The anamnesis should be conducted as described by the *Padova Charter on personal injury and damage* [1], but with a particular focus and in-depth analysis on the work-related, emotional-sexual, cultural, and social-recreational aspects of life.

Recent diseases are not of interest, being relevant to the identification of the "Current Social-Psycho-Somatic State," of subsequent ascertainment.

Table 30.1 Step 4.1—Psychodiagnostic tests

	Test	Sensibility	Specificity	Malingering Cut-offs
Floor effect	Rey 15-item Test	70 %	92 %	≤9/15
	Rey Word Recognition (RWR)	70 %	92 %	≤6/15
	Dot counting Test	100 %	>90 %	180 e 130 s
	The b Test	68 %	99 %	See interpretation manual
Self-report Inventory	Structured Interview of Reported Symptoms -2 (SIRS-2)	67 %	98 %	Specific for each scale
	Structured Inventory of Malingered Symptomatology (SIMS)	52 %	100 %	>14
	Minnesota Multiphasic Personality Inventory—2 (MMPI-2)	>80 %	>90 %	Specific for each scale
	Minnesota Multiphasic Personality Inventory Restructured Form (MMPI-RF)	92	97	Specific for each scale
Forced choice	Test Of Memory Malingering (TOMM)	91 %	95 %	≤16/50
	Letter Memory Test (LMT)	73 %	100 %	≤93 %
	Word Memory Test (WMT)	64 %	100 %	≤75
	Portland Digit Recognition Test (PDRT)	70 %	100 %	≤44
	Victoria Symptom Validity Test (VSVT)	88 %	100 %	≤50 %
	Computerized Assessment of Responce Bias (CARB)	56 %	83 %	≤50 %
	Coin In the Hand Test (CIH)	93 %	88 %	<8,50

B. *Circumstantial, Clinico-Documental-Instrumental Data*

B.1—Somatic Data

All data identifying preexisting somatic integrity (with determination of any preexisting pathological features) can be deduced from the documents described by the *Padova Charter on personal injury and damage—Steps 1a and 1b* [1].

Particular attention should be paid to any previous ascertainments and/or evaluations carried out by legal and/or medical professionals.

B.2—Cognitive-Personological Data

The data identifying the preexisting cognitive functions (perception, expression, attention, executive functions, memory, comprehension, and orientation) and personological structures (personality traits/disturbances; psychiatric disturbances/pathologies) can be deduced from the sources listed below.

- *Public/Private Healthcare Structures*

The data emerging from the healthcare structures in which the examinee was admitted in the period prior to the injuring event include medical records, nursing reports, reports of the clinical specialist, clinical-instrumental analysis reports, diagnostic-prognostic-therapeutic prescriptions, etc.

- *Public/Private Attendant Care Facilities*

Data emerging from attendant care facilities in which the examinee was admitted in the period prior to the injuring event adhere to the prescribed and completed assistance and/or rehabilitative programs, etc.

- *Healthcare Professionals and Paramedics*

This concerns the collection of diagnostic-prognostic-therapeutic certifications and/or clinical reports prepared by healthcare professionals and paramedics in the period prior to the injuring event.

- *Legal and Medical Professionals*

This concerns the collection of certifications regarding any previous ascertainments and/or evaluations carried out by legal and/or medical professionals.

- *Scholastic and Academic Structures*

This concerns the collection of data pertaining to scholastic and/or academic performance, educational qualifications acquired, level achieved, etc.

- *Employment Certifications*

This concerns the collection of data pertaining to aptitude for work, chronology of professional duties undertaken, level of responsibility conferred, level of professional development achieved, stress levels tolerated, etc.

- *Insurance Entities*

Insurance data includes settled claims (civil responsibility, motor third-party liability, private insurance), contracts of insurance (risk categories, pathologies, and declared activities), social security, etc.

- *Police and Judicial Bodies*

Judicial data include highway code disputes, illicit use of drugs of abuse, and previous investigations/proceedings of a civil and/or criminal nature.

B.3—Social-Relational

Data relating to preexisting social and relational structures can be deduced from the sources set out below.

- *Certifications of Family Structure*

This concerns certifications pertaining to the composition of the family unit in the period prior to the injuring event.

- *Scholastic and Academic Structures*

This concerns the collection of data pertaining to any disciplinary/behavioral reports, programs of psychological support undertaken, patterns of identified behavior, scholastic and/or academic progression attained, etc.

- *Employment Certifications*

This concerns the collection of data pertaining to work aptitude, responsibility assumed, relationship with colleagues, stress management, etc.

- *Insurance Entities*

This concerns the collection of data deriving from previous incidents and/or insurance contracts and pertaining to regular employment and/or social activities.

- *Economic-Profitable Entities*

This concerns data pertaining to the financial situation in the period prior to the injuring event.

- *Social-Cultural and Recreational Structures*
  This concerns the collection of data pertaining to social-cultural and ludic-recreational activities performed in the period prior to the injuring event, of a continual, habitual, episodic, or occasional character.

30.2.1.2 Step 1.2: Epicrisis

Having completed the collection and related analysis of the above data, one proceeds to the *epicrisis* (Fig. 30.4), aimed at defining the preexisting somatic, cognitive-personological, and social-relational state, as explained below.

Epicrisis

A. *Somatic*
One proceeds to the identification and description of the "state of health" prior to the facts and/or the "preexisting pathological framework."
B. *Cognitive and Personological*

- *Cognitive Structure*
  Concerns the nosographic classification inclusive of qualitative/quantitative descriptions
- *Personological Structure.*
  Concerns the nosographic classification inclusive of qualitative/quantitative descriptions
- *Peak Functioning*
  The differentiated cognitive functions are subject to age-related qualitative/ quantitative physiological decrease. It is therefore essential to take account of the average values of age-related performance.

C. *Social-Relational*
This involves taking into consideration emotional state, family and social relationships, and the academic/employment, cultural, and recreational spheres.

30.2.1.3 Step 1.3: Clinical-Psychosocial Synthesis

The clinical-psychosocial synthesis is the expression of the collected data and the related epicrisis.

30.2.2 Step 2. Injuring Event

The second Methodological Ascertainment Step, aiming at the objectification of the injuring event, includes the collection and analysis of the anamnestic and documental data, the epicrisis, and the detailed description of the characteristics of the event, as set out below.

30.2.2.1 Step 2.1: Data Collection and Analysis

The collection and related analysis of the data of probative value, derived from specific "documentary sources," aim at the objective demonstration of the injuring event (Fig. 30.5).

A. *Anamnestic Data*

Anamnestic data can be collected directly from the examinee and/or close relatives.

B. *Documentary Data*

Documentary data, identifying the nature and characteristics of the event, can be deduced from the sources described below.

- *Public/Private Healthcare Structures*
  Data extrapolated from health structures where the examinee was admitted as a result of the injuring event include anamnesis and objective examinations, records of admittance to emergency ward facilities, medical records, nursing reports, reports of the clinical specialist, clinical-instrumental analysis reports, histopathological findings, diagnostic-prognostic-therapeutic prescriptions, etc.
- *Public/Private Attendant Care Facilities*
  Data emerging from attendant care facilities in which the examinee was admitted as a result of the injuring event include medical records, nursing reports, reports of rehabilitation performance, clinical-care report, assistance and/or rehabilitative programs, etc.
- *Healthcare Professionals and Paramedics*
  This concerns the collection of diagnostic-prognostic-therapeutic certifications and/or clinical reports prepared by healthcare professionals and paramedics.
- *Legal and Medical Professionals*
  This involves the collection of certificates regarding ascertainments and/or assessments carried out by legal and/or medical professionals.
- *Insurance Entities*
  This involves the collection of insurance documentation (civil responsibility, motor third-party liability, private insurance) pertaining to the event, as well as any social security certifications.
- *Police and Judicial Bodies*
  This involves the collection of the circumstantial/testimonial data related to the event, as well as any documents relating to investigations/proceedings of civil and/or criminal nature.

30.2.2.2 Step 2.2: Epicrisis

Having completed the collection and related analysis of the above data, one proceeds to the epicrisis, aimed at defining the characteristics of the event.

Characteristics of the Event
This involves defining the characteristics of the event, such as *type* (nature of the trauma-acute and/or chronic somatic, acute and/or chronic emotional, somatic-emotional), *time, chronological evolution, means of production,* and *dynamics.*

30.2.3 Step 3. Current Social-Psycho-Somatic State

The third Methodological Ascertainment Step, aiming at the ascertainment of the "Current Social-Psycho-Somatic State", includes the collection and analysis of anamnestic and documentary data, systematic clinical examination, as well as the epicrisis and clinical-psychosocial synthesis, as set out below.

This step must be performed after at least 1 year from the injuring event.

30.2.3.1 Step 3.1: Data Collection and Analysis

The collection and related analysis of the data of probative value, derived from specific "documentary sources," aims at the objective demonstration of the current social-psychosomatic state (Fig. 30.6).

A. *Somatic Data*

Data identifying somatic integrity subsequent to the injuring event and in the current period are derived from the sources set out below.

- *Public/Private Healthcare Structures*
  Data derived from the healthcare structures in which the examinee was admitted in the period subsequent to the injuring event include anamnesis and objective examinations, records of admittance to emergency ward facilities, medical records, nursing reports, reports of the clinical specialist, clinical-instrumental analysis reports, histopathological findings, diagnostic-prognostic-therapeutic prescriptions, etc.
- *Public/Private Attendant Care Facilities*
  Data emerging from attendant care facilities in which the examinee was admitted in the period subsequent to the injuring event include medical records, nursing reports, reports of rehabilitation performance, clinical-care report, assistance and/or rehabilitative programs, etc.
- *Healthcare Professionals and Paramedics*
  This concerns the collection of diagnostic-prognostic-therapeutic certifications and or clinical reports prepared by healthcare professionals and paramedics.
- *Legal and Medical Professionals*
  This concerns the collection of certifications and documents relating to the ascertainments and/or evaluations carried out by legal and/or medical professionals.

B. *Cognitive-Personological Data*

The data identifying the cognitive functions (perception, expression, attention, executive functions, memory, comprehension, and orientation) and personological structure (personality traits/disturbances; psychiatric disturbances/pathologies), subsequent to the injuring event and in the current period, can be deduced from the sources listed below.

- *Public/Private Healthcare Structures*
  Data extrapolated from health structures where the examinee was admitted subsequent to the injuring event include medical records, nursing reports, reports of the clinical specialist, clinical-instrumental analysis reports, histopathological findings, diagnostic-prognostic-therapeutic prescriptions, etc.
- *Public/Private Attendant Care Facilities*
  Data derived from attendant care facilities in which the examinee was admitted in the period subsequent to the injuring event include medical records, nursing reports, reports of rehabilitation performance, clinical-care reports, assistance and/or rehabilitative programs, etc.
- *Healthcare Professionals and Paramedics*
  This concerns the collection of diagnostic-prognostic-therapeutic certifications and or clinical reports prepared by healthcare professionals and paramedics.
- *Legal and Medical Professionals*
  This concerns the collection of certifications and documents relating to the ascertainments and/or assessments carried out by legal and/or medical professionals.
- *Scholastic and Academic Structures*
  This concerns the collection of data pertaining to scholastic and/or academic status in the period subsequent to the injuring event.
- *Employment Certifications*
  This concerns the collection of data pertaining to the *quoad laborem* prognosis subsequent to the injuring event, type of professional commitments undertaken, responsibility assumed, prospects for professional advancement, etc.
- *Insurance Entities*
  This involves the collection of any data pertaining to insurance contract reviews (classes of risk, pathologies, and declared activities), as well as any social insurance documentation.
- *Police and Judicial Bodies*
  Judicial data include highway code disputes, illicit use of drugs of abuse, and previous investigations/proceedings of a civil and/or criminal nature.

C. *Social-Relational Data*

Data identifying social and relational structures subsequent to the injuring event or in the current period are derived from the following sources.

- *Certifications of Family Structure*

  This concerns certifications relating to the composition of the family unit in the period subsequent to the injuring event.
- *Scholastic and Academic Structures*

  This concerns the collection of data pertaining to any disciplinary/behavioral reports, programs of psychological support undertaken, patterns of identified behavior, scholastic and/or academic progression attained, etc.
- *Employment Certifications*

  This concerns the collection of data pertaining to work aptitude, responsibility assumed, relationship with colleagues, stress management, etc.
- *Insurance Entities*

  This involves the collection of any data pertaining to insurance contract reviews (classes of risk, pathologies, and declared activities), as well as any social insurance documentation.
- *Economic-Profitable Entities*

  This involves the collection of data pertaining to the financial situation in the period subsequent to the injuring event.
- *Social-Cultural and Recreational Structure*

  This concerns the collection of data pertaining to social-cultural and ludic-recreational activities performed in the period subsequent to the injuring event, of a continual, habitual, episodic, or occasional character.

30.2.3.2 Step 3.2: Systematic Clinical Examination

The systematic clinical examination (Fig. 30.7) must be carried out according to the indications of the "International Guidelines on Medico-Legal Methods of Ascertainment and Criteria of Evaluation of Personal Injury and Damage Under Civil-Tort Law" [1].

In the medical anamnesis, one must particularly focus on the work-related, emotional-sexual, cultural, and social-recreational aspects of life.

Crucial value must be attributed to the **neuropsychological and psychopathological examinations**, which aim at the survey of clinical objective data and are an

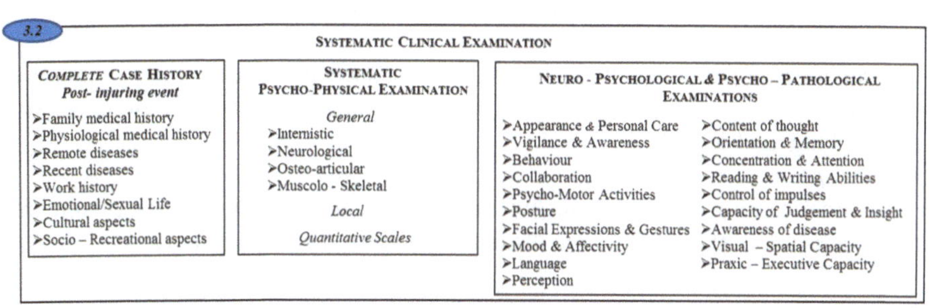

Fig. 30.7 Step 3.2—Systematic clinical examination

essential tool for the clinical diagnosis, the quantitative/qualitative definition of cognitive skills, as well as the differential diagnosis of any neurological and/or psychopathological pathologies.

The examinations must be conducted in accordance with the neuropsychological and psychopathological methodologies and protocols indicated by international literature. For these specific ascertainment purposes, the use of rating scales for clinical diagnosis should be avoided, as they are not appropriate for the attainment of objectivity in the forensic field.

Objective-Clinical Data

The objective data of interest, to be obtained by means of accurate clinical examination, are as follows.

- *Appearance and Personal Care*

Data concerning appearance and self-care include habitus, clothing, personal hygiene, and esthetic care.

- *Vigilance and Awareness*

Data pertaining to vigilance and awareness include degree of vigilance, level of consciousness, and any pathological alterations (e.g., drowsiness, somnolence).

- *Behavior*

Data pertaining to behavior include gaze, level of confidence, tendency to manipulate, eccentricity, and others.

- *Collaboration*

Data concerning collaboration with the examiner include helpfulness toward the examiner and exhibition of autonomy vs. need of the assistance of third parties.

- *Psychomotor Activities*

Data pertaining to psychomotor activities include composure, agitation, gestures, and others.

- *Posture*

Data pertaining to posture include physical vicinity, tension, and relaxation.

- *Facial Expressions and Gestures*

Data pertaining to facial expressions and gestures include expressiveness of the face, nods of the head, body language, and others.

- *Mood and Affectivity*

Data pertaining to mood and affectivity include euthymia, sadness, depression, anxiety, restlessness, euphoria, appropriateness of affectivity, and others.

- *Language*

Data pertaining to language include fluency of speech, expressiveness, richness of vocabulary, syntactical-semantic correctness, stuttering, echolalia, schizophasia, sidetracking, and others.

- *Perception*

Data concerning perception include any pathological alterations (e.g., hallucinations, delusions, others). Describe the nature, intensity, and frequency.

- *Content of thought*

Data on the content of thought include the description of the nature, intensity, and frequency of any pathological alterations (e.g., delusional contents, insertions, tangentiality, sidetracking).

- *Orientation and Memory*

  Data pertaining to space-time-person orientation and memory include the description of the nature, intensity, and frequency of any pathological alterations (e.g., mnestic deterioration, confabulation).
- *Concentration and Attention*

  Data pertaining to concentration and attention include the ability to focus attention on specific stimuli and shift attention from one stimulus to another.
- *Reading and Writing Abilities*

  Data pertaining to reading and writing abilities include the definition of the cultural level and any pathological alterations (e.g., dyslexia, dysgraphia).
- *Control of Impulses*

  Data pertaining to the control of impulses include the description of the ability to retain aggressive impulses and reaction to frustrating/stressful situations.
- *Capacity of Judgment and Insight*

  . Data pertaining to the capacity of judgment and insight include concern, indifference, etc.
- *Awareness of Disease*

  This notes the level of awareness of the disease.
- *Visual-Spatial Capacity*

  One proceeds to qualitative/quantitative descriptions of visual-spatial capacity.
- *Praxic-Executive Capacity*

  One proceeds to qualitative/quantitative descriptions of praxic-executive capacity.

30.2.3.3 Step 3.3: Epicrisis and Synthesis

One proceeds to the clinical-documental epicrisis and the related somatic, cognitive, psychopathological, and social-relational synthesis.

30.2.4 Step 4. Detection of Examinee's Level of Cooperation

The present methodological Step aims at the detection of the examinee's level of cooperation, in order to verify the validity of data generated by the previous steps, identifying the suspicion of malingering (Fig. 30.8).

Nosographic Framework

Malingering is defined by DSM 5 (V65.2, "Additional conditions that may be a focus of clinical attention") as the "intentional production of false or grossly

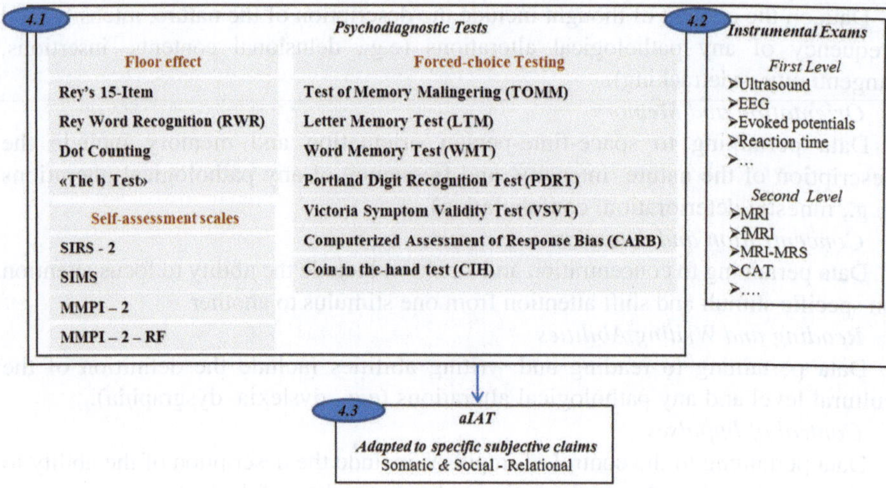

Fig. 30.8 Step 4—Detection of Examinee's level of cooperation

exaggerated physical or psychological symptoms, motivated by external incentives such as avoiding military duty, avoiding work, obtaining financial compensation, evading criminal prosecution, or obtaining drugs" (Chap. 29).

As described by DSM 5, malingering is not a "diagnosable disorder," and the ultimate decision regarding the truthfulness of the examinee is a question for the court to decide [2, 3].

In terms of the nosographic framework, malingering is distinguished as follows.

- "General": production and/or amplification of typical symptoms of differentiated psychopathological areas (e.g., depression, anxiety, psychosis, cognitive deficit).
- "Specific": description of precise pathological data (e.g., post-traumatic stress disorder—PTSD postwar mission).

So-called coaching is also widely described within the category of the specialist neuropsychological literature, in reference to the preparation of the examinee by an expert (e.g., lawyer, psychologist) for the psychodiagnostic evaluation of the official technical consultant, in order to effectively change the results of the examination, making the identification of simulation on a solely clinical basis more difficult.

Contexts/Areas with a Higher Frequency of Malingering

Higher frequency rates of malingering are registered in institutionally relevant contexts/areas, i.e., *criminal law* (ability to understand and/or will, compatibility with the prison regime, social dangerousness), *civil law* (personal injury, ability to provide for own interests, parenting skills), *social insurance* (working capacity, disability, accompaniment), and *administrative* (fitness to drive, fitness to carry firearms).

Differential Diagnosis

The main psychiatric pathologies which are characterized by "behaviors of simulation/dissimulation" are conversion disorder and/or other forms of somatoform disorder (algic disorders, somatization, undifferentiated somatoform),[1] dissociative disorder,[2] factitious disorder,[3] Münchausen syndrome,[4] Münchausen syndrome by proxy,[5] and Ganser syndrome.[6]

Methodology of Evaluation

The proposed methodology for the detection of lack of cooperation, incongruent and/or aberrant responses on the part of the examinee, is outlined as follows.

30.2.4.1 Step 4.1: Psychodiagnostic Tests

The first phase is substantiated by the administration of a panel of neuropsychological tests, defined as a result of the examination of the specialized national and international literature [4–16] and treaties [17–20], with the related selection of categories of tests (and individual tests for each category).

The synopsis of the average data of specificity (correct identification of "non-malingerers") and sensitivity (correct identification of "malingerers") of each test and its related interpretative cutoff are shown in Table 30.1.

The synthetic description of each proposed test is reported as follows.

Floor Effect

This involves the evaluation of the examinee's ability to properly perform extremely easy tasks. Malingering is identified when the result is less than that obtained from individuals actually suffering from cognitive disorders.

---

[1] Simulation differs from conversion disorder and other somatoform disorders for the *intentional* production of symptoms.

[2] It is possible that a patient suffering from dissociative disorder or dissociative state attributable to another neuropsychiatric disease "produces," on clinical observation, psychological symptoms (e.g., disorientation, memory loss, lack of reasoning and understanding, disorders of ideation, pseudodementia) that are not based on an actual decrease in cognitive and/or another objectivizable organic dysfunction.

[3] Simulation differs from factitious disorder in that the motivation as to the production of the symptom is constituted by an external stimulus, whereas in factitious disorder external incentives are absent.

[4] Intentional production of symptoms and physical complaints aimed at achieving attention and specialized healthcare.

[5] Similar to the preceding, it is distinguished by the characteristic that the perpetrator induces disorders in another person.

[6] Psychogenic pseudodementia or hysterical twilight state, typically observed in prisons. It was initially recognized in prisoners awaiting execution, with marked decrease of higher cognitive functions (absurd and evasive language, serious amnesia, dissolution of each semantic competence, inability to perform logical-deductive reasoning, also basic), as against apparently preserved consciousness, understanding, and orientation.

– *Rey's 15-Item Test*

This is a test that identifies a tendency to simulate or to aggravate memory deficits. A grid of 15 visual elements, "apparently" difficult to memorize, is presented for 10 s (letters, numbers, geometric shapes) and is then withdrawn for a further 10 s. The examinee is then asked to reproduce the memorized stimuli on a sheet of paper. The rating is calculated based on the total number of items recalled.[7] The majority of patients with severe head injury or mental retardation obtain results in the standard range [4, 5, 18–20].

– *Rey Word Recognition*

This is a test in which a list of 15 words is read at a frequency of 1/s. After a break of 5 s, a list of 15 "targets" (words read previously) and 15 "distractors" (new words) is proposed, for each of which the examinee must respond affirmatively or negatively (remember/do not remember).[8] The score is calculated based on the number of words recalled correctly [4, 18–20].

– *Dot Counting*

This is a test that identifies a tendency to simulate or to aggravate learning difficulties or specific visual-perceptual deficits.

It consists of two parts:

1. "Ungrouped dots," points in a random configuration
2. "Grouped dots," points in a specific configuration

The second part is simpler than the first. The examinee is required to count the number of points present on some sheets of paper and to provide the response as quickly as possible. The rating is calculated based on the time taken to respond to every item. For both tests the response times of the collaborating subjects increase gradually with the increase of the number of points.[9] Two or more deviations from the average of the response times indicate malingering [4, 6, 18–20].

– *The b Test*

This is a test that involves the reading of letters of the alphabet. It is indicated to reduce the possibility of false-positive results, also in patients with brain injuries [7, 8, 18–20].

Self-assessment Scales

Questionnaires consisting of a variable number of items that detect the existence, frequency, and intensity of psychopathological disorders

– *Structured Interview of Reported Symptoms-2 (SIRS-2)*

---

[7] Cutoff validated by experimental studies amounting to 9/15, below which malingering is identified

[8] Cutoff validated by experimental studies amounting to 6/15, below which malingering is identified

[9] Cutoff validated by experimental studies amounting to 180 s for counting the ungrouped dots and 130 s for the grouped dots

This is a reference standard for the assessment of simulated psychiatric disorders. Organized in the form of a structured interview substantiated by 172 questions, it is designed to detect 13 response profiles commonly associated with malingering [9, 18, 20].

The interview is structured as follows:

- *Detailed Information I* (items from 1 to 16)
- *General Information I* (items from 17 to 70)
- *Repeated Information I* (items from 71 to 86)
- *Detailed Information II* (items from 87 to 102)
- *General Information II* (items from 103 to 156)
- *Repeated Information II* (items from 157 to 172)

The results are summarized through 13 evaluative scales.

- "Rare Symptoms": rare symptoms in psychiatric patients
- "Symptom Combinations": combinations of symptoms of dissimilar nature and etiology
- "Improbable or Absurd Symptoms": improbable and/or absurd symptoms, also for psychiatric subjects
- "Blatant Symptoms": obvious symptoms, typical of major psychiatric disorders, that malingerers tend to attribute to themselves to a quantitatively superior extent
- "Subtle Symptoms": typical psychiatric symptoms that could be omitted by malingerers
- "Severity of Symptoms": numerousness of symptoms classified as "severe" (tend to be excessive in malingerers)
- "Selectivity of Symptoms": degree of selectivity of symptoms (reduced in malingerers)
- "Reported vs Observed Symptoms": items for which the examiner has the immediate possibility of verifying on the basis of direct observation

Cutoff scores are provided for each of the eight "primary" scales reported above, which permit the classification of the description according to the categories "honest," "dubious," "probable fiction," and "certain fiction."

The test is also able to calculate the scores of the following five additional scales.

- "Direct Appraisal of Honesty": items in which the examinee is explicitly asked to indicate their "honesty" in describing themselves
- "Defensive Symptoms": daily symptoms typical of the experience of the great majority of people (worries, issues, negative non-pathological situations)
- "Symptom Onset": items that identify aspects of sudden and/or atypical onset of mental disorders, which, as such, could signal doubts as to the veracity of the reports
- "Overly Specified Symptoms": items in which the examinee identifies symptoms with an excessive degree of precision (e.g., duration and/or frequency of appearance)

- "Inconsistency of Symptoms": 32 repeated items, which can identify inattention and/or inaccuracy of response

– *Structured Inventory of Malingered Symptomatology (SIMS)*

Consisting 75 questions (true/false), the subject must respond affirmatively or negatively and identify any worsening "distortions" of the answers [9, 10, 18, 20]. The test focuses on the following domains: low intelligence (LI), affective disorders (AF), neurological impairment (N), psychosis (P), and amnestic disorders (AM).[10]

– *Minnesota Multiphasic Personality Inventory-2 (MMPI-2)*

This consists of 567 dichotomous items of true/false response. It provides guidance on personality and on the correspondence of the profile of responses with different psychiatric nosographic features. It consists of 10 "basic clinical scales" (and related subscales), 15 "scales of content," as well as multiple "supplementary or experimental clinical scales" and other secondary indexes [11, 18, 20].

The limit of the test is substantiated by the inability to detect malingering limited to a symptom and/or to a specific feature.

– *Minnesota Multiphasic Personality Inventory-2-RF (MMPI-2-RF)*

This is the latest version of the aforementioned MMPI-2, articulated in 51 scales (divided into "substantial" and "valid") aimed at identifying salient and clinically relevant personological variables [12, 20].

Forced-Choice Testing

Questionnaires involve the unavoidability for the examinee of choosing between alternative answers to each question. Malingerers provide a number of correct answers significantly lower than the level of correct answers attributable to chance.

– *Test of Memory Malingering (TOMM)*

This is one of the neuropsychological reference standards for detecting the simulation of mnesic disorders. It specifies a "learning," "recognition," and "deferred retention" test. In the learning test 50 figures are shown, each for 3 s. In the recognition test, 50 cards are shown, on each of which is drawn a figure seen previously and a new figure of which the examinee must indicate the figure seen previously. The deferred retention test (not mandatory) is only applied if the score is less than 45 (the maximum score is 50).

Considering a total of 50 items, the statistical-epidemiological data identify a cutoff of 16/50 for the diagnosis of malingering [13, 18–20].

– *Letter Memory Test (LTM)*

This is a test in which some letters are projected onto a monitor for 3 s. The examinee is asked to memorize and subsequently transcribe the largest possible number of letters [4, 14, 18–20].[11]

---

[10] Cutoff > 14 for the identification of malingering

[11] Cutoff <93 % for the identification of malingering

– *Word Memory Test (WMT)*
This is a computerized test based on the recognition of semantically related word couplings (20-item word list). Words appear in pairs: one word is presented, followed by the next, 1 s later. The pair disappears and another set is presented 2 s later. The list is presented twice, and then the examinee is asked to recall as many word pairs as possible [17–20].[12]
– *Portland Digit Recognition Test (PDRT)*
This consists of a series of 72 tests. In each of them, five digits in sequence are reported verbally. Thereafter, the examinee is invited to perform an "interfering" task (e.g., count from 10 to 1). A series of numbers is then presented visually, out of which the examinee must recognize those reported verbally at the beginning of the test [4, 15, 18, 20].[13]
– *Victoria Symptom Validity Test (VSVT)*
This is a computerized test consisting of 48 items presented in 3 blocks of 16 each. It involves presenting a sequence of stimuli to be memorized (visual, verbal, numerical, acoustic, etc.) and subsequently recognized [4, 18, 20].
The type and number of items answered correctly and the related latency times are measured, in order to ascertain any exaggerations or simulations of cognitive deficits (perfect performance = 100 %; minimum performance = 50 %). The reliability of the answer is always calculable statistically.[14]
– *Computerized Assessment of Response Bias (CARB)*
This is a computerized test consisting of 75 trials. A string of five digits is presented to be memorized. Following the memorization phase, the examinee must identify one of the alternatives as correct (forced choice) [18, 20].[15]
– *Coin-in-the-hand test (CIH)*
This is a test in which a coin is placed in one hand for 2 s. Following an "interfering" task (e.g., counting with eyes closed from 10 to 0), the examinee is asked to indicate the hand in which the coin was placed. There are ten tests with the money equally distributed in the two hands [16, 19].[16]

30.2.4.2 Step 4.2: Instrumental Exams

The verification of the "veracity" of the findings derived from the systematic clinical objective examination is also performed through the use of targeted instru-

[12] Cutoff ≤ 75 for the identification of malingering
[13] Cutoff ≤ 44 for the identification of malingering
[14] Cutoff <50 % for the identification of malingering
[15] Cutoff ≤ 50 % for the identification of malingering
[16] Cutoff < 8.50 for the identification of malingering

mental tests. They are divided into two macro-categories, namely, first and second-level examinations, as explained below.

These tests contribute to increase the probative value of the clinical objective findings.

"First-Level" Exams

This involves noninvasive and low-cost instrumental exams, such as echography, electroencephalography, evoked potentials, reaction times, etc.

"Second-Level" Exams

This involves invasive and/or high-cost instrumental exams, such as CAT, MRI, functional MRI, magnetic resonance spectroscopy (MRS), electromyography, etc.

30.2.4.3 Step 4.3: Autobiographical Implicit Association Test

The Autobiographical Implicit Association Test (aIAT) is based on the innovative modification of the method proposed by Greenwald et al. [21] that, on the basis of the survey of latency of response to predefined questions, indirectly establishes the association between concepts. The examinee is exposed to a random order of "items" relating to four concepts, which he/she is required to classify according to category (two categories corresponding to as many motor responses). In the event that two concepts are associated with each other at the cognitive level, a response time faster than that employed for responses relating to concepts that are not associated with each other (and therefore requiring dissimilar motor responses) will be detected. When two concepts require the same response, this is defined as the "congruent condition"; when, by contrast, two concepts require differing answers, this is defined as the "incongruent condition." The difference observed in the reaction time (or between the "incongruent condition" (slow) and the "congruent condition" (fast)) is defined as the "IAT effect."

Sartori et al. [22, 23] proposed a variant of the method described above, referred to as "autobiographical IAT," aimed at ascertaining "punctual" autobiographical memories (episodic memory). In particular, the method allows the examiner to distinguish which of the two alternative versions relating to the same "thematic" (or object of investigation) is true. This is accomplished by requiring the examinee to complete two critical blocks of categorization trials, each of which pairs a different potentially autobiographical event with true events. Because pairing of a truly autobiographical event with true events should facilitate responses, the specific pattern of response times (RTs) in the two blocks indicates which autobiographical event is true and which is false [24–26].

The application of the aIAT method is used to identify, with high probability (91 % accuracy), the veracity of punctual subjective references (somatic and/or social-relational) that are significant in the evaluation of subjective aspects of damage (e.g., disabling pain to a specific area of the body, causing significant reduction of the quality of life).

30.3 Conclusions

As outlined by the *Padova Charter on Personal Injury and Damage Under Civil-Tort Law* [1], the ascertainment of non-pecuniary losses must be based on meticulous scientific methods that guarantee objectivity, reproducibility, and rigor, aiming at the achievement of "scientific evidence."

In relation to the state of the art, particular difficulties still exist in the process of ascertaining impairments and/or disabilities which pertain to the "personal sphere" of the individual, such as pain and suffering, loss of amenity, and/or psycho-existential damage, which pose critical issues deriving from the high prevalence of malingering in legally relevant contexts (criminal law, civil law, insurance).

This chapter presents a novel interdisciplinary methodology, based on the *integration* of *systematic medical semeiotics*, *clinical neuropsychological ascertainment*, *specific psychological testing*, as well as a *new method for memory detection*, aimed at the attainment of greater objectivity and accuracy in the ascertainment of peculiar aspects of nonpecuniary damage, overcoming the limitations related to malingering.

References

1. Ferrara SD, Baccino E, Boscolo-Berto R, Comandè G, Domenici R, Hernàndez-Cueto C, Gulmen MK, Mendelson G, Montisci M, Norelli GA, Pinchi V, Ranavaya M, Shokry DA, Sterzik V, Vermylen Y, Vieira DN, Viel G, Zoja R (2016) Padova Charter on personal injury and damage under civil-tort law: medico-legal guidelines on methods of ascertainment and criteria of evaluation. Int J Legal Med 130(1):1–12
2. Mendelson G, Mendelson D (1996) Malingering. Aust Lawyer 31(7):26–27
3. Mendelson G, Mendelson D (1993) Legal and psychiatric aspects of malingering. J Law Med 1:28–34
4. Inman TH, Berry DT (2002) Cross-validation of indicators of malingering a comparison of nine neuropsychological tests, four tests of malingering, and behavioral observations. Arch Clin Neuropsychol 17(1):1–23
5. Morse CL, Douglas-Newman K, Mandel S, Swirsky-Sacchetti T (2013) Utility of the Rey-15 recognition trial to detect invalid performance in a forensic neuropsychological sample. Clin Neuropsychol 27(8):1395–1407
6. Boone KB, Lu P, Back C, King C, Lee A, Philpott L, Shamieh E, Warner-Chacon K (2002) Sensitivity and specificity of the Rey Dot Counting Test in patients with suspect effort and various clinical samples. Arch Clin Neuropsychol 17(7):625–642
7. Boone KB, Lu P, Sherman D, Palmer B, Back C, Shamieh E, Warner-Chacon K, Berman NG (2000) Validation of a new technique to detect malingering of cognitive symptoms: the b Test. Arch Clin Neuropsychol 15(3):227–241
8. Roberson CJ, Boone KB, Goldberg H, Miora D, Cottingham M, Victor T, Ziegler E, Zeller M, Wright M (2013) Cross validation of the b Test in a large known groups sample. Clin Neuropsychol 27(3):495–508
9. Edens JF, Poythress NG, Watkins-Clay MM (2007) Detection of malingering in psychiatric unit and general population prison inmates: a comparison of the PAI, SIMS, and SIRS. J Pers Assess 88(1):33–42

10. Rogers R, Robinson EV, Gillard ND (2014) The SIMS Screen for feigned mental disorders: the development of detection-based scales. Behav Sci Law 32(4):455–466
11. Lange RT, Sullivan KA, Scott C (2010) Comparison of MMPI-2 and PAI validity indicators to detect feigned depression and PTSD symptom reporting. Psychiatry Res 176(2–3):229–235
12. Mason LH, Shandera-Ochsner AL, Williamson KD, Harp JP, Edmundson M, Berry DT, High WM Jr (2013) Accuracy of MMPI-2-RF validity scales for identifying feigned PTSD symptoms, random responding, and genuine PTSD. J Pers Assess 95(6):585–593
13. Gierok SD, Dickson AL, Cole JA (2005) Performance of forensic and non-forensic adult psychiatric inpatients on the Test of Memory Malingering. Arch Clin Neuropsychol 20 (6):755–760
14. Greub BL, Suhr JA (2006) The validity of the letter memory test as a measure of memory malingering: robustness to coaching. Arch Clin Neuropsychol 21(4):249–254
15. Greve KW, Bianchini KJ, Heinly MT, Love JM, Swift DA, Ciota M (2008) Classification accuracy of the Portland digit recognition test in persons claiming exposure to environmental and industrial toxins. Arch Clin Neuropsychol 23(3):341–350
16. Kelly PJ, Baker GA, van den Broek MD, Jackson H, Humphries G (2005) The detection of malingering in memory performance: the sensitivity and specificity of four measures in a UK population. Br J Clin Psychol 44(3):333–341
17. Hom J, Denney RL (2002) Detection of response bias in forensic neuropsychology. Haworth Medical Press, New York
18. Morgan JE, Sweet JJ (2009) Neuropsychology of malingering casebook. American Academy of Clinical Neuropsychology/Psychology Press, New York
19. Stracciari A, Bianchi A, Sartori G (2010) Neuropsicologia forense. Il Mulino Editore, Bologna
20. Young G (2014) Malingering, feigning, and response bias in psychiatric/psychological injury. Springer Science + Business Media, Dordrecht
21. Greenwald AG, Nosek BA, Banaji MR (2003) Understanding and using the implicit association test: I. An improved scoring algorithm. J Pers Soc Psychol 85(2):197–216
22. Sartori G, Agosta S, Zogmaister C, Ferrara SD, Castiello U (2008) How to accurately detect autobiographical events. Psychol Sci 19(8):772–780
23. Agosta S, Sartori G (2013) The autobiographical IAT: a review. Front Psychol 4:519
24. Hu X, Rosenfeld PJ (2012) Combining the P300-complex trial-based Concealed Information test and the reaction time-based autobiographical Implicit Association Test in concealed memory detection. Psychophysiology 49:1090–1100
25. Hu X, Rosenfeld JP, Bodenhausen GV (2012) Combating automatic autobiographical associations: the effect of instruction and training in strategically concealing information in the autobiographical implicit association test. Psychol Sci 23:1079–1085
26. Freng S, Kehn A (2013) Determining true and false witnessed events: can an eyewitness-implicit association test distinguish between the seen and unseen? Psychiatry Psychol Law 20:761–780

Chapter 31
International Guidelines on the Methods of Ascertainment of Personal Injury and Damage Under Civil-Tort Law

Santo Davide Ferrara, Eric Baccino, Rafael Boscolo-Berto, Giovanni Comandè, Ranieri Domenici, Claudio Hernàndez-Cueto, Mete Korkut Gulmen, George Mendelson, Massimo Montisci, Gian Aristide Norelli, Vilma Pinchi, Mohammed Ranavaya, Dina A. Shokry, Vera Sterzik, Yvo Vermylen, Duarte Nuno Vieira, Guido Viel, and Riccardo Zoia

Abstract Compensation for personal damage, defined as any pecuniary or non-pecuniary loss causally related to a personal injury under civil-tort law, is strictly based on the local jurisdiction and therefore varies significantly across the world. This manuscript presents the first "International Guidelines on Medico-Legal Methods of Ascertainment and Criteria of Evaluation of Personal Injury and Damage under Civil-Tort Law". This consensus document, which includes a step-by-step illustrated explanation of flow charts articulated in eight sequential steps and a comprehensive description of the ascertainment methodology and the criteria of evaluation, has been developed by an International Working Group

Electronic supplementary material: The online version of this chapter (doi:10.1007/978-3-319-29812-2_31) contains supplementary material, which is available to authorized users.

S.D. Ferrara (✉) • R. Boscolo-Berto • M. Montisci • G. Viel
Department of Legal and Occupational Medicine, Toxicology and Public Health, University-Hospital of Padova, Via Falloppio 50, 35128 Padova, Italy
e-mail: santodavide.ferrara@unipd.it; rafael.boscoloberto@unipd.it; massimo.montisci@unipd.it; guido.viel@unipd.it

E. Baccino
Service de Médecine Légale, University of Montpellier, Hôpital Lapeyronie, 191 Av. du Doyen Gaston Giraud, 34295 Montpellier Cedex, France
e-mail: e-baccino@chu-montpellier.fr

G. Comandè
LIDER-Lab, University Scuola Superiore Sant'Anna, Piazza Martiri della Libertà 33, 56127 Pisa, Italy
e-mail: giovanni.comande@sssup.it; gico@sssup.it

R. Domenici
Department of Clinical, Surgical, and Molecular Pathology, Unit of Legal Medicine, University of Pisa, Via Roma 55, 56126 Pisa, Italy
e-mail: ranieri.domenici@med.unipi.it

S.D. Ferrara et al. (eds.), *Personal Injury and Damage Ascertainment under Civil Law*, DOI 10.1007/978-3-319-29812-2_31

composed of juridical and medicolegal experts and adopted as Guidelines by the International Academy of Legal Medicine (IALM). This chapter represents a slightly modified version of an article published in the International Journal of Legal Medicine.

C. Hernàndez-Cueto
Department of Legal Medicine, Forensic Toxicology and Anthropology, University of Granada, Avda. de Madrid 11, 18071 Granada, Spain
e-mail: chc@ugr.es

M.K. Gulmen
Department of Forensic Medicine, Medical Faculty, Cukurova University, Adli Tip Anabilim Dali, 01330 Balcali, Adana, Turkey
e-mail: mete.gulmen@gmail.com

G. Mendelson
Department of Psychiatry, School of Clinical Sciences, Faculty of Medicine, Nursing and Health Sciences, Monash University, c/ PO Box 2499, 3161 Caulfield Junction, Melbourne, VIC, Australia
e-mail: george.mendelson@monash.edu

G.A. Norelli • V. Pinchi
Department of Health Sciences, Forensic Sciences Section, Institute of Legal Medicine, University of Florence, Largo Brambilla 3, 50134 Florence, Italy
e-mail: ganorelli@unifi.it; vilma.pinchi@unifi.it

M. Ranavaya
Division of Disability Medicine, Joan C. Edwards School of Medicine, Marshall University, 1600 Medical Center Drive, Huntington 25701, WV, USA
e-mail: mranavayamd@abime.org

D.A. Shokry
Department of Forensic Medicine and Clinical Toxicology, Faculty of Medicine, Cairo University, Kasr Al Ainy St. Cairo, 11562 Cairo, Egypt
e-mail: dinashokry_2004@hotmail.com

V. Sterzik
Institute of Forensic Medicine, Kantonsspital St. Gallen, Rorschacher Str. 95, 9007 St. Gallen, Switzerland
e-mail: v.sterzik@me.com

Y. Vermylen
Department of Dentistry, Faculty of Medicine, The Catholic University Leuven, Capucijnenvoer 7, 3000 Leuven, Belgium
e-mail: yvovermylen@skynet.be

D.N. Vieira
Department of Forensic Medicine, Ethics and Medical Law, Faculty of Medicine, University of Coimbra, Pólo das Ciências da Saúde - Unidade Central, Azinhaga de Santa Comba, Celas, 3000-354 Coimbra, Portugal
e-mail: dnvieira.pt@gmail.com; dnvieira@fmed.uc.pt

R. Zoia
Department of Health and Biomedical Sciences, Section of Legal Medicine, University of Milan, Via Luigi Mangiagalli 37, 20133 Milan, Italy
e-mail: riccardo.zoia@unimi.it

31.1 Introduction

Personal injury is a legal term for a physical or psychological injury suffered by the plaintiff under civil and/or tort law or statute [1]. Damages related to the injury can be *pecuniary* or *non-pecuniary* in nature [2–4].

Although several comparative studies and research projects on civil/tort law and personal injury claims, aimed at developing new tools for promoting harmonisation of civil law, have been performed at an international level, heterogeneity and divergences still exist in the definition and compensation of personal injuries/damages across different national legislative systems [3, 4] and in some instances across various provinces/states within the same country such as Canada and the USA. It is noteworthy that the compensation in these countries for the same personal injury might be significantly different based on whether the injury was work related and arose out of and in the course of employment versus motor vehicle accident or medical malpractice [5]. Several countries categorise non-pecuniary or non-material damages using defined medical criteria and award damages on the basis of specified Barèmes and Compensation Tables. Other national systems rely on the discretion of the judge (or juries made out of common citizens as in USA), and damages are awarded according to legal practice [4], which in common-law countries is based mainly on principle of precedent (i.e. same outcome for same and similar cases of the past).

Although the regulations in various countries are extremely heterogeneous, as indeed are the operational procedures, clinicians and/or medicolegal experts are involved in the majority of cases. Apart from the specific framework (extrajudicial or judicial) in which the professional works, whether the expert acts a consultant for the judge, insurance company, injured party or other institution or figure, the methods of ascertainment to be followed should be the same, including analysis of clinical and documentary data and execution of clinical and instrumental exams.

The starting point for any awarding procedure, indeed, should be a clinical and medicolegal ascertainment, gaining evidence on the trauma/event causing the injury, the mechanism of injury, the pre-existing health status of the injured party and the health consequences of the injury (temporary and permanent impairment, work incapacity, mental and behavioural impairment, loss of amenity, etc.) [4, 5].

An international literature survey on this issue retrieved research efforts (i.e. Rothley Group, Trier 2000 Group) and publications aimed at rationalising the clinical/medicolegal assessment of non-pecuniary damages and proposing different Barémes or evaluation scales, consisting of systems of percentage points for each category of physical and/or mental impairment [2–4].

In the USA the gold standard for personal damage assessment is the *The American Medical Association's Guides to the Evaluation of Permanent Impairment (AMA Guides)*, created as a systematic process whereby disability determinations require that an initial physical or psychological impairment rating be made according to the scientific standard and specific medical criteria converting human pathology (illness/injury) to a number expressed as a percentage of the whole person (WPI unit), with a 0 % WPI reflecting a normal functioning and a 100 % approaching death. Since the clinician (medical doctor) is empowered by the knowledge, skills and abilities due to professional training, he/she is thus charged to render such whole person impairment ratings by the American Medical Association using this rating manual (*AMA Guides*) that is a standardised, objective reference for this purpose, originally published in 1971 and periodically updated and revised to the most current AMA Guides, 6th ed., published in 2008 [6]. The AMA Guides is recognised nationally and globally as the preferred reference for medical impairment ratings and has been adopted and used nationally in the USA (both at Federal and States level) as well as internationally in 16 countries for adjudications of personal injury claims in workers' compensation and civil/tort claims including all Canadian provinces and all three Canadian territories, the Netherlands, Australia, New Zealand, Fiji, Hong Kong and Korea, Colombia, Middle East, Malaysia, South Africa, Botswana and Namibia [6]. American Board of Independent Medical Examiners has formally trained and certified, by examination, thousands of professionals including medical doctors, lawyers and judges in the use of the AMA Guides across these jurisdictions.

In Europe, in May 2003 a group of medical experts supported by the *Confederation Europeen d'Experts en evalutation et reparation du Dommage Corporel* (CEREDOC) presented a "recommendation" to the European Commission, the European Parliament and the Council of Europe proposing European Evaluation Baremés inspired by the French, Belgian, Italian and Spanish compensation tables, which, however, failed to be adopted [4, 7]. Although commendable, the above efforts were probably premature given the absence of a shared clinical and medicolegal ascertainment methodology. Prior to setting any impairment rating criteria, indeed, it is of upmost importance to define the quality requirements for the ascertainment methodology and the evaluation criteria,[1] which are essential to guarantee the objectivity, rigour and reproducibility of the data/evidence collection procedure [7–9]. Currently, other than the AMA Guides as described above, there are no supranational and/or national clinical/medicolegal guidelines dealing specifically with the ascertainment methodology of personal injury and damage under civil/tort law [9, 10]. Therefore, following a scientific initiative by the President of the *International Academy of Legal Medicine* (IALM), an International Working Group composed of medical experts and jurists was created in order to analyse at an intercontinental level the methodological rules, regulations and procedures currently used in the ascertainment and evaluation phases of a personal injury/damage. This comparative, critical and scientific study gave rise to a Consensus Conference held at the University of Padova where the *Padova Charter on Methods of Ascertainment and Criteria of Evaluation of Personal Injury/Damage in Civil/Tort Law*

[1] Evaluation criteria are intended as "*logical steps*" to be followed for the assessment of any impairment and/or disability, *not* as "Baréme" or "Compensation Table" or "Guide" for expressing an impairing rating as percentage on the entire psychic and anatomo-functional value of the person.

was elaborated. This effort is part of a more extensive project including the authors and other experts on personal injury and damage ascertainment, all members of an IALM Working Group, from 21 countries spread over 5 continents as listed below in alphabetical order: Argentina, Australia, Belgium, China, Egypt, Estonia, France, Germany, Hungary, India, Italy, Japan, Lithuania, Nigeria, Portugal, Spain, the Netherlands, the UK, Turkey, United Arab Emirates and the USA.[2]

31.2 Itemisation of the Guidelines

The guidelines were subdivided into the following *items*:

1. *Expert Definition and Essential Knowledge*
2. *Methods of Ascertainment*

[2] **Osama Mohammed Al Madani**, Forensic Medicine, SCFHS Riyadh, Kingdom of Saudi Arabia; **Manal S. Bamousa**, Forensic Medicine, SCFHS Riyadh, Kingdom of Saudi Arabia; **Peter Banczerowski**, Semmelweis University, Department of Neurosurgery, Budapest, Hungary; **Wout E. L. De Boer**, Academy of Swiss Insurance Medicine, ASIM, Basel, Switzerland; **Jan Buitenhuis**, Dutch Academic Center for Insurance Medicine, DACIM Groningen, the Netherlands; **Krisztian Csapó**, Semmelweis University Department of Neurosurgery, Budapest, Hungary; **Agnes Dósa**, Semmelweis University Department of Forensic and Insurance Medicine, Budapest, Hungary; **Uwom O. Eze**, Forensic Pathology, University College Hospital, Ibadan, Nigeria; **Ahmet Hilal**, Cukurova University, Medical Faculty Department of Forensic Medicine, Istanbul, Turkey; **Ping Huang**, Shanghai Key Laboratory of Forensic Medicine, Institute of Forensic Science, Ministry of Justice, Shanghai, P.R. China; **Haluk Ince**, Istanbul University, Medical Faculty Department of Forensic Medicine and Public Health, Istanbul, Turkey; **Eva Keller**, Semmelweis University Department of Forensic and Insurance Medicine, Budapest, Hungary; **Magdy A. Kharoshah**, Forensic Medicine, SCFHS Riyadh, Kingdom of Saudi Arabia; **Adarsh Kumar**, Chairman Medical Disability Evaluation Board, JPNA Trauma Centre, All India Institute of Medical Sciences, New Delhi, India; **Marta Beatriz Maldonado**, Faculty of Odontology, Institute of Forensic Sciences, University of Buenos Aires, Argentina; **Danuta Mendelson**, School of Law, Faculty of Business and Law, Deakin University, Burwood, Australia; **Katja De Munnynck**, Centre of Forensic Medicine, University Hospital of the Catholic University of Leuven, Leuven, Belgium; **Axel Muttray**, Institute of Occupational, Community and Environmental Medicine, Johannes Gutenberg University of Mainz, Mainz, Germany; **Elisabeth Mützel**, Institute of Forensic Medicine, Ludwig Maximilian University of München, München, Germany; **William O. Odesanmi**, Forensic Pathology, Ekiti State University, Ado Ekiti, Nigeria; **Romas Raudys**, State Forensic Medicine Service under the Ministry of Justice of the Republic of Lithuania, Mykolo Romerio Universitetas, Vilnius, Lithuania; **Jean-Sebastien Raul**, Institut de Médecine Légale, Strasbourg, France; **Andras Sarvary**, Semmelweis University Department of Forensic and Insurance Medicine, Budapest, Hungary; **Toshiko Sawaguchi**, Department of Legal Medicine, Tokyo Women's Medical University, Tokyo, Japan; **Marika Väli**, Estonian Forensic Science Institute, University of Tartu, Tartu, Estonia; **Peter Vanezis**, Department of Clinical Pharmacology, Cameron Forensic Medical Sciences, William Harvey Research Institute, Barts and the London, Queen Mary University of London, London, UK; **Ya-hui Wang**, Shanghai Key Laboratory of Forensic Medicine, Institute of Forensic Science, Ministry of Justice, Shanghai, P.R. China; **Peter Weiß**, Department of Public Prosecution, Würzburg, Germany.

- *Step 1. Collection of circumstantial, clinico-documental and instrumental data*
- *Step 2. Systematic clinical examination*
- *Step 3. Clinical synthesis*
- *Step 4. Instrumental exams and/or specialist consultation*

3. *Evaluation Criteria*

- *Step 1. Verification of maximal medical improvement/stabilisation*
- *Step 2. Clinical and medicolegal epicrisis*

(a) Pre-existing health status
(b) *Reconstruction of the damaging event*
(c) *Identification of physiopathological features*
(d) Identification of injury, temporary and permanent impairment

- *Step 3. Causal value and link*
- *Step 4. Impairment and disability description*

31.3 Expert Definition and Essential Knowledge

Currently there is a lack of consensus of a universal definition and or qualification of specialist in Legal Medicine or personal injury and damage evaluator leading to a lack of an international recognition of such authority. Additionally, these skills are generally not taught during the formal professional training.

In several countries the ascertainment and evaluation of personal injury and damage is carried out by clinicians, specialists in Insurance Medicine and/or other professionals. In the USA subspecialty of *Disability Medicine* is an emerging field described as a clinical medical practice which encompasses the identification, prediction, prevention, assessment, evaluation and management of impairment and disability in both human individuals and populations [5, 6].

This consensus document recommends that the "Expert" (from now on referred to as such) demonstrates the essential knowledge set out below.

(a) Notions of civil/tort and administrative laws regarding personal injury and damage, with particular reference to the regulations in the healthcare and insurance sectors.
(b) Theoretical and practical notions of clinical and medicolegal semeiotics devoted to the assessment of psychophysical validity in relation to civil/tort and insurance laws.
(c) Theoretical notions on the subject of material causality, ascertainment methodology and criteria for the identification of the causal value/link between the event and the injury and between this latter and the temporary/permanent impairment.

31.4 Methods of Ascertainment

Flow Chart 1 depicts the four fundamental logical steps to be followed during the ascertainment methodology for any personal injury and/or damage and is described in detail in the following sections.

31.4.1 Step 1. Collection of Circumstantial, Clinico-documental-instrumental Data

The first step is the collection of circumstantial, clinico-documental and instrumental data, with the retrieval of all information believed to be useful for a diagnostic framework, for the reconstruction of the injuring event, the identification of the clinico-pathological features, injuries, impairments and disabilities *(Flow Chart 1)*.[3]

All documentary data relating to the circumstances and the mechanism of injury (e.g. records drafted by the police, complaint forms relating to the event, etc.) should be acquired.

In cases of *traumatic events*, adjunctive documentary data describing the *type* and characteristics of the *involved means*, the *role* of the *injured person*, the presence of correctly used *protection safeguards* (belt, helmet), the *material damages to the involved means* and the report on the *dynamics of the accident* should be collected.

The clinical and instrumental documents of prime importance to be examined are depicted in Fig. *31.1* and described below (Step 1a and 1b).

31.4.1.1 Step 1a. In Case of Previous Hospital Admission

- *Anamnesis and Physical Examination*

This is essential to evaluate the initial clinical picture and early psychophysical modification due to the claimed event.

- *Medical Orders Sheet*

The decisions made by doctors attending the patient, according to how the case develops, are noted on this sheet.

- *Emergency Room Assistance Sheet* or *Emergency Room Report*

This document is compiled when the patient has requested care in the emergency room: it includes the reason for consultations, the results of any examinations and tests requested, clinical opinion and diagnosis. As a result, the following decisions

[3] In several countries, in the private law framework, it is not always possible (even with a judge's authorisation) to integrate the medical and healthcare documentation presented by the plaintiffs and defendants, and the examination is limited to the documents presented by the parties.

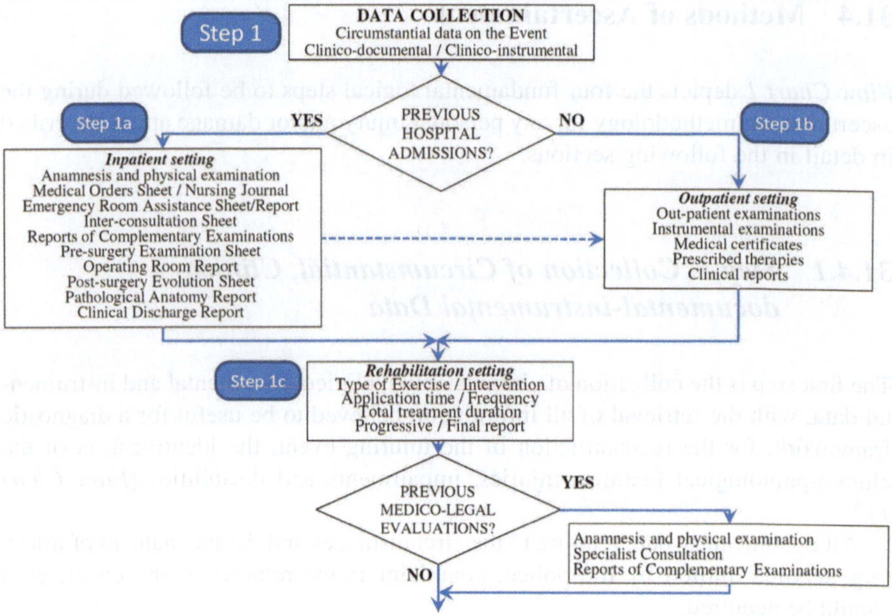

Fig. 31.1 Flow chart 1. Methods of ascertainment. Steps 1a–c

are made to request inter-consultation or collaboration with a specialist (according to pathology), to start treatment and to send the patient home or to indicate admission to the hospital.

– *Inter-consultation Sheet*

This sheet records all actions by other specialists who may examine the patient at the request of the doctor responsible for that patient. It is compiled when the patient's state, other than that for which that patient was admitted to hospital, is documented by a specialist from another discipline.

– *Reports of Complementary Examinations*

These refer to diagnostic tests, the results of which are interpreted and reported by the specialists who made them, e.g. imaging, neurophysiological, psychological tests, etc.

– *Pre-surgery Examination Sheet*

This document is compiled when surgical intervention is necessary. Pre-surgery examinations are carried out by an anaesthetist, according to established procedures, and patients are classified with respect to their ASA index or risk level.

– *Operating Room Report*

This report records the nature of the surgical intervention, all incidents related to the technique used and specific patient findings. It is therefore a patient document which is usually illustrated with simple drawings showing what actions were taken in the surgical field, e.g. sutures, drains, etc.

- *Post-surgery Evolution Sheet*

  This sheet describes monitoring of the patient with respect to general conditions and the specific surgical operation performed.
- *Pathological Anatomy Report*

  This report describes any histological or histopathological examination on bioptical or surgical specimens.
- *Nursing Journal*

  This sheet covers all incidents relating to vital signs, administration of medicines and medications, requests for care and any unusual decisions (including, requests to doctors on duty made by nurses for extra medicines, especially analgesics, etc.), outside usual working hours. Detailed notes which may be of interest are frequently found in nursing sheets.
- *Clinical Discharge Report*

  This is issued when the patient is discharged from the medical viewpoint and goes home or to another hospital. It summarises the period in which the patient was hospitalised, and, although specific, it should be a complete document which includes the cause of hospitalisation, with precise diagnoses, treatments administered, evolution, state of the patient at discharge, and treatment(s) to be followed, with indications of any future examinations and whether the family doctor should carry out monitoring.

31.4.1.2 Step 1b. In Case of Outpatient Care, Without Hospital Admission or After Hospital Discharge

- *Outpatient Examination*

  All clinical evaluations where a subject has undergone an outpatient procedure, in order to ascertain the state of health or disease, or the trend of the same, must be taken into consideration in order to reconstruct a picture as complete as possible of the story and its evolution over time.
- *Instrumental Examinations*

  All of the instrumental evaluations that a subject has undergone during an outpatient procedure, in order to ascertain the state of health or disease, or the performance of the same, must be taken into consideration in order to reconstruct a picture as complete as possible of the story and the its evolution over time.
- *Medical Certificates*

  Each certification on the health status for diagnostic, prognostic, therapeutic or work purposes must be taken into consideration in order to render the estimation of the periods of temporary impairment and the evaluation of permanent impairment as precise as possible.
- *Prescribed Therapies*

  All therapeutic prescriptions (i.e. drug treatments, medical devices, etc.) must be checked and evaluated at the end of the periods of temporary impairment for a realistic estimate of the severity of the clinical condition and its evolution over time.

– *Clinical Reports*

The clinical reports eventually produced in communication between general practitioners and specialist colleagues as well as between physicians and other institutions (private and social insurance, employer, etc.) must be examined in order to create the most accurate clinical picture possible.

31.4.1.3 Step 1c. Rehabilitation Documents

In any case, one must also take into account any rehabilitation documents produced during the clinical evolution of the injury and the healing/stabilisation process. These documents will be explanations/summaries of the type of exercise and/or treatment scheduled, execution times and/or application and their frequency on a daily/weekly/monthly basis, encompassing the total duration of the treatment and the progressive and final reports produced in relation to it.

31.4.2 Step 2. Systematic Clinical Examination

In case that the subject has already received previous advice/ascertainment, both in extrajudicial and judicial phases, that report must be collected and taken into account. Any previous medical findings, related to the anamnesis, physical examination as well as any specialist consultations and reports of complementary evaluations, must be collected and examined, considering that the above assessments could be consistently spaced in time, being referred also to moments in the distant past. After this documental acquisition, case history collection and psychophysical examination must be conducted directly (Fig. *31.2*).

31.4.2.1 Step 2a. Case History

The first operation is to identify the examined person collecting his/her name, surname, date of birth, marital status, address, telephone, e-mail, information regarding his/her education and any eventual personal insurance cover.

Prior to the medical anamnesis, any information on the damaging event and the mechanism of injury must be collected. The injury/damage is generally the consequence of a traffic accident, a medical malpractice case [9], or other types of traumatic events (i.e. sport-related accidents, work-related accidents, domestic accidents, etc.). In order to properly reconstruct the event and the mechanism of injury, all of the available circumstantial and clinical information, including immediate symptoms and signs after the injury, treatments administered and intermediate/final outcomes, must be collected.

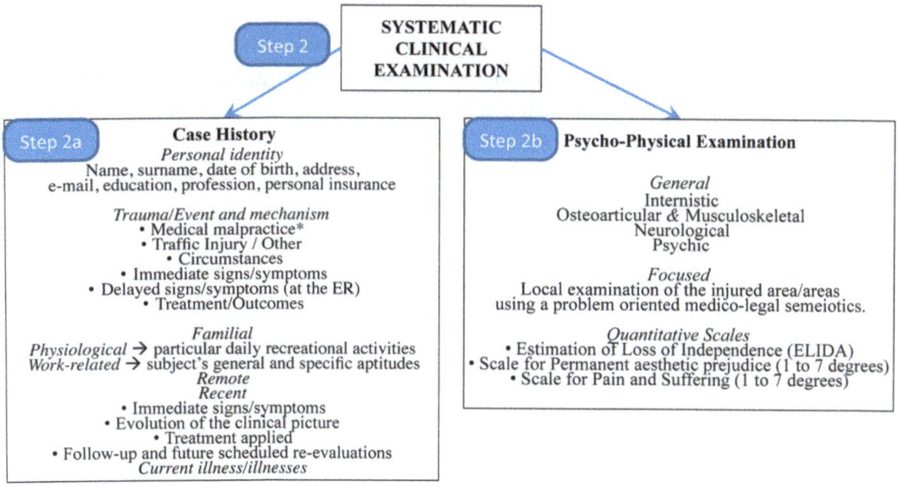

Fig. 31.2 Flow chart 1. Methods of ascertainment. Steps 2a–b

The anamnesis should include the:

1. *Family medical history*, recording any health information of the relatives of the examined person (up to the third generation).
2. *Physiological medical history*, recording information on psychomotor development, lifestyle, sexual habits, allergies, diuresis, defecation and sleep schedule.
3. *Remote diseases*, with a comprehensive list of previous sicknesses, operations, traumatic accidents, prostheses and/or orthoses.
4. *Recent diseases*, with a focus on the immediate signs/symptoms after the event, the evolution of the clinical picture, the treatments applied, the follow-up pathways and any future scheduled re-evaluations. Subsequently, a detailed account of current problems, complaints and symptoms must be collected.
5. *Work-related and social life aspects*, detailing general/specific working aptitudes, education, previous (listed in chronological order) and current occupation and daily recreational activities, such as hobbies and domestic, sport and leisure activities.

31.4.2.2 Step 2b. Psychophysical Examination

The psychophysical examination should be performed in a consulting room equipped with dressing room, bathroom and medical bed and provided with measurement instruments and provoking tests (e.g. goniometer, inclinometer, ruler, sphygmomanometer, sterile needles, stethoscope, etc.).

The psychophysical examination consists of a comprehensive clinical and medicolegal visit, including internistic, osteoarticular-musculoskeletal, neurological, psychic and local examination of the injured/damaged area/s.

Internistic Examination
This examination should include the inspection and palpation of all body systems, the palpation and percussion of the thorax and abdomen and the auscultation of the lungs, heart and bowel sounds with a stethoscope. It aims at identifying any disease or impairment of the internal organs. If any signs of internistic disease emerge during that examination, a specialist consultation with possible first-/second-level instrumental investigations should be carefully considered.

Osteoarticular and Musculoskeletal Examination
This examination, aimed at identifying any impairment of the active and/or passive range of motion of the examinee's joints, should include the head, spine, chest, pelvis, upper and lower limbs, and any eventual prostheses and orthoses, being performed both by active and passive movements. The active range of motion should be recorded with a goniometer and/or inclinometer.

Neurological Examination
This examination, aimed at identifying any impairment of the nervous system, should include the examination of higher functions (gait, speech), mental status (memory and orientation), cranial nerves, noncortical and cortical sensory systems, motor system (trophic state, muscle tone and strength, involuntary movements), reflexes (primitive, superficial, deep tendon), sensory and cerebellar functions.

Psychic Examination
This examination includes the observation of the general aspect, behaviour, mood and affect, perception, thought and awareness of the examinee. It utilises psychometric tests, neuropsychological tests and assessment scales aimed at identifying and measuring intelligence and personality abnormalities, brain damage and the extent of any psychic, behavioural and socio-relational changes. Laboratory and instrumental exams including biochemical and imaging studies can be performed for identifying/excluding potential causes of mental disorders and/or verifying and monitoring the psychopharmacological treatment. The interpretative *epicrisis* of data involves the comparative evaluation of circumstantial-clinical-behavioural-objective-testistic-laboratory and instrumental data, with the aim of formulating a nosographic diagnosis, establishing its severity in relation to the size and intensity of symptoms and the impact on the scholastic, work and relational functions.[4]

Local Examination
After the aforementioned systematic general examination, a focus should be made on the injured area/areas performing an *analytical local examination* using a *problem-oriented clinical and medicolegal semeiotics*.

Any visible injuries or sequelae will be photographed (overview picture followed by a detailed picture with scale) and analytically described with regard

[4] A dedicated International IALM Working Group is drafting an adjunctive methodological flow chart for the ascertainment and evaluation of psychic impairment, pain and suffering and existential damage.

to their localisation (using landmarks), mutual distribution and morphometric characteristics. Inspection will be followed by palpation, percussion and auscultation where applicable. The local examination must identify any impairment of the articular, muscular and/or neurological function differentiating true disorders, from malingering and/or simulation [11, 12].

Quantitative Scales for Pain, Aesthetic Prejudice and Loss of Independence
It is recommended to use only widespread scales, which have been previously validated and published on peer-reviewed journals for the objective identification and quantification of suspected impairments, as pain, aesthetic prejudice and loss of independence.

The *Visual Analogue Scale* (VAS) formed of a horizontal line, 10 cm in length, anchored by word descriptors at each end on which the patient marks the point that he/she feels to represent his/her perception is a valid instrument for measuring pain (VAS is not very useful in forensic environment as it is all self-report).

The quantification of the aesthetic prejudice should be performed with the *Orofacial Aesthetic Scale* (OAS), developed especially for prosthodontic patients, including eight items investigating the appearance of the examinee: face, profile, mouth, tooth alignment, tooth shape, tooth colour, gums as well as overall impression measured on an 11-point numeric rating scale (0 “Very dissatisfied”, 10 “Very satisfied” with appearance) [13].

The *Estimation of Loss of Independence Scale* (ELIDA), an adaptive behaviour scale, should be used to measure the need for assistance in daily living activities. Fifty activities, within ten subscales, are rated on a yes/no basis, with higher scores reflecting a higher need of assistance [14].

31.4.3 Step 3. Clinical Synthesis

A synthesis of all the collected data with verification of sufficiency for reconstructing a comprehensive clinical picture must be performed (Fig. 31.3).

31.4.4 Step 4. Instrumental Exams and/or Specialist Consultation

In the case that further anatomo-functional data are needed, a specialist can be consulted, or instrumental exams can be prescribed.[5]

[5] In some countries, indeed, if the instrumental exams have only medicolegal purposes and not a clear clinical and therapeutic indication, they cannot be performed.

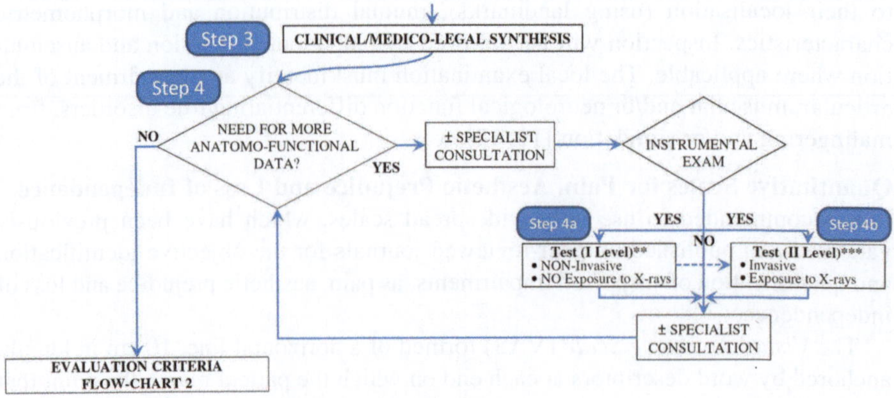

Fig. 31.3 Flow chart 1. Methods of ascertainment. Steps 3–4

Instrumental exams of first and second level can be prescribed directly by the expert or by the consulted specialist.

31.4.4.1 First-Level Exams: Step 4a

First-level exams are ultrasound, magnetic resonance, electrocardiography, electroencephalography and any other investigations which are not harmful for the examinee.

31.4.4.2 Second-Level Exams: Step 4b

Any exams based on the use of ionising radiation or those who could pose a risk for the examinee belong to the second level (e.g. computed tomography, positron emission tomography, electromyography, endoscopy, etc.).

The interpretation of the instrumental results can be performed by the expert with sufficient experience and/or expertise in that specific field or by the specialist.

31.5 Evaluation Criteria

The *Flow Chart 2* depicts the four fundamental logical steps to be followed during the evaluation phase for any personal injury and/or damage and is described in detail in the following sections.

31.5.1 Step 1. Verification of Maximal Medical Improvement/Stabilisation

The evaluation process can start only if the injury/disease has reached its maximal medical improvement, which means that healing or stabilisation to a permanent sequela/e occurred (Fig. 31.4).

In the event that the clinical situation is still evolving (i.e. ongoing disease), it is necessary to postpone the ascertainment until healing or stabilisation occurs.

31.5.2 Step 2. Clinical and Medicolegal Epicrisis

This step consists of a comparative analysis of all the collected data aimed at assessing the pre-existing health status (*Step 2a*), reconstructing the damaging event (*Step 2b*) and identifying the clinico-pathological diagnosis (*Step 2c*) and the corresponding medicolegal diagnosis (*Step 2d*), in terms of temporary/permanent impairment or other damages (e.g. sexual dysfunction, aesthetic prejudice, decrease of the quality of life, etc.).

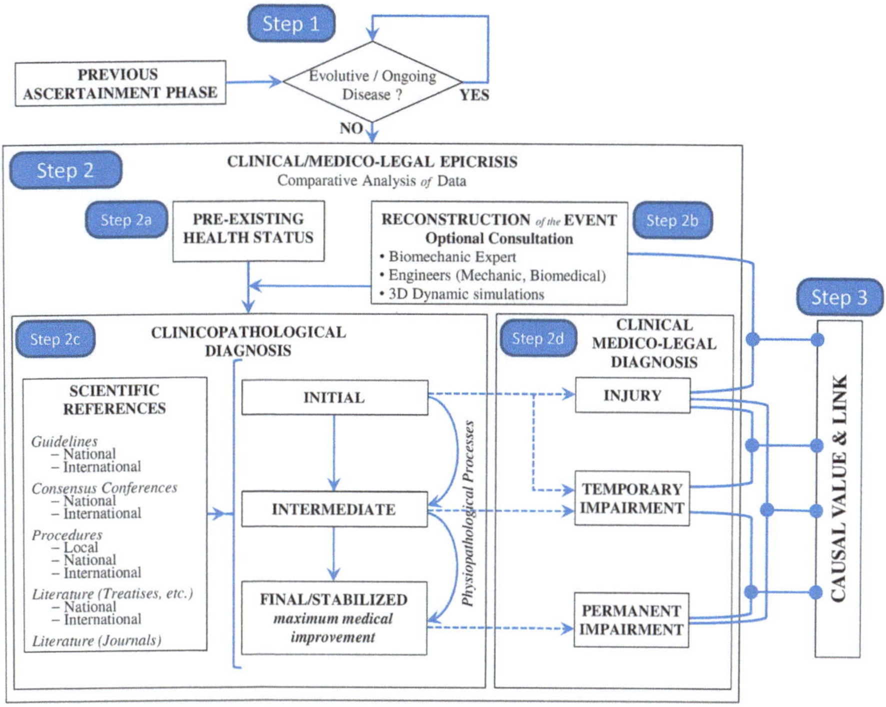

Fig. 31.4 Flow chart 2. Evaluation criteria. Steps 1–2

31.5.2.1 Step 2a. Pre-existing Health Status

It is essential to reconstruct the pre-existing health status in order to detect any changes that occurred as a result of the damaging event. This step will permit the identification of any differential damages attributable to the event itself, according to the principle of personalisation of the ascertainment.

31.5.2.2 Step 2b. Reconstruction of the Damaging Event

Basing on the available circumstantial data, the recorded medical history and the clinical objective data, the dynamics of the damaging event and the mechanism of injury must be reconstructed. For that purpose, if the event is characterised by an impact, a *biomechanical expert* could be consulted, in order to analyse all the available information regarding the scenario before and after the questioned event, and elaborating a finite element model (FEM) taking into account the main aspects of interest (i.e. velocity, trajectory, energy, etc.). A number of experimental data, hypotheses and computations will be necessary to calibrate and validate the model, verifying the required accuracy and precision. The three-dimensional (3D) dynamic simulation reconstructed by the biomechanical expert must then be compared with the injury/disorders ascertained on the victim.

31.5.2.3 Step 2c. Identification of the Clinico-pathological Features

The clinico-pathological features of the injury/disorder must be reconstructed in order to reach a clinical diagnosis of the initial, intermediate and final stages.

A thorough analysis and clear description of the physiopathological pathways, which connect the diverse evolutive phases of the injury/disease, must be performed.

The physiopathological features and pathways are examined on the basis of scientific sources, such as guidelines, consensus documents, operational procedures, evidence-based publications (Cochrane Reviews, meta-analysis, etc.) and other literature, composed of treatises and articles published in peer-reviewed journals (PubMed-MEDLINE, Embase, Scopus, Ovid, ISI Web of Science, etc.), preferably with *Impact Factor*.

These scientific sources of nonequivalent importance must also be graded according to the source hierarchy as shown below:

- Guidelines (international and/or national)
- Consensus documents (international and/or national)
- Procedures (international, national and/or local)
- Literature (treatises, journals)

31.5.2.4 Step 2d. Identification of Injury, Temporary and Permanent Impairment

After examining the scientific sources and reconstructing the physiopathological processes linking the identified clinico-pathological features, as described in *Step 2c*, the following have to be determined:

- Injury and temporary impairment related to the initial clinico-pathological features
- Temporary impairment related to the intermediate clinico-pathological features
- Permanent impairment related to the final/stabilised clinico-pathological features

Moreover, the presence of any other types of impairments with clinical and medicolegal relevance, such as sexual sphere modifications, aesthetic prejudice, alteration of daily activities and relational and social life, must be identified.

31.5.3 *Step 3. Causal Value and Causal Link*

The causal value/link between the event and the injury and between that injury and the temporary/permanent impairment must be verified (Fig. 31.5). This verification must be based on "criteria of scientific probability", such as (a) Universal Laws, by

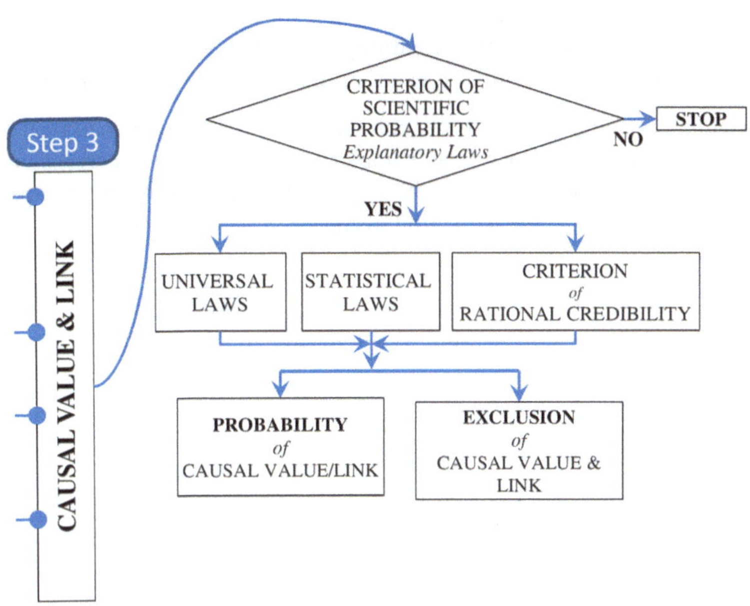

Fig. 31.5 Flow chart 2. Evaluation criteria. Step 3

means of deduction and (b) Statistical Laws, by means of inference, or, in the absence of such laws, according to (c) the criterion of rational credibility. If this is not possible, due to the absence of "explanatory laws", the ascertainment must be interrupted.

The standard of proof required in civil/tort cases varies according to the national laws but is generally based on the rule of "more probable, than not" (i.e. enough evidence does exist to make the scientific explanation more likely than not that the fact the claimant seeks to prove is true).

The identification of the degree of probability of the causal link should always be performed and, when possible, expressed as an estimated percentage of probability.

31.5.4 *Step 4. Impairment and Disability Description*

This final step foresees the analytical description of the temporary/permanent impairment, the disability and any other pecuniary or non-pecuniary losses of medicolegal relevance (Fig. 31.6).

Pecuniary Losses

Damages are awarded for the injury actually sustained by the victim, and for all the consequential expenses, which flow from the injury. Pecuniary losses may be classified under two different headings:

- The first concerns the additional expenses incurred as a result of the damaging event (*damnum emergens*).
- The second concerns the loss of earnings and other benefits which the injured person would have received as a result of the damaging event (*lucrum cessans*).

The technical and expert analysis, consisting of an objective analytical description of the temporary and permanent impairments, and their repercussion on the work capacity, will be utilised by the judge for better estimating the pecuniary losses causally related to the damaging event.

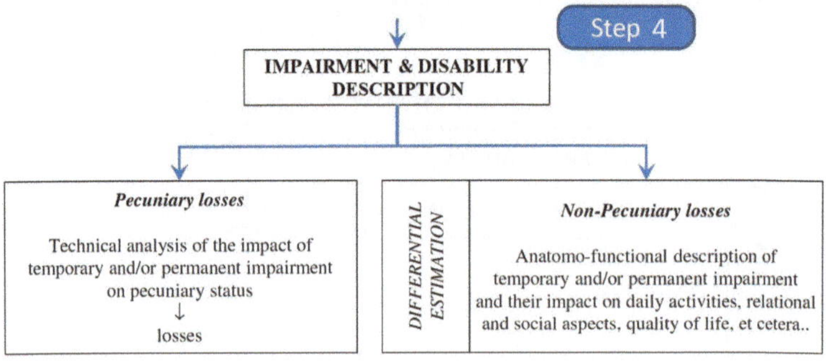

Fig. 31.6 Flow chart 2. Evaluation criteria. Step 4

Non-pecuniary Losses

A detailed and motivated description of any aesthetic prejudice, sexual dysfunction and/or temporary/permanent functional impairment, specifying their impact and repercussion on the leisure and social activities, must be furnished.

This analytical and objective description will be utilised by the judge for estimating the non-pecuniary losses causally related to the damaging event.

The present guidelines do not provide harmonised Baremes or Compensation Schemes for quantifying the impairment/disability and refer to national systems for rating rules and criteria.

31.6 Conclusions

"Personal Injury Ascertainment, Evaluation and Compensation" are very complex issues, from both clinical, medicolegal and juridical points of view. Huge heterogeneity still exists in the legislative frameworks and compensation schemes adopted at different national levels but also in the methodology used to verify the existence and extent of the injury/damage. These procedures must be based on sound scientific methods that guarantee objectivity, reproducibility and rigour in the collection of scientific evidence, worthy as credible evidence at civil court and accepted as scientific proof [15].

However, the current non-homogeneous competences, know-how and expertise of the different professionals involved in the process (from insurance professionals, claims adjusters to clinicians and medicolegal experts and lawyers/judges, etc.), in the absence of a universal personal injury assessment guideline, make the quality and reliability of personal injury/damage assessment and compensation susceptible to great variability across various jurisdictions.

The *Padova Charter* on the "Methods of Ascertainment and Criteria of Evaluation of Personal Injury and Damage under Civil-Tort Law", being the first international consensus document focussing on the very initial phase of the compensation procedure (i.e. the ascertainment of the injury/damage), paves the way for a future harmonisation of the impairment rating and the assessment of any pecuniary and non-pecuniary losses causally related to the personal injury.

References

1. Warren Neocleous M (1997) Personal injury: practice and procedure in Europe. Routledge-Cavendish, London
2. Holding JH, Kaye P (1993) Damages for personal injuries: a European perspective. Chancery Law Pub, Chichester
3. Hureau J (2006) Harmonisation of personal injury compensation in the European Union. Application to medical liability case law. Bull Acad Natl Med 190:725–746
4. Bona M, Mead P (2003) Personal injury compensation in Europe. Kluwer, Deventer

5. Ranavaya MI, Rondinelli R (2000) The major US disability and compensation systems: origins and historical overview. In: Rondinelli RD, Katz RT (eds) Impairment rating and disability evaluation. WB Saunders, Philadelphia, pp 3–16
6. Rondinelli RD, Ranavaya M (2008) American Medical Association: guides to the evaluation of permanent impairment, 6th edn. AMA Press, Chicago
7. Gerin C (1953) Medicolegal evaluation of personal physical damage in civil liability. Riv Infort Mal Prof 40:371–424
8. Chappuis G, Soltermann B (2008) Number and cost of claims linked to minor cervical trauma in Europe: results from the comparative study by CEA, AREDOC and CEREDOC. Eur Spine J 17(10):1350–1357
9. Ferrara SD, Bajanowski T, Cecchi R, Snenghi R, Case C, Viel G (2010) Bio-medicolegal guidelines and protocols: survey and future perspectives in Europe. Int J Legal Med 124 (4):345–350
10. Ferrara SD, Bajanowski T, Cecchi R, Boscolo-Berto R, Viel G (2011) Bio-medicolegal scientific research in Europe: a comprehensive bibliometric overview. Int J Legal Med 125 (3):93–402
11. Giusti G (2009) Semeiotica medico-legale. In: Giusti G (ed) Trattato di Medicina Legale e Scienze Affini, 2nd edn. CEDAM, Padova
12. Hartlage LC (2012) Clinical detection of malingering. In: Reynolds CR, MacNeill A (eds) Detection of malingering during head injury litigation, 2nd edn. Springer, Heidelberg, pp 333–350
13. Larsson P, John MT, Nilner K, Bondemark L, List T (2010) Development of an Orofacial Aesthetic Scale in prosthodontic patients. Int J Prosthodont 23(3):249–256
14. Brusselmans W (1992) The ELIDA-scale. Estimation of loss of independence. Acta Physiother 47:51–54
15. Ferrara SD, Baccino E, Bajanowski T, Boscolo-Berto R, Castellano M, De Angel R, Pauliukevičius A, Ricci P, Vanezis P, Vieira DN, Viel G, Villanueva E, EALM Working Group on Medical Malpractice (2013) Malpractice and medical liability. European guidelines on methods of ascertainment and criteria of evaluation. Int J Legal Med 127(3):545–557

Chapter 32
International Guidelines on the Methods of Ascertainment of Whiplash-Associated Disorders

Santo Davide Ferrara, Viviana Ananian, Eric Baccino, Peter Banczerowski, Daniele Bordignon, Rafael Boscolo-Berto, Ranieri Domenici, Javier Gorriz Quevedo, Matthias Graw, Wolfram Hell, Claudio Hernandez-Cueto, Peter Juel Thiis Knudsen, Stefano Masiero, Massimo Montisci, Gian Aristide Norelli, Vilma Pinchi, Romas Raudys, Jean Sebastien Raul, Vera Sterzik, Enrico Tessitore, Jana Tuusov, Peter Vanezis, Yvo Vermylen, Duarte Nuno Vieira, Guido Viel, Alessia Viero, Enrique Villanueva, and Riccardo Zoia

Abstract This chapter presents the International Guidelines developed by the Working Group on Personal Injury and Damage under the patronage of the International Academy of Legal Medicine (IALM) regarding the Methods of Ascertainment of any suspected Whiplash-Associated Disorders (WAD).

The online version of this chapter (doi:10.1007/978-3-319-29812-2_32) contains supplementary material, which is available to authorized users.

S.D. Ferrara (✉) • V. Ananian • R. Boscolo-Berto • M. Montisci • G. Viel • A. Viero
Department of Legal and Occupational Medicine, Toxicology and Public Health, University-Hospital of Padova, Via Falloppio 50, 35128 Padova, Italy
e-mail: santodavide.ferrara@unipd.it; ananian.viviana@gmail.com; rafael.boscoloberto@unipd.it; massimo.montisci@unipd.it; guido.viel@unipd.it; alessia.viero85@gmail.com

E. Baccino
University of Montpellier, Hôpital Lapeyronie, 191 Av. du Doyen Gaston Giraud, 34295 Montpellier, Cedex, France
e-mail: e-baccino@chu-montpellier.fr

P. Banczerowski
Department of Neurosurgery, Semmelweis University, Amerikai út 57, 1145 Budapest XIV, Hungary
e-mail: idegsebeszet@med.semmelweis-univ.hu

D. Bordignon
Private Medico-Legal Practice, Strada Marosticana 333, 36100 Vicenza, Italy
e-mail: d.bordignon@libero.it

S.D. Ferrara et al. (eds.), *Personal Injury and Damage Ascertainment under Civil Law*, DOI 10.1007/978-3-319-29812-2_32

This chapter includes a detailed description of the logical and methodological steps of the ascertainment process as well as a synoptic diagram in the form of a flow-chart. This chapter represents a slightly modified version of an article published in the International Journal of Legal Medicine.

R. Domenici
Department of Clinical, Surgical, and Molecular Pathology, Unit of Legal Medicine, University of Pisa, Via Roma 55, 56126 Pisa, Italy
e-mail: ranieri.domenici@med.unipi.it

J. Gorriz Quevedo
Gorriz Hernando Médicos, Avda/Diagonal, 612 5° 9a Barcelona, Spain
e-mail: 20478jgq@comb.cat

M. Graw • W. Hell
Institut für Rechtsmedizin, Ludwig-Maximilians-University of München, Nussbaumstrasse 26, 80336 Munich, Germany
e-mail: matthias.graw@med.uni-muenchen.de; wolfram.hell@med.uni-muenchen.de

C. Hernandez-Cueto
Department of Legal Medicine, Forensic Toxicology and Anthropology, University of Granada, Avda. de Madrid 11, 18071 Granada, Spain
e-mail: chc@ugr.es

P.J.T. Knudsen
Institute of Forensic Medicine, University of Southern Denmark, J.B. Winsløws Vej 17, DK-5000 Odense C, Denmark
e-mail: pthiis@health.sdu.dk

S. Masiero
Department of Neurosciences, Physical and Rehabilitation Medicine, University-Hospital of Padova, Via Giustiniani 1, 35128 Padova, Italy
e-mail: stef.masiero@unipd.it

G.A. Norelli • V. Pinchi
Department of Health Sciences, Forensic Sciences Section, Institute of Legal Medicine, University of Florence, Largo Brambilla 3, 50134 Florence, Italy
e-mail: ganorelli@unifi.it; vilma.pinchi@unifi.it

R. Raudys
State Forensic Medicine Service under the Ministry of Justice of the Republic of Lithuania, Mykolo Romerio Universitetas, Didlaukio g. 86E, Vilnius 08303, Lithuania
e-mail: romas.raudys@vtmt.lt

J.S. Raul
Institut de Médecine Légale, Faculté de Médecine, Université de Strasbourg, 11 Rue Humann, 67085 Strasbourg, France
e-mail: jeanseb.raul@gmail.com

V. Sterzik
Institute of Forensic Medicine, Kantonsspital St. Gallen, Rorschacher Str. 95, 9007 St. Gallen, Switzerland
e-mail: v.sterzik@me.com

32.1 Introduction

The term Whiplash-Associated Disorders (WAD) was introduced for the first time in 1995 by the Quebec Task Force [1, 2], which published the first systematic review on the subject of whiplash injuries.

The term "Whiplash" indicates the harmful mechanism of acceleration and deceleration with the transfer of energy to the structure of the neck, while "Associated Disorders" represent the related syndromic features of that injury.

The aforementioned harmful mechanism usually occurs in road accidents involving motor vehicles, in particular in the case of collisions or side impacts, and can cause a plurality of bone and soft tissue injuries that may result in a variety of clinical conditions.

Within the category of Personal Injury and Damage compensation under Civil-Tort Law, WAD are a paradigmatic example of "disorder" easy to be simulated,

E. Tessitore
Département de Neurosciences Cliniques, Service de Neurochirurgie, Faculté de Médecine, Hôpitaux Universitaires de Genève, Rue Gabrielle-Perret-Gentil 4, 1211 Geneva 14, Switzerland
e-mail: enrico.tessitore@hcuge.ch

J. Tuusov
Department of Pathological Anatomy and Forensic Medicine, University of Tartu, Ravila 19, 50411 Tartu, Estonia
e-mail: jana.tuusov@ekei.ee

P. Vanezis
Department of Clinical Pharmacology, Cameron Forensic Medical Sciences, William Harvey Research Institute, Barts and the London, Queen Mary University of London, Charterhouse Square, London EC1M 6BQ, UK
e-mail: p.vanezis@qmul.ac.uk

Y. Vermylen
Department of Dentistry, Faculty of Medicine, The Catholic University Leuven, Capucijnenvoer 7, 3000 Leuven, Belgium
e-mail: yvovermylen@skynet.be

D.N. Vieira
Department of Legal Medicine, Ethics and Medical Law, Faculty of Medicine, University of Coimbra, Pólo das Ciências da Saúde—Unidade Central, Azinhaga de Santa Comba, Celas 3000-354, Coimbra, Portugal
e-mail: dnvieira.pt@gmail.com; dnvieira@fmed.uc.pt

E. Villanueva
Department of Legal Medicine, Toxicology and Physical Anthropology, University of Granada, Avda Madrid 11, 18071 Granada, Spain
e-mail: guadalfeo40@telefonica.net

R. Zoia
Department of Health and Biomedical Sciences, Section of Legal Medicine, University of Milan, Via Luigi Mangiagalli 37, 20133 Milan, Italy
e-mail: riccardo.zoia@unimi.it

whose determination, in most cases, is based only on the subjective symptoms complained, and thus hard to objectify. For these reasons, WAD have been a continuous source of controversy due to their association with compensatory litigation claims [3].

Whiplash-Associated Disorders are a controversial issue also in the scientific literature [4] because they are not universally recognized as a nosographic entity in their own right, being considered by several authors as a man-made illness and a medicolegal illusion [3–5].

The 2008 comparative study carried out by the Comitè Europeen des Assurances (CEA), by the Association pour l'étude de la Réparation du Dommage Corporel (AREDOC), and by the Confederation Europeen d'Experts en valutation et reparation du Dommage Corporel (CEREDOC) [6] further indicates that the number of disputes related to WAD varies depending on the legislative, operational, and insurance framework in force in each European State [3].

The issue of medicolegal interest related to the assessment of WAD is, in fact, more prevalent in Germany, Britain, and Italy, while in France, Greece, Lithuania, and Portugal claims related to this issue have only minimal impact [6].

Therefore, WAD constitute, especially in some European Jurisdictions, an issue of increasing importance, involving very high costs for society, as well as health consequences in the medium and long term.

The International interest in the topic under discussion is also evident from the growing number of publications by authors from different countries concerning the legal [7], medical, and biomechanical aspects of minor trauma of the cervical spine [8].

The review of the International Literature and the comparison among Experts with regard to the different National realities has detected the presence of Clinical Guidelines related to the diagnosis and treatment of WAD produced by authoritative International Scientific Societies, in the absence of International Medicolegal Guidelines on WAD Ascertainment Methodology.

Therefore, the need to produce a Consensus Charter, based on rigorous and sound scientific data, shared by International Clinical and Medicolegal Experts, in order to arrive at a strict and objective methodology to serve as standard procedure and to introduce an interdisciplinary approach that includes accident-analytic and biomechanical findings [3, 6]. It would also be useful to provide specialized training for Medical Experts, characterized by strict methodology that ensures its formal exactness and defines the objective quality standards to be applied by those responsible for settling personal injury claims and to ensure better collaboration between physicians, lawyers, insurers, and Experts in bio-dynamics.

This document, which is the result of a scientific initiative promoted by the President of the International Academy of Legal Medicine, illustrates the International Medicolegal Guidelines on the Ascertainment Methodology in cases of suspected Whiplash-Associated Disorders.

These Guidelines have been proposed and reviewed by a *board* of International juridical, clinical, and Medicolegal Experts from the following countries: Belgium, Denmark, Estonia, France, Germany, Hungary, Italy, Lithuania, Portugal, Spain, Switzerland, and the UK.

32.2 Structure of the Guidelines

The Guidelines are subdivided into the following *items*.

Expert Definition and Essential Knowledge.

Methods of Ascertainment.

1. *Acute Phase.*
   (a) *Clinical Examination.*
      – *Case History.*
      – *Accident and Biomechanical analysis.*
   (b) *Identification of high-risk factors.*
   (c) *Objective examination.*
2. *Chronic phase.*
   (a) *Collection of circumstantial, clinical, and instrumental data.*
   (b) *Systematic Clinical Examination.*
      – *Case History.*
      – *Psychophysical examination.*
      – *Pain Drawing.*
   (c) *Instrumental exams and/or specialist consultation.*
      – *First-level exams.*
      – *Second-level exams.*
   (d) *Medicolegal Epicrisis.*

32.3 Expert Definition and Essential Knowledge

Depending on the country in which the whiplash injury takes place, the Expert performing the ascertainment of Whiplash-Associated Disorders can be a Medico-legal Examiner, a Clinician, a Specialist in Insurance Medicine, or even not a physician.

The present guidelines recommend that a clinical examination is mandatory and that the medical examiner, regardless of his/her basic training, should demonstrate the essential knowledge set out below.

– Notions of civil and administrative laws regarding personal injury and damage, with particular reference to the regulations in the healthcare and insurance sectors.

- Theoretical and practical notions of Medicolegal semeiotics as well as Medicolegal ascertainment of psychophysical validity in relation to civil and insurance laws.
- Theoretical notions on the subject of material causality, ascertainment methodology, and criteria for the identification of the causal value/link between the traumatic event and the injury and between this latter and the temporary/permanent impairment.

In addition, cervical spine injuries show the need for a multidisciplinary approach enabling the problem to be viewed in its entirety, and, therefore, the Medical Expert must avail him/herself of other Specialists and of interdisciplinary collaborations, such as those with Biomechanical Experts for the reconstruction of the dynamics of the harmful event.

32.4 Methods of Ascertainment

Although the regulations in various countries are extremely heterogeneous—as, indeed, are the operational procedures—Clinicians or Medicolegal Experts are involved in the majority of cases.

Apart from the specific framework (extrajudicial or judicial) in which the professional works, and apart from the fact that person acts as a consultant for the judge, the insurance company, the injured party, or other Institutions or figures, the methods of ascertainment to be followed are the same, including analysis of clinical and documentary data and execution of clinical and instrumental examinations, described in detail in the following sections.

32.4.1 Acute Phase

32.4.1.1 Clinical Examination

The medical ascertainment in the acute phase regards adult patients (i.e., over 14 years of age with fully developed spines [9, 10]) who undergo the initial ascertainment within 6 months from the trauma (Fig. 32.1).

- *Case History*

The first operation that the ascertaining Clinical or Medicolegal Expert must perform is the complete and detailed collection of all the available clinical and documentary data [11], including the medical history provided during the consultation between the doctor and the patient, clinical data deduced from the analysis of medical records, reports, and/or instrumental images that may be present, believed to be useful for a diagnostic framework and for later identification of the clinicopathological features, injuries, impairments, and other damages. In particular, the Expert will have to investigate what is listed below.

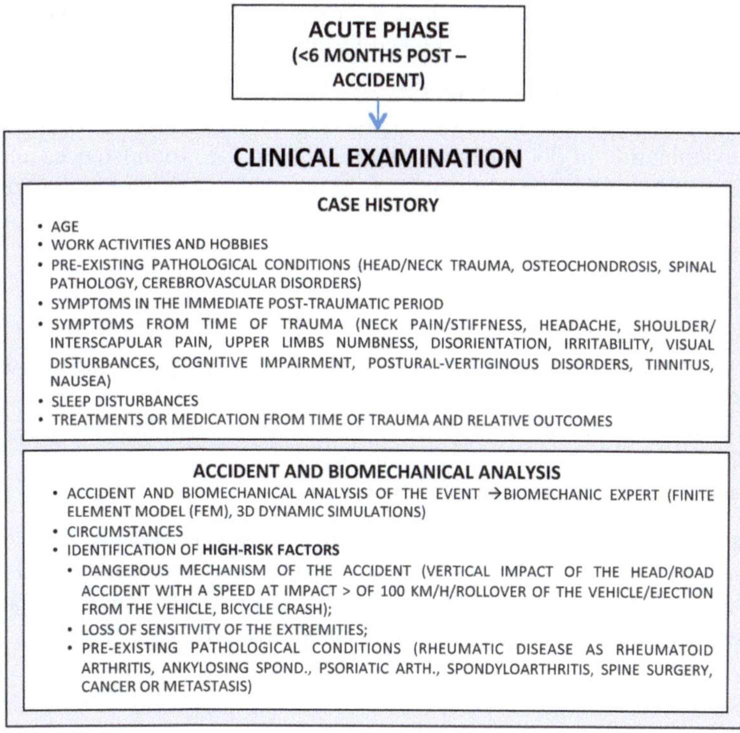

Fig. 32.1 Medical ascertainment in the acute phase. Clinical examination, including case history, accident, and biomechanical analyses

- *Age* of the patient at the time of the accident.
- *Work activities* performed by the patient before the accident and at the time of the medical ascertainment.
- Any *hobbies*.
- Possible *preexisting diseases*, such as previous cerebral and/or cervical trauma, osteochondrosis, spinal disease, and/or cerebrovascular disease.
- *Symptomatology* reported by the patient in the *immediate posttraumatic period*.
- *Symptomatology* arising in the period between the *time of the trauma* to the *time of the ascertainment*, with particular attention to the symptoms, such as pain (using the visual analogue scale) and/or cervical stiffness, headache, pain in the shoulders and in the interscapular area, disorientation, irritability, visual disturbances, cognitive impairments, postural impairments, dizziness, tinnitus, nausea, dorsal and/or lumbar pain, paresthesia, dysesthesia and a tingling sensation in the upper arms, swallowing impairments, and disturbances at the level of the temporo-mandibular joint [12].
- Any *sleep disturbances*.
- Any *pharmacological treatment* taken from the time of the trauma to the time of the ascertainment and the related results.

- Any *physio-rehabilitative treatments* from the time of the trauma to the time of the ascertainment and the related results.

– *Accident and Biomechanical Analysis*

The Medical Expert will then have to proceed, through dialogue with the patient and the examination of documentary data relating to the circumstances and to the mechanism of injury [13] (e.g., records of the accident investigation drafted by the Police, complaint forms relating to the accident, etc.), to the acquisition of all the information related to the traumatic event, as listed below.

- *Date and place* of the event.
- *Type of vehicles* involved.
- *Role of the patient* (e.g., driver, front or back passenger, cyclist, pedestrian, etc.).
- Presence of correctly used *protection safeguards* (belt, helmet).
- *Material damages to the vehicles* involved.
- Description of the *dynamics of the accident.*

The acquisition of such data is essential for the *biomechanical reconstruction of the traumatic event* (with the help of an *Expert in Biomechanics*) and for the identification of possible *high-risk factors* of damage to the cervical anatomical structures, described in detail in the following paragraph.

32.4.1.2 Identification of High-Risk Factors

Included among *high-risk factors* [14–16] are:

– The traumatic mechanisms with high potential for harm, such as vertical blows at the level of the head, road accidents with an impact speed of over 100 km/h, rollovers of vehicles, and/or ejection of the victim outside of the passenger compartment;
– Loss of sensitivity of the extremities;
– The presence of preexisting pathologies, particularly rheumatic diseases (e.g., rheumatoid arthritis, ankylosing spondylitis, psoriatic arthritis, seronegative spondyloarthritis, etc.), previous spinal surgeries, and neoplastic diseases with or without metastases.

The identification of *at least one high-risk* factor entails a specialized clinical ascertainment or a specialized clinical re-ascertainment (Fig. 32.2).

According to the guidelines of the American College of Radiology [10], the presence *of at least one high-risk factor* [14] among those described above, in patients older than 14 years, entails the performance of instrumental tests, such as Computerized Axial Tomography (CT) of the cervical area [17].

In the absence of high-risk factors, the clinico-medico-legal ascertainment can be performed, evaluating the ability to actively rotate the head bilaterally by 45 degrees. If an inclinometer is available, such a manual ascertainment may be

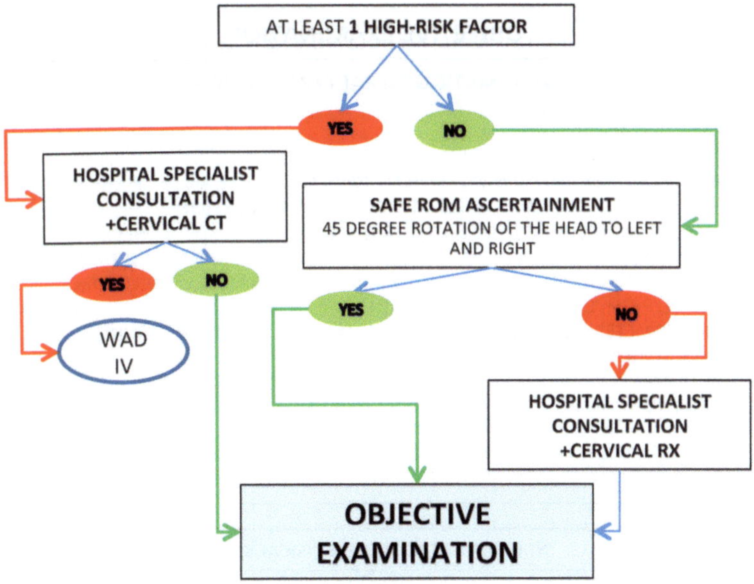

Fig. 32.2 Medical ascertainment in the acute phase. Identification of high-risk factors and description of the clinical pathway

replaced by an instrumental ascertainment (using the inclinometer), which must be regarded as positive if reduced by more than 40 %.

In cases where the patient is not able to actively rotate the head bilaterally by 45 degrees, or presents a mobility reduction of ≥40 %, he will have to undergo a specialized clinical ascertainment of the cervical area, with possible instrumental investigation [18].

32.4.1.3 Objective Examination

The *Objective Examination* (Fig. 32.3) consists of a comprehensive visit, including general, neurological, osteo-articular, and musculoskeletal examinations and evaluation of the possible presence of injuries to each of the individual parts of the body (head, neck, chest, back, pelvis, upper and lower limbs), specifying for each injury where it is located, the type of injury, and its morphometric characteristics.

Subsequently, the Expert must focus on the injured area/areas performing a local osteo-articular and neurologic examination, including inspection, palpation, and ascertainment of mobility, sensitivity, and strength of the areas described below, using a problem-oriented Medicolegal semeiotics (Fig. 32.3).

During the *inspection*, the physician must, in particular, observe the patient's posture, with attention to the position of the head and neck.

The *palpation*, performed using digital pressure, must be performed in order to evaluate the presence of any algic reactions at the level of the spinous and

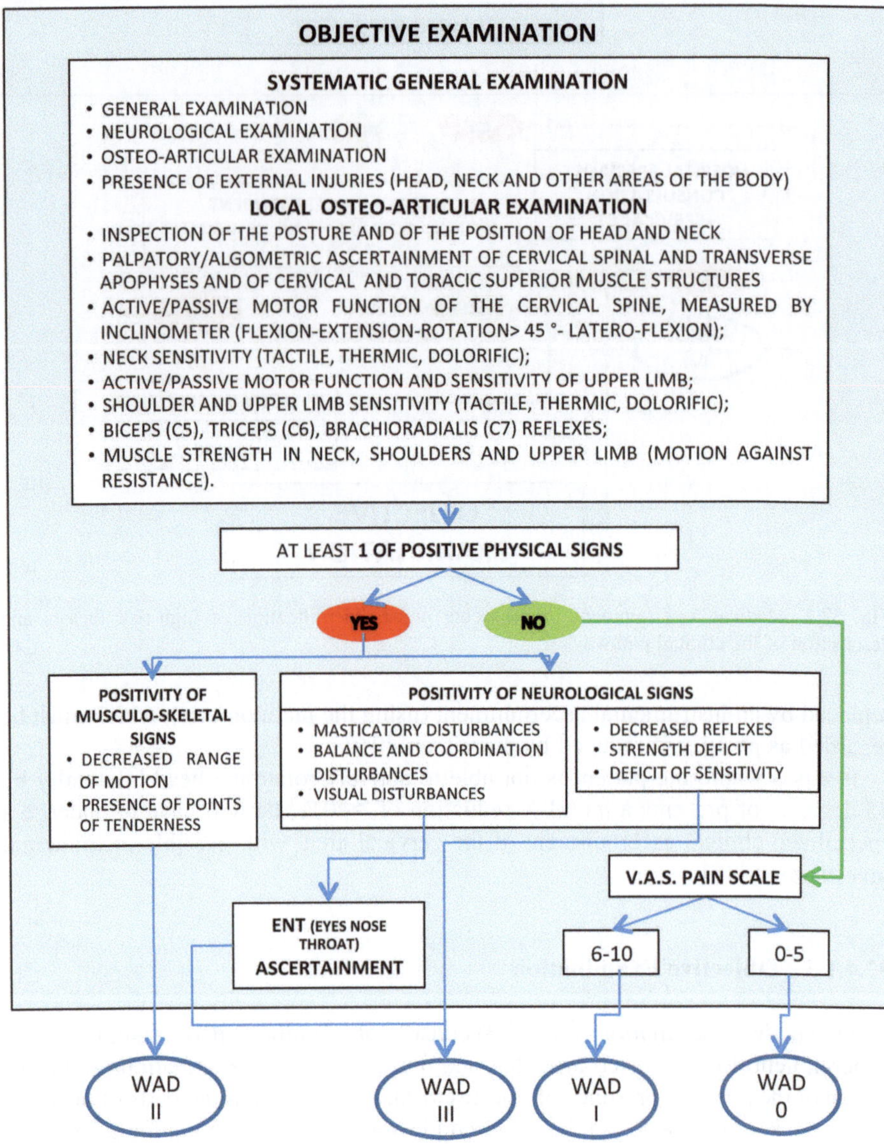

Fig. 32.3 Medical ascertainment in the acute phase. Objective examination

transverse processes of the cervical and dorsal rachis and at the level of the cervical muscular structures, the trapezius muscles and chest muscles. The present Guidelines recommend the routine utilization of quantitative "scales" for the objective recording of pain.

At the level of these algic areas, it is also appropriate to perform an instrumental evaluation with an algometer using the Visual Analogue Scale (VAS) to define pain, construing the algometric ascertainment as positive only at values above 5. The use of this scale also allows for comparison with subsequent algometric ascertainment.

Subsequently, the following must be carried out:

- Complete examination of *active and passive motor function of the cervical spine*, possibly using an inclinometer, of the flexion and extension movements of the head and neck with simultaneous rotation and lateral-flexion;
- Examination of *tactile, thermal, and pain sensitivity* in the neck;
- Examination of *active and passive motor function* and *tactile, thermal, and pain sensitivity* in the neck, shoulders, and upper limbs;
- Examination of the bicipital (C5), tricipital (C6), and stiloradial (C7) *bone tendon reflexes;*
- Examination of *muscle strength* in the *muscles of the neck, shoulders, and upper limbs* by ascertainment of the movements against resistance.

In the event that the examination is negative, one proceeds only to the evaluation of pain according to the VAS and the classification of the injury according to the score obtained.

In particular, in the case of a score between 0 and 5, the injury is classified as a *Whiplash-Associated Disorder (WAD) of degree 0* (absence of symptoms of the neck), while in case of a VAS score between 6 and 10, the injury is classified as a *WAD grade I* (neck pain), as indicated by the Quebec Task Force 1995 (QTF).

In the event that the *objective musculoskeletal loco-regional examination* detects the presence of positive signs and symptoms, such as *decreased range of cervical motion* or the presence of *points of tenderness*, the injury is classified as *WAD Grade II*.

In the event that, during the *objective neurological examination*, there is evidence of reduced reflexes and/or the presence of loss of strength or sensitivity, the injury is classified as *WAD grade III*. In the examination of objective neurological disorders, even *chewing, swallowing, balance, and/or coordination impairments, including visual disturbances,* can be detected, which must be evaluated with particular attention and confirmed through the performance of specialist ascertainment (Eye Nose Throat—E.N.T. Ascertainment) with any further instrumental details indicated by the specialist. The discovery of the above disorders involves the classification of the injury as *WAD grade III*.

Evidence of fractures/dislocations from the cervical CT entails the classification of the injury as *WAD grade IV* according to the Quebec Task Force Classification 1995 (QTF) [1].

For *WAD grade 0, where no treatment is necessary*, the Expert will have to reexamine the patient once stabilization has occurred (6 months).

For *WAD Grade I–III* the Expert must send the patient back to the attending physician for any prescription of drug treatments and/or physical therapy, advising the maintenance of an active lifestyle and indicating the performance of a *subsequent Medicolegal ascertainment* in the event of persistence and chronicity of symptoms or, in any case, *once Maximum Medical Improvement* has been reached (i.e., healing or stabilization to a permanent sequela/e).

32.4.2 *Chronic Phase*

The ascertainment in the chronic phase must be performed on patients over 14 years of age who undergo the ascertainment for the first time after six months from the trauma and in patients who, despite drug and rehabilitation therapy prescribed during the acute phase, continue to complain about the persistence of symptoms *once* the achievement of *Maximal Medical Improvement has been reached* (i.e., healing or stabilization to a permanent sequela/e).

In the event that the clinical situation is still evolving (i.e., ongoing disease), it is necessary to postpone the ascertainment until healing or stabilization occurs.

32.4.2.1 Collection of Circumstantial, Clinical, and Instrumental Data

In the event that a previous ascertainment has already been carried out in the acute phase, the first operation which the Expert must perform is the collection of all circumstantial, clinical-documental (certificates of rehabilitation therapies performed, specifying the type of treatment carried out and the duration, medical expenses incurred, and any medicolegal reports), and instrumental available data (reports of specialist visits and instrumental tests with relevant radiographs), retrieving all medical and healthcare information believed to be useful for a diagnostic framework and for later identification of the clinicopathological features, injuries, impairments, and other damages (Fig. 32.4). If, instead, it involves a first ascertainment, the Expert will proceed directly to the systematic clinical examination (Fig. 32.4).

32.4.2.2 Systematic Clinical Examination

– *Case History*

The Expert must carry out the complete and detailed collection of all clinical data and documents available to the examinee, related to the trauma and traumatic mechanism, as well as the familial, physiological, work, remote (e.g., preexisting pathologies, such as any previous traumatic brain and/or neck trauma, osteochondrosis, spinal diseases, and cerebrovascular diseases), and recent case history of the subject examined [19].

In particular, an in-depth investigation must be made of the circumstances of the trauma (with identification of any high- and low-risk factors), the symptoms arising immediately after the trauma, and those arising at a distance as well as, more recently, specifying the periods of cervical collar immobilization, drug therapies, and/or rehabilitation services performed.

– *Psychophysical examination*

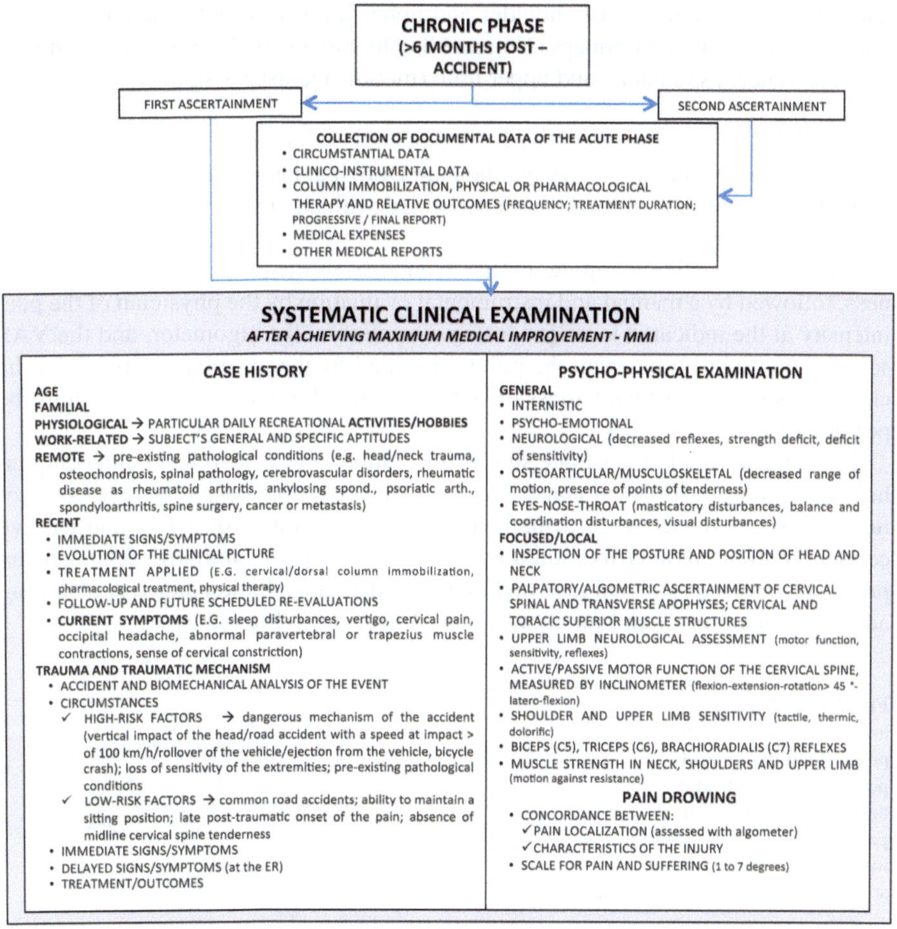

Fig. 32.4 Medical ascertainment in the chronic phase. Data collection and systematic clinical examination, including case history, psychophysical examination, and pain drawing

The psychophysical examination consists of a comprehensive Medicolegal visit, including internistic, psycho-emotional, neurological, osteo-articular, musculo-skeletal, and eyes–nose–throat examinations, paying attention to any decreased reflexes, strength deficit, deficit of sensitivity, decreased range of motion, presence of points of tenderness, masticatory disturbances, balance and coordination disturbances, and visual disturbances.

After the aforementioned systematic clinical examination, the Expert must focus on the injured area/areas performing an analytical local examination using a problem-oriented Medico-legal semeiotics, including inspection of the posture and position of the head and neck, palpatory/algometric ascertainment of cervical spinal and transverse apophyses, cervical and thoracic superior muscle structures, upper limb neurological ascertainment (motor function, sensitivity, reflexes), active/passive motor function of the cervical spine measured by inclinometer (flexion-extension-rotation;

latero-flexion), evaluation of shoulder and upper limb sensitivity (tactile, thermic, dolorific) of biceps (C5), triceps (C6), and brachioradialis (C7) reflexes, and muscle strength in neck, shoulders, and upper limb (motion against resistance).

– *Pain Drawing*

The Expert must finally carry out the Pain Drawing, namely the ascertainment of correlation between pain localization (assessed with an algometer) and the characteristics of the injury.

This is a subjective mapping, by the examinee, of the points of greatest tenderness, followed by a manual and instrumental evaluation by the physician of the pain intensity at the indicated locations, using acupressure, the algometer, and the VAS scale. A comparison between the points specified by the examined person and the characteristics areas of tenderness in WAD (i.e., myofascial trigger points) must be performed.

In the presence of at least one significant symptom (e.g., cervical pain, occipital headache, sense of cervical constriction) or sign (e.g., paraspinal muscle contractures, trapezius muscle contractures, alteration in the range of active and passive cervical motion possibly measured by inclinometer), the examining physician can proceed to any instrumental tests and/or any Expert consultation aimed at obtaining additional anatomical and functional data, if necessary (Fig. 32.5).

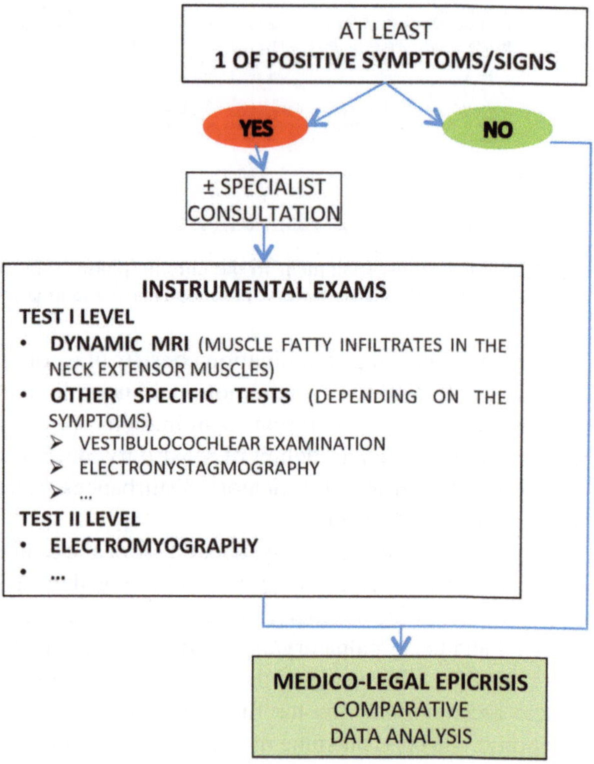

Fig. 32.5 Medical ascertainment in the chronic phase. Identification of positive symptoms and description of the clinical pathway, including instrumental exams and/or specialist consultations

32.4.2.3 Instrumental Exams and/or Specialist Consultation

In the case that further anatomo-functional data are needed, the Expert can involve a Specialist and advise the performance of instrumental exams, which can be divided into two categories (First and Second level) and can be prescribed directly by the Expert or by the Specialist (Fig. 32.5).

First-Level Exams

Non-invasive exams, not based on the use of ionizing radiation, are categorized as first level.

- *Magnetic Resonance Imaging* (MRI) to be performed in order to highlight the presence of fatty infiltration [20, 21] at the level of the extensor muscles of the neck. MRI can also detect any disk abnormalities, fractures, ligament damage or bone marrow injury.
- Other instrumental tests, such as *cochleovestibular examination*, *electro-nystagmography*, and *angio-magnetic resonance*, indicated on the basis of a clinical suspect.

Second-Level Exams

Exams based on the use of ionizing radiation and other invasive exams, such as the *Electromiography (EMG)*, to be performed in order to confirm the clinical suspicion of radiculopathy, loss of sensitivity, weakness/lack of muscle strength, and inability to elicit biceps, triceps, and stiloradial deep tendon reflexes.

In both cases (first- and second-level exams), the interpretation of the results can be performed by the Expert only if he/she has proven experience and expertise in that specific field.

32.4.2.4 Medicolegal Epicrisis

At this point, the Expert must collect all the available data and perform a comparative analysis aimed at assessing the preexisting health status, reconstructing the damaging event with the help of a Biomechanical Expert, and identifying the clinicopathological diagnosis and the corresponding Medicolegal diagnosis in terms of temporary/permanent impairment or other damages (e.g., pain and suffering, etc.), for the detailed illustration of which see the General Guidelines on the subject of Personal Injury and Damage.

Acknowledgments The authors are grateful to Drs. Francesco Pravato and Sarah Nalin for their comments.

References

1. Spitzer WO, Skovron ML, Saqlmi LR et al (1995) Scientific Monograph of the Quebec Task Force on whiplash Associated Disorders: redefining "whiplash" and its management. Spine 20(8 Suppl):1S–73S
2. Bono G, Antonaci F, Ghirmai S et al (2000) Whiplash injuries: clinical picture and diagnostic work-up. Clin Exp Rheumatol 18(2 Suppl 19):S23–8
3. Represas C, Vieira DN, Magalhães T, Dias R, Frazão S, Suárez-Peñaranda JM, Rodríguez-Calvo MS, Concheiro L, Muñoz JI (2008) No cash no whiplash?: Influence of the legal system on the incidence of whiplash injury. J Forensic Leg Med 15(6):353–5
4. Worsfold C (2014) When range of motion is not enough: towards an evidence-based approach to medico-legal reporting in whiplash injury. J Forensic Leg Med 25:95–9
5. Jansen GB, Edlund C, Grane P, Hildingsson C, Karlberg M, Link H, Måwe U, Portala K, Rydevik B, Sterner Y (2008) Whiplash injuries: diagnosis and early management. The Swedish Society of Medicine and the Whiplash Commission Medical Task Force. Eur Spine J 17(Suppl 3):S355–417
6. Chappuis G, Soltermann B (2008) Number and cost of claims linked to minor cervical trauma in Europe: results from the comparative study by CEA. AREDOC and CEREDOC. Eur Spine J 17(10):1350–7
7. Castro W, Lemcke H, Schilgen M, Lemcke L (1998) So-called "whiplash trauma" legal and medical considerations. Chirurg 69:176–184
8. Cassidy JD, Carroll L, Côté P, Lemstra M, Berglund A, Nygren A (2000) Effects of eliminating pain and suffering on the incidence and prognosis of whiplash claims. N Engl J Med 342:1179–1186
9. Rondinelli RD (2006) The spine and pelvis. In: Guides to the evaluation of permanent impairment, 6th edn. American Medical Association, pp 557–593
10. Daffner RH et al.—Expert Panels on Musculoskeletal and Neurologic Imaging (2012) ACR Appropriateness Criteria® suspected spine trauma. American College of Radiology (ACR)
11. TRACsa: Trauma and Injury Recovery (2008) Clinical guidelines for best practice management of acute and chronic whiplash-associated disorders. TRACsa, Adelaide
12. Häggman-Henrikson B, List T, Westergren HT, Axelsson SH (2013) Temporomandibular disorder pain after whiplash trauma: a systematic review. J Orofac Pain 27(3):217–26
13. American Medical Association (2007) Cervical whiplash: assessment, treatment and impairment. The Guides Newsletter
14. Stiell IG et al (2001) The Canadian C-Spine Rule for radiography in alert and stable trauma patients. JAMA 286(15):1841–1848
15. Bussières AE, Taylor JA, Peterson C (2007) Diagnostic imaging practice guidelines for musculoskeletal complaints in adults-an evidence-based approach-part 3: spinal disorders. J Manipulative Physiol Ther 31(1):33–88
16. Griffith B, Bolton C, Goyal N, Brown ML, Jain R (2011) Screening cervical spine CT in a Level I Trauma Center: overutilization? Am J Roentgenol 197(2):463–487
17. Bailitz J et al (2009) CT should replace three-view radiographs as the initial screening test in patients at high, moderate, and low risk for blunt cervical spine injury: a prospective comparison. J Trauma 66(6):1605–1609
18. Nordin M et al (2008) Assessment of neck pain and its associated disorders: Results of the bone and joint decade 2000–2010 Task Force on Neck Pain and Its Associated Disorders. Eur Spine J 17(Suppl 1):101–122

19. Kerry R (2011) Examination of the upper cervical region. In: Petty JN (ed) Neuromusculoskeletal examination and assessment, 4th edn. Elsevier, Churchill Livingstone
20. Elliott J (2011) The evidence for pathoanatomical lesions. In: Sterling M, Kenardy J (eds) Whiplash: evidence base for clinical practice, 1st edn. Churchill Livingstone Elsevier, Australia, pp 29–40
21. Elliott JM, Pedler AR, Jull GA, Van Wyk L, Galloway GG, O'Leary SP (2014) Differential changes in muscle composition exist in traumatic and nontraumatic neck pain. Spine (Phila Pa 1976) 39(1):39–47

Part VIII
Final Statements

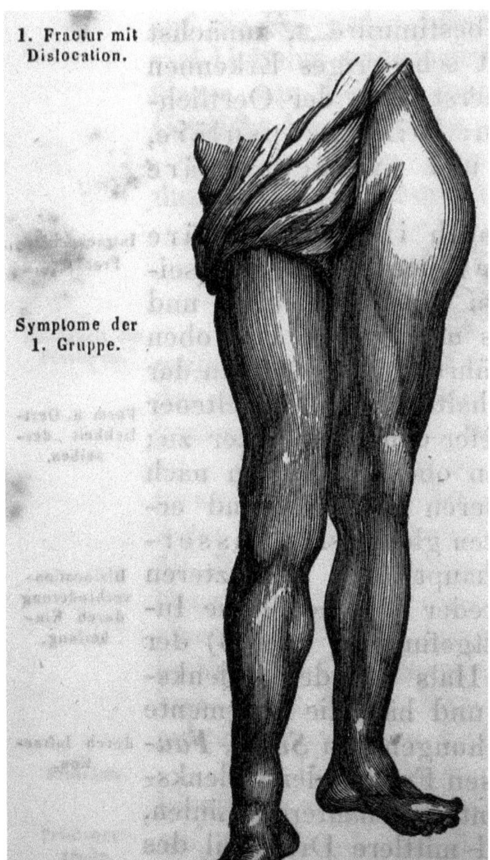

Lehrbuch der Fracturen, Luxationen und Bandagen / von dr. Ravoth. Berlin: A. von Hirschwald, 1856. Courtesy of historical section of the "Vincenzo Pinali" Medical Library of the University of Padova

Chapter 33
Requirements and Final Recommendations

Santo Davide Ferrara, Rafael Boscolo-Berto, and Guido Viel

Abstract This chapter sets out in summarized form the requirements and the final recommendations regarding the ascertainment and evaluation of personal injury and damage under civil-tort law following the methodology described in detail in Chaps. 30, 31, and 32.

The recommendations, which are listed in numerical order, pertain to the cultural background and minimum level of expertise and competence that the ascertaining clinical and/or medicolegal expert and his/her co-advisors must possess and the logical and procedural steps indispensable for the ascertainment and evaluation of any impairment, disability, and/or pecuniary/nonpecuniary losses causally related to a personal injury.

33.1 Recommendation 1 - Essential Expertise and Competence of the Ascertaining Expert

Currently, there is a lack of consensus on a universal definition and/or qualification of specialist in legal medicine or personal injury and damage evaluator, leading to a lack of an international recognition of such authority.

Therefore, it is recommended that the clinical and/or medicolegal expert who deals with cases of personal injury and damage ascertainment and evaluation demonstrates the essential knowledge set out below:

(a) Notions of tort/civil and administrative laws regarding personal injury and damage, with particular reference to the regulations in the healthcare and insurance sectors.

S.D. Ferrara (✉) • R. Boscolo-Berto • G. Viel
Department of Legal and Occupational Medicine, Toxicology and Public Health, University-Hospital of Padova, Via Falloppio 50, 35128 Padova, Italy
e-mail: santodavide.ferrara@unipd.it; rafael.boscoloberto@unipd.it; guido.viel@unipd.it

S.D. Ferrara et al. (eds.), *Personal Injury and Damage Ascertainment under Civil Law*, DOI 10.1007/978-3-319-29812-2_33

(b) Theoretical and practical notions of clinical and medicolegal semeiotics devoted to the assessment of psychophysical validity in relation to tort/civil and insurance laws.
(c) Theoretical notions on the subject of material causality, ascertainment methodology, and criteria for the identification of the causal value/link between the event and the injury and between this latter and the temporary/permanent impairment.

33.2 Recommendation 2 - Essential Knowledge of the Consultant

The clinician, surgeon, radiologist, biomechanical engineer, or any other consultant who assists the ascertaining expert in cases of personal injury and damage should possess the title of specialist in their particular field of study, obtained at the university level.

He/she is required to demonstrate theoretical and practical competence in the specialist subdiscipline, which is the object of the case under examination.

33.3 Recommendation 3 - Collection of Circumstantial, Clinico-Documental-Instrumental Data

It is recommended that the ascertaining expert collects the circumstantial, clinico-documental, and instrumental data related to the case, retrieving all information believed to be useful for a diagnostic framework, for the reconstruction of the injuring event, and for the identification of the clinicopathological features, injuries, impairments, and disabilities.

All documentary data relating to the circumstances and the mechanism of injury (e.g., records drafted by the police, complaint forms relating to the event, etc.) should be acquired.

In cases of traumatic events, adjunctive documentary data describing the type and characteristics of the involved means, the role of the injured person, the presence of correctly used protection safeguards (belt, helmet), and the material damages to the involved means, and the report on the dynamics of the accident should be collected.

The clinical documents of prime importance to be collected and examined are described in detail in the Guidelines, Chaps. 31–32. In cases of hospitalization, they should include the anamnesis and physical examination, medical order sheet, emergency room assistance sheet or emergency room report, inter-consultation sheet, reports of complementary examinations, presurgery examination sheet, operating room report, postsurgery evolution sheet, nursing journal, and clinical discharge report. In case of outpatient care, without hospital admission or after hospital discharge, they should include all clinical evaluations where a subject has undergone an outpatient procedure, any instrumental examinations, medical certificates, and/or prescribed therapies.

In any case, any rehabilitation documents produced during the clinical evolution of the injury and the healing/stabilization process must be collected and examined. These documents will be explanations/summaries of the type of exercise and/or treatment scheduled, execution times and/or application, and their frequency on a daily/weekly/monthly basis, encompassing the total duration of the treatment and the progressive and final reports produced in relation to it.

33.4 Recommendation 4 - Systematic Clinical Examination for Any Personal Injury/Damage

It is recommended that the clinical examination involves collection of the anamnesis and a careful psychophysical examination, including internistic, osteoarticular, musculoskeletal, neurological, psychic, and local examinations.

After identifying the examined person collecting his/her name, surname, date of birth, marital status, address, telephone, e-mail, information regarding his/her education, and any eventual personal insurance cover, the examiner investigates the date and place of the event, the type of means involved, and the dynamics of the event.

The anamnesis should include the *family medical history*, recording any health information of the relatives of the examined person (up to the third generation); the *physiological medical history*, recording information on psychomotor development, lifestyle, sexual habits, allergies, diuresis, defecation, the sleep schedule, and remote diseases, with a comprehensive list of previous sicknesses, operations, traumatic accidents, and prostheses and/or ortheses; *recent disease history*, with a focus on the immediate signs/symptoms after the event, the evolution of the clinical picture, the treatments applied, the follow-up pathways and any future scheduled reevaluations, and a detailed account of current problems, complaints, and symptoms; *work-related and social life aspects*, detailing general/specific working aptitudes, education, previous (listed in chronological order) and current occupation, and daily recreational activities, such as hobbies and domestic, sport, and leisure activities.

The *psychophysical examination* should be performed in a consulting room equipped with a dressing room, bathroom, and medical bed and provided with measurement instruments and provoking tests (e.g., goniometer, inclinometer, ruler, sphygmomanometer, sterile needles, stethoscope, etc.). The psychophysical examination consists of a comprehensive clinical and medicolegal visit, including internistic, osteoarticular-musculoskeletal, neurological, psychic, and local examination of the injured/damaged area/s.

Any visible injuries or sequelae will be photographed (overview picture followed by a detailed picture with scale) and analytically described with regard to their localization (using landmarks), mutual distribution, and morphometric characteristics. Inspection will be followed by palpation, percussion, and auscultation where applicable. The local examination must identify any impairment of the articular, muscular, and/or neurological function differentiating true disorders from malingering and/or simulation.

It is recommended to use widespread quantitative scales, previously validated and published in peer-reviewed journals, for the objective identification and quantification of suspected impairments, such as pain, esthetic prejudice, and loss of independence.

33.5 Recommendation 5 - Systematic Clinical Examination for Psychic-Existential Damage

In cases of suspected psychic-existential damage, the ascertaining expert should collect all documentary and anamnestic data useful for the definition of the *preexisting* and *current* "*social-psycho-somatic state*," including all *somatic*, *cognitive* (perceptual, expressive, attentional, executive, memory, comprehension, and orientational functions), *personological* (personality traits/disturbances, psychiatric disturbances/pathologies), and *socio-relational* data.

Apart from the data set out in Recommendation 4, it is recommended that the *medical history* comprises also work-related, emotional, sexual, cultural, social, and recreational aspects of life. The *clinical examination* should collect *objective data* on appearance and personal care, vigilance and awareness, behavior, collaboration, psychomotor activity, posture, facial expressions and gestures, mood and affectivity, language, perception, content of thought, orientation and memory, concentration and attention, reading and writing abilities, control of impulses, capacity of judgment and insight, awareness of disease, visual and spatial capacity, and praxic and executive capacity. The verification of the "veracity" of the findings derived from the systematic clinical objective examination can be performed through targeted instrumental examinations and neuropsychological tests.

In cases of suspected malingering, the expert should refer to Recommendation 7.

33.6 Recommendation 6 - Systematic Clinical Examination for Whiplash-Associated Disorders

It is recommended that in cases of suspected whiplash injury, the *anamnesis* includes information on preexisting diseases (e.g., cerebral and/or cervical trauma, osteochondrosis, spinal or cerebrovascular diseases), immediate post-traumatic symptoms, and symptomatology between the time of the trauma and the time of the ascertainment. Particular attention should be paid to cervical stiffness and pain (registered using the visual analogue scale), headache, pain in the shoulders and interscapular area, disorientation, irritability, visual disturbances, cognitive impairments, postural impairments, dizziness, tinnitus, nausea, dorsal and/or lumbar pain, paraesthesia, dysesthesia and a tingling sensation in the upper arms, swallowing impairments and disturbances at the level of the temporomandibular joint, and any sleep disturbances. Information on the periods of cervical collar immobilization, drug therapies, and/or rehabilitation services must be collected.

The psychophysical examination should include a comprehensive medicolegal visit, with internistic, psycho-emotional, neurological, osteoarticular, musculoskeletal, and eyes-nose-throat examinations, paying attention to any decreased reflexes, strength deficit, deficit of sensitivity, decreased range of motion, presence of points of tenderness, masticatory disturbances, balance and coordination disturbances, and visual disturbances.

The local examination should include the inspection of the posture and position of the head and neck, palpatory/algometric ascertainment of cervical spinal and transverse apophyses, cervical and thoracic superior muscle structures, upper limb neurological ascertainment (motor function, sensitivity, reflexes), active/passive motor function of the cervical spine measured by inclinometer (flexion-extension-rotation, latero-flexion), and evaluation of the shoulder and upper limb sensitivity (tactile, thermic, dolorific) of biceps (C5), triceps (C6), brachioradialis (C7) reflexes, and muscle strength in the neck, shoulders, and upper limb (motion against resistance).

33.7 Recommendation 7 - Neuropsychological Tests for Detecting Malingering

The detection of simulating and/or dissimulating behaviors consisting of the intentional exhibition of false or exaggerated symptoms motivated by external incentives is one of the most difficult challenges encountered by the clinical or forensic expert during the ascertainment of personal injury and damage.

It is recommended, therefore, that in case of suspected simulation/dissimulation, the ascertaining expert utilizes multiple sources of independent data, integrating the clinical interview and systematic objective examination with tests and tools specifically devoted to the detection of malingering. The most important instruments to be used are the *discrepancy method* (i.e., analyzing the consistency between the exhibited symptoms and the syndrome), the *symptom validity testing*, the *floor effect strategy*, the *structured inventory of malingered symptomatology* (SIMS), the *test of memory malingering* (TOMM), and the *aIAT*, a novel variant of the *implicit association test*, which evaluates the trueness of a referred autobiographical event.

33.8 Recommendation 8 - Instrumental Exams and/or Specialist Consultation

In the case that after the systematic clinical examination further anatomo-functional data are needed, a specialist can be consulted or instrumental exams can be prescribed. Instrumental exams of first and second level can be prescribed directly by the ascertaining expert or by the consulted specialist.

First level exams are ultrasound, magnetic resonance imaging (MRI), electrocardiography, electroencephalography, and any other investigations, which are not harmful for the examinee.

Any exams based on the use of ionizing radiation or those which could pose a risk for the examinee belong to the second level (e.g., computed tomography, positron emission tomography, electromyography, endoscopy, etc.).

For whiplash-associated disorders, first level examinations are MRI for highlighting fatty infiltration at the level of the extensor muscles of the neck, cochleovestibular examination, and electronystagmography. Second level examinations are electromyography (EMG) to confirm a clinical suspicion of radiculopathy, loss of sensitivity, or lack of muscle strength and any exams based on the use of ionizing radiation or those who could pose a risk for the examinee.

The interpretation of the instrumental results can be performed by the ascertaining physician with sufficient experience and/or expertise in that specific field or by the consulted specialist.

33.9 Recommendation 9 - Verification of Stabilization

It is recommended that the evaluation process starts only if the injury/disease has reached its maximal medical improvement, which means that healing or stabilization to a permanent sequela/e occurred.

In the event that the clinical situation is still evolving (i.e., ongoing disease), it is necessary to postpone the ascertainment until healing or stabilization occurs.

33.10 Recommendation 10 - Clinical and Medicolegal Epicrisis

It is recommended that the comparative analysis of all the collected data aims at assessing the preexisting health status (a), reconstructing the damaging event (b), identifying the clinicopathological diagnosis (c), and the corresponding medicolegal diagnosis (d), in terms of temporary/permanent impairment or other damages (e.g., sexual dysfunction, esthetic prejudice, decrease of the quality of life, etc.).

(a) *Preexisting health status*. The reconstruction of the preexisting health status is fundamental in order to detect any changes that occurred as a result of the damaging event and for evaluating any differential damages attributable to the event itself, according to the principle of personalization of the ascertainment.
(b) *Reconstruction of the damaging event*. Based on the available circumstantial data, the recorded medical history, and the clinical objective data, the dynamics of the damaging event and the mechanism of injury must be reconstructed. For that purpose, if the event is characterized by an impact, a biomechanical expert could be consulted, in order to analyze all the available information regarding the scenario before and after the questioned event and elaborating a finite element model (FEM) taking into account the main aspects of interest (i.e., velocity, trajectory, energy, etc.).
(c) *Identification of the clinicopathological features*. The clinicopathological features of the injury/disorder must be reconstructed in order to reach a clinical diagnosis of the initial, intermediate, and final stages. A thorough analysis and clear description of the physiopathological pathways, which connect the diverse evolutive phases of the injury/disease, must be performed. The physiopathological features and pathways are examined on the basis of scientific sources, such as guidelines, consensus documents, operational procedures, evidence-based publications (Cochrane reviews, meta-analysis, etc.), and other literature sources composed of treatises and articles published in peer-reviewed journals (PubMed-Medline, Embase, Scopus, Ovid, ISI Web of Science, etc.), preferably with impact factor.
(d) *Identification of injury, temporary, and permanent impairment*. After examining the scientific sources and reconstructing the physiopathological processes linking the identified clinicopathological features, the following have to be determined:

  - Injury and temporary impairment related to the initial clinicopathological features.
  - Temporary impairment related to the intermediate clinicopathological features.
  - Permanent impairment related to the final/stabilized clinicopathological features.

Moreover, the presence of any other types of impairments with clinical and medicolegal relevance, such as sexual sphere modifications, esthetic prejudice, alteration of daily activities, relational and social life, must be identified.

33.11 Recommendation 11 - Impairment and Disability Characterization

It is recommended that an analytical characterization of the temporary/permanent impairments, the disability and any other pecuniary or nonpecuniary losses of medicolegal relevance, be performed. Pecuniary losses may be classified under two different headings, the first concerning the additional expenses incurred as a result of the damaging event ("damnum emergens") and the second concerning the loss of earnings and other benefits the injured person would have received but for the damaging event ("lucrum cessans"). Nonpecuniary losses comprise any esthetic prejudice, sexual dysfunction, and/or temporary/permanent functional impairment, with their impact and repercussion on the leisure and social activities.

The objective analytical characterization of the impairments and their repercussion on the work-capacity and leisure activities furnished by the ascertaining expert will be utilized by the judge for better estimating the pecuniary and nonpecuniary losses causally related to the damaging event.

33.12 Recommendation 12 - Evaluation of the Causal Value and Link

It is recommended that the causal value/link between the event and the injury and between that injury and the temporary/permanent impairment be verified. This verification must be based on "criteria of scientific probability," such as (a) universal laws, by means of deduction; (b) statistical laws, by means of inference, or, in the absence of such laws, according to (c) the criterion of rational credibility. If this is not possible, due to the absence of "explanatory laws," the ascertainment must be interrupted. The standard of proof required in tort/civil cases varies according to the national laws, but is generally based on the rule of "more probable, than not" (i.e., enough evidence does exist to make the scientific explanation more likely than not that the fact the claimant seeks to prove is true). It is recommended, however, due to the identical nature of the medicolegal reasoning in criminal and civil court cases (i.e., the demonstration of the *condition sine qua non*) that the ascertaining expert adopts the same evaluation criteria, meaning the search for evidence as an affirmation of "evidence-based medicine." Moreover, the identification of the degree of probability of the causal link should always be performed and expressed as an estimated percentage of probability.

Part IX
Iconography

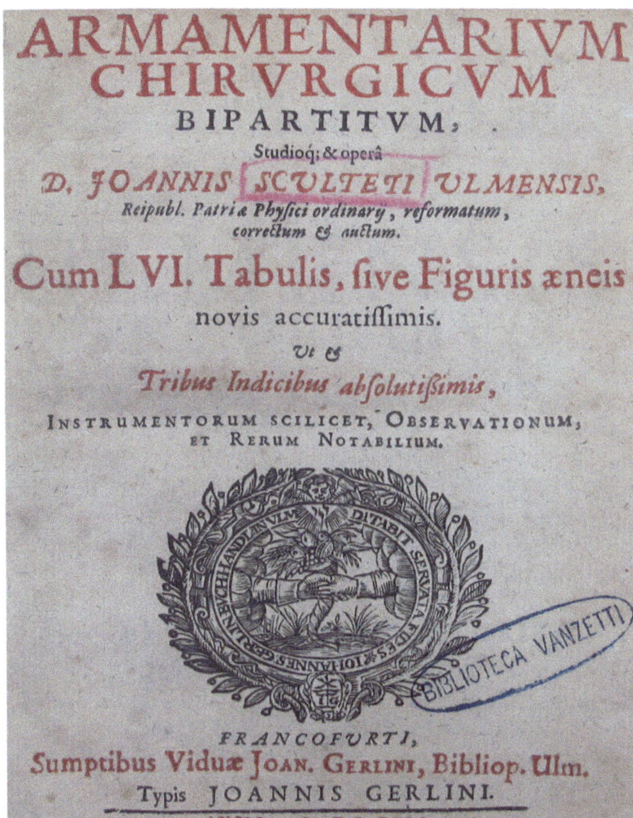
ARMAMENTARIVM
CHIRVRGICVM
BIPARTITVM,
Studioq; & operâ
D. JOANNIS SCULTETI ULMENSIS,
Reipubl. Patriæ Physici ordinarÿ, reformatum,
correctum & auctum.
Cum LVI. Tabulis, ſive Figuris æneis
novis accuratiſſimis.
Ut &
Tribus Indicibus abſolutiſſimis,
INSTRUMENTORUM SCILICET, OBSERVATIONUM,
ET RERUM NOTABILIUM.

FRANCOFURTI,
Sumptibus Viduæ JOAN. GERLINI, Bibliop. Ulm.
Typis JOANNIS GERLINI.
ANNO M DC LXVI.

Schultes, Johann 1595–1645 (Scultetus). Armamentarium chirurgicum bipartitum, studioque & opera D. Joannis Sculteti Ulmensis … reformatum, correctum & auctum. Cum 56 tabulis, sive figuris aeneis novis accuratissimis. Ut & tribus indicibus absolutissimis, instrumentorum scilicet, obseruationum, et rerum notabilium Francofurti: sumptibus viduae Joan. Gerlini, Bibliop. Ulm. typis Joannis Gerlini, 1666. Courtesy of historical section of the "Vincenzo Pinali" Medical Library of the University of Padova

Chapter 34
Historical Iconography on Personal Injury and Damage from the "Vincenzo Pinali" Antique Medical Library

Santo Davide Ferrara, Guido Viel, and Rafael Boscolo-Berto

Abstract This chapter proposes a historical overview of antique iconography, taken from the historical section of the "Vincenzo Pinali" Medical Library of the University of Padova. The icons, dating from the fourteenth and eighteenth centuries, demonstrate the evolution of biomedical knowledge and of the constant presence of profiles of responsibility in the performance of medical and surgical practices.

A brief overview of historical iconography is proposed to the reader, concerning works in which profiles of personal injury and damage can be identified.

In particular, these works are part of the heritage of the Historical Section of the "Vincenzo Pinali" Medical Library of the University of Padova. The Historical "Vincenzo Pinali" Medical Library derives from the bequests of valuable collections transmitted by professors N. D'Ancona (1875–1931), A. De Giovanni (1838–1916), F. Fanzago (1764–1835), L. Lucatello (1863–1926), V. Pinali (1802–1875), A. Tebaldi (1833–1895), and T. Vanzetti (1809–1888). The collection has been enriched by the donation of approximately 2,000 works of the physiologist V. Ducceschi (1871–1952), a passionate historian of medicine. The "Sala Pinali" collects together around 7,500 works, mostly related to editions comprised between 1480 and 1830, including 7 incunables, over 600 from the sixteenth century, and more than 20,000 contributions of biology and medicine of the past centuries. The adjoining "Sala Ducceschi" contains the fund derived from the homonymous donor and a part of the bequests mentioned previously, a collection of 165 manuscripts autographed in part, dated to periods comprised between the fourteenth and eighteenth centuries, as well as a series of valuable anatomical waxes depicting aspects of anatomy and ocular pathology (Figs. 34.1, 34.2, 34.3, 34.4, 34.5, 34.6, 34.7, 34.8, 34.9, 34.10, 34.11, 34.12, 34.13, 34.14, 34.15, 34.16, 34.17, 34.18, 34.19, 34.20, 34.21, 34.22, 34.23, 34.24, 34.25, 34.26, 34.27, 34.28, 34.29, 34.30, 34.31, 34.32, 34.33, 34.34, 34.35, 34.36, 34.37, 34.38, 34.39, 34.40, 34.41, 34.42, 34.43, 34.44, 34.45, 34.46, 34.47, and 34.48).

S.D. Ferrara (✉) • G. Viel • R. Boscolo-Berto
Department of Legal and Occupational Medicine, Toxicology and Public Health, University-Hospital of Padova, Via Falloppio 50, 35128 Padova, Italy
e-mail: santodavide.ferrara@unipd.it; guido.viel@unipd.it; rafael.boscoloberto@unipd.it

S.D. Ferrara et al. (eds.), *Personal Injury and Damage Ascertainment under Civil Law*, DOI 10.1007/978-3-319-29812-2_34

Fig. 34.1 Schultes, Johann 1595–1645 (Scultetus). Armamentarium chirurgicum bipartitum, studioque & opera D. Joannis Sculteti Ulmensis … reformatum, correctum & auctum. Cum 56 tabulis, sive figuris aeneis novis accuratissimis. Ut & tribus indicibus absolutissimis, instrumentorum scilicet, obseruationum, et rerum notabilium Francofurti : sumptibus viduae Joan. Gerlini, Bibliop. Ulm. typis Joannis Gerlini, 1666. Courtesy of historical section of the "Vincenzo Pinali" Medical Library of the University of Padova

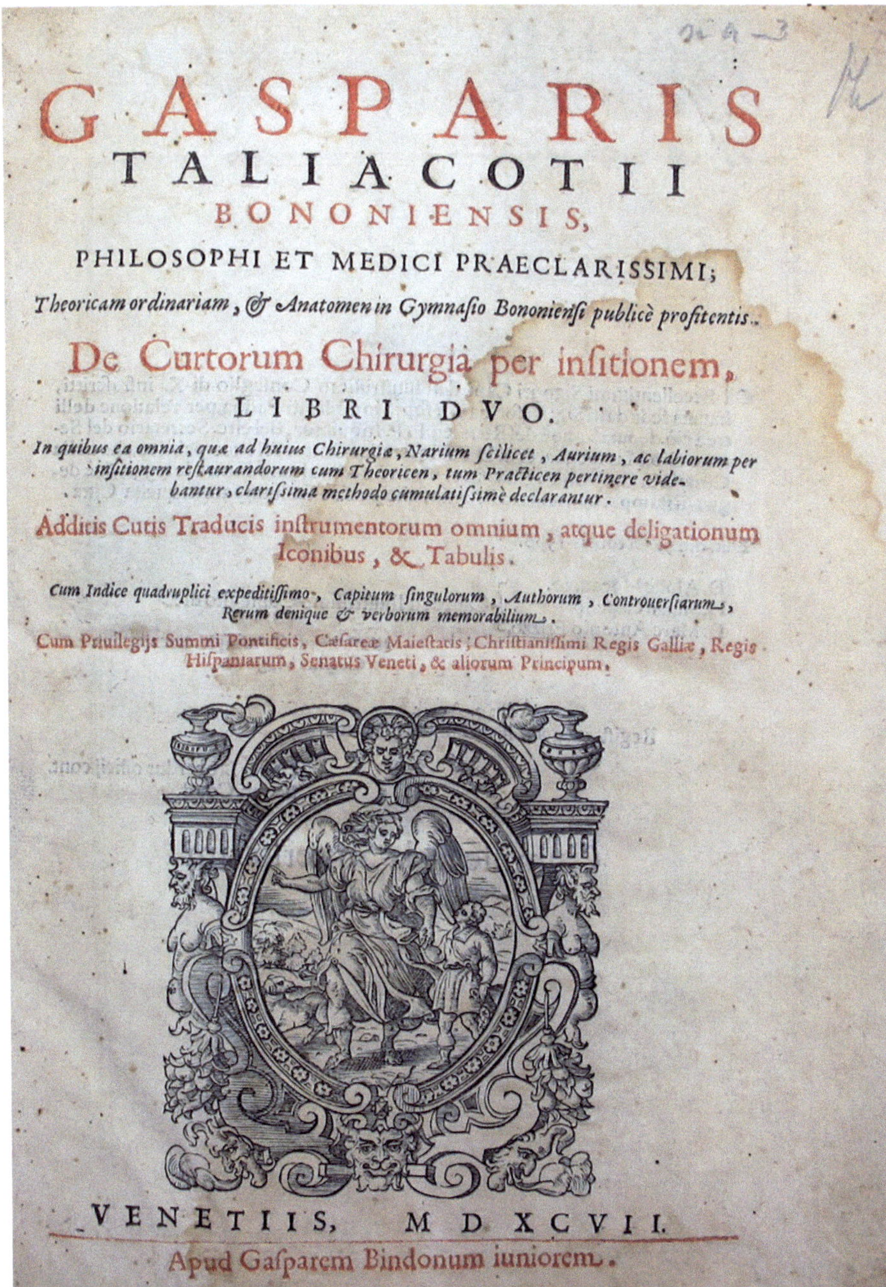

GASPARIS
TALIACOTII
BONONIENSIS,
PHILOSOPHI ET MEDICI PRAECLARISSIMI;
Theoricam ordinariam, & Anatomen in Gymnasio Bononiensi publicè profitentis.
De Curtorum Chirurgia per insitionem,
LIBRI DVO.
In quibus ea omnia, quæ ad huius Chirurgiæ, Narium scilicet, Aurium, ac labiorum per insitionem restaurandorum cum Theoricen, tum Practicen pertinere videbantur, clarissima methodo cumulatissimè declarantur.
Additis Cutis Traducis instrumentorum omnium, atque deligationum Iconibus, & Tabulis.
Cum Indice quadruplici expeditissimo, Capitum singulorum, Authorum, Controuersiarum, Rerum denique & verborum memorabilium.
Cum Priuilegijs Summi Pontificis, Cæsareæ Maiestatis, Christianissimi Regis Galliæ, Regis Hispaniarum, Senatus Veneti, & aliorum Principum.
VENETIIS, M D X C V I I.
Apud Gasparem Bindonum iuniorem.

Fig. 34.2 Tagliacozzo, Gaspare (1545–1599). De curtorum chirurgia per insitionem libri duo. In quibus ea omnia, quae ad huius chirurgiae, narium scilicet, aurium, ac labiorum per insitionem restaurandorum cum theoricen, tum practicen pertinere videbantur, clarissima methodo cumulatissime declarantur. Additis Cutis traducis instrumentorum omnium, atque deligationum iconibus, & tabulis. ... Venetiis : apud Gasparem Bindonum iuniorem, 1597. Courtesy of historical section of the "Vincenzo Pinali" Medical Library of the University of Padova

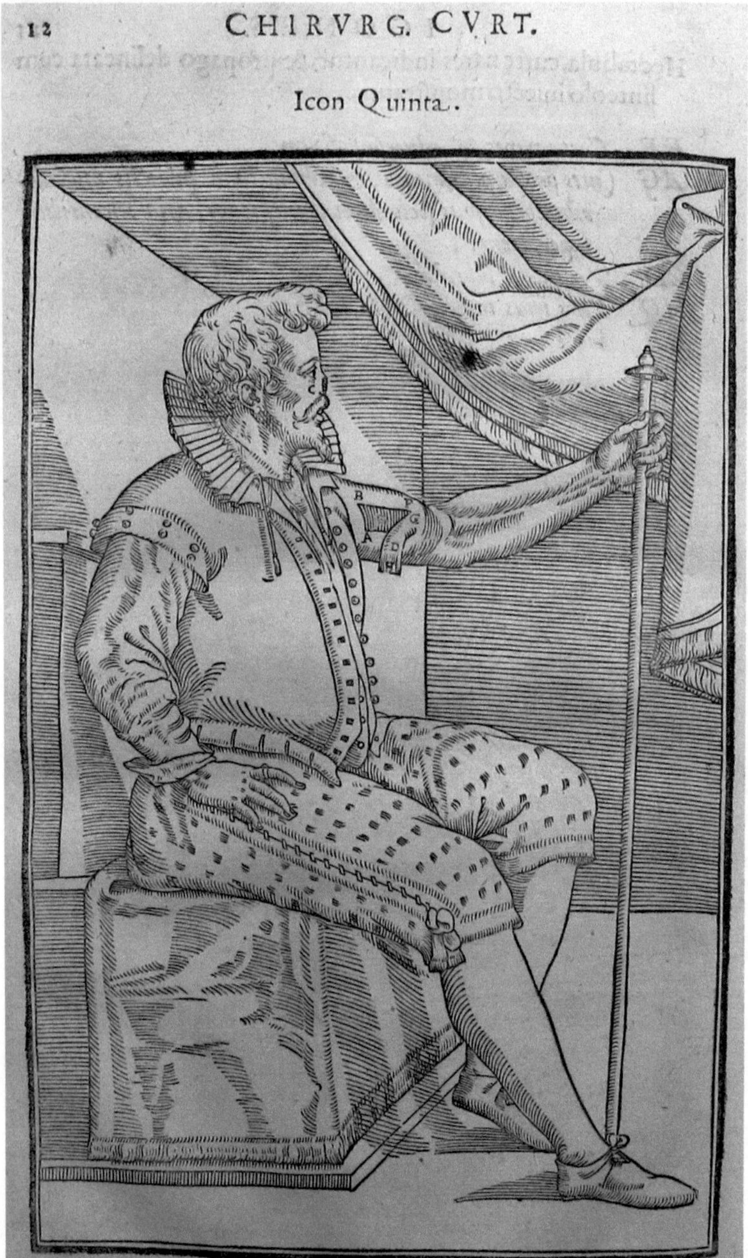

Fig. 34.3 Tagliacozzo, Gaspare (1545–1599). De curtorum chirurgia per insitionem libri duo. In quibus ea omnia, quae ad huius chirurgiae, narium scilicet, aurium, ac labiorum per insitionem restaurandorum cum theoricen, tum practicen pertinere videbantur, clarissima methodo cumulatissime declarantur. Additis Cutis traducis instrumentorum omnium, atque deligationum iconibus, & tabulis. ... Venetiis : apud Gasparem Bindonum iuniorem, 1597. Courtesy of historical section of the "Vincenzo Pinali" Medical Library of the University of Padova

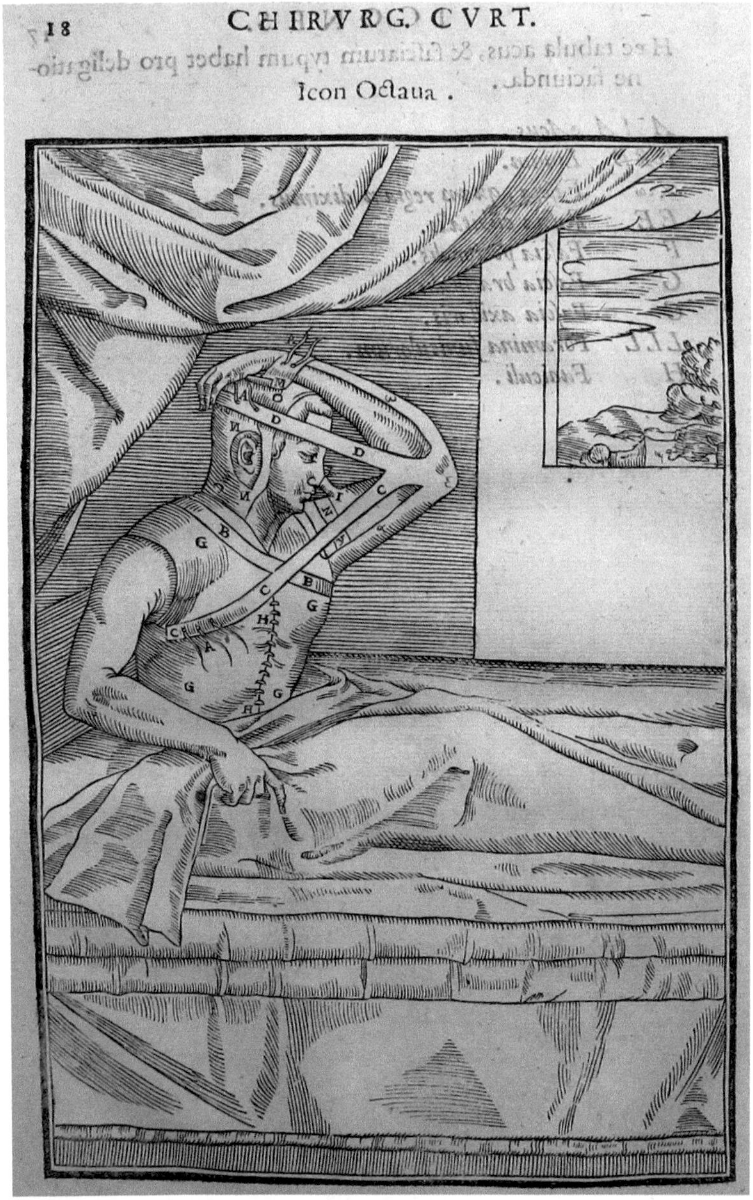

Fig. 34.4 Tagliacozzo, Gaspare (1545–1599). De curtorum chirurgia per insitionem libri duo. In quibus ea omnia, quae ad huius chirurgiae, narium scilicet, aurium, ac labiorum per insitionem restaurandorum cum theoricen, tum practicen pertinere videbantur, clarissima methodo cumulatissime declarantur. Additis Cutis traducis instrumentorum omnium, atque deligationum iconibus, & tabulis. ... Venetiis : apud Gasparem Bindonum iuniorem, 1597. Courtesy of historical section of the "Vincenzo Pinali" Medical Library of the University of Padova

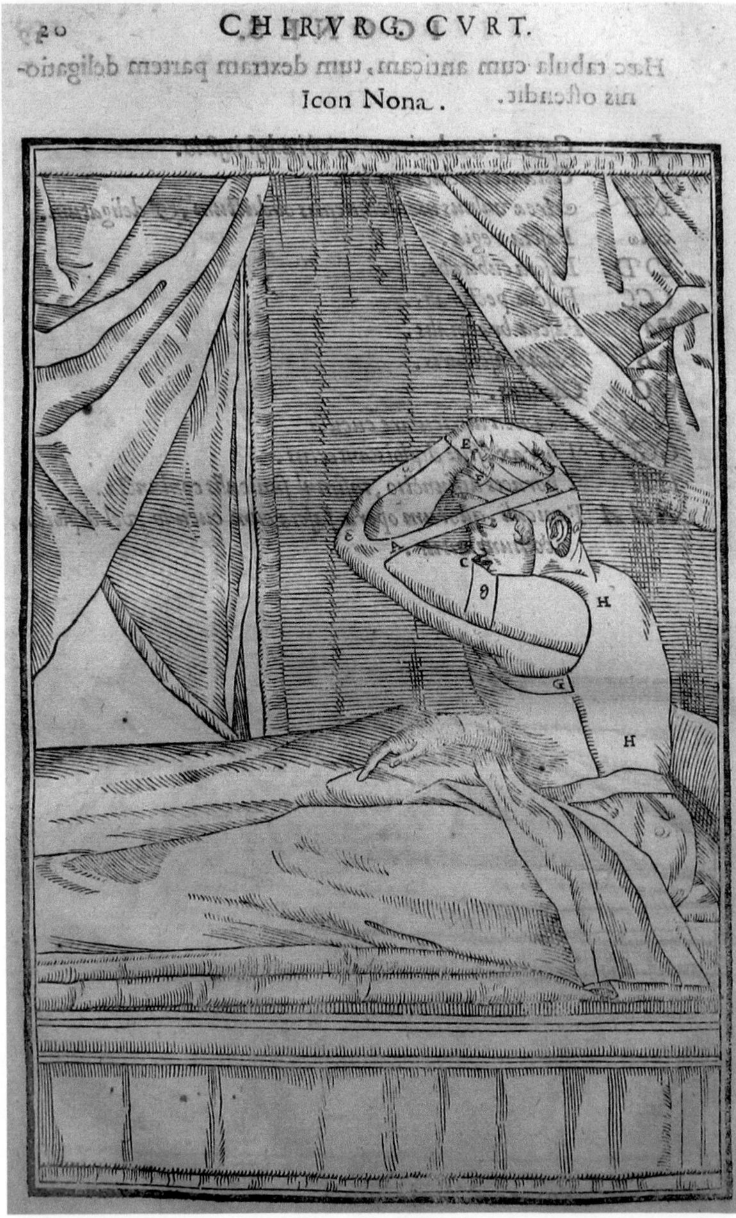

Fig. 34.5 Tagliacozzo, Gaspare (1545–1599). De curtorum chirurgia per insitionem libri duo. In quibus ea omnia, quae ad huius chirurgiae, narium scilicet, aurium, ac labiorum per insitionem restaurandorum cum theoricen, tum practicen pertinere videbantur, clarissima methodo cumulatissime declarantur. Additis Cutis traducis instrumentorum omnium, atque deligationum iconibus, & tabulis. ... Venetiis : apud Gasparem Bindonum iuniorem, 1597. Courtesy of historical section of the "Vincenzo Pinali" Medical Library of the University of Padova

Fig. 34.6 Tagliacozzo, Gaspare (1545–1599). De curtorum chirurgia per insitionem libri duo. In quibus ea omnia, quae ad huius chirurgiae, narium scilicet, aurium, ac labiorum per insitionem restaurandorum cum theoricen, tum practicen pertinere videbantur, clarissima methodo cumulatissime declarantur. Additis Cutis traducis instrumentorum omnium, atque deligationum iconibus, & tabulis. ... Venetiis : apud Gasparem Bindonum iuniorem, 1597. Courtesy of historical section of the "Vincenzo Pinali" Medical Library of the University of Padova

Fig. 34.7 Tagliacozzo, Gaspare (1545–1599). De curtorum chirurgia per insitionem libri duo. In quibus ea omnia, quae ad huius chirurgiae, narium scilicet, aurium, ac labiorum per insitionem restaurandorum cum theoricen, tum practicen pertinere videbantur, clarissima methodo cumulatissime declarantur. Additis Cutis traducis instrumentorum omnium, atque deligationum iconibus, & tabulis. . . . Venetiis : apud Gasparem Bindonum iuniorem, 1597. Courtesy of historical section of the "Vincenzo Pinali" Medical Library of the University of Padova

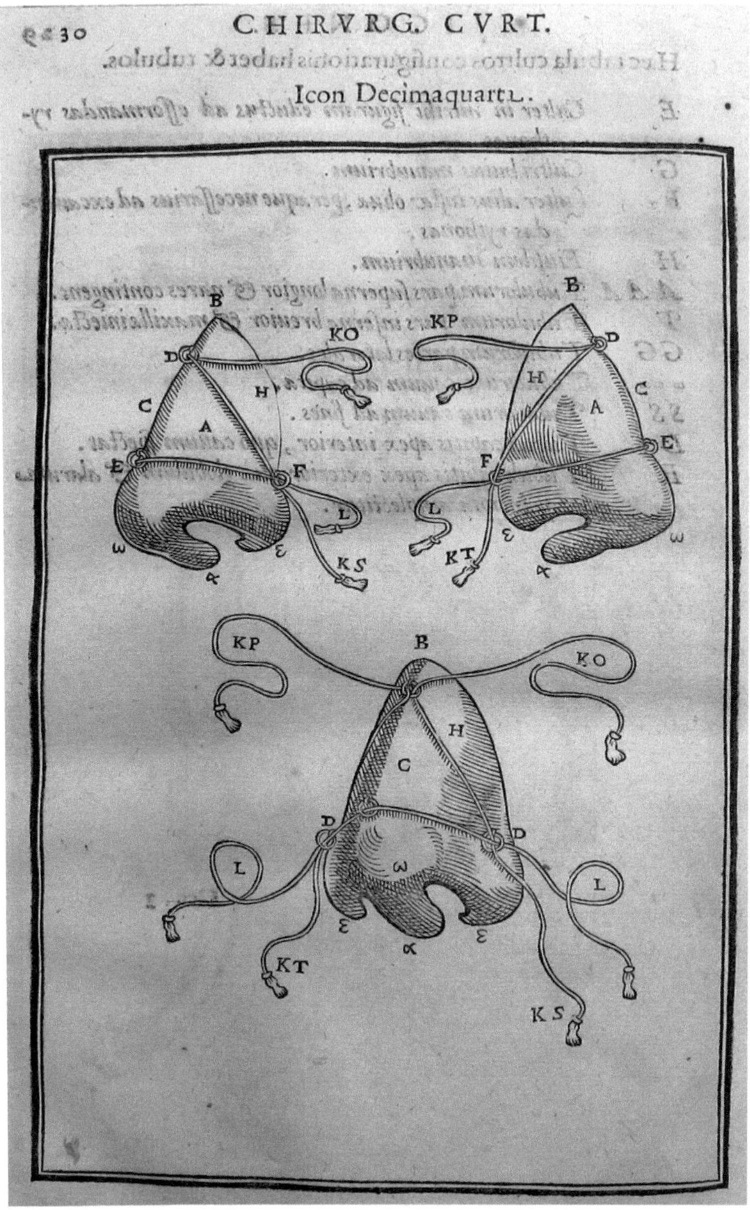

Fig. 34.8 Tagliacozzo, Gaspare (1545–1599). De curtorum chirurgia per insitionem libri duo. In quibus ea omnia, quae ad huius chirurgiae, narium scilicet, aurium, ac labiorum per insitionem restaurandorum cum theoricen, tum practicen pertinere videbantur, clarissima methodo cumulatissime declarantur. Additis Cutis traducis instrumentorum omnium, atque deligationum iconibus, & tabulis. ... Venetiis : apud Gasparem Bindonum iuniorem, 1597. Courtesy of historical section of the "Vincenzo Pinali" Medical Library of the University of Padova

Fig. 34.9 Tagliacozzo, Gaspare (1545–1599). De curtorum chirurgia per insitionem libri duo. In quibus ea omnia, quae ad huius chirurgiae, narium scilicet, aurium, ac labiorum per insitionem restaurandorum cum theoricen, tum practicen pertinere videbantur, clarissima methodo cumulatissime declarantur. Additis Cutis traducis instrumentorum omnium, atque deligationum iconibus, & tabulis. ... Venetiis : apud Gasparem Bindonum iuniorem, 1597. Courtesy of historical section of the "Vincenzo Pinali" Medical Library of the University of Padova

Fig. 34.10 Tagliacozzo, Gaspare (1545–1599). De curtorum chirurgia per insitionem libri duo. In quibus ea omnia, quae ad huius chirurgiae, narium scilicet, aurium, ac labiorum per insitionem restaurandorum cum theoricen, tum practicen pertinere videbantur, clarissima methodo cumulatissime declarantur. Additis Cutis traducis instrumentorum omnium, atque deligationum iconibus, & tabulis. ... Venetiis : apud Gasparem Bindonum iuniorem, 1597. Courtesy of historical section of the "Vincenzo Pinali" Medical Library of the University of Padova

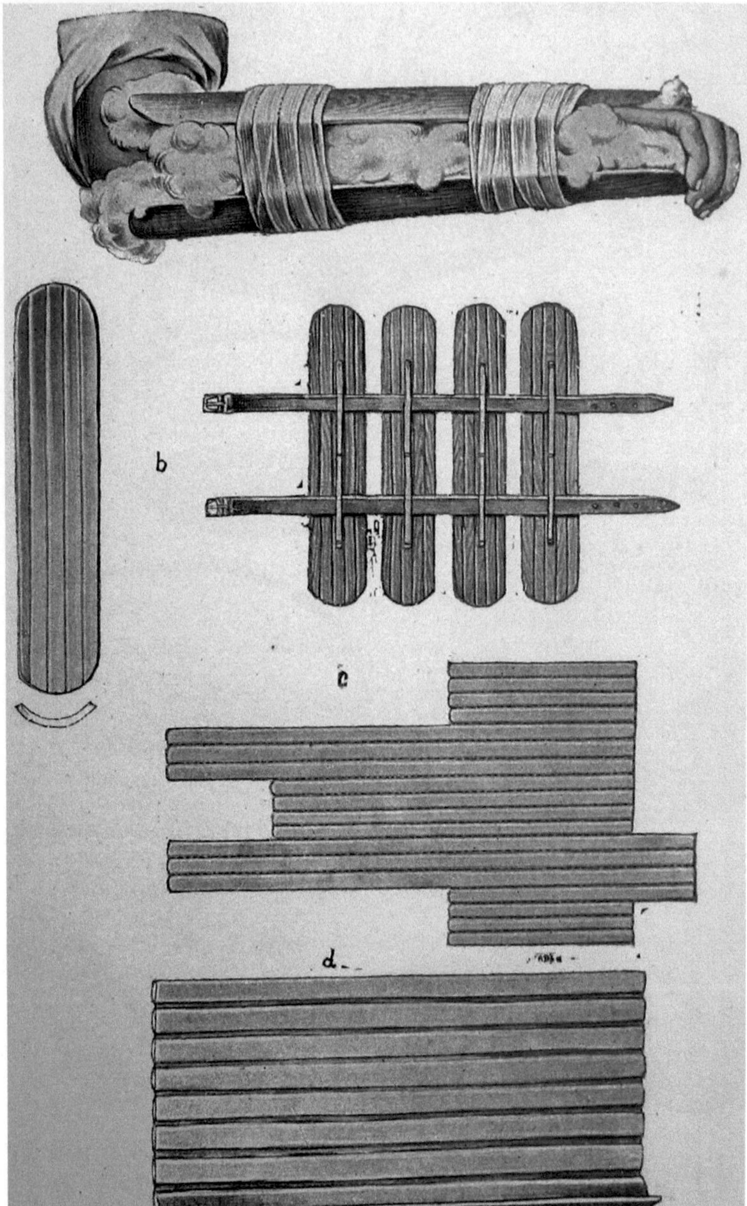

Fig. 34.11 Hoffa, Albert. Atlante ed elementi di tecnica delle fasciature e degli apparecchi per medici e studenti di Albert Hoffa. Milano : Società Editrice Libraria, 1899. Courtesy of historical section of the "Vincenzo Pinali" Medical Library of the University of Padova

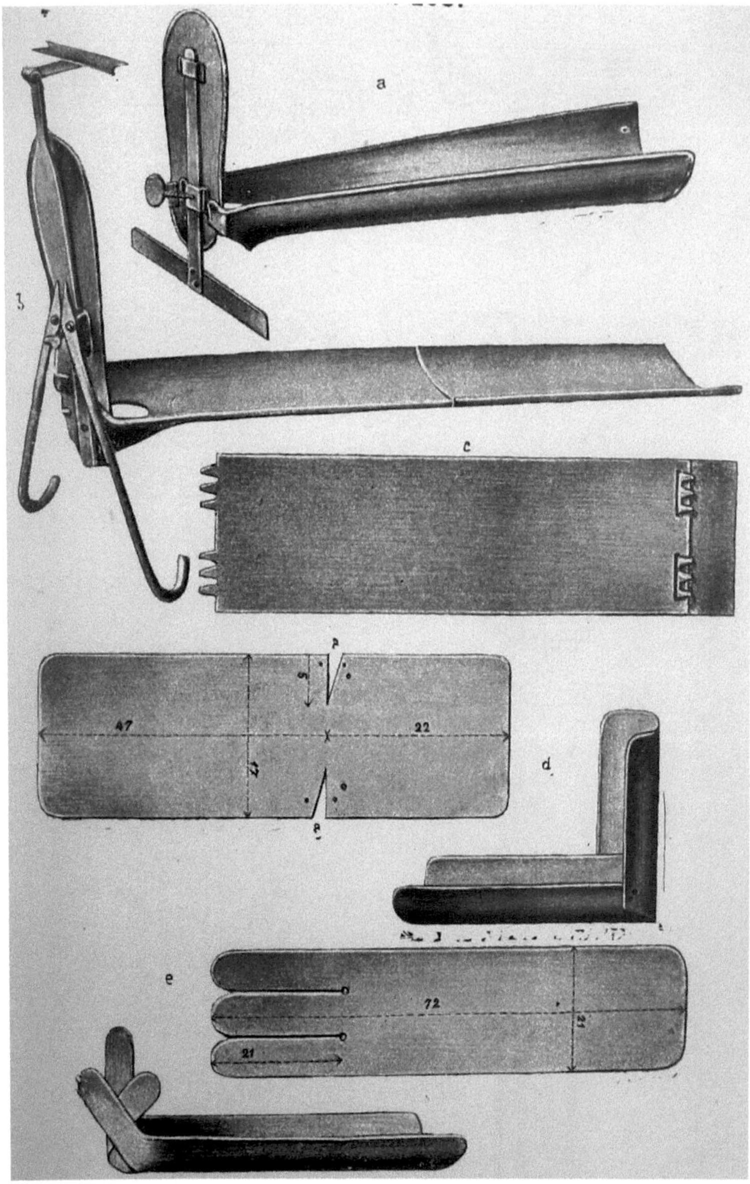

Fig. 34.12 Hoffa, Albert. Atlante ed elementi di tecnica delle fasciature e degli apparecchi per medici e studenti di Albert Hoffa. Milano : Società Editrice Libraria, 1899. Courtesy of historical section of the "Vincenzo Pinali" Medical Library of the University of Padova

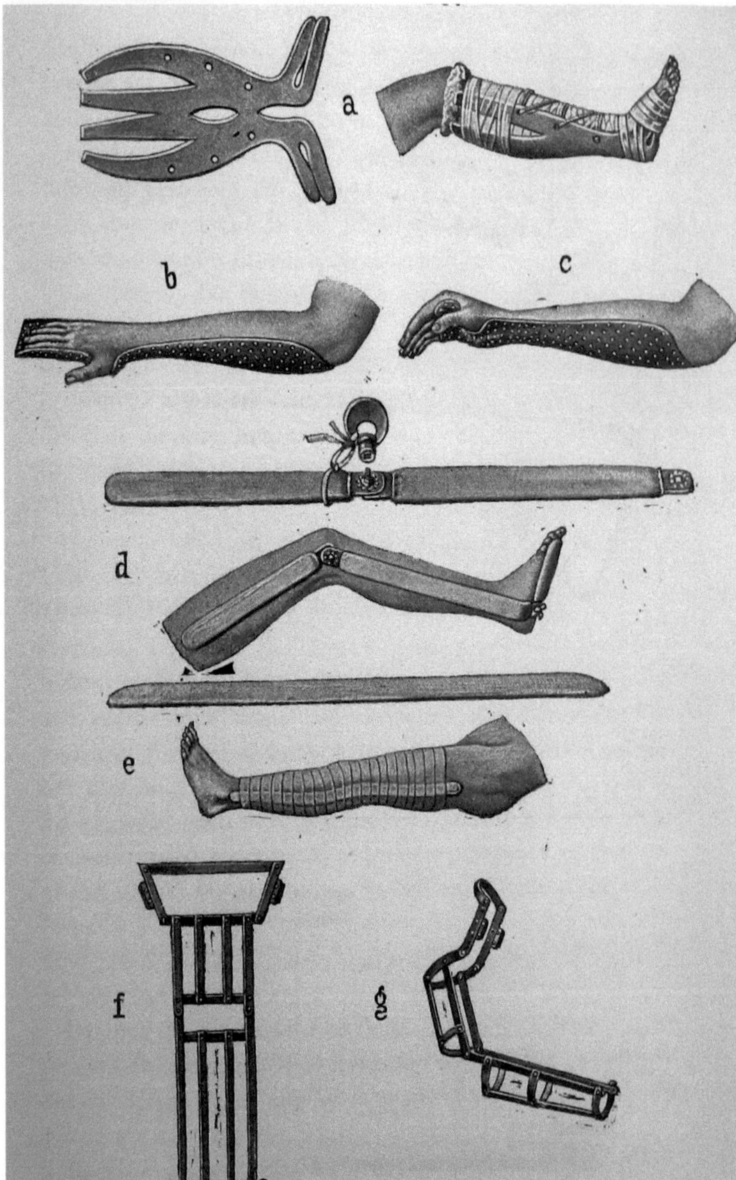

Fig. 34.13 Hoffa, Albert. Atlante ed elementi di tecnica delle fasciature e degli apparecchi per medici e studenti di Albert Hoffa. Milano : Società Editrice Libraria, 1899. Courtesy of historical section of the "Vincenzo Pinali" Medical Library of the University of Padova

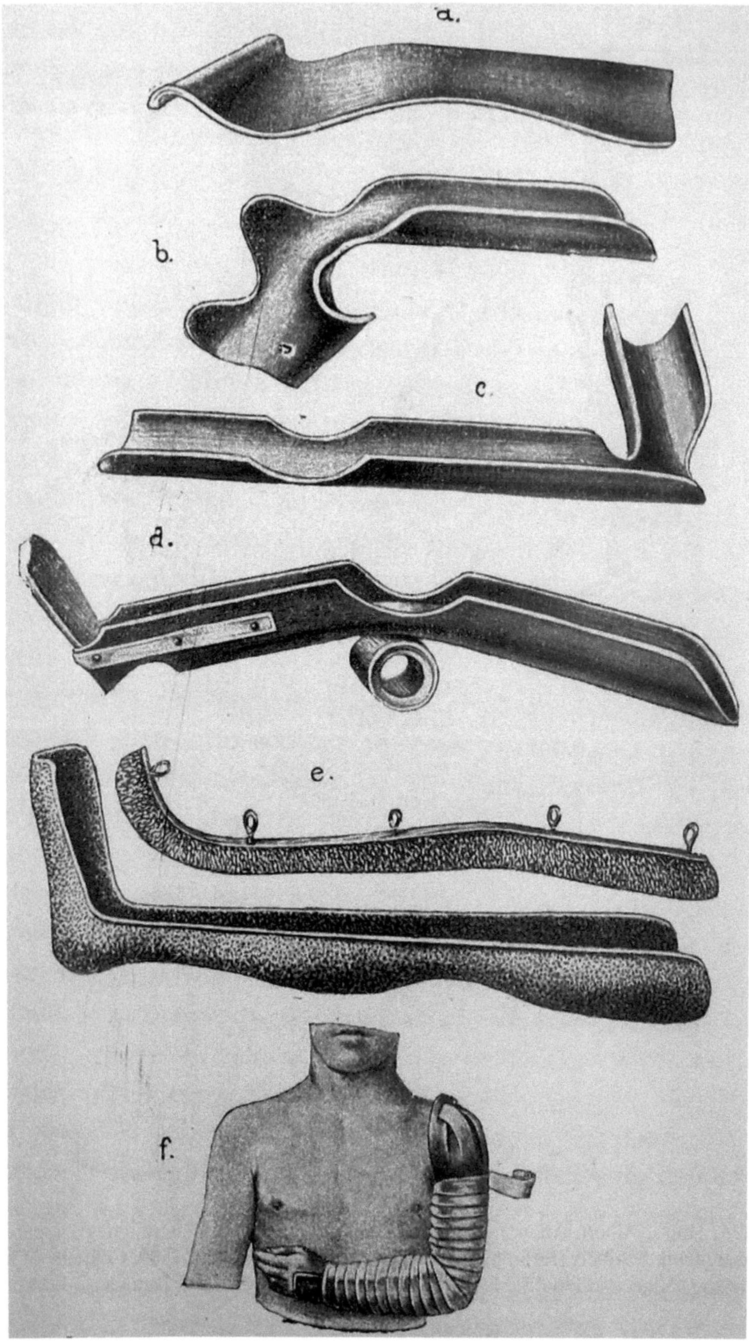

Fig. 34.14 Hoffa, Albert. Atlante ed elementi di tecnica delle fasciature e degli apparecchi per medici e studenti di Albert Hoffa. Milano : Società Editrice Libraria, 1899. Courtesy of historical section of the "Vincenzo Pinali" Medical Library of the University of Padova

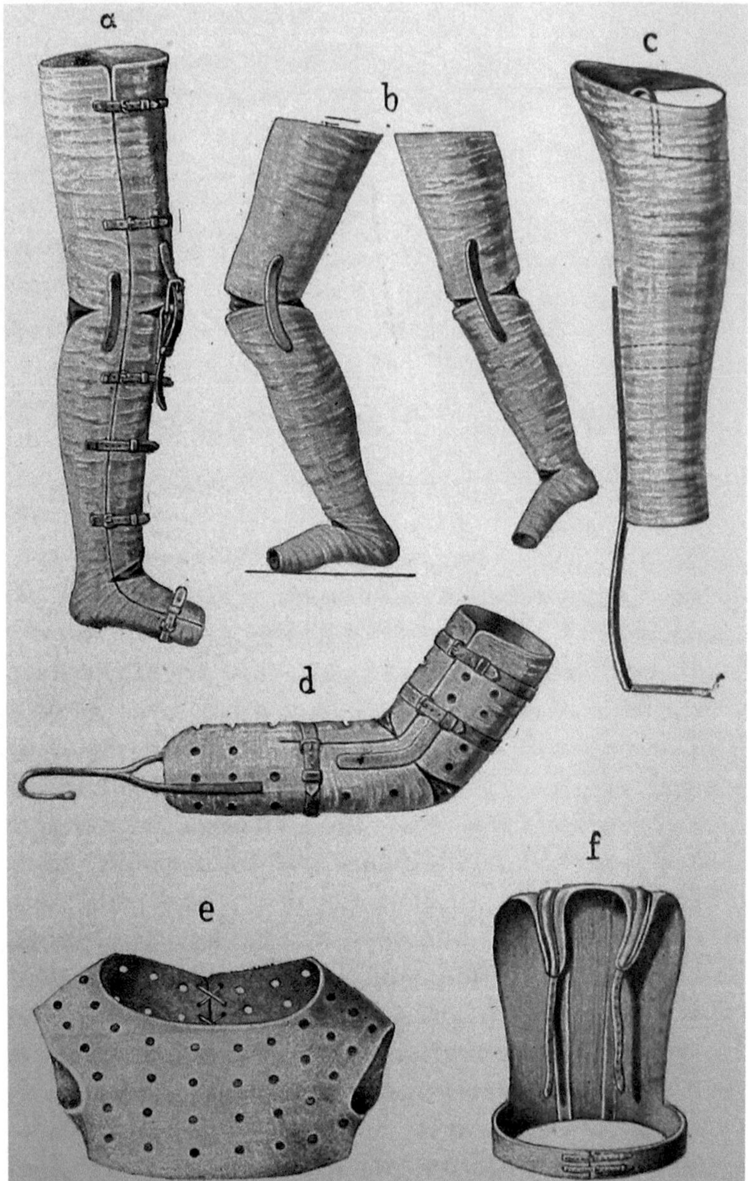

Fig. 34.15 Hoffa, Albert. Atlante ed elementi di tecnica delle fasciature e degli apparecchi per medici e studenti di Albert Hoffa. Milano : Società Editrice Libraria, 1899. Courtesy of historical section of the "Vincenzo Pinali" Medical Library of the University of Padova

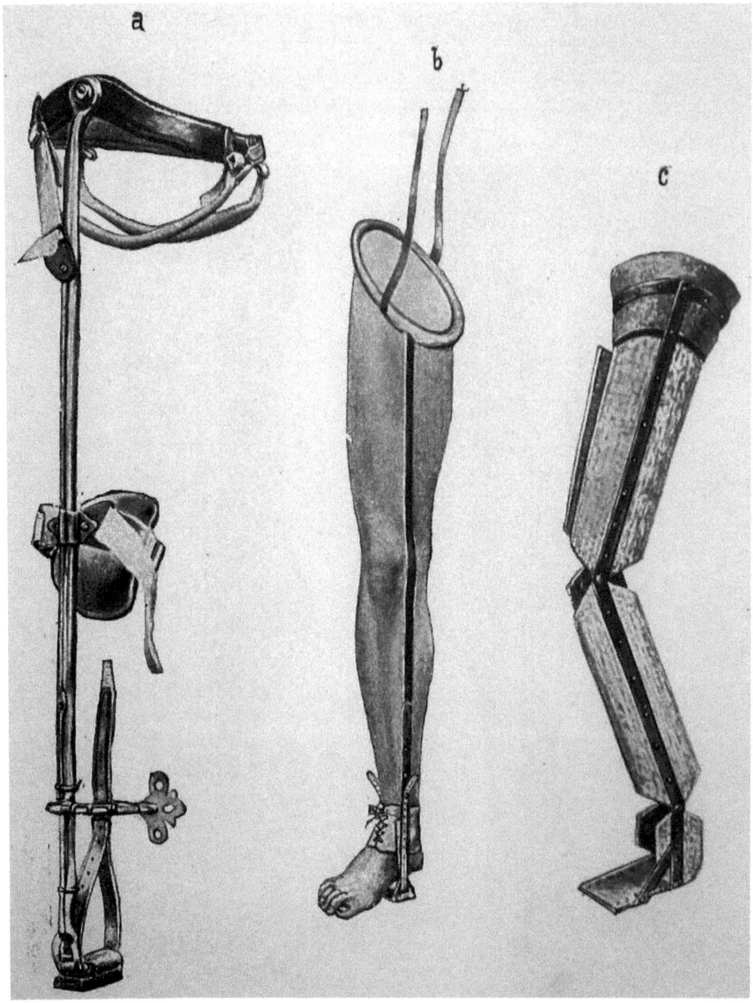

Fig. 34.16 Hoffa, Albert. Atlante ed elementi di tecnica delle fasciature e degli apparecchi per medici e studenti di Albert Hoffa. Milano : Società Editrice Libraria, 1899. Courtesy of historical section of the "Vincenzo Pinali" Medical Library of the University of Padova

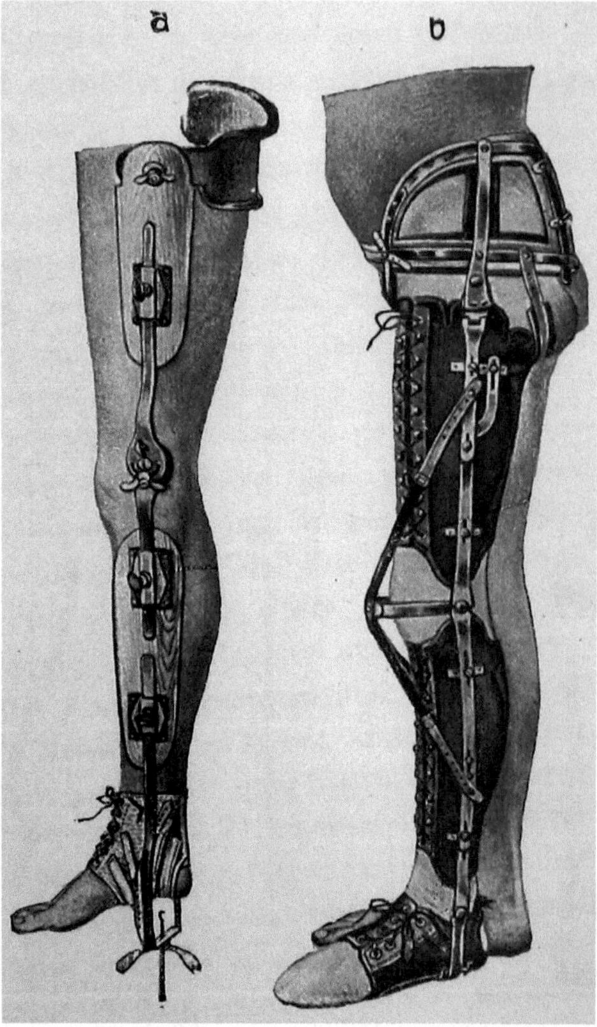

Fig. 34.17 Hoffa, Albert. Atlante ed elementi di tecnica delle fasciature e degli apparecchi per medici e studenti di Albert Hoffa. Milano : Società Editrice Libraria, 1899. Courtesy of historical section of the "Vincenzo Pinali" Medical Library of the University of Padova

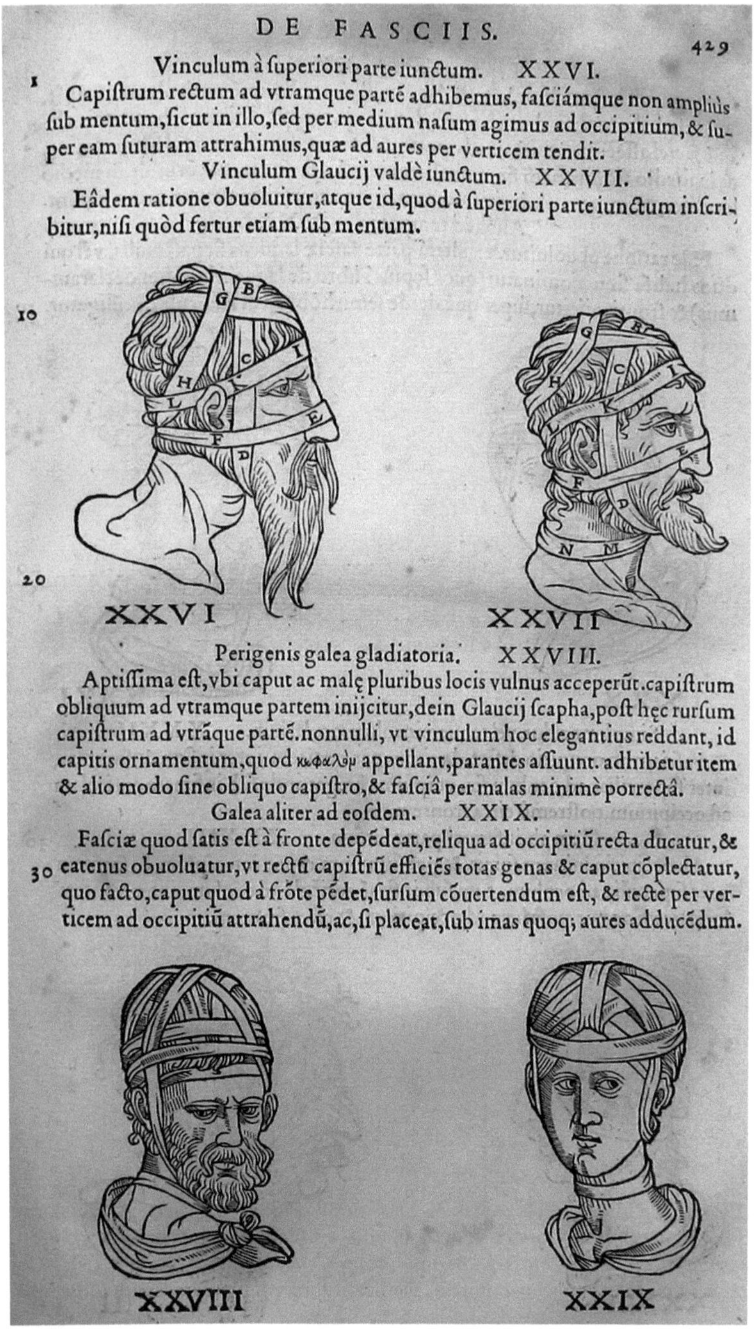

DE FASCIIS. 429

Vinculum à ſuperiori parte iunctum. XXVI.

Capiſtrum rectum ad vtramque partẽ adhibemus, faſciámque non amplius ſub mentum, ſicut in illo, ſed per medium naſum agimus ad occipitium, & ſuper eam ſuturam attrahimus, quæ ad aures per verticem tendit.

Vinculum Glaucij valdè iunctum. XXVII.

Eâdem ratione obuoluitur, atque id, quod à ſuperiori parte iunctum inſcribitur, niſi quòd fertur etiam ſub mentum.

Perigenis galea gladiatoria. XXVIII.

Aptiſſima eſt, vbi caput ac malę pluribus locis vulnus acceperũt. capiſtrum obliquum ad vtramque partem inijcitur, dein Glaucij ſcapha, poſt hęc rurſum capiſtrum ad vtrãque partẽ. nonnulli, vt vinculum hoc elegantius reddant, id capitis ornamentum, quod κεφαλὴν appellant, parantes aſſuunt. adhibetur item & alio modo ſine obliquo capiſtro, & faſciâ per malas minimè porrectâ.

Galea aliter ad eoſdem. XXIX.

Faſciæ quod ſatis eſt à fronte depẽdeat, reliqua ad occipitiũ recta ducatur, & eatenus obuoluatur, vt rectũ capiſtrũ efficiẽs totas genas & caput cõplectatur, quo facto, caput quod à frõte pẽdet, ſurſum cõuertendum eſt, & rectè per verticem ad occipitiũ attrahendũ, ac, ſi placeat, ſub imas quoq; aures adducẽdum.

Fig. 34.18 Guidi, Guido <il vecchio> ca. 1500–1569. Chirurgia è Graeco in Latinum conuersa, Vido Vidio Florentino interprete, cum nonnullis eiusdem Vidij commentarijs. ... Lucetiae [] Parisiorum : excudebat Petrus Galterius, pridie Calendas Maij [30 IV] 1544. Courtesy of historical section of the "Vincenzo Pinali" Medical Library of the University of Padova

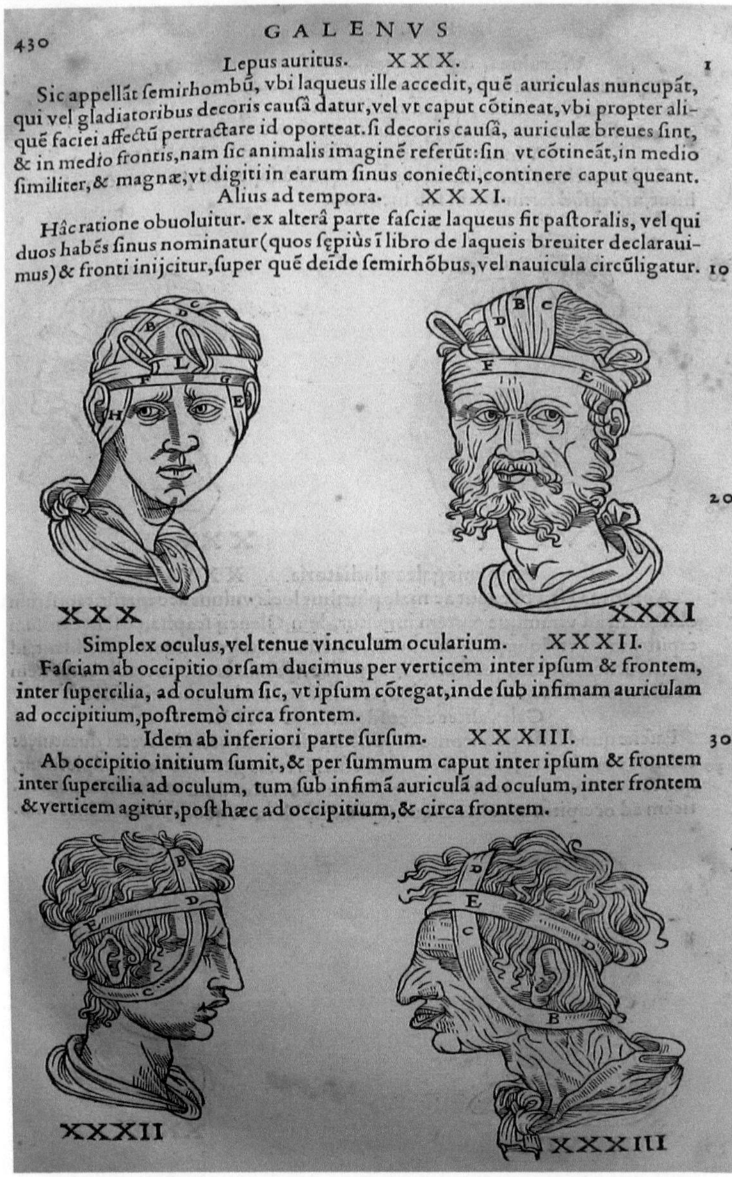

430 GALENVS

Lepus auritus. XXX.

Sic appellãt ſemirhombũ, vbi laqueus ille accedit, quẽ auriculas nuncupãt, qui vel gladiatoribus decoris cauſã datur, vel vt caput cõtineat, vbi propter aliquẽ faciei affectũ pertractare id oporteat. ſi decoris cauſã, auriculæ breues ſint, & in medio frontis, nam ſic animalis imaginẽ referũt: ſin vt cõtineãt, in medio ſimiliter, & magnæ, vt digiti in earum ſinus coniecti, continere caput queant.

Alius ad tempora. XXXI.

Hâc ratione obuoluitur. ex alterâ parte faſciæ laqueus fit paſtoralis, vel qui duos habẽs ſinus nominatur (quos ſępiùs ĩ libro de laqueis breuiter declarauimus) & fronti inijcitur, ſuper quẽ deĩde ſemirhõbus, vel nauicula circũligatur.

XXX XXXI

Simplex oculus, vel tenue vinculum ocularium. XXXII.

Faſciam ab occipitio orſam ducimus per verticem inter ipſum & frontem, inter ſupercilia, ad oculum ſic, vt ipſum cõtegat, inde ſub infimam auriculam ad occipitium, poſtremò circa frontem.

Idem ab inferiori parte ſurſum. XXXIII.

Ab occipitio initium ſumit, & per ſummum caput inter ipſum & frontem inter ſupercilia ad oculum, tum ſub infimã auriculã ad oculum, inter frontem & verticem agitur, poſt hæc ad occipitium, & circa frontem.

XXXII XXXIII

Fig. 34.19 Guidi, Guido <il vecchio> ca. 1500–1569. Chirurgia è Graeco in Latinum conuersa, Vido Vidio Florentino interprete, cum nonnullis eiusdem Vidij commentarijs. ... Lucetiae [] Parisiorum : excudebat Petrus Galterius, pridie Calendas Maij [30 IV] 1544. Courtesy of historical section of the "Vincenzo Pinali" Medical Library of the University of Padova

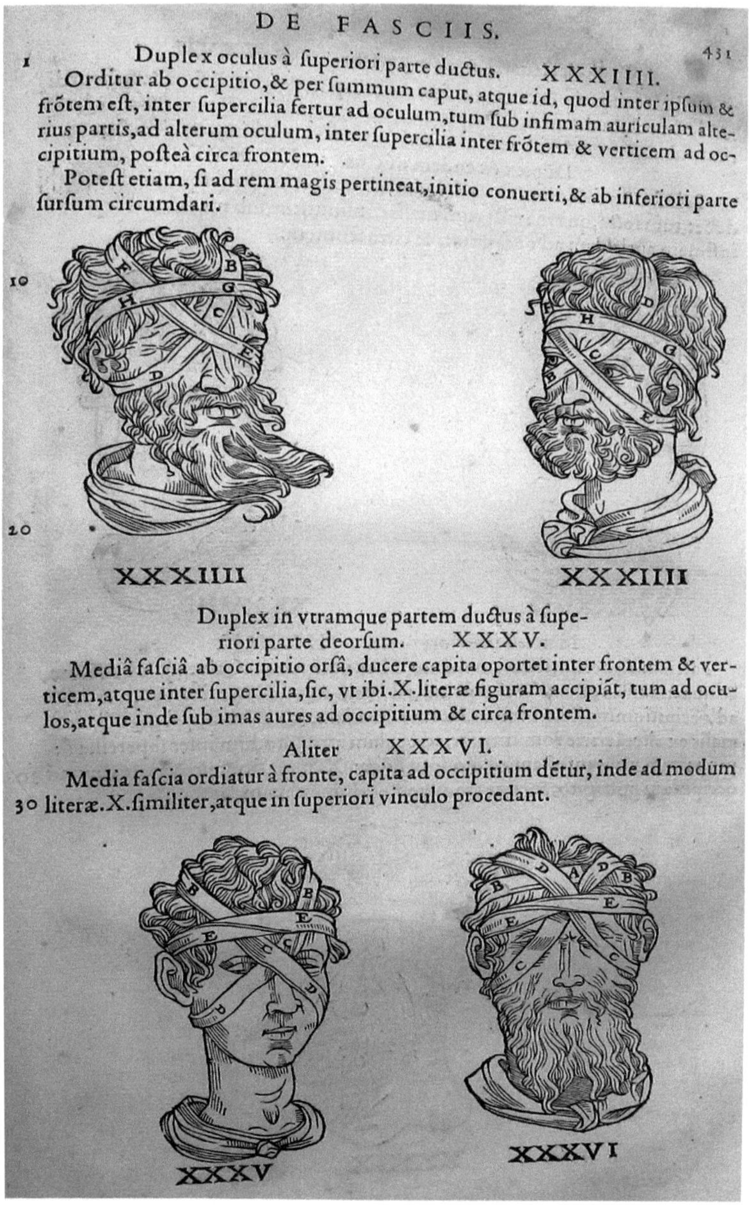
DE FASCIIS. 431

Duplex oculus à ſuperiori parte ductus. XXXIIII.

Orditur ab occipitio,& per ſummum caput, atque id, quod inter ipſum & frõtem eſt, inter ſupercilia fertur ad oculum,tum ſub infimam auriculam alterius partis,ad alterum oculum, inter ſupercilia inter frõtem & verticem ad occipitium, poſteà circa frontem.

Poteſt etiam, ſi ad rem magis pertineat,initio conuerti,& ab inferiori parte ſurſum circumdari.

XXXIIII XXXIIII

Duplex in vtramque partem ductus à ſuperiori parte deorſum. XXXV.

Mediâ faſciâ ab occipitio orſâ, ducere capita oportet inter frontem & verticem,atque inter ſupercilia,ſic, vt ibi.X.literæ figuram accipiãt, tum ad oculos,atque inde ſub imas aures ad occipitium & circa frontem.

Aliter XXXVI.

Media faſcia ordiatur à fronte, capita ad occipitium dẽtur, inde ad modum literæ.X.ſimiliter,atque in ſuperiori vinculo procedant.

XXXV XXXVI

Fig. 34.20 Guidi, Guido <il vecchio> ca. 1500–1569. Chirurgia è Graeco in Latinum conuersa, Vido Vidio Florentino interprete, cum nonnullis eiusdem Vidij commentarijs. ... Lucetiae [] Parisiorum : excudebat Petrus Galterius, pridie Calendas Maij [30 IV] 1544. Courtesy of historical section of the "Vincenzo Pinali" Medical Library of the University of Padova

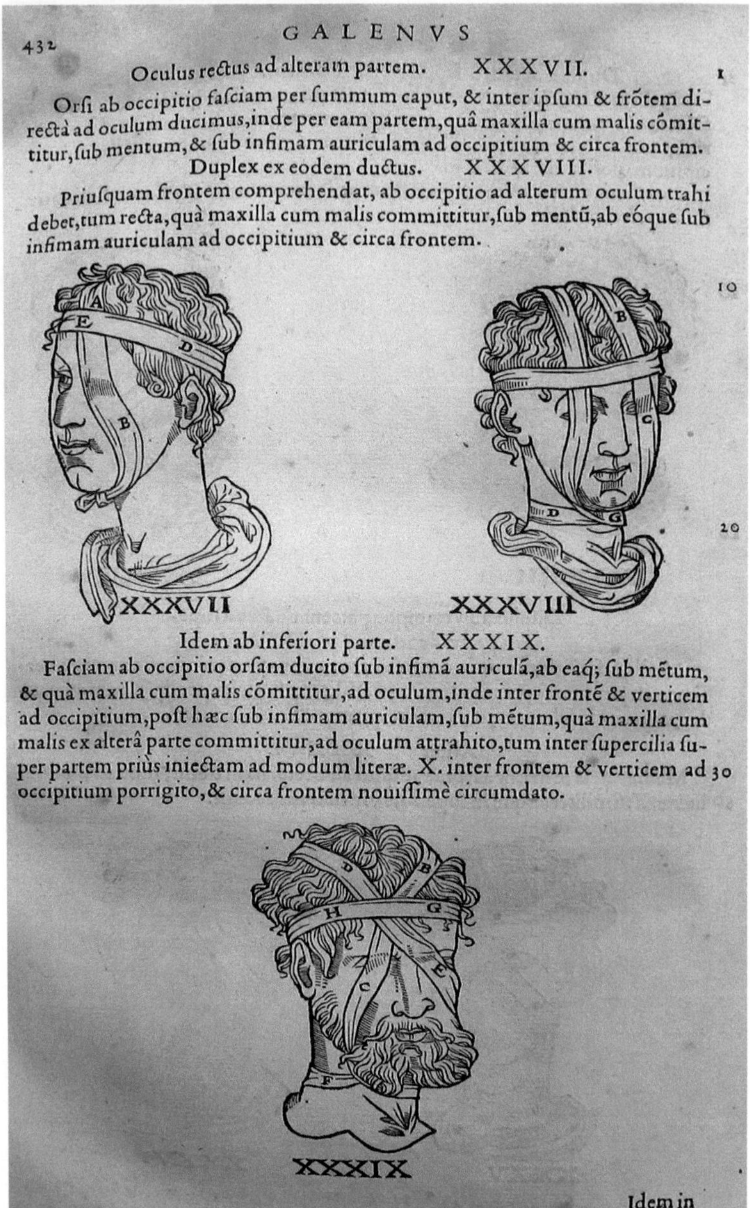

432 GALENVS

Oculus rectus ad alteram partem. XXXVII.

Orſi ab occipitio faſciam per ſummum caput, & inter ipſum & frõtem directà ad oculum ducimus, inde per eam partem, quâ maxilla cum malis cõmittitur, ſub mentum, & ſub infimam auriculam ad occipitium & circa frontem.

Duplex ex eodem ductus. XXXVIII.

Priuſquam frontem comprehendat, ab occipitio ad alterum oculum trahi debet, tum recta, quà maxilla cum malis committitur, ſub mentũ, ab eóque ſub infimam auriculam ad occipitium & circa frontem.

XXXVII XXXVIII

Idem ab inferiori parte. XXXIX.

Faſciam ab occipitio orſam ducito ſub infimã auriculã, ab eaq; ſub mẽtum, & quà maxilla cum malis cõmittitur, ad oculum, inde inter frontẽ & verticem ad occipitium, poſt hæc ſub infimam auriculam, ſub mẽtum, quà maxilla cum malis ex alterâ parte committitur, ad oculum attrahito, tum inter ſupercilia ſuper partem priùs iniectam ad modum literæ. X. inter frontem & verticem ad occipitium porrigito, & circa frontem nouiſſimè circumdato.

XXXIX

Idem in

Fig. 34.21 Guidi, Guido <il vecchio> ca. 1500–1569. Chirurgia è Graeco in Latinum conuersa, Vido Vidio Florentino interprete, cum nonnullis eiusdem Vidij commentarijs. ... Lucetiae [] Parisiorum : excudebat Petrus Galterius, pridie Calendas Maij [30 IV] 1544. Courtesy of historical section of the "Vincenzo Pinali" Medical Library of the University of Padova

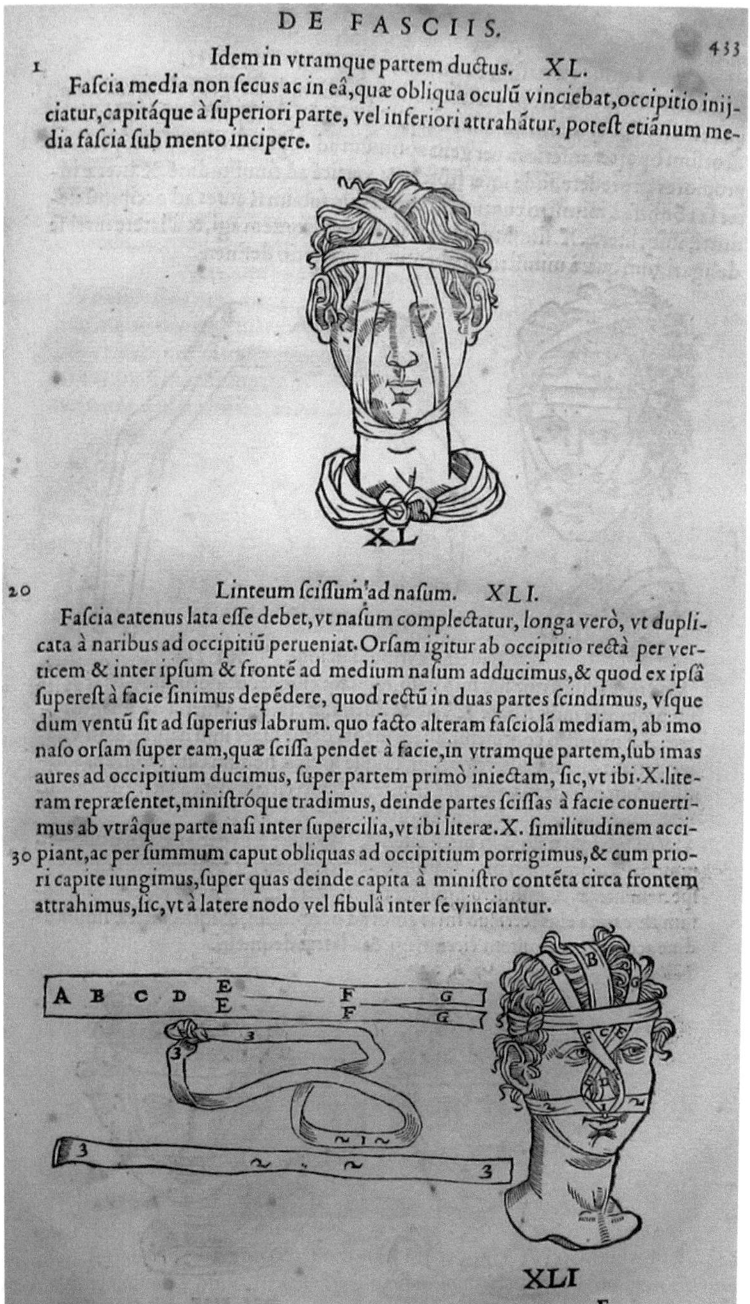

DE FASCIIS. 433

Idem in vtramque partem ductus. XL.

Faſcia media non ſecus ac in eâ,quæ obliqua oculũ vinciebat,occipitio inijciatur,capitáque à ſuperiori parte, vel inferiori attrahãtur, poteſt etiãnum media faſcia ſub mento incipere.

XL

Linteum ſciſſum ad naſum. XLI.

Faſcia eatenus lata eſſe debet,vt naſum complectatur, longa verò, vt duplicata à naribus ad occipitiũ perueniat.Orſam igitur ab occipitio rectà per verticem & inter ipſum & frontẽ ad medium naſum adducimus,& quod ex ipſâ ſupereſt à facie ſinimus depẽdere, quod rectũ in duas partes ſcindimus, vſque dum ventũ ſit ad ſuperius labrum. quo facto alteram faſciolã mediam, ab imo naſo orſam ſuper eam,quæ ſciſſa pendet à facie,in vtramque partem,ſub imas aures ad occipitium ducimus, ſuper partem primò iniectam, ſic,vt ibi X.literam repræſentet,miniſtróque tradimus, deinde partes ſciſſas à facie conuertimus ab vtrâque parte naſi inter ſupercilia,vt ibi literæ.X. ſimilitudinem accipiant,ac per ſummum caput obliquas ad occipitium porrigimus,& cum priori capite iungimus,ſuper quas deinde capita à miniſtro contẽta circa frontem attrahimus,ſic,vt à latere nodo vel fibulã inter ſe vinciantur.

XLI

E

Fig. 34.22 Guidi, Guido <il vecchio> ca. 1500–1569. Chirurgia è Graeco in Latinum conuersa, Vido Vidio Florentino interprete, cum nonnullis eiusdem Vidij commentarijs. ... Lucetiae [] Parisiorum : excudebat Petrus Galterius, pridie Calendas Maij [30 IV] 1544. Courtesy of historical section of the "Vincenzo Pinali" Medical Library of the University of Padova

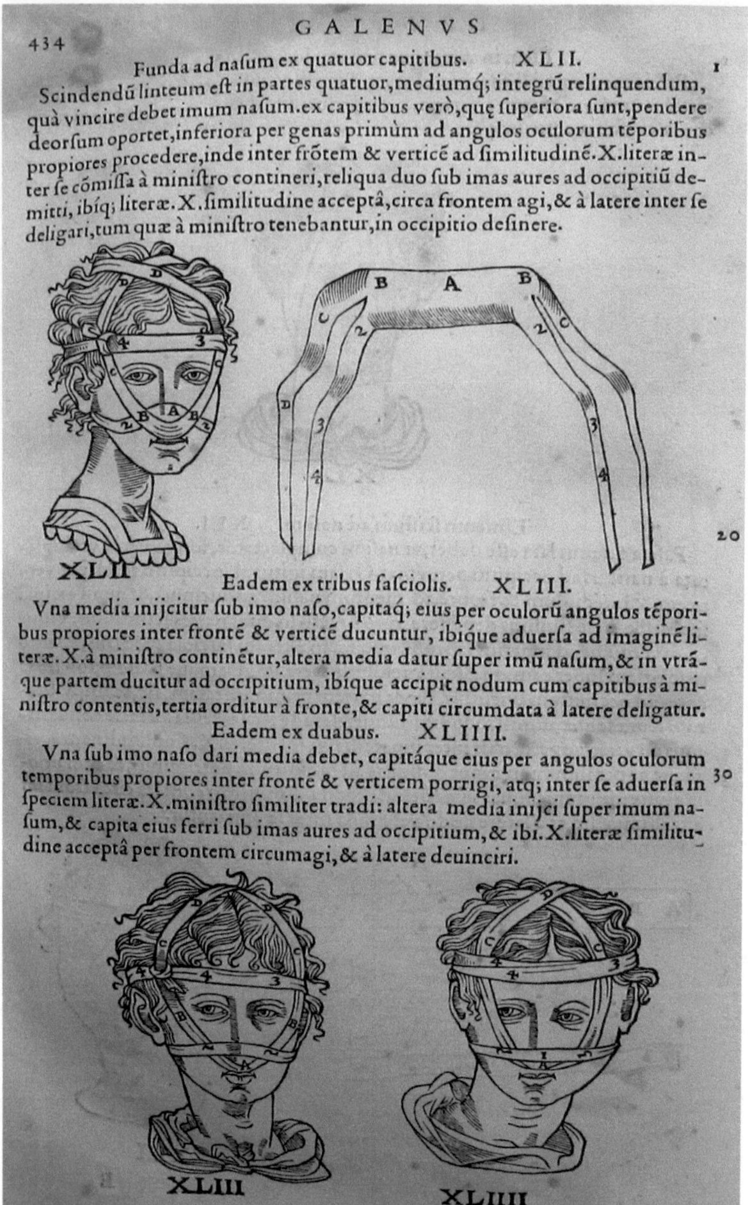

434 GALENVS

Funda ad naſum ex quatuor capitibus. XLII.

Scindendũ linteum eſt in partes quatuor,mediumq́; integrũ relinquendum, quà vincire debet imum naſum.ex capitibus verò,quę ſuperiora ſunt,pendere deorſum oportet,inferiora per genas primùm ad angulos oculorum tẽporibus propiores procedere,inde inter frõtem & verticẽ ad ſimilitudinẽ.X.literæ inter ſe cõmiſſa à miniſtro contineri,reliqua duo ſub imas aures ad occipitiũ demitti, ibíq; literæ.X.ſimilitudine acceptâ,circa frontem agi,& à latere inter ſe deligari,tum quæ à miniſtro tenebantur,in occipitio deſinere.

Eadem ex tribus faſciolis. XLIII.

Vna media inijcitur ſub imo naſo,capitaq́; eius per oculorũ angulos tẽporibus propiores inter frontẽ & verticẽ ducuntur, ibíque aduerſa ad imaginẽ literæ.X.à miniſtro continẽtur,altera media datur ſuper imũ naſum,& in vtrãque partem ducitur ad occipitium, ibíque accipit nodum cum capitibus à miniſtro contentis,tertia orditur à fronte,& capiti circumdata à latere deligatur.

Eadem ex duabus. XLIIII.

Vna ſub imo naſo dari media debet, capitáque eius per angulos oculorum temporibus propiores inter frontẽ & verticem porrigi, atq; inter ſe aduerſa in ſpeciem literæ.X.miniſtro ſimiliter tradi: altera media inijci ſuper imum naſum,& capita eius ferri ſub imas aures ad occipitium,& ibi.X.literæ ſimilitudine acceptâ per frontem circumagi,& à latere deuinciri.

Fig. 34.23 Guidi, Guido <il vecchio> ca. 1500–1569. Chirurgia è Graeco in Latinum conuersa, Vido Vidio Florentino interprete, cum nonnullis eiusdem Vidij commentarijs. ... Lucetiae [] Parisiorum : excudebat Petrus Galterius, pridie Calendas Maij [30 IV] 1544. Courtesy of historical section of the "Vincenzo Pinali" Medical Library of the University of Padova

468 ORIBASIVS

Quomodo laqueus Nauticus debeat adhiberi.

Ex medio ſinu duplicatæ habenę duos item ſinus facere oportet,eóſque inter ſe permutatos ità collocare,vt interior extrinſecus, exterior ab ĩteriori parte ſitus ſit. hâc enim viâ nexus laquei ab vnâ parte,capita ab alterâ procedunt. Eſt autẽ idoneus ijs,quæ extendi inæqualiter debent: valet item ad continendas ferulas, quæ fracturis accommodantur . iuncturâ namque adhibitâ vnum habenæ caput ſiniſtrâ manu teneatur, alterum verò per affectã partem voluatur,ſic,vt vnus & alter ſinus fiat, per quos reliquum habenæ caput traijciatur, vt ab eâ parte,quæ in nos ſpectat, verſus contrariam porrectum ſiniſtrâ rurſus contineatur.quo iniecto ferulæ in ſinus demiſſæ ad vitioſum membrum dentur,capitáque attrahantur,& inter ſe alligentur, vt ferulas teneant. Valet item ad cubitum ſuſtinendum, non ſecus atque ad intentionem,aut ad ferulas continendas,imponitur enim,implicatúrque ad cubitum ſuſpendendum,vbi lata faſcia non eſt.in quo caſu ſinus ità inter ſe diducendi ſunt,vt alter prope cubitum ſit,iuxta manum alter, capita verò ad ceruicem adducenda ſunt , ibíque nodo inter ſe deliganda.

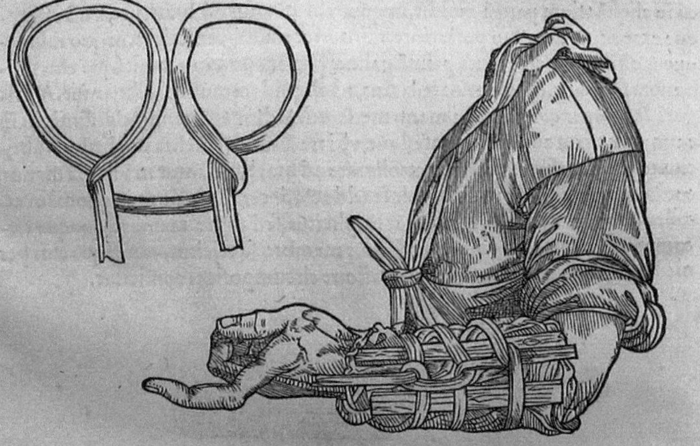

Laqueus χιαστὸς quomodo implicetur.

Ad χιαστὸν habena duplicanda eſt,cuius vtrumque caput ſiniſtrâ manu continendum:ſinus verò dextrâ prehenſus conuertendus eſt,ſic,vt capita ad ſimilitudinem literæ.X.aduerſa inter ſe ſint, inde enim nomen habuit χιαστός. quo facto ſinus capitibus.X. literam referentibus ſuperinijciendus , quódque ex his ſubiectum eſt,per medium ſinum attrahẽdum. eóque fit, vt medius laquei nexus appareat : à lateribus verò,hinc ſinus vnus,inde duo capita ſe oſtendãt. Valet autem,vbi oportet inæqualiter diſtendere.

Paſtoralis

Fig. 34.24 Guidi, Guido <il vecchio> ca. 1500–1569. Chirurgia è Graeco in Latinum conuersa, Vido Vidio Florentino interprete, cum nonnullis eiusdem Vidij commentarijs. ... Lucetiae [] Parisiorum : excudebat Petrus Galterius, pridie Calendas Maij [30 IV] 1544. Courtesy of historical section of the "Vincenzo Pinali" Medical Library of the University of Padova

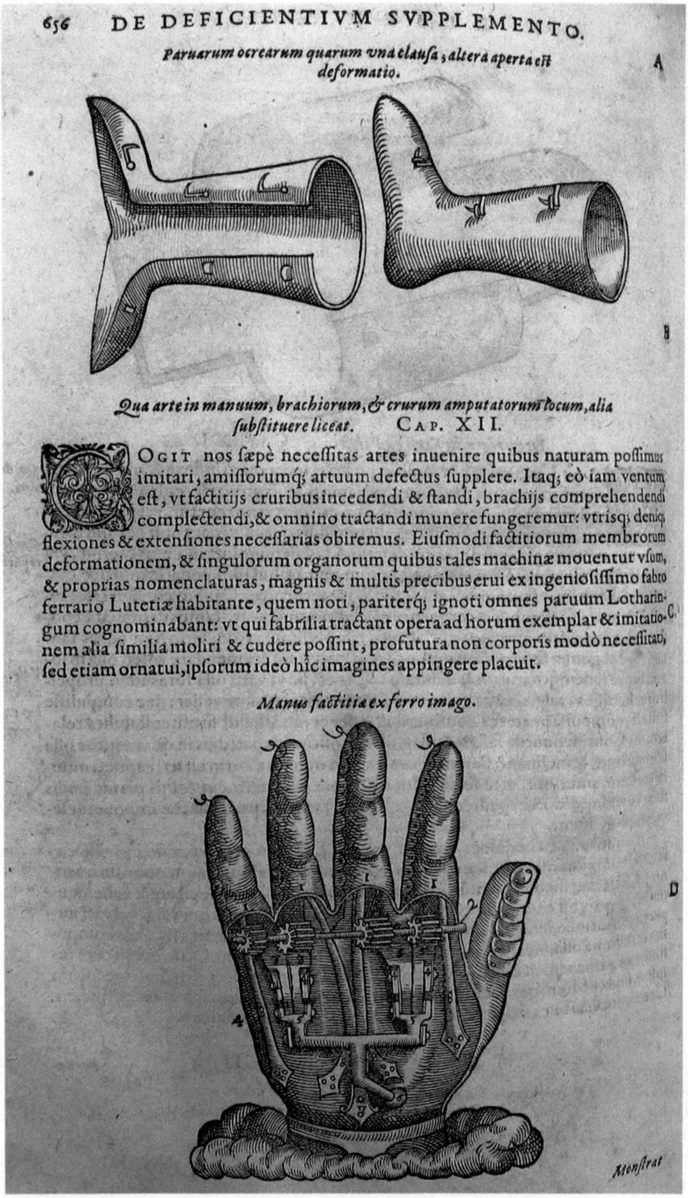

656 DE DEFICIENTIVM SVPPLEMENTO.

Paruarum ocrearum quarum vna clausa, altera aperta est deformatio. A

B

Qua arte in manuum, brachiorum, & crurum amputatorum locum, alia substituere liceat. CAP. XII.

COGIT nos sæpè necessitas artes inuenire quibus naturam possimus imitari, amissorumq; artuum defectus supplere. Itaq; eò iam ventum est, vt factitijs cruribus incedendi & standi, brachijs comprehendendi complectendi, & omnino tractandi munere fungeremur: vtrisq; deniq; flexiones & extensiones necessarias obiremus. Eiusmodi factitiorum membrorum deformationem, & singulorum organorum quibus tales machinæ mouentur vsum, & proprias nomenclaturas, magnis & multis precibus erui ex ingeniosissimo fabro ferrario Lutetiæ habitante, quem noti, pariterq; ignoti omnes paruum Lotharingum cognominabant: vt qui fabrilia tractant opera ad horum exemplar & imitationem alia similia moliri & cudere possint, profutura non corporis modò necessitati, sed etiam ornatui, ipsorum ideò hîc imagines appingere placuit. C.

Manus factitia ex ferro imago.

D

Monstrat

Fig. 34.25 Paré, Ambroise (1510?-1590). pera chirurgica Ambrosii Paraei, Galliarum regis primarii, et Parisiensis chirurgi. Quibus continentur, non solum perfectissima curandi ratio tumores praeter naturam, vulnera, ulcera, luxationes, & fracturas: . . . A docto viro, plerisque locis recognita: & latinitate donata. Iacobi Guillelmeau, . . .labore & diligentia. Omnia nunc demum magno studio elimata: et novis iconibus elegantissimis illustrata. Francofurti ad Moenum : Ioannem Feyrabend, impensis Petri Fischeri, 1594 (Impressum Francofurti ad Moenum : typis Ioannis Feyrabend, impensis Petri Fischeri, 1594). Courtesy of historical section of the "Vincenzo Pinali" Medical Library of the University of Padova

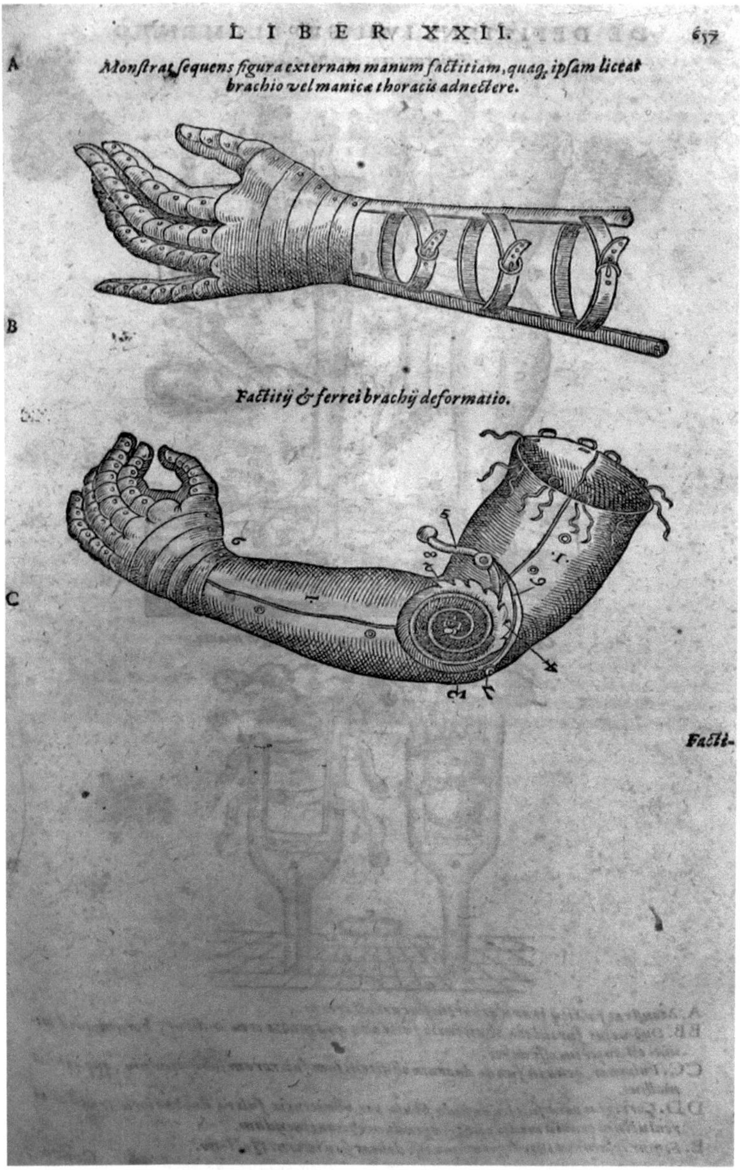

Fig. 34.26 Paré, Ambroise (1510?-1590). pera chirurgica Ambrosii Paraei, Galliarum regis primarii, et Parisiensis chirurgi. Quibus continentur, non solum perfectissima curandi ratio tumores praeter naturam, vulnera, ulcera, luxationes, & fracturas: ... A docto viro, plerisque locis recognita: & latinitate donata. Iacobi Guillelmeau, ...labore & diligentia. Omnia nunc demum magno studio elimata: et novis iconibus elegantissimis illustrata. Francofurti ad Moenum : Ioannem Feyrabend, impensis Petri Fischeri, 1594 (Impressum Francofurti ad Moenum : typis Ioannis Feyrabend, impensis Petri Fischeri, 1594). Courtesy of historical section of the "Vincenzo Pinali" Medical Library of the University of Padova

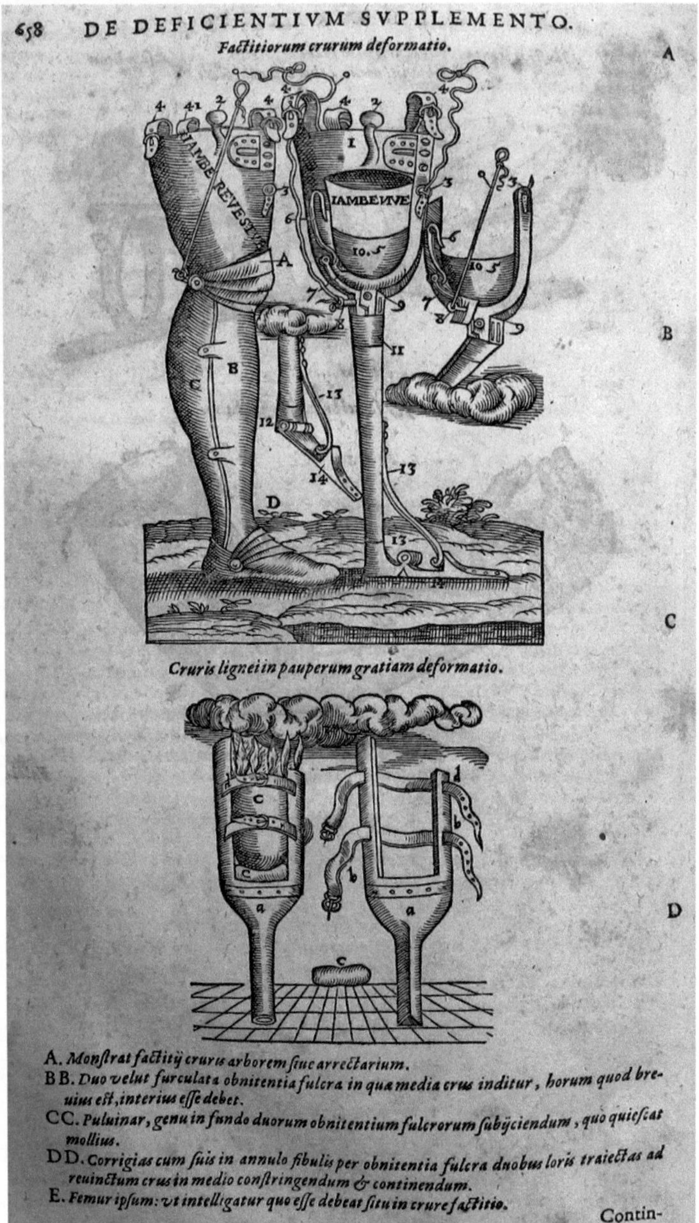
658 DE DEFICIENTIVM SVPPLEMENTO.

Factitiorum crurum deformatio.

A

B

Cruris lignei in pauperum gratiam deformatio.

C

D

A. *Monstrat factitij cruris arborem siue arrectarium.*

BB. *Duo velut furculata obnitentia fulcra in quæ media crus inditur, horum quod breuius est, interius esse debet.*

CC. *Puluinar, genu in fundo duorum obnitentium fulcrorum subijciendum, quo quiescat mollius.*

DD. *Corrigias cum suis in annulo fibulis per obnitentia fulcra duobus loris traiectas ad reuinctum crus in medio constringendum & continendum.*

E. *Femur ipsum: vt intelligatur quo esse debeat situ in crure factitio.*

Contin-

Fig. 34.27 Paré, Ambroise (1510?-1590). pera chirurgica Ambrosii Paraei, Galliarum regis primarii, et Parisiensis chirurgi. Quibus continentur, non solum perfectissima curandi ratio tumores praeter naturam, vulnera, ulcera, luxationes, & fracturas: ... A docto viro, plerisque locis recognita: & latinitate donata. Iacobi Guillelmeau, ...labore & diligentia. Omnia nunc demum magno studio elimata: et novis iconibus elegantissimis illustrata. Francofurti ad Moenum : Ioannem Feyrabend, impensis Petri Fischeri, 1594 (Impressum Francofurti ad Moenum : typis Ioannis Feyrabend, impensis Petri Fischeri, 1594). Courtesy of historical section of the "Vincenzo Pinali" Medical Library of the University of Padova

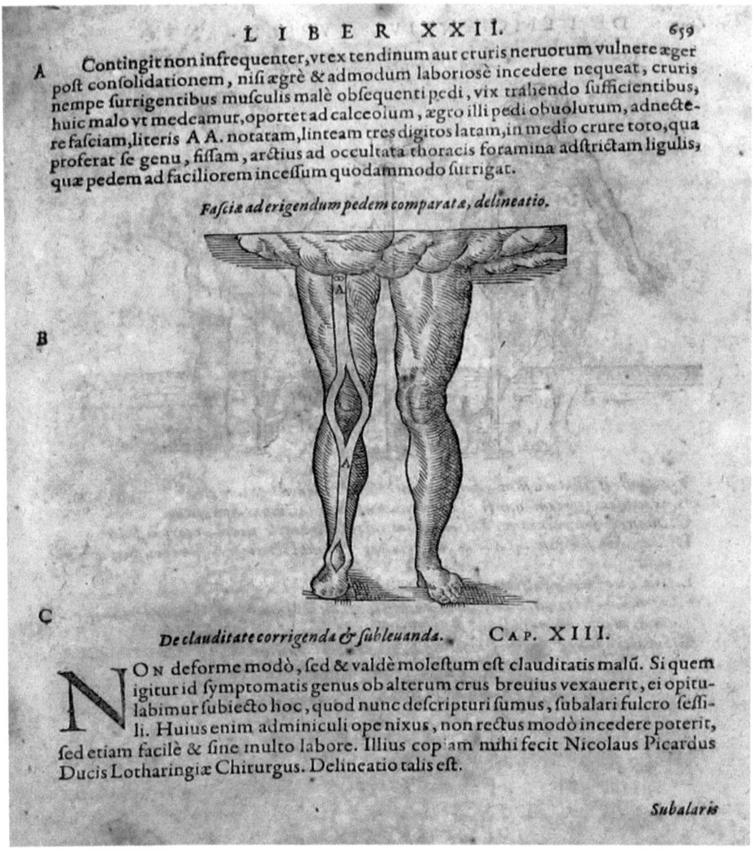

LIBER XXII. 659

A Contingit non infrequenter, vt ex tendinum aut cruris neruorum vulnere æger poſt conſolidationem, niſi ægrè & admodum laborioſè incedere nequeat, cruris nempe ſurrigentibus muſculis malè obſequenti pedi, vix trahendo ſufficientibus, huic malo vt medeamur, oportet ad calceolum, ægro illi pedi obuolutum, adnectere faſciam, literis A A. notatam, linteam tres digitos latam, in medio crure toto, qua proferat ſe genu, fiſſam, arctius ad occultata thoracis foramina adſtrictam ligulis, quæ pedem ad faciliorem inceſſum quodammodo ſurrigat.

Faſciæ ad erigendum pedem comparatæ, delineatio.

B

C

De clauditate corrigenda & ſubleuanda. CAP. XIII.

NON deforme modò, ſed & valdè moleſtum eſt clauditatis malũ. Si quem igitur id ſymptomatis genus ob alterum crus breuius vexauerit, ei opitulabimur ſubiecto hoc, quod nunc deſcripturi ſumus, ſubalari fulcro ſeſſili. Huius enim adminiculi ope nixus, non rectus modò incedere poterit, ſed etiam facilè & ſine multo labore. Illius copiam mihi fecit Nicolaus Picardus Ducis Lotharingiæ Chirurgus. Delineatio talis eſt.

Subalaris

Fig. 34.28 Paré, Ambroise (1510?-1590). pera chirurgica Ambrosii Paraei, Galliarum regis primarii, et Parisiensis chirurgi. Quibus continentur, non solum perfectissima curandi ratio tumores praeter naturam, vulnera, ulcera, luxationes, & fracturas: ... A docto viro, plerisque locis recognita: & latinitate donata. Iacobi Guillelmeau, ...labore & diligentia. Omnia nunc demum magno studio elimata: et novis iconibus elegantissimis illustrata. Francofurti ad Moenum : Ioannem Feyrabend, impensis Petri Fischeri, 1594 (Impressum Francofurti ad Moenum : typis Ioannis Feyrabend, impensis Petri Fischeri, 1594). Courtesy of historical section of the "Vincenzo Pinali" Medical Library of the University of Padova

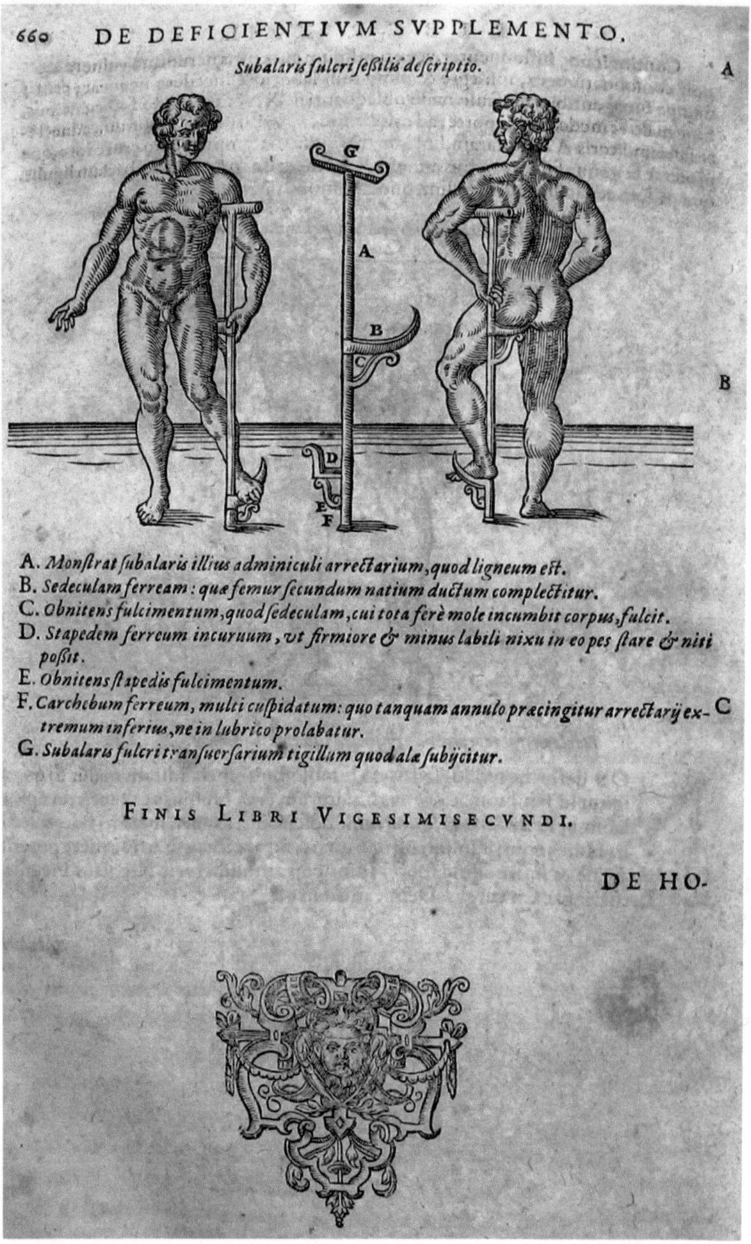

660 DE DEFICIENTIVM SVPPLEMENTO.

Subalaris fulcri sessilis descriptio.

A. *Monstrat subalaris illius adminiculi arrectarium, quod ligneum est.*
B. *Sedeculam ferream: quæ femur secundum natium ductum complectitur.*
C. *Obnitens fulcimentum, quod sedeculam, cui tota ferè mole incumbit corpus, fulcit.*
D. *Stapedem ferreum incuruum, vt firmiore & minus labili nixu in eo pes stare & niti possit.*
E. *Obnitens stapedis fulcimentum.*
F. *Carchebum ferreum, multi cuspidatum: quo tanquam annulo præcingitur arrectarij extremum inferius, ne in lubrico prolabatur.*
G. *Subalaris fulcri transuersarium tigillum quod alæ subijcitur.*

FINIS LIBRI VIGESIMISECVNDI.

DE HO-

Fig. 34.29 Paré, Ambroise (1510?-1590). pera chirurgica Ambrosii Paraei, Galliarum regis primarii, et Parisiensis chirurgi. Quibus continentur, non solum perfectissima curandi ratio tumores praeter naturam, vulnera, ulcera, luxationes, & fracturas: . . . A docto viro, plerisque locis recognita: & latinitate donata. Iacobi Guillelmeau, . . .labore & diligentia. Omnia nunc demum magno studio elimata: et novis iconibus elegantissimis illustrata. Francofurti ad Moenum : Ioannem Feyrabend, impensis Petri Fischeri, 1594 (Impressum Francofurti ad Moenum : typis Ioannis Feyrabend, impensis Petri Fischeri, 1594). Courtesy of historical section of the "Vincenzo Pinali" Medical Library of the University of Padova

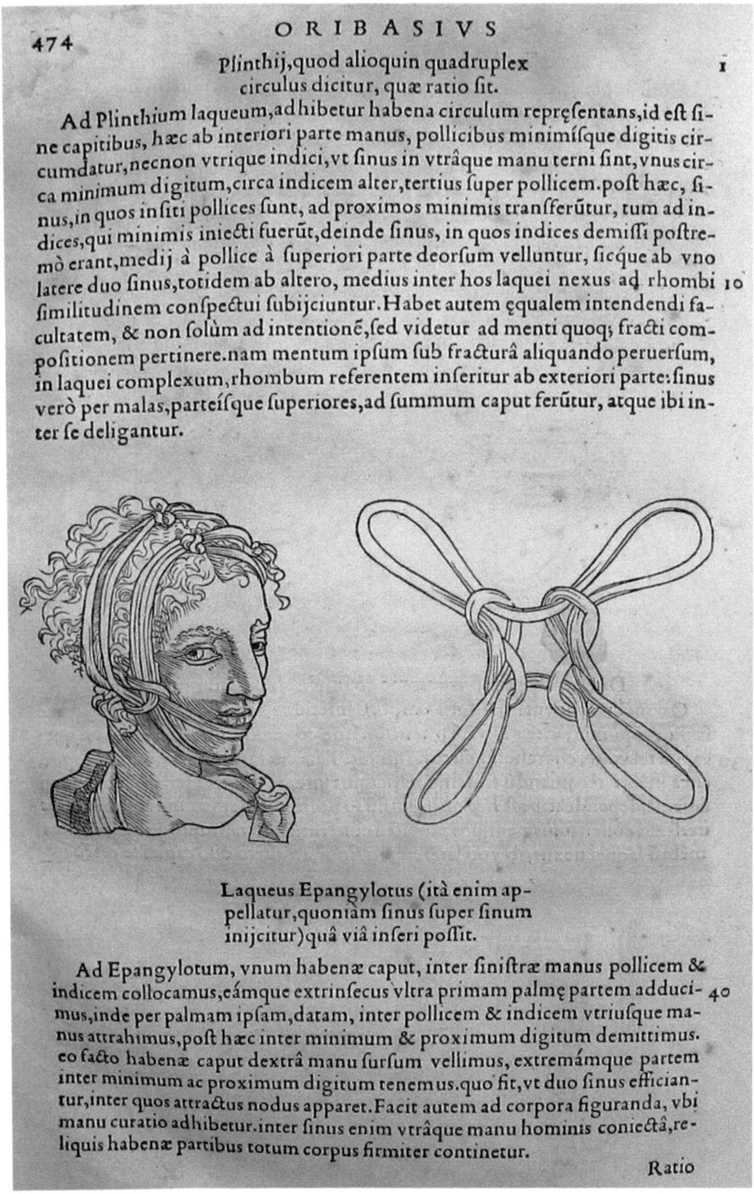

474 ORIBASIVS

Pſinthij,quod alioquin quadruplex circulus dicitur, quæ ratio ſit.

Ad Plinthium laqueum,adhibetur habena circulum repręſentans,id eſt ſine capitibus, hæc ab interiori parte manus, pollicibus minimíſque digitis circumdatur,necnon vtrique indici,vt ſinus in vtrâque manu terni ſint,vnus circa minimum digitum,circa indicem alter,tertius ſuper pollicem.poſt hæc, ſinus,in quos inſiti pollices ſunt, ad proximos minimis tranſferũtur, tum ad indices,qui minimis iniecti fuerũt,deinde ſinus, in quos indices demiſſi poſtremò erant,medij à pollice à ſuperiori parte deorſum velluntur, ſicq́ue ab vno latere duo ſinus,totidem ab altero, medius inter hos laquei nexus ad rhombi ſimilitudinem conſpectui ſubijciuntur.Habet autem ęqualem intendendi facultatem, & non ſolùm ad intentionẽ,ſed videtur ad menti quoq; fracti compoſitionem pertinere.nam mentum ipſum ſub fracturâ aliquando peruerſum, in laquei complexum,rhombum referentem inſeritur ab exteriori parte:ſinus verò per malas,parteíſque ſuperiores,ad ſummum caput ferũtur, atque ibi inter ſe deligantur.

Laqueus Epangylotus (ità enim appellatur,quoniàm ſinus ſuper ſinum inijcitur)quâ viâ inſeri poſſit.

Ad Epangylotum, vnum habenæ caput, inter ſiniſtræ manus pollicem & indicem collocamus,eámque extrinſecus vltra primam palmę partem adducimus,inde per palmam ipſam,datam, inter pollicem & indicem vtriuſque manus attrahimus,poſt hæc inter minimum & proximum digitum demittimus. eo facto habenæ caput dextrâ manu ſurſum vellimus, extremámque partem inter minimum ac proximum digitum tenemus.quo fit,vt duo ſinus efficiantur,inter quos attractus nodus apparet.Facit autem ad corpora figuranda, vbi manu curatio adhibetur.inter ſinus enim vtrâque manu hominis coniectâ,reliquis habenæ partibus totum corpus firmiter continetur.

Ratio

Fig. 34.30 Guidi, Guido <il vecchio> ca. 1500–1569. Chirurgia è Graeco in Latinum conuersa, Vido Vidio Florentino interprete, cum nonnullis eiusdem Vidij commentarijs. ... Lucetiae [] Parisiorum : excudebat Petrus Galterius, pridie Calendas Maij [30 IV] 1544. Courtesy of historical section of the "Vincenzo Pinali" Medical Library of the University of Padova

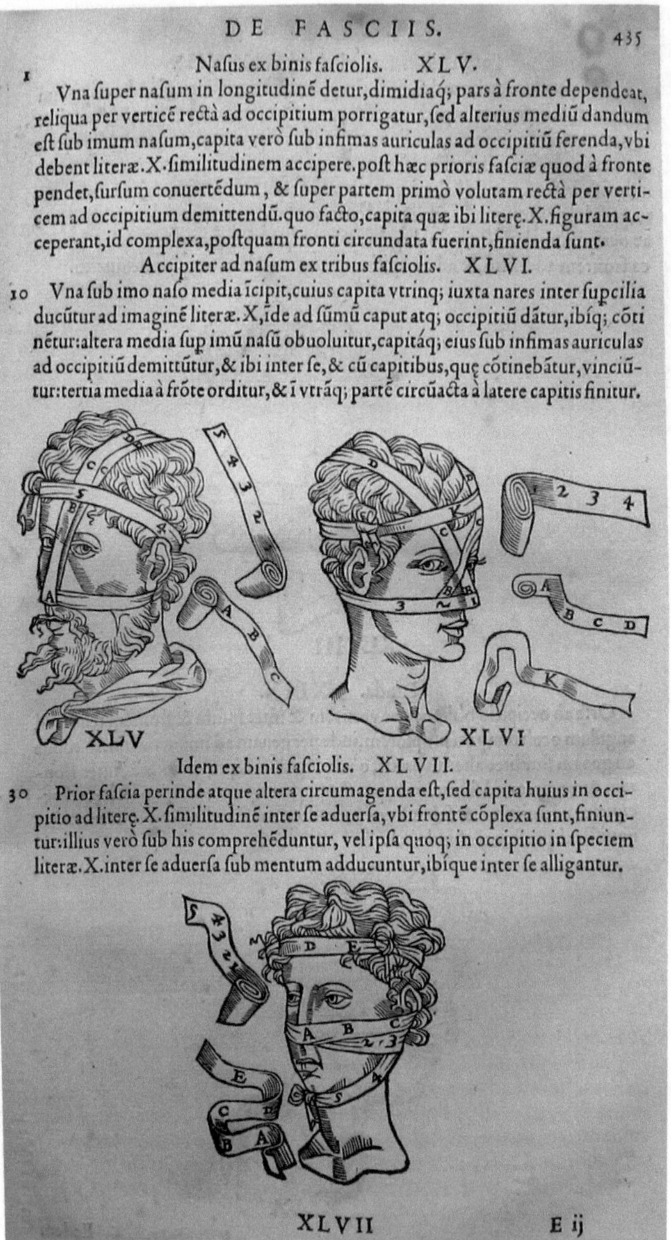

DE FASCIIS. 435

Naſus ex binis faſciolis. XLV.

Vna ſuper naſum in longitudinē detur, dimidiaq; pars à fronte dependeat, reliqua per verticē rectà ad occipitium porrigatur, ſed alterius mediū dandum eſt ſub imum naſum, capita verò ſub infimas auriculas ad occipitiū ferenda, vbi debent literæ. X. ſimilitudinem accipere. poſt hæc prioris faſciæ quod à fronte pendet, ſurſum conuertēdum, & ſuper partem primò volutam rectà per verticem ad occipitium demittendū. quo facto, capita quæ ibi literę. X. figuram acceperant, id complexa, poſtquam fronti circundata fuerint, finienda ſunt.

Accipiter ad naſum ex tribus faſciolis. XLVI.

Vna ſub imo naſo media īcipit, cuius capita vtrinq; iuxta nares inter ſupcilia ducūtur ad imaginē literæ. X, īde ad ſūmū caput atq; occipitiū dātur, ibiq; cōtinētur: altera media ſup imū naſū obuoluitur, capitáq; eius ſub infimas auriculas ad occipitiū demittūtur, & ibi inter ſe, & cū capitibus, quę cōtinebātur, vinciūtur: tertia media à frōte orditur, & ī vtrāq; partē circūacta à latere capitis finitur.

XLV XLVI

Idem ex binis faſciolis. XLVII.

Prior faſcia perinde atque altera circumagenda eſt, ſed capita huius in occipitio ad literę. X. ſimilitudinē inter ſe aduerſa, vbi frontē cōplexa ſunt, finiuntur: illius verò ſub his comprehēduntur, vel ipſa quoq; in occipitio in ſpeciem literæ. X. inter ſe aduerſa ſub mentum adducuntur, ibíque inter ſe alligantur.

XLVII E ij

Fig. 34.31 Guidi, Guido <il vecchio> ca. 1500–1569. Chirurgia è Graeco in Latinum conuersa, Vido Vidio Florentino interprete, cum nonnullis eiusdem Vidij commentarijs. ... Lucetiae [] Parisiorum : excudebat Petrus Galterius, pridie Calendas Maij [30 IV] 1544. Courtesy of historical section of the "Vincenzo Pinali" Medical Library of the University of Padova

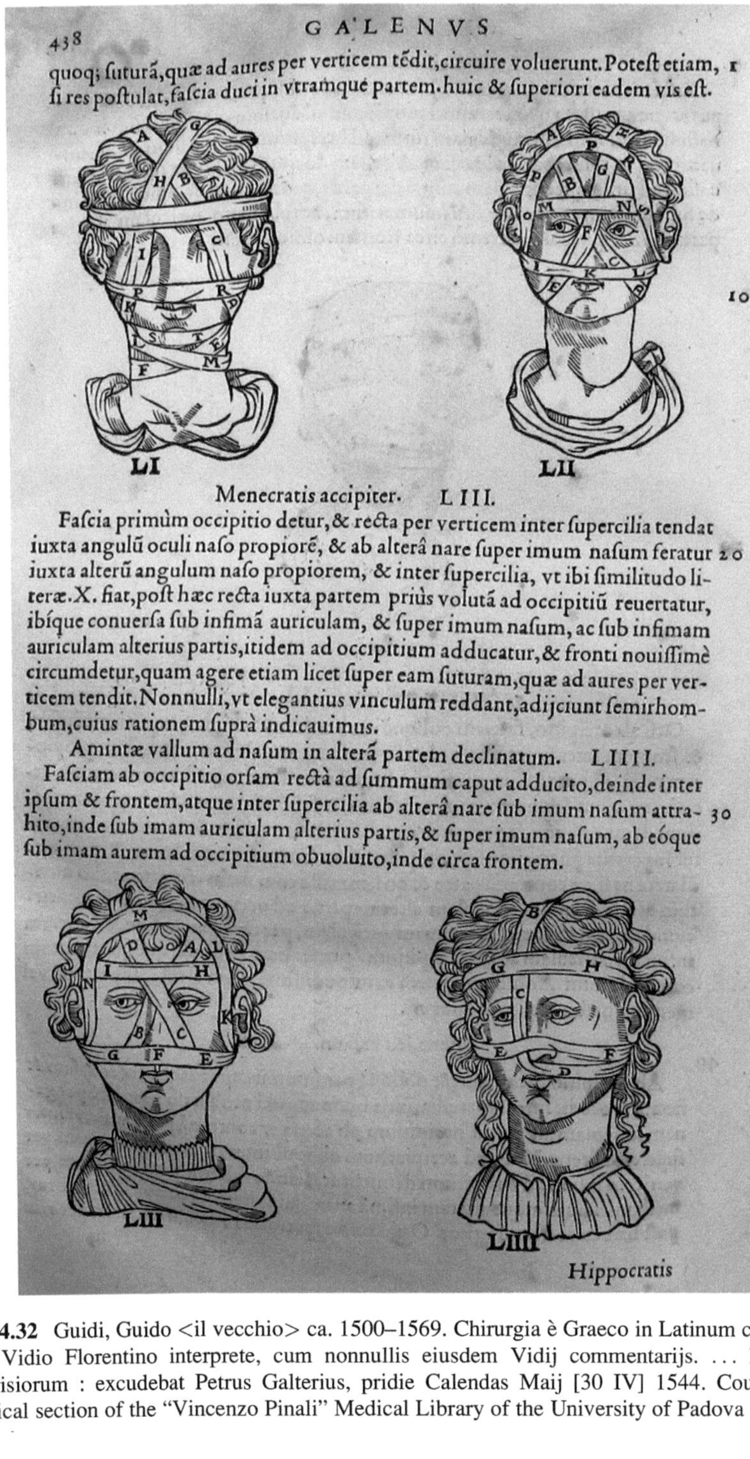
GALENVS

438

quoq; ſuturã,quæ ad aures per verticem tẽdit,circuire voluerunt. Poteſt etiam, ſi res poſtulat,faſcia duci in vtramquẽ partem. huic & ſuperiori eadem vis eſt.

LI LII

Menecratis accipiter. LIII.

Faſcia primùm occipitio detur,& recta per verticem inter ſupercilia tendat iuxta angulũ oculi naſo propiorẽ, & ab alterâ nare ſuper imum naſum feratur iuxta alterũ angulum naſo propiorem, & inter ſupercilia, vt ibi ſimilitudo literæ.X. fiat,poſt hæc recta iuxta partem priùs volutã ad occipitiũ reuertatur, ibíque conuerſa ſub infimã auriculam, & ſuper imum naſum, ac ſub infimam auriculam alterius partis,itidem ad occipitium adducatur,& fronti nouiſſimè circumdetur,quam agere etiam licet ſuper eam ſuturam,quæ ad aures per verticem tendit. Nonnulli,vt elegantius vinculum reddant,adijciunt ſemirhombum,cuius rationem ſuprà indicauimus.

Amintæ vallum ad naſum in alterã partem declinatum. LIIII.

Faſciam ab occipitio orſam rectà ad ſummum caput adducito,deinde inter ipſum & frontem,atque inter ſupercilia ab alterâ nare ſub imum naſum attrahito,inde ſub imam auriculam alterius partis,& ſuper imum naſum, ab eóque ſub imam aurem ad occipitium obuoluito,inde circa frontem.

LIII LIIII

Hippocratis

Fig. 34.32 Guidi, Guido <il vecchio> ca. 1500–1569. Chirurgia è Graeco in Latinum conuersa, Vido Vidio Florentino interprete, cum nonnullis eiusdem Vidij commentarijs. ... Lucetiae [] Parisiorum : excudebat Petrus Galterius, pridie Calendas Maij [30 IV] 1544. Courtesy of historical section of the "Vincenzo Pinali" Medical Library of the University of Padova

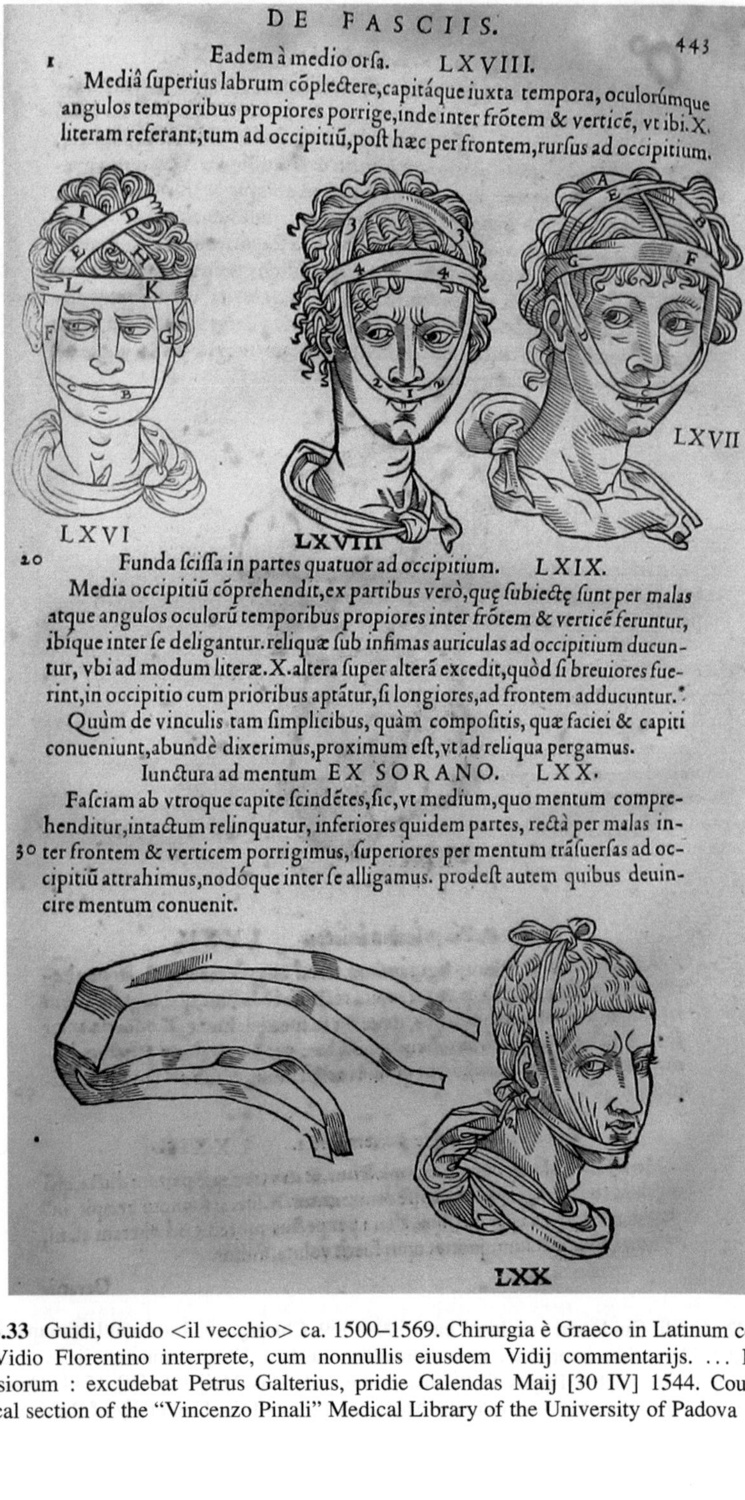

DE FASCIIS. 443

Eadem à medio orſa. LXVIII.

Mediâ ſuperius labrum cõplectere,capitáque iuxta tempora, oculorúmque angulos temporibus propiores porrige,inde inter frõtem & verticẽ, vt ibi. X. literam referant,tum ad occipitiũ,poſt hæc per frontem,rurſus ad occipitium.

LXVI LXVIII LXVII

Funda ſciſſa in partes quatuor ad occipitium. LXIX.

Media occipitiũ cõprehendit,ex partibus verò,quę ſubiectę ſunt per malas atque angulos oculorũ temporibus propiores inter frõtem & verticẽ feruntur, ibíque inter ſe deligantur. reliquæ ſub infimas auriculas ad occipitium ducuntur, vbi ad modum literæ. X. altera ſuper alterã excedit,quòd ſi breuiores fuerint,in occipitio cum prioribus aptãtur,ſi longiores,ad frontem adducuntur.

Quùm de vinculis tam ſimplicibus, quàm compoſitis, quæ faciei & capiti conueniunt,abundè dixerimus,proximum eſt,vt ad reliqua pergamus.

Iunctura ad mentum EX SORANO. LXX.

Faſciam ab vtroque capite ſcindẽtes,ſic,vt medium,quo mentum comprehenditur,intactum relinquatur, inferiores quidem partes, rectà per malas inter frontem & verticem porrigimus, ſuperiores per mentum trãſuerſas ad occipitiũ attrahimus,nodóque inter ſe alligamus. prodeſt autem quibus deuincire mentum conuenit.

LXX

Fig. 34.33 Guidi, Guido <il vecchio> ca. 1500–1569. Chirurgia è Graeco in Latinum conuersa, Vido Vidio Florentino interprete, cum nonnullis eiusdem Vidij commentarijs. … Lucetiae [] Parisiorum : excudebat Petrus Galterius, pridie Calendas Maij [30 IV] 1544. Courtesy of historical section of the "Vincenzo Pinali" Medical Library of the University of Padova

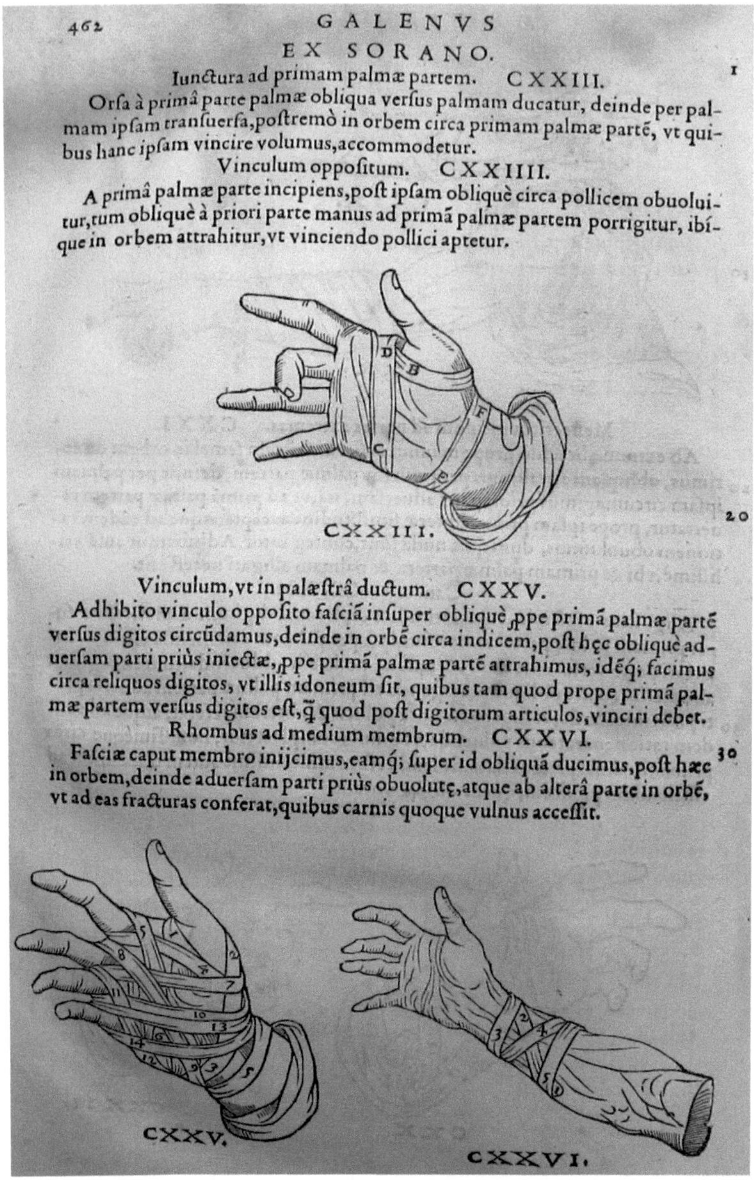

462 GALENVS
EX SORANO.

Iunctura ad primam palmæ partem. CXXIII.

Orſa à primâ parte palmæ obliqua verſus palmam ducatur, deinde per palmam ipſam tranſuerſa, poſtremò in orbem circa primam palmæ partẽ, vt quibus hanc ipſam vincire volumus, accommodetur.

Vinculum oppoſitum. CXXIIII.

A primâ palmæ parte incipiens, poſt ipſam obliquè circa pollicem obuoluitur, tum obliquè à priori parte manus ad primã palmæ partem porrigitur, ibíque in orbem attrahitur, vt vinciendo pollici aptetur.

CXXIII.

Vinculum, vt in palæſtrâ ductum. CXXV.

Adhibito vinculo oppoſito faſciã inſuper obliquè, ꝑpe primã palmæ partẽ verſus digitos circũdamus, deinde in orbẽ circa indicem, poſt hęc obliquè aduerſam parti priùs iniectæ, ꝑpe primã palmæ partẽ attrahimus, idẽq; facimus circa reliquos digitos, vt illis idoneum ſit, quibus tam quod prope primã palmæ partem verſus digitos eſt, q̃ quod poſt digitorum articulos, vinciri debet.

Rhombus ad medium membrum. CXXVI.

Faſciæ caput membro inijcimus, eamq; ſuper id obliquã ducimus, poſt hæc in orbem, deinde aduerſam parti priùs obuolutę, atque ab alterâ parte in orbẽ, vt ad eas fracturas conferat, quibus carnis quoque vulnus acceſſit.

CXXV. CXXVI.

Fig. 34.34 Guidi, Guido <il vecchio> ca. 1500–1569. Chirurgia è Graeco in Latinum conuersa, Vido Vidio Florentino interprete, cum nonnullis eiusdem Vidij commentarijs. ... Lucetiae [] Parisiorum : excudebat Petrus Galterius, pridie Calendas Maij [30 IV] 1544. Courtesy of historical section of the "Vincenzo Pinali" Medical Library of the University of Padova

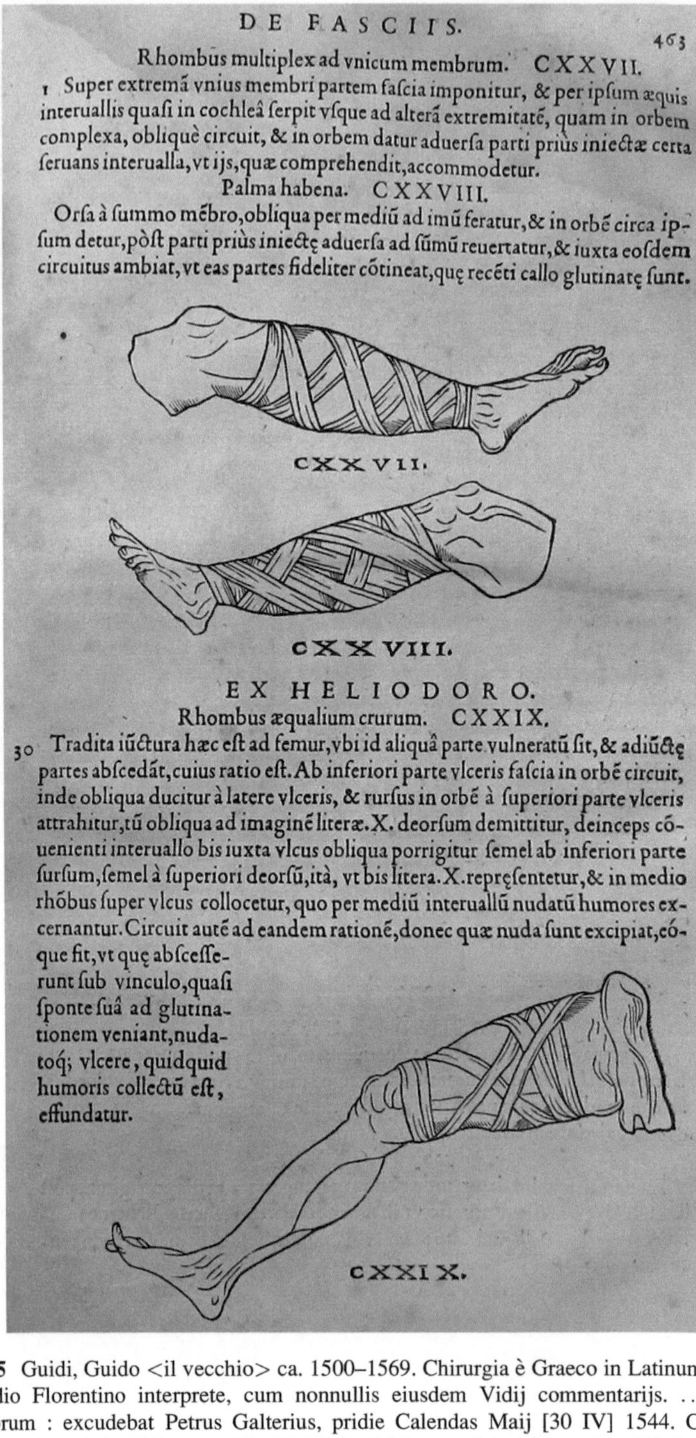

DE FASCIIS. 463

Rhombus multiplex ad vnicum membrum. CXXVII.

1 Super extremã vnius membri partem faſcia imponitur, & per ipſum æquis interuallis quaſi in cochleã ſerpit vſque ad alterã extremitatẽ, quam in orbem complexa, obliquè circuit, & in orbem datur aduerſa parti priùs iniectæ certa ſeruans interualla, vt ijs, quæ comprehendit, accommodetur.

Palma habena. CXXVIII.

Orſa à ſummo mẽbro, obliqua per mediũ ad imũ feratur, & in orbẽ circa ipſum detur, pòſt parti priùs iniectę aduerſa ad ſũmũ reuertatur, & iuxta eoſdem circuitus ambiat, vt eas partes fideliter cõtineat, quę recẽti callo glutinatę ſunt.

CXXVII.

CXXVIII.

EX HELIODORO.

Rhombus æqualium crurum. CXXIX.

30 Tradita iũctura hæc eſt ad femur, vbi id aliquâ parte vulneratũ ſit, & adiũctę partes abſcedãt, cuius ratio eſt. Ab inferiori parte vlceris faſcia in orbẽ circuit, inde obliqua ducitur à latere vlceris, & rurſus in orbẽ à ſuperiori parte vlceris attrahitur, tũ obliqua ad imaginẽ literæ. X. deorſum demittitur, deinceps cõuenienti interuallo bis iuxta vlcus obliqua porrigitur ſemel ab inferiori parte ſurſum, ſemel à ſuperiori deorſũ, ità, vt bis litera. X. reprę ſentetur, & in medio rhõbus ſuper vlcus collocetur, quo per mediũ interuallũ nudatũ humores excernantur. Circuit autẽ ad eandem rationẽ, donec quæ nuda ſunt excipiat, cóque fit, vt quę abſceſſerunt ſub vinculo, quaſi ſponte ſuâ ad glutinationem veniant, nudatoq; vlcere, quidquid humoris collectũ eſt, effundatur.

CXXIX.

Fig. 34.35 Guidi, Guido <il vecchio> ca. 1500–1569. Chirurgia è Graeco in Latinum conuersa, Vido Vidio Florentino interprete, cum nonnullis eiusdem Vidij commentarijs. ... Lucetiae [] Parisiorum : excudebat Petrus Galterius, pridie Calendas Maij [30 IV] 1544. Courtesy of historical section of the "Vincenzo Pinali" Medical Library of the University of Padova

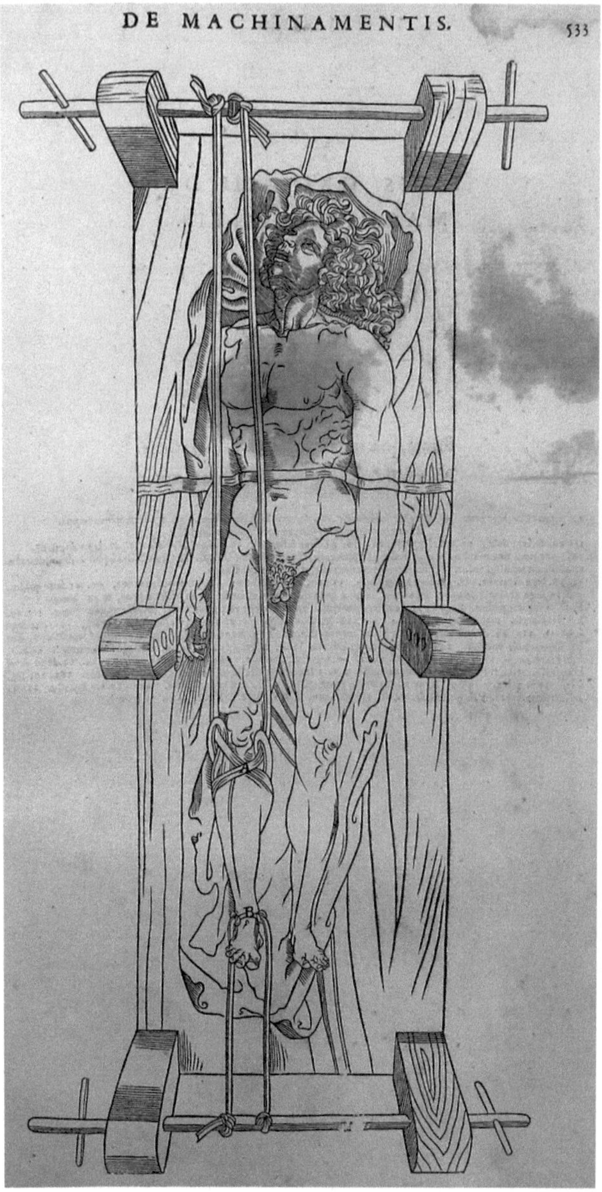

Fig. 34.36 Guidi, Guido <il vecchio> ca. 1500–1569. Chirurgia è Graeco in Latinum conuersa, Vido Vidio Florentino interprete, cum nonnullis eiusdem Vidij commentarijs. ... Lucetiae [] Parisiorum : excudebat Petrus Galterius, pridie Calendas Maij [30 IV] 1544. Courtesy of historical section of the "Vincenzo Pinali" Medical Library of the University of Padova

Fig. 34.37 Guidi, Guido <il vecchio> ca. 1500–1569. Chirurgia è Graeco in Latinum conuersa, Vido Vidio Florentino interprete, cum nonnullis eiusdem Vidij commentarijs. ... Lucetiae [] Parisiorum : excudebat Petrus Galterius, pridie Calendas Maij [30 IV] 1544. Courtesy of historical section of the "Vincenzo Pinali" Medical Library of the University of Padova

Fig. 34.38 Guidi, Guido <il vecchio> ca. 1500–1569. Chirurgia è Graeco in Latinum conuersa, Vido Vidio Florentino interprete, cum nonnullis eiusdem Vidij commentarijs. ... Lucetiae [] Parisiorum : excudebat Petrus Galterius, pridie Calendas Maij [30 IV] 1544. Courtesy of historical section of the "Vincenzo Pinali" Medical Library of the University of Padova

Fig. 34.39 Guidi, Guido <il vecchio> ca. 1500–1569. Chirurgia è Graeco in Latinum conuersa, Vido Vidio Florentino interprete, cum nonnullis eiusdem Vidij commentarijs. … Lucetiae [] Parisiorum : excudebat Petrus Galterius, pridie Calendas Maij [30 IV] 1544. Courtesy of historical section of the "Vincenzo Pinali" Medical Library of the University of Padova

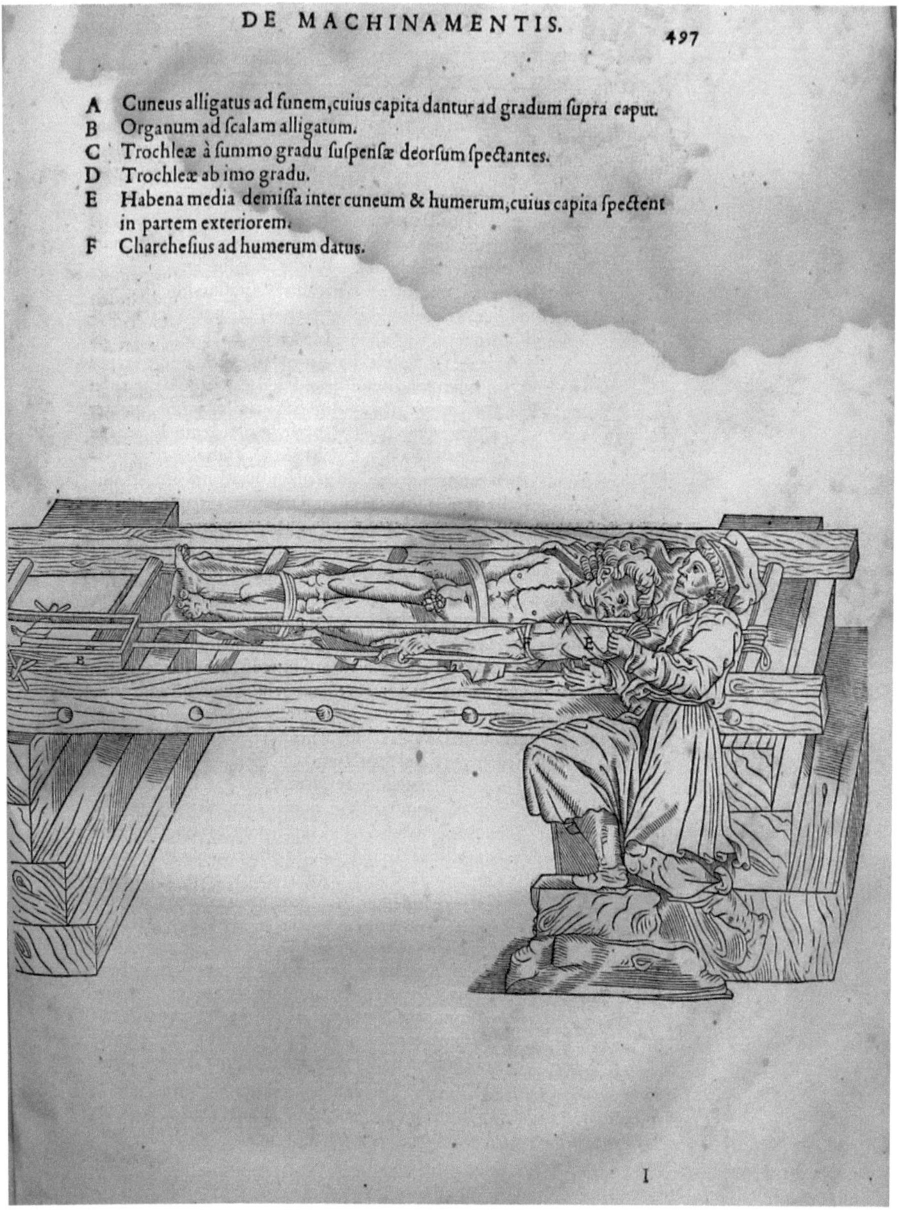
DE MACHINAMENTIS. 497

A Cuneus alligatus ad funem, cuius capita dantur ad gradum ſupra caput.
B Organum ad ſcalam alligatum.
C Trochleæ à ſummo gradu ſuſpenſæ deorſum ſpectantes.
D Trochleæ ab imo gradu.
E Habena media demiſſa inter cuneum & humerum, cuius capita ſpectent in partem exteriorem.
F Charcheſius ad humerum datus.

I

Fig. 34.40 Guidi, Guido <il vecchio> ca. 1500–1569. Chirurgia è Graeco in Latinum conuersa, Vido Vidio Florentino interprete, cum nonnullis eiusdem Vidij commentarijs. … Lucetiae [] Parisiorum : excudebat Petrus Galterius, pridie Calendas Maij [30 IV] 1544. Courtesy of historical section of the "Vincenzo Pinali" Medical Library of the University of Padova

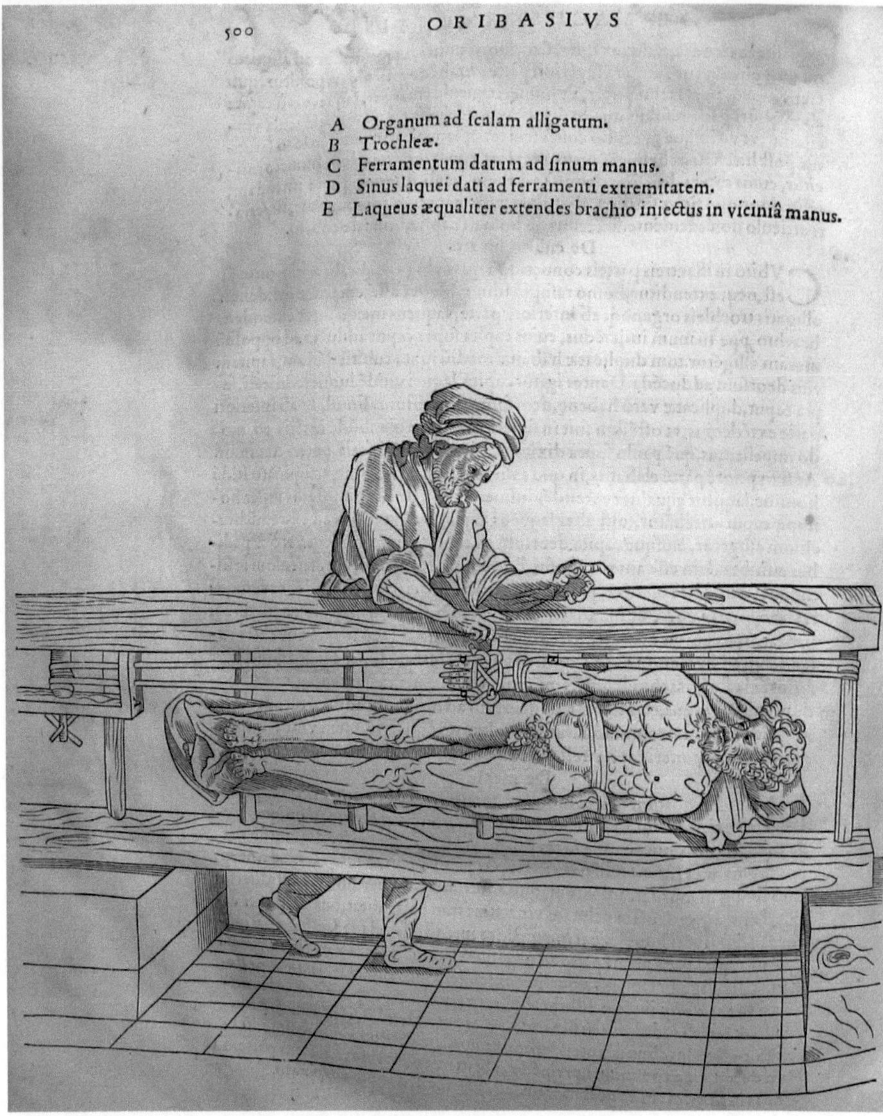

Fig. 34.41 Guidi, Guido <il vecchio> ca. 1500–1569. Chirurgia è Graeco in Latinum conuersa, Vido Vidio Florentino interprete, cum nonnullis eiusdem Vidij commentarijs. … Lucetiae [] Parisiorum : excudebat Petrus Galterius, pridie Calendas Maij [30 IV] 1544. Courtesy of historical section of the "Vincenzo Pinali" Medical Library of the University of Padova

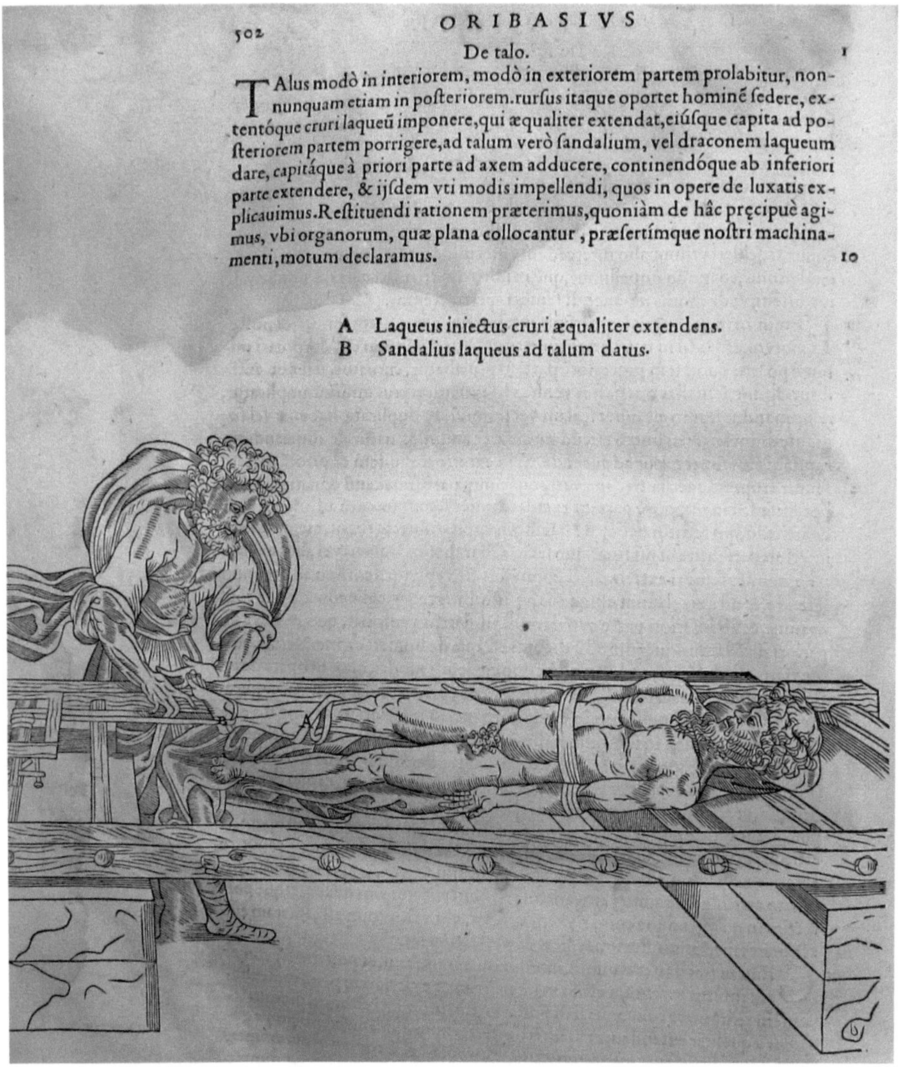

502 ORIBASIVS

De talo.

TAlus modò in interiorem, modò in exteriorem partem prolabitur, nonnunquam etiam in poſteriorem. rurſus itaque oportet hominē ſedere, extentóque cruri laqueū imponere, qui æqualiter extendat, eiúſque capita ad poſteriorem partem porrigere, ad talum verò ſandalium, vel draconem laqueum dare, capitáque à priori parte ad axem adducere, continendóque ab inferiori parte extendere, & ijſdem vti modis impellendi, quos in opere de luxatis explicauimus. Reſtituendi rationem præterimus, quoniàm de hâc præcipuè agimus, vbi organorum, quæ plana collocantur, præſertímque noſtri machinamenti, motum declaramus.

A Laqueus iniectus cruri æqualiter extendens.
B Sandalius laqueus ad talum datus.

Fig. 34.42 Guidi, Guido <il vecchio> ca. 1500–1569. Chirurgia è Graeco in Latinum conuersa, Vido Vidio Florentino interprete, cum nonnullis eiusdem Vidij commentarijs. ... Lucetiae [] Parisiorum : excudebat Petrus Galterius, pridie Calendas Maij [30 IV] 1544. Courtesy of historical section of the "Vincenzo Pinali" Medical Library of the University of Padova

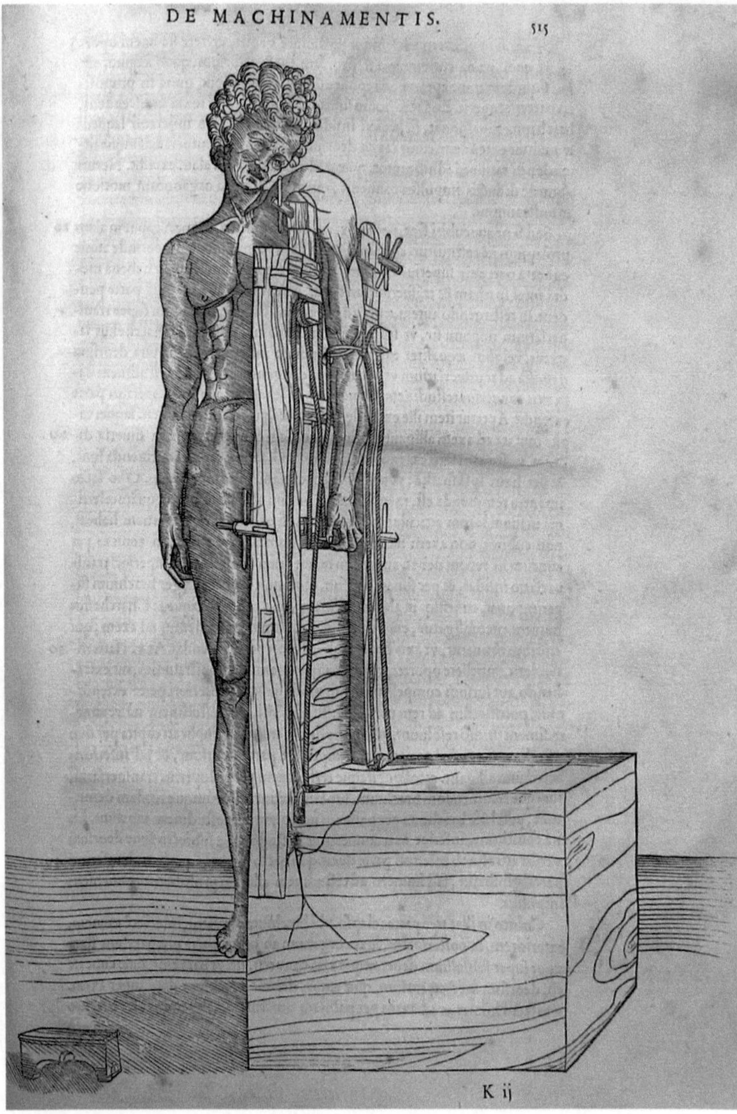

Fig. 34.43 Guidi, Guido <il vecchio> ca. 1500–1569. Chirurgia è Graeco in Latinum conuersa, Vido Vidio Florentino interprete, cum nonnullis eiusdem Vidij commentarijs. ... Lucetiae [] Parisiorum : excudebat Petrus Galterius, pridie Calendas Maij [30 IV] 1544. Courtesy of historical section of the "Vincenzo Pinali" Medical Library of the University of Padova

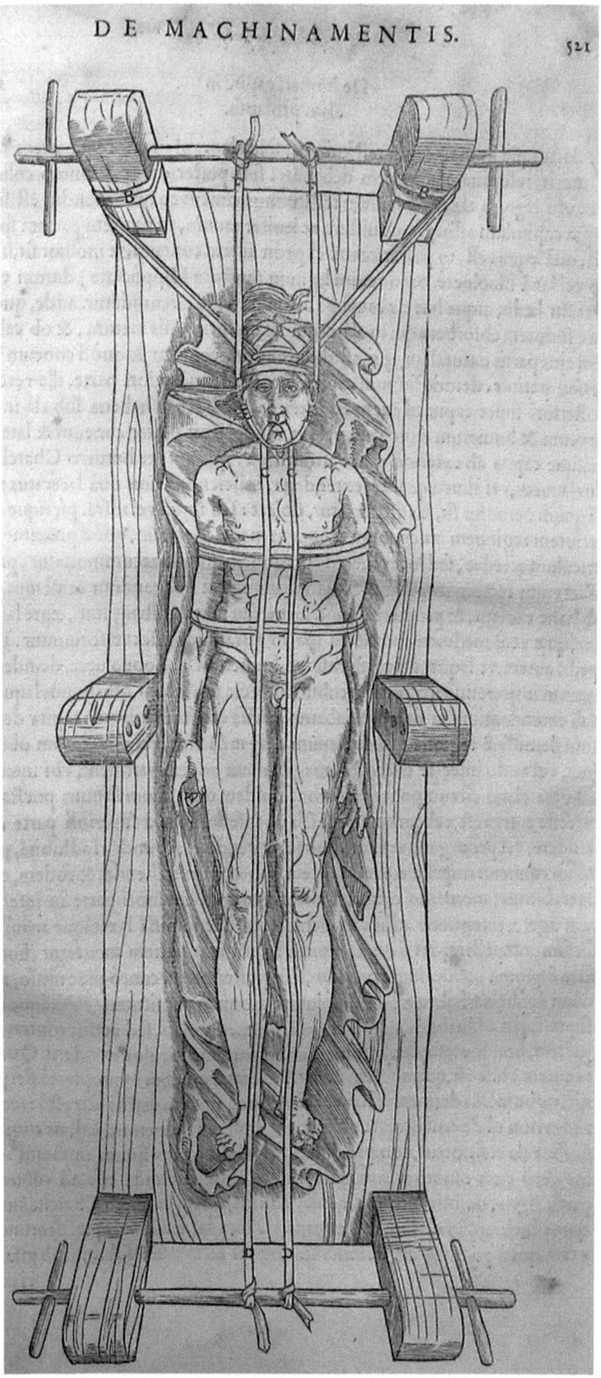

Fig. 34.44 Guidi, Guido <il vecchio> ca. 1500–1569. Chirurgia è Graeco in Latinum conuersa, Vido Vidio Florentino interprete, cum nonnullis eiusdem Vidij commentarijs. ... Lucetiae [] Parisiorum : excudebat Petrus Galterius, pridie Calendas Maij [30 IV] 1544. Courtesy of historical section of the "Vincenzo Pinali" Medical Library of the University of Padova

Fig. 34.45 Guidi, Guido <il vecchio> ca. 1500–1569. Chirurgia è Graeco in Latinum conuersa, Vido Vidio Florentino interprete, cum nonnullis eiusdem Vidij commentarijs. ... Lucetiae [] Parisiorum : excudebat Petrus Galterius, pridie Calendas Maij [30 IV] 1544. Courtesy of historical section of the "Vincenzo Pinali" Medical Library of the University of Padova

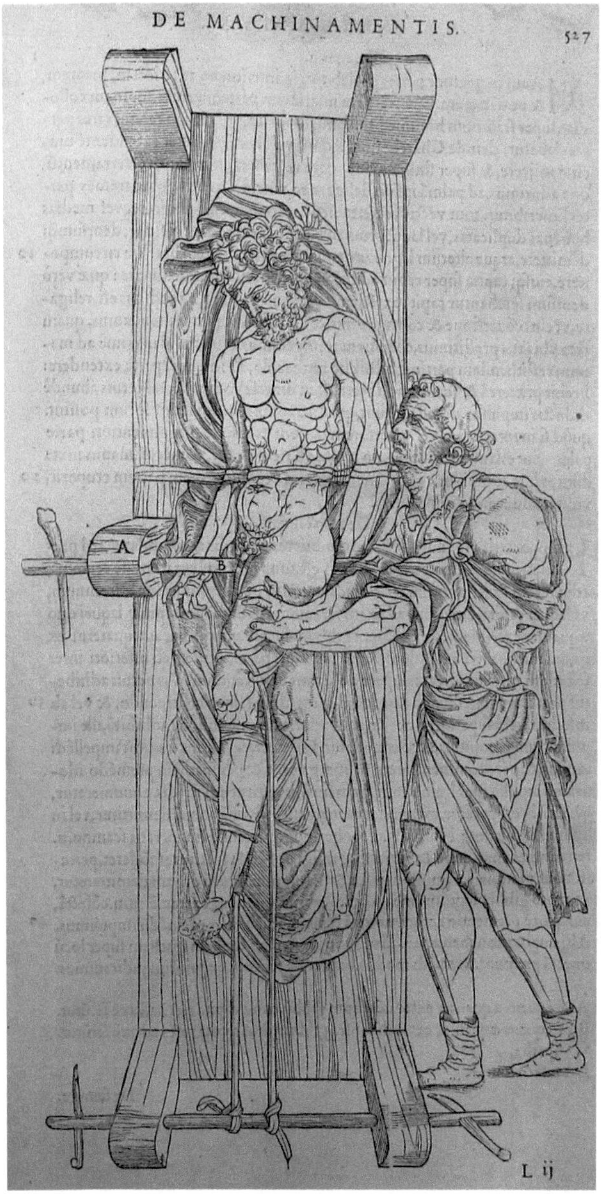

Fig. 34.46 Guidi, Guido <il vecchio> ca. 1500–1569. Chirurgia è Graeco in Latinum conuersa, Vido Vidio Florentino interprete, cum nonnullis eiusdem Vidij commentarijs. ... Lucetiae [] Parisiorum : excudebat Petrus Galterius, pridie Calendas Maij [30 IV] 1544. Courtesy of historical section of the "Vincenzo Pinali" Medical Library of the University of Padova

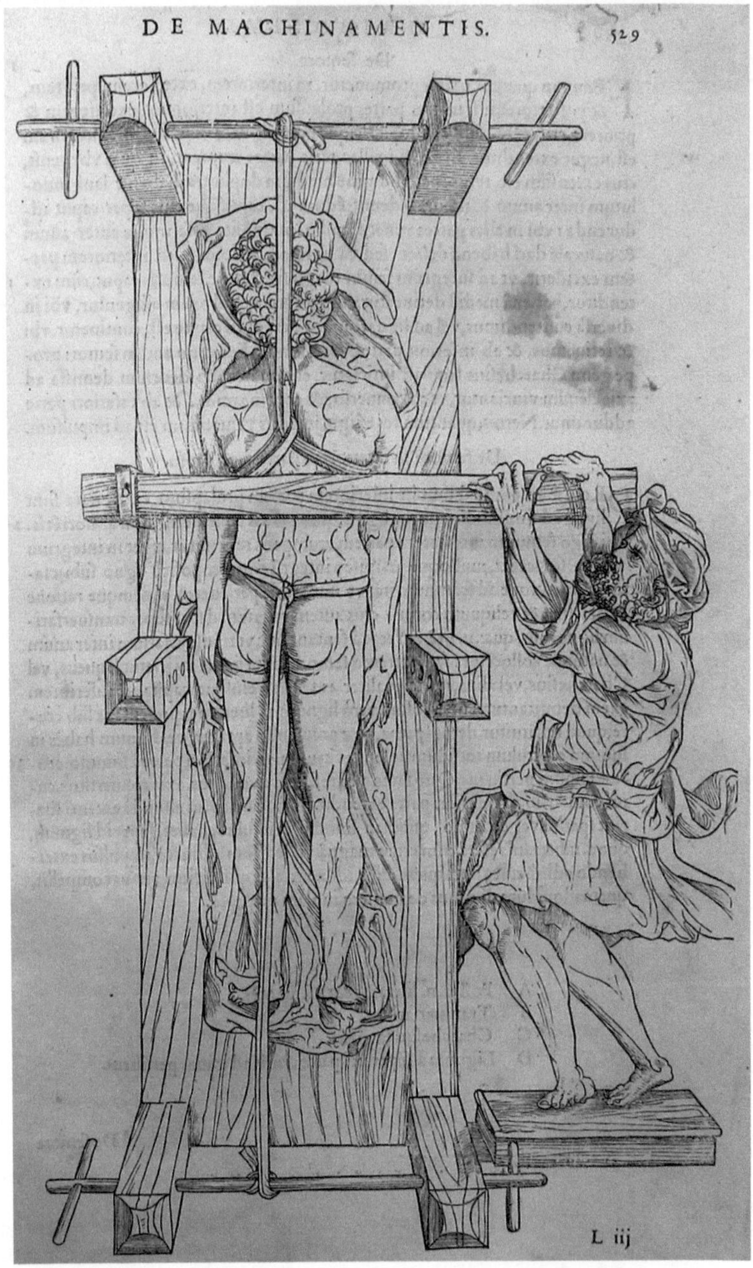

Fig. 34.47 Guidi, Guido <il vecchio> ca. 1500–1569. Chirurgia è Graeco in Latinum conuersa, Vido Vidio Florentino interprete, cum nonnullis eiusdem Vidij commentarijs. ... Lucetiae [] Parisiorum : excudebat Petrus Galterius, pridie Calendas Maij [30 IV] 1544. Courtesy of historical section of the "Vincenzo Pinali" Medical Library of the University of Padova

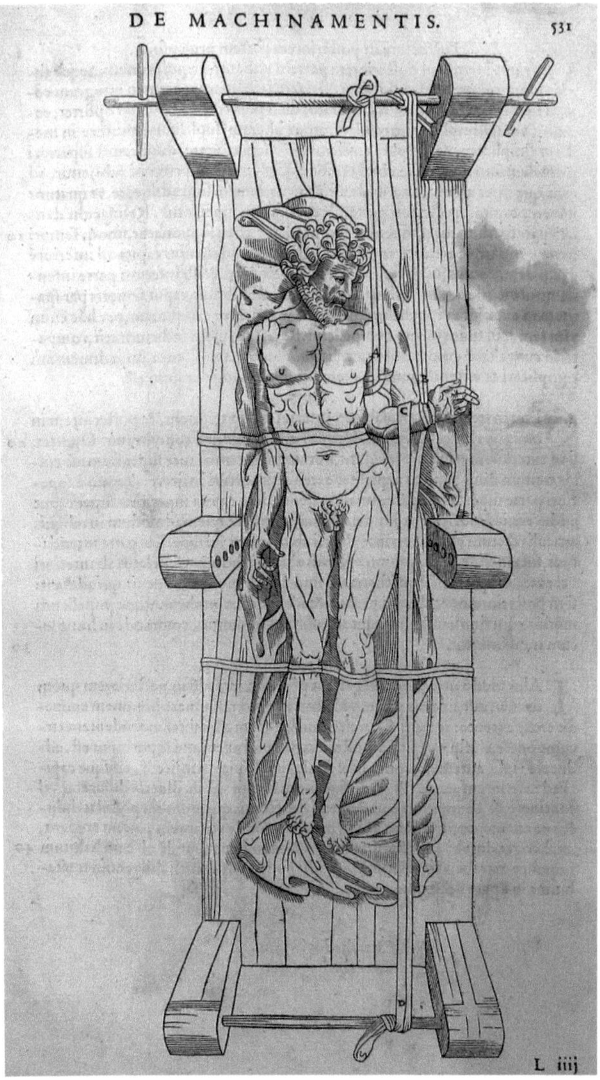

Fig. 34.48 Guidi, Guido <il vecchio> ca. 1500–1569. Chirurgia è Graeco in Latinum conuersa, Vido Vidio Florentino interprete, cum nonnullis eiusdem Vidij commentarijs. ... Lucetiae [] Parisiorum : excudebat Petrus Galterius, pridie Calendas Maij [30 IV] 1544. Courtesy of historical section of the "Vincenzo Pinali" Medical Library of the University of Padova

Note on References-Bibliography

The editors have proposed to the authors the adoption of bibliographical references in the guise of "references" or "bibliography" in accordance with their citation needs in relation to the specific chapter.

S.D. Ferrara et al. (eds.), *Personal Injury and Damage Ascertainment under Civil Law*, DOI 10.1007/978-3-319-29812-2

Acknowledgments

The editor and coeditors are grateful to the International Academy of Legal Medicine (IALM), its Presidium, Scientific Committee, and all of the Members of the National Societies of Legal Medicine who collaborated for the realization of this Monograph. A special appreciation goes to Dr. Thomas M. Dewis for the thorough and courteous language editing of the volume.

Further thanks go to Dr. Giuseppina Sonia Zecchin, Head of Libraries at the Faculty of Medicine of the University of Padova, and to Mrs. Giulia Rigoni Savioli for the assistance provided to the editors in the selection of the historical iconography from the Historical Section of "Vincenzo Pinali" Medical Library.

S.D. Ferrara et al. (eds.), *Personal Injury and Damage Ascertainment under Civil Law*, DOI 10.1007/978-3-319-29812-2

Glossary

Anaesthesia Report This report comprises all information on the physiopathological state of the patient during anaesthesia and surgery.

Ascertainment Methodology This is the methodology for ascertaining any personal injury and/or damage under civil-tort law.

Authorization for admission Consent form signed by patient or patient's legal representative if the patient is physically or psychologically incapable of doing so.

Barème The term refers to the evaluative reference tables of permanent impairment. From the practical point of view, these are presented as a collection in tabular form of the main physical and psychic impairments, divided by organs and apparatuses, to each of which is assigned a numerical value expressed as percentage representing, indicatively, the degree of impairment of the psychophysical integrity.

Capability of causing harm (Ex Ante Criterion of) This is the capability of a specific action/event to cause harm or disease. Such a capability must be ascertained by comparing the nature and strength of the action/event to the effects observed.

Causal Link/Causal Value This is the connection between the "event—possible cause" and the "injury—effect") or between the injury (possible cause) and the related pecuniary/non-pecuniary damage (effect), where the latter is understood to be a consequence of the first.

Chronological criterion This indicates the possible correlation between the moment of action of the causal factor (which may involve the omission of an action) and the moment when the injury becomes manifest.

Clinical Discharge Report This is issued when the patient is discharged, from the medical point of view, and goes home or to another hospital. It summarizes the period in which the patient was hospitalized and should be a complete document,

S.D. Ferrara et al. (eds.), *Personal Injury and Damage Ascertainment under Civil Law*, DOI 10.1007/978-3-319-29812-2

which includes the cause of hospitalization, with precise diagnoses, treatments administered, evolution, the state of the patient when discharged, and treatment (s) to be followed, with indications of any future examinations and whether the family doctor should carry out monitoring.

Clinical Synthesis This is the summary of the clinical, documentary, and objective data before the phase of analysis and evaluation.

Compensation Payment of a sum of money in proportion to the pecuniary and non-pecuniary losses suffered by the damaged person.

Conditio sine qua non This is the juridical theory concerning the essential requisite existing between a specific antecedent and the fact in the case where the fact would not have occurred without the antecedent. It is also known as the *but-for* rule and is the minimum indispensable for the objective imputation of harmful events in Criminal Law.

Consent Documents Such documents have to demonstrate that the patient was properly informed and that he has fully understood the implications of the given medical intervention and has agreed to it. They are generally compulsory by law.

Counterfactual Reasoning This is a type of hypothetical reasoning in which, regarding the causal link, one tries to answer the question as to whether, without the conduct of the actor—contrary to the facts—a certain event would have taken place in any case. If the ascertainment indicates a negative answer (the event would have taken place), one may conclude that the action, or omission, is a necessary condition for the event to take place. If instead the answer is positive (the event would have taken place in any case), the behavior of the actor was not a necessary condition and there is no causal link.

Criterion of exclusion of other causes The cause of juridical relevance may act alone or together with other preexisting or simultaneous causes (co-causes) that took place later and which, if they are true co-causes, do not interrupt the causal link. Instead, the criterion of exclusion of other causes, if satisfied, leads to the opposite consequence, i.e., interruption of the causal link. In order for interruption of the causal link to occur, "other causes" must be identified, either alone or necessary and sufficient to produce the event, or producing it completely autonomously.

Criterion of Phenomenological Continuity This indicates the possible correlation between the moment of action of the causal factor (which may involve the omission of an action) and the moment when the injury becomes manifest.

Criterion of Rational/Logical Credibility This is the criterion used for evaluating the causal value of the event and the relationship of an actual causal link between the event and the injury when universal or statistical explanatory laws are lacking.

Damnum emergens A type of pecuniary loss. Expenses incurred as a direct result of the damaging event. It can be represented by the amounts disbursed for the purchase of medicines and/or aids or for the necessary therapies, as well as treatment costs to be incurred in the coming years.

Degree of Probability of Causal Value and Causal Link The ascertainment of the causal value and causal link between the traumatic event and injury/damage, which is identified by applying counterfactual reasoning and then medicolegal criteria, expressed in terms of certainty, high probability/quasi-certainty, average probability, low probability, possibility, or exclusion of the causal value–causal link.

Disability As stated by the World Health Organization (WHO) and the International Classification of Impairments, Disabilities and Handicaps (ICF), the disability is defined as any restriction or lack resulting from an impairment of ability to perform an activity in the manner or within the range considered normal for a human being.

Emergency Room Assistance Sheet or Emergency Room Report This is compiled when the patient has requested care in the Emergency Room, including the reason for consultations, the results of any examinations and tests that have been requested, clinical opinion, and diagnosis.

Explanatory Law This expresses regularity in the succession of events observed in nature, from which it is possible to infer a known or still unknown fact (in which case it is predicted). The applicable laws are subdivided into universal and statistical laws.

Falsificationism This is the theory that falsifiability is an essential characteristic of any scientific hypothesis, which must be capable of being falsified by scientific observation and empirical experiments.

Force Majeure An extraordinary event or circumstance beyond the control of the parties.

Health status According to the definition developed by the World Health Organization, this refers to a state of complete physical, mental, and social well-being and not merely the absence of disease.

Injury Anatomical and/or functional evolutive alteration (i.e., lesion, diasease, etc.) resulting from an event.

Insurance premium The amount of money that the contracting party pays to the insurance company as payment for the service provided.

Inter-consultation Sheet This sheet records all actions by other specialists who may examine the patient at the request of the doctor responsible for that patient. It is compiled when the patient's state, other than that for which that patient was admitted to hospital, is documented by a specialist from another discipline.

Lucrum cessans Income foregone, or the loss of utilities that the subject would have procured if the harmful event had not occurred.

Medical Orders Sheet This is the sheet on which doctors attending the patient are obliged to record their decisions.

Necessary Condition A necessary condition is a single condition that must be satisfied in order for an event to take place. The necessary condition is examined through counterfactual reasoning.

Non-Pecuniary losses Any immaterial damage affecting the physical, psychological, and/or existential integrity of the person (e.g., aesthetic prejudice, sexual dysfunction, and/or temporary/permanent functional impairment).

Nursing Journal This sheet covers all incidents relating to vital signs, administration of medicines and medications, requests for care, and any unusual decisions (including, for example, requests to doctors on duty made by nurses for extra medicines, especially analgesics, etc., outside usual working hours). Detailed notes which may be of interest are frequently found in nursing sheets.

Operating Room Report This report records the nature of the surgical intervention, all incidents related to the technique used, and specific patient findings. It is, therefore, a patient document which is usually illustrated with a simple drawing showing what actions were taken in the surgical field, e.g., sutures, drains, etc.

Ordinary activities Professional and nonprofessional activities (recreational, cultural, athletic, social, etc.) ordinarily carried out by the subject.

Pain and suffering A form of non-pecuniary damage consisting of subjective suffering related to the temporary and/or permanent impairment/disability.

Pathological Features These are features of the disease recognized in living persons/cadavers, divided into *initial*, *intermediate*, and *final* clinical pictures, resulting in restoration to health, death, chronic pathological state, or permanent injury.

Patient's journal This document records daily changes in the hospitalized patient's condition, response to treatment, recommended tests and their results, and clinical evaluation of the patient's state until discharged.

Pecuniary losses Prejudice characterized by damage of patrimonial interests, which may undergo evaluation and monetary quantification. It includes *damnum emergens* and *lucrum cessans*.

Permanent impairment Following the statments of the World Health Organization (WHO) and the International Classification of Impairments, Disabilities and Handicaps (ICF), the permanent impairment can be defined as a permanent loss or abnormality of psychological or anatomical structure or function. It is a definitive loss or diminution of physical and psychological integrity with respect to the state that existed before the damaging event. *Coexisting impairments* are defined as impairments which affect different organs or functional systems. *Concurrent impairments* are defined as impairments which affect the same organ or system.

Personal injury insurance This is a contract whereby the insurer, against payment of a premium, undertakes to pay an amount to the insured person, in case of injury due to an accidental, violent, and external cause.

Personal damage Any pecuniary or non-pecuniary losses causally related to a personal injury under civil-tort law.

Physiopathological Pathway This is the actual chain of events which took place and links the initial pathological features with the intermediate and final ones.

Post-surgery Evaluation Sheet This sheet describes monitoring of the patient with respect to general conditions and the specific surgical operation performed.

Pregnancy Monitoring Sheet In cases of pregnancy, this document indicates all examinations, records of vital signs, incidents occurring to the mother, development of the fetus (size, weight, heartbeat, etc.), results of screening for chromosomopathies and malformations, etc.

Pre-surgery Examination Sheet This document is compiled when surgical intervention is necessary. Pre-surgery examinations are carried out by an anaesthetist, according to established procedures, and patients are classified with respect to their ASA index or risk level.

Private insurance Consists of the transfer of risk from one subject (the insured) to another (the insurer). It is a contract entered into whereby the insurer, subject to payment of a premium, undertakes to pay to the insured person, within established limits, a sum of money in compensation for the damage produced by an accident.

Record of Assistance at Birth This is a clearly compiled record of the phases of the birth clarifying problems, the time when they are detected, and at which moment each professional intervened.

Reports of Complementary Examinations These refer to diagnostic tests, the results of which are interpreted and reported by the specialists who made them, e.g., imaging, neurophysiological, psychological tests, etc.

Specific work incapacity This is the incapacity of performing a specific work activity as a consequence of the damaging event.

Source Hierarchy This is the gradation of scientific sources of nonequivalent importance into 1. Guidelines, 2. Consensus Documents, 3. Operational Procedures, 4. Literature (Treatises), and 5. Literature (Journals).

Statistical Law This is limited to stating that the occurrence of an event is accompanied by the occurrence of another event in a certain percentage of cases and with relative frequency.

Sufficient Condition This is a single condition which, if verified, guarantees that a particular occurrence will take place.

Temporary impairment Temporary loss or decrease of psychophysical integrity with respect to the state that existed before the damaging event. It accounts only for a specific period regarding the lives of the injured and ends with clinical cure or with the consolidation to permanent sequelae. It is usually indicated in days.

Topographic Criterion This describes the correlation between the injury and the anatomo-functional location at which the hypothesized causal factor acted; it takes on importance mainly in the framework of the injuriousness of physical energy, i.e., mechanical, electrical, radiating, baric, or chemical energy, or due to bacterial or viral agents. The criterion may be deemed to be satisfied in the case of direct topographic correspondence (e.g., fracture of the skull due to a fall), indirect (counter-coup), or at a distance (pulmonary embolism after contusion of lower limbs).

Universal Law This law derives from consolidated and unanimously shared scientific knowledge.

Work capacity This is the ability to perform one or more working activities and is subject to the existence of biological, attitudinal, and technical-professional characteristics.

Index

S.D. Ferrara et al. (eds.), *Personal Injury and Damage Ascertainment under Civil Law*, DOI 10.1007/978-3-319-29812-2

MIX
Papier aus verantwortungsvollen Quellen
Paper from responsible sources
FSC® C105338

If you have any concerns about our products, you can contact us on
ProductSafety@springernature.com

In case Publisher is established outside the EU, the EU authorized representative is:
Springer Nature Customer Service Center GmbH
Europaplatz 3, 69115 Heidelberg, Germany

Printed by Libri Plureos GmbH
in Hamburg, Germany